Contributions to Operations Research and Economics

Contributions to Operations Research and Economics:
The Twentieth Anniversary of CORE

edited by Bernard Cornet and Henry Tulkens

The MIT Press
Cambridge, Massachusetts
London, England

This book was set in Times Roman by Asco Trade Typesetting Ltd., Hong Kong and printed and bound in the United States of America

Library of Congress Cataloging-in-Publication Data

Contributions to operations research and economics: the twentieth
  anniversary of CORE / edited by Bernard Cornet and Henry Tulkens.

   p. cm.
  ISBN 0-262-03149-3
  1. Economics, Mathematical—Congresses. 2. Operations research—
Congresses. 3. Econometrics—Congresses. 4. Université catholique
de Louvain (1970–   ). Center for Operations Research and
Econometrics—Congresses. I. Cornet, B. II. Tulkens, Henry.
HB135.C646   1989
330'.01'1—dc20   89-12905
                                                      CIP

Contents

List of Contributors

Robert Aumann, The Hebrew University, Jerusalem

Michael O. Ball, University of Maryland

Anton P. Barten, Katholieke Universiteit Leuven, and CORE

Robin Boadway, Queen's University and CORE, Université Catholique de Louvain

Paul Champsaur, Direction de la Prévision, Paris

Bernard Cornet, Université Paris I, and CORE, Université Catholique de Louvain

Claude d'Aspremont, CORE, Université Catholique de Louvain and Facultés Universitaires Saint-Louis, Brussels

Jean-Pierre Florens, Université de Toulouse

Roger Guesnerie, Ecole des Hautes Etudes en Sciences Sociales, Paris

Peter Hammond, Stanford University, and CORE, Université Catholique de Louvain

David F. Hendry, Oxford University

Werner Hildenbrand, Universität Bonn

Olivier Janssens de Bisthoven, CORE, Université Catholique de Louvain

Peter Kooiman, Central Bureau of Statistics, The Netherlands

Wei-Guo Liu, University of Waterloo

Etienne Loute, Facultés Universitaires Saint-Louis, Brussels, and CORE

Thomas L. Magnanti, Massachusetts Institute of Technology

Pierre Malgrange, CNRS and CEPREMAP, Paris

John E. Mitchell, Cornell University

Jean-François Mertens, CORE, Université Catholique de Louvain

Michel Mouchart, CORE, Université Catholique de Louvain

Adrian Pagan, University of Rochester

William R. Pulleyblank, University of Waterloo

Jean-François Richard, CORE, Université Catholique de Louvain, and Duke University

Alexander H. G. Rinnooy Kan, Erasmus Universiteit, Rotterdam

John Roberts, Stanford University

Michael J. Todd, Cornell University

Jean Waelbroeck, Université Libre de Bruxelles, and CORE

Introduction

We conceived of the celebration marking the twentieth anniversary of the foundation of CORE, the Center for Operations Research and Econometrics, as an opportunity for the scientific community in mathematical economics, game theory, operations research and econometrics to both take stock of its achievements over the last two decades, and to promote some of its recent research. Although CORE's part in these achievements and new developments was the pretext that triggered the initiative, the aim was wider, namely, to serve all who have contributed, and/or are contributing today to the fields involved.

The format of this volume reflects the organization of the symposium held at Louvain-la-Neuve, Belgium, in January 1987. Its division into three parts corresponds to CORE's tradition of holding, during each academic year, three series of weekly seminars in mathematical economics and game theory, operations research, and econometrics.

First, within each part, one or two invited survey chapters set the stage. The authors were asked to write these chapters in such a way that nonspecialist, but mathematically inclined readers could grasp the main developments in the field. The comments of discussants were solicited to complete the picture.

Next, an invited research chapter is offered, which is presented as a major example of the activities taking place at CORE seminars. The chairmen in charge of these seminars, Professors Claude d'Aspremont, Laurence Wolsey, and Jacques Drèze have selected the contributors. The topics chosen include "equilibria in large economies" for mathematical economics, "projective algorithms in linear programming" for operations research, and "encompassing theory" for econometrics.

Finally, a collection of specialized research chapters provide examples of current research in the respective fields.

The rationale for gathering the chapters in this way, rather than publishing them in various specialized journals, is to promote interactions among economic theory, game theory, econometrics, and operations research — interactions that occur through the common use of mathematics. All of these fields belong to the decision sciences, a domain of knowledge in which both mathematical concepts and the mathematical language are the common thread supporting the reasoning.

Over its twenty years of existence, CORE has systematically endeavored to keep the interdependence of these disciplines clearly in view. This was the case both in its policy regarding permanent faculty members and visitors and in its publication programs. Above all, this policy was grounded in the belief that such interaction is only possible through direct and personal contacts between the scientists on the occasion of academic visits on common premises.

All the authors contributing to this volume have shared that experience at the Center. We take the very fact of their papers appearing here as a testimony on their part that this interaction indeed contributed to their own scientific achievements and is worthwhile pursuing in the future.

In the preparation of this volume, the editors have benefited from both the expertise and the tireless cooperation of the CORE administrative and secretarial staff. They wish to express their sincere thanks to this staff, and especially to its head, Sheila Verkaeren.

Bernard Cornet   Henry Tulkens
Research Director of CORE   Chairman of the XXth Anniversary
1986–1988   Program Committee

I GAME THEORY AND MATHEMATICAL ECONOMICS

Introduction to Part I

The Survey Chapters

In game theory the period 1967 to 1987 has witnessed important developments, both in the theory and in the uses of game-theoretic methodology for the modeling of economic phenomena. Chapter 1 by Robert Aumann surveys several of these contributions in nontechnical terms; its aim is to bring to light the essence of the ideas on which these contributions rest. The chapter begins with a list of the various areas of game theory and their economic applications to which contributions have been made at CORE during the period under review. It then deals with three topics in greater detail: the Shapley value and its application to economies with public goods, repeated games with incomplete information and the issue of information revelation over time, and finally the application of the Shapley value to the study of fixed price economies and, in particular, of Drèze equilibria.

In his comment Claude d'Aspremont characterizes Aumann's view of game theory as going beyond a structuralist one. He makes this point by showing its implications for the relationships between truth and theory, as well as between justice and theory. The further comment by Jean-François Mertens draws three lessons from the history of ideas in game theory, as they have been developed by Aumann: retaining knowledge, not praxis, as the aim; realizing the importance of preliminary technical work; and concentrating on basic questions.

Next, in mathematical economics, chapter 2 by Paul Champsaur offers a broad synthesis on information exchange, incentive compatibility, and general equilibrium. Economic efficiency requires gathering and exchanging a lot of information that is inherently decentralized. Individual agents have to be provided with adequate incentives to release their private information. The interplay between information dispersion and individual incentives limits the kind of allocations that can be reached. The development, during the past fifteen years, of a literature on incentive-compatible mechanisms has endowed economists with an adequate tool for the formal study of information and incentive constraints. What these constraints are in a general equilibrium context—for finite and infinite economies, with and without public goods—is Paul Champsaur's topic.

Robin Boadway's comment on this chapter elaborates on the related theme of asymmetric information within the competitive price mechanism. He traces its consequences for the validity of the two fundamental theorems of welfare economics. In a further comment Peter Hammond identifies and expounds no less than eight reasons why differential information must drastically change the whole discipline of economics, in its analyses of both equilibrium and efficiency.

The Mathematical Economics Seminar Chapters

Chapter 3, by Werner Hildenbrand, deals with two themes that are central issues in the mathematical study of large economies: (1) the main theorems on the core of such economies, namely, the core-equivalence theorem and the limit theorem on the core, which originated in the celebrated works by Aumann, and Debreu-Scarf, respectively; (2) the properties of the market (or excess) demand function of private ownership economies with a large number of consumers. Recognizing the need for more structure on the description of the economy, if one wants to go beyond existence theorems, the chapter explores the implications of making assumptions on the distribution of the agent's characteristics.

Chapters 4, 5, and 6 deal with more specific topics of current research in mathematical economics and game theory.

The presence and importance of increasing returns in production are widely recognized in the economics literature. Yet attempts to incorporate their study in models with the generality of the Walrasian model are only recent. Two research papers are presented as examples of this endeavor.

Chapter 4, by Bernard Cornet, considers the existence problem of equilibria when firms follow the so-called marginal cost pricing doctrine. The author proposes to formalize this notion with Clarke's normal cone and, in the appendix, this choice is justified on economic grounds.

Chapter 5, by Roger Guesnerie, focuses on the first-best approach and, as the previous one, is guided by normative theory. The author discusses the nature of nonconvexities encountered in production and presents various resource allocation processes, focusing mainly on the marginal cost pricing doctrine.

Finally, combining recent conceptual developments in both game theory and mathematical economics, John Roberts presents in chapter 6 a model of a Walrasian economy where quantity-constrained equilibria are subgame perfect equilibria of a noncooperative game in extensive form. An existence theorem for nonmarket-clearing equilibria is proved. A main novelty of the model is the specification of processes through which prices are formed and transactions are organized.

1 CORE as a Macrocosm of Game-Theoretic Research, 1967–1987

Robert J. Aumann

It's really a tremendous pleasure to participate in this birthday celebration. My first visit to CORE was in 1969, and I was immediately captivated by the dynamism of the place and the people who constitute it. Since then there have been many visits, and I have come to feel about CORE as my European home.

When Henry Tulkens asked me for a title for this talk, I first thought of something like "CORE as a Center for Game-Theoretic Research." But after all, CORE has been much more than such a center. It is not only that important game-theoretic research has been going on here at CORE for the last twenty years. It is that most of the central, most interesting, and most vital strands of game theory have been represented here. So I considered "CORE as a Microcosm of Game Theory." But this doesn't do justice to the subject either. "Microcosm" means "small world." For game theory, CORE has been not a small world but a big world. In the last ten or fifteen years the influence of game theory on economics has been growing steadily. CORE has played a very important part in this development, both in creating the game theory itself and in working out its applications to economics. CORE looms very large in the world of game theory. It is a macrocosm, not a microcosm.

Let me mention here just some of the important areas in game theory to which CORE has made major, central contributions:

1. Economies with large indivisible units (syndicates) (Drèze, Gabszewicz, Gepts, Mertens; Shitovitz, Greenberg, Postlewaite)

2. Economies with many goods (Mertens, Gabszewicz; Bewley)

3. Core of an economy (Hildenbrand, Bohm, Champsaur, Gepts; Schmeidler, Zamir, Bergstrom, Roberts, Vind)

4. Repeated and stochastic games (Mertens, Sorin, Forges, Waternaux, Lefevre; Zamir, Neyman, Hart, Ponssard)

5. Shapley value, both abstract theory and applications to economics (Mertens, Drèze; Neyman, Tauman, Mirman, Aumann)

6. Strategic equilibria (Moulin, Vial, Mertens; Kohlberg, Schmeidler, Aumann)

7. Coalitions, coalitional games, and coalition structures (Drèze, Delbaen, Tulkens, d'Aspremont; Sondermann, Zamir, Schmeidler, Greenberg, Aumann)

8. Incentives, incomplete information, mechanisms (d'Aspremont, Gerard-Varet, Schoumaker)

9. Oligopoly (Gabszewicz, Deschamps, Jacquemin, Vial, d'Aspremont; Hansen, Roberts, Sonnenschein)

10. Public goods (Drèze, de la Vallée Poussin, Champsaur, Tulkens; Henry, Roberts, Rosenthal, Weber, Zamir)

This is a very impressive list. The centrality of CORE's work in these areas is difficult to overestimate. If one wants to know what the classic contributions are, it is enough to look at the list of CORE reprints. The seminal contribution that started area 1—economies with atoms—is the classic paper of Drèze, Jaskold-Gabszewicz, and Gepts; and since then most of the work in this area has been done right here at CORE, both by local researchers and by visitors. Similar statements can be made for the theory of repeated games, Shapley value, Core, and many of the other areas mentioned above. I vividly remember the excitement in the air at the time of my first visit, on the subject of Cores and equilibria of economies with a continuum of goods *and* a continuum of agents. Does the equivalence principle still hold? The question is still very much with us. That work in the late 1960s was the forerunner of a stream of research that has continued to occupy researchers to this day.

I could go on reminiscing in this way. (It is, I suppose, a sign of age; CORE may be a vigorous twenty, but some of the rest of us are a little older.) Instead, let me speculate a little on what it is that makes CORE so unique. There are, after all, several great centers in the world in the areas of mathematical economics and game theory, staffed by extremely able, original, friendly, and cooperative people. But at CORE there is a quality of intensity and excitement that is difficult to find elsewhere. Why?

The reason appears to be a very unusual mix of outstanding permanent staff and visitors. Many institutions have excellent permanent staff, as well as a budget for a few visitors, and perhaps an occasional emphasis year. Other institutions are built primarily on visitors. CORE, with its strong permanent core plus a considerable stream of visitors, provides a unique breeding ground: a place where cross-fertilization leads to the conception of new ideas, as well as a womb—a warm, supportive environment in which these ideas can grow and mature.

For what it may be worth, much of my own best work is inextricably tied up with this place. Perhaps an appropriate modesty would have called for the omission of my name from the above summary. But I am both grateful and proud to have been associated with CORE, and to continue to be; I have no desire to hide the association, or to make light of it.

Ladies and gentlemen, we must get to some substance. The most substantial evidence of CORE's success is in its accomplishments. One cannot hope to survey game theory at CORE in one lecture. What I propose to do here is to take two or three ideas that were generated at CORE and see where they have led on the intuitive level.

One of the areas in which CORE has made very important, central contributions is the theory and applications of the Shapley value. The Shapley value is a kind of index of the power of each participant in an interactive situation—each player in a game. It is to a game what the mean is to a distribution; without making any specific predictions, it gives one an idea of how the land lies. Since 1974 much of the most important theoretical work on values of large games has been done at CORE; worthy of particular mention in this connection is a very important piece that appeared in the *International Journal of Game Theory* in early 1988, in which Jean-François Mertens solves a difficult problem that had been open for many years—the existence of a value on an extremely large class of games, including all market games, differentiable or not. In the applications, too, CORE has been very active. Jacques Drèze and I spent seven years working on the value of fixed price markets; the results appeared in the November 1986 issue of *Econometrica*—just in time for CORE's birthday. More about that later. First I would like to discuss an application of the value to public goods, which is another subject on which CORE has been very active. This represents joint work of M. Kurz and A. Neyman with me, which appeared in the *Journal of Economic Theory* in June 1987. The particular aspects that I will discuss now were mostly generated at the time of a short visit of Mordecai Kurz to CORE in 1978, when I was spending half a year here.

The situation we were considering is that of a country in which the choice of public goods is determined by a majority vote of the citizens. There may, however, be residents of the country who are not citizens; they pay taxes but are not allowed to vote. The public goods we are talking about are nonexclusive. Once produced, they may be used by anybody, citizens as well as noncitizens, and, in the case of citizens, quite independently of how they voted.

In this kind of situation it seems obvious that it is very important what the tastes of the citizens are, and that the tastes of the noncitizens count for nothing. But value analysis leads to precisely the opposite conclusion

—that it does not matter who the citizens are. For a given distribution of tastes of all residents, value analysis leads to the same outcome no matter what tastes the citizens have.

To bring this point home, let me illustrate with an example. There are two kinds of agents in the country: one kind prefers public libraries; the other prefers television. We can think of the country as equally divided on this score. Then the value of a library lover—his power, so to speak—is not only independent of whether he is a citizen but also of whether there is any library lover at all who is a citizen. The value outcome is the same whether all the citizens are library lovers or all are television fans.

Now this is totally unexpected, it sounds absurd. But the value has a very good track record. There have been several instances in which the value seemed strange at first but very few, if any, where this strangeness survived closer examination. Indeed, if theory always yields expected results, it is neither very interesting nor very important. The best kind of theory is that which sounds strange at first but on closer examination turns out to be "right" after all, to yield an important *unexpected* insight.

When we look at the voting situation more carefully, the result under discussion makes perfectly good economic sense. In a cooperative game people may be bribed to vote in one way or another. The individual voter knows that no matter how he votes, he will be able to use the public goods that will in fact be produced. He knows that his vote may influence the decision as to which public goods will be produced, but he also knows that this influence is quite small. For the right price, he might be willing to sell his vote.

What is the minimal price at which a citizen will sell his vote? In any case it has to be more than the expected result of his voting in the way he wants. If there are ten million citizens in the country, his expected influence on the voting process is, for him, worth about one ten-millionth of *his* expected usage of the public goods; if he is a television fan, say, this is about one ten-millionth of *his* television viewing, which is a quite negligible amount. So he should be willing to sell his vote for next to nothing.

What will the resulting market price of a vote be? Well, one needs only 51 percent of the voters to put through any public goods program one wants. It doesn't take very long to realize that in such a situation, cutthroat competition will develop among the voters, and the price of a vote will go down to practically nothing. So the tastes of the *voters* (as distinguished from plain residents) don't make a difference.

If the vote doesn't determine the shape of the public goods program, what does? It is the taxes paid by the taxpayer; it is who *pays* for the public goods, not who votes for them. All this is set out in the above-mentioned JET paper.

Very good. So the value of a vote makes economic sense after all. But it probably sounds quite strange to the man in the street. "If that is economic sense," he will say, "so much the worse for economics."

The cynics among us will say that this just confirms what they have always said, that democracy is a sham, that all that counts is money. But how do the rest of us make common sense, not just "economic sense," of the result? Can the vote really count for next to nothing in determining the mix of public goods?

The explanation of the paradox lies in the underlying assumption that a vote can be sold. I am not talking about legal, "administrative" restrictions; those can always be overcome in some way, and usually they are. I am talking about something that is more effective, namely, informational restrictions. In most countries the vote is secret. You can't sell a vote because there is no way that you can guarantee delivery. So the result collapses. It's not a cooperative game; the contracts are unenforceable (recall that a *cooperative* game is one in which agreements are enforceable). The economic argument behind the result also collapses.

Does that make the result useless, a waste of time? Not at all; on the contrary, it becomes more beautiful. It has always been assumed that the reason for the secret vote is to protect the voter from the pressure of others to influence his vote. But it turns out that there is a more intrinsic reason: to protect the voter from himself, or rather to protect the voters from themselves. If we would enable a vote to be sold (note that I say "enable," not "allow"), all voters would want to sell their votes, and then because of the competition effect, they would get next to nothing for them.

This line of reasoning also has some implications for the rules of voting in a legislature. Most voting in a legislature is required to be open. Is this good or bad? Well, it would seem to be bad, because it does enable a vote to be sold, not necessarily for money but for other votes. This is what makes logrolling possible. But logrolling is not altogether a bad thing; it enables the legislators (and indirectly, the voters) to express the strengths of their preferences and have them taken into account. In some sense the open vote is a more perfect expression of democracy just *because* it blunts the tyranny of the majority.

The bottom line is that game theory cannot tell you what kind of social effects to seek. But it *can* tell you what kind of effects to expect from the social system that you build, and sometimes they are far from obvious.

The next idea I will discuss is taken from the theory of repeated games with incomplete information. Repeated games are game theory's tool for dealing with informational effects over time: teaching and learning, reputations, mutual help, establishing cooperative or inimical relationships, signaling, revealing or concealing substantive information, and so on.

One of the earliest insights yielded by the theory was that in the case of incomplete information—when one side has substantive information that the other side does not—the informed side cannot make use of its special information without eventually revealing it. The revelation is indirect; if one side makes use of its information, the other side will eventually infer the information from the actions of the first side.

This is a gross effect; it is true "in the large." But there are some very interesting second-order effects, which I would like to discuss now, that indicate that "in the small" perhaps the informed side *can* make use of its information. The work I am talking about was started by Jean-François Mertens and Shmuel Zamir in a 1976 paper published in the *International Journal of Game Theory* (CORE reprint 312), and I understand that it has recently been developed further. The optimal strategy when you don't want to reveal your information often calls for randomization, "confusing the enemy" by sometimes doing one thing, sometimes the other. The way in which one randomizes—the relative frequency with which one takes the one action or the other—must not depend on the substantive information that one is trying to conceal, for otherwise, the other side could read the information from the relative frequency. But when one randomizes, there is a natural random variation in the series of outcomes. Could the informed side "hide" behind this natural random variation and get a result that is a little better for it than could be obtained if it made no use of its information?

A good parable for this situation is a story I heard many years ago while still in high school. By law, the bread that bakeries sell must weigh what it is claimed to weigh; a 1-kilo loaf must weigh a kilo, and so on. But in baking bread, it is difficult to be that precise. So the law permits some leeway: the standard deviation of weight that might occur in the normal course of events is estimated, and a shortfall is allowed by that amount.

A customer of a certain bakery noticed that he was consistently getting bread that was slightly underweight. The baker seemed to be within his rights because the shortfall was within the legal limits. So what the customer did was to keep a record of the weights of the loaves he bought. Although each one was within the legal limit, the record did not have the distribution it should have had (approximately normal). With this information the customer went to the police, and because of the way the law was worded, the police were eventually able to obtain a conviction of the baker for deliberately selling underweight bread.

This parable seems to indicate that the informed player cannot hide behind randomness in order to take advantage of his information. Curiously, that is not always the case. There are games in which the informed player can take advantage of his special information, up to the order of magnitude of one standard deviation (approximately the square root of the number of repetitions). The reason is that though the uninformed player will eventually "catch on," by the time he does, it is too late to do anything about it. These are fairly "flat" games in which revealing information will not significantly harm the informed player. In other games, which are not "flat," the extent to which the informed player can use his information to get a second-order advantage, while still concealing it, is much smaller.

We return finally to the subject of values of fixed price economies, to which I alluded earlier. As we all know, Jacques Drèze has made fundamental contributions to this subject, including what is known as the "Drèze equilibrium" for such markets. I have done some work on the theory and applications of the Shapley value. So when I arrived at Louvain-la-Neuve in the winter of 1978 to spend a semester at CORE, Jacques and I decided to join forces to have a look at what the Shapley value has to say about fixed price markets. This led to seven years of some of the most intense, frustrating, and rewarding work that I have ever done, and I am confident that for Jacques it was much the same.

Let me try to give you just a flavor of our investigation. It has been known for a long time that in ordinary economies that are "free" (not constrained by fixed prices) and competitive (have many individually insignificant agents), the Shapley value leads to the competitive equilibrium. In other words, the a priori power of each agent in such an economy is precisely what is dictated by the law of supply and demand; what an agent can "expect" to get in the game of free, unconstrained exchange is whatever his net worth will buy him, at prices determined so that total supply matches total demand.

Fixing prices means constraining the set of trades—and therefore of consumptions—available to each agent. An agent can now consume only what he can buy (at the fixed prices) with the worth (at the fixed prices) of his endowment. Thus a fixed price market looks much like an ordinary market—not the originally given market, but one derived from it by replacing each consumption set by the set of all consumptions that are attainable from the endowment by trading at the fixed prices.

So, calculating Shapley values for the original market, with fixed prices, should be equivalent to calculating Shapley values for the derived market, but without fixing prices in the derived market. By the principle enunciated above, one would expect to be led to the competitive equilibria of the derived market. These equilibria of course have nothing to do with competitive equilibria in the original market, and the prices arising endogenously in the derived market have nothing to do with prices in the original market. They are in a different currency, somewhat like the rationing coupons that governments issue to achieve a "fair" or at least orderly distribution of scarce commodities in times of crisis (such as war).

Much of this had been realized already by Drèze and Müller ("Optimality Properties of Rationing Schemes," *Journal of Economic Theory*, 1980), who gave the name "coupons" to the currency that arises endogenously in the derived market. But their work was not in the context of Shapley values.

The analogy with rationing coupons is particularly apt in several ways. Rationing coupons do not replace money, they come in addition to money; purchases are paid for in both ordinary money *and* coupons. Moreover the shortages that necessitate rationing are impossible in a "free" market; the prices of scarce commodities are simply driven so high that there is no excess demand for them. Shortages (and surpluses) are *created* by fixed prices; since the prices are not set to equate supply and demand, excess demands and supplies ensue, and this is what leads to rationing.

In other ways, though, the analogy is less apt. Rationing coupons are usually issued separately for each of many scarce commodities (oil, sugar, gasoline, etc.); here there is only one kind of coupon, which is used for all commodities. (The usual kind of rationing, in which different goods are rationed separately, is what lies at the basis of the "Drèze equilibrium" for fixed price markets.) Moreover coupon "prices" (the coupon amount to be paid per unit of each commodity) are normally fixed themselves; they are set exogenously. By contrast, in the equilibrium discussed above (to which the Shapley value appears to lead), the coupon prices are endogenous; they are set by market forces. Finally, in the usual kind of rationing, each citizen is granted some positive amount of coupons to start with, a "coupon endowment." Here, however, this seems not to be the case, since in equilibrium, each citizen may spend in coupons at most what he receives from the goods that he sells.

The problem with this analysis was that one of the classical Arrow-Debreu conditions that guarantees the existence of a competitive equilibrium—the nonsatiation condition—fails for the derived market, and indeed most of these markets do not have any competitive equilibria. This had already been realized by Drèze and Müller. In the context of Shapley values, this seemed at the time very odd because we did not see how the association of values with competitive equilibria depends on nonsatiation, and we *were* able to prove that a value exists (as it does in just about all applications, which is one of its advantages). This was only the first in a series of "contradictions in mathematics" that appeared to block our path, and it was a long time before we began to see, even dimly, what is going on with the values of these markets.

The whole story, with all its twists and turns, is too long to be told here. Here is the conclusion we eventually reached: When the derived market does not have a competitive equilibrium, one gives each trader a positive coupon endowment after all; his budget then consists of this coupon endowment *plus* the coupon proceeds from the sale of his goods endowment, and he may buy what he wants with this budget. (One must remember that purchases must be "legal": They must be paid for in money, at the fixed prices, as well as in coupons.) For appropriately chosen coupon endowments and coupon prices, supply then matches demand. Each Shapley value of the original fixed price market corresponds to some such "equilibrium."

This may not look like much at first. The Shapley value is by definition Pareto optimal (given that one must trade at the fixed money prices), and the second law of welfare economics implies that *every* such outcome can be "supported" by appropriate coupon prices and endowments. But in general, the coupon endowments of some agents may be negative, of others zero, and of still others positive. What is asserted here is that when the derived market has no competitive equilibrium, each Shapley value can be supported by coupon endowments that are *positive* for all traders.

Even more can be said about the coupon endowments corresponding to Shapley values. Most important, the (endogenous) coupon endowment of each trader depends only on the (exogenous) goods endowment of that trader, not on his tastes (utility function). Two traders with the same goods endowment but different tastes will get the same coupon endowment. And the dependence is monotonic: If trader Adams starts out with at least as much of each good as trader Brown, then Adams's coupon endowment will be at least as large as Brown's.

For example, fixed wages may lead to an oversupply of labor. To correct this, various rationing schemes that involve cutting down on working hours have been proposed. In the scheme implied by the Shapley value, the maximum work week for any worker would depend on his time endowment —on how much time he has. A worker who for some reason can only work part-time might be assigned a quota smaller than the average, even though he may be able to fill the average quota.

Perhaps the most important conclusion to be drawn from all this is the following: Although the Shapley values of fixed price markets are not generally associated with competitive equilibria, they have one important property in common with competitive equilibria. At a competitive equilibrium each trader is assigned a choice set—the budget set—from which he chooses an element that he most prefers. Of course the element chosen by the trader depends on his tastes; traders with the same budget set but with different utilities will in general wind up with different consumptions. But the *choice set* itself does not depend on the trader's tastes; it depends only on his endowment. I mean by this that agents with the same endowments have the same choice set, irrespective of their utilities. Of course budget sets depend on prices, and in a sense prices "depend" on everyone's utilities. Nevertheless, once determined, they are the same for everyone.

It is this basic property that is shared by the Shapley values of fixed price markets. Each trader is assigned a choice set, namely, the "coupon budget set," defined as the set of all consumptions that the trader can legally purchase with the sum of his coupon endowment and the proceeds of the sale of his goods endowment at the going coupon prices. From this choice set the trader chooses a bundle that he most prefers according to his tastes. But the choice set itself does not depend on his tastes, it depends on his goods endowment only, in exactly the same sense that in an ordinary market, a trader's budget set depends on his goods endowment only.

Lest you think that this is a rather common phenomenon, let me assure you that it is not. In many situations the Shapley value depends on the *cardinal* utility function of an agent, on his attitude toward risk; two agents who differ only in their attitudes toward risk—have the same ordinal preferences and the same physical and legal characteristics (endowment, right to vote, etc.)—may yet be assigned considerably different outcomes by the Shapley value. This can even happen when the situation under consideration involves no explicit element of risk—when the only elements of risk are "strategic," that is, due to uncertainty as to how other players will behave. When it does happen, the outcome cannot be represented as the result of optimizing over a choice set that is independent of tastes, since such optima would be independent of attitudes toward risk.

Some examples where the Shapley value depends crucially on attitudes toward risk are ordinary markets with finitely many traders, the public goods economies with many agents considered above, and taxation models with many agents (like those that Kurz and I consider in *Econometrica*, 1977). In these and other cases, agents who are "fearful," or risk averse, are often penalized by being assigned smaller choice sets. It is then impossible to "decouple" the Shapley value, to represent it as the outcome of each trader choosing from a choice set that is independent of his tastes. I venture to say that where this kind of decoupling is impossible is the "normal," expected case—that the decoupling occurring in ordinary, or fixed price, markets with many traders constitutes a very special phenomenon.

What is the significance of this phenomenon? It has to do with the ideas of nondiscrimination, of equal opportunity, of anonymity, and these in turn are closely associated with "perfect competition." When you bargain for a purchase, the price may well depend on your tastes or your attitudes toward risk. But the very fact that you are bargaining indicates that the situation is not perfectly competitive. In a perfectly competitive situation, you tastes don't matter; it you don't get the "right" price from one agent, you will get it from another. Discrimination—distinguishing agents by their tastes—is widely considered an anticompetitive practice. Of course agents with different physical endowments should not expect equal opportunities. But the requirement that agents with the same physical endowments be allowed to choose from the same choice set does appear nicely to capture the idea of equal opportunity.

The point is not to give such agents equal opportunity by fiat. Rather, the situation itself should be intrinsically nondiscriminatory: The opportunities for each agent that are implicit in the situation should be independent of his tastes. This is exactly what the above condition on the Shapley value says. We thus conclude that whereas fixing prices does restrict consumption sets, and changes outcomes drastically, it does not change the inherently competitive nature of the market.

One often thinks of perfect competition in terms of large numbers of small agents. This condition complements the above nicely; without it, we are unlikely to get nondiscrimination. But the presence of many small agents is not sufficient by itself to ensure perfect competition; it does not rule out imperfections like public goods, increasing returns, transactions costs, and so on. Moreover, it is perhaps better to think of many small agents as a physical condition leading to perfect competition, whereas the idea of intrinsic nondiscrimination is more like a definition, it is close to what we *mean* by perfect competition.

The thrust of my remarks has been to give you some examples of how has game-theoretic work at CORE yielded practical and theoretical insights of a general nature that are expressible in words rather than formulas. That is about all that game theory—or for that matter, economic theory—is good for anyway: qualitative insights. I don't think we are going to get much that is quantitatively useful from our disciplines.

Let me close with a word of appreciation and gratitude that transcends the personal. CORE has been very hospitable not only to me but to a large number of Israeli game theorists. For us, the relationship has been enormously fruitful. I can only hope that it has not all been one way.

Thank you.

COMMENTS: WHAT IS BOB AUMANN TRYING TO ACCOMPLISH?
CLAUDE D'ASPREMONT

My comments are meant to thank Bob Aumann for what he has said and for all he has done for CORE. I would like to limit myself to just a few philosophical remarks. My question could be "What is Bob Aumann trying to accomplish?" since, for all of us at CORE, that amounts to asking "What is game theory trying to accomplish?" I would like first to recall some of his ideas and then to expand to some others germane to today's presentation.

Rightly, Bob Aumann insists that the fundamental purpose of game theory—as an application of mathematics to the social world, based on a rationality hypothesis—is our understanding of this world. Practical applications and correct predictions, whenever possible, are only by-products. Comprehension is the essential aspect. Comprehension consists in recognizing a structure in which, as he says, "we feel at home," or in "organizing our thoughts and observations in a useful manner." And this can be done in a number of ways: there are several game-theoretic models and several solution concepts.

One difficulty, with which this structuralist conception deals, is the relationship between theory and truth. Clearly, here we go beyond the mere recognition of structures. There is a "fundamental interest" motivating the theorist. In the real world individuals do not behave as they do in models. The solution concepts are not real; people are not really rational. However, "our interest" is to organize our observations in a unifying and clarifying way, and this is done in an "as if" mode. It is useful to think *as if* the individual were rational. In Kantian terminology, we are not only making "determinative" judgments, going from the general to the specific, but also "reflexive" judgments, using analogy as a means for unification. As Aumann says, "In judging utility maximization, we must not ask 'Is it plausible?' but 'What does it tie together, where does it lead?'" In other words, in our quest for scientific truth, we are not interested in simple verifiability (or falsifiability or whatever) but in the fruitfulness of our constructs.

There have been many fruitful concepts in game theory (and for most of these, Aumann's contributions have been crucial). This is the case for the notion of core and its usefulness in understanding economic competition; the use of repeated games to deal with informational effects over time; and the von Neumann-Morgenstern solution to express the idea of social organization. Another particularly striking example is John Harsanyi's introduction of the incomplete information theoretical apparatus. This has permitted the notion of Nash equilibrium not only to be generalized to situations of differential information (with many applications like the ones in incentive theory); it has led Bob Aumann to the crucial definition of "common knowledge" and to a new view of the Nash equilibrium—as an expression of Bayesian rationality—and to a new interpretation of the use of mixed strategies. Beliefs about the other players' choices are determined endogenously and each player can then be seen as choosing a definite pure strategy in an incomplete information setup. Considering all the applications of the Nash equilibrium, one easily realizes the importance of such a theoretical unification.

Another difficulty with the conception of game theory is its relation to the conception of social justice. Rawls says, "Justice is the first virtue of social institutions as truth is of systems of thought." Game theory, as a discipline inserted in the normative-descriptive circle, deals explicitly with institutions, either as basic assumptions (like the possibility of binding agreements) or as final conclusions (when solutions are just particular kinds of contracts). Models and solution concepts are not ethically neutral.

Rationality does not imply ethical independence. It is therefore essential that ethical implications be made explicit. The progress here has been, for instance, with respect to some views on the compensation principle of the New Welfare Economics that realize (thanks to Bob Aumann) that the assumption of perfectly transferable utilities does not imply interpersonal comparisons. Likewise there has been progress (by Shapley, Harsanyi, and Aumann) in realizing that the λ-transfer value as a solution notion implies an endogenous determination of interpersonal comparisons. Zero λ-weights for some individuals hence are not pathological per se but may reveal the pathology of the situation.

Finally, as for the relationship between truth and theory, the relationship between justice and theory is not simple: constraints expressing equity as nonenvy are analogous to incentive compatibility constraints; symmetry assumptions in bargaining theory have an ambiguous status, and so on. However, here we also have a "fundamental interest" motivating the theorist, but a practical one. In our quest for just institutions, we are not interested in ethical neutrality but in the implementability of our construct, in "public good and power" as today's presentation has reminded us.

COMMENTS
JEAN-FRANÇOIS MERTENS

For us at CORE, the frequent visits of Bob Aumann and other Israeli game theorists have been extremely beneficial as well. It suffices to have a look at the list of areas of activity he just presented to see that major contributions were made by Israeli visitors, alone or more often in coauthorship. It is indeed those frequent, outstanding visitors who contributed enormously to the shape of activity at CORE.

This is further underscored by the fact that Bob Aumann's own work lies at the origin of most of those areas of interest:

His celebrated core-equivalence theorem (*Econometrica*, 1964) lies at the root of all work on economies with large, indivisible units: The absence of such syndicates being the basic assumption of his theorem, the intention was to see in what direction the distortion—if any—would go.

Similarly, the work on economies with many goods was motivated by the desire to understand whether equivalence depends just on all traders being individually negligible or on the fact that many more traders than commodities are involved.

Also the other work on the core of an economy was motivated by this theorem—as is probably any interest by economists in the core concept: The driving question was whether the limiting result also held approximately for approximately competitive economies.

Similarly, Bob Aumann's path-breaking Arms Control and Disarmament Agency papers with Maschler and Stearns on repeated games with incomplete information, together with his classic work on supergames and on the folk theorem, opened this field of research and started all interest in it. Personally, I remember vividly and most gratefully how during a summer workshop at the Rand Corporation he spent long hours explaining to me all the basics and tricks of the trade, after my interest had been sparked by a seminar he gave at CORE the spring before. As we have just heard, beautifully explained and straight from the horse's mouth, the question is about the strategic use of differential information in dynamic situations. By now, this type of question has become central to large parts of economic theory and has led to tremendous developments, but in the late sixties, Bob Aumann was really the forerunner of all those developments.

In the same way, all developments of the Shapley value—both abstract theory and applications to economics—were started by Aumann's work—through his book with L. Shapley on *Values of Non-Atomic Games* and his value-equivalence theorem (*Econometrica*, 1975).

And I could go on and on, mentioning, for example, his paper on correlated equilibria ("Subjectivity and Correlation in Randomized Strategies," *Journal of Mathematical Economics*, 1974), which is relative to the area of strategic equilibria, and so on. Obviously, we are proud to count Bob Aumann as a member of the CORE family. But what ought we to learn from such an impressive track record?

A first lesson to be drawn, on which he has so justly insisted in his lecture as well as on other occasions, is the importance of the insight a theory may yield, and that scientific work has ultimately to be judged according to that criterion: The proper aim of science, as expressed already by the meaning of the word itself, is knowledge, understanding—not praxis. A theory is interesting and important when it leads to seemingly paradoxical results, the thorough understanding of which yields new insights.

The public goods result with Mordecai Kurz and Abraham Neyman which Bob Aumann just presented is an excellent illustration, and the more so because the explanation itself leads to further paradoxes and more questions: For instance, he just convinced us how this is not a cooperative game, because "the essential, most important contracts (to vote in this or that way) are unenforceable." But the theory itself showed that even if the contracts were enforceable, they would be completely worthless, so no one would care much about their enforceability. Can an "independence of irrelevant alternatives" type of argument lead us so astray? What then about the NTU value? If a cooperative analysis is not applicable here, then certainly it cannot be made in other political and politico-economic applications, where the vote was proved to be important, including the work of Bob Aumann and Mordecai Kurz on "power and taxes." Yet in those cases the analysis was found to yield valuable insights. Are we not throwing out the baby with the bathwater? We would probably not have jumped to those conclusions had we found a positive value for the vote. And surprisingly, the Shapley value does yield a positive value for the vote in this public goods model, so long as the majority required is strictly larger than 50 percent. Indeed, a random coalition of half the population will enjoy exactly the same total utility as the opposing coalition, whatever the public goods produced and hence whatever the vote: the vote is irrelevant. But a random coalition of 60 percent of the population will, due to the size difference, enjoy an edge over the opposing coalition, if it can vote a public good to be produced; on the other hand, if the opposing coalition votes down any public good project, both will get the same utility: zero. Here the voting power counts.

What is going on? The above is not an explanation but merely a verbal translation of the essential aspects of the proof. It depends crucially on all specific (and perhaps less palatable) aspects of the value: random coalitions, total utilities for coalitions, and their differences with the corresponding totals for the opposing coalitions, and so on. The puzzling thing is that, whichever way one turns it, Bob Aumann's explanation seems equally true if his 51 percent is replaced by 61 percent... And those paradoxes remain even in situations of open voting: Perhaps, before throwing out the baby with the bathwater, we should look for an insight that explains the results both for 50 percent and for higher quotas. The real reason seems to hinge more on this difference than on the ability to bribe voters, or to sell votes.

Is the explanation of "open voting" that Bob Aumann just presented then not true? Certainly, no. It is definitely a deep and insightful analysis of that situation, and I fully agree with it. But why does the Shapley value disagree with it for quotas larger then one-half? Perhaps the Shapley value is wrong? But it has a very good track record, as Bob Aumann just reminded us ...

Similarly, the claim that such games cannot be analysed as cooperative games when voting is secret is in principle completely correct, and an important and clear warning shot (and perhaps even more applicable in principle in other situations than in the present one). Still, cooperative analysis has a good track record even in such borderline cases.

As Bob Aumann has told us, such is theory at its best: it should be deep, brilliant, insightful, and tought provoking. His public goods example was a perfect illustration.

A second lesson to be drawn from Bob Aumann's record is that often such breakthroughs require a painstaking preliminary effort in constructing the mathematical apparatus required for the analysis. His introduction, in his 1964 and 1966 *Econometrica* papers, of a nonatomic measure space of agents as the right model for individually negligible traders, and his proof of the core-equivalence principle, were accompanied by his "Intergrals of Set-Valued Functions" (*J. Math. Analysis App.*, 1965), his 1965 paper with M. Perles in the same journal on "A Variational Problem Arising in Economics," and his measurable choice theorem in *La Décision* (1969). Similarly, his value-equivalence theorem (*Econometrica*, 1975) took as additional preliminaries the entire book with L. Shapley on *Values of Non-Atomic Games.*

Finally, it must be difficult for the layman to appreciate how perplexing and frustrating the struggle with examples must have been (and is still so in much current work) prior to the first results on repeated games with incomplete information in the ACDA papers. But this discussant can attest to that: It is quite possible in such work to sit for months on a single, simple example, trying idea after idea and one computation after another, without seeing anything or having the slightest cue about what is going on. This is what insight is about. When situations that are completely paradoxical and unintelligible to anyone, even in the simplest cases, become nearly self-evident when the results are understood. But to gain such insights, Bob Aumann never retreated before the required painful and less glamorous groundwork.

A last lesson I wish to draw is that Bob Aumann's research has been always motivated by and centered on the most important and fundamental questions of economics: trying to understand Adam Smith's mysterious "invisible hand"—how can social order and a well-functioning society emerge from a situation where individuals all pull and push in different directions, each maximizing his own selfish objectives?

The first insight was gained through the core-equivalence theorem. In Aumann's model for individually negligible traders, the core would justify the competitive equilibria, based on individual preferences (the core of a game depends only on its characteristic function), not on some assumed market mechanism. And he proved that competitive equilibria indeed do exist for this model. But this was not sufficient for him: Perhaps the core concept was geared too much toward markets, since the core is empty for most games that are not market games. Clearly, an analogous theorem with some all-purpose solution concept was required—so followed the value-equivalence theorem (and this line of research was recently brought to completion when Andreu Mas Colell proved an equivalence theorem for Aumann and Maschler's bargaining set). Yet this was still not sufficient for him. In some sense, any cooperative solution concept assumes that co-operation will eventually emerge. In addition, phenomena related to imperfect competition, to externalities and public goods, and to asymmetric information, among other things, will make the assumptions of the theorems inapplicable in many cases. A still deeper explanation was clearly called for, both more general and explaining cooperation itself. Hence his work on supergames and on the folk theorem (1959, 1960, 1961, 1967, 1976), showing that just the repetitive aspect present in most situations was sufficient to enable cooperation to emerge as a Nash equilibrium, that is, justified on fully individualistic, noncooperative grounds alone. Even this was not satisfactory for him: Aumann went on to consider the case of asymmetric information—in the Arms Control and Disarmament Agency papers (1966, 1967, 1968) with Maschler and recently with Hart (1986). He also wanted some explanation of why repetition not only enabled cooperation but in some sense forced it (with Sorin 1986).

This is an admirable lesson for each of us, and for CORE as a whole: not to dissipate our efforts, but to keep focused on the most important questions. In doing so, Bob Aumann provided the root of much of today's economic theory.

Thank you, Bob.

2 Information, Incentives, and General Equilibrium

Paul Champsaur

Economists have recognized early on that the social pursuit of efficiency can run into serious obstacles whenever some of the conditions for a good functioning of markets are not satisfied. Three conditions are especially important:

A large number of relatively small economic agents.

The absence of externalities (let us say for simplicity, the absence of public goods).

The absence of public interventions aiming at income redistribution.

Moreover most of the economists agree that the main obstacle to efficiency pertains to the difficulty of obtaining, notably at a central level, the information necessary either to remedy market failures or to minimize the distortions provoked by income redistribution. Therefore economists have endeavoured to devise procedures for the exchange and gathering of information. An essential part of this information is dispersed: this is the information pertaining to the characteristics (preferences, initial resources, cost functions, etc.) of individual agents. This information is private in the sense that an agent knows its own characteristics which are not, at least completely, observable. Until the 1970s the procedures that had been proposed did not take into account the strategic nature of information exchange: agents were supposed to answer truthfully questions concerning their private information. Most of these procedures took the form of iterative planning procedures, and they displayed very satisfactory properties: Significant income redistribution could be achieved without jeopardizing efficiency; similarly, efficient production levels of public goods could be financed. Research done at CORE and by people associated with CORE has played a leading role in the corresponding literature.

At the beginning of the 1970s, however, there came a growing awareness that the properties of information exchange among agents were in a sense too satisfactory: Truthful reporting is an optimistic behavioral assumption. What good are the above procedures if the agents are no longer thought to report their true private information but to select their answers according to their perceived best interests? Is it possible to design procedures or mechanisms that deliver adequate incentives to report truthfully? What kind of allocations can be reached through such incentive-compatible mechanisms? An important literature devoted to these questions has emerged over the past fifteen years. And in this research area CORE members and CORE visitors have been very active and successful.

The development of the literature on this subject has been so explosive that to review it all would be an impossible task. Furthermore there are two recent remarkable and complete surveys that will appear in a volume in the honor of Leonid Hurwicz. One was written by J. Roberts. Its title is "Incentives, Information and Iterative Planning." The other was written by T. Groves and J. Ledyard. Its title is "Incentive Compatibility Ten Years Later." The purpose of this chapter is limited in consequence. It will say nothing on iterative planning. The attention will be concentrated on information and incentive constraints in a general equilibrium framework and on what these constraints become when the number of agents is large. The reader should also be warned that this chapter is a personal walk through the literature rather than a faithful survey.

We will use as a benchmark situations where markets work well, that is, economies with a large number of agents and without public goods or income redistribution. We have to understand first what incentives stimulate, in such situations, the efficient exchange of information that takes place at a competitive equilibrium. Noncooperative game theory is the natural tool for this. The next step is to characterize the information-gathering mechanisms that deliver similar incentives. Then we are able to look for what can be achieved with such mechanisms when the production of public goods has to be financed or when income redistribution is sought.

Indeed, economists did not wait for such a systematic and explicit analysis of incentive-compatible mechanisms before guessing what allocations could be reached under information and incentive constraints. Second-best theory, especially when concerned with income redistribution, had to rely on such a guess since its development (see, for example, Mirrlees 1971 and Atkinson 1973) preceded the formal analysis of incentive compatible mechanisms. The latter theory has confirmed the intuitions of second-best theorists and determined under which assumptions they are right.

The chapter is organized as follows. The economic model is presented in section 2.1. Various assumptions concerning the individual agents' information and the initial information available at the central level are introduced in section 2.2, together with the corresponding noncooperative game equilibrium concepts. Incentive properties of finite economies are examined in section 2.3. Section 2.4 is devoted to economies with a large number of agents. Section 2.5 leaves the realm of the existing literature for open questions and conjecture, with a particular emphasis on the social value of prior statistical information.

2.1 The Economic Model

There are $m + 1$ private goods and n public goods indexed $h = 0, 1, \ldots,$ $m + n$. The first private good ($h = 0$) is the numeraire. A net trade for an agent is a couple (x, y), where x in $\mathbb{R}^{m+1}$ is the net trade in private goods and y in $\mathbb{R}_+^n$ is the vector of public goods quantities available for everybody. For simplicity, we assume that the set of feasible net trades is the same for every agent and is equal to $X \times \mathbb{R}_+^n$, where X is a standard set of individual feasible trades in $\mathbb{R}^{m+1}$ (closed, convex, etc.).

The names of the agents are the elements of a measure space $(T, \mathscr{T})$. $\mathscr{T}$ is the σ-algebra of coalitions. The relative weights of the various coalitions are given by a probability measure λ on $(T, \mathscr{T})$. If T is finite, λ will be the counting measure. If T is infinite, λ will be a nonatomic measure on $(T, \mathscr{T})$.

An *allocation* d is a couple $(\mathbf{x}, y)$ where $\mathbf{x}$ is an integrable function from T into X and y in $\mathbb{R}_+^n$ is a vector of public goods quantities. An allocation is *feasible* if

$(\bar{x}, y)$ belongs to Z,

where $\bar{x} = \int_T \mathbf{x} d\lambda$ is the aggregate net trade vector in private goods and Z, a subset of $\mathbb{R}^{m+1} \times \mathbb{R}_+^n$, is the aggregate production set of the economy. Again, for simplicity, we assume that Z is a closed convex cone that satisfies the usual assumptions. Let D be the set of all feasible allocations.

The tastes of an agent are represented by a von Neumann-Morgenstern concave utility function from $X \times \mathbb{R}_+^n$ into $\mathbb{R}$ which C^2 and strictly monotonic. We will consider a parametrized family of agents' characteristics. The space A of parameters is a subset of $\mathbb{R}^l$. The parametrization is given by a C^2 function u from $A \times X \times \mathbb{R}_+^n$ into $\mathbb{R}$. For every element a in A, we have a standard utility function $u(a, \cdot)$ from $X \times \mathbb{R}_+^n$ into $\mathbb{R}$.

Sometimes, because either the general model is too difficult to handle or a partial equilibrium analysis suffices, it becomes convenient to simplify the formalization by considering *quasi-linear utility functions*. Then the utility function $u(a, \cdot)$ can be decomposed into the sum of x_0, the net trade in the numeraire, and of a function $v(a, \cdot)$ from $\mathbb{R}^m \times \mathbb{R}_+^n$ into $\mathbb{R}$ which retains all the properties previously assumed for u:

$$u(a, \cdot) = v(a, \cdot) + x_0.$$

An *economy* is defined by a measurable function from T onto A (or profile). $\alpha(t)$ is the characteristics of agent t in the sense that $u(\alpha(t), \cdot)$ is its utility function. Let M be the set of probability measures defined on A. The distribution of characteristics of economy α is an element μ_α of M defined by

$$\mu_\alpha = \lambda \circ \alpha^{-1}.$$

To be properly interpreted, an economy with a continuum of agents can be thought of as an approximation of an economy with a large but finite number of agents. Let us consider a sequence of finite economies (T, α^k) with $|T^k| \to \infty$ when $k \to \infty$. The above sequence converges to a continuum economy (T, α) if the sequence of distributions of characteristics $\mu^k = \lambda^k \circ (\alpha^k)^{-1}$ converges in M to μ. Of course, M, the space of probability measures on A, is supposed to be endowed with an appropriate topology (for example, the topology of weak convergence).

An allocation $(\mathbf{x}, y)$ is *Pareto optimal or efficient* if it is feasible and if there exists no feasible allocation $(\mathbf{x}', y')$ such that

$$u(\alpha(t), \mathbf{x}'(t), y') > u(\alpha(t), \mathbf{x}(t), y) \qquad \text{for almost all } t \text{ in } T.$$

An allocation $(\mathbf{x}, y)$ is *privately efficient* if it is feasible and if there exists no feasible allocation $(\mathbf{x}', y)$ such that

$$u(\alpha(t), \mathbf{x}'(t), y) > u(\alpha(t), \mathbf{x}(t), y) \qquad \text{for almost all } t \text{ in } T.$$

Private efficiency corresponds to the usual efficiency concept restricted to the allocation of private goods for fixed quantities of public goods. It is clearly a much weaker condition than (full) efficiency.

An allocation $(\mathbf{x}, y)$ is *individually rational* if no agent is worse off than in the initial no-trade situation:

$$u(\alpha(t), \mathbf{x}(t), y) \geqq u(\alpha(t), 0, 0) \qquad \text{for almost all } t \text{ in } T.$$

If $u(\alpha(t), \mathbf{x}(t'), y) > u(\alpha(t), \mathbf{x}(t), y)$, we say that agent t is *envying* agent t'. Agent t is envious at allocation $(\mathbf{x}, y)$ if the set of agents it is envying has a strictly positive measure. An allocation is *equitable* if the set of envious agents is negligible. Formally, let $E(\mathbf{x}, y)$ be the set of couple (t, t') such that t is envying t':

$E(\mathbf{x}, y) = \{(t, t') \text{ in } T \times T, u(\alpha(t), \mathbf{x}(t'), y)) > u(\alpha(t), \mathbf{x}(t), y)\}.$

The allocation $(\mathbf{x}, y)$ is equitable if

$\lambda \otimes \lambda(E(\mathbf{x}, y)) = 0,$

where $\lambda \otimes \lambda$ is the product measure on $T \times T$.

A private goods price vector p is an element of $\mathbb{R}_+^{m+1}$ with $\pi_0 = 1$. Let p be the set of all such price vectors. A personalized public goods price system is an integrable function π from T into $\mathbb{R}_+^n$, $\pi(t)$ being the personalized price vector of agent t.

A *Lindahl equilibrium* is composed of a feasible allocation $(\mathbf{x}, y)$ (called the "Lindahl allocation") and of a price system (p, π) such that, for almost all t in T,

(i) $(\mathbf{x}(t), y)$ maximizes $u(\alpha(t), \cdot)$

on $\{(x', y') \text{ in } X \times \mathbb{R}_+^n, px' + \pi(t)y' = 0\};$

(ii) $p\bar{x} + \bar{\pi}y = 0$

where $\bar{x} = \int_T \mathbf{x}(t)d\lambda$ and $\bar{\pi} = \int_T \pi(t)d\lambda$ is the aggregate public goods price vector

An *egalitarian competitive equilibrium* is composed of a feasible allocation $(\mathbf{x}, y)$ (called "egalitarian competitive allocation") and of a couple (p, π) in $P \times \mathbb{R}_+^n$ such that, for almost all t in T,

(i) $\mathbf{x}(t)$ maximizes $u(\alpha(t), \cdot, y)$

on $\{x \text{ in } X, px = -\pi y\};$

(ii) $p\bar{x} + \pi y = 0.$

In other words, an egalitarian competitive equilibrium is a competitive (or Walrasian) equilibrium for the private goods economy which is obtained when the public goods quantities are fixed and their production cost in shared equally among the agents. Of course, in the absence of public goods $(n = 0)$, the two concepts of egalitarian competitive equilibrium and of Lindahl equilibrium coincide with the concept of competitive (or Walrasian) equilibrium.

It is well known that every Lindahl allocation is efficient. Similarly, every egalitarian competitive allocation is privately efficient but not, in general, fully efficient. A Lindahl allocation is generally not egalitarian competitive.

2.2   The Information Is Limited

The most compelling limitation concerns the information available at the central level. We distinguish between three degrees of information for the Center:

C1. The Center is *completely informed* of the characteristics of the economy, that is of the profile α. For each agent t, the Center knows its characteristics $\alpha(t)$.

C2. The Center has only a *statistical information* about the characteristics of the economy. The Center believes that each of the agents is drawn independently from a population with a distribution of characteristics μ. The Center's beliefs are supposed to be accurate in the sense that when the number of agents is large, the actual distribution of characteristics is close to the hypothetical one. They coincide in the limit case where $(T, \mathcal{T}, \lambda)$ is a nonatomic measure space.

C3. The Center is *ignorant* of the distribution of characteristics even if the number of agents is large.

Of course, each individual agent t is supposed to know its own characteristics $\alpha(t)$. But its information concerning the other agents might be limited. Again, as for the Center, we distinguish between three possible states of information for the agents. Of course their information with respect to each other is symmetric: all the agents are in the same information state. Let us describe these states.

A1. *Complete information.* Every agent t knows not only $\alpha(t)$ but the entire profile, that is, $\alpha(t')$, $t' \neq t$.

A.2. *A statistical information.* Every agent believes that each of the other agents is drawn independently from a population with a distribution of characteristics μ. It means that all the agents share the same statistical information. This information is supposed to be accurate like the statistical information that the Center might have. Indeed, if both the Center and the agents have some statistical information, their corresponding beliefs are supposed to be identical.

A3. *Ignorance.* The agents do not have any reliable information on other agents' characteristics. They may nevertheless form beliefs in a Bayesian way. But these beliefs are diverse, and the Center does not know how they are formed.

If the Center is completely informed, there are no informational limitations to the set of allocations that can be reached. Then potential limitations come from the bargaining power of the agents and coalitions; they are the subject of cooperative game theory. We are interested in situations where the Center has *at most* some statistical information. In such situations there is necessarily an asymmetry of information between the Center and the agents since each agent knows at least its own characteristics. The combination of two information states for the Center and three information states for the agents yields six possible information states for the economy. However, they are not equally interesting, and the literature has focused on particular combinations. These combinations appear in the following table:

		Agents		
		A1	A2	A3
Center	C2		X	X
	C3	X		X

These cases will be examined in the order of decreasing information for the agents. Each case corresponds to some information limitations restricting the set of allocations that can be reached. These restrictions arise because of the exchange and gathering of information necessary to explore and agree upon welfare-improving departures from the initial no-trade allocation. This is usually modeled as a noncooperative game based on a decentralized *mechanism*.

A mechanism is composed first of a message (or action) space S. Every agent t has to select a message in S. A *play* is a measurable function s from T into S, $s(t)$ being the message selected by agent t. A mechanism f associates with a play s a feasible allocation $d = f(s)$. We will restrict our attention to mechanisms such that the net trade assigned to an agent does not depend on its name t, that is, depends only on its message and on the distribution of messages on the message space. Such mechanisms are called *anonymous*. The focus on anonymous mechanisms is justified by three main reasons. First, the Center's information concerning the agents is symmetric. Since its information is at most statistical, the Center has no a priori information that might serve as a basis for a discrimation in favor or against a particular agent. Second, we assume that when comparing the performances of two mechanisms, the Center will use a symmetric welfare criterion. Indeed, the only welfare criterion introduced so far—Pareto domination—is too weak to disqualify wildly asymmetric mechanisms. But the reader should have in mind more specific welfare criterions like the social welfare functions used in second-best analysis. Last but not least, in computing its best-reply strategy, an agent need not know the message $s(t')$ of every other agent $t' \neq t$ but only the message distribution. Therefore the standard concept of Nash equilibrium under complete information remains meaningful even if the agents' information is limited to the knowledge of the distribution of characteristics, a more reasonable assumption especially in large economies.

In order to define precisely an anonymous mechanism, we use the formalism introduced by Dubey, Mas-Colell, and Shubik (1980). Let N be the set of probability measures on S and $v_{\mathbf{s}} = \lambda \circ \mathbf{s}^{-1}$ be the probability measure on S induced by play $\mathbf{s}$. An anonymous mechanism f is composed of a couple of function (f_x, f_y), where

1. f_x is a function from $S \times N$ into X such that $f_x(\mathbf{s}(t), v_{\mathbf{s}})$ is the net trade in private goods assigned to agent t, and

2. f_y is a function from N into $\mathbb{R}^n_+$ such that $f_y(v_{\mathbf{s}})$ is the vector of public goods quantities enjoyed by everybody.

For a given mechanism, the nature of the game in which the agents are consciously involved depends on their information. Let us skip from the formal description of the game corresponding to each of the three possible states of information to the associated noncooperative equilibrium concept.

If the information is complete (A1), the relevant equilibrium concept is the standard *Nash equilibrium*. The strategy space is simply the message space S. At such an equilibrium, every agent t chooses the best message, knowing the messages $\mathbf{s}(t')$ choosen by the other agents $t' \neq t$.

If the information is statistical (A2), we have a game of incomplete information and the corresponding concept of *Bayesian Nash equilibrium*. The strategy space is the set of functions from A into S. At such an equilibrium an agent knows only what each other agent would choose for every possible characteristics it may have. Therefore its message is chosen so as to maximize its expected utility given the probability distribution μ on every other agent's characteristics.

It is important to notice that the two preceding equilibrium concepts coincide for anonymous mechanisms in infinite economies.

In the ignorance situation (A3) it is not possible to predict what will happen unless, for every agent and every characteristic, there exists a message that is a best reply for every possible play chosen by the other agents, that is, a dominant strategy. If this is the case, we get an *equilibrium in dominant strategies*. Then beliefs or guesses concerning other agents, characteristics, or choices do not matter. Notice that the existence of a dominant strategy for each agent is a very demanding property for a mechanism.

When the agents' information is not complete (A2 or A3), it is possible to simplify drastically the formalization by

1. identifying the message space S with the space of possible characteristics A, that is, by considering only *direct mechanisms*, and

2. restricting our attention to equilibria such that every agent's strategy is to announce its true characteristics (*truth-telling equilibria*). That the set of allocations that can be obtained as equilibrium outcomes is not reduced by such restrictions on the mechanisms we consider is a consequence of the well-known *revelation principle*.

In some contexts the Center may lack the power to force some agents to engage themselves knowingly into a game that will make them worse off. In other words, the proposed mechanism has to be designed in such a way that each agent can secure a utility level at least as high as its initial one. The mechanism has to satisfy a condition of *individual rationality*. For our purpose, a simple interpretation of this condition will suffice: Nash allocations have to be individually rational. Such a condition might also be justified by the Center's implicit welfare criterion (a Rawlsian criterion, for example).

2.3   Finite Economies

Throughout this section we consider finite economies with a fixed number of agents $|T|$.

Agents' Information Is Complete

In the complete information case, it is possible to devise mechanisms whose *Nash equilibria correspond to efficient allocations*. This was shown first by Groves and Ledyard (1977), Hurwicz (1979a), and Schmeidler (1980). Even though the Center has no information on the distribution of characteristics, efficiency can nevertheless be reached noncooperatively, provided that each agent knows exactly the characteristics of the other agents.

Then the question is whether the set of efficient allocations that can be reached in such a way is large. A *negative answer* has been given by Hurwicz (1979b). Hurwicz provided a remarkable characterisation of the efficient allocations that can be obtained noncooperatively. Let us consider a mechanism such that all its Nash equilibria yield *individually rational and efficient allocations*. Then these allocations are necessarily *Lindahl allocations* (*competitive allocations* in economies without public goods). This is true even if the mechanism is not anonymous. In short, if the Center is very ignorant and insists nevertheless on getting individually rational Nash allocations different from Lindahl (or competitive) allocations, then it must accept allocations that are not efficient.

Some conditions are required for this result to hold. From an economic point of view, they are technical and not really restrictive, except for one: the set of all possible preferences generated by the utility function $u(a, \cdot)$: $X \times \mathbb{R}^n_+ \to \mathbb{R}$ for all possible values of a in A has to be "large" enough. A formal definition of this "variety" condition is outside the scope of this chapter. Let us just say that it is compatible with the quasi-linearity assumption. The knowledge of the set of possible preferences is the only information possessed by the Center when designing a mechanism. The "variety" condition means that this information has to be imprecise enough to qualify the state of ignorance (C3) which the Center is supposed to be in.

Several mechanisms that illustrate Hurwicz's characterization have been exhibited either for private goods economies (Hurwicz 1979a; Schmeidler 1980) or for economies with public goods (Hurwicz 1979a; Walker 1981). In the public goods case none of them are anonymous mechanisms. We doubt that there exists an anonymous mechanism whose Nash allocations are individually rational and exactly efficient. However, if the set of possible preferences A is compact, there always exist anonymous mechanisms whose Nash allocations are sufficiently close to Lindahl allocations (see Champsaur and Laroque 1981a).

The case where the Center has some statistical information—the information state (A1, C2)—has not been considered explicitly in the literature. Indeed, it seems that as long as the "variety" condition remains valid for the set of likely (as opposed to potential) preferences, the above analysis will not be altered. The set of likely preferences is generated by the support of the measure μ in A (rather than A itself).

Statistical Information Is Available

The Center and the agents share the same statistical information. If the corresponding concept of Bayesian Nash equilibrium is assuming a central role in the literature on incentives, the characterization of the Bayesian Nash allocations has proved difficult. The main results obtained so far are due to d'Aspremont and Gerard-Varet (1979) under the quasi-linearity assumption. They were able to exhibit and characterize mechanisms whose *Bayesian Nash allocations are efficient.* These efficient allocations are generally not Lindahl allocations. Furthermore the characterization indicates that in economies with public goods and only one private good ($m = 0$), none of these efficient mechanisms are individually rational (see also Laffont and Maskin 1979 on this point).

The quasi-linearity assumption plays an essential role in the existence proof. In the case of a more general set of possible preferences, it seems very unlikely that any efficient Bayesian mechanism will exist at all.

Agents Have No Information

The existence of nontrivial mechanisms with equilibria in dominant strategies is far from evident. Pioneer work on that subject goes back to Vickrey (1961). A series of remarkable results by Groves (1970), Clarke (1971), Green and Laffont (1978), and Walker (1978) have provided a more precise characterization of the dominant strategy mechanisms for the case of quasi-linear preferences. These results have led to a clear negative result. There does not exist any dominant strategy mechanism that yields *efficient allocations.*

This impossibility result is a fortiori true for more general preferences as shown by Hurwicz (1972, 1975) and Lydyard and Roberts (1974).

Whether or not the Center has some statistical information does not play any role in the above results.

Temporary Conclusions

At first sight it is tempting to draw two main conclusions from this brief review of the incentive properties of finite economies. First, among the two components of an information state—the agents information and the Center's information—only the former one seems to have a decisive influence on the possibility to obtain efficient allocations noncooperatively and on the nature of the efficient allocations that may be reached. Second, and this is rather surprising, information and incentive constraints seem to have similar effects on finite economies with or without public goods.

However, as pointed out early by Hurwicz (1972), both problems—the role of the Center's information and the incentive differences between public and private goods—become really meaningful only when the number of agents is large. Since the mid-1970s an important effort has been made to understand the incentive properties of large economies. As we shall see in the next section, our temporary conclusions will need to be seriously modified in the light of the many results that have been obtained.

2.4   Infinite Economies

The Central Role of Equitable Allocations

When the set of agents $(T, \mathcal{T}, \lambda)$ is a nonatomic measure space, every agent t is negligible, and its message (or strategy) $\mathbf{s}(t)$ cannot affect the message distribution $v_\mathbf{s}$. Let us consider an anonymous mechanism f. It selects a vector of public goods quantities $f_y(v_\mathbf{s})$ that is independent of agent t's message. Furthermore the opportunity set $f_x(S, v_\mathbf{s})$ for the private goods net trades is the same for every agent. Therefore, at the Nash equilibrium of an anonymous mechanism, (almost) every agent prefers its net trade to that of other agents: a Nash allocation of *an anonymous mechanism is necessarily equitable*. Of course, what is true for standard Nash equilibria is also true for equilibria in dominant strategies (and for Bayesian equilibria).

A converse assertion, as shown by Hammond (1979), is that *every equitable allocation can be obtained as the outcome of a dominant strategy equilibrium*. In other words, the *equality* property subsumes the information and incentives constraints in infinite economies. The exact nature of the information limitations, especially for the individual agents, does not seem to matter. This is exactly what second-best theorists like Mirrlees (1971) and Atkinson (1973) had guessed at the beginning of the 1970s. Hammond's result looks like a justification of the standard second-best analysis which consists in maximizing a symmetric social welfare function over the set of equitable allocations. For a thorough examination of the relationship between the second-best analysis and incentive compatible mechanisms in infinite economies, see Guesnerie (1987).

Clearly, the effort we have made to distinguish between various information states and equilibrium concepts is not particularly relevant to large economies. However, as we shall see later, there appear to be serious contradictions between properties of finite and infinite economies, so we have to be more cautious in interpreting them.

To proceed further, we have to know what the equity property implies, especially when combined with efficiency requirements. First, it is easy to verify that every *egalitarian competitive allocation is equitable*. Works by Varian (1976), Hammond (1979), and Champsaur and Laroque (1981b) have shown that *every equitable allocation that is privately efficient is egalitarian competitive*. This characterization supposes that the set of preferences that actually appears in the economy enjoys some topological properties. These properties can be expressed directly on the parameters' space. They amount essentially to the connectedness in $\mathbb{R}^l$ of the support of μ_α. Although this "connectedness" condition excludes economies with "types" for which the support of μ_α is discrete, it is a very mild restriction. It is compatible with all of the conditions that have already been introduced (for example, the variety condition).

The implications are quite different for economies with or without public goods. Let us begin with the latter ones ($n = 0$).

Private Goods Economies

Then private efficiency is full efficiency and an egalitarian-competitive allocation is simply a standard competitive allocation. The characterization by Hurwicz (1979b) of the efficient allocations that can be obtained as the outcome of a Nash equilibrium is confirmed. Moreover individual rationality, which was a condition for obtaining this characterization, becomes a consequence of incentive compatibility: efficiency and equity imply individual rationality in infinite economies without public goods.

The concept of *competitive mechanism* can be used to summarize what an efficiency-seeking Center can do in infinite economies. This is a direct and anonymous mechanism that associates with every economy, finite or infinite, a competitive allocation. Let us consider such a competitive mechanism and denote it by f^c, $f^c(\alpha)$ being a competitive allocation for the economy (T, α). In short, f^c selects for each distribution of characteristics μ_α an equilibrium price vector. Any such mechanism f^c is a dominant strategy mechanism for infinite economies. Does it imply that this competitive mechanism will deliver approximately the same incentives (the gain any individual agent can expect from misreporting its preferences is small) in large but finite economies? As shown by Postlewaite and Roberts (1976), the answer is no, unless f^c is continuous, that is, unless the equilibrium price system selected by f^c is continuous with respect to the distribution of characteristics μ_α. Incentive properties for infinite economies are *meaningful only if the corresponding mechanisms enjoy adequate continuity properties* (see also Champsaur and Laroque 1982 on this point).

As a consequence the aforementioned incentive properties of infinite economies are approximately valid for large but finite economies only if the set of possible preferences generated by the utility function $u(a, \cdot)$ for all possible values of a in A is restricted so as to guarantee the existence of a continuous selection in the competitive equilibrium correspondence. For example, let us assume that the *preferences are quasi linear*. Then there exists a unique competitive mechanism f^c that is, of course, continuous. As explained earlier, f^c is *approximately a dominant strategy mechanism in large economies*. If the preferences are quasi linear and if the Center has no other aim than mere efficiency (in this context it means that the Center's welfare criterion is *utilitarian*; that is, it is the sum of agents' utility levels), then the influence of the information state vanishes in large private goods economies.

On the other hand, if the set of possible preferences is *rich enough*, we know that any competitive mechanism f^c will be discontinuous. Then what the Center can achieve in large but finite economies depends crucially on the information state. In particular, if the Center has no a priori accurate information on the distribution of characteristics (C3), the agents' information matters a lot. If the agents also have no information (A3), the Center has to resort to dominant strategies. Then *not only will efficiency not be reached in finite economies, but it cannot even be approached in large but finite economies*. If the agents are in the state of complete information (A1), efficiency can be reached through Nash equilibria of indirect mechanisms in both finite economies, as indicated earlier, and infinite economies (see Dubey, Mas-Colell, and Shubik 1980). The picture is different if the Center has an accurate statistical information (C2). Then it is reasonable to conjecture that *efficiency can be approached through approximately dominant strategies* when the number of agents is large. In other words, if the Center has accurate statistical information, we can expect the influence of the agents' information to be negligible in large economies if efficiency alone is pursued.

We can also say that the second-best analysis, in its standard practice, is definitively well founded when the Center has a priori statistical information.

Public Goods Economies

Equity has dramatic consequences for the distribution of the production cost of public goods. For example, in an economy (finite or infinite) with only one private good ($m = 0$), an allocation is equitable if and only if all agents contribute an equal amount of private goods for the production of public goods: $\mathbf{x}(a)$ is independent of a. A generalization of this simple observation is that an equitable and privately efficient allocation is egalitarian competitive in a "connected" economy. A differentiation of the shares of the public goods cost is analogous to income redistribution. In a connected economy such differentiation is possible only if there are several private goods ($m > 0$) and if private efficiency is abandoned.

Whenever the agents' preferences differ, *efficient and equitable allocations will typically not be individually rational* since agents that derive little utility from the public goods contribute as much as agents that value them a lot. In infinite economies with public goods, information and incentive constraints forbid efficiency if the Center lacks either the power or the wish to impose involuntary trades, that is, allocations that are not individually rational. This is certainly the main difference between economies with public goods and economies with only private goods.

How does such an incompatibility fit with the incentive properties of finite economies? It depends on the agents' information. The properties of Bayesian equilibria in finite economies mentioned above agree with this incompatibility. Similarly, Roberts (1976) showed that, in large but finite public goods economies, a mechanism cannot yield efficient and individually rational allocations with strategies that are approximately dominant. However, the state of complete information for the agents (A1) leads to an apparent contradiction: in finite economies, Lindahl allocations can be obtained as Nash allocations (or approached as Nash allocations of anonymous mechanisms). Lindahl allocations are generally far from being equitable. Their very definition implies that agents with different preferences are asked for different contributions: the latter are proportional to the marginal rate of substitution between public and private goods.

How should we interpret this discontinuity between the properties of finite and infinite economies? We have already noted that the two concepts of Nash equilibrium under complete information, on the one hand, and of Bayesian equilibrium, on the other hand, coincide in infinite economies for anonymous mechanisms. Therefore we can expect that in large but finite economies, the additional information provided by the exact knowledge of the distribution of characteristics (A1) as compared with a slightly imprecise knowledge (A2) will make little difference. This is what has happened in private goods economies. The problem we encounter for public goods economies is certainly due to a lack of continuity among the mechanisms that were used to get individually rational and efficient (or approximately efficient) Nash allocations. Attempting to define such a continuity requirement is outside the scope of this chapter. However, we still have to be suspicious about the interpretation of results obtained in finite economies under the assumption of complete information (A1).

Let us return to equitable and (fully) efficient allocations. Such allocations are called *fair allocations*. Following Groves and Ledyard (1985), let us call a *fair-efficient mechanism* a direct and anonymous mechanism that associates with every economy, finite or infinite, a fair allocation. In an economy without public goods, a fair-efficient mechanism is simply a competitive mechanism. Let us consider a fair-efficient mechanism and denote it by f^e, $f^e(\alpha)$ being is a fair allocation for the economy (T, α). f^e selects, for each distribution of characteristics μ_α, a private goods price vector and a public goods production vector. Any such mechanism f^e is a dominant strategy mechanism for infinite economies. As in the case of private goods economies, this is not enough to infer that large but finite economies have approximately the same incentive properties as infinite economies. In addition we have at least to assume either that the Center has an accurate statistical information or that the fair-efficient mechanism f^e is continuous with respect to the distribution of characteristics. If the first condition is satisfied, that is, if the Center is in the information state C2, then, in large but finite economies with public goods, it seems reasonable that efficiency should be attained through approximately dominant strategies, and this does not seem more difficult to show than for private goods economies.

If the Center is *ignorant (C3)*, and if the set of possible preferences is *rich enough*, then there does not exist any continuous fair-efficient mechanism. Of course, the discontinuity of any fair-efficient mechanism might be due, in the presence of several private goods, to the discontinuity of the equilibrium private goods price vector correspondence. However, the discontinuity persists even if there is only private good. Then, as in the case of private goods economies, we conjecture a negative result: Efficiency cannot be approached by dominant strategy mechanism in finite economies even if the number of agents becomes large.

A final case remains to be examined. The set of possible preferences can be restricted in such a way as to guarantee the existence of a continuous fair-efficient mechanism. For example, if the preferences are quasi linear, as we will assume in the rest of the chapter, there exists a unique and continuous fair-allocation mechanism f^e. Are we in a position to reiterate a statement that is the exact extension to public goods economies of what has already been written for private goods economies? There is in fact a difficulty that points to another important difference between public and private goods. For simplicity, let us assume that there is only one private good ($m = 0$). An equitable allocation is composed of a public goods vector and of a private goods contribution that is the same for everyone. Therefore the net trade is the same for all agents. In other words, a dominant strategy mechanism assigns an agent a net trade that, in infinite economies, is completely independent of the message sent by that agent. Truthfulness is a dominant strategy: there is no incentive to lie. But any other message is also a best strategy: *There is no incentive to tell the truth.* This indifference of the agents—which is an inherent feature of collective public decision making for infinite nonatomic set of agents—contrasts with what happens in private goods economies. In private goods economies an agent is strongly induced to announce its true utility function since, if it reports another utility function, it will get a net trade that maximizes, under an unchanged budget constraint, the latter function. This is the second important difference between private goods economies and public goods economies. As a consequence, if the fair-efficient mechanism is used in a large but finite public goods economy, the best strategy of an agent may be very far from truthtelling (even if the other agents tell the truth). A fortiori a Nash equilibrium may lead to very inefficient allocations even if the strategies are almost dominant strategies. That such an unfortunate phenomenon may occur has been pointed out by Groves and Ledyard (1985).

The preceding discussion leads to a reformulation of the desirable incentive properties of large economies. Can a dominant strategy mechanism be found that yields approximately efficient allocations in large but finite economies? If the answer is yes, it means that an a priori ignorant Center

(C3) should be able, when the number of agents is large, *to extract an accurate information from the agents* and *simultaneously to exploit this information to attain efficiency*. In short, the value of prior statistical information (C2) would become negligible when the number of agents increases (at least if the preferences are quasi linear). This problem is examined in the next section.

2.5   The Social Value of Prior Statistical Information

As far as we know, the problem we want to discuss has not been treated in the existing literature. However, it is beyond to scope of this chapter to provide a complete formal analysis. Therefore we shall only try to formulate conjectures and to explain, in a simplified framework, why they look reasonable.

The number of public goods is reduced to one, the same as for private goods. The parameters' space is one dimensional ($l = 1$) and A is a *bounded* interval of $\mathbb{R}$. The unit costs of the public good can be taken equal to one. Then an allocation $(\mathbf{x}, y)$ is feasible if

$$\int_T x d\lambda + y \leqq 0.$$

Finally, we assume that the function v—we have $u(a, x, y) = v(a, y) + x$— is such that the marginal rate of substitution between the public and the private goods is monotonic with respect to a, or, for example,

$$\frac{\partial^2 v}{\partial y \, \partial a} > 0.$$

This assumption, which is often made in the literature, simplifies the characterization of dominant strategy mechanisms.

Let us consider a direct anonymous mechanism, that is, a couple of functions $f_x : A \times N \to \mathbb{R}$ and $f_y : N \to \mathbb{R}_+$. The function f_y which determines the public goods quantity is also called a *public decision function*. In principle, a mechanism is defined for economies that have the same set of agents $(T, \mathcal{T}, \lambda)$, that is, for all economies of the same size. Let us call k the size of the economy, with $k = |T|$. We will index by k the mechanisms that we consider by the size of the economy to which they are adapted. For example, f_y^k will denote a symmetric function from A^k into $\mathbb{R}_+$. Of course, a mechanism (f_x^∞, f_y^∞) for infinite economies defines also a mechanism for finite economies of any size.

Within the set of anonymous direct mechanisms, we want to characterize the dominant strategy mechanisms. For infinite economies, this is easy. Consider an arbitrary public decision function $f_y^\infty : N \to \mathbb{R}_+$. Let us add the following function f_x^∞ defined by

$$f_y^\infty(a, \mu) = -f_y(\mu), \qquad \text{for all } a \text{ in } A \text{ and } \mu \text{ in } N.$$

The couple (f_y^∞, f_x^∞) is a dominant strategy mechanism, and in this way we get all of the dominant strategy mechanisms for infinite economies. We say that a public decision function f_y^k is *k-implementable in dominant strategies* if it is possible to find a function f_x^k such that the couple (f_x^k, f_y^k) is a dominant strategy mechanism for economies of size k. We have just seen that an arbitrary public decision function is ∞-implementable in dominant strategies. What about implementability for a finite k?

It is well known that, under our assumptions, k-implementable public decision functions have a simple characterization: a public decision function f_y^k is k-implementable if and only if it is *nondecreasing with respect to each of its arguments*. Hence, as a consequence, a general public decision function $f_y^\infty : N \to \mathbb{R}_+$ is k-implementable for all k if and only if *it is weakly increasing* in the following sense:

$$\{\mu' \gtrsim \mu\} \Rightarrow \{f_y^\infty(\mu') \geq f_y^\infty(\mu)\},$$

where $\gtrsim$ denotes the relation of stochastic dominance on the set N of probability measures on $A : \mu' \gtrsim \mu$ if and only if, for all a in A, $\mu'((-\infty, a]) \leq \mu((-\infty, a])$.

We are in a position to formulate the following *technical conjecture*: Let f_y^∞ be a general public decision function that is continuous on N and weakly increasing. Then, for every finite k, there exists a function f_x^k such that

1. the couple (f_x^k, f_y^∞) is a dominant strategy mechanism for economies of size k, and

2. $|f_x^k + f_y^\infty|$ tends uniformly to zero when $k \to \infty$.

In other words, the sequence of dominant strategy mechanisms (f_x^k, f_y^∞) converges when $k \to \infty$ toward the dominant strategy mechanism for infinite economies (f_x^∞, f_y^∞) with $f_x^\infty(a, \mu) = -f^\infty(\mu)$

After these technical preliminaries, we return to the question raised at the end of the preceding section. We want to find dominant strategy mechanisms that yield approximately efficient allocations in large economies. Since the utility functions are quasi linear, an allocation $(\mathbf{x}, y)$ is efficient if and only if it maximizes the sum of the utility levels:

$$\int_T (v(\alpha(t), y) + \mathbf{x}(t))d\lambda.$$

Of course, all efficient allocations of a given economy have the same public goods level, which is defined by the public decision rule corresponding to the fair-efficient mechanism f_y^e. It is easy to verify that the unique efficient public decision function f_y^e is weakly increasing and continuous. Then, if we accept the preceding technical conjecture, we believe in the following statement: for economies of size k, there exists *a dominant strategy mechanism yielding allocations that are approximately fair when k is large.*

This conjecture answers the connected question about the value for the Center of any accurate statistical information available before designing a mechanism for large economies. This value is negligible as far as the Center is concerned only with mere efficiency, which means, in this framework, that its welfare criterion is the *utilitarian Social Welfare Function* (SWF) equal to the sum of the utility levels. However, the preceding analysis invites us to broaden the question: What about the social value of prior statistical information for other SWF? Let us, for example, introduce the following family of SWF:

$$\int_T h(v(\alpha(t), y) + \mathbf{x}(t))d\lambda,$$

where h is a strictly increasing and concave function from $\mathbb{R}$ into $\mathbb{R}$. The standard second-best analysis amounts to maximizing a SWF (which often belongs to the above family) over the set of equitable allocations in infinite economies. By analogy with the utilitarian case, let us denote by f_y^h the public decision function that results from the maximization of the SWF (corresponding to the function h) over the set of equitable allocations. If h is linear, f_y^h coincide with the efficient decision function f_y^e. But, when h is strictly concave, f_y^h will typically differ from f_y^e. Hence we call it a *second-best public decision function*. In infinite economies the dominant strategy mechanism (f_y^h, f_x^∞), with $f_x^\infty(a, \mu) = -f_y^h(\mu)$, subsumes what the Center can do, taking into account the incentive constraints and its welfare criterion. However, when h is strictly concave, f_y^h is generally not weakly increasing. Therefore we conjecture that it is not possible to devise a dominant strategy mechanism yielding approximately second-best allocations in large but finite economies. It also means that prior statistical information keeps a positive social value: if the Center has enough statistical information, it can design a dominant strategy mechanism that approaches the second-best optimum in large economies with a distribution of preferences close to the expected one.

Similar phenomena can also arise in private goods economies ($m > 0$, $n = 0$). Then second-best analysis leads to nonlinear pricing. When the nonlinear pricing scheme does not discriminate completely among consumers with different characteristics—consumers with different characteristics are "bunched" into the same net trade—it is likely that prior statistical information remains valuable even in large private goods economies.

Johansen (1981), when reviewing the book by Green and Laffont (1979), expressed the opinion that the literature on incentive-compatible mechanisms, to which Green and Laffont had made a major contribution, had underestimated the value, for public decision making, of a priori information on the distribution of agents preferences. Because the literature in question was narrowly concerned with mere efficiency under the assumption of quasi-linear preferences, such a neglect was justified. But the analysis of this section supports Johansen's intuition in any context where public decision is doomed to stay within second-best limits.

References

d'Aspremont, C., and L. A. Gérard-Varet. 1979. "On Bayesian Incentive Compatible Mechanism." In *Aggregation and Revelation of Preferences*, edited by J.-J. Laffont, Amsterdam: North Holland, 269–288.

Atkinson, A. B. 1973. "How Progressive Should Income Tax Be?" In *Essays in Modern Economics*, edited by J. M. Parkin, and A. Nobay, New York: Macmillan.

Champsaur, P., and G. Laroque. 1981a. "Le plan face aux comportements stratégiques des unités décentralisées." *Annales de l'INSEE* 42:3–29.

Champsaur, P., and G. Laroque. 1981b. "Fair Allocations in Large Economies." *Journal of Economic Theory* 25:269–282.

Champsaur, P., and G. Laroque. 1982. "A Note on Incentives in Large Economies." *Review of Economic Studies* 49:627–635.

Clarke, E. H. 1971. "Multipart Pricing of Public Goods." *Public Choice* 8:19–23.

Dubey, P., A. Mas-Colell, and M. Shubik. 1980. "Efficiency Properties of Strategic Market Games: An Axiomatic Approach." *Journal of Economic Theory* 22:339–362.

Green, J., and J.-J. Laffont. 1979. *Incentives in Public Decision Making.* Amsterdam: North Holland.

Groves, T., and J. Ledyard. 1977. "Optimal Allocation of Public Goods: A Solution to the 'Free Rider' Problem." *Econometrica* 45:783–809.

Groves, T., and J. Ledyard. 1985. "Incentive Compatibility Ten Years Later." Northwestern University and California Institute of Technology.

Guesnerie, R. Forthcoming. "A Contribution in the Theory of Taxation." In *The Series of Econometric Society Monographs.*

Hammond, P. 1979. "Straightforward Individual Incentive Compatibility in Large Economies." *Review of Economic Studies* 40:263–282.

Hurwicz, L. 1972. "On Informationally Decentralized Systems." In *Decision and Organization: A Volume in Honor of Jacob Marschak,* edited by R. Radner, and C. B. McGuire, Amsterdam: North Holland, 297–336.

Hurwicz, L. 1975. "On the Existence of Allocation Systems Whose Manipulative Nash Equilibria are Pareto-Optimal." Paper presented at the Third World Congress of the Econometric Society in Toronto.

Hurwicz, L. 1979a. "Outcome Functions Yielding Walrasian and Lindahl Allocations at Nash Equilibrium Points." *Review of Economic Studies* 46:217–225.

Hurwicz, L. 1979b. "On Allocations Attainable Through Nash Equilibria." In *Aggregation and Revelation of Preferences,* edited by J.-J. Laffont, Amsterdam: North Holland, 337–419.

Johansen, L. 1981. "Review and Comments on 'Incentives in Public Decision Making' by J. R. Green and J.-J. Laffont." *Journal of Public Economics* 16:123–128.

Laffont, J.-J., and E. Maskin. 1979. "A Differential Approach to Expected Utility Maximizing Mechanisms." In *Aggregation and Revelation of Preferences,* edited by J.-J. Laffont, Amsterdam: North Holland, 289–308.

Ledyard, J., and J. Roberts. 1974. "On the Incentive Problem with Public Goods." Discussion Paper 116, Center for Mathematical Studies in Economics and Management Science, Northwestern University.

Mirrlees, J. A. 1971. "An Exploration in the Theory of Optimal Income Taxation." *Review of Economic Studies* 38:175–208.

Postlewaite, A., and J. Roberts. 1976. "The Incentives for Price-taking Behavior in Large Economies." *Econometrica* 44:115–128.

Roberts, J. 1976. "The Incentives for the Correct Revelation of Preferences and the Number of Consumers." *Journal of Public Economics* 6:359–374.

Schmeidler, D. 1980. "Walrasian Analysis via Strategic Outcome Functions." *Econometrica* 48:1585–1593.

Varian, H. R. 1976. "Two Problems in the Theory of Fairness." *Journal of Public Economics* 5:249–260.

Vickrey, W. 1961. "Counterspeculation, Auctions, and Competitive Sealed Tenders." *Journal of Finance* 16:8–37.

Walker, M. 1978. "A Note on the Characterization of Mechanisms for the Revelation of Preferences." *Econometrica* 46:147–158.

Walker, M. 1981. "A Simple Incentive Compatible Scheme for Attaining Lindahl Allocations." *Econometrica* 49:65–71.

COMMENTS
ROBIN BOADWAY

Sitting through the first half of this three-day symposium listening to a very distinguished group of speakers recount the contributions of CORE members to economic theory, one might come away with the impression that, at CORE, economic theory is game theory. This, I think, would be a mistaken impression of the breadth of the work that has gone on here over the past two decades. The contributions to game theory and its applications have obviously been outstanding. So too have been CORE's contributions in a number of other areas.

I cite as only one example of this the important fields of public and welfare economics. A similarly impressive list of contributions to that compiled by Professor Aumann this morning for game theory could well have been replicated for public and welfare economics. The list would include, among other items, such areas as public enterprise economics, second-best theory, social choice (both positive and normative), fiscal federalism, public goods theory, project evaluation, income distribution, and tax theory. It would not be completely isolated from game theory (no area of economics can be), but it would not be dependent on its methods. Its collaborators would include the usual mix of strong permanent members and distinguished visitors, many of whom are present at this symposium. Its work would be characterized by an extraordinary degree of joint authorship, reflecting something about the special atmosphere of CORE, as well as an overriding interest in normative and policy-related economics.

One manifestation of this diversity lies in the fact that the title of this session "Information, Incentives and General Equilibrium," means quite different things to different people. The relevance of informational constraints depends upon the question one is interested in addressing. When I was told the title of the session for which I would be a discussant, I drafted a rough set of comments I thought appropriate to the title. As it turned out, my comments addressed a completely different area of information, that of asymmetric information, than what Paul Champsaur so ably surveyed. Since my prepared comments complement those of the paper, and since this session is designed to be in the nature of a survey, I think the audience would be much better served by them than by any, essentially peripheral, comments I could add to those of Peter Hammond's about Paul Champsaur's splendid synthesis.

I would particularly like to highlight some of the unfortunate consequences that the existence of asymmetric information has for traditional welfare economics. I would also like to suggest that these consequences leave us with plenty to fill the research agenda of CORE's public finance economists for the next twenty years!

There is a wide literature on the properties of different allocation mechanisms under informational constraints, a literature into which Paul Champsaur's chapter would fall. My comments will be restricted to a particular mechanism—the competitive price system. I intend to indicate the sorts of results that exist on the welfare economics of competitive allocations in the presence of asymmetric information. My comments can be brief because, despite the fundamental problems that asymmetric information poses for welfare economics, the literature is small and substantive results have only been obtained on a piecemeal basis for a number of specific cases.

As an organizing principle, let me refer to the two fundamental theorems of welfare economics that apply in models of full information with conventional restrictions on preferences and technology:

THEOREM 1   Every competitive equilibrium attained as one varies initial endowment patterns is Pareto optimal.

THEOREM 2   Any Pareto-optimal allocation of resources can be obtained by some competitive equilibrium with a suitable initial allocation of endowments.

Loosely speaking, theorem 1 refers to the efficiency properties of competitive equilibria, whereas theorem 2 is relevant for equity considerations. Put differently, instances of failure of the first theorem (so-called market failures) give rise to efficiency arguments for market intervention. Thus the existence of externalities, public goods, and nonconvexities may be used to justify corrective taxes and subsidies, public provision, or regulation. We rule out these sources of market failure in what follows. In accordance with the second theorem, equity concerns can be attended to by appropriate lump-sum redistributions of endowments or income in an otherwise decentralized economy. In this way any point on society's efficiency or Pareto frontier can be reached.

What happens to these two theorems is a world of asymmetric information? The answer to that question depends upon the circumstances under consideration. The essence of asymmetric information is that agents possess some private information about themselves that is denied to other agents (including the government) with whom they trade. This information can be characterized as one of two types:

1. It may concern an individual characteristic that differs across persons, such as ability, tastes, and health. Private information of this sort gives rise to problems of adverse selection.

2. It may concern the behavior or activities of an individual (preventive activity, smoking or drinking habits, levels of effort, etc.). The inability to observe these publicly gives rise to problems of moral hazard.

In either case the information concerned is private both to other agents and to the government, although both are typically assumed to have statistical information. Furthermore the private information may or may not involve phenomena for which there is social risk, although most applications assume there is not. Given this informational disadvantage of other agents and government, we must refine our notion of Pareto optimality. Since full information Pareto-optimal allocations are no longer feasible, we defined a restricted notion of efficiency called *constrained Pareto optimality*. It refers to the set of allocations that maximizes a weighted sum of utilities subject to both a resource constraint and an information constraint (a self-selection or an incentive constraint).

At this time there does not exist a general theory of welfare economics under asymmetric information. Instead, there are a series of specific results. In the following, I report the sort of results obtained according to which of the fundamental theorems they affect, and according to type of private information.

Theorem 1 (Every Competitive Equilibrium Is Pareto Optimal)

Consider first the case of moral hazard. It has been demonstrated in the literature that there are certain cases in which competitive equilibria are constrained Pareto optimal in the presence of moral hazard. Unfortunately, the restrictions required are quite severe. For example, the theorem applies in single commodity economies where the moral hazard affects the size of contingent outcomes, but not their probabilities, and where insurers can observe total purchases. When any of these requirements are not satisfied, market failure occurs. Pauly (1974) has shown this for the case in which total purchases are not observable, and Marshall (1976) has shown it for the case in which the person with the private information can influence the probability of outcomes. Recently, Arnott and Stiglitz (1986) have demonstrated how market failure occurs in multicommodity settings and how differential commodity taxation can be welfare improving. On the other hand, Prescott and Townsend (1984) have shown that if trading takes place in contingent markets ex ante, and if no trading is allowed ex post (after the state of nature has been revealed), Arrow-Debreu competitive markets are Pareto optimal despite moral hazard. Obviously, these conditions are quite stringent as well.

The results for adverse selection are somewhat more promising, once we have settled on an appropriate equilibrium concept. The most explicit results have been obtained in the context of insurance markets, though similar phenomena exist in other contexts, such as durable goods markets or labor markets, both with unobserved quality.

For some equilibrium concepts, such as that of Rothschild and Stiglitz (1976), an equilibrium may not exist. In such cases market intervention through, say, compulsory public insurance may be welfare improving. However, it has been shown by Wilson (1977) that for his concept of equilibrium, which generally exists, allocations are constrained Pareto optimal. Furthermore Wilson claims that for other behavioral assumptions, he could always devise an equilibrium concept that would satisfy existence and be constrained Pareto optimal. If this is the case, no efficiency case for public sector intervention exists.

Theorem 2 (Every Pareto-Optimal Allocation Can Be Attained by a Competitive Equilibrium)

Here we must be much more pessimistic, especially when viewed from the point of view of the ability to implement policy. In general, the set of constrained Pareto optima attainable under asymmetric information will depend upon the initial allocation of endowments (of wealth, abilities, etc.). When there are many goods and activities, any of the constrained Pareto-optimal allocations can only be attained with highly nonlinear tax or price schedules, regardless of whether the source of imperfect information is moral hazard or adverse selection (see Mirrlees 1974). What we have is a generalization of the theory of second best allowing for the possibility of nonlinear instruments. Given the desirability of nonlinear pricing, constrained Pareto optima cannot be construed as competitive equilibria in the usual sense of the word.

Something is retrieved in certain special circumstances. For example, under rather weak restrictions, aggregate productive efficiency is desirable, so decentralization of production decisions is optimal, and nonlinear pricing occurs only in the consumption sector (see Diamond and Mirrlees 1971). Note, however, that the aggregate production efficiency results requires that the government be otherwise choosing its policy instruments optimally. Also, in an economy with many consumer goods and leisure, separability of leisure from goods allows one to avoid non-linear prices on the goods (Atkinson and Stiglitz 1980).

The demanding nature of optimal intervention rules under asymmetric information partly reflects the fact that the notion of constrained Pareto optimality is a very strong requirement. It assumes that the only thing the planner does not know is the private information of each agent. The planner has statistical information available and knows everything else about the economy (including consumer preferences). The strength of this informational requirement is demonstrated by the fact that, if actually implemented, the optimal policy would induce people to reveal their true characteristics by their behavior. The planner could then use that to achieve the first-best or unconstrained Pareto optimum. So far, no natural way has been proposed to weaken this requirement.

One common procedure for avoiding these complications is to restrict the policy instruments in some arbitrary away. For example, as in the traditional theory of second best, one might restrict taxes to be linear, whether they be commodity or income taxes. One might also restrict the economic variables that can be observed. For example, the planner may observe earnings but not wage rates. However, imposing restrictions such as linearity can have unfortunate policy consequences. As Roger Guesnerie and Kevin Roberts (1987) makes clear, if restrictions such as linearity are imposed on some instruments so that the constrained Pareto optimum is not attained, the use of other non-tax instruments such as quantity rationing or price fixing (for example, minimum wages) can be welfare improving.

It seems to me that we are still a long way off from obtaining convincing policy implications for models with asymmetric information. More to the point, it seems that the informationally constrained Pareto optimum is an impossible goal for the planner to achieve. Perhaps more informationally based constraints are waiting to be discovered which will move policy into the realm of the possible. This should provide more than enough work to keep CORE's public economists busy for the next twenty years.

References

Arnott, R., and J. E. Stiglitz. 1986. "Moral Hazard and Optimal Commodity Taxation." *Journal of Public Economics* 29:1–24.

Atkinson, A. B., and J. E. Stiglitz. 1980. *Lectures in Public Economics*. New York: McGraw-Hill.

Diamond, P. A., and J. A. Mirrlees. 1971. "Optimal Taxation and Public Production: I. Production Efficiency." *American Economic Review* 61:8–27.

Guesnerie, R., and K. Roberts. 1987. "Minimum Wage Legislation as a Second Best Policy." *European Economic Review* 31:490–498.

Marshall, J. M. 1976. "Moral Hazard." *American Economic Review* 66:880–890.

Mirrlees, J. A. 1974. "Notes on Welfare Economics, Information and Uncertainty." In *Essays on Economic Behaviour under Uncertainty*, edited by M. S. Balch, D. L. McFadden, and S. Y. Wu. Amsterdam: North Holland, ch. 9.

Pauly, M. 1974. "Overinsurance and Public Provision of Insurance." *Quarterly Journal of Economics* 88:44–62.

Prescott, E. C., and R. M. Townsend. 1984. "Pareto Optima and Competitive Equilibria with Adverse Selection and Moral Hazard." *Econometrica* 52:21–45.

Rothschild, M., and J. E. Stiglitz. 1976. "Equilibrium in Competitive Insurance Markets: An Essay in the Economics of Imperfect Information." *Quarterly Journal of Economics* 90:629–649.

Wilson, C. 1977. "A Model of Insurance Markets with Incomplete Information." *Journal of Economic Theory* 16:167–207.

COMMENTS
PETER J. HAMMOND

It is an honor to be invited to speak on such an auspicious occasion, and to be allowed to discuss a paper so worthy of the occasion. I have to say that I feel not only like a newcomer, but like a son who is asked to speak at his parents' wedding anniversary. One is aware of celebrating not only an event that has had great influence—not entirely understood—on one's career as an economist but also of the privilege of spending some time as a welcome guest at Europe's premier research center in economics.

Paul Champsaur's admirable paper represents a bridge linking, on one side, the theoretical work on continuum economies which Werner Hildenbrand discusses elsewhere in this volume and on game theory which is Robert Aumann's subject, with, on the other side, more practical issues of economic policy.

First, recall that in principle Paul faced the impossible task of surveying twenty years of progress in economic theory at CORE during the space of just sixty minutes. He entered the realm of the possible by confining himself to a single topic, entirely appropriate for a member of the French "Direction de la Prévision." I believe that later historians of economic thought are very likely to see the last twenty years as marking the beginning of an "information revolution" in the evolution of mathematical economics. There has been an explosion in our understanding of the problems created when agents differ in their information about certain relevant aspects of the economic environment—problems of differential information.

Historical Background

Before CORE's foundation, the formal analysis of differential information was almost inexistant. There were good informal discussions, of course, and Kenneth Arrow's work on the welfare economics of medical care (if one may be permitted to cite work by a colleague). Yet, in general equilibrium theory, almost nothing had been done. Indeed, Roy Radner published an important paper in *Econometrica* in 1968. There he took the view that an agent unable to distinguish between two possible events at a given date must have the same contingent net trade vector in these two events. This corresponds with the natural restriction in game theory that if an agent cannot tell apart two different nodes of an extensive game tree because they are in the same set of his information partition, then his strategy choices at those two nodes must coincide. But this ignores the possibility of communication before or during the game (possibilities which, in the theory of games, extend greatly the set of equilibria, as Françoise Forges has been discovering in an important series of papers). In economic environments there is also the possibility that agents may be able to infer much or all of the information originally unavailable to them simply by observing market prices—a possibility that Roy Radner himself has, among others, done much to explore in the course of the last ten years.

Around the time that CORE was founded, much interest was aroused in iterative, planning procedures through the work of Edmond Malinvaud (notably in the volume edited by Malinvaud and Bacharach in the *Review of Economic Studies*) and Geoffrey Heal (in his Ph.D. thesis, the *Review of Economic Studies*, and his book on *The Theory of Economic Planning*). An important paper by J. Drèze and D. de la Vallée-Poussin also appeared in the *Review*, and the MDP procedure received its name. Yet, as later papers by John Roberts, Claude Henry, Henry Tulkens, and Françoise Schoumaker served to show, the success of the MDP procedure is somewhat problematic in economics with differential information even if agents are myopic. When agents start to anticipate the allocation where the procedure will finally come to rest, Paul Champsaur, himself, in collaboration with Guy Laroque, and also Michel Truchon, showed a few years ago that the MPD procedure has rather serious problems associated with it. Their work forces us to turn attention first toward characterizing those truly feasible allocations to which an iterative procedure might be expected to converge.

This literature on planning procedures promised to shed light on a highly significant question for the design and comparison of economic systems— whether to use prices as quantities, markets, or a command economy. Yet, with fully information and increasingly powerful techniques of mathematical optimization, this is hardly an interesting question. It is *precisely* when information differs between agents that both market and command economies experience difficulties, so that comparison of economic systems becomes meaningful. And, before discussing iterative planning procedures, one first needs a new understanding of what allocations are *feasible* when planners, market participants, or other institutions and agencies, are incompletely informed about other participants in the economy.

The next developments I have to report prove that CORE does not quite have a monopoly of good ideas. In fact, Leo Hurwicz and Ted Groves in particular were working elsewhere on incentive compatible mechanisms. John Harsanyi had devised a fundamental methodology for creating games on incomplete information, of which economies with differential information effectively form a subset. George Akerlof wrote a famous paper on the market for "lemons" (thus teaching European speakers of English a slang term for dud secondhand cars) or, more important, rural credit markets in India and other less developed countries. Joe Stiglitz, on his own and in collaboration with numerous others, wrote a series of papers on markets with incomplete information and also participated in editing two symposia on the subject in the mid-1970s (in the *Quarterly Journal of Economics* and the *Review of Economic Studies*). Jerry Green and Jean-Jacques Laffont collaborated on a series of papers and then their book on *Incentive in Public Decision Making*. The explosion was well under way. Enough material was produced to make Paul Champsaur's task of surveying some of what has happened since then still far from easy.

Recurrent Position

After this discussion of some of the background to Paul Champsaur's chapter, let us move to some observations as to where we stand now.

Champsaur, together with other economists whose work he reports, and some he does not, seems to me to establish that differential information—in particular, privacy of information about tastes, endowments, and productive capacities—changes the whole discipline of economics rather drastically, because of the following eight observations:

1. *Allocation mechanisms.* In general, differential information can only occur when there is uncertainty about the economic environment itself. Thus the economic allocation will vary with the environment, usually, and one must then describe the *allocation mechanism* that specifies the economic allocation as a function of the environment. A notable exception, of course, is the special case that receives much attention in the literature when the following three conditions are all met. First, the differential information should concern only each individual's personal characteristics—tastes, endowments, productive capacities, assets, and all other features of the individual that are pertinent to the economic allocation. This is the case of private information regarding individual characteristics. Second, the distribution of individual characteristics in the population should have been known—perhaps through a very carefully constructed anonymous sampling procedure that encourages truthful revelation of individual characteristics. Third, the mechanism should treat all individuals symmetrically so that the allocation of public goods depends only on the distribution of personal characteristics and that of private goods on both this distribution and the individual characteristic of the recipient (or supplier). In this special case the allocation is determined as a function that maps personal characteristics to their net demand vectors, and all that is uncertain is who is who and so who gets what net demand vector for private goods. It is hard to see how this special case could ever occur except in a continuum economy, as the limit of a sequence of increasingly large finite economics.

2. *Implementing mechanisms.* An obvious way of trying to implement an allocation mechanism is to ask everybody to report directly what they know, and then arrange the corresponding economic allocation. This has the obvious defect that individuals are likely to find advantages in concealing their private information or being deceptive. Thus theorists have been led to consider more indirect approaches. And of course actual economic systems nearly always use indirect approaches. These are immensely complicated games of buying, selling, haggling, bargaining, price determination, trading strategies, drawing up production and investment plans. Thus an

economic system amounts to a game of incomplete information, far too complicated to describe, let alone analyze fully. In this game of incomplete information we may presume that agents choose Harsanyi equilibrium strategies based upon their private information and also on what they understand of how the economic system works. This game is really the economic system that determines the economic allocation mechanism. Often, the game is called a "mechanism," as in Champsaur's chapter. I prefer to call it an *implementing mechanism*. It is presumed to determine the allocation mechanism as a function of economic agent's *strategy rules*, each of which maps their information into a strategy in the implementing mechanism.

3. *The revelation principle and incentive constraints.* Consider a Harsanyi equilibrium profile of strategy rules in the implementing mechanism for each agent in the economy. These strategy rules give rise to an allocation mechanism in the economic system. Say that the resultant allocation mechanism is *implemented* through the Harsanyi equilibrium of the implementing mechanism. Now, in the implementing mechanism, it is always open to the agent to use deceptive strategies, behaving exactly as if their information were different. This is true even if their information is not exclusive; for instance, the economy must be able to function even if somebody tries to behave as though he were much more wealthy than he is known to be. Consider, then, any alteration in the information of an individual, and the resulting change (if any) in the allocation that emerges from the allocation mechanism that is implemented by the Harsanyi equilibrium in the implementing mechanism. This change of allocation cannot be to the individual's advantage; otherwise he would want to upset the Harsanyi equilibrium by using the deceptive strategy of pretending that his information had altered. This means that the allocation mechanism itself must deter such deception. Viewed, then, as a direct implementing mechanism, the allocation mechanism must not discourage the honest revelation of information. This is the famous *revelation principle*, in a rather more general form than has usually been considered (see Myerson, *Journal of Mathematical Economics*, 1982, and the recent book edited by Hurwicz, Schmeidler, and Sonnenschein, 1985). It requires the allocation mechanism to be *incentive compatible*, or to satisfy *incentive constraints* that prevent the agents gaining from being deceptive. Meeting such constraints is a necessary condition for an allocation mechanism to be truly feasible in as much as, if they are violated, then any attempts to implement the

allocation mechanism will result in a different allocation mechanism. In principle, the condition is sufficient because the allocation mechanism can be used to implement itself, but in practice, there may be other restrictions because of complexity, multiple equilibria, dynamic considerations, the difficulty of eliciting reasonable summaries of information (Green, *Journal of Economic Theory*, 1983), and so on.

4. *Second best.* If incentive constraints did nothing to prevent the attainment of full information, "first-best" Pareto-efficient allocations, one could perhaps afford to neglect them. In fact, as Champsaur points out, if one insists on both full information Pareto efficiency and incentive compatibility, there is rarely much scope, if any, for income redistribution. Typically, one is reduced to selecting Walrasian equilibria without lump-sum redistribution in private goods economies, or Lindahl equilibria with public goods production financed by a uniform poll tax. An obvious corollary is that almost all of the allocation mechanisms that produce first-best allocations are incentive incompatible, because they do have to rely on lump-sum redistribution. One enters the world of the second best.

5. *Incentive incompatibility of Walrasian allocations.* Not even Walrasian allocation mechanisms may be incentive compatible, however. These mimic perfectly competitive equilibrium in complete markets without any lump-sum redistribution. The problem is that any agent is usually able to turn the terms of trade in his own favor by a deceptive strategy that implicitly understates his true willingness to trade. There are three exceptional cases where this power can be made to disappear. The first is a continuum economy in which no agent is powerful enough to affect the apparent equilibrium price vector. The second is an economy in which there is no private information, because all agents know everything about each other. Then, even though a market organizer may know nothing about the agents, a Hurwicz mechanism can be used to implement Walrasian allocations through Nash equilibrium strategies in the agents' game of complete information. The third case is when there are quasi-linear preferences, as discussed by Champsaur and in the original work by Claude d'Aspremont and Louis-André Gérard-Varet.

6. *Constrained Pareto efficiency and desirable "distortions."* Attempts to implement Walrasian or other allocation mechanism yielding first-best Pareto-efficient allocations have been numerous, but they have been seriously misleading. Incentive constraints prevent the attainment of at

most a few points of the first-best Pareto frontier, which implies the existence of a "second-best" frontier, subject to incentive constraints. Most of its points lie below those on the first-best frontier. Second-best Pareto efficiency relative to incentive constraints requires what first-best welfare theory regards as "distortions," such as taxes, rationing, or even minimum wage legislation (as in a recent paper by Guesnerie and Roberts). Thus true optimality may well imply what first-best welfare economics has come to call, very misleadingly, "deadweight loss," or the "excess burden" of taxation. It is time to abandon such terminology. The losses and burdens are illusory, at least in part. Elementary textbooks tell us how, in a one consumer world, they can be replaced by a lump-sum tax that is better for the consumer. They imply, and advanced textbooks state, that the Pareto improvement is also possible with many consumers with differential lump-sum taxation. But such taxation is almost always incentive incompatible, so not truly feasible.

That is not to say that *all* taxes are Pareto efficient relative to incentive constraints. Many, of course, are very inefficient. But welfare economists and public finance theorists need to turn their attention to Pareto and welfare improvements in *incentive-compatible* taxation schemes. Indeed, may one yet hope for a Drèze iterative procedure for improving incentive-compatible allocation mechanisms (even it comes from Jean rather than Jacques)?

7. *Markets as constraints.* Enforcing allocation mechanisms, even if they are incentive compatible, typical requires restraints on the freedom of agents to trade as they please. Typical second-best mechanisms require taxes, rationing, market controls, minimum wages, usury laws, and so on. They create obvious temptations for tax evasions, black marketing, and generally for trading in a hidden economy. In the extreme, unless such activities can be monitored and controlled, only laissez-faire is possible. By now one has entered a third-best world. In first-best welfare theory, free markets are usually seen as the instruments of good economic policy. In third-best welfare theory, "market forces" become additional constraints on the attainment of a second-best Pareto-efficient economic allocation mechanism—constraints even more restrictive than the incentive constraints discussed above. It turns out that the true cost of "market distortions" is often the administrative cost of restricting market forces, and not the alleged efficiency loss that is contructed on the pretence that there are no incentive constraints.

8. *Emigration and credit constraints.* In an economy where no attempt is made to redistribute real income, and where are no externalities, public goods, or obstacles to complete markets, a Walrasian allocation mechanism *may* be incentive compatible and first-, second-, and third-best Pareto efficient (see observation 5 above). With public goods, and an emigration constraint (which is surely rather more plausible than individual rationality, which cannot necessarily even be interpreted as a constraint preventing suicide), not even the fair and efficient mechanism which Champsaur has discussed may be feasible. Then first-best Pareto efficiency is lost irretrievably. Another fundamental obstacle to first-best efficiency occurs in simple sequence economies, where Keynesian moral hazard associated with the repayment of debt intervenes.

Conclusion

In my reflections on the topics covered in Paul Champsaur's chapter, I have tried to include more of the historical background to explain why this is a highly significant area of research in economic theory, likely to have profound implications for future research and even, I would hope, for the way more practically minded economists discuss policy. The substitution of my "Pareto efficiency" for the "general equilibrium" of Champsaur's title is no accident; the implications of this work go far beyond recognized general equilibrium theory.

Finally, Champsaur points to a glaring gap in literature, which I feel especially acutely. There are many quite elegant and general results for continuum economies, together with some useful positive results for rather special finite economies. But those elegant results for continuum economies need to be given more practical expression as limiting results for incentive-compatible mechanisms in large finite economies. At present the best we have are the results of Roberts and Postlewaite (1976), Roberts (1976), and Palfrey and Srivastava (1986) on approximate incentive compatibility. Perhaps this is the best one can hope for. But I hope for a fuller analysis soon of this important question, preferably from one of CORE's sons or daughters, such as Paul Champsaur.

References

Champsaur, P., and G. Laroque. 1982. "Strategic Behavior in Decentralized Planning Procedure." *Econometrica* 50(2): 325–344.

d'Aspremont, C. and L. A. Gérard-Varet. 1979. "On Bayesian Incentive Compatible Mechanisms." In *Aggregation and Revelation of Preferences*, edited by J.-J. Laffont, Amsterdam: North Holland.

Hurwicz, L., Schmeidler, D., and H. Sonnenschein. 1985. *Social Goals and Social Organization: Essays in Memory of Elisha Pazner*. Cambridge: Cambridge University Press.

Palfrey, T. R., and S. Srivastava. 1986. "Private Information in Large Economies." *Journal of Economic Theory* 39:34–58.

Roberts, J., and A. Postlewaite. 1976. "The Incentives for Price Taking Behavior in Large Exchange Economies." *Econometrica* 44:115–128.

Roberts, J. 1976. "The Incentives for Correct Revelation of Preferences and the Number of Consumers." *Journal of Economics* 6:359–374.

Truchon, M. 1984, "Nonmyopic Strategic Behavior in the MDP Planning Procedure." *Econometrica* 52(5):1179–1190.

3 CORE and Equilibria of a Large Economy

Werner Hildenbrand

3.1

Usually one begins a birthday address for an old friend with a joke. This address, however, is announced in the program as an "Advanced Seminar in Mathematical Economics." Hence I have to be serious. Before I explain the difference between the core with capital and lowercase letters, let me begin with a very personal remark.

I remember still very well when in the fall of 1968 we moved into the new CORE-building in Heverlee. The building was not yet completely finished, but we could not wait, indeed important problems waited to be solved. At that time, in October 1968, I began to organize the weekly CORE Seminar in Mathematical Economics. Some of my colleagues at CORE were quite sceptical; how would I find every week a speaker with an original research paper? Where would these speakers come from? Remember in the 1960s there was not much going on in mathematical economics in Europe. The first speaker, if I remember well, was Jean Gabszewicz who reported on his thesis that he had just finished. Today he is the president of CORE and the CORE Seminar in Mathematical Economics became well-known in the profession and enjoys high prestige. No doubt, today CORE is known as one of the outstanding research institutes in the world. How was this success possible?

Surely many people, in particular, many distinguished visitors contributed to this extraordinary success of CORE. However, there was one person without whom CORE would not have been founded and would not have survived.

If today we celebrate "Twenty years of CORE," then this event means to me, and I am certain to many others in the audience, that we celebrate the extraordinary achievement of Jacques Drèze.

Dear Jacques, I would like to thank you, personally and in the name of many visitors of CORE, I would like to thank you for all what you did for the economic profession and, in particular, for mathematical economics.

When I accepted with great pleasure the invitation to speak at the present occasion I was considering to summarizing and surveying what has been

This is the written version of the invited paper presented at the CORE Mathematical Economics Seminar, January 19, 1987.

done at CORE in mathematical economics in the least twenty years. Yet quickly I realized that this is an impossible task. There are 681 CORE reprints in this period, a large fraction of which is in mathematical economics! How could *one* person in *one* hour do justice to all these contributions?

Obviously, I had to revise my plan and become more modest. I decided to take the other extreme and to tell the story of my personal affair with CORE. My view is partial and, I am afraid, most likely, controversial.

Let me recall the situation of mathematical economics in 1968. Mathematical economists at that time, and, I emphasize, in my view, were a well-defined group of people. Whatever was the academic background of the members of that group, the *absolute authority* in all questions of doubt was *Theory of Value*. Consequently the price system of an economy was a *hyperplane* in a linear space, and economic equilibrium was a *fixed point* of a suitably defined upper semicontinuous correspondence. Calculus was considered as a technique suitable for engineers since it was written in the *book* that the new developments "freed mathematical economics from its traditions of differential calculus and compromises with logic." All assumptions had to be placed exclusively on the *primitive concepts* of the model; in short, it was the period of the absolute reign of the *axiomatic method* where "the theory, in the strict sense, is logically entirely disconnected from its interpretations."

The group—I may reveal them as disciples of Gérard Debreu—not only shared the same strict methodological position, but there was also absolute agreement among the members of the group about the importance and relevance of the contributions after *Theory of Value*. Among them two fundamental papers played a decisive role. Debreu-Scarf's and Aumann's contributions to the core of an economy. This consensus on the right methodological position and the judgment what is important in mathematical economics created a unique atmosphere in the first years at CORE.

3.2

Let me begin by refreshing your memory and explaining the two fundamental contributions, I referred to before, which influenced so deeply the research in the first years at CORE.

The economic model is that of an exchange economy. Thus we consider a set A of economic agents, and every agent a is simply described by a

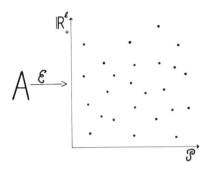

Figure 3.1

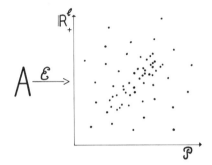

Figure 3.2

preference relation $\precsim$ on R^l_+ and a vector $e_a \in R^l_+$ of initial endowments. More formally, an exchange economy with l commodities is defined by a mapping $\mathcal{E}$ from the set A of agents into the set of agents' characteristics $\mathcal{P} \times R^l_+$, where $\mathcal{P}$ denotes the set of individual preferences and R^l the commodity space. We always assume that the vector of total endowments $e = \sum_{a \in A} e_a$ is strictly positive. (See figure 3.1.)

The "cloud" of points $(\precsim_a, e_a)$ in the space of agents' characteristics $\mathcal{P} \times R^l_+$ describes the distribution $\mu_{\mathcal{E}}$ of agents' characteristics of the economy $\mathcal{E}$ which will play an important role later, but for the moment any configuration of the "cloud" (e.g., as in figure 3.2) is allowed.

Here are the definitions of the familiar equilibrium concepts.

A *redistribution* for the economy $\mathcal{E}$ is a function f of A into R^l_+ such that

$$\sum_A f_a = \sum_A e_a.$$

A redistribution f^* is called *Walras allocation* if there exists a price vector p^* such that for every agent $a \in A$ expenditure equals income, that is, $p^* \cdot f^*(a) = p^* \cdot e_a$, and no commodity bundle x that is preferred to $f^*(a)$ belongs to the budget set, that is, $x \succ_a f^*(a)$ implies $p^* \cdot x > p^* \cdot e_a$. $W(\mathscr{E})$ denotes the set of Walras allocations.

A redistribution $\hat{f}$ is in the core $C(\mathscr{E})$ of the economy $\mathscr{E}$ if there is *no coalition* B (nonempty subset of A) such that

1. there are $y_a \in R^l_+$ for $a \in B$ with $y_a \succ_a \hat{f}(a)$, and

2. $\sum_{a \in B} y_a = \sum_{a \in B} e_a$.

From these definitions follows trivially the remarkable inclusion

$$W(\mathscr{E}) \subset C(\mathscr{E}).$$

As we know from familiar figures in the Edgeworth box the inclusion is typically strict. Since Edgeworth's famous book of 1881 we also know that the "difference" between these two equilibrium concepts becomes small or even negligible if the economy becomes competitive, that is to say, becomes large in a certain sense.

Let us make this precise. Define the difference between the two equilibrium concepts $C(\mathscr{E})$ and $W(\mathscr{E})$ by the smallest number $\delta(\mathscr{E})$ with the property: for every allocation $f \in C(\mathscr{E})$ there exists an allocation $f^* \in W(\mathscr{E})$ such that

$$|f(a) - f^*(a)| \le \delta(\mathscr{E}) \qquad \text{for every } a \in A.$$

Thus, if $\delta(\mathscr{E})$ is small, then from *every* agent's point of view *any* core allocation is like a competitive equilibrium.

We consider now a sequence of economies

$$\mathscr{E}_n : A_n \to \mathscr{P} \times R^l_+$$

with the obvious condition that the number $\# A_n$ of agents in the economy $\mathscr{E}_n$ tends to infinity. Then we ask the question, Under what circumstances do we obtain

$$\delta(\mathscr{E}_n) \to 0?$$

THEOREM (Debreu-Scarf, 1963)   *Given any economy*

$$\mathscr{E} : \{1, \dots, r\} \to \mathscr{P} \times R^l_+$$

with strictly convex and monotone preferences. Then for the sequence $\mathscr{E}_n$: $A_n \to \mathscr{P} \times R_+^l$ of replica economies, defined by

$$A_n = \{(i,j) | 1 \leq i \leq r, 1 \leq j \leq n\} \quad \text{and} \quad \precsim_{ij} = \precsim_i, e_{ij} = e_i,$$

it follows that $\delta(\mathscr{E}_n) \to 0$.

Let us pause for a moment and admire the simplicity and the beauty of this result. Our admiration would even be greater if I had the time to show the elegance of the proof. The only objection one can make—and, indeed, should make—is the assumed rigidity and symmetry in the way the sequence becomes large. Observe that the "cloud" of points in $\mathscr{P} \times R_+^l$, that is, the distribution of agents' characteristics remains the same throughout the sequence. Obviously, one would like to know whether the conclusion remains valid for sequences that become large in a less symmetric way. But before I pursue this idea, let me come to Aumann's contribution, which decisively influenced my own work, actually my interest in mathematical economics.

If asymptotically we have the equivalence of the two equilibrium concepts, then we might expect that "in the limit," that is to say, for an economy with an infinite number of agents, the two equilibrium concepts actually coincide. The important contribution of Aumann is that he has chosen the right definition of a "limit economy." It is not sufficient to consider an economy with an infinite number of agents, but one where the influence of every agent on collective actions is strictly negligible, that is to say, an atomless measure space of economic agents. To make the point simple, Aumann has chosen the unit interval $[0, 1]$ with Lebesgue measure.

Thus we define an *exchange economy with a continuum of agents* as a mapping $\mathscr{E}_\infty$ of the unit interval $[0, 1]$ into the space of agents' characteristics. For technical reasons, one has to assume that this mapping $\mathscr{E}_\infty$ is "measurable" in a certain sense. For such an economy, a redistribution, a Walras allocation and the core can be defined analogously by replacing the summation by an integral.

THEOREM (Aumann 1964) *For every economy $\mathscr{E}_\infty : [0, 1] \to \mathscr{P} \times R_+^l$ with a continuum of agents and monotone preferences it follows that*

$$W(\mathscr{E}_\infty) = C(\mathscr{E}_\infty).$$

Again I propose to pause and admire the beauty of this theorem. With the right definition of a perfectly competitive economy the two, conceptually quite different, equilibrium concepts coincide. This is neat!

I emphasize that in Aumann's theorem no convexity assumption of preferences and no restriction on the distribution of agents' characteristics is required; preferences and endowments of the participating agents can be very different or identical.

It should be clear from what I have said, even for the nonspecialist in mathematical economics that these two fundamental contributions inspired a great research activity at CORE. The two theorems were extended (e.g., to economies with atoms or with production) and were related to each other. The CORE Reprint Series contains 28 publications on this subject or related topics.

I cannot refrain from stating quickly, as an example, a simple version of a limit theorem on the core which shows that the symmetry built in a replica sequence is not essential for the shrinking of the core to the set of competitive equilibria.

Let $T = \{\precsim_i, e_i\}_{i=1,\ldots,r}$ be a finite set of agents' characteristics. Consider a sequence

$$\mathscr{E}_n : A_n \to T, \qquad n = 1, 2, \ldots,$$

of economies where $\#A_n \to \infty$. In addition we want to require that the distribution $\mu_{\mathscr{E}_n}$ of agents' characteristics of the economy $\mathscr{E}_n$ (the "cloud" in figure 3.1) converges to a "limit distribution." Since we assumed that T is a finite set, this can be made precise quite easily. In every economy we count the number of agents which are of type i, that is, we define

$$v_n(i) = \frac{1}{\#A_n} \# \{a \in A_n | \mathscr{E}_n(a) = (\precsim_i, e_i)\}.$$

Thus the distribution of agents' characteristics of the economy $\mathscr{E}_n$ is described by the frequences $v_n(i)$. The distribution $v_n(\cdot)$ can be identified with a point in the simplex $\Delta = \{x \in R_+^r | x_i > 0 \text{ and } \sum_{i=1}^r x_i = 1\}$.

We assume now that $v_n(i) \to v(i) > 0$. Thus the limit distribution $v(\cdot)$ is again a point in Δ, and defines in an obvious manner an economy $\mathscr{E}_\infty$ with a continuum of agents.

One might expect that for such sequences $(\mathscr{E}_n)$ we obtain the desired result $\delta(\mathscr{E}_n) \to 0$. Yet this is not the case. The limit economy $\mathscr{E}_\infty$ might have too many equilibria. Limit theorems of the first generation overcome this difficulty by weakening the definition $\delta(\mathscr{E})$ of "difference" between $C(\mathscr{E})$ and $W(\mathscr{E})$. Today I prefer another approach, which became possible after the development of the theory of regular economies, initiated by CRS #67 of

G. Debreu. Let us call the sequence $(\mathscr{E}_n)$ "sleek" if the set Π_n of equilibrium prices of the economy $\mathscr{E}_n$ converges to the set Π_∞ of equilibrium prices of the limit economy $\mathscr{E}_\infty$.

Obviously, replica sequences are always sleek. For sleek sequences one can, indeed, prove the desired result $\delta(\mathscr{E}_n) \to 0$, yet one cannot exclude, even under strong assumptions on the individual characteristics in T, that some sequences are not sleek. The reason for this is the fact, that the set Π of equilibrium prices of an economy does not, in general, depend continuously on the distribution $\mu_\mathscr{E}$ of agents' characteristics. This lack of determinateness, however, can be shown to be an "exceptional" case. For this claim I rely, of course, on the theory of regular economies. Perhaps I should mention here that with CRS #67 calculus became again acceptable in general equilibrium analysis; preferences were again smooth, and hence demand functions differentiable.

To be more precise about the "exceptional" cases, let us call a subset C in the simplex Δ *negligible* if it is closed and of Lebesgue measure zero. Then we obtain the following second generation

LIMIT THEOREM ON THE CORE   *Let T be a finite set of characteristics with smooth preferences. Then there exists a negligible subset C in Δ such that for every sequence $\mathscr{E}_n : A_n \to T$ whose limit distribution v does not belong to C it follows that*

$$\delta(\mathscr{E}_n) \to 0.$$

3.3

Since I decided to tell of my own affair with CORE, I took the liberty of discussing in some detail the development of limit theorems on the core of exchange economies. In the 1970s, naturally, other research topics in mathematical economics became central at CORE. I will give no details here. Let me just indicate the main research areas:

Walrasian equilibrium theory. Existence theorems for Walrasian equilibria were proved for more and more general models, with and without production; they included infinitely many agents or infinite dimensional commodity spaces, incomplete and nonconvex or nontransitive preferences, even random preferences were considered. General equilibrium analysis under uncertainty was further developed, and the theory of regular economies was initiated.

Temporary equilibrium analysis. A shift from Walras to Hicks started with a series of contributions in temporary equilibrium analysis. Many CRS papers were written on this subject.

Price rigidity, the fix-price model. The shift from Walras to Hicks went on to Keynes and received definite macroeconomic features. CRS # 225 by J. Drèze (1975) on price rigidity initiated many contributions on the fix-price model, and the "microeconomic foundations" of macroeconomics was for some time a big theme.

Equilibrium à la Cournot. This field of research was initiated by CRS # 106 by Gabszewicz and Vial (1972).

To complete the list I should also mention the contributions to allocation processes and incentive mechanism as well as contributions to utility theory with or without uncertainty and to demand analysis.

I hope that my friends, colleagues, and the visitors at CORE pardon me if I do not explain their contributions in any detail. These papers are well-known today by the profession. They were written in a stimulating atmosphere here at CORE, it was a productive and exciting period for mathematical economics.

3.4

It became quite clear in the 1970s that the problem in Walrasian, as well as in non-Walrasian, equilibrium analysis is not that equilibrium too rarely exists; just the opposite creates problems. What had been thought to be true only in specific economic circumstances turned out to be the rule, not the exception.

Indeed, in order to decide whether a system of equations

$$E_1(p_1,\ldots,p_l) = 0$$

$$\vdots \qquad\qquad \vdots$$

$$E_l(p_1,\ldots,p_l) = 0$$

has a solution it does not require much specific knowledge about the functions $E_h(\cdot)$. In what follows I interpret $E(\cdot)$ as an excess demand function of a private ownership economy. Thus I again refer to Walrasian equilibrium analysis.

For example, it is not essential that the excess demand function be derived from utility-maximizing agents; continuity and suitable "boundary behavior" of E are sufficient for existence.

In contrast to the problem of existence of economic equilibria, the determinateness of these equilibria (the solution of $E(p) = 0$) turned out to be quite an intractable problem. Obviously, determinateness can have different meanings. I have already mentioned a weak concept of determinateness when I discussed the limit theorems on the core, namely, that the set of equilibrium prices depends continuously on the parameters of the economy. The theory of regular economies gives a satisfactory answer. Again, as for existence, the theory of regular economies does not require a specific structure of the excess demand function. Differentiability is sufficient if we are satisfied with results that hold generically.

Existence theorems and the theory of regular economies definitely are great intellectual achievements; the results are deep and the arguments are beautiful. Yet economists before the Arrow-Debreu-McKenzie area had a different view of general equilibrium analysis and, in particular, of the determinateness of equilibria. Here are two typical quotations:

To some people (including, no doubt, Walras himself) the system of simultaneous equations, determining a whole price system, seems to have vast significance. They derive intense intellectual satisfaction from the contemplation of such a system of subtly interrelated prices; and the farther the analysis can be carried ... the better are they pleased, and the profounder insight into the working of a competitive economic system they feel they get.... Nevertheless, in spite of these merits, it is clear that many economists (perhaps most, even of those who have studied Walras seriously) have felt in the end a certain sterility about this approach.... Now the reason for this sterility of the Walrasian system is largely, I believe, that he did not go on to work out the laws of change for his system of General Equilibrium. He could tell what conditions must be satisfied by the prices established with given resources and given preferences; but he did not explain what would happen if tastes or resources changed. (Hicks 1946, p. 60)

It is the task of comparative statics to show the determination of the equilibrium values of given variables under postulated conditions with various data being specified.... If no more than this could be said, the economist would be truly vulnerable to the gibe that he is only a parrot taught to say "supply and demand." ... In order for the analysis to be useful it must provide information concerning the way in which our equilibrium quantities will change as a result of changes in the parameters taken as independent data. (Samuelson 1947, p. 257)

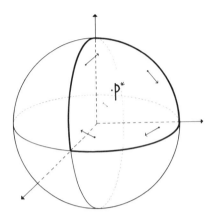

Figure 3.3

Expectations, as we all have experienced in our life, have sometimes to be revised. Since the work of Sonnenschein, Mantel, and Debreu, we all know that expectations about uniqueness and stability of Walrasian equilibria have definitely to be revised for the beloved *exchange* economies.

Let me recall the facts. The excess demand function $E_{\mathscr{E}}(\cdot)$ of an exchange economy $\mathscr{E}$, as defined earlier, is continuous, homogeneous ($E_{\mathscr{E}}(\lambda_p) = E_{\mathscr{E}}(p)$, $\lambda > 0$) and satisfies Walras identity ($p \cdot E_{\mathscr{E}}(p) = 0$). Hence an excess demand function defines a vector field on the positive sphere S_+. (See figure 3.3.) The Walrasian equilibria of the economy $\mathscr{E}$ are then called by mathematicians the singularities of the vector field.

The crucial fact now is that we cannot expect these "excess-demand" vector fields $E_{\mathscr{E}}(\cdot)$ to have any specific structure. Scarf's famous example was a first indication; he gave an example of an exchange economy whose associated vector field leads to a phase diagram (solution path of the differential equation $\dot{p} = E_{\mathscr{E}}(p)$) like that in figure 3.4. Here is what we know today.

THEOREM   *Given any continuous vector field f on S_+. For every compact subset $K \subset S$, there exists an exchange economy $\mathscr{E} : A \to \mathscr{P} \times R_+^l$ such that*

$$E_{\mathscr{E}}(p) = f(p) \quad \text{on } K.$$

The economy $\mathscr{E}$ has no pathological features, that is to say, individual preferences can be chosen to be strictly convex and monotone or smooth; they

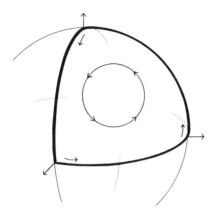

Figure 3.4

can even be chosen to be identical for all agents in A. Furthermore the individual endowment vectors can be chosen to be collinear.

What is left from our expectations about uniqueness and stability in the face of this result? The answer is clear: a purely mathematical problem. The mathematical theory, fortunately, is well developed. Indeed, the index theorem and the theory of dynamical systems give us the (weakest possible) conditions on the excess demand function (or vector field) which lead to uniqueness and stability. The problem is that these mathematical conditions have no obvious and easy economic interpretation. For example, uniqueness of equilibria (up to normalization) follows if

$$\mathrm{Det}\begin{bmatrix} -\partial p_1 E_1(p), \ldots, & -\partial p_{l-1} E_1(p) \\ \vdots & \vdots \\ -\partial p_1 E_{l-1}(p), \ldots, & -\partial p_{l-1} E_{l-1}(p) \end{bmatrix}$$

is positive (at every equilibrium price vector). Somewhat stronger conditions are easier to interpret, for example, if the matrix JE in the above determinant is either negative definite or has a negative dominant diagonal. Yet there remains the fundamental problem: How do we justify the required structure of the Jacobian matrix of the excess demand function?

In principle, there are three approaches: the academic, the pragmatic, and the scientific approach. The first one I recommend to those who want to publish, say, in *Econometrica* or *Journal of Mathematical Economics*. The second one is used by most people who do applied work. The third approach is still waiting to be pursued seriously.

An example of the academic approach is the following. Stay within the familiar exchange economies. Formulate assumptions on individual characteristics $(\precsim, e)$ such that the required structure can be derived. This approach must lead to extremely restrictive assumptions. For example, homothetic and identical individual preferences or homothetic preferences (more general, preferences that lead to monotone individual demand functions) and collinear individual endowments. I do not expect very interesting new results along these lines. Either we ask the wrong question in the right model or, more likely, the right question in the wrong model (to be clear, I refer to exchange economies). The pragmatic approach stands on its own feet; it does not need much explanation.

3.5

You might now expect me to say something about the scientific approach. I will try, but I have to be modest. During the whole of my period at CORE every time I went to the lounge, the blackboards were covered with mysterious econometric calculations, estimates, and even pictures of such real life phenomena as income distributions. I have to admit that this first disturbed me and later had a strong positive influence on my thinking.

Let us stipulate that market (or mean) demand of a private ownership economy is a continuous or differentiable function $F(p)$ in the price system p. We are interested in useful properties of the function $F(p)$, which can be expressed by properties of the Jacobian matrix $\partial F = (\partial p_j F_i(p))_{i,j=1,\dots,l}$.

The most useful property of F, which comes to my mind, is that the Jacobian matrix ∂F is negative (semi)definite. This property, however, is unfulfillable if the function F is homogeneous. In this case it suffices to require that the matrix ∂F be negative definite on a hyperplane. However, is there any empirical evidence that the market demand function F will satisfy this hope?

Market demand refers to a large population of households. Therefore let us define the market demand function F directly by

$$F(p) = \int f(p,b)\rho(p,b)db,$$

where f denotes the *statistical Engel function*, that is, $f(p, b)$ is the mean demand vector at the price system p of all households with expenditure b, and $\rho(p, \cdot)$ denotes the *density* of the distribution of expenditure at the price system p.

Then we obtain for the Jacobian matrix ∂F of F the following decomposition:

$$\partial F(p) = S - A + D,$$

where

$S = $ the mean Slutzky substitution matrix of the Engel function $f(p, \cdot)$,

$A = $ the mean income effect matrix,

$$A = \left(\int f_j(p, b) \partial_b f_i(p, b) \rho(p, b) db \right)_{i,j},$$

$D = $ the matrix of the income distribution effects,

$$D = \left(\int f_i(p, b) \partial_{p_j} \rho(p, b) db \right)_{i,j}.$$

In the following I want to argue that we have good reasons to assume that the matrix A is positive definite. For the moment, I have not much to say on the structure of the other two matrices. Let me just mention that the matrix S is negative (semi)definite if the statistical Engelfunction $f(p, b)$ satisfies the weak axiom of revealed preference. The matrix D will create great difficulties if the density $\rho(p, \cdot)$ depends very sensitively on the price system—as it does, in general, in exchange economies.

Let me start by stating a mathematical result: *The matrix A is positive semidefinite if the density $\rho(p, \cdot)$ is decreasing on R_+. For this we need no assumption on the form of the Engel function $f(p, \cdot)$ other than $f(p, 0) = 0$.* Unfortunately, this result is not very useful since, fortunately, in reality the estimations of these densities are not everywhere decreasing.

Consequently the desired property of the matrix A becomes an empirical problem. The shape of the statistical Engel curves and the form of the density of the expenditure distribution becomes relevant.

In order to decide whether the matrix A is positive definite, one has to estimate from empirical data the functions in question. At this point one has to decide on parametric or nonparametric estimations.

As an example for a *parametric estimation,* one assumes—without theoretical justification, of course—that the Engel curves for every commodity h are of the "working" type,

$$f_h(b) = \alpha_h b + \beta_h b \log b,$$

and that the distribution of expenditure is lognormal. Under these *ad hoc* assumptions one can prove that the matrix A is positive definite provided that the variance of the normalized distribution of expenditure is greater than 0.28!

I emphasize that this conclusion is independent of the estimation of the coefficients α_h and β_h. I should mention that the estimated variance of the normalized expenditure distribution for the years 69 to 83 is always greater than 0.4.

For alternative functional forms of the Engel curves (e.g., polynomials, say, of degree 3) one obtains analogous results. In all these cases, sufficient, yet realistic, dispersion in the distribution of expenditure leads to a positive definite matrix A.

I have to admit that I have difficulties with the parametric approach. Therefore I estimated with nonparametric methods (kernel estimator) for 9 aggregated commodities the Engel curves and the density of the expenditure distribution. Figure 3.5 illustrates the kernel estimator for food and for alcohol plus tobacco. With these estimates one can compute the matrix A and check whether it is positive definite. For the data of the Family Expenditure Survey of the U.K. during the years 69 to 83 it turned out that the matrix A has, indeed, the desired structure.

Let me come back quickly to the matrix D. There would be no difficulties with this matrix if the rank of D is less or equal to one. This is the case if the dependence of the expenditure density $\rho(p, \cdot)$ on the price vector p is described only by an index $s(p)$ (e.g., mean expenditure), that is, $\rho(p, b) = \eta(s(p), b)$, where $\eta(s, b)$ is a one-parameter family of densities. This assumption implies that the normalized (i.e., mean equal to one) densities $\rho^*(p, \cdot)$ must be identical for all p. Of course, one cannot estimate in a given year the density for different price vectors. Therefore we look at the normalized densities in different years. In figures 3.6 and 3.7 we show these normalized densities (parametric and nonparametric estimation) for the years 69 to 83.

I hope you will agree with me that the questions I have been discussing are important for general equilibrium analysis. Surely the answers are not

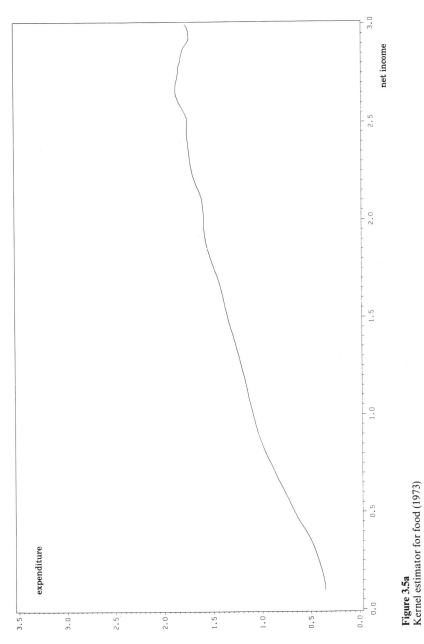

Figure 3.5a
Kernel estimator for food (1973)

Figure 3.5b
Kernel estimator for alcohol and tobacco (1973)

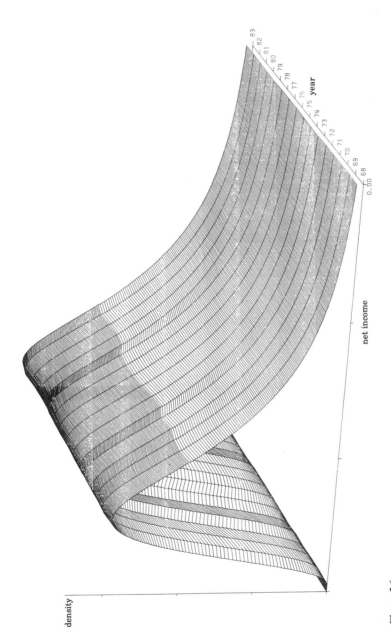

Figure 3.6
Density estimation, 1968–1983: lognormal fit

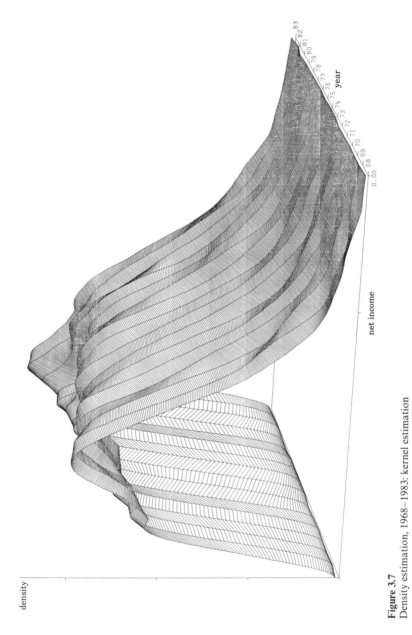

Figure 3.7
Density estimation, 1968–1983: kernel estimation

yet satisfactory but the approach, I hope, is sound. We need general equilibrium models with specific structure if we want to go beyond existence theorems. One part of the strategy that we can use to obtain some structure consists in making assumptions on the distribution of agents' characteristics and this is motivated by the fundamental development in general equilibrium theory which I have tried to sketch in this talk. Many of these results have been developed to a large extent at CORE.

The impact of CORE on my work is only too obvious. There are many other mathematical economists in this audience who could tell a similiar story.

I am very grateful that I had the chance to spend many years at CORE. I hope that other economists will have the same fortune.

References

Family Expenditure Survey. 1968–1983. Annual Base Tapes and Reports. London: Department of Employment, Statistics Division, Her Majesty's Stationary Office. (The data were made available by the ERSC Data Archive at the University of Essex.)

Hicks, J. R. 1946. *Value and Capital.* London: Oxford University Press.

Samuelson, P. A. 1947. *Foundations of Economic Analysis.* Cambridge: Harvard University Press.

4 Existence of Equilibria in Economies with Increasing Returns

Bernard Cornet

In this chapter we consider a general equilibrium model, in which the usual assumptions are made on the consumption side, but no convexity assumption is made either on the total production set or on the production sets of the firms. A marginal cost pricing equilibrium is a state that consists of a price vector, a list of consumption plans, a list of production plans that satisfy the usual conditions of the competitive equilibrium (Debreu 1959) except for the behavior rule of the producers who are supposed to fulfill the first-order necessary condition for profit maximization.

The welfare implications and the decentralized properties of marginal cost pricing equilibria have been studied by several authors, coming back to Hotelling (1938), and more recently by Guesnerie (1975), and then by Brown and Heal (1979, 1980). The existence problem has been considered by Beato (1979), (1982) and by Mantel (1979).

The purpose of this chapter is to give sufficient conditions for the existence of a marginal cost pricing equilibrium that will encompass, in particular, the result of Beato (1982) and Mantel (1979). Our definition of a marginal cost pricing equilibrium differs from the one in Beato (1982) and Guesnerie (1975) only in the way we formalize the behavior rules of the producers. We do not assume here that the total production set or the production sets of the firms have a smooth boundary. We use Clarke's definition of the cone of normals to an arbitrary subset of a Euclidean space, whereas in Beato (1982) and Guesnerie (1975) the negative polar of the cone of interior displacement (Dubovickii and Miljutin 1965) was considered. The proof of the existence theorem rests heavily upon recent results by Rockafellar (1979) and the author (1987).

The chapter is organized as follows. In section 4.1 we give the definition and some properties of Clarke's normal cone, and we make the main assumptions of the chapter. In section 4.2 existence theorems of a marginal cost pricing equilibrium are stated, first, when a fixed structure of revenue is given, and second, with a general structure of revenue. The proofs of the theorems are given in section 4.3.

4.1 Notation and Assumptions

We consider an economy with l goods, m consumers, and n producers. We denote by ω in $\mathbb{R}^l$ the vector of total initial endowments, by $X_i \subset \mathbb{R}^l$ the consumption set of the ith consumer $(i = 1, \ldots, m)$, by $Y_j \subset \mathbb{R}^l$ the production set of the jth producer ($j = 1, \ldots, n$), by $Y = \{\sum_{j=1}^{n} y_j |$ for all j, $y_j \in Y_j\}$ the total production set of the economy, and we suppose that the preferences of the ith consumer are represented by a utility function $u_i : X_i \to \mathbb{R}$. Let $x = (x_h)$, $y = (y_h)$ be vectors in $\mathbb{R}^l$. We denote by $x \cdot y = \sum_{h=1}^{l} x_h y_h$ the scalar product of $\mathbb{R}^l$, and by $\|x\| = (x \cdot x)^{1/2}$ the Euclidean norm of $\mathbb{R}^l$; the notation $x \geq y$ (respectively, $x \gg y$) means $x_h \geq y_h$ (respectively, $x_h > y_h$) for all $h \in \{1, \ldots, l\}$. We denote by $\mathbb{R}_+^l = \{x \in \mathbb{R}^l | x \geq 0\}$ the closed positive cone of $\mathbb{R}^l$, and we let $\mathbb{R}_{++}^l = \{x \in \mathbb{R}^l | x \gg 0\}$. We posit the following assumptions.

(A.1)
- i. For all h, $\omega_h > 0$;

- ii. for all i, $X_i = \mathbb{R}_+^l$;

- iii. for all i, u_i is continuous, strictly quasi concave, and monotonic (that is, for all x, x' in $\mathbb{R}_+^l$ such that $x \leq x'$, $x \neq x'$, then $u_i(x) < u_i(x')$).

(A.2)
- i. For all j, Y_j is a closed subset of $\mathbb{R}^l$;

- ii. Y is a closed subset of $\mathbb{R}^l$;

- iii. 0 belongs to Y;

- iv. $Y - \mathbb{R}_+^l \subset Y$ (free disposal);

- v. let $\hat{Y} = [\{\omega\} + Y] \cap \mathbb{R}_+^l$; then $\hat{Y}$ is a compact subset of $\mathbb{R}^l$.

Before stating the next assumption, we need to introduce some definitions. Let A be a nonempty subset of $\mathbb{R}^l$, and let x be an element of $\mathbb{R}^l$; we denote by $\bar{A}$ the closure of A, by int A the interior of A, by $\overline{\text{co}}\, A$ the closed convex hull of A, and by $d_A(x) = \inf\{\|x - a\| | a \in A\}$ the distance from x to A.

DEFINITION 1 (Clarke 1975). *Let Y be a closed subset of $\mathbb{R}^l$, and let y be an element in Y. The cone of normals to Y at y, also called the normal cone to Y at y, denoted by $N_Y(y)$, is the set*

$$\overline{\text{co}} \left\{ \lim_q \lambda_q (y_q' - y_q) \right\},$$

where we consider all sequences $\{\lambda_q\} \subset [0, \infty)$, $\{y_q\} \subset Y$, $\{y_q'\} \subset \mathbb{R}^l$ such that $y_q' \to y$, and, for all q, $\|y_q' - y_q\| = d_Y(y_q')$.

The next proposition shows that the above definition coincides with the usual notion of normals to a set in the two following cases:

C.1. *Y is a closed convex subset of $\mathbb{R}^l$ and y is an element in Y.*

C.2. *There exist two finite subsets E and I and continuously differentiable functions $g_k : \mathbb{R}^l \to \mathbb{R}, k \in E \cup I$, such that Y can be written as follows:*

$$Y = \left\{ y \in \mathbb{R}^l \,\middle|\, \begin{array}{l} \text{for all } k \in E, g_k(y) = 0 \\ \text{for all } k \in I, g_k(y) \leq 0 \end{array} \right\},$$

and y is an element in Y such that the gradient vectors $\nabla g_k(y)$, for $k \in E \cup I(y)$, are linearly independent, where $I(y) = \{k \in I \mid g_k(y) = 0\}$.

Let Y be a closed subset of $\mathbb{R}^l$, and let y be an element in Y. We define the cone of perpendicular vectors as follows:

$$\perp_Y(y) = \{\lambda(y' - y) \mid \lambda \geq 0, y' \in \mathbb{R}^l, \|y' - y\| = d_Y(y')\}.$$

Note that

$$\perp_Y(y) = \left\{ p \in \mathbb{R}^l \,\middle|\, \exists \lambda \geq 0, \forall y' \in Y : p \cdot y \geq p \cdot y' - \left(\frac{\lambda}{2}\right) \|y - y'\|^2 \right\}$$

so that Clarke's normal cone can be equivalently defined as the closed convex hull of the set

$$\limsup_{y' \to y} \perp_Y(y') \overset{\text{def}}{=} \{p = \lim p_q \mid \exists (y_q) \subset Y, (y_q) \to y, p_q \in \perp_Y(y_q), \text{ for all } q\}.$$

PROPOSITION 1

(i) Under assumption (C.1),

$$N_Y(y) = \perp_Y(y) = \{p \in \mathbb{R}^l \mid p \cdot y \geq p \cdot y' \text{ for all } y' \text{ in } Y\}.$$

(ii) Under assumption (C.2),

$$N_Y(y) = \perp_Y(y) = \left\{ \sum_{k \in E \cup I(y)} \lambda_k \nabla g_k(y) \,\middle|\, \begin{array}{l} \text{for all } k \text{ in } E, \lambda_k \in \mathbb{R} \\ \text{for all } k \text{ in } I(y), \lambda_k \geq 0 \end{array} \right\}.$$

For the proof of proposition 1, see, for example, Clarke (1983). We now introduce the next assumption:

For all $y \in \partial Y$ such that $y + \omega \geq 0$, for all $p \in N_Y(y), p \neq 0$, (A.3)
then $p \cdot (y + \omega) > 0$.

This assumption is satisfied, in particular, in the two cases given by the next proposition.

PROPOSITION 2   *Suppose that $\omega \gg 0$ and that (A.2) holds, together with one of the two following conditions:*

(i) For all $y \in \partial Y$ such that $y + \omega \geq 0$, then $N_Y(y) \subset \mathbb{R}^l_{++} \cup \{0\}$.

(ii) Y is a convex subset of $\mathbb{R}^l$.

4.2   Statement of the Results

We now formally define a marginal cost pricing equilibrium, and we first suppose that a fixed structure of revenue is given. Denoting $\Delta = \{\delta = (\delta_i) \in \mathbb{R}^m \,|\, \text{for all } i, \, \delta_i \geq 0, \text{ and } \sum_{i=1}^m \delta_i = 1\}$ as the simplex of $\mathbb{R}^m$, and for $(\delta, p, y) \in \Delta \times \mathbb{R}^l \times Y$, we let

$$r_i(p, y) = \delta_i p \cdot (y + \omega), \qquad i = 1, \dots, m.$$

In other words, the revenue $r_i(p, y)$ of the ith consumer is supposed to be a fixed proportion of $p \cdot (y + \omega)$, the total profit of the economy added to the value of the initial endowment at the current price system.

DEFINITION 2   *Let $\delta \in \Delta$ be fixed. We say that $((x_i^*), (y_j^*), p^*) \in \mathbb{R}^{lm} \times \mathbb{R}^{ln} \times \mathbb{R}^l$ is a marginal cost pricing equilibrium (with respect to δ) if the following four conditions are satisfied:*

(i) $p^* \gg 0$.

(ii) For all i, $x_i^* \in \mathbb{R}^l_+$, $p^* \cdot x_i^* \leq r_i(p^*, \sum_{j=1}^n y_j^*)$, and $u_i(x_i^*) = \max\{u_i(x_i) \,|\, x_i \in \mathbb{R}^l_+, \, p^* \cdot x_i \leq r_i(p^*, \sum_{j=1}^n y_j^*)\}$.

(iii) $\sum_{i=1}^m x_i^* = \sum_{j=1}^n y_j^* + \omega$.

(iv) For all j, $y_j^* \in Y_j$, and $p^* \in N_{Y_j}(y_j^*)$.

The only difference between the above definition and the one in Guesnerie (1975) and Beato (1982) comes from the choice of the sets $N_{Y_j}(y_j)$. Here we take Clarke's cone of normals, whereas Guesnerie and Beato take the cone of interior displacements of Dubovickii and Miljutin (1965).

In the following, we will also consider the related condition at the aggregate level:

(iv') For all j, $y_j^* \in Y_j$, and $p^* \in N_Y(\sum_{j=1}^n y_j^*)$.

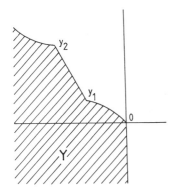

Figure 4.1

REMARK 1   When, for all j, Y_j is a closed convex subset of $\mathbb{R}^l$, by proposition 1, (iv) is satisfied if and only if, for all j, $y_j^* \in Y_j$ and $p^* \cdot y_j^* = \max\{p^* \cdot y_j | y_j \in Y_j\}$, that is, if and only if, at the price system p^*, for all j, at y_j^* the jth producer maximizes its profit.

REMARK 2   If for all j, Y_j is a closed convex subset of $\mathbb{R}^l$, one easily deduces from proposition 1 that the conditions *(iv)* and *(iv')* are equivalent. However, for arbitrary closed subsets Y_j of $\mathbb{R}^l$, in general, neither *(iv)* implies *(iv')*, nor *(iv')* implies *(iv)* (see figures 4.2 and 4.3). The first example in figure 4.2 was communicated to us by Andreu Mas-Colell (see also Beato and Mas-Colell 1985).

The next theorem gives sufficient conditions for the existence of $((x_i^*),(y_j^*),p^*)$ satisfying conditions *(i)*, *(ii)*, *(iii)*, and *(iv')*.

THEOREM 1   *Under assumptions* (A.1), (A.2), *and* (A.3), *for all* $\delta \in \Delta$, *there exists* $((x_i^*),(y_j^*),p^*) \in \mathbb{R}^{lm} \times \mathbb{R}^{ln} \times \mathbb{R}^l$ *satisfying the conditions (i), (ii), (iii), and (iv').*

Clearly, for $n = 1$ (a unique producer), the triple $((x_i^*),(y_j^*),p^*)$ given by theorem 1 is a marginal cost pricing equilibrium. For $n > 1$, we need to assume some additional assumptions to guarantee the existence of a marginal cost pricing equilibrium.

THEOREM 2   *Under assumptions* (A.1), (A.2), (A.3), *and* (A.4), *for all* $\delta \in \Delta$, *there exists a marginal cost pricing equilibrium with respect to* δ.

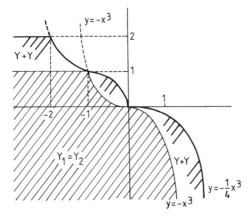

Figure 4.2

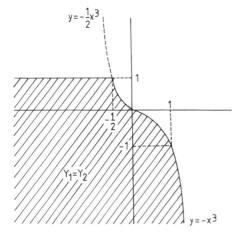

Figure 4.3

We now want to consider a more general structure of revenues. We first recall that, if $r_i(p, y)$ is a fixed structure of revenue, then there exists a fixed element δ in Δ and for $(p, y) \in \mathbb{R}^l_+ \times Y$, $r_i(p, y) = \delta_i p \cdot (y + \omega)$, $i = 1, \ldots, m$. Thus the following assertions hold:

(i) For all i, the function $r_i : [\mathbb{R}^l_+ \setminus \{0\}] \times Y \to \mathbb{R}_+$ is continuous.

(ii) $\sum_{i=1}^m r_i(p, y) = p \cdot (y + \omega)$.

Now let $r_i : [\mathbb{R}^l_+ \setminus \{0\}] \times Y \to \mathbb{R}^l_+$, $i = 1, \ldots, m$, by arbitrary functions.

DEFINITION 3   *We say that the functions $r_1, \ldots, r_m$ define a structure of revenue if the above conditions (i) and (ii) are satisfied, and that $((x_i^*), (y_j^*), p^*) \in \mathbb{R}^{lm} \times \mathbb{R}^{ln} \times \mathbb{R}^l$ is a marginal cost pricing equilibrium with respect to the structure of revenue $r_1, \ldots, r_m$ if the four conditions of definition 2 are satisfied.*

Before stating the analogue of theorems 1 and 2 for an arbitrary structure of revenue, we modify assumption (A.3) as follows:

For all $y \in \partial Y$ such that $y + \omega \geq 0$, for all $p \in N_Y(y)$, $p \neq 0$, then for all i, $r_i(p, y) > 0$.   (A.3')

At this point it is worth noticing that for every structure of revenue $r_1, \ldots, r_m$, (A.3') implies (A.3) since $\sum_{i=1}^m r_i(p, y) = p \cdot (y + \omega)$. In other words, among all the structures of revenue, assumption (A.3') is the weakest in the case of a fixed structure of revenue.

We can now state the main theorem of this chapter.

THEOREM 3   *Let $r_1, \ldots, r_m$ be a structure of revenue.*

(i) Under assumptions (A.1), (A.2), and (A.3'), there exists $((x_i^*), (y_j^*), p^*)$ satisfying the conditions (i), (ii), (iii) of definition 2 and (iv').

(ii) Under assumptions (A.1), (A.2), (A.3'), and (A.4), there exists a marginal cost pricing equilibrium with respect to the structure of revenue $r_1, \ldots, r_m$.

Clearly, theorems 1 and 2 are direct consequences of theorem 3. The proof of theorem 3 is given in the next section.

REMARK 3   Let $\omega_i \in \mathbb{R}^l_{++}$, $i = 1, \ldots, m$, such that $\omega = \sum_{i=1}^m \omega_i$. Let δ be a fixed element in Δ, and for $(p, y) \in \mathbb{R}^l_+ \times Y$, let

$r_i(p, y) = \delta_i p \cdot y + p \cdot \omega_i, \qquad i = 1, \ldots, m.$

Clearly, $r_1, \ldots, r_m$ is a structure of revenue.

It is worth noticing that, under, assumption (A.1), assuming that the ith consumer has the vector $\omega_i \gg 0$ for initial endowment, then the existence of a competitive equilibrium in this pure exchange economy can be deduced from theorem 3 by taking $Y = -\mathbb{R}^l_+$. Indeed, assumption (A.2) is clearly satisfied. By proposition 1, $p \in N_Y(y)$ if and only if $p \geq 0$ and $p \cdot y = 0$; hence (A.3$'$) is also satisfied. By theorem 3 (i), there exists $((x_i^*), (y_j^*), p^*)$ satisfying the conditions *(i)*, *(ii)*, *(iii)* of definition 2 and *(iv$'$)*.

4.3   Proof of Theorem 3

We first prove a lemma and recall some results that will be used in the proof of theorem 3. Let S be the simplex of $\mathbb{R}^l$, that is,

$$S = \left\{ x = (x_h) \in \mathbb{R}^l \middle| \text{for all } h, \, x_h \geq 0, \text{ and } \sum_{h=1}^{l} x_h = 1 \right\}.$$

For $x = (x_h) \in \mathbb{R}^l$, let $\|x\|_1 = \sum_{h=1}^{l} |x_h|$, and let $\phi : \mathbb{R}^l_+ \setminus \{0\} \to S$ be the mapping defined by

$$\phi(x) = \frac{x}{\|x\|_1} = \frac{x}{\sum_{h=1}^{l} x_h}.$$

LEMMA 1   *Suppose that $\omega \gg 0$, that (A.2) and (A.3) hold, and let $A = [\{\omega\} + \partial Y] \cap \mathbb{R}^l_+$. Then the mapping $\phi|_A$, the restriction of ϕ to A, is a homeomorphism from A to S.*

Proof   For $\phi|_A$ to be well defined, we first verify that 0 does not belong to A, or equivalently, that $-\omega$ does not belong to ∂Y. Indeed, $\omega \in \text{int } \mathbb{R}^l_+$, and by (A.2), one has $-\text{int } \mathbb{R}^l_+ \subset Y$. Hence $-\omega \in \text{int } Y$.

We now prove that $\phi|_A$ is injective. Let y_1, y_2 in ∂Y such that $y_1 + \omega \geq 0$, $y_2 + \omega \geq 0$ and $\phi(y_1 + \omega) = \phi(y_2 + \omega)$; then there exists $\lambda > 0$ such that $\omega + y_1 = \lambda(\omega + y_2)$. We show that $\lambda = 1$ by contraposition. Suppose that $\lambda > 1$ (and the proof is similar if $\lambda < 1$). We introduce the following sets, for all element y in Y,

$T_Y(y) = \{v \in \mathbb{R}^l \mid \forall p \in N_Y(y) : p \cdot v \leq 0\},$

$k_Y(y) = \{v \in \mathbb{R}^l \mid \exists \varepsilon > 0, \, \forall t \in (0, \varepsilon) : y + tB(v, \varepsilon) \subset Y\},$

(i.e., Clarke's tangent cone and the cone of interior displacement).

As we have already noted, assumption (A.3′) implies assumption (A.3). Using a separation argument, on easily deduces from (A.3) that $-(\omega + y_1) \in$ int $T_Y(y_1)$. From Cornet (1987) and Rockafellar (1979), int $T_Y(y_1) \subset k_Y(y_1)$. Let us denote by e the vector in $\mathbb{R}^l$ that has all its coordinates equal to one. Since $-(\omega + y_1) \in k_Y(y_1)$, for $\alpha > 0$, $t > 0$ small enough, $z = y_1 + t[-(\omega + y_1) + \alpha e]$ belongs to Y. In the following, we further suppose that $t < (\lambda - 1)/\lambda$. An easy calculation shows that $-y_2 + z = (\omega + y_2)(-1 + \lambda - t\lambda) + t\alpha e \gg 0$. Hence $y_2 \in \{z\} - \text{int } \mathbb{R}^l_+$. Since $z \in Y$, by assumption (A.2), $y_2 \in \text{int } Y$, which contradicts $y_2 \in \partial Y$. This shows that $\phi|_A$ is injective.

We now show that $\phi|_A$ is onto. For $s \in S$, let $\Lambda(s) = \{\lambda \geq 0 \,|\, \lambda s - \omega \in Y\}$. From (A.2) and the assumption $\omega \gg 0$, the set $\Lambda(s)$ is nonempty compact, and we let $\lambda(s) = \max\{\lambda \,|\, \lambda \in \Lambda(s)\}$. Clearly, for all s in S, $s = \phi(\lambda(s)s)$, and it only remains to show that $\lambda(s)s \in A = [\{\omega\} + \partial Y] \cap \mathbb{R}^l_+$, or equivalently, that $\lambda(s)s - \omega \in \partial Y$. Suppose that it is not true, then $\lambda(s)s - \omega \in \text{int}(Y)$ for some s, and for $\varepsilon > 0$ small enough, $s[\lambda(s) + \varepsilon] - \omega \in Y$ which contradicts the definition of $\lambda(s)$.

Clearly, the mapping $\phi|_A$ is continuous. We have previously shown that $\phi|_A$ is one-to-one. Since S is a compact subset of $\mathbb{R}^l$, then $\phi|_A$ is a homeomorphism. ∎

The next lemma states the properties of demand functions that are needed in the following (see Debreu 1981 for the proof of the lemma).

LEMMA 2 *Let us assume that (A.1) holds. Then for all i, for all $p \gg 0$, for all $w > 0$, there exists a unique solution—denoted by $d_i(p, w)$—of the following maximization problem:*

$$\begin{cases} \text{maximize } u_i(x) \\ \text{subject to } p \cdot x \leq w \text{ and } x \geq 0, \end{cases}$$

which satisfies the following properties:

(i) For all $p \gg 0$, for all $w > 0$, one has $p \cdot d_i(p, w) = w$.

(ii) The mapping $d_i \colon \mathbb{R}^{l+1}_{++} \to \mathbb{R}^l$ is continuous.

(iii) For any sequence $\{p_q\} \subset S \cap \mathbb{R}^l_{++}$ that converges to some element p_0 in S that has some zero coordinates, for any sequence $\{w_q\} \subset (0, \infty)$ that converges to some element $\omega_0 > 0$, then $\|d_i(p_q, w_q)\| \to \infty$ when $q \to \infty$.

LEMMA 3   (Rockafellar 1979). *Let Y be a nonempty closed subset of $\mathbb{R}^l$ and let y be an element of Y. Then y belongs to the interior of Y if and only if $N_Y(y) = \{0\}$.*

LEMMA 4   *Let Y be a nonempty closed subset of $\mathbb{R}^l$ such that $Y - \mathbb{R}^l_+ \subset Y$, then the following conditions hold:*

(i) $N_Y(y) \subset \mathbb{R}^l_+$ for every $y \in Y$.

(ii) The correspondence $N_Y(\cdot)$ from Y to $\mathbb{R}^l$ is closed at every $y \in Y$, that is, for all sequences $\{y_q\} \subset Y, \{p_q\} \subset \mathbb{R}^l$ such that $\{y_q\}$ converges to y and $\{p_q\}$ converges to some element p in $\mathbb{R}^l$, then p belongs to $N_Y(y)$.

Proof   (i) Recalling that $N_Y(y) = \overline{\text{co}} \lim \sup_{y' \to y} \perp_Y(y')$, it suffices to show that $\perp_Y(y) \subset \mathbb{R}^l_+$ for every $y \in Y$. Let $p \in \perp_Y(y)$, then there exists $\lambda \geq 0$ such that $p \cdot y \geq p \cdot y' - (\lambda/2)\|y - y'\|^2$ for every $y' \in Y$. Let $v \in \mathbb{R}^l_+$, then taking in the previous inequality, for $t > 0$, $y' = y - tv$ [which belongs to Y by assumption (A.2)], one gets $p \cdot v \geq (\lambda/2)t\|v\|^2$. Passing to the limit, when $t \to 0_+$, one gets $p \cdot v \geq 0$. Since v is an arbitrary vector of $\mathbb{R}^l_+$, we have thus shown that $p \in \mathbb{R}^l_+$.

(ii) For the proof of the second part, see Rockafellar (1979) or the appendix. ∎

Proof of theorem 3   (i) Let $A = [\{\omega\} + \partial Y] \cap \mathbb{R}^l_+$, and let S be the simplex of $\mathbb{R}^l$. We denote by ∂S the relative boundary of S, that is, the set of elements in S having some zero coordinates. By lemma 1, the mapping $\phi|_A : x \to x/\|x\|_1$ is a homeomorphism from A to S, and we denote by ψ its inverse. Hence $\psi : S \to A$. We now define the correspondences F, G from $S \times S$ to $\mathbb{R}^l$ as follows: Let $V = \{(p, s) \in S \times S | \text{for all } i, r_i(p, \psi(s) - \omega) > 0\}$, then V is an open subset of $S \times S$. For $(p, s) \in S \times S$, let

$$F(p, s) = N_Y(\psi(s) - \omega) \cap S;$$

$$G(p, s) = \left\{ \frac{\sum_{i=1}^{m} d_i(p, r_i(p, \psi(s) - \omega))}{\|\sum_{i=1}^{m} d_i(p, r_i(p, \psi(s) - \omega))\|_1} \right\}, \qquad \text{if } p \gg 0 \text{ and } (p, s) \in V,$$

$$= \{u \in S | p \cdot u = 0\}, \qquad \text{if } p \in \partial S \text{ and } (p, s) \in V,$$

$$= S \qquad \text{if } (p, s) \notin V.$$

Step 1   *We claim that, for all (p, s) in $S \times S$, $F(p, s)$ and $G(p, s)$ are nonempty, convex, compact subsets of S and that the correspondences F and G are upper semicontinuous.*

Let (p, s) be an element in $S \times S$. By lemma 4, $F(p, s)$ is a convex, compact subset of S; by lemma 3, it is nonempty. Again, by lemma 4, the correspondence F is upper semicontinuous.

We now verify that the correspondence G is well defined, that is, if $p \gg 0$ and $(p, s) \in V$, then $\sum_{i=1}^{m} d_i(p, r_i(p, \psi(s) - \omega)) \neq 0$. Suppose, on the contrary, that it is null. By lemma 2 (i), using the fact that $r_1, \ldots, r_m$ is a structure of revenue, we get

$$0 = p \cdot \left[\sum_{i=1}^{m} r_i(p, \psi(s) - \omega) \right] = p \cdot \psi(s).$$

Recall that $\psi(s) \in [\{\omega\} + \partial Y] \cap \mathbb{R}_+^l$ and $p \gg 0$, then $\psi(s) = 0$ and $-\omega \in \partial Y$. From (A.2), $-\mathbb{R}_+^l \subset Y$. Since $\omega \gg 0$, we deduce that $-\omega \in \text{int } Y$, which contradicts the fact that $-\omega \in \partial Y$.

Clearly, for all (p, s) in $S \times S$, $G(p, s)$ is a nonempty, convex, compact subset of S, and the correspondence G is upper semicontinuous at every element $(\bar{p}, \bar{s})$ in $S \times S$ such that $(\bar{p}, \bar{s}) \notin V$. Let $(\bar{p}, \bar{s}) \in S \times S$ such that $\bar{p} \gg 0$ and $(\bar{p}, \bar{s}) \in V$; by lemma 2 (ii) the correspondence G is also upper semicontinuous at $(\bar{p}, \bar{s})$.

Now let $(\bar{p}, \bar{s})$ be an element of $S \times S$ such that $\bar{p} \in \partial S$ and $(\bar{p}, \bar{s}) \in V$, and let $\{s_q\} \subset S$, $\{p_q\} \subset S$, and $\{u_q\} \subset \mathbb{R}^l$ be sequences such that, for all q, $u_q \in G(p_q, s_q)$, $s_q \to \bar{s}$, $p_q \to \bar{p}$, and $\{u_q\}$ converges to some element $\bar{u}$ in $\mathbb{R}^l$. To show that G is upper semicontinuous at $(\bar{p}, \bar{s})$, it suffices to prove that $\bar{u}$ belongs to $G(\bar{p}, \bar{s})$. Since $(\bar{p}, \bar{s})$ belongs to the open subset V of $S \times S$, for q large enough $(p_q, s_q) \in V$, and we have the following alternative:

a. There exists an infinite number of q such that $p_q \in \partial S$, or

b. There exists an infinite number of q such that $p_q \gg 0$.

In the first case, passing to the limit when $q \to \infty$, we get $\bar{p} \cdot \bar{u} = 0$; hence $\bar{u} \in G(\bar{p}, \bar{s})$. In the second case, without any loss of generality, we can suppose that, for all q, $p_q \gg 0$. For q large enough, for all i, $r_i(p_q, \psi(s_q) - \omega) > 0$; hence, by Lemma 2 (i), using the fact that $r_1, \ldots, r_m$ is a structure of revenue,

$$p_q \cdot u_q = \frac{\sum_{i=1}^{m} r_i(p_q, \psi(s_q) - \omega)}{\| \sum_{i=1}^{m} d_i(p_q, r_i(p_q, \psi(s_q) - \omega)) \|_1}$$

$$= \frac{p_q \cdot (\psi(s_q) - \omega)}{\| \sum_{i=1}^{m} d_i(p_q, r_i(p_q, \psi(s_q) - \omega)) \|_1}.$$

Since $(\bar{p},\bar{s}) \in V$, that is, for all i, $r_i(\bar{p},\psi(\bar{s})-\omega) > 0$, by lemma 2 (iii), $\bar{p}\cdot\bar{u} = \lim_q p_q \cdot u_q = 0$. Hence $\bar{u} \in G(\bar{p},\bar{s})$. This ends the proof of Step 1.

Step 2 Let H be the correspondence from $S \times S$ to $S \times S$ defined by $H(p,s) = F(p,s) \times G(p,s)$. From Kakutani's theorem and step 1 there exists a fixed point (p^*,s^*) of the correspondence H, that is, $p^* \in F(p^*,s^*)$ and $s^* \in G(p^*,s^*)$. Let $y^* = \psi(s^*) - \omega$, then $y^* \in \partial Y$, $y^* + \omega \geq 0$ and $p^* \in N_Y(y^*) \cap S$. Therefore by assumption (A.3'), for all i, $r_i(p^*,\psi(s^*)-\omega) > 0$. Hence $(p^*,s^*) \in V$. We now claim that $p^* \gg 0$. Suppose, on the contrary, that $p^* \in \partial S$. From the fixed-point property, $s^* \in G(s^*,p^*)$ or equivalent $p^* \cdot s^* = 0$. Recall that, from the definition of the mapping ψ, there exists $\lambda^* > 0$ such that $\psi(s^*) = \lambda^* s^*$. Hence $p^* \cdot \psi(s^*) = 0$. But since $r_1, \ldots, r_m$ is a structure of revenue, $0 = p^* \cdot \psi(s^*) = \sum_{i=1}^m r_i(p^*,\psi(s^*)-\omega) > 0$, a contradiction.

Thus $p^* \gg 0$ and $(p^*,s^*) \in V$; from the definition of G,

$$s^* = \frac{\sum_{i=1}^m d_i(p^*, r_i(p^*,\psi(s^*)-\omega))}{\|\sum_{i=1}^m d_i(p^*, r_i(p^*,\psi(s^*)-\omega))\|_1}.$$

Hence by lemma 2 (i), using the fact that $r_1, \ldots, r_m$ is a structure of revenue,

$$p^* \cdot s^* = \frac{p^* \cdot \psi(s^*)}{\|\sum_{i=1}^m d_i(p^*, r_i(p^*,\psi(s^*)-\omega))\|_1}.$$

Recall that there exists $\lambda^* > 0$ such that $\psi(s^*) = \lambda^* s^*$. From this fact and the two above equalities, we get

$$y^* + \omega = \psi(s^*) = \sum_{i=1}^m d_i(p^*, r_i(p^*,y^*)).$$

For all i, let $x_i^* = d_i(p^*, r_i(p^*,y^*))$, then we have proved that $((x_i^*),(y_j^*), p^*)$ satisfies the conditions *(i)*, *(ii)*, *(iii)* of definition 2 and *(iv')*. This ends the proof of part (i) of theorem 3.

The proof of part (ii) is a consequence of part (i) and the following lemma.

LEMMA 5 *Let Y_1, Y_2 be closed subsets of $\mathbb{R}^l$, and let Y be the closure of $Y_1 + Y_2$, then*

$$\perp_{Y_1+Y_2}(y_1 + y_2) \subset \perp_{Y_1}(y_1) \cap \perp_{Y_2}(y_2) \qquad \text{for every } y_1 \in Y_1, y_2 \in Y_2.$$

Proof Let $p \in \perp_{Y_1+Y_2}(y_1 + y_2)$, then there exists $\lambda \geq 0$ such that $p \cdot (y_1 + y_2) \geq p \cdot (y_1' + y_2') - (\lambda/2)\|y_1 + y_2 - y_1' - y_2'\|^2$ for every $y_1' \in Y_1$, and

$y_2' \in Y_2$. Taking $y_2' = y_2$, one deduces that $p \in \perp_{Y_1}(y_1)$, and similarly, $p \in \perp_{Y_2}(y_2)$. ∎

Appendix

This appendix provides further justifications for the choice of Clarke's normal cone in the formalization of the marginal cost pricing rule in the study of the existence problem.[1] We also investigate the relationship with the rule proposed in 1975 by Guesnerie, who used Dubovickii-Miljutin's cone of interior displacement; we point out, however, that Clarke's paper, published in 1975, was not available at the time of Guesnerie's work. As we shall see, Clarke's normal cone allows us to enlarge the class of economies that admit marginal cost pricing equilibria without weakening the equilibrium notion. This formalization has since been adopted by all the papers devoted to the existence problem.

We have chosen to present the first version of our paper, which was written as a Berkeley Discussion Paper in 1982, and which takes Clarke's normal cone as the primary concept.[2] Besides the simplicity of the presentation, another justification is given in the next section.

The Closed Graph Property of Clarke's Normal Cone

We come back to the closed graph property of Clarke's normal cone (lemma 4), which plays a key role in the existence proof. This property is a direct consequence of the following lemma, which allows us to give a simple and direct proof of lemma 4, different from the original one by Rockafellar (1979). Incidentally, the lemma also shows that, under the free disposal assumption, the "closure" is superfluous in the definition of Clarke's normal cone.

LEMMA   *Let Y be a closed subset of $\mathbb{R}^l$, let F be a correspondence from Y to $\mathbb{R}_+^l$ such that, for every y, $F(y)$ is a cone (i.e., $p \in F(y)$ and $\lambda \geq 0$ imply $\lambda p \in F(y)$), we define the correspondence N, from Y to $\mathbb{R}_+^l$, by*

$$N(y^*) = \text{co} \limsup_{y \to y^*} F(y),$$

where $\limsup_{y \to y^*} F(y) \overset{\text{def}}{=} \{p = \lim p_q | \exists (y_q) \subset Y, (y_q) \to y^*, \text{ and } p_q \in F(y_q) \text{ for all } q\}$.

Then the correspondence N has a closed graph (and, in particular, the set $N(y^*)$ is closed).

Proof Let $(y_q) \subset Y$ and $(p_q) \subset \mathbb{R}^l$ be sequences converging, respectively, to some elements $y^* \in Y$ and $p^* \in \mathbb{R}^l$, and such that $p_q \in N(y_q)$ for every q. We have to show that $p^* \in N(y^*)$. Indeed, from Caratheodory's theorem, for every q, one can write $p_q = \sum_{i=1}^{l+1} \lambda_q^i p_q^i$ for some elements $p_q^i \in \limsup_{y \to y^*} F(y)$, and for some real numbers $\lambda_q^i \geq 0$ $(i = 1, \ldots, l+1)$ such that $\sum_{i=1}^{l+1} \lambda_q^i = 1$. But $p^* \geq 0$ since $F(y) \subset \mathbb{R}_+^l$ for every y, and we can suppose that $p^* \neq 0$ (since 0 clearly belongs to $N(y^*)$). Thus, denoting $e = (1, \ldots, 1)$, one deduces that $p^* \cdot e > 0$. Consequently, for q large enough, $p_q \cdot e > 0$, and $p_q = (p_q \cdot e) \sum_{i=1}^{l+1} \pi_q^i$, where $\pi_q^i = (\lambda_q^i / p_q \cdot e) p_q^i$. But the sequence (π_q^i) remains in a fixed compact set since $\pi_q^i \in \mathbb{R}_+^l$ and $\pi_q^i \cdot e \leq 1$. Without any loss of generality, we can suppose that, for every $i = 1, \ldots, l+1$, the sequence (π_q^i) converges to some element π^i that belongs to $\limsup_{y \to y^*} F(y)$, since this set is a cone, and since the correspondence $y^* \limsup_{y \to y^*} F(y)$ has a closed graph (from its definition). Taking the limit when $q \to \infty$, one deduces that $p^* = (p^* \cdot e) \sum_{i=1}^{l+1} \pi^i$, with $\pi^i \in \limsup_{y \to y^*} F(y)$. This shows that $p^* \in N(y^*)$. ∎

A Counterexample

We now show that theorem 3 is no longer true, in general, if, in the definition of a marginal cost pricing equilibrium, Condition (iv) of definition 2 is replaced by either one of the following stronger conditions:

(iv'') for all j, $y_j^* \in Y_j$ and $p^* \in \hat{N}_{Y_j}(y_j^*) \overset{\text{def}}{=} \limsup_{y \to y_j^*} \perp_{Y_j}(y)$ (i.e., if "$\overline{\text{co}}$," the closed convex hull, is removed in the definition of Clarke's normal cone);

(iv''') for all j, $y_j^* \in Y_j$ and $p^* \tilde{N}_{Y_j}(y_j^*) \overset{\text{def}}{=} [k_{Y_j}(y_j^*)]^o$ (Dubovickii-Miljutin's normal cone)[3].

We consider an economy with two commodities, a single producer having for production set Y, the sum of the two sets Y_1 and Y_2 defined, respectively, by $Y_1 = \{(y^1, y^2) \in \mathbb{R}^2 | y^1 \leq 0$ and $y^2 \leq -y^1\}$ (which is convex), and $Y_2 = \{(y^1, y^2) \in \mathbb{R}^2 | y^1 \leq 0$ and $y^2 \leq (1/16)(y^1)^2\}$ (which admits increasing returns to scale), and two consumers, with consumption sets $X_1 = X_2 = \mathbb{R}_+^2$, utility functions $u_1(x^1, x^2) = x^2$, $u_2(x^1, x^2) = \min\{6x_1, x_2\}$, initial endowments $\omega_1 = (0, 50)$, $\omega_2 = (20, 0)$, and revenue functions $r_1(p, y) = p \cdot \omega_1 + p \cdot y$, $r_2(p, \pi_1, \pi_2) = p \cdot \omega_2$. This economy is obtained from the example of Beato and Mas-Colell (1985) by merging their two firms (whose production sets are exactly Y_1 and Y_2) into a single one.

We now show that this economy has a unique marginal cost pricing equilibrium (x_1^*, x_2^*, y^*, p^*) (in the sense of definition 2), which does not

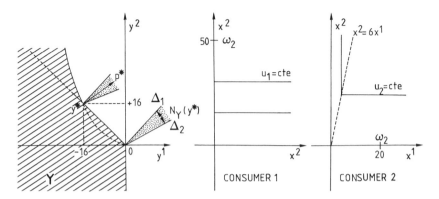

Figure 4.4
Clarke's normal cone and Dubovickii-Miljutin's normal cone

satisfies conditions (iv″) and (iv‴). We first notice that $p_2^* > 0$, otherwise the consumption of the first consumer would be unbounded and, without any loss of generality, we can suppose that $p_2^* = 1$. Given the production plan $y = (y_1, y_2) \in \partial Y$ and the price vector $p = (p_1, 1)$, the demand of the first consumer is $(0, 50 + p_1 y_1 + p_2)$, and the demand of the second consumer is $(20p_1/[p_1 + 6], 120p_1/[p_1 + 6])$. The market clearing condition for the first good then implies that

$$\frac{0 + 20p_1}{p_1 + 6} \leq 20 + y_1, \qquad \text{with equality if } p_1 > 0.$$

But the marginal cost pricing rule (condition (iv) definition 2) fixes the price p_1 as follows: $p_1 \geq 1$ if $y_1 = 0$, $p_1 = 1$ if $-16 < y_1 < 0$; $2 \geq p_1 \geq 1$ if $y_1 = -16$; $p_1 = -(1/8)y_1$ if $y_1 < -16$. One then clecks that the unique solution is given by

$$y^* = (-16, 16), \quad p^* = (1.5, 1), \quad x_1^* = (0, 42), \quad \text{and} \quad x_2^* = (4, 24).$$

Clearly, p^* does not belong to the cone $\hat{N}_Y(y^*)$, which is the union of the two closed half-lines $\Delta_1 = \{\lambda(1, 1) | \lambda \geq 0\}$ and $\Delta_2 = \{\lambda(2, 1) | \lambda \geq 0\}$ (and recall that Clarke's normal cone $N_Y(y^*)$ is the convex hull of Δ_1 and Δ_2). Furthermore p^* does not belong to Dubovickii-Muljutin's normal cone at y^*, which is reduced to $\{0\}$ (cf. figure 4.4). Actually this economy does not satisfy assumptions (A.2) and (A.3), but it is the case after a slight modification of the utility functions and the initial endowments.

Clarke's Normal Cone and Dubovickii-Miljutin's Normal Cone

We now discuss the relationship between theorem 3 and the previous existence result by Beato (1979, 1982) in which the marginal cost pricing rule is formalized with the cone of interior displacement, that is, condition (iv) of definition 2 is replaced by condition (iv''').

We have seen previously that condition (iv''') is stronger than (iv), hence the associated equilibrium notion is a priori stronger than ours. We will show, however, that under the assumptions made by Beato (1982) the two formalizations are equivalent. In her existence result, Beato assumes that (A.1) and (A.2) hold and that, for every $y \in \partial Y \cap \{y \in \mathbb{R}^l | y + \omega \geq 0\}$, then ($\alpha$) $k_Y(y)$ is convex, (β) the correspondence $y \to [k_Y(y)]^o \cap B(0, 1)$ is upper semicontinuous at y, and (γ) $[k_Y(y)]^o \subset \mathbb{R}^l_{++} \cup \{0\}$.

The following proposition shows that, under assumption (β), Dubovickii-Miljutin's normal cone coincide with Clarke's cone. Hence Beato's assumptions imply (A.3), without weakening the equilibrium notion.

PROPOSITION (Cornet 1987)   *Let Y be a closed subset of $\mathbb{R}^l$, let $y^* \in Y$, then the three following conditions are equivalent*:

(i) $N_Y(y^*) = [k_Y(y^*)]^o$;
(ii) the correspondence $y \to [k_Y(y)]^o \cap \overline{B(0, 1)}$ is upper semicontinuous at y^*;
(iii) the correspondence $y \to [k_Y(y)]^o$ is closed at y^*.

Furthermore, if one of the conditions (i), (ii), or (iii) is satisfied, then $k_Y(y)$ is convex.

Thus the convexity assumption (α) made by Beato is, in fact, a consequence of assumption (β). We point out that these two assumptions are quite stringent. In particular they both exclude cases of paticular economic interest such as firms with a fixed cost and then a linear one, and firms having production sets as in figure 4.4.

The "Price Decentralization Property" and the "Disaggregated Approach"

The first existence approach by Beato (1979, 1982), Brown and Heal (1982), Mantel (1979), and our previous paper exhibits equilibria that are aggregate productive efficient, that is, the total equilibrium production belong to $\partial(\sum_{j=1}^{n} Y_j)$. In these papers the existence proof consists in two steps. It is first shown the existence of a marginal cost pricing equilibrium of the aggregate economy $\mathcal{E} = ((X_i, u_i, r_i), Y, \omega)$, and it is then shown that this equilibrium is also a marginal cost pricing equilibrium of the original economy. The second step relies on the following "price decentralization property", that is, the inclusion:

$$N_Y\left(\sum_{j=1}^{n} y_j^*\right) \subset \bigcap_{j=1}^{n} N_{Y_j}(y_j^*).$$

However, this inclusion is not true, in general, as shown by figure 4.4; consider the production sets Y_1 and Y_2 as defined in the above counterexample, and let $y_1^* = 0$, $y_2^* = (-16, +16)$, and $p^* = (1.5, 1)$. Then $p^* \in N_Y(y_1^* + y_2^*)$, but p^* does not belong to $N_{Y_1}(y_1^*) \cap N_{Y_2}(y_2^*)$.

It is worth pointing out the following weaker "price decentralization property" (Cornet and Rockafellar 1990). If Y_j ($j = 1, \ldots, n$) are closed subsets, and if $Y = \sum_{j=1}^{n} Y_j$ is closed and satisfies the free disposal assumption, that is, $Y - \mathbb{R}_+^l \subset Y$, then

$$N_Y(\textstyle\sum_{j=1}^{n} y_j^*) \cap \bigcap_{j=1}^{n} N_{Y_j}(y_j^*) \neq \{0\} \qquad \text{for every } y_j^* \in Y_j.$$

However, to perform the second step of the existence proof presented above, one needs the strong property (with the inclusion) that is only satisfied under very strong assumptions: assumption (A.4), or the stronger assumption that $\sum_{j=1}^{n} Y_j$ has a smooth boundary (Brown and Heal 1982; Mantel 1979), or the upper semicontinuity assumption (β) (Beato 1982).

These assumptions on the total production set are quite stringent, as shown before, and they are ruled out in the next approach, the "so called disaggregated approach," which was considered by (1): Dierker, Guesnerie, and Neuefeind (1985), Beato and Mas-Colell (1985), Brown et al. (1986), by Bonnisseau (1988), Bonnisseau-Cornet (1988a), Kamiya (1988), and Vohra (1988) in the special issue of the *Journal of Mathematical Economics* on increasing returns, and (2) by Bonnisseau-Cornet (1985, 1988b). The papers in (1) have all in common to allow for more general pricing rules than marginal cost, whereas the two last papers by Bonnisseau-Cornet only consider the existence of marginal cost pricing equilibria (and their results are not true, in general, for more general rules).

Notes

This research was done partly at the Center for Operations Research and Econometrics, Belgium, and partly while the author was visiting the Group for the Applications of Mathematics and Statistics to Economics at the University of California, Berkeley, Summer 1982. The author thanks Gerard Debreu for his hospitality and Paulina Beato and Andreu Mas-Colell for helpful discussions. The appendix is the only major modification to the paper, which has been circulating since 1982 as a Berkeley Discussion Paper.

1. The situation may be different for other questions, and, in particular, for the generalization of the second welfare theorem in the absence of convexity assumptions (cf., Ali Khan 1987, Cornet 1988, and the references in these papers).

2. The second version, which appeared as a CORE Discussion Paper in 1984, takes the interior of Clarke's tangent cone as the primary concept and then defines the normal cone by polarity, as in the definition of Dubovickii-Muljutin's cones. The existence theorems, however, are the same in both papers.

3. $[k_{Y_j}(y_j^*)]^o = \{p \in R^l | p \cdot v \leq 0 \text{ for all } v \in k_{Y_j}(y_j^*)\}$ denotes the negative polar of the cone of interior displacements $k_{Y_j}(y_j^*)$, as defined in the proof of lemma 1. We recall that we have shown previously that $T_{Y_j}(y_j^*) \stackrel{\text{def}}{=} [N_{Y_j}(y_j^*)]^o \subset k_{Y_j}(y_j^*)$; hence, $N_{Y_j}(y_j^*) \subset [k_{Y_j}(y_j^*)]^o$.

References

Beato, P. 1979. "Marginal Cost Pricing Equilibria with Increasing Returns." Ph.D. dissertation, University of Minnesota.

Beato, P. 1982. "The Existence of Marginal Cost Pricing Equilibria with Increasing Returns." *Quarterly Journal of Economics* 389:669–688.

Beato, P., and A. Mas-Colell. 1983. "Gestion au coût marginal et efficacité de la production agrégée: un exemple." *Annales de l'INSEE* 51:39–46.

Beato, P., and A. Mas-Colell. 1985. "On Marginal Cost Pricing with Given Tax-Subsidy Rules." *Journal of Economic Theory* 37:356–365.

Bonnisseau, J.-M. 1988. "On Two Existence Results of Equilibria in Economies with Increasing Returns." *Journal of Mathematical Economics* 17, 193–207.

Bonnisseau, J.-M., and B. Cornet. 1988. "Existence of Equilibria when Firms Follow Bounded Losses Pricing Rules." *Journal of Mathematical Economics* 17, 119–147.

Bonnisseau, J.-M., and B. Cornet. 1989. "Existence of Marginal Cost Pricing Equilibrium in an Economy with Several Non-Convex Firms." *Econometrica* (forthcoming).

Bonnisseau, J.-M., and B. Cornet. 1988. "Existence of Marginal Cost Pricing Equilibria: The Nonsmooth Case." CORE Discussion Paper 8815, Louvain-la-Neuve: CORE.

Brown, D., and G. Heal. 1979. "Equity, Efficiency and Increasing Returns." *Review of Economic Studies* 46:571–585.

Brown, D., and G. Heal. 1980. "Two-part Tariffs, Marginal Cost Pricing and Increasing Returns in a General Equilibrium Model." *Public Economics* 25–49.

Brown, D., G. Heal, A. Kahn, and R. Vohra. 1986. "On a General Existence Theorem for Marginal Cost Pricing Equilibrium." *Journal of Economic Theory* 38:371–379.

Clarke, F. 1975. "Generalized Gradients and Applications." *Transactions of the American Mathematical Society* 205:247–262.

Clarke, F. 1983. *Optimization and Nonsmooth Analysis.* New York: Wiley.

Cornet, B. 1987. "Regularity Properties of Open Tangent Cones." *Mathematical Programming Studies* 30:17–33.

Cornet, B. 1988. "Tarification an coût marginal et Pareto optimalité" In *Mélanges économiques: Essais en l'honneur de Edmond Malinvaud*, P. Champsaur et al. (eds.). Paris: Economica. English translation, The MIT Press, 1990, to appear.

Cornet, B. 1988. *General Equilibrium Theory and Increasing Returns*, Special Issue of the *Journal of Mathematical Economics*. Amsterdam: North Holland.

Cornet, B., and R. T. Rockafellar. 1990. "Separation Theorems and Supporting Price Theorems for Nonconvex Sets." Working paper, University of Paris I.

Debreu, G. 1959. *Theory of Value*. New York: Wiley.

Debreu, G. 1981. "Existence of Competitive Equilibrium." In *Handbook of Mathematical Economics*, edited by K. Arrow, and M. Intriligator, New York: North Holland.

Dierker, E., R. Guesnerie, and W. Neuefeind. 1985. "General Equilibrium When Some Firms Follow Special Pricing Rules." *Econometrica* 53:1369–1393.

Dubovickii, A. J., and A. Miljutin. 1965. "Extremum Problems in the Presence of Restrictions." *Zh. Vychisl. Mat. Fiz.* 5:395–453, *USSR Comp. Math. and Math. Physics* 5:1–80.

Guesnerie, R. 1975. "Pareto Optimality in Non-Convex Economies." *Econometrica* 43:1–30.

Hotelling, H. 1938. "The General Welfare in Relation to Problems of Taxation and of Railway and Utility Rate." *Econometrica* 6:242–269.

Kakutani, S. 1941. "A Generalization of Brouwer's Fixed Point Theorem." *Duke Mathematical Journal* 8:457–459

Kamiya, K. 1988. "Existence and Uniqueness of Equilibria with Increasing Returns." *Journal of Mathematical Economics* 17:149–178.

Khan, Ali M. 1987. "Ioffe's Normal Cone and Foundations of Welfare Economics." Discussion Paper, University of Illinois.

Mantel, R. 1979. "Equilibrio con Rendimientos Crecientes a Escala." *Anales de la Associacion Argentina de Economia Politica* 1:271–282.

Rockafellar, R. T. 1979. "Clarke's Tangent Cone and the Boundary of Closed sets in $\mathbb{R}^n$." *Nonlinear Analysis* 3:145–154

Vial, J. -Ph. 1983. "Strong and Weak Convexity of Sets and Functions." *Mathematics of Operations Research* 8:231–259.

5 First-Best Allocation of Resources with Nonconvexities in Production

Roger Guesnerie

Although it is generally agreed that production technologies often display increasing returns to scale, the theory of resource allocation has mainly developed under the assumption of convexity of the production sector. This situation may receive a number of explanations.

First, convexity has proved to be the adequate structure for an elegant synthesis of the ideas that have emerged in the last century of economics. Out of convex structures we have a less well-behaved mathematical world and less explored economic universe. However, compensation in gains of relevance for losses in elegance can be expected from its study.

Second, it can be argued that some key results obtained under the convexity assumption[1] remain (approximately) relevant in circumstances where convexity fails. For example, in economies with a large consumption side, nonconvexities in preferences do not destroy the standard results of, say, Debreu's theory of value. In the same way, if indivisibilities in the production sector are small with respect to the size of the economy, such as when the "efficient" production scale of a production unit is small with respect to the size of the product market, then standard results are affected in only a minor way. There is no doubt, however, that large indivisibilities and natural monopolies (although the terms are not synonymous) require specific treatment.[2]

A third reason for the attention given to the convexity assumption in formalized theory may be found in the biases toward monopolistic competition introduced by increasing returns to scale in production. The situation is likely to call for a positive theory significantly different from the Walrasian one and which we know to be difficult. A symmetric argument can be drawn for normative theory; it is intuitively plausible that the "large" organizations often needed for the management of techniques displaying large indivisibilities raise incentive compatibility questions that are more acute than they are in a convex world with smaller units. However, the progressive attack of difficulties—a characteristic of the analytic method—should prove as helpful in this field as in others.

With these general remarks in mind, I found it reasonable to delimitate this chapter according to the following lines: First, I will be concerned only with nonconvexities in the production sector of an economy without public goods and externalities and I will assume convexity of preferences.[3] I have already mentioned that in an economy with many consumers, this restriction is not likely to have much effect. Second, I will emphasize the general equilibrium aspects of the problem, that is, pure theory rather than its applications. Finally, my approach will be guided by normative theory and remain in the "first-best" spirit. That means that the organizational problems I raise here partly neglect the informational constraints that are often at the source of second-best analysis. The introduction into the theory of the incentives questions generated by asymmetric information is a promising subject that has passed the state of infancy but remains in an exploratory phase. The reader interested in the subject is invited to refer to a survey by Caillaud, Guesnerie, Rey, and Tirole (1988), the first version of which was written in parallel with the present chapter.

Section 5.1 presents a brief review of the types of nonconvex production sets encountered in the literature and attempts to give a brief description of nonconvexities. Section 5.2 reviews the conditions of a (first-best) Pareto optimal allocation of resources and comments on several issues of decentralization (two-part tariffs, etc.). Section 5.3 continues discussing conditions of first-best efficiency. It stresses that the presence of nonconvexities endangers the principle of separation between efficiency and equity issues as it has solidified in the economists' intuition from the experience of a convex world. Also a general equilibrium version of surplus maximization is presented and is shown to provide a correct nonlinear scheme for decentralization. Section 5.4 concerns the so-called resource allocation processes. It mentions briefly some planning algorithms and discusses at length the concept of marginal cost pricing equilibrium. This concept formalizes the description of the outcome of economic activity when it is organized according to the principles of the so-called marginal cost pricing doctrine. A number of studies have been devoted to this subject (concerning existence, optimality), and they are reviewed in this section. Section 5.5 considers other directions of research: study of the core of economies with increasing returns to scale, public control of natural monopolies through taxation, and approximate efficiency.

5.1 Nonconvexities in Production

Preliminary Remarks

Convex production sets are regular bodies familiar to the economist. Nonconvex sets belong to a much broader category of mathematical objects, and we would like to know whether the large variety of irregularities that can a priori be found can be restricted by considerations drawn from the economic theory of production. In discussing this issue, it is useful to review some well-known facts relative to the justification of the convexity assumption for production.

In the following, the commodity space is $\mathbf{R}^n$, and we now introduce two axioms on the production set Y, a subset of $\mathbf{R}^n$. The first, *additivity*, holds for a production set Y if for every couple of production plans y_1, y_2 that are elements of Y, the sum $y_1 + y_2$ belongs to Y. The second, *Divisibility* (or *nonincreasing returns to scale*) holds if for every production plan y belonging to Y, ty also belongs to Y, with $0 \leq t \leq 1$. In other words, divisibility holds if every production plan can be "miniaturized" to the extent desired. It is generally argued that although additivity may fail when production is formalized in a setting where the number of commodities has been fixed a priori, it can nevertheless be an economically meaningful property once all factors of production have been identified. In some sense we could base production theory upon the following axiom, which we will call AO: "within some (possibly) enlarged commodity space, additivity is an economically meaningful property." Divisibility is a much more debatable property and a number of reasons of its failure have been discussed in the literature (a thorough exposition of the subject can be found in Arrow-Hahn 1971). However, if one accepts AO and if divisibility holds (in the enlarged space), it is well known that the production set is necessarily a convex cone in the enlarged commodity space, and consequently it is a convex set in the original commodity space.

If the justifications of the convexity assumption for production briefly sketched above are accepted, then nonconvexities should be attributed to the failure of divisibility and hence be associated with indivisibilities, that is, in the present terminology, with increasing returns to scale. There then arises the question of what are the implications, if any, of accepting axiom AO for production theory when in some areas of production there are increasing returns to scale. A "fundamentalist" view of this would suggest that pure analysis be conducted in the commodity space where additivity holds. Such an approach, which has been advocated in classical contexts by McKenzie (among others), would apply, in particular, to the theory of resource allocation and to the study of general equilibrium of the core. More pragmatically one should recommend the intellectual exercise of trying to figure out whether in each case the failure of additivity may be attributed to some "hidden" factors.

On Some Classes of Nonconvex Production Sets

Let us present a number of classes of nonconvex production sets considered in the literature. The statement of definitions will be neither completely informal (they are sketched) nor completely formal (notation is not fully explicit). Note that free disposal, that is, $Y\text{-}\mathbf{R}^n_+ \subset Y$, is always implicitly assumed.

The first category we single out consists of production sets *with convex iso output sections*. They come naturally into the picture in the study of decentralization. Assuming that an output space and an input space can be identified, the output vector y^0 (with all positive components) is distinguished from the input vector y^I (with all negative components), hence the production plan is $y = (y^0, y^i)$. A production set Y has convex iso output sections if $Y \cap (y^0 = \bar{y}^0)^4$ is a convex set, for every $\bar{y}^0$ belonging to the range of possible output vectors. Similarly, we could define production sets with convex iso input sections (see Guesnerie 1975).

A second category often considered in the literature consists of production sets having *strictly increasing returns to scale* everywhere. Formally, this means that the production set Y is such that, for every efficient point y (belonging to the efficiency frontier of Y), and for every $t < 1$, ty does not belong to Y. A slightly different definition, perhaps more convenient, is the following: for every efficient point $y \neq 0$, and every $t < 1$, $(1/t)y$ belongs to the interior of Y.

The concept of natural monopoly is much discussed in the literature. The tentative formal definition I propose here follows Allais' definition of *secteur différencié*. It also conforms with the definition of natural monopolies, based on cost functions, advocated by Baumol and his collaborators. However, Baumol's definitions are local, that is, relative to a given scale of market demand and to fixed input prices when the following one is global, referring to a strong form of natural monopoly. *Strong natural monopoly* is said to hold for a set Y if for every nonzero efficient point of Y, it is impossible to find two nonzero-elements of Y, y_1, y_2 such that $y \leq y_1 + y_2$. In other words, there is always a *strict* loss in duplicating production between two different firms. Note that the property defined here is stronger than the additivity property discussed above: it could be termed *subadditivity* (of production sets and not of cost functions as in Baumol).

At this point we could compare the different concepts just introduced. This comparison is facilitated if we consider the distinction emphasized by

Baumol (1977), Panzar-Willig (1977) and others concerning "ray" and "transray" properties. Let me explain the distinction in the case of production sets describing the production of several outputs from one input.[5] Given the output vector y^0, the production set is defined by the function with associates to y^0 the minimal input level that allows to produce it, that is, $\Phi(y^0)$. The shape of the production set can be understood by looking at it first along a ray, along a fixed direction of y^0, and then by looking at deformations from ray to ray. It can already be understood from this remark that there is no simple relationship between the concept of increasing returns to scale and the concept of natural monopoly. The first one is ray-specific when the second one implies transray comparisons. Now let us forget for a moment the transray aspects of the confrontation and consider the restriction of a production set along a ray. Increasing returns to scale are roughly equivalent to *decreasing ray average costs*, that is, to the fact that the function $\lambda \mapsto (\Phi(\lambda \bar{y}^0)/\lambda$ is increasing. This implies subadditivity (along a ray), but the converse is not true: a subadditive firm does not necessarily have a decreasing ray average cost. Figure 5.1 provides the standard counterexample: returns to scale are not strictly increasing, although the duplication of production between firms is never justified, so we have natural monopoly. Note indeed that any point $M(\alpha, \beta)$ passes the test of natural monopoly proposed by D. Fisher (see Baumol 1977): The production frontier never meets its mirror image with respect to $M'(OM' = (1/2)OM)$ in the input interval $(\alpha, \alpha/2)$.

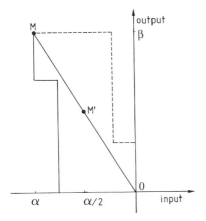

Figure 5.1

Things are getting worse when transray considerations are introduced. It turns out that according to Baumol (1977), we have "the most unexpected finding" of the theory, "that scale economies are neither necessary nor sufficient for monopoly to be the least costly form of organization" (p. 809). The reasons why increasing return are not necessary have been discussed. The fact that they are not sufficient comes from the fact that increasing returns to scale only impose ray specific properties but a priori few restrictions on transray deformations. With this in mind, it is easy to construct examples of strictly increasing returns to scale sets that are not strong natural monopolies. Take, for example, a production set Y which has iso output sections that are not convex; that y_1, y_2 two iso output production plans, so that $(y_1 + y_2)/2$ does not belong to Y; if along the corresponding intermediate ray returns are not "too much" increasing, then it understandable that $y_1 + y_2$ may not belong to Y. Let us go now further in the discussion of transray properties.

First, the concept of *transray convexity* which is central to the argument of "sustainability" given By Baumol-Bailey-Willig (1977) will be briefly presented. This is a local concept (relative to some output vector $\bar{y}^0$) involving the shape of the production possibility set (or the graph of the cost function if one considers cost functions rather than one-input production sets). Transray convexity holds if there exists an hyperplane in $\mathbf{R}^n$ through $\bar{y}^0$, with a normal in the positive orthant of the output space, such that the intersection of this hyperplane with the epigraph of the cost function is convex. In particular, transray convexity implies that if two output vectors of the given hyperplane correspond to the same cost (or input level) then any convex combination of these vectors is cheaper. It corresponds to "economies of scope" in Panzar-Willig's suggestive terminology.[6]

The second question concerning economies of scope can be formulated as follows: What does additivity (which reflects a weak form of "economies of scope") imply for the structure of the production set when it is combined with economies of scale? It turns out that when two technologies with increasing returns to scale use the same input or produce the same output, the production set deriving from their juxtaposition (under the additivity assumption) may have badly behaved sections. An example of this phenomenon has first been given by Arrow-Hurwicz (1960). It goes as follows. Take two production processes. The first one, associated with the production set Y^A allows the transform of one input into an output with a strictly increasing returns to scale technology. The second one associated with the production set Y^B, allows the transform of another input into the *same* output through another strictly increasing returns to scale technology. Consider now $Y^A + Y^B$ and an iso output section $y^0 = \bar{y}^0$. Both production plans $(\bar{y}^0, 0, y_A^I)$, $(\bar{y}^0, y_B^I, 0)$ (which I assume to be efficient in Y^A and Y^B, respectively, and for which I take straightforward notation) belong to the section. However, $(\bar{y}^0, ty_B^I, (1 - t)y_A^I)$ cannot belong to $Y_A + Y_B$: to produce $t\bar{y}^0$ requires more than ty_B^I and to produce $(1 - t)\bar{y}^0$ requires (strictly) more than $(1 - t)y_A^I$. This example hence shows that the iso output section of the production set $Y^A + Y^B$ is not convex, although the iso output section of each production set Y^A, Y^B is convex. The example could be adapted in order to obtain nonconvex iso input sections from the addition of production sets having convex iso input sections.

The above example can be viewed in terms of merging processes for firms. Taking two firms whose both production sets belong to one of the categories introduced above, one may wonder whether they will remain in the same category after merging. In mathematical terms one is considering whether the categories introduced above are closed for the operation of addition of sets. The preceding example actually shows that the category of production sets with convex iso output sections is not. I leave to the reader to pursue the reflection for the other categories that have been introduced.

The concept of distributive set due to H. Scarf (1981) (and to which we will return in section 5.5) can also be viewed as involving some kind of economies of scope. Consider production plans $y^k \in Y$. The set Y is said to be distributive, if every positive combination $y = \sum \alpha^k y^k$, $\alpha^k > 0$ belongs to Y provided the quantity of any input of y is larger (in absolute value) than the quantity of the same input in any of the y^k. This definition implies increasing returns to scale and also convex iso input sections, but more than that it implies that the restriction of the production set to input vectors smaller than some a priori given input vector is below the cone generated by the convex iso input section associated with the given vector. Dehez-Drèze (1988) proposed a symmetrical definition of distributive sets (although equivalent in the one-input, one-output case) that reverses the role that inputs and outputs have in Scarf's definition.[7]

As a final parenthesis, one should note here that the work of H. Scarf (1981) (which has no relationship with his work on the core) represents one important step in the direction of improving basic production theory with indivisibilities. This work is, however, beyond the scope of this survey here, as the reader will have recognized; the emphasis is rather on what has been called the "shape aspects" of nonconvexities (Calsamiglia 1977).

5.2   Pareto Optimality in a Nonconvex Economy: Characterization

The subject we turn to now has had a long history that can be traced back as far as to Dupuit (1844) in his discussion of public utility pricing. In the same context of public pricing, the idea that an optimum of welfare "corresponds to the sale of everything at marginal cost" was developed by Hotelling (1938). A previous recognition of the failure of the competitive mechanism when increasing returns to scale are present is usually attributed to Marshall (1920) and "a theory of marginal cost pricing" was later elaborated by Pigou (1933), Lange (1936), Lerner (1937), and Allais (1943), among others.

An history of ideas in this field would certainly be fascinating, but neither the purpose of this survey nor the competence of the author justify more than the above brief review. The state of the art on the characterization of Pareto optimum in nonconvex economies will now be presented in the abstract model of the economy à la Arrow-Debreu. For this presentation I rely much on my own article on this subject (Guesnerie 1975), although other models of an abstract economy (Brown-Heal 1980) could have been used. (For an emphasis on the differentiability techniques, see also Smale 1976.)

Characterization of Pareto Optima

Consider an abstract Arrow-Debreu economy. The commodity space is $\mathbf{R}^n$. Consumers are indexed by i ($i = 1, \ldots, m$). For each consumer, there exists a complete preordering $\lesssim_i$ over his (her) consumption set X_i, and this preordering is represented by a utility function U_i. Production sets Y_j are subsets of $\mathbf{R}^n$ ($j = 1, \ldots, q$). Total initial endowments define a vector ω of $\mathbf{R}^n_+$.

Let us assume that consumption sets and preferences are convex so that we can focus on nonconvexity in the production sector. In this abstract economy a set of feasible states can be defined and assumed to be nonempty (otherwise we do not have an interesting problem). We expect in most nonpathological problems to get a compact set of feasible states.

Also we expect that the Pareto preordering has maximal elements, Pareto optima, on the characterization of which we are now focusing on.

At this point we make no special assumption about production sets. We know that either (1) they can be approximated in a satisfactory way, around each point of their frontier, by some kind of (convex) "tangent cone" (we do not provide any formal definition; there are several different candidates for such "cones" to which we will come back later), (2) or we require that at each point there be defined some (convex) "normal cone," the cone of "outward normals." (Note that if a "tangent cone" exists, the "normal cone" may be defined as its negative polar cone.) The just mentioned regularity conditions are not too demanding. They allow us to derive characterization theorems that typically have the flavor of the following statement:

THEOREM 1 Given a Pareto optimal feasible state $(x_i^*)(x_j^*)$ in which one consumer is not satiated, there exists a vector of "prices" or "social values" $\rho^* \neq 0$ such that

(i) x_i^* minimizes $\rho^* \cdot x_i$ subject to $x_j \gtrsim x_i^*$, $\forall i$, and

(ii) ρ^* belongs to the "normal cone" of Y_j, in y_j^*, $\forall j$.

Versions of this statement that make precise the nonsatiation condition and condition (ii) are found in Guesnerie (1975) where the "tangent cone" used is the cone of interior displacements introduced by the Russian mathematicians Doubovitsky-Millioutine (1965). The "normal cone" is the negative polar cone of the cone of interior displacements. If the latter one is denoted $k(Y_j, y_j^*)$ and the former one k^+, condition (ii) can be equivalently rewritten as follows:

(ii) $\rho^* \in k^+(Y_j, y_j^*)$.

The concept of the *cone of interior displacements* was later adopted by Beato (1976) in her thesis. Cornet (1988) has convincingly argued that the appropriate concept for the analysis is rather the "Clarke's cone of normals." Besides technical advantages, this new tool allows us to consider production sets with inward kinks and to remove the convexity of local approximations needed in Guesnerie (1975). Versions of the above theorems using this different concept have been obtained. (See Cornet 1986, 1988b and Bonnisseau-Cornet 1988a.) More recently, another variant has been obtained by Ali M. Khan (1987) using the Ioffe's cone (which is smaller than the Clarke's cone).

Whatever the technicalities involved, the meaning of the above statement is straightforward. In a (first-best) Pareto optimal state, some minimal coordination is required between the plans of the agents; "optimal" production plans must be such that the "normal cones" of the associated production sets have a common vector of "social values" in their intersection.

When the production set Y_j has a smooth frontier, the "normal cone" coincides with the outward normal vector of the surface (whatever the concept of normal cone used), and condition (ii) coincides with

(ii) a) ρ^* is an outward normal vector at y_j^* to the surface limiting Y_j (denoted $V(Y_j, y_j^*)$ in the following).

This latter condition means that when the frontier of Y_j is smooth around y_j^*, any infinitesimal move dy_j around y_j^*, satisfies $\rho^* \cdot dy_j = 0$. In other words, Pareto optimality implies that at the optimal production plan, the profit for each smooth firm is extremal (for a characterization of Pareto optimality under smoothness assumptions (see also Smale 1976).

First Comments

As already stressed, the basic idea behind the above theorems has a long history. However, the above formal approach sheds more light on a number of issues.

First, the above theorem actually constitutes a generalization of the second theorem of welfare economics: if Y_j is convex, condition (ii) is equivalent to

(ii) b) $\rho^* \cdot y_j^* > \rho^* \cdot y_j, \forall y_j \in Y_j,$

that is, the optimal production plans are profit maximizing with respect to the vector of social values ρ^*. Some of the subsequent discussions relate to other extensions of the theory of value to nonconvex economies.

Second, because profit in extremum is y_j^*, in a sense price equals marginal cost. Consider the firm producing one output (the argument straightforwardly extends to several outputs); the production plan y^* (drop j) can be written down, distinguishing output from inputs (y^{*0}, y^{*I}). Taking dy^0 an (infinitesimal) change in output and dy^I a corresponding (infinitesimal) change in inputs, we get from the fact that profit is extremum that $\rho^{*0} \cdot dy^0 = |\rho^{*I} \cdot dy^I|$ or $\rho^{*0} = |\rho^{*I} \cdot dy^I|/dy^0$ (with the obvious notation). Hence the social value (or price) of the output equals the increment of cost associated, in the neighborhood of the optimal production plan, with an increment of one unit of the output level. However, it is somewhat misleading to interpret this equality as the equality of price and marginal cost;[8] y^{*I} is not necessarily an input combination leading to the production of the output target at *minimum* cost, cost being measured with respect to the social values (or prices) of inputs ρ^{*I}. In other words, if one considers the usual cost function of production theory $C(y^0, p)$, and assumes it to be differentiable with respect to y^0, condition (iia) does *not* imply that $\rho^{*0} = \partial C / \partial y^0 (y^{0*}, \rho^{*I})$.

It is easy to see that cost minimization can fail. Take the example of the production of one output with two inputs in which the section of the production set at some given level of output has the shape indicated on figure 5.2. If indifference curves of social welfare have the shape suggested by the dotted line, then the social optimum will be C when cost minimization necessary leads to A or B. The example suggests that the convexity of the section output $= C^{\text{ste}}$ would be enough to restore necessity of cost minimization. It is easy to show that this is indeed the case. Assuming that the production set is such that iso output sections are convex and the cost function is differentiable, then condition (ii) takes the form

(ii) d) $\rho^{*0} = \dfrac{\partial C}{\partial y^0}(y^{*0}, \rho^{*I}).$

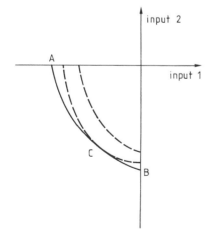

Figure 5.2

Only in this latter case, efficiency unambiguously requires that prices equal marginal costs.

The latter considerations provide an unusual challenge to cost minimization as a management rule. It should be noted that its failure may depend on the way technologies are grouped into firms: for example, in the example of section 5.1 of two increasing returns to scale firms producing the same output with two different inputs, cost minimization is a satisfactory management rule provided the two firms are independent, but it is not desirable when two firms are merged (since the total production set has nonconvex iso output sections, having the shape indicated in figure 5.2). In other words, the conditions of decentralization may significantly be affected by the way production technologies are assigned to centers of decisions. Note that the distinction thus introduced between "technologies" and "center of decision" is meaningless in the traditional welfare analysis of the decentralization of convex economies.

The fact that cost minimization does not necessarily select the "right" techniques even if the "right" price system is used is, however, not surprising: it seems contradictory to expect to find a broad enough environment in which profit maximization is inadequate for the choice of output levels, when cost minimization would be a correct selection procedure for techniques.

Third, let $\rho^* \cdot y_j^*$, be the profit of firm j, evaluated at the adequate price vector ρ^*, for example, with a technology with iso output convex section. If the firm has strictly increasing returns in the sense of the definition of section 5.1, then its marginal cost is a decreasing function (with respect to the output quantity) and the equality $\rho^{*0} = \partial C/\partial y^0(y^{*0}, \rho^{*1})$ implies that $\rho^* \cdot y_j^*$ is negative. (Note, however, that the same is not necessarily true for a strong natural monopoly in the sense of section 5.1.)

This is a first well-known disturbing fact for the implementation of marketlike mechanisms for decentralization; firms with nonpositive profit are not supposed to survive in a market context. However, there is room in the interpretation of the above abstract theorem. Necessary conditions of optimality only imply that each consumer faces marginal cost for the price to be paid for the marginal quantity he demands.[9] (Personalized) nonlinear pricing that meets this last condition is not a priori incompatible with decentralization. In particular, one may wonder whether the optimum can be sustained by *personalized two-part tariffs* that induce correct decisions for consumers and ensure a positive profit for the firm. Two-part tariffs rely on a fixed fee (entrance fee) plus a proportional fee. One can imagine different two-part tariffs equilibria according to whether

1. the entrance fee is aggregate (this gives access to any commodity produced by the nonconvex sector) or disaggregate (this gives access to all the outputs of a given firm or to a single output);

2. the entrance fees are sufficient to balance the budget of a given firm, of a given sector, or of the nonconvex sector as a whole; and

3. the firm's behavior, for given entrance fees, is or is not compatible with profit maximization. (We leave it to the reader to consider different possible formal definitions.)

The intuition for the sustainability of the optimum via an aggregate entrance fee is clear when one considers increasing returns coming from the existence of a fixed cost for only one firm. In a first-best Pareto optimum the Scitovsky indifference surface is entirely above the set of aggregate feasible consumption plans. The aggregate budget set associated with the optimum (OAB in figure 5.3) looks like a budget set associated with a two-part tariff and can actually be viewed as the sum of individual budget sets having the same shape as the aggregate budget set and being below individual indifference curves associated with the given optimum. The sharpest conclusion going into the direction just suggested by this example is that of Brown-Heal (1980) who assert that the adequate entrance fee is

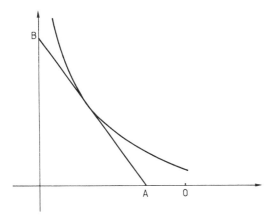

Figure 5.3

aggregate and commodity based. However, the criterion obtained—that the consumption bundle would be outside some linear subspace—seems somewhat cumbrous. (See the quoted authors for a more precise analysis.)

The difficulty in obtaining general results may not be surprising if one notes that the graphical argument of figure 5.3 is somewhat misleading in higher-dimensional spaces. In a three-commodity world with two different outputs, one produced by a decreasing returns firm and the other one with a technique involving fixed cost, decentralization via an entrance fee may be impossible (see Quinzii 1988).

Finally, the analysis of first-order conditions of Pareto optimality stressed in the preceding analysis should be completed with an analysis of second-order conditions. This subject does not seem to have attracted much attention. Allais contributed to this problem in his 1943 book, and a number of expressions of second-order conditions were obtained in his more recent book (1979) which returned to a comprehensive analysis of the concept of *surplus distribuable*. We will not consider in detail the second-order conditions but only stress the effects that the "coexistence" of convex and nonconvex firms has on the optimal production of the same good. The first effect was pointed out by Allais himself: In a two-commodity economy (one input, one output) optimality requires that at most one firm operate in an area of "local increasing returns to scale." An extension of Allais' argument to a n commodity world was obtained by Beato (1976) using differentiability techniques (then at most $n - 1$ firms are outside a "locally convex" area of their production set). The results have a flavor reminiscent of those obtained with the powerful Shapley-Folkman lemma which has been much exploited in the theoretical literature of the 1970s (see Starr 1969 and Arrow-Hahn 1971 for an analysis that considers small indivisibilities).

5.3   Pareto Optimality in a Nonconvex Economy: Further Developments

Income Distribution and Pareto Optimum in a Nonconvex Economy

The study of convex economies has accustomed economists to the idea that equity and efficiency can be separated. This sort of principle can be given different meanings. To discuss it in more detail, we have to refer to a more precise formulation. (The one chosen here is convenient but is only one among others.)

Consider the abstract economy of section 5.2, we further assume that, for every i, $X_i = \mathbf{R}^n_+$. Let α denote a specific Pareto optimum. Noting that (under weak conditions) the set of Pareto optima is homeomorphic[10] to the simplex of $\mathbf{R}^m$ denoted ζ^m, we can identify α with a vector of ζ^m (recall that m is the number of consumers). Let $(x_i(\alpha), y_j(\alpha))$ be the allocation and $\rho(\alpha)$ be the price vector associated with the optimum.

Compute $r_i(\alpha) \overset{\text{def}}{=} (\rho(\alpha) \cdot x_i(\alpha))/\sum \rho(\alpha) \cdot x_i(\alpha))$; this is in fact the share of "national income"[11] given to consumer i (note that $\sum_i r_i(\alpha) = 1$), an income indicator that is taken here for convenience. The mapping r: $\alpha \to (r_1(\alpha), \ldots, r_m(\alpha))$ can be viewed as a mapping from the simplex into itself. In this framework separation between equity and efficiency issues can take a number of forms:

1. A weak form. With every Pareto optimum one can associate shares of national incomes that allow to "decentralize" the optimum. This assertion is true in convex economies where it appears as a version of the second theorem of welfare economics. As we have seen above, this assertion also holds in a nonconvex economy, with a less demanding concept of decentralization.

2. A strong form according to which there exists a one-to-one correspondence between Pareto optima and shares of national income. This strong form is generally wrong even in a convex economy.

3. An intermediate form that assumes that in addition to (1), which determines the existence of the mapping r, we have $r(\zeta^m) = \zeta^m$, that is, the mapping r is surjective (S). In other words, every share of national income is reached as decentralized income when one goes over the set of Pareto optima.

This intermediate separation principle holds in a convex economy. It obtains, for example, as a combination of an existence theorem of "Walras' equilibria" (which ensures the existence of an equilibrium for every share of national income) and of the first theorem of welfare economics (which ensures that the exhibited price equilibrium belongs to the set of Pareto optima).

The equality $r(\zeta^m) = \zeta^m$ (which again is conditional on the possibility of defining a mapping r, i.e., on weak decentralization properties), necessarily incorporates existence theorems, for equilibria of the Walras type in a convex setting and of marginal cost pricing type in a nonconvex one. In fact, mappings analogous to r have been used for some time in solving existence problems. Negishi (1960) is credited for the first existence study based on a mapping starting from the set of Pareto optima. Many existence proofs of Walrasian equilibria rely on this device, and without any claim to exhaustivity, one may mention Arrow-Hahn (1971), Fabre-Sender and Guesnerie (1973), Mantel (1979) and, to quote a more recent article on an economy with an infinite horizon, Kehoe-Levine (1982).

The surjectivity property (S) incorporates an optimality assessment: it asserts that among the set of equilibria (for a given structure of incomes), one is Pareto optimal. This can be viewed as a weak generalization of the first welfare theorem to the case of nonconvex economies (naturally, in such economies the first welfare theorem *stricto-sensu* remains true but is often empty) supporting the standard economic intuition of separation between equity and efficiency issues. Hence a natural and conceivable generalization of the theory of value to nonconvex economies, besides the generalization of what has been called the weak separation principle incorporated in the statement of section 5.2, would consist in the generalization of the surjectivity result (S).

Note that the result is not a priori hopeless. In particular, the fact that among the marginal cost pricing equilibria one is Pareto optimal is true in a one-consumer economy. It may, however, be wrong in a nonconvex economy with several consumers. The counterexample given in Guesnerie (1975) considers an economy whose set of feasible consumption bundles has the shape indicated in figure 5.4. A two-consumer economy is considered. Preferences are exhibited such that the income distribution $(\frac{1}{2},\frac{1}{2})$ (each obtains half of national income) is never associated with a Pareto optimum. To show that, it is enough to consider the "distribution economies" (in the sense of Malinvaud 1969) associated with A and B, to compute their equilibrium, with income distributed in the proportion $(\frac{1}{2},\frac{1}{2})$, and to draw the associated Scitovsky indifference curves through A and B. The counterexample obtains when the Scitovsky indifference curves have the shape depicted on figure 5.4.

The counterexample presented later by Brown-Heal (1979) has a very similar flavor. The aggregate production set has exactly the same shape but a simplified computation and a more suggestive interpretation comes from a more systematic treatment of Edgeworth boxes and of the set of feasible utilities associated with the distribution economies A and B (depicted on

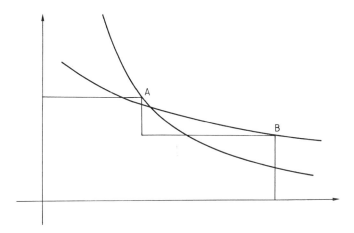

Figure 5.4

figure 5.5) associated with A and B. A counterexample obtains for an income distribution, giving rise to equilibria associated with C and D.

Hence the surjectivity of the mapping r cannot be expected in general. This has a certain number of consequences to which we will come back later. There are, however, nonconvex economies where the surjectivity of r, and in some sense the separation of equity and efficiency issues, obtain. This is the case of (1) economies that are in some sense homeomorphic to convex economies (for a precise statement see Brown-Heal 1981) and (2) economies with homothetic preferences where Scitovsky indifference surfaces do not intersect.

In fact, the problem is intimately related with the continuity properties of the mapping r. The surjectivity property actually follows from the continuity of r (Guesnerie 1981, ch. 2, prop. 17; for a related analysis, see Tillman 1982) and, upstream, from the continuity of the mapping that associates production (and consumption) plans to every Pareto optimum, a property that clearly fails in the above example. Hence the paradoxical phenomenon of "inefficient" income distributions crucially *depends upon the fact the socially optimal production plan may jump when the weights attributed to consumers in the social evaluation criterion change slightly.*[12]

Let us take advantage of this discussion to mention an idea that has often been presented at least informally. It consists in an analogy between the production scale of an increasing returns to scale firm and a public good.

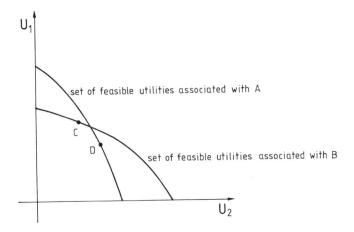

Figure 5.5

Actually Dierker (1984) has been able to exploit this idea. His argument rests on a clever trick that would be too long to report here. It is, however, interesting to note that the original equilibria of the private good economy, later called marginal cost pricing equilibria, become in Dierker's transformed economy Lindhal equilibria. More interestingly, the nonconvexities in preferences of the transformed economy do not vanish in the aggregate with a large number of consumers. And an originally inefficient equilibrium corresponds to an inefficient Lindhal equilibrium, with inefficiency then having a classical origin.

The Decentralized Attainment of Pareto Optima through "Surplus Maximization": A General Equilibrium Approach

The immediate implication of the preceding characterization theorem is that signals of correct prices do not bring enough information to the firm for the choice of its production plan. Do more complex signals, for example, nonlinear price schedules, provide sufficient information?[13] In partial equilibrium analysis it is assumed that the maximization of (consumers' + producers') surplus leads to "optimal" decisions. This fact has been used in applied analyses involving nonconvex technologies (see, for example, Gastaud-Grandmont 1967) and in many partial equilibrium theoretical models for example, those used in incentives theory (Baron-Myerson 1982).[14] In this section I will attempt to describe a general equilibrium version of the surplus criterion, that is, to find an economically significant decision criterion that, if used by a firm, would lead it to socially optimal decisions. Two preliminary remarks come out straightforwardly.

First, for each first-best Pareto optimum (α), one would like to find some "meaningful" function $\phi_j(\cdot, \alpha)$ such that the optimal production plan of firm j appears as the maximum of such a function under technological constraints, that is, such that $(A_j)y_j^*$ max $\phi_j(y_j, \cdot)$, $y_j \in Y_j$. Given that y_j^* is efficient (for firm j), a separating surface between Y_j and $(y_j^* + \mathbf{R}_+^n)$, which exists under a very weak assumption, provides a "germ" for such a function (see Brown-Heal 1980).

Second, assume that there exists some function ϕ such that $(A)y^*$ maximize $\phi(y, \cdot)$, over the set Y, that is, we have found some function the maximization of which over the global production set Y leads to the choice of the optimal production plan y^* (again from the above remark this should not be too difficult). Then it is easy to see that (A_j) holds with $\phi_j = \phi(y_{-j}^* + y_j, \cdot)$ and with

$$y_{-j}^* \overset{\text{def}}{=} \sum_{i \neq j} y_i^*.$$

In other words, firm j can use the global criterion ϕ in considering as fixed the production of all other firms. This point also is stressed in Brown-Heal (1980) who argue that (after translation) the corresponding functions can be taken as homogeneous.

The question is, however, not exhausted; we look for functions ϕ and ϕ_j that have economic meaning. To find them, we proceed as follows (Guesnerie 1980, ch. 2): First, we consider the maximization problem for fixed $y \in \mathbf{R}^n$, $\alpha \in \zeta^m$:

Maximize λ

subject to $U_i(x_i) \geq \lambda \alpha_i$

and $\sum_i x_i \leq y + \omega$.

This is a maximization of social welfare, subject to the constraint that the vector of utilities be in the direction α and that global production is fixed at y. Call $V(y, \alpha)$ the maximum of this problem. It is a concave function which whenever differentiable, satisfies the property that $\partial_y V = \theta(y, \alpha)p(y, \alpha)$, where $p(y, \alpha)$ is vector price of $\mathbf{R}^n$ that is normalized in such a way that the numéraire (commodity 1) has price 1 and $\theta(y, \alpha)$ is a number that gives the marginal "social utility" of the numéraire. From the second welfare theorem, $p(y, \alpha)$ is an equilibrium price vector associated with adequate individual incomes $R_i(y, \alpha)$. It follows from this analysis that

1. $\phi(y, \alpha)$ of formula (A) can be taken as $V(y, \alpha)$ and ϕ_j of formula (A_j) can be taken as $V(y^*_{-j} + y_j, \alpha)$, and

2. $V(y, \alpha)$ can be written, up to a constant, $\int \theta(u, \alpha)p(u, \alpha)du$, the integral being taken along any line from 0 to y (meeting, however, the condition $y + \omega \gg 0$).

Summarizing and dropping notation α, we have the following assertion:

THEOREM 2   Given a Pareto optimum (x^*_i, y^*_j) of an economy, there exists functions $p^*(y), \theta^*(y), R^*_i(y)$ such that $p^*(y)$ is a (normalized) equilibrium price vector when incomes are $R^*_i(y)$ and such that

(i) x^*_i maximizes $U_i(x_i)$ under the constraint $p^*(y^*) \cdot x_i \leq R^*_i(y^*)$,

(ii) y^* maximizes $\int_0^y \theta^*(u)p^*(u) \, du$, under the constraint $y \in Y$;

(iii) y^*_j maximizes $\int_0^{y_j} \theta^*(y^*_{-j} + u_j)p^*(y^*_{-j} + u_j)du_j$, under the constraint $y_j \in y_j$.

(All integrals can be computed along *any* path where the integrand is defined, going from its origin to its extremity.)

Theorem 2 asserts that there is a criterion of the surplus type that provides a "correct" decision rule for each convex or nonconvex firm. This "general equilibrium surplus" calls for some comment. First, note that there are of course many different social welfare functions $V(y, \alpha)$ that could have been taken without modifying the analysis. In other words, $V(y, \alpha)$ is one social welfare function that has its maximum in y^*, but there are others from which a different function $p(y, \alpha)$ could have been drawn. Second, condition (iii) points out several differences with the general equilibrium surplus function and the partial equilibrium surplus function:

1. The utility of the numéraire may be variable along the path of integration.

2. $p^*(y)$ is an equilibrium price vector (depending upon the production plan y) that is associated with some income distribution that itself depends upon y.

3. In distinguishing between inputs and outputs $(y_j = y^0_j, y^I_j)$ then condition (iii) *does not imply*, in general, that

$$y_j^{*0} \max \int_0^{y_j^0} y_j \theta^*(y_j^0) p^*(y_j^0) dy_j^0 - C_j(p^{*I}(y^*), y_j^0),$$

where the above maximand is the difference between some (sophisticated) version of the standard consumer surplus and a cost. It cannot even be asserted that y_j^{*0} is an extremum of such an expression.

Hence the general equilibrium surplus considered here and the partial equilibrium surplus only coincides in very special circumstances (which I leave to the reader to make more explicit). This is not surprising, and it conforms to the conclusions obtained from the examination of the compatibility of partial equilibrium measures of surplus with social welfare maximization. Studies on the subject, such as by Blackorby-Donaldson (1983) and Roberts (1982), complement the analysis of this subsection.

5.4 Marginal Cost Pricing as a Resource Allocation Process

Characterizing the first-best Pareto optimum is a natural first step in our reflection. The second step involves looking at what Hurwicz (1972) called the resource allocation process. Resource allocation processes (in the Hurwicz terminology as used by Calsamiglia 1977) have the purpose of making explicit the information channels, then the procedures within which the agents' interaction takes place, and finally the outcome(s) they induce. In the first subsection I will describe briefly Hurwicz' framework and planning algorithms and then I will present a result due to Calsamiglia (1977) concerning the minimum dimensionality of the message space to be used in a nonconvex economy. In the second and third subsections I will discuss marginal cost pricing (MCP) equilibria. (Since MCP equilibria can be viewed as the outcome of some kind of resource allocation process organized along the lines of the precepts of Lerner, Hotelling, Allais, and others, precepts that I will refer to as the *marginal cost pricing doctrine*.)

Resource Allocation Processes, Planning Algorithms, and the Dimensionality of the Message Space

Mount and Reiter (1974) introduced the well-known triangular diagram reported in figure 5.6. The analysis suggested by this diagram distinguishes the set of characteristics of the agent θ (technologies, preferences), the set of messages M, and the set of outcomes (feasible allocations). For given

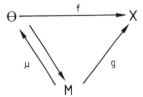

Figure 5.6

characteristics θ, the exchange of messages leads to an equilibrium set of messages, depending upon θ, the vector of characteristics, and possibly upon g; $f = g \circ \mu$ is the performance function. Consider, for example, the case where θ consists of the technological characteristics of the production sector and X is the space of allocations of a given input bundle between firms. A resource allocation process is associated with a message space M, a function g from the message space into X, and an equilibrium set of messages.[17] f can be, for example, a function that associates an efficient allocation of inputs between firms with every state of characteristics. If the diagram of figure 5.5 commutes, then the corresponding allocation process is said to *realize f*. Note that, as defined here, allocation processes take into account the dispersion of information but ignore incentives questions. They assume explicitly or implicitly, that the information, in particular, the information on technologies, is truthfully revealed. Indeed most of this section rules out incentives questions.

Planning algorithms are not only resource allocation processes in the sense defined here; besides a message space and an equilibrium concept, they also incorporate an iterative computational method. There is a large literature on planning algorithms, and its review is beyond the scope of this chapter (for a partial survey, see Heal 1971). In fact two types of algorithms are considered. The first type generates small moves in the right direction by reallocating resources among agents at the margin. These algorithms relate more or less closely with gradient processes (see Aoki 1968; Arrow-Hurwicz 1960; Heal 1975). They perform well locally but not necessarily globally: they climb the closest hill not necessarily the highest. For example, in the context of the allocation of inputs between different competing firms, the algorithm that reallocates at the margin inputs proportionately to the difference between the marginal productivity of a firm and the average marginal productivity across firms[16] generally converges to a local optimum, and not to a global one. Algorithms of the second type are not based on marginal conditions and are expected to perform better in terms of global convergence. But they rely on complex set of messages (see, for example, the algorithm in Hurwicz 1960).[17]

A comparison of the properties and characteristics of the two different types of algorithms suggests that the dimensionality of the message space plays a key role in the performance of the process. Indeed, Calsamiglia shows that in nonconvex environments, an efficient allocation of resources between firms cannot be realized by a process with a finitely dimensional message space, unless the space of characteristics is sufficiently restricted. Calsamiglia's argument is abstract and technical, but it rests on the existence of situations of the kind described in the following example. There are two firms and a unit quantity of a primary input; an allocation can be described by a real number t between 0 and 1, which is, for example, the allocation to the first firm. Suppose now that technologies are such that the production of the first firm writes down

$$\sum_1^N \frac{l_{1n} t^n}{l_{1n}} > 0$$

when the production of the second firm writes down

$$l_2 - \sum_1^N l_{2n} t^n.$$

If technologies are convex, the sum of the two functions is concave, and optimality can be checked from the equality of marginal productivities (i.e., with one-dimensional messages). When technologies are nonconvex, then no test of optimality can be designed that ignores some of the N numbers l_{1n} (and l_{2n}). (To show that rigorously, Calsamiglia uses a reshuffling argument that is frequent in the literature on "realization."). But N can be chosen large enough so that it exceeds the dimensionality given a priori of message space, a contradiction to the finite dimensionality of the message space.

Cremer's algorithm (Cremer 1977) may be viewed as lying somewhere between the two types of algorithms previously described. The firm is asked to send at each step a finite dimensional message, that is an efficient production plan whose coordinates are smaller than those of some announced vector From the answer received, the Center constructs, step by step, an upper approximation of the production set and announces, as a new bound for the firm's message, the social maximum over the current upper approximation of the production set. Note, however, that Cremer's result of convergence toward the full optimum does not contradict Calsamiglia's theorem. Cremer's algorithm crucially relies on the memory of the Center of all previous steps, and it is infinite dimensional in Calsamiglia's terminology.

Note that a marginal cost pricing mechanism based on the principles that we are now going to define, although not modeled as a planning process but as a decentralized mechanism, is a resource allocation process in Calsamiglia's sense. However, it has a finite dimensional message space and cannot realize in Calsamiglia's sense a first-best allocation of resources.

Marginal Cost Equilibrium: Definition and Existence

Let us reintroduce the consumption sector in an economy in which the allocation of resources takes place through market mechanisms. Let us assume that the distribution of incomes follows exogenously fixed rules. We formalize this idea in the following way: Given p the price system and w the "national wealth," there is some distribution function $d_i(p, w)$ that determines the wealth of agent i as a function of p and w. Although this formalization of fixed rules ideas is not the most general, it compromises between generality and simplicity. Let us now define a *marginal cost pricing equilibrium* as a set of production plans $\bar{y}_j$ consumptions plans $\bar{x}_i$ and a price system $\bar{p}$ such that

(i) $\bar{x}_i$ maximizes $U_i(x_i)$ under the constraint $\bar{p} \cdot x_i < d_i(\bar{p}, \bar{w})$;
(ii) $\bar{p} \in k^+(Y_j, \bar{y}_j), \forall j$;
(iii) $\bar{w} = \bar{p} \cdot \omega + \sum_j \bar{p} \cdot \bar{y}_j$; and
(iv) $\sum_i \bar{x}_i = \sum_j \bar{y}_j + \omega$.

Condition (i) is the standard utility maximization under the budget constraint. The income of consumer i is determined by the income formation rule, given that the total wealth $\bar{w}$ is defined by (iii)—where (only) the aggregate profit in the production sector appears as an argument of $\bar{w}$; (ii) is nothing else than the relationship between $\bar{p}$ and $\bar{y}_j$ which was obtained in section 5.2 as a necessary condition for Pareto optimality. In cases of "convex iso output sections," it implies marginal cost pricing. Condition (iv) is the usual market clearing condition.

The concept so introduced (or a slightly different version) was called QA-equilibrium in Guesnerie (1975), where it was argued that it was a natural generalization of Walras' equilibrium. The terminology of marginal cost pricing (MCP) equilibrium used by Beato and Brown-Heal is certainly more appealing, although not fully correct in view of the above remarks on condition (ii). Let me sketch briefly the justification of the concept of MCP equilibrium; a more critical assessment will be postponed until the end of this section. (1) It is the adequate equilibrium concept for a market economy in which the rules of income formation are exogenously determined and in which the behavioral rules of nonconvex firms are transformed in order to make them compatible with the attainment of first-best optima. Firms are instructed to equalize prices and marginal costs rather than to maximize profits (the two rules coincides under convexity). Such an organization seems to follow the recommendations we can extract from the reading of the economists who popularized the marginal cost ideas. In short, MCP equilibrium is a natural concept for the formalization of the marginal cost pricing doctrine. (2) Equivalently, an MCP equilibrium can be viewed as the outcome of a system that mixes planning on the production side with rigid market rules for the distribution of income and the allocation of produced goods within the consumption sector.

Note at this point that the first characterization theorem of section 5.2 can be restated now more concisely: a first-best Pareto optimum is a marginal cost pricing equilibrium with respect to some adequate distribution function.

The study of *existence* of marginal cost pricing equilibrium has been the subject of a number of contributions over the last ten years.

First, it should be stressed again as in Guesnerie (1975) that if efficiency and equity issues can be separated in the sense made precise in section 5.3, then the solution to the existence problem would follow easily from the optimization analysis. For example, the surjectivity of the function r of section 5.2 implies that an MCP equilibrium, with respect to any distribution functions of the form $d_i(\ ) = \theta_i \bar{w}(\sum_i \theta_i = 1)$, exists (the one detected in the proof is a Pareto optimum). And this result could be extended to any distribution function that is reasonable (see below) and *continuous* in p, w.

Hence the difficulty in the existence problem relates with the non-separability of efficiency and equity issues. This difficulty was faced by Guesnerie, Brown-Heal, Beato, and Mantel, but the first two significant results have to be attributed to Beato (1982) and Mantel (1979). Beato,

Mantel, and then Cornet (1982) show that an MCP equilibrium exists for an aggregate production sector, that is, for condition (ii) being (iie), $p \in k^+(Y, \bar{y})$, and under the assumption that the frontier of Y is smooth. We will come back to these assumptions later.

The argument is elegant and easy to understand. Consider the feasible production set (aggregate production set plus vector of initial endowment, $(Y + \omega)$). Consider in the positive orthant of the commodity space a simplex that is "above" the feasible production set. Take a point x in this simplex. The line Ox meets the frontier of the production set at $M(x)$. Let $p(x)$ be one outward normal vector of the production frontier in $M(x)$. Consider now the hyperplane normal to $p(x)$ going through $M(x)$. (Its equation is $p(x) \cdot z = p(x) \cdot M(x)$.) Take a point $N(x)$ on this hyperplane that represents the aggregate consumption chosen by consumers, when their individual wealth is determined by the distribution function given total wealth $p(x) \cdot M(x)$. Consider the half line starting from 0 and passing through $N(x)$, and call $\phi(x)$ the point where it meets the simplex. Consider now $\phi : x \to \phi(x)$. It is easy to see that (1) the mapping ϕ is continuous, $Y + \omega$ being smooth and preferences being strictly convex, and (2) MCP equilibria are fixed points of the mapping. Since the mapping is continuous from the simplex into itself, it has a fixed point, a MCP must exist.

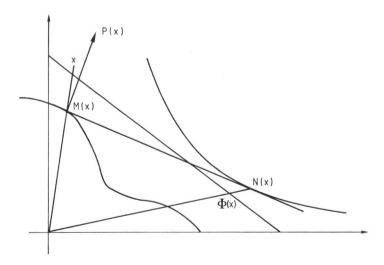

Figure 5.7

In this informal sketch of the proof, some technicalities have been hidden. In particular, there are several conditions to be imposed on the distribution function. The following conditions used by Dierker-Guesnerie-Neuefeind (1985) in a different context would be sufficient: (1) d_i is continuous; (2) if $w > \text{Inf}\, p \cdot X$, then $d_i(p, w) > \text{Inf}\, p \cdot X_i$ (i.e., if the economy is not bankrupt, then no individual is pushed to his survival level). Another assumption should be introduced to ensure that the whole economy does not go bankrupt. One possibility is to ensure that the deficit under MCP never becomes "too high"; another one is to modify MCP under such circumstances (see Dierker-Guesnerie-Neuefeind 1985).

The Beato-Mantel argument has been improved in several ways (proof of local uniqueness by Brown-Heal 1982, for example). But the most significant contribution is due to Cornet (1982). As mentioned above, Cornet uses "Clarke's cone of normals," which allows him to eliminate the smoothness assumption of the global production set.[19] Furthermore Cornet derived a decentralized version of the theorem:

$$(\text{ii}) \Rightarrow \bar{p} \in k^+ (Y_j, \bar{y}_j), \forall_j.$$

Nevertheless, it should be made clear that in the case of several firms (i.e., if we give up the aggregate point of view), the Cornet assumption for decentralization may not be satisfied. Take, for example, the case (to which we will often come back later) of two firms, both producing commodity 2 from commodity 1. The first firm has strictly increasing returns to scale when the second has constant returns to scale. Then the aggregate production set has the shape shown in figure 5.8 and does not meet Cornet's regularity assumptions. Thus, to have general validity in the multifirm case, the proof must follow another route.

I will first show that great care must be given to boundary conditions if one expects MCP equilibria to exist for several firms. Let us turn to the example where a strictly increasing returns to scale firm (firm A) and a constant returns to scale firm (firm B) coexist. We draw on a Marshallian diagram "pseudosupply" curves: at p, the pseudosupply of the nonconvex firm is the output level (assumed here unique) where marginal cost equals price. The pseudosupply of firm A, as defined, has a behavior completely opposite to the supply behavior of a convex firm (see figure 5.9a). The pseudosupply of firm B consists of an horizontal half line, one vertical segment of the vertical axis and one vertical half line at plus infinity. The total pseudosupply has the shape indicated in figure 5.9b. It is clear from

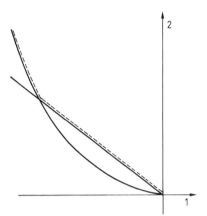

Figure 5.8

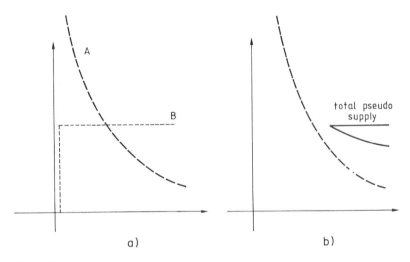

Figure 5.9

this diagram that the demand curve does not intersect the total pseudo-supply curve, that is, there does not exist MCP equilibrium (from now on called MCPE).

It should, however, be clear that the possible absence of MCPE depends on the fact that the increasing returns to scale firm is (implicitly) unable to quit. To restore MCPE, we must create an exit possibility for the non-convex firm. Obviously, if one closes a priori the nonconvex firm, the MCPE is restored, but the problem has been suppressed. What is needed is a possibility of *endogenous* closing of the increasing returns to scale firm, which would be compatible with the idea that we have of marginal cost pricing. Dierker-Guesnerie-Neuefind (1985) have argued that the boundary problem considered here is common to a broad class of "pricing rules" (marginal cost pricing belongs to this category) and that a boundary condition for pricing rules is crucial for the existence of equilibria in a more general setting. Here a natural endogenous closing down of the increasing returns to scale firms obtains when one assumes that O can be announced for any p such that $p \in k^+(Y, O)$ (which in fact corresponds to the formal definition we have given of MCPE but not to the informal and more frequent one used in the above discussion).[19]

Existence of MCPE with several firms in a fully disaggregated framework has been addressed by several authors: in particular, Beato–Mas-Colell (1985) showed how the Beato-Mantel argument could be modified for the multifirm case. Brown-Heal-Khan-Vohra (1986) obtained an existence result in the case where there is a convex sector and *one* nonconvex firm.

More recent results on the existence of marginal cost pricing equilibria include those of Kamiya (1988), Bonnisseau-Cornet (1989, 1988b), and Vohra (1988). Bonnisseau-Cornet (1989) provide the most general existence results for the multifirm case. Finally, the result obtained by Dierker-Guesnerie-Neuefeind (1985) concerns general pricing rules. It covers marginal cost pricing in a fully disaggregate (although on the most general) case as well other pricing rules (pricing rule à la Boiteux considered in the next chapter, average cost pricing, etc.). Further results for general pricing rules have been obtained by Bohm V. (1988) and Bonnisseau-Cornet (1988b).

Marginal Cost Pricing: Optimality

Clearly, among the set of MCP equilibria, some may be rather bad because they select the wrong production scale. The question of optimality raised here is whether some are "good."

The discussion of the separation between equity and efficiency issues (section 5.3) has already suggested a couple of answers which we will briefly review:

1. For some continuous income formation rules d, there exist MCP equilibria, but none of them is first-best Pareto optimum. In other words, the corresponding income formation rules are Pareto dominated by other rules; hence some rules of income formation should be changed for efficiency reasons.

2. There exist, however, continuous income formation rules that generate MCP equilibria, one of them at least being a first-best Pareto optimum. Furthermore there is a subset of economies (which includes the convex economies) for which all continuous "reasonable" income formation rules generate at least one efficient MCP equilibrium. We can refer to such economies, which we analyzed in section 5.3, as "well behaved." Now for a given economy that does not belong to the class of well-behaved economies, both cases can occur, and it is a priori difficult to say how big are the "efficient" income formation rules compared to the inefficient ones.

In the example of section 5.3 (recall the rule of income formation, $d_i = r_i w$ and $r_i = \frac{1}{2}, i = 1, 2$) every MCPE although not Pareto optimal was production efficient. But production efficiency itself is not guaranteed. It turns out that, as shown by Beato–Mas-Colell (1983, 1985), we can find economies such that none of the MCPE associated with a given income formation rule is production efficient. Hence in the subset of income formation rules incompatible with efficiency, inefficiencies may be qualitatively more or less severe; the case where non-MCPE is production efficient is particularly disturbing.

Some idea of the Beato–Mas-Colell example can now be obtained from figure 5.10. It comes within the framework of the two-firm economy which has served to illustrate our previous discussion. Again, we draw the pseudo-supply curves but identify the subset of efficient supplies. When the production level is within the segment Oq_0, efficiency requires that only the constant-returns-to-scale firm operate, and the corresponding part of the supply curve is the segment $C'D'$. For production levels above q_0, the increasing-returns-to-scale firm should produce alone; the corresponding part of pseudosupply starts in D''. Consumption theory does not rule out a graph of the demand function that would coincide with the full line EIF of figure 5.10. In such a case there would no be production-efficient MCP.

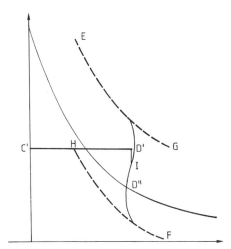

Figure 5.10

In fact, in the example of Beato–Mas-Colell, the graph of demand would be viewed as having the form suggested by *EGHF*. The discontinuity from *G* to *H* reflects the switch from the constant-returns-to-scale firm to the increasing-returns-to-scale firm—a switch from a budget-balanced firm to a firm with deficit—which induces an income loss (for consumers) and is responsible for the sudden decrease in demand. The nature of the phenomenon is different from the one analyzed in section 5.3 but still reflects a discontinuity across the set of Pareto optima: the discontinuity concerns not the optimal production plan itself (at least in the example) but the first-order characteristics—the outward normal of this optimal plan.

The previous analysis may seem negative for what I have called before the "marginal cost pricing doctrine." When rules of income formation are fixed, and even if one assumes that one can pick among MCP equilibria, there is no insurance that the outcome will be first-best Pareto efficient or even production efficient. This criticism should not be confused with the one according to which MCP equilibria cannot choose the right "scale" because they only rely upon local information; here MCP equilibria that are inefficient because of obvious scale mistakes are ruled out.

These facts may be viewed as very dramatic for the MCP doctrine. This seems likewise to be the opinion of Beato–Mas-Colell (1983) as it appears from their introduction. I would be more cautious. On the one hand, the theory does not say much about the size of "inefficient" income distributions in a given economy. On the other hand, it is not true that all nonconvexities give rise to these phenomena. Let us mention two classes of problems for which they do not occur:

1. If nonconvexities are only due to fixed costs, and if the subset of nonconvex technologies that should be used is invariant when individuals are weighted differently in the social welfare function, then there exist efficient MCP equilibria whatever the income distribution (This is straightforward consequence of a statement already given in section 5.3.) The marginal cost pricing doctrine is reasonable then once the subset of efficient techniques can be unambiguously identified (see my monograph, 1980, for a less sketchy discussion).

2. Dierker (1986) has identified a class of increasing-returns-to-scale technologies and convex preferences for which MCP equilibria are first-best Pareto efficient. I will not describe the model in detail (I have alluded to it previously), but its main features are the following: there coexists a convex sector with a nonconvex sector, whose production frontier is smooth. Dierker assumes that

a. Consumer preferences are such that total expenditures (in the sense of the expenditure function) of all the convex sector (consumers + convex producers) for the goods produced by the nonconvex sector is nondecreasing with respect to the price level. In other words, expenditures are somewhat inelastic and increase when the price level increases.

b. Technologies are such that total receipts of the increasing-returns-to-scale sector *when it sells at marginal cost* are an increasing function of the scale of production, correctly defined. When scale can actually be meaningfully defined, the assumption is not unreasonable. It means that marginal cost do not decrease too fast. These assumptions seem acceptable for a number of standard cases of increasing returns and they give a much less negative picture of MCP equilibria.

As we will see later, Quinzii (1988) in her study of the core has independently proposed conditions on elasticities of supply and demand that are satisfied when Dierker's conditions are. The Quinzii's version of Dierker's result provides the *most general result on the optimality of MCP equilibria.*

The section will be concluded by a critical assessment of the concept of MCP equilibria. Let us sort out two main criticisms:

1. Although the concept provides a formal generalization of the concept of Walras' equilibrium, there is no clear way in which one can argue that it is the outcome of a marketlike mechanism.[20] In particular, it is difficult to associate it with converging *tâtonnement* processes à la Walras.

2. There is an asymmetry in the treatment of the consumption and the production sector that may be hard to justify. This is particularly true from the point of view of incentives theory, where economic organization is determined from basic informational and observational constraints. With MCP equilibria, it is implicitly assumed that the information on technologies transmitted from the firm to the Planner can be checked costlessly. But it is not clear how informational and delegation constraints can justify the modeling options adopted for the comsumption side. If the Planner knew individual characteristics and tastes, he would not be bound to use a rigid income structure and the distribution function would only be provisional (MCP being perhaps provisional outcomes along a sequence of algorithms à la Champsaur-Drèze-Henry 1974). Now, if the Planner has no information on the characteristics and individual tastes of consumers, the use of anonymous taxation (excise taxes, VAT) to finance the deficit of increasing returns to scale firms and to redistribute income is suggested by basic incentives theory (see Hammond 1979; Guesnerie 1981; Roberts 1983).

Although these criticisms should be taken seriously, the contributions on existence and optimality of MCP equilibria have brought unavoidable facts on the scene and have given useful views on how nonconvexities in production affect the general equilibrium mechanics of complex economies.

5.5 Other Research Directions

Among the possible outcomes of economic activity in a nonconvex economy, the previous analysis has focused attention on MCP equilibria. The pure theory of economic organization in presence of increasing returns to scale has also gone in different directions. The models that have been considered rely on different implicit or explicit assumptions on the role of government in the allocation of resources and/or on behavior of different agents. Studies on the core, which will be considered first, naturally fit the framework of a private ownership economy.

Studies on the Core of a Nonconvex Economy

Consider a production economy where initial endowments are privately owned. Has such an economy a nonempty core? The question is not well defined until we have made precise which production sets are available to coalitions. One may assume that either coalitions have access to different production sets or the same production set Y is available to each coalition. On pure theoretical grounds, the issue relates to the discussion of additivity of section 5.1, and preferences about modeling options should reflect the views one has concerning the marketability of hidden factors. I will mention the existence result obtained by Sonderman (1974) who considers production sets $Y(S)$ specific to coalitions (see also Bohm 1974). Although these production sets are not necessarily convex, the production set of the grand coalition that contains them is assumed to be convex. However, $Y(S)$ grows in a way that displays increasing returns to size across coalitions. The existence proof uses the fact that the side payments games, obtained from the initial game through profit maximization relative to some given price system, are convex.

Let us now consider the case where the global production set Y is available to every coalition. It is known that the existence proof available for an exchange economy extends to a production economy when Y is a convex cone. What happens when Y displays increasing returns to scale? Let me attempt an informal discussion about the nature of the difficulties. One could think that increasing returns to scale reinforce the power of the grand coalition relatively to other coalitions and hence that it makes more likely the existence of the core. This intuition had indeed some truth. Consider, for example, an economy with two goods, the first one, the input, being transformed into the second one according to a technology with strictly increasing returns to scale (and hence increasing average returns). Assume that consumers only have endowments in inputs. Clearly, if their preferences only concerned the output, the game would be Scarf balanced and then would have a nonempty core. It turns out that the conclusion remains true when the input is desired and preferences are convex (see Mas-Colell 1980). However, the conclusion relies on the fact that endowments are only in inputs, as shown by the following counterexample, which I owe to M. Quinzii: The production function is $y = x^2$, and there are three consumers who have the same utility function $u(x, y)$ but different endowments $(6, 0)$, $(0, 6)$, $(6, 0)$ (the endowment of the second consumer being in output); this game can be transformed into a side payment game, and it can be checked that the balanced family (12, (23), (13) does not meet Scarf conditions.[21]

Hence even in two-commodity economies, increasing returns to scale do not guarantee the existence of the core. When there are more than two commodities, other phenomena come in superposition with the preceding ones. In the terminology of Baumol, "transray" properties are likely to play a role in conjunction with "ray-specific" properties. Some degree of economies of scope is needed to give an improved position to the grand coalition.

In fact Scarf (1986) has shown that the distributive set concept plays a central role in the analysis. When inputs are not desired, distributivity of the production set is sufficient and in some sense necessary to get nonemptiness of the core. This result is intimately related to the properties of distributive sets which were emphasized after it was defined in section 5.1.

The model considered by Quinzii (1982) has two inputs and one output. The production set, available to all coalitions, has both increasing returns to scale and iso output convex sections in the sense of section 5.1. The proof proceeds by associating with every Pareto optimal utility levels (v) a side payment game, whose characteristic function $v(S)$ is the value of the program:

$$\inf p \cdot \sum_{i \in S} x_i + C\left(p, \sum_{i \in S} y_i\right), \qquad u_i(x_i, y_i) \geq v_i,$$

where (x_i, y_i) is the consumption bundle of consumer i and $C(p, y)$ is the cost function associated with Y. Quinzii shows that if the allocation solution of a program $v(N)$ is always unique, then the game actually has a nonempty core. She argues that this is indeed the case when some relationship between the product of the derivative of marginal cost by the derivative of compensated demand is smaller than one (a condition that has already been related to the one proposed by Dierker).

It is worth mentioning that the condition emphasized by Quinzii guarantees the surjectivity of the mapping considered in section 5.3. This remark deserves further clarification, but it suggests that the wrong behavior of nonconvex economies in terms of either inefficient incomes or emptiness of the core can in certain cases be found to have a common origin in the "jumps" of optimal production plans when one goes over the set of Pareto optima.

Restoring Effiency through Public Control of Natural Monopolies

The organization of the production side of the economy which is implicit to the concept of MCP equilibria has two features: First, information on production possibilities can be obtained without cost by the planner; second, the planner can enforce the adoption of the "right" behavior by the firm. Although these two assumptions are related, it is possible to have them dissociated: What happens if the planner does not control the behavior of the firm, although he has information on its technological capabilities? We will look at this problem for a firm with fixed costs (which are the only source of increasing returns to scale) and which is managed as a private monopolist. Actually, we have a natural monopoly as well. The question arises of whether government policy can restore efficiency. Indeed, it has often been argued that an adequate subsidy on a good produced by a monopoly can do the job; this argument has been clearly articulated in a well-defined, although simple, second-best framework by Bohm (1967).

A flavor of the argument can easily be given in the partial equilibrium context. Let q be the production of the monopoly, and let p be the price of the good such that $p = D(q)$. The profit of the monopolist associated with the production level q and with a cost function C is $qD(q) - C(q)$ and is assumed to define a quasi-concave function of q. The optimal production level q is such that $D - qD' = C'$. If a "specific" tax is to be levied on the good, the first-order condition obtains with $D - t_0$ instead of D.

Routine calculations shows that the optimal tax to levy on the good in order to restore optimal production, that is, to induce the monopoly to produce q^* such that $D(q^*) = C'(q^*)$ is

$$\frac{-t_0^*}{D(q^*)} = q^* \frac{D'(q^*)}{D(q^*)}.$$

The optimal tax is a subsidy and the subsidy rate equals the inverse of the demand elasticity in q^*.

Guesnerie-Laffont (1978) have considered the problem in an abstract second-best framework similar to the one previously considered by Guesnerie (1976) for the study of optimal government policies in presence of deviant price takers. Here the "deviance" originates in the presence of price makers on the market of one commodity (commodity 0). Commodities on other markets are delivered either by private competitive firms or by government-controlled firms. Consumers are price takers. The government is assumed to be able to redistribute income in a lump-sum fashion and to disconnect consumption and production prices through linear taxes. The price-taking behavior is formalized through a correspondence that generates the price of commodity zero as depending on the production prices of other goods, the set of taxes and individual (lump-sum) incomes. Monopolistic behavior appears as a particular case of this price-taking formalization. It is shown that the solution of the second-best program falls into two different cases. In the "regular" case the first-best Pareto optimality obtains. Particularly, in the monopoly case, the optimal subsidy conforms with the inverse elasticity rule mentioned above. In the "nonregular" case the optimal solution is an actual second-best; taxes have a much more complex structure and prices (either production prices or consumption prices) diverge from the "social values" of commodities. Contrary to the conventional wisdom drawn from example in previous literature on the control of monopolies, it is asserted that the regular case is *not* generic. In particular, a simple economy is exhibited in which the nonregular case always occurs. An example is illustrated in figure 5.11 where the graph of the profit function is shown for different values of the tax on the good.

For small subsidies (or for taxes), the profit of the monopolist is maximal for low values of $q(\varepsilon)$. Increasing the subsidy in an attempt to encourage higher levels of production is at first useless and leads (after some critical valued is reached) to a very high production level. If, as is the case, the

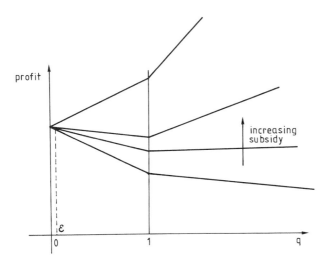

Figure 5.11

first-best Pareto optimal level of production of the considered commodity is somewhere between 0 and 1, it cannot be reached via a subsidy.

Hence, returning to our original problem, even with well-behaved non-convex techniques, the use of linear taxes does not correct the monopolistic deviance and does not restore first-best Pareto optimality. The analysis has been extended to the case where the firm is managed, not by a private monopolist, but by a self-managed monopolist in the Ward-Vanek tradition (Guesnerie-Laffont 1984). However, the analysis calls for some discussion that goes beyond our present purpose.

1. The restrictive choice of linear taxes influences the negative result obtained above. With nonlinear taxes the first-best optimum is actually decentralizable, even under asymmetric information (see Caillaud-Guesnerie-Rey-Tirole 1988).

2. The example depends heavily on the concavity of the profit function, which has also been a source of difficulties in the study of existence of monopolistic general equilibrium (see Roberts-Sonnenschein 1977). This nonconcavity has the consequence that the behavior of the monopoly cannot be described from the first-order conditions. Similarly, the reaction of the monopolist is not a continuous function of parameters. The Guesnerie-Laffont article emphasised a point made independently in the context of a moral hazard principal-agent problem by Mirrlees (1975). The point can be generally expressed as follows: *there is nothing pathological in getting the second-best optimum trapped in a point where the reaction function of some agent is discontinuous.* This is indeed a central difficulty in the study of the principal-agent problem with moral hazard (see, for example, Grossman-Hart 1983), as well as in the problem of monopoly control.

Approximate Efficiency under Increasing Returns to Scale

If obtaining full optimality in our economy with increasing returns to scale is difficult, there may be a case for paying attention to solutions that, although not optimal, meet "satisficing" standards, for example, by guaranteeing that the welfare loss does not go beyond some computable (and reasonable) bound. I will speak briefly of two studies in this direction.

The first one is due to Dierker (1980). He starts with the (correct) remark that MCP equilibria may lead to bad outcomes. Even if we are in the case where the income distribution is such that at least one MCP equilibrium is efficient, others associated with the same income distribution may be very inefficient because they select production scales that are "socially" wrong. Furthermore it may be difficult to estimate welfare loss. Dierker suggests that the pricing rule be modified in such a way that, although losing, in general, the possibility of full optimality, one obtains, instead, the insurance that welfare loss can be evaluated.

Because the shortcomings of MCP doctrine can in some sense be attributed to marginal cost behaving erratically as a function of scale, Dierker suggests that asymptotic cost pricing be adopted, that is, that goods be priced at marginal cost and computed as if the production scale were very large. Note that asymptotic cost pricing is not more incentive compatible than MCP and that, like MCP, it generally leads to a deficit. Dierker shows that the welfare loss tends to zero when the size of the economy increases (which is not surprising given the definition of asymptotic cost pricing), but its main result is that welfare loss is smaller than the deficit of the firm, hence providing an observable bound for welfare loss.

Another idea of approximate efficiency is explored in Guesnerie-Hart (1982) in a stylized general equilibrium model with only two commodities. Here increasing-returns-to-scale firms are oligopolies that face the threat of entry. A Cournot-Nash equilibrium with entry (with quantities as strategies) is assumed to obtain: When the economy is replicated, the Cournot-Nash equilibrium converges toward a first-best optimum, independently of the existence of fixed costs. (For a comprehensive analysis of convergence results in a partial equilibrium framework, see Ushio 1983.) However, the speed of convergence is much higher with convex technologies than in the case of a fixed cost. In the first case welfare loss is in $1/r$ (r = the replication rate) when it is in $1/\sqrt{r}$ in the second case. Replication ensures in both cases the emergence of a (quasi)price-taking behavior, but the number of firms in the market is much too large in the second case (it increases indefinitely but at a speed that is much smaller than r). Although the implications of this convergence result for finite economies are somewhat unclear, it shows that there is still a great deal of difference between convex and nonconvex economies, even in the case where a similar convergence results holds for both of them.

5.6 Conclusion

In this chapter I have attempted at a coherent presentation of the state of the art on the subject of resource allocation. I do not claim the survey to be exhaustive. Its reading would certainly benefit from the complementary views taken in recent papers such as those by Cornet (1988c) and Dehez (1988) who provide more detailed assessment of the work that has developed since 1984 when the first version of this chapter was prepared. In particular, Cornet (1988c) provides a comprehensive account of the analytical efforts aimed at improving the statements of the second welfare theorems and of existence theorems for marginal cost pricing equilibria. Dehez (1988) describes efforts in a new direction, which he has explored with Drèze, that aim at a better positive theory. Also the special issue of the *Journal of Mathematical Economics* (see Cornet 1988d) devoted to nonconvexities witnesses the present vitality of the field and presents new material that has not been analyzed in depth here.

Knowledge often progresses in cycles in which conceptual breakthroughs and analytical achievements alternate. The success of the recent analytical effort may then suggest that the time is ripe for conceptual innovations that would put the subject in better perspective.

Notes

An early version of this chapter was prepared for a lecture given during the IMSS Stanford summer seminar, on July 31, 1984. This lecture was part of a one-day workshop on public production which was organized by E. Sheshinski and me. I benefited from very helpful comments on this paper from J. M. Bonnisseau, X. Calsamiglia, P. Dehez, M. Quinzii, and J. Tirole. Remaining errors are mine.

1. The derivation of those results in general form has been one of the major achievements of the postwar economic theory.

2. Introducing space and externalities into the analysis also leads to intriguing basic nonconvexities (see Starrett 1977).

3. For an example of the "convexification effect" of aggregation, see Hildenbrand (1974) and Aumann (1964).

4. This notation is, strictly speaking, incorrect. In the following we will often embed y^0 in the commodity space when there is no ambiguity, as we have done here.

5. The distinction remains the same for several inputs, although it yields less insight. In fact the natural monopoly literature does not assume one input but discusses ray and transray properties with respect to cost functions.

6. It is not clear why the property defining transray convexity is plausible. It is true, however (and satisfactory because the term "economies of scale" implies subadditivity), that economies of scale in the sense of transray convexity (though y^0), together with ray decreasing average cost (along any ray), implies local subadditivity in y^0 (see Baumol 1977, prop. 12).

7. This definition should provide a rigorous general equilibrium treatment of the questions of supportable cost functions for natural monopolies. See also Sharkey (1982).

8. Price rather equals the "marginal displacement cost" in the sense of Lerner.

9. See Kolm (1970) for a discussion of this idea.

10. This is a well-known fact; see, for example, Arrow-Hahn (1971) and de Montbrial (1972).

11. In economic terms, note that national income as measured here includes the consumption of leisure.

12. In particular, this is not related to the financing problem and to the fact that firms may have a deficit.

13. This question differs from the one raised in section 5.2 where nonlinear prices (two-part tariffs) aimed at obtaining a balanced budget for the firm.

14. The incentive aspects of the control of nonconvex economies are studied in a different chapter. Note, however, that in these models giving total surplus as a nonlinear money payment defines an incentive-compatible mechanisms that implement the first best.

15. In the sense of Calsamiglia's definition 2, μ must be locally threaded (i.e., rule out inadmissible compression of information) and g "compatible" with μ, this latter condition meaning that μ selects one equilibrium message when there are several.

16. In another context this is the principle on which are based the algorithms known as MDP processes (see Malinvaud, Drèze, and de la Vallee Poussin).

17. This is the point emphasized by Calsamiglia's "set-valued processes."

18. Beato followed Guesnerie in using the Dubovitsky-Millioutine cone of interior displacements.

19. Note that, although important on technical grounds, the difficulty due to the boundary behavior rests upon the fact that the commodities produced by the convex and nonconvex firms have the same *name* and hence are constrained to have the same price in equilibrium.

20. Unless we are in conditions when the mapping price, MCP production plan is unique.

21. $v(1,2) = v(2,3) = 6$, $v(13) = 9$, $v(1,2,3) = 10$. Very loosely, one could say that coalition that has its endowments in output has "too much power" because of the increasing return to scale technology.

References

Allais, M. 1943. *Economie et intérêt*. Paris.

Allais, M. 1977. "Théorie générale des surplus." *Publications de l'ISMEA*, Paris.

Aoki, M. 1968. "Dynamic Processes and Social Planning under Increasing Returns." Stanford University. Mimeo.

Arrow, K., and F. Hahn. 1971. *General Competitive Analysis*. San Francisco: Holden Day.

Arrow, K., and L. Hurwicz. 1960. "Decentralization and Computation in Resource Allocations." In *Essays in Economics and Econometrics*, edited by R. W. Pfouts. Chapel Hill: University North Carolina Press, 34–104.

Aumann, R. 1964. "Markets with a Continuum of Traders." *Econometrica* 32:39–54.

Baron, D., and R. Myerson. 1982. "Regulating a Monopolist with Unknown Costs." *Econometrica* 911–930.

Baumol, W. 1977. "On the Proper Cost Tests for Natural Monopoly in a Multiproduct Industry." *American Economic Review* 67(5):809–822.

Baumol, W., E. Bailey, and R. Willig. 1977. "Weak Invisible Hand Theorems and the Sustainability of a Multiproduct Natural Monopoly." *American Economic Review* 67:350–365.

Beato, P. 1976. "Marginal Cost Pricing Equilibria with Increasing Returns." Ph.D. Dissertation, University of Minnesota.

Beato, P. 1982. "The Existence of Marginal Cost Pricing with Increasing Returns." *Quarterly Journal of Economics* 97:669–689.

Beato, P., and A. Mas-Colell. 1983. "Gestion au coût marginal et efficacité de la production agrégée: un exemple." *Annales de l'INSEE* 51:39–45.

Beato, P., and A. Mas-Colell. 1985. "On Marginal Cost Pricing with Given Tax-Subsidy Rules." *Journal of Economic Theory* 37:356–365.

Beato, P., and A. Mas-Colell. 1984. "The Marginal Cost Pricing Rule as a Regulation Mechanism in Mixed Markets." In: *The Performance of Public Enterprises. Concepts and Measurement*, edited by M. Marchand, P. Pestieau, and H. Tulkens. Amsterdam: North Holland. 81–100.

Böhm, V. 1974. "The Core of an Economy with Production. *Review of Economic Studies* 61:429–436.

Böhm, V. 1988. "Existence of Equilibria with Price Regulation." In *Contribution to Mathematical Economics. Essays in Honor of Gérard Debreu*, edited by W. Hildenbrand and A. Mas-Colell. Amsterdam: North Holland.

Bohm, P. 1967. "On the Theory of Second Best." *Review of Economic Studies* 41:301–314.

Bonnisseau, J. M., and B. Cornet. 1988a. "Valuation Equilibrium and Pareto Optimum in Non-Convex Economies." *Journal of Mathematical Economics* 17, 293–308.

Bonnisseau, J. M., and B. Cornet. 1988b. "Existence of Equilibria when Firms Follow Bounded Losses Pricing Rules." *Journal of Mathematical Economics* 17:119–147.

Bonnisseau, J. M., and B. Cornet. 1989. "Existence of Marginal Cost Pricing Equilibrium in an Economy with Several Non-Convex Firms." *Econometrica* (forthcoming).

Brown, D., and G. Heal. 1979. "Equity Efficiency and Increasing Returns." *Review of Economic Studies* 46:571–585.

Brown, D., and G. Heal. 1980. "Two Part Tariffs, Marginal Cost Pricing and Increasing Returns in a General Equilibrium Model." *Journal of Public Economics* 13:25–49.

Brown, D., and G. Heal. 1981. "Welfare Theorems for Economies with Increasing Returns." Essex University. Mimeo.

Brown, D., and G. Heal. 1982. "Existence, Local Uniqueness, and Optimality of a Marginal Cost Pricing Equilibrium in an Economy with Increasing Returns." Working Paper, California Institute of Technology.

Brown, D., G. Heal, Ali M. Kahn, and R. Vohra. 1986. "On a General Existence Theorem for Marginal Cost Pricing Equilibrium." *Journal of Economic Theory* 38:371–379.

Calsamiglia, X. 1977. "Decentralized Resource Allocation and Increasing Returns." *Journal of Economic Theory* 14:263–283.

Calsamiglia, X. 1982. "On the Size of the Message Space under Non-Convexities." *Journal of Mathematical Economics* 10:197–203.

Caillaud, B., R. Guesnerie, P. Rey, and J. Tirole. 1988. "Production and Incentives Theory: A Review of Recent Contributions." *Rand Journal of Economics* 19:1–26.

Champsaur, P., J. Drèze, and C. Henry. 1974. "Stability Theorems with Economic Applications." *Econometrica* 45, 273–294.

Cornet, B. 1986. "The Second Welfare Theorem in Non-Convex Economies." CORE Discussion Paper 8630, Louvain-la-Neuve.

Cornet, B. 1988a. "Existence of Equilibria in Economies with Increasing Returns." Revised from Berkeley Working Paper 1982, this volume.

Cornet, B. 1988b. "Tarification au coût marginal et Pareto optimalité." In *Mélanges économiques: Essais en l'honneur de Edmond Malinvaud*, Paris: Economica, 29–70.

Cornet, B. 1988c. "General Equilibrium Theory and Increasing Returns: Presentation." *Journal of Mathematical Economics* 17, 103–118.

Cornet, B. 1988d. "*General Equilibrium Theory and Increasing Returns*. Special Issue of the *Journal of Mathematical Economics*. Amsterdam: North Holland.

Cremer, L. 1977. "A Quantity-Quantity Algorithm for Planning under Increasing Returns to Scale." *Econometrica* 45:1339–1345.

Dehez, P., and J. Drèze. 1988. "Competitive Equilibria with Quantity-Taking Producers and Increasing Returns." *Journal of Mathematical Economics* 17, 209–230.

Dehez, P., and J. Drèze. 1988. "Distributive Production Sets and Equilibria with Increasing Returns." *Journal of Mathematical Economics* 17, 231–248.

Dierker, E. 1980. "Natural Monopolies and Asymptotic Cost Pricing." Working Paper, Bonn University.

Dierker, E. 1986. "When Does Marginal Cost Pricing Lead to Pareto Efficiency?" *Zeitschrift für Nationalökonomie* 5:41–66.

Dierker, E., C. Fourgeaud, and W. Neuefeind. 1976. "Increasing Returns to Scale and Productive Systems." *Journal of Economic Theory* 13:428–438.

Dierker, E., R. Guesnerie, and W. Neuefeind. 1985. "General Equilibrium When Some Firms Follow Special Pricing Rules." *Econometrica* 53:1369–1393.

Dierker, E., and W. Neuefeind. 1988. "Quantity Guided Price Setting." *Journal of Mathematical Economics* 17, 249–259.

Dubovickii, A. J., and A. Miljutin. 1965. "Extremum Problems in the Presence of Restrictions." *USSR Comp. Math. and Math. Physics* 5:1–80.

Faber-Sender, F., and R. Guesnerie. 1973. "Etude des structures de revenus associées aux optima paretiens d'une économie convexe." *Bulletin de mathématiques économiques*.

Fourgeaud, C., B. Lenclud, and P. Sentis. "Equilibre, optimum et décentralisation dans un cas de rendement croissant." *Cahiers du Séminaire d'Econométrie* 15:29–46.

Grossman, S., and O. Hart. 1983. "An Analysis of the Principal Agent Problem." *Econometrica* 51(1):7–45.

Guesnerie, R. 1969. "Optimum de Pareto et ensembles de production non-convexes." *Bulletin de mathématiques économiques* 2:31–60.

Guesnerie, R. 1975a. "Pareto Optimality in Non-Convex Economies." *Econometrica* 43:1–30.

Guesnerie, R. 1975b. "Public Production and Taxation in a Simple Second Best Model." *Journal of Economic Theory* 10(2):127–153.

Guesnerie, R. 1980. "Modèles de l'économie publique." Monographie du Séminaire d'Econométrie. Editions du CNRS: Paris.

Guesnerie, R. 1981. "On Taxation and Incentives: Further Reflections on the Limits to Redistribution." CEQC Discussion Paper. To appear as chapter 1 in *A Contribution to the Theory of Taxation*.

Guesnerie, R., and J.-J. Laffont. 1978. "Taxing Price Makers." *Journal of Economic Theory* 19:423–455.

Guesnerie, R., and J.-J. Laffont. 1984. "Indirect Public Control of Self-Managed Monopolies." *Journal of Comparative Economics* 8:139–158.

Guesnerie, R., and O. Hart. 1985. "Welfare Losses due to Monopolistic Competition. Asymptotic Results for Cournot-Nash Equilibria with and without Free Entry." *International Economic Review* 26:525–545.

Hammond, P. 1979. "Straightforward Individual Incentive Compatibility in Large Economies." *Review of Economic Studies Symposium* 46:263–282.

Heal, G. 1971. "Planning, Prices and Increasing Returns." *Review of Economic Studies* 38:281–294.

Heal, G. 1972. *The Theory of Economic Planning*. Amsterdam: North Holland.

Hildenbrand, W. 1974. *Core and Equilibria of a Large Economy*. Princeton: Princeton University Press.

Hotelling, H. 1938. "The General Welfare in Relation to Problems of Taxation and of Railways Utility Rates." *Econometrica* 6:142–269.

Hurwicz, L. 1960. "Optimality and Informational Efficiency in Resource Allocation Processes." In *Mathematical Methods in Social Sciences*, edited by K. Arrow, S. Karlin, and P. Suppes, 27–46.

Hurwicz, L. 1972. "On Informationally Decentralized Systems." In *Decision and Organization*, edited by C. D. McGuire and R. Radner, Amsterdam: North Holland, ch. 14.

Ischiichi, T., and M. Quinzii. 1983. "Decentralization for the Core of a Production Economy with Increasing Returns." *International Economic Review* 24:397–412.

Kamiya, K. 1988. "Existence and Uniqueness of Equilibria with Increasing Returns." *Journal of Mathematical Economics* 17, 149–178.

Khan, Ali M. 1987. "Ioffe's Normal Cone and Foundations of Welfare Economics." Discussion Paper, University of Illinois.

Khan, Ali M., and R. Vohra. 1987. "An Extension of the Second Welfare Theorem to Economies with Non-Convexities and Public Goods." *Quarterly Journal of Economics* 102:223–241.

Malinvaud, E. 1969. *Leçons de théorie microéconomique*. Paris: Dunod.

Mantel, R. 1979. "Equilibria con Rendimientos Crecientes a Escala." *Anales de la Associacion Argentina de Economia Politica* 1:271–282.

Mas-Colell, A. 1980. "Remarks on the Game Theoretic Analysis of a Simple Redistribution of Surplus Problem." *International Journal of Game Theory* 9:125–140.

Mirrlees, J. 1977. "The Theory of Moral Hazard and Unobservable Behaviour." Nuffield College. Mimeo.

Mount, K., and S. Reiter. 1974. "The Informational Size of Message Spaces." *Journal of Economic Theory* 8:161–192.

Panzar, J., and R. Willig. 1977. "Economies of Scale in Multi Output Production." *Quarterly Journal of Economics* 91:481–493.

Quinzii, M. 1982. "An Existence Theorem for the Core of a Productive Economy with Increasing Returns." *Journal of Economic Theory* 28:32–50.

Quinzii, M. 1982. "Définition et existence du noyau dans un modèle d'économie où la production présente des rendements croissants." *Cahiers du Séminaire d'Econométrie* 23.

Quinzii, M. 1988. "*Rendements croissants et équilibre général.*" Paris: Editions du CNRS.

Rader, T. 1970. "Resource Allocation with Increasing Returns to Scale." *American Economic Review* 60:814–825.

Roberts, J. and H. Sonnenschein. 1977. "On the Foundations of the Theory of Monopolistic Competition." *Econometrica* 45:101–103.

Roberts, J. 1980. "Price-Independent Welfare Prescriptions." *Journal of Public Economics* 13:277–297.

Roberts, J. 1984. "The Theoretical Limits to Redistribution." *Review of Economic Studies* 1: 177–195.

Scarf, K. 1981. "An Outline of Some Results on Production and Core." Mimeo.

Scarf, K. 1981. "Production Sets with Indivisibilities, Part I: Generalities." *Econometrica* 49:1–32.

Scarf, K. 1986. "Notes on the Core of a Productive Economy." In *Contributions to Mathematical Economics. Essays in Honor of Gerard Debreu*, edited by W. Hildenbrand and A. Mas-Colell, Amsterdam: North Holland.

Sharkey, W. 1982. *The Theory of Natural Monopoly.* Cambridge: Cambridge University Press.

Silvestre, J. 1978. "Increasing Returns in General Non-Competitive Analysis." *Econometrica* 46:397–402.

Smale, S. 1976. "Global Analysis and Economics IV: Equilibrium with Boundaries and Production Sets." *Journal of Mathematical Economics.*

Starr, R. 1969. "Quasi Equilibria in Economies with Non-Convex Preferences." *Econometrica* 37:25–39.

Starrett, D. 1977. "Measuring Returns to Scale in the Aggregate and the Scale Effect of Public Goods." *Econometrica* 45:1439–1455.

Sonderman, D. 1974. "Economies of Scale and Equilibria in Coalition Production Economies." *Journal of Economic Theory* 8:259–291.

Tillman, G. 1981. "Efficiency in Economies with Increasing Returns." University of Bonn. Mimeo.

Ushio, Y. 1983. Cournot-Nash Equilibria in Large Markets. The Case of Declining Average Cost Curves." *Review of Economic Studies* 50:347–354.

Vohra, R. 1988. "On the Existence of Equilibria in Economies with Increasing Return: A Synthesis." *Journal of Mathematical Economics* 17, 179–192.

Yun, K. 1984. "Pareto-Optimality in Non-Convex Economies and Marginal Cost Pricing Equilibria." *Proceedings of the First International Conference of Korean Economists.*

6 Equilibrium without Market Clearing

John Roberts

Two of the major themes in the twenty years of research in mathematical economics at CORE have been the study of quantity-constrained equilibria as an approach to macroeconomic issues and the use of game-theoretic methodology in modeling economic phenomena. While both of these themes are represented in the proceedings of this symposium, the latter has probably received somewhat more attention. This chapter will only partially correct this imbalance because, although its subject matter is equilibria that involve rationing and involuntary unemployment, the methods used are those of noncooperative game theory.

In particular, the object of this chapter is to report on and extend a line of work[1] that demonstrates that quantity-constrained equilibria can arise, even when all agents are fully rational and correctly forecast the full implications of their actions in all circumstances and when all prices and wages and all quantities are endogenously determined under a set of market institutions that are consistent with the emergence of unconstrained, full employment equilibria. In fact, the unemployment equilibria can arise at the Walrasian prices and wages.

Obtaining these results involves modeling much more explicitly than is usual the institutions under which prices, wages, and the quantities transacted by each individual arise. Modeling the economic environment of preferences, endowments, and production possibilities in the usual fashion, and combining this with the model of market institutions, yields a game in extensive form. Examination of the subgame perfect equilibria of this game then produces the desired result: There are multiple equilibria in which prices and wages are set at their Walrasian levels while quantities vary across these equilibria from the Walrasian full-employment levels down to a zero level of general economic activity. In all of these equilibria—except the full employment one—at least some agents perceive binding quantity constraints on their transactions. Moreover, despite the rationing, there is no inherent tendency for prices and wages to adjust because these have been set (at their Walrasian levels) by self-interested agents who correctly forecast the full implications of each price and wage choice they might make and who see no private gain to altering these choices.

6.1 The Coordination Problem, Markets, and Economic Models

At least since Adam Smith, economists have recognized the importance of markets as coordinating devices. Individuals have diverse, selfish interests. Realizing these at more than the most minimal level requires that the individuals' actions be coordinated. Markets are a mechanism by means of which coherence is achieved: Responding in a self-interested fashion to "market signals" and disciplined by "market forces," individuals take actions that advance not only their own interests but also those of their trading partners. In fact this market-mediated activity may even yield a socially efficient outcome.

The first fully rigorous formalization of this insight came with the development of competitive general equilibrium theory in the 1950s. This formulation is one of the major accomplishments of economic science. Upon it have been built most of the contributions of the last three decades to understanding the economy as a general, interconnected system. In particular, almost all of modern macroeconomic theory is couched in terms of variants, specializations, and extensions of this modeling. For example, although the recent treatises on macro theory by Böhm (1988) and Sargent (1987) differ radically in content, both analyses fundamentally derive from competitive general equilibrium theory.

Yet a few moments' reflection on the evident, manifold successes of this modeling must lead to some sense of wonderment. A remarkable feature of this theory, as presented, for example, in Debreu (1959), is that markets, *per se*, have no formal role in it: The elements of the formal theory are a commodity space, producers (defined by their production sets), consumers (defined by their consumption sets, preferences, endowments and ownership shares), price systems (elements of the dual of the commodity space), and allocations (an element of the commodity space for each agent that individually and jointly satisfy feasibility conditions). Formally, the term "market" does not appear.[2] This is thus a theory that seeks to explain prices and the patterns of production, exchange, and consumption in the economy, yet it is a theory that has no treatment of how prices are set by the agents in the economy or of how actual transactions are realized, let alone of what might happen if the unmodeled mechanisms for determining prices and quantities should fail or if agents should adopt something other than the price-taking maximizing behavior that is assumed.

Of course, much of the work in general equilibrium theory over the last thirty years has been aimed at filling these lacunae, and members of CORE have made seminal contributions to these efforts. Two of the more prominent examples are by Jaskold-Gabszewicz and Vial (1972), one of the earliest treatments of imperfect competition in a closed multimarket model, and by Drèze (1975), the first general equilibrium analysis of quantity rationing necessitated by prices failing to adjust to equate supply and demand.

Contributions of this sort, and these ones in particular, are important: They have introduced significant elements of realism to the basic model, they have given insight, and they have had a major impact on subsequent work. For example, the fix-price approach to Keynesian macroeconomics that has been developed to such a large extent by current and former CORE members, students, visitors, and friends (see Böhm 1988 for references) grows largely out of the Drèze paper. Nevertheless, a number of the less plausible aspects of the Walrasian story and less satisfactory elements of competitive general equilibrium theory remain largely unexplored.

If we stop and think about actual markets, the contrast with the story embodied in competitive general equilibrium theory is striking. Few markets feature publicly announced and mechanistically adjusted prices. Instead, prices are determined directly by interested parties. Whether buyers or sellers post prices at which they will transact, or bargaining and negotiation occurs between buyers and sellers, or a double oral auction is used, the prices that actually emerge in real markets are the result of self-interested strategic behavior. These prices are not always freely known to all but rather must be discovered by search, and there is ample evidence that goods that are apparently identical in all respects can carry differing prices. Moreover simple, costless mechanisms for matching buyers and sellers are rare. Even in financial markets, brokers differ in their efficiency of order execution, and there are occasional suggestions that this activity is carried out strategically. In other markets, such as those for labor or housing, it is often necessary to search for potential trading partners. As well, in most markets, actual transactions are not determined by some impersonal mechanism: self-interested individuals decide with whom they will trade, and this may potentially affect final allocations. This is especially the case when rationing occurs.

Given all this, the success of analyses that derive from the competitive general equilibrium model is remarkable, even when these analyses replace one or another of its less realistic assumptions. Still, this success should not deter us from considering models that are apparently more descriptively accurate to see if the high degree of coordination achieved in the competitive general equilibrium model and its offshoots also obtains when there is no disinterested auctioneer publicly announcing prices and no impersonal, efficient mechanism for determining transactions.

The natural way to do this is to describe (model) explicitly the institutions for price and quantity determination in terms of the actions available to agents at different points, the information they have when acting, and the results that follow from their various possible actions. In partial equilibrium analysis it has become standard to employ the methods of the theory of noncooperative games in extensive form to construct such models. These same methods would seem equally appropriate for general equilibrium analysis, although they have rarely been employed in this context.[3]

As we demonstrate in the following section, it is in fact possible not only to use game theory to construct closed models of economies that incorporate explicit, more or less realistic descriptions of actual institutions but also to solve these models to generate interesting patterns of equilibrium behavior, including the failure of markets to clear.

Of course, once one thinks of the economy in game-theoretic terms, one recalls the large literature in game theory on coordination problems. Coordination games are ones with multiple, Pareto-comparable Nash equilibria. (See Aumann and Sorin 1989 for a recent discussion of coordination games.) As is well known, there is no existing theory that would indicate that a Pareto-superior equilibrium must be the result of rational individual behavior: If everyone somehow becomes convinced that others will run up the "down" escalator and run down the "up" escalator, and if the escalators are too narrow to permit passing in opposite directions, each is individually best off to mimic this forecast behavior, despite its gross social inefficiency.

As the following section will show, "reasonable" market institutions can give rise to coordination games, that is, seeming reasonable representations of the sort of stories we tell in introductory courses about how markets work can yield efficient solutions to the problem of coordinating individual economic behavior, but they need not do so. In fact equilibria may involve gross inefficiencies, with markets failing to clear and yet prices not adjusting despite the assumed hyper-rationality of all individuals, despite their acting optimally in all circumstances while correctly forecasting the full effects of each of their possible actions, and despite the possibility of their adjusting prices and wages being built into the model.

6.2 Economies, Institutions, and Equilibria

In this section we first specify the set of economies and the economic institutions under consideration. A key special feature of these economies is that there is a measure of separation and specialization between consumers in input supply, output consumption, and ownership of firms. Specifically, if a consumer is capable of supplying an input that is productive in some firms' technology or if the consumers' utility function is increasing in a good that the firm can supply, then the consumer does not own a positive share of this firm. Also a consumer can supply an input that is productive to some firm only if the consumer's utility is not increasing in any output of that firm. Finally, if a consumer's utility is increasing in the output of some firm, the consumer cannot supply any input that is productive for that firm. Thus a firm's owners do not overlap with its potential customers or suppliers, and these latter two groups are disjoint.

The assumed institutions involve prices being set by firms, consumers' responding with output demand orders from the individual firms and output supply offers to them, and then firms' deciding how much of these various orders and offers to accept and fill.[4]

The economy and institutions together define a game in extensive form. We then examine the subgame perfect equilibria of this game. These have the crucial property indicated above that equilibrium in this strong sense does not imply market clearing. Subgame perfection implies that consumers are price-takers. However, they may be subject to quantity rationing and thus be unable to buy and sell their Walrasian, utility-maximizing quantities at a given vector of prices. This rationing arises because other consumers' output orders are inadequate to justify firms hiring the Walrasian input quantities, even if they are offered, or because others' input supply offers will not allow firms to meet the Walrasian demands. Crucially, however, there may be no incentive for any firm to change prices for its inputs and outputs, despite this rationing.

Consider then a private ownership economy $\langle (U^i, \omega^i, \theta^i)_{i=1}^H, (Z^j)_{j=1}^F \rangle$, where U^i is the utility function, $\omega^i \in R_+^N$ is the endowment and $\theta^i = (\theta^{i1}, \ldots, \theta^{iF})$ is the vector of ownership shares of consumer i, $i = 1, \ldots, H$, and Z^j is the production set of firm j, $j = 1, \ldots, F$.

Assume that goods $1, \ldots, M$ are inputs, $(1 < M < N - 1)$, that goods $M + 1, \ldots, N - 1$ are outputs, $(M + 1 < N - 1)$, and that good N is neither an input nor an output. Also assume that there is free disposal in each Z^j for inputs and outputs. Formally, if $z \in Z^j$ for some $j \in \{1, \ldots, F\}$, then

$z_m \leq 0$ for $m \in \{1, \ldots, M\}$;

if $n \in \{M + 1, \ldots, N - 1\}$, then $[z_n < 0]$ implies $[(z - z_n e^n) \in Z^j]$;

$z_N = 0$; and

$z' \equiv (z - \varepsilon e^n) \in Z^j$ for all $\varepsilon > 0$, all $n \in \{1, \ldots, N - 1\}$,

where $e^n \in R^n$ has 1 in the nth place and zero elsewhere.

Also assume that $\omega_N^i > 0$ for all $i \in \{1, \ldots, H\}$, that $\sum_{i=1}^{H} \omega_n^i > 0$ for $n \in \{1, \ldots, M\}$, and that $\sum_{i=1}^{H} \omega_n^i = 0$, $n \in \{M + 1, \ldots, N - 1\}$, so each consumer is endowed with good N, there is a positive total endowment of each input, and there is no endowment of outputs. Likewise assume that if $z \in Z^j$ for some $j \in \{1, \ldots, F\}$ and if $z \neq 0$, then $z_m < 0$ for some $m \in \{1, \ldots, M\}$, so there is no free production, and that each Z^j shows constant returns to scale (i.e., Z^j is a convex cone, $j \in \{1, \ldots, F\}$).

Assume that each U^i is continuous, nondecreasing, and quasi concave on R_+^N, that $U^i(x) = -\infty$ if $x_n < 0$ for any n, so that negative quantities are arbitrarily distasteful, and that $U^i(x) < U^i(x + \varepsilon e^N)$ for all $x \in R_+^N$ and all $\varepsilon > 0$, so that preferences are strictly increasing in good N.

Define input $m \in \{1, \ldots, M\}$ to be productive for firm j if for each $z \in Z^j$ there exists $n \in \{M + 1, \ldots, N - 1\}$, $\varepsilon > 0$ and $\delta > 0$ such that $z - \delta e^m + \varepsilon e^n \in Z^j$: Using more of input m allows increased production of some output n.

To capture the separation mentioned above, assume that

if $\omega_m^i > 0$ and input m is productive for firm j, then $U^i(x) = U^i(x - \delta x_n e^n)$ for all $\delta \leq 1$, all $x \in R_+^N$, and all n such that there exists $z \in Z^j$ with $z_n > 0$;

if $U^i(x) < U^i(x + \varepsilon e^n)$ for some $x \in R_+^N$, $\varepsilon > 0$ and $n \in \{M + 1, \ldots, N - 1\}$, if input m is productive for firm j, and if there exists $z \in Z^j$ with $z_n > 0$, then $\omega_m^i = 0$; and

if $\theta^{ij} > 0$, then $\omega_m^i = 0$ for all inputs m that are productive for firm j and $U^i(x) = U^i(x - \delta x_n e^n)$ for all $x \in R_+^N$, all $\delta \leq 1$ and all $n \in \{M + 1, \ldots, N - 1\}$ such that there exists $z \in Z^j$ with $z_n > 0$.

The separation of customers and suppliers is intended to correspond to the feature of modern economies that individuals generalize in consumption but specialize in employment. However, the present formulation clearly goes beyond this. The separation between owners and customers or employees is made largely to avoid feedbacks through a firm's profits to its demand. It may be a reasonable approximation, but perhaps is becoming less so with the growth of Employee Stock Ownership Plans, pension funds that hold ownership claims on the employing firm, profit-sharing programs, and worker-managed organizations.

For the sake of simplicity, assume that if a consumer is not endowed with an input, then the consumer does not derive utility from that good (i.e., $\omega^i_m = 0$ for $m \in \{1, \ldots, M\}$ implies $U^i(x) = U^i(x - \delta x_m e^m)$ for all $x \in R^N_+$ and $\delta \le 1$). Thus there will be no basis for direct exchange between consumers. Finally, to avoid triviality, assume that each input is productive for some firm and that for each output n there is a firm $j \in \{1, \ldots, F\}$ and $z \in Z^j$ with $z_n > 0$.

Firms will be announcing prices under the assumed institutions. However, because good N is the only universally desired good and is not an input or output, we will normalize its price at unity[5] and will treat its price as beyond the influence of the firms.

The institutions being considered are meant to be moderately descriptive representations of markets in which firms post prices, then hire and produce to order. One obviously unrealistic assumption is that the economy (preferences, endowments, ownership shares, and production sets) and institutions are common knowledge. However, one would conjecture that uncertainties about any of these would not improve the performance of the institutions.

An important issue is whether the firms should be considered as independent entities (players) with their own objective functions or whether instead they should be modeled as agents of their owners, with only consumers' utilities being ultimately considered. From a positive point of view, the former has much to recommend it, but the latter is more standard in general equilibrium theory and welfare economics. Of course, either approach raises difficult problems of what the behavior of the firm should be. In the papers referenced above I finessed these issues by assuming that each firm was solely owned by an agent who supplied no input and consumed only good N, the numeraire. This meant that profit maximization for the firm and utility maximization for its owner were identical. Here the firms will be taken to be profit-maximizing entities. However, given the separation of each firm's owners from its customers and suppliers, profit maximization might well be a sensible solution to the owners' group decision problem of selecting the firm's strategies.

As noted above, the assumed institutions involve each firm j first selecting a price vector $p^j \in R^{N-1}$. These choices are made simultaneously and independently. Next, knowing the vector $(p^1, \ldots, p^F)$, each consumer i announces a vector of orders and offers $(y^{i1}, \ldots, y^{iF})$, $y^{ij} \in R^{N-1}$, where y^{ij}_m, $m \in \{1, \ldots, M\}$, is the amount of input m that i offers to sell to firm j ($y^{ij}_m \le 0$), and y^{ij}_n, $n \in \{M + 1, \ldots, N - 1\}$ is the amount of output n that i orders from j ($y^{ij}_n \ge 0$). Then $y^{ij}_N \equiv -\sum_{n=1}^{N-1} p^j_n y^{ij}_n$ is the net change in the amount of numeraire that the consumer would realize if the orders and offers made to this firm were executed. Again, the consumers' choices are made simultaneously and independently. These orders and offers are taken to be *bona fide* proposals to transact, and this leads to the requirements $\sum_{j=1}^F y^{ij}_n + \omega^i_n \ge 0$ for all $n = 1, \ldots, N - 1$. Finally, each firm j, knowing the prices p^1, $\ldots, p^F$, and all the orders and offers y^{ij}, $i = 1, \ldots, H$, $j = 1, \ldots, F$, selects a vector $z^{ij} \in R^{N-1}$, for each $i = 1, \ldots, H$, where $0 \ge z^{ij}_m \ge y^{ij}_m$, $m \in \{1, \ldots, M\}$ and $0 \le z^{ij}_n \le y^{ij}_n$, $n \in \{M + 1, \ldots, N - 1\}$. The z^{ij} vectors are the amounts of consumer i's orders and offers that firm j accepts. The inequalities relating the z^{ij}_n and y^{ij}_n values, $n \in \{1, \ldots, N - 1\}$, reflect voluntary exchange conditions. Feasibility requires that the vector $(\sum_{i=1}^H z^{ij}_1, \ldots, \sum_{i=1}^H z^{ij}_{N-1}, 0)$ belong to Z^j.

The resultant allocation then has firm j use inputs $\sum_{i=1}^H z^{ij}_n$, $n = 1, \ldots, M$ to produce outputs $\sum_{i=1}^H z^{ij}_n$, $n \in \{M + 1, \ldots, N - 1\}$, earning profits of $\sum_{n=1}^{N-1} p^j_n \sum_{i=1}^H z^{ij}_n$. The final consumption of consumer i is $x^i_m \equiv \omega^i_m + \sum_{j=1}^F z^{ij}_m$ of input m, $x^i_n \equiv \sum_{j=1}^F z^{ij}_n$ of output n (recall $\omega^i_n = 0$), and $x^i_N \equiv \omega^i_N - \sum_{j=1}^F \sum_{n=1}^{N-1} p^j_n z^{ij}_n + \sum_{j=1}^F \theta^{ij} \sum_{n=1}^{N-1} p^j_n \sum_{h=1}^H z^{hj}_n$ of numeraire. Note that we allow $x^i_N < 0$, but that this brings infinitely negative utility: Negative holdings of money are "unreasonable" but will not arise in equilibrium. Apart from this factor, every possible specification of choices for the firms and consumers yields a feasible allocation.

Evaluating these allocations according to the consumers' utility functions and firms' profits gives a game. A strategy for firm j in this game is first a choice of p^j and then a function mapping $(R^{N-1})^F \times (R^{N-1})^{HF}$ into $(R^{N-1})^H$, giving the quantities of each order and offer it received that it accepts, as depending on all the firms' price vectors and all the consumers' orders and offers. A strategy for consumer i is a map from $(R^{N-1})^F$ into $(R^{N-1})^F$, giving the consumer's orders and offers to the various firms as depending on the announced prices. The strategies of both the firms and the consumers are subject to the feasibility and voluntary exchange constraints given above. An "equilibrium" is a subgame perfect equilibrium of the game, that is, a strategy for each agent (firm or consumer), with the properties that

1. for each $(N-1)F$-vector of prices that could be announced and each $(N-1)HF$-vector of possible orders and offers from consumers, the $(N-1)H$-vector of acceptances for each firm j specified by its strategy maximizes the firm's profits (subject to the feasibility and voluntary exchange constraints);

2. for each $(N-1)F$-vector of possible price announcements, the $(N-1)F$-vector of orders and offers of each consumer i that are specified by the consumer's strategy maximizes U^i, given that the other consumers' orders and offers will be those specified by their strategies and that the firms' acceptances of whatever orders and offers are made will be those specified by their strategies; and

3. the price choice of each firm j specified by the firm's strategy maximizes its profits, given that other firms' price choices will be those specified by their strategies, that the resultant consumer orders and offers will be determined by their strategies, and that the firms' acceptances will be given by their strategies.

Note that, in equilibrium, prices are set in full understanding of actual response of quantities to any price choice. Thus, if rationing occurs (i.e., some consumer is not able to realize his or her utility-maximizing, competitive consumption at the prevailing prices[6]), then it is not because prices are not free to adjust. We will demonstrate that rationing can occur, and may even do so at equilibrium prices that not only permit full market clearing but actually are perfectly competitive.

Given an economy satisfying our assumptions, consider any K-fold replication of the economy, that is, an economy with KH consumers and KF firms, where there are K firms with the same technology as each of the firms in the original economy and K consumers with the same preferences and endowments as each of the consumers in the original economy and where the kth consumer of each type, $k = 1, \ldots, K$, holds positive ownership shares only in the kth firm of each type. Consider a symmetric Walrasian outcome[7] for this replica economy, that is, a price vector $\bar{p} = (\bar{p}_1, \ldots, \bar{p}_{N-1}, 1)$ for the inputs and outputs (recall that $p_N = 1$), a consumption vector $\bar{x}^i$ for each type of consumer, and a production vector $\bar{z}^j$ for each type of firm such that

$\bar{z}^j$ maximizes $\bar{p} \cdot z$ on Z^j for each j;

$\bar{x}^i$ maximizes $U^i(x)$ subject to $\bar{p} \cdot x \le \bar{p} \cdot \omega^i + \sum_{j=1}^{F} \theta^{ij} \bar{p} \cdot \bar{z}^j$ for each i; and

$K \sum_{i=1}^{H} (\bar{x}^i - \omega^i) = K \sum_{j=1}^{F} \bar{z}^j$.

(Note that our assumptions ensure that a Walrasian solution exists.) Then we have

THEOREM   If $K \ge 2$, then for any integer k, $0 \le k \le K$, there exists an equilibrium in which all firms announce the Walrasian price vector $\bar{p}$; k of the consumers of each type i, $i \in \{1, \ldots, H\}$, receive their Walrasian consumption vectors $\bar{x}^i$ and k of the firms of each type j produce their Walrasian production vectors $\bar{z}^j, j \in \{1, \ldots, F\}$, while the remaining $K - k$ consumers of each type consume their initial endowment vectors ($x^i = \omega^i$, $i = 1, \ldots, H$), and the remaining $K - k$ firms of each type produce zero ($z^j = 0, j = 1, \ldots, F$).

Proof   Note first that if no consumer offers to sell inputs to a particular firm, it is optimal for no one to place orders with the firm, and that if no one places orders with a firm, then it is optimal not to offer inputs to it. Thus, given any prices, there is always an equilibrium in the resulting subgame in which any given firm is inactive, receiving zero orders and offers. This result is clearly dependent on each firm's owners, suppliers, and customers being disjoint groups.

   Given the assumed symmetry, $(\bar{p}, \bar{z}^1, \ldots, \bar{z}^F, \bar{x}^1, \ldots, \bar{x}^H)$ constitutes a Walrasian solution for the base economy with F firms and H consumers. Thus there exist $(N - 1)HF$ real numbers ξ_n^{ij} such that $\bar{x}_n^i = \omega_n^i + \sum_j \xi_n^{ij}$, and $\bar{z}_n^j = \sum_i \xi_n^{ij}$, $i = 1, \ldots, H$, $j = 1, \ldots, F$ and $n = 1, \ldots, N - 1$. Thus the Walrasian allocation can be achieved in the replica economy by having K "subeconomies," each identical to the base economy, with no transactions between subeconomies. Further we can select these subeconomies so that the owners of the firms in each are exclusively the consumers in this subeconomy.

   Now suppose each firm announces the Walrasian price vector $\bar{p}$, that the ith consumer, $i = 1, \ldots, H$, in each of k of the subeconomies announces orders and offers ξ_n^{ij} to firm $j, j = 1, \ldots, F$, in this subeconomy and orders and offers of 0 to all firms in the other subeconomies, that the ith consumer, $i = 1, \ldots, H$, in the remaining $K - k$ subeconomies orders and offers 0 to all firms, and finally that each firm accepts all orders and offers placed with it. These actions will yield the specified outcomes. We now must ensure that no agent wishes to deviate from this behavior.

Note that no firm can gain by changing its acceptances: These yield zero profits, and at the Walrasian prices no technologically feasible input–output vector yields positive profits. A consumer who realizes his Walrasian consumption obviously cannot benefit by any change in his orders and offers, given the price vector. To ensure that a consumer who transacts zero also cannot benefit by any deviation, we must specify the firms' response to such a deviation.

Note that the assumed separation means that no consumer can supply inputs to a firm from which he might buy outputs. Thus a firm receiving an input supply offer from an inactive consumer does not have the demand to justify purchasing more inputs: The only source of demand is other consumers, and their offers and orders are taken as given. Also, by the same logic, a firm that receives an extra output order does not have access to the inputs that allow extra production. Thus we can specify that if any inactive consumer makes orders and offers different from those specified, he receives no acceptances. Consequently no deviation is worthwhile.

Thus we have an equilibrium in the subgame given the Walrasian prices. We must now ensure that no firm wishes to deviate from these prices. To do so, we specify that a firm announcing $p \neq \bar{p}$ receive zero orders and offers. Any consumers who would have dealt with this firm instead place the orders and offers they would have placed with it with the corresponding firm in another subeconomy. All other orders and offers are unchanged from those specified to follow the Walrasian price announcements, and the firms accept all orders and offers received.

Because of the constant returns assumption, the firm receiving the orders and offers that would have gone to the deviating firm can accept these. Further, since profits are zero at the Walrasian price, both with and without the extra business, it will be willing to do so. Thus the consumers still receive the same consumption vectors as they would absent a price deviation, and the firms' profits are unchanged. Finally, because (as argued above) it is equilibrium behavior for all consumers to shun a given firm, no consumer can gain from deviating from the specified behavior.

We thus have described the strategies following selection of the Walrasian prices by all firms and by all but one firm. If more than one firm announces prices differing from the Walrasian, then we can specify any pattern of subgame equilibrium behavior.[8] This completely describes the set of strategies, and these constitute a subgame perfect equilibrium. The actual equilibrium outcome will then be as specified in the statement of the theorem. ■

The preceding proof illustrates clearly the nature of the coordination problem that the Walrasian auctioneer solves but which is not automatically solved by the market institutions assumed here. The rationing involves self-confirming conjectures, just as does the full-employment equilibrium. Expectations of rationing lead to behavior that results in rationing; expectations of being unconstrained generate orders and offers that require no quantity constraints. Moreover prices are set in light of correct forecasts of the quantity responses that any possible price choice would generate, and even when rationing is forecast, in equilibrium there are no incentives to change prices.

A key question is the extent to which other institutions would yield better performance. My papers cited above and the Jones-Manuelli paper begin exploring this robustness question, at least in the context of specific examples. The main results of my papers suggest that so long as the separation of owners, consumers, and suppliers holds, the existence of equilibria both with and without rationing is robust to a variety of alterations in the behavior (e.g., announcing effective demands) and institutions (e.g., having input market transactions completed before output orders are placed, or allowing consumers to set input prices). On the other hand, Jones and Manuelli (1987) find that certain other modifications are important (e.g., having firms with lexicographic preferences on profits and then output).

A separate line of work that posits quite distinct institutions but that also employs noncooperative game-theoretic methods to explore general equilibrium issues leads to similar conclusions regarding the possibility of rationing with flexible prices. In particular, Rubinstein and Wolinsky (1986) consider a model with one good plus the numéraire, B buyers, and S sellers, each of whom owns one indivisible unit of the good. Buyers and sellers meet, one random pair at a time, and bargain over price. If no bargain is struck, both agents return to the pool; otherwise, they complete the agreed transaction and leave the market. Assuming $B > S$, there is a unique Walrasian price equal to r, the common reservation price of the buyers. However, any value between 0 (the seller's reservation value) and r can be the common price at which exchange occurs in a perfect equilibrium. Thus equilibrium features a failure of market clearing: Demand (B) exceeds supply (S) and yet prices do not adjust.

Clearly much remains to be done. Yet the possibility of market equilibrium with flexible competitive prices but with rationing seems sufficiently important—both for macro and for micro—that further work should be worthwhile.

Notes

The research reported here was supported by grants from the US National Science Foundation. This chapter is respectfully dedicated to Jacques Drèze in gratitude not only for his many contributions to the science and the profession of economics but also, more personally, for his contributions to my own scientific and professional development. As a scientist maintaining the highest standards of rigor, as a practical man in touch with the real and pressing problems of actual economies, and as an institution-builder supporting others' work, even at the cost of his own, Jacques Drèze represents standards of behavior and accomplishment that are an inspiration to all who know him.

1. The major references are Roberts (1987a, 1989). See also Roberts (1987b, 1987c) and Jones and Manuelli (1987).

2. Even in less austere treatments (e.g., Arrow and Hahn 1971), the "market" appears to be a common meeting place wherein all trade occurs, with prices set by a disinterested auctioneer who adjusts prices if and only if zero is not an element of the image of the excess demand correspondence.

3. The work on game-theoretic models of exchange beginning with Shubik (1972) is an important exception. A particularly relevant recent contribution is the literature on general equilibrium models of bargaining. See, for example, Rubinstein and Wolinsky (1986).

4. Variants of these institutions are considered in Jones-Manuelli (1987) and my papers cited above.

5. See Jaskold-Gabszewicz and Vial (1972) for a discussion of the importance of the choice of numeraire in non-Walrasian models.

6. Note that subgame perfection requires consumers to be price-takers.

7. A "Walrasian outcome" is not an equilibrium of the game, since it is not a set of strategies. Thus the nonstandard terminology.

8. Consider, for example, zero orders and offers by all consumers to all firms.

References

Arrow, K. J., and F. H. Hahn. 1971. *General Competitive Analysis.* San Francisco: Holden-Day.

Aumann, R. J., and S. Sorin. 1989. "Cooperation and Bounded Recall." *Games and Economic Behavior* 1:5–39.

Böhm, V. 1988. *Disequilibrium and Macroeconomics*. Oxford: Basil Blackwell.

Debreu, G. 1959. *Theory of Value: An Axiomatic Analysis of Economic Equilibrium*. New York: Wiley.

Drèze, J. 1975. "Existence of an Exchange Equilibrium Under Price Rigidities." *International Economic Review* 16:301–320.

Jaskold-Gabszewicz, J., and J. -Ph. Vial 1972. "Oligopoly 'a la Cournot' in General Equilibrium Analysis." *Journal of Economic Theory* 4:380–400.

Jones, L., and R. Manuelli. 1987. "The Coordination Problem and Equilibrium Theories of Recessions." Mimeo, Kellogg Graduate School of Management, Northwestern University.

Roberts, J. 1987a. "An Equilibrium Model with Involuntary Unemployment at Flexible, Competitive Prices and Wages." *American Economic Review* 77:856–874.

Roberts, J. 1987b. "General Equilibrium Analysis of Imperfect Competition: An Illustrative Example." *In Arrow and the Ascent of Modern Economic Theory*, edited by G. Feiwel. London: Macmillan, 415–438.

Roberts, J. 1987c. "Unemployment as a Coordination Failure: Importance to Micro-Institutions for Macro Performance." Mimeo, Graduate School of Business, Standford University.

Roberts, J. 1989. "Involuntary Unemployment and Imperfect Competition: A Game Theoretic Macro Model." In *The Economics of Imperfect Competition and Employment: Joan Robinson and Beyond*, edited by G. Feiwel. London: Macmillan.

Rubinstein, A., and A. Wolinsky, 1986. "Decentralized Trading, Strategic Behavior and the Walrasian Outcome." Technical Report 497, The Economics Series, Institute for Mathematical Studies in the Social Sciences, Stanford University.

Sargent, T. J. 1987. *Dynamic Macroeconomic Theory*. Cambridge, MA: Harvard University Press.

Shubik, M. 1972. "Commodity Money, Oligopoly, Credit and Bankruptcy in a General Equilibrium Model." *Western Economic Journal* 10:24–38.

II OPERATIONS RESEARCH

Introduction to Part II

The Survey Chapter

Chapter 7, by Thomas Magnanti, "Twenty Years of Mathematical Programming," begins with a brief discussion of the history of mathematical programming before 1967, which includes some recent state-of-the-art applications to underline the practical developments in the field since 1967. The author then chooses five important research themes of the last twenty years: (1) the foundations of convex analysis and duality theory, (2) the development of computational fixed point theorems, (3) emergence of combinatorial optimization, (4) interfaces with computer science and numerical analysis, and (5) new discoveries in linear programming. He discusses the first three in some detail, and cites references for the last two.

The first discussant, Etienne Loute, focuses on the fourth topic (interfaces with computer science and numerical analysis) through a discussion of the development of (linear) mathematical programming systems, through experimental computer implementations and the recent development of software for microcomputers.

The second discussant, Alexander H. G. Rinnooy Kan, addresses the next twenty years and raises several puzzling questions about our understanding of algorithms, of which the simplex method is a prime example. The quality of algorithms, the effectiveness of randomization, and the development of algorithms for parallel computation are cited as areas in which our understanding is still in its infancy.

The Mathematical Programming Seminar Chapters

Karmarkar's projective linear programming algorithm is one of the exciting new discoveries in linear programming, mentioned in section 7.5 of the survey chapter. This algorithm has led to a wealth of research, and various authors have proposed affine variants of the algorithm, which are in some ways simpler but do not lead to polynomial algorithms. In the invited chapter 8, John Mitchell and Michael Todd compare such variants and establish conditions under which the affine algorithms are also polynomial.

Chapter 9, by Michael Ball, Wei-Guo Liu, and William Pulleyblank on "Two-Terminal Steiner Tree Polyhedra," is typical of one very rich area of research in combinatorial optimization (see section 7.3 of the survey chapter), namely, the study of polyhedral combinatorics. The goal of the authors is to describe a linear programming formulation whose optimal solution solves the Steiner tree problem. Starting from the initial graphical problem, they give several such formulations that involve either additional constraints or additional variables, and discuss the relationships between them.

Finally, chapter 10, "Solving Arborescent Linear Programs with Nested Decomposition" by Olivier Janssens de Bisthoven and Etienne Loute, describes an algorithm for large-scale linear programs that arise typically when there is a joint effect of a multiregional structure and a time-phased structure, or when uncertainty leads to large stochastic linear programs. The authors discuss an implementation of the algorithm, based on a commercial mathematical programming system, as well as the data structures and computational strategies used.

7 Twenty Years of Mathematical Programming

Thomas L. Magnanti

Mathematical programming is a broad scientific field with exciting intellectual content and with diverse applications cutting across numerous problem domains. The field has many roots: optimization problems in agriculture solved by the ancient Greeks; the work of many of the great mathematicians of the eighteenth and nineteenth centuries, including such luminaries as Euler, Gauss, and Lagrange; fundamental results on linear inequality systems developed by the noted mathematicians Julius Farkas, Jean-Batiste Fourier, and T. S. Motzkin; analysis of economic problems conducted by John von Neumann and by Abraham Wald. As mathematical programming evolved, these contributions provided rich intellectual foundations. But mathematical programming as we know it today is quite young. If we take the 1947 discovery of the simplex method, and its subsequent rapid development, as the field's inception, then mathematical programming is a mere forty years old—very much an infant when compared to many other fields in the physical, social, and life sciences. And yet the mathematical programming community can point with considerable pride to the field's rapid growth: to its substantial body of accumulated knowledge, to its wide-ranging contributions to many problem contexts, and to the far-reaching impact that it has had on education and on practice. Just the fact that mathematical programming is taught in hundreds of universities throughout the world and in such varied departments as agriculture, business, economics, engineering, mathematics, and urban studies, among others, attests to the field's success.

These sentiments raise a fascinating question: What is the status of mathematical programming and what have been the field's major scientific and practical accomplishments? Providing a thorough answer to this question would be an enormous undertaking, far too ambitious for any brief account of the field. This chapter has a more limited purpose: Suppose we look back only twenty years. What have been some major intellectual themes during this period? The choice of twenty years seems appropriate for several reasons. First, 1967 was the founding date of CORE, the Center for Operations Research and Econometrics, a center that has been a rallying point for much research in operations research and mathematical programming, and thus this choice of a date reflects the twentieth-anniversary celebration that this book commemorates. Second, if we accept 1947 as the origin of mathematical programming, through 1987, twenty years is exactly the half-life of the field. And, from a more personal perspective, twenty years ago I began graduate studies in mathematical programming. Thus this time frame captures my own professional involvement with the field.

The discussion in this chapter is intended for nonspecialists with some modest background in optimization or allied fields such as economics or engineering. We assume that the reader recognizes the importance of linear programming and the simplex method for its solution. Rather than trying to be encyclopedic, we will examine a small number of main ideas, for the most part using illustrative geometry and avoiding technical details. To help the reader who might wish to pursue some of the material in this chapter in more depth, in a concluding section we cite several basic textbooks and monographs that should serve as a guide to the rich and extensive literature on mathematical programming. These references contain citations to original research contributions.

Our discussion is limited. It focuses on constrained finite-dimensional optimization problems that are deterministic and static and have single objective functions. Therefore, except for a few passing remarks, we do not describe many related developments in allied fields such as optimal control theory, dynamic programming, Markov decision theory, graph theory, or multicriterion optimization.

7.1 Background

Before beginning to discuss developments from 1967 to 1987, we might reflect upon what was already in place in 1967. The simplex method of linear programming was firmly established as the computational work-horse of the field, and linear programming itself had become demonstrably the field's intellectual core. In particular, the ideas of linear programming pivoting and of linear programming duality theory had already become central constructs that were, to this day, to stimulate many developments in the field that have attempted to explain, emulate, or extend these ideas. As discussed in Abraham Charnes and William Cooper's influential book *Management Models and Industrial Applications of Linear Programming*, by the early 1960s linear programming had already had a significant impact on practice, mostly through applications in industrial settings, particularly large oil and chemical companies. In addition by 1967 computer manufacturers had already developed major computer systems for linear programming, including the noted IBM system MPSX. And linear programming had had a very substantial influence on economic theory as reflected in Robert Dorfman, Paul Samuelson, and Robert Solow's, David Gale's, and Gerard Debreau's pathbreaking books *Linear Programming and Economic Analysis*, *The Theory of Linear Economic Models*, and *Theory of Value*. In addition mathematical programmers had already developed many results other than the theory and algorithms of linear programming. These included

1. theory and specialized algorithms for problems in network optimization, as reported in Lester Ford and D. R. Fulkerson's classic book, *Flows in Networks*, as well as the development of fundamental connections between this field and other branches of combinatorial mathematics;

2. branch and bound and basic cutting plane methods of integer programming, and applications of branch and bound in many problem settings;

3. the foundations of nonlinear programming solution methods, including linear programming like pivoting methods for quadratic programming, and both gradient-based feasible direction methods, and basic barrier and penalty methods for more general problems;

4. fundamental theoretical constructs of nonlinear programming, including local optimality conditions, most notably the fundamental Karush-Kuhn-Tucker conditions, and the theory of convex analysis;

5. the theory of mathematical programming decomposition, especially the seminal method known as Dantzig-Wolfe decomposition, and several other basic results in the theory of large-scale optimization;

6. the central constructs of game theory including the discovery of intimate connections between this theory and mathematical programming, and the development of the important underlying theory of saddlepoints and minimax optimization;

7. basic theory and algorithms for a topic known as linear complementarity that was to serve as the precursor to the general theory of computational fixed points (see section 7.4); and

8. early work in the field of combinatorial optimization including algorithms and theory for fields known as matching and matroid optimization.

In addition related fields had laid many similar foundations, for example,

1. the Pontryagin maximum principle of optimal control theory, basic methods for solving optimal control problems (particularly the well-known "quadratic loss function" problem), and the theory of Kalman filtering;

2. the "principle of optimality" and methods for solving many core models, both deterministic and stochastic, in dynamic programming; and

3. many basic models, much underlying theory, and several fundamental solution procedures for stochastic optimization, particularly policy iteration and value iteration methods of Markov decision theory, and the basic models ("wait-and-see" and "two-stage") of stochastic programming.

Mathematical programming methods were central to these developments, and they in turn motivated many results for the type of deterministic mathematical programming to be considered in this chapter.

These lists are very impressive. Clearly by 1967 mathematical programming had already arrived as a legitimate and fertile field of scientific inquiry. It may appear that the research community had already discovered many of the most important results in mathematical programming. Certainly the field had firmly planted its roots, but much was still to come. The status of textbooks might provide just one measure of the field's status at the time. In 1963 George Dantzig published his landmark book, *Linear Programming and Extensions*, which brought together many known results to that date, summarized numerous contributions from the literature, and provided many historical perspectives. By 1967 authors had written many texts in linear programming (Saul Gass's and Michel Simmonard's books, both entitled *Linear Programming*, were other notable contributions). But much less had appeared on other topics. Although in 1960 G. Zoutendijk had published one of the first books on nonlinear programming, many of the now standard references in nonlinear programming had yet to appear. These included influential books by Anthony Fiacco and Garth McCormick (*Nonlinear Programming: Sequential Unconstrained Minimization Techniques*), Olvi Mangasarian (*Nonlinear Programming*), Tyrrell Rockafellar (*Convex Analysis*), and Willard Zangwill (*Nonlinear Programming: A Unified Approach*), published in rapid succession in 1968 through 1970, and later books by Mordecai Avriel (*Nonlinear Programming: Analysis and Methods*), Mokhtar Bazarra and S. M. Shetty (*Nonlinear Programming Theory and Algorithms*), and David Luenberger (*Introduction to Linear and Nonlinear Programming*). In addition the first comprehensive mathematical programming textbook on large-scale optimization, Leon Lasdon's *Opti-*

mization for Large Systems, did not appear until 1971. One year later Robert Garfinkel and George Nemhauser published *Integer Programming,* one of the first comprehensive treatments of this field. As reflected by this flurry of important, seminal textbooks in the late 1960s and early 1970s, 1967 was about the time when mathematical programming had matured considerably; the field had attracted a cadre of top flight scholars; these researchers not only wrote what became the field's basic textbooks for years to come, but many of them were to become among the most influential and leading researchers and practitioners of the 1970s and 1980s; moreover the field now had a rich knowledge base that was to serve as the intellectual foundation for its second two decades.

7.2   Mathematical Programming Practice

One of the most important distinguishing features of mathematical programming is that it provides a fertile domain both for theoretical discoveries and for meaningful practice. Practical challenges have inspired much of the field's key methodological advances, and new theory has often extended the frontiers of practice. For example, many years ago practical challenges in the distribution of natural gas led to the development of Dantzig-Wolfe decomposition. More recently, problems posed by energy distribution, monetary markets, agricultural markets, and other spatially separated economic markets (including natural gas again) and by urban traffic equilibrium have prompted new theory in computational fixed points and for systems of inequalities known as variational inequalities. On the other hand, as an example in the other direction, novel theory for integer programming decomposition has permitted practitioners to solve a wide range of new problems. In the discussion to follow, which focuses on methodological developments over the last two decades, we describe several of these advances in underlying theory. But discussion of theory alone would not adequately reflect activities in mathematical programming. Therefore the brief description in this section of a few applications will provide at least a hint of how mathematical programming has recently contributed to practice. (In the following sections we will treat a few additional application domains.)

Normally, since the applications of mathematical programming are so diverse, choosing a few selected examples would be an impossible task. Fortunately, however, since 1972, the Institute of Management Sciences has conducted a yearly competition (now known as the Edelman Prize Competition) for the best application of management science/operations research as measured by documented savings or contributions to the client of the study. The following studies, which draw heavily on mathematical programming, have recently won this competition:[1]

• *Improving distribution systems planning at Air Products.* In the distribution of industrial gases, customers store inventory at its point of consumption. Suppliers therefore face a complex decision problem. When should they replenish the inventory in a customer's tank, and how should the supplier manage its distribution system, in particular, route its vehicles to effectively blend its inventory management and vehicle-routing decisions. Because of the time element required to account for the inventory replenishment decisions and the combinatorial nature of the routing decisions, this type of application easily becomes a very large, complex optimization problem. In the early 1980s Air Products and Chemical Corporation, a major supplier of industrial gases, developed an integar programming based decision support system for this application to be used as an operational planning tool. In a number of applications the mixed integer programming model contained up to 800,000 variables and 200,000 constraints. Using a sophisticated method of integar programming decomposition, known as Lagrangian relaxation (see section 7.3), the company was able to solve the problem to near optimality and save between 6 to 10 percent of operating costs.

• *Cutting logs optimally at Weyerhauser.* In harvesting trees, a lumber company must make decisions on how to cut felled trees into logs that it then transports to its plants for processing into end products. This decision is important: the value of a tree can vary by 50 percent or more depending upon how it is cut. The cutting decision is complicated, though, because it depends upon the characteristics of the felled trees—their length, curvature, diameter, and impurities (knots)—as well as on the economic value of the end products. Moreover the "wood buckers" who cut the trees must make their cutting decisions in real time in the field. In a novel application of optimization, analysts at Weyerhauser Company formulated this problem as a dynamic program and developed an interactive video game that permitted wood buckers, by "playing" against the dynamic program, to test and refine their mental heuristics for choosing how to cut trees (solving the dynamic program in the field was not feasible). The company credits this optimization-based learning approach as contributing over $100 million in increased profits in the last ten years.

• *Managing the Netherlands' water resources.* National water management is a complex problem that must strike a balance between a variety of technical, political, and economic considerations, as well as address uncertainty in the availability and consumption of water. The problem is particularly important for a country like the Netherlands that relies so heavily on irrigated crop production for its economic well-being. To address this problem, in the late 1970s through the mid 1980s the Dutch government developed and applied a sophisticated set of integrated models, including six mathematical programs (both linear and nonlinear) and two heuristic optimization procedures. These optimization models assisted planners in several ways: by providing operating strategies and price and regulation strategies for distribution surface and ground water, by reallocating electricity generation among power plants, by determining the type of irrigation system to be used, and by estimating maximum possible algae populations. The integrated system, which resulted in a new national water management system, is credited with saving hundreds of million dollars in investment expenditures and reducing agricultural damage by about $15 million per year, while also decreasing thermal and algae pollution.

• *Improving business planning at Citgo Petroleum Corporation.* Since the early days of mathematical programming in the 1950s, oil companies have always been among the most conspicuous and leading users of linear and nonlinear programming and of network optimization. Linear programming models of refineries help to guide crude selections and acquisitions, refinery operating levels, and blending decisions; nonlinear programming aids in process control and energy utilization; network models support supply decisions, including exchange agreements with other suppliers, distribution decisions, and marketing decisions. During 1984 and 1985 Citgo Petroleum Company embarked upon a major management science effort, combining mathematical programming, statistics, artificial intelligence, and organizational theory, to redesign and better integrate its business planning systems. Linear programming, network optimization, and nonlinear programming were central to this effort, which the company credits with changing the way it does business and with improving profits by approximately $70 million per year.

These examples, though among the best success stories for operations research/management science, only begin to touch upon how mathematical programming contributes to practice. Mathematical programming is used every day in the context of engineering design, communication systems, transportation, logistics, manufacturing, and numerous other problem domains. These examples and many others demonstrate that mathematical programming has not only matured into a rich scientific discipline with many theoretical subfields but has also successfully sustained its original practical impetus.

7.3 Research Themes

Mathematical prgramming is an enormous field, with thousands of researchers and thousands of research contributions each year. Therefore, to make the task of discussing research contributions of the last twenty years more manageable, I have imposed the following stipulation: limit the discussion to five major research themes.[2] My choices are

1. setting foundations of convex analysis and duality theory,
2. inception and maturation of computational fixed point theory,
3. emergence of combinatorial optimization,
4. interfaces with computer science and numerical analysis, and
5. new discoveries in linear programming.

These (somewhat overlapping) themes are not intended to encompass all research conducted over the last twenty years. Nevertheless, the list does capture many important general topics and research thrusts that have attracted a large constituency of researchers from within the mathematical programming community. If asked to prepare a similar list of five topics, other members of the mathematical programming would undoubtedly choose differently, categorize past research in other ways, and/or place different emphasis on the topics included. Most members of this community would quite likely agree, however, that these topics represent important or influential research thrusts.

Figure 7.1 gives further rationale for the choices on this list. The time line in this figure shows topics in mathematical programming that have won major research awards given either by the mathematical programming community itself or by the broader operations research and mathematics

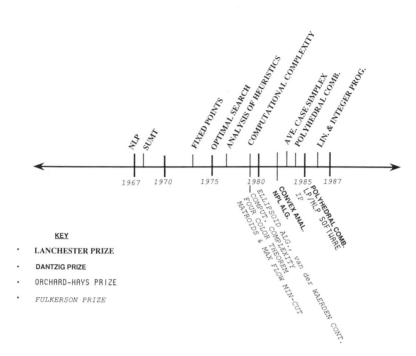

Figure 7.1
Prizes for mathematical programming

communities. The awards referred to in this figure are the Lanchester Prize, an award given annually by the Operations Research Society of America for best research publication in the English language; the Dantzig Price, given every three years by the Mathematical Programming Society and the Society for Industrial and Applied Mathematics for an original contribution to the field of mathematical programming; the Fulkerson Prize, given every three years by the American Mathematical Society and Mathematical Programming Society for outstanding papers in the field of discrete mathematics; and the Orchard-Hays Prize, given every three years by the Mathematical Programming Society for excellence in computational mathematical programming.

Setting Foundations in Convex Analysis and Duality Theory

One of the major achievements of modern mathematical programming—the unification and extension of mathematical programming duality theory—has been prompted by the research community's recognition of the central role played by convexity. Indeed, the research agenda in modern duality theory has to a large extent systematically replaced differentiability requirements with convexity. The seeds for this development are quite old, dating from discoveries in mathematics (e.g., various separation theorems for convex bodies including the celebrated Hahn-Banach theorem), in optimal control, and in statistics, as well as in economics and game theory. In fact, beginning with the seminal work of Werner Fenchel in the 1950s, researchers had conducted much of the work on this topic during the early and mid-1960s. Nevertheless, this body of research provides so much of the essential underlying mathematics of mathematical programming, and has continued to attract so much attention from researchers, that it definitely deserves emphasis in this exposition.

A Problem in Geometry   Figure 7.2a, which is taken from the book jacket of David Luenberger's well-known textbook, *Optimization by Vector Space Methods*, nicely embodies the essence of duality theory in nonlinear programming. This figure shows a convex set C (i.e., a set containing all line segments connecting any two points in the set), a point X not in the set, and a line L that lies between (separates) the set and the point: the point and set lie on opposite sides of the line. The perpendicular line segment joining the point X and the line L in this figure measures the (shortest) distance between the point and the line. We might formulate the following geometric optimization problem:

FARTHEST LINE PROBLEM   From among all lines L that separate a set C and a point X that is not in the set, find the line that is farthest from the given point.

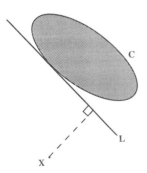

Figure 7.2a
Separating a point and a set

Now consider the following seemingly unrelated problem (at least on the surface):

CLOSEST POINT PROBLEM   Find the point in a set C that is closest to a point X that is not in that set.

Since every point in the set C lies on the side of the separating line opposite from the point X, every point in the set is at least as far from X as *any* separating line. Therefore we have the following inequality, which has become known in the mathematical programming community as "weak duality":

WEAK DUALITY   The distance d from any specified point X to the farthest line L separating X and a set C is no more than the distance D from X to the closest point in the C.

Like most such weak duality results in mathematical programming, this conclusion is immediate from the problem description. A much deeper result is valid as well:

STRONG DUALITY   The distance d from a specified point X to the farthest separating line *equals* the distance D from this point to the closest point Y in a specified convex set, that is, $d = D$.

Note that we can establish this result geometrically by choosing the separating line so that it (see figure 7.2b)

1. passes though the point Y in the set that is closest to X, and

2. is perpendicular to the line segment from X to Y.

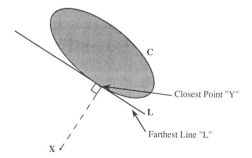

Figure 7.2b
Geometric duality

Therefore the farthest separating line "supports" (is tangent to) the set C at the nearest point Y in C to the point X. This type of separating and supporting line argument underlies most results in nonlinear programming duality theory; in three dimensions a separating line becomes a separating plane, and in higher dimensions the line becomes an analog of the plane (the solution, known as a hyperplane, to a linear equation). Conceptually, the geometry remains much the same, though in many instances the argument becomes much more intricate.

The type of minimum distance problem considered in this simple geometrical example embodies a number of "minimum norm" applications that arise in optimal control, for example what is the minimum fuel expenditure needed to send a rocket to the moon. This model also captures the essence of quadratic programming (i.e., minimizing a quadratic function), since minimizing distance is the same as minimizing the square of the distance, which is a quadratic function. And yet this minimum distance example might seem far removed from the general mathematical programming problem.

Nevertheless, to those familiar with the rudiments of linear programming or mathematical programming, these results may seem suspiciously familiar. What may be a bit more surprising is that a modest twist on this problem formulation embodies the most fundamental results of general duality theory of mathematical programming. To describe the modified problem, let us consider figure 7.3. Now instead of measuring distance from the point X to any separating line L by the usual Euclidean distance, suppose we do the following. As shown in the figure, take any "target line" TL that both passes through the point X and intersects the set C; now measure the

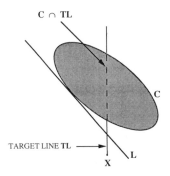

Figure 7.3
Separating a point and a set along a target line

distance from X to any separating line L as the distance from X to the intersection of L and the target line TL (see figure 7.3). Also, instead of finding the closest point in C to X, we now seek the closest point Y to X that lies in both C and on the line TL. Again, weak duality is an easy consequence of the problem formulation; moreover choosing the separating line L as a line that is tangent to the set C at the closest point Y to X in $C \cap TL$ establishes strong duality.

Duality in Mathematical Programming   Let us now add some contextual richness to the last observation to see how the same geometric interpretation provides both connections with mathematical programming and useful economic interpretations (and hence provides an important linkage between mathematical programming and economic theory). Consider the general mathematical programming problem:

$$v = \text{minimum } f(x)$$

$$\text{subject to } g(x) = b \qquad\qquad\qquad\qquad\qquad \text{(MP)}$$

$$x \in S.$$

In this formulation, x is a vector of decision variables, b is a specified "target" resource level, $g(x)$ is the resource used by the decision vector x, and S is a specified set that restricts the choice of the decisions. The function $f(x)$ measures the cost of operating at decision level x. For simplicity for the moment, assume that b and $g(x)$ are scalars (the same interpretation applies if they are vectors, but in higher dimensions). Now make the following associations:

$C = \{(\gamma, y) : \gamma = f(x) \text{ and } y = g(x) \text{ for some } x \in S\}$,

$X = (0, b)$,

and

$TL = \{(\gamma, b) : \gamma \text{ any real number}\}$.

Note that we are embedding the problem data in a space that jointly represents both costs and resources.[3] The target line fixes the resources at the target value b. C represents the set of *attainable* combinations of costs and resource outcomes, *ignoring* the resource constraint $g(x) = b$. Note that any point (γ, y) in $C \cap TL$ satisfies $\gamma = f(x)$, $y = g(x) = b$ for some $x \in S$. Also, since the line TL is vertical (see figure 7.4), the closest such point to

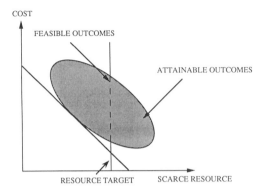

COST

FEASIBLE OUTCOMES

ATTAINABLE OUTCOMES

RESOURCE TARGET   SCARCE RESOURCE

Figure 7.4
Nonlinear programming duality

X achieves the minimum value of $\gamma = f(x)$ among such choices; that is, it solves the mathematical programming problem MP. Therefore the closest point problem is the same as this mathematical program.

Now, let us interpret the farthest line problem. Write any separating line as follows:

$$\gamma = \text{constant} - uy. \tag{1}$$

(We have chosen to use the minus sign before the term uy to facilitate subsequent interpretation.) In this expression the constant and the slope $-u$ of the line are fixed; γ and y are variables. Observe that the u has the units of cost/unit resource; that is, *it is a price*. Moreover, by our prior geometric observations the farthest line (with slope $-u^*$) passes through the optimal combination of cost and resource usage of the mathematical program, that is, passes though the point $(\gamma = f(z), y = g(z))$ corresponding to the optimal solution z to the mathematical program. Also, since the set C lies above this separating line, any point $(\gamma = f(x), y = g(x))$ with $x \in S$ must lie above the corresponding point $(\gamma, y = g(x))$ on the line; that is, it must satisfy the inequality

$$\gamma = \text{constant} - u^*g(x) \le f(x)$$

and, since z lies on this line,

$$\gamma = f(z) = \text{constant} - u^*g(z).$$

Combining these two expressions shows that

$$f(z) + u^*g(z) = \min_{x \in S} \{f(x) + u^*g(x)\}. \tag{2}$$

Note that this optimization problem does not include the resource constraint $g(x) = b$. Rather, it places a price u^* on resources and adds a resource cost $u^*g(x)$ to the original cost $f(x)$. Nevertheless, the optimal solution z to the original mathematical program solves both problems! Therefore this expression embodies a fundamental notion in economics (and one that has also had significant practical implications for computational mathematical programming).

PRICING PRINCIPLE   For some particular choice $u = u^*$ of prices u, the optimal solution z to a (convex) mathematical programming problem can be obtained by solving a modified problem that eliminates the resource constraint and simply charges an amount $u^*g(x)$ for any resource usage.

In economic terms, the pricing system "supports" the resource allocation problem. Note that since $g(z) = b$, if we substract ub from both sides of (2), then at $u = u^*$ the resulting problem,

$$L(u) = \min_{x \in S} \{f(x) + u[g(x) - b]\}, \tag{LaP}$$

has the same optimal objective value, $L(u^*)$, as the original problem MP. Mathematical programmers refer to the function $f(x) + ug(x)$ as the *Lagrangian* and to the prices u as *Lagrangian (dual) variables*. They also refer to the optimization problem

$$d = \max_u L(u)$$

as the *Lagrangian dual* to the original problem. Weak duality implies that for any choice of prices, or dual variables u, $L(u) \le v = f(z)$, and therefore

$$d \le v.$$

Strong duality asserts that the values of the original minimization problem and the Lagrangian dual maximization problem are the same, that is,

$$d = v.$$

(The Lagrangian value $L(u)$ has a nice geometric interpretation. Suppose that $z(u)$ solves the Lagrangian problem LaP for a given value of u; then since the line $\gamma = \text{constant} - uy$ defined by u passes through the point $(f(z(u)), g(z(u)))$, the constant term equals $f(z(u)) + ug(z(u))$. Substituting

$y = b$ to find the intersection of this line with the target line TL gives its vertical intercept as $\gamma = f(z(u) + ug(z(u)) - ub = L(u).$)

In concluding this discussion, we should note that the underlying geometry and its mathematical and economic interpretation requires that the set C be convex (in our discussion of combinatorial optimization in section 7.3, we illustrate the complications that arise in other situations). This requirement, in turn, implies some restrictions on the functional form of the mathematical program. For example, consider a typical mathematical program formulated in inequality form:

minimize $f(w)$

subject to $g(w) \leq b$.

If we introduce additional (slack) variables to reformulate the problem in the form described previously, it becomes

minimize $f(w)$

subject to $g(w) + s = b$

$$s \in S = \{s : s \geq 0\}.$$

Now $x = (w, s)$ and C will be convex whenever the functions $f(w)$ and $g(w)$ are convex; that is, the line segment joining any two values of the functions lies on or above the functions.

Our discussion has also glossed over one important technical point. In writing the equation (1) of the separating line L, we assumed that the coefficient of γ was nonzero (geometrically, the line is not vertical, that is, of the form $y = $ constant) so that by scaling we could set this coefficient to 1. In some instances this choice might not be possible (there may be no farthest line but rather a sequence of lines that approaches the farthest distance; thus the dual problem has no optimal solution—it has a sequence of solutions that approach the optimal value). Although this possibility adds some technical complications, it does not alter the basic results or their interpretation.

Other Interpretations and Implications   The ideas and interpretations expressed thus far have become recognized as important to the mathematical programming community for several reasons. They have

1. provided firm mathematical foundations and considerable geometric insight for duality in mathematical programming;

2. formalized connections between mathematical programming and economic theory;

3. led to new algorithms for solving mathematical programming problems in practice;

4. provided new interpretations and insight concerning standard results in mathematical programming (even for linear programming, despite the fact that it had been studied so thoroughly previous to the development of these results) as well as new insight and interpretations for such important ideas as problem decomposition; and

5. stimulated new fields of inquiry within mathematical programming.

The remainder of this section briefly touches upon these last two points, and hints at a few algorithmic possibilities (see section 7.5 as well).

Linear Programming   Suppose that we apply the duality constructs to the linear programming problem:

minimize $c^T x$

subject to $Ax = b$ (LP)

$\qquad x \geq 0.$

In this formulation, A is an m by n matrix and b and c are m-dimensional and n-dimensional column vectors. If we let $S = \{x : x \geq 0\}$, then the outcome set C has a very special form. In this instance

$C = \{(c^T x, Ax) : x \geq 0\},$

which can be viewed as those outcomes that can be expressed as nonnegative combinations (with weights $x_1, x_2, \ldots, x_n$) of the columns of the stacked matrix

$$\begin{bmatrix} c^T \\ A \end{bmatrix}.$$

Note that this set is just the convex cone generated by the rays emanating from the origin through each column of this matrix. (Figure 7.5 shows an example with $n = 5$ decision variables and $m = 2$ rows in the matrix A.) Since any supporting plane to this set must pass through the origin, the constant term in (1) must be zero (note that since the example requires a

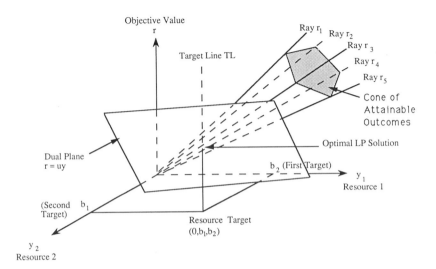

Figure 7.5
Linear programming duality

plane instead of the line, we use the term plane for the rest of this discussion). Moreover any cost-resource combination lies above any supporting plane; thus if we set $x_j = 1$ and $x_k = 0$ for all $k \neq j$, the outcome point (c_j, A_j) must lie above any supporting plane $\gamma = -uy$ at $y = A_j$; equivalently, if we set $\mu = -u$, this point must satisfy the inequality

$$\gamma = \mu(A_j) \leq c_j.$$

When written for each column j of A, these conditions are exactly the linear programming dual feasibility constraints. Moreover, since any supporting plane passes though the origin, the height of its intersection with the target line $\{(\gamma, b) : \gamma \text{ a real number}\}$ is $\gamma = -ub = \mu b$. Consequently the geometric dual problem of finding the supporting plane that intersects the target line as far from the point $(0, b)$ as possible has the algebraic representation:

maximize μb

subject to $\mu A \leq c$,   (DLP)

which is the standard linear programming dual to the original linear program LP.

This identification is more than incidental. The geometry illustrates the interpretation of linear programming dual variables as prices on the scarce resources. Moreover the geometry demonstrates how the optimal dual variables need not be unique: for example, if the target line $\{(\gamma, b) : \gamma$ a real number$\}$ happens to pass through one of the rays $\{(c_j x_j, A_j x_j) : x_j \geq 0\}$, then several optimal dual supporting planes will also pass through this ray. Each of them provides a lower bound approximation to how the optimal value to the linear programming varies with b. Moreover note that the value of the linear program LP as a function of b is always the lowest point in the cone C of attainable outcomes. Therefore, along any line segment $\theta b^1 + (1 - \theta) b^2$ the value of the linear program will be piecewise linear and convex. This result provides a geometric interpretation of the same familiar result in parametric linear programming.

In concluding this discussion, we might note that even though the duality theory described in this section has provided new insight about linear programming and about its connections to duality for other types of mathematical programs, the use of this geometry predates the last twenty years. Indeed, this geometry (or a slightly modified version of it in which the set $S = \{x : \Sigma_j x_j = 1$ and $x \geq 0\}$ replaces the set $S = \{x : x \geq 0\}$) is what prompted George Dantzig to give the simplex method its name. The geometry is very rich. For example, note from figure 7.5 that no matter how we might reconfigure the rays, the target line always has its lowest intercept with the attainable set C on a face of C, which is always defined by at most two rays. Thus every optimal solution has the property that at most two variables (in this case $m = 2$) are positive. This geometrical observation shows why linear programs always have a basic solution. (In fact, it is instructive to interpret the simplex method in this geometry.)

Approximations, Nondifferentiable Optimization, and Other Dual Constructs Duality theory, and its geometric interpretation, provides many linkages between apparently disparate concepts in mathematical programming. In this subsection we very briefly summarize three such topics.

For simplicity, let us return to the geometric version of the dual problem with a target line TL, as shown in figure 7.3. Suppose, as indicated in figure 7.6a, we replace the set C by a polygonal approximation P lying inside it. Then we solve the problem over P instead of C to obtain an approximate solution to the problem as well as an approximate solution to the dual problem (the line APP in the figure). Previously, we saw that the optimal solution to the dual problem supports the set C, interesting it at the target line TL. This observation suggests that we move the approximate line

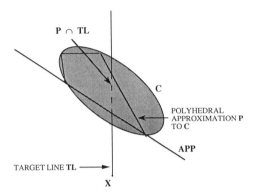

Figure 7.6a
Polyhedral approximation algorithm

APP parallel to itself until it supports *C*. If the point of support of this line happens to intersect the target line, we have solved the problem over *C*. If not, then we can use this point to refine (enlarge) the polygonal approximation (see figure 7.6b) and repeat the procedure. As we can see by continuing the procedure for more steps, in the limit it converges: The separating lines converge to the optimal separating line, and the points of support of these lines to *C* converge to the closest point in *C* to *X*. In fact this lovely geometry and convergence result is quite general; it applies in higher dimensions, and any limiting line and limiting point always solve the dual geometric problems.

In mathematical programming terms this solution method is known as generalized linear programming, or as Dantzig-Wolfe decomposition. Recall that in this setting the corner point p_1 (and p_2, p_3, p_4, p_5 as well) of the polygon *P* represents a combination $(f(x_1), g(x_1))$ of cost and resource usage for some point x_1 in *S*. Since every point in the polygon is a weighted combination of these corner points (with weights w_1, w_2, w_3, w_4, w_5), the mathematical program defined over *P* becomes (with the shorthand notation $f_j = f(x_j), g_j = g(x_j)$ for each j):

minimize $w_1 f_1 + w_2 f_2 + w_3 f_3 + w_4 f_4 + w_5 f_5$

subject to $w_1 g_1 + w_2 g_2 + w_3 g_3 + w_4 g_4 + w_5 g_5 = b$

$$w_1 \quad + w_2 \quad + w_3 \quad + w_4 \quad + w_5 \quad = 1$$

$$w_1 \geq 0, w_2 \geq 0, w_3 \geq 0, w_4 \geq 0, w_5 \geq 0.$$

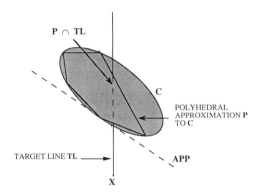

Figure 7.6b
Refining the polyhedral approximation

This problem is a linear program in the weighting variables! The linear programming dual variable u for the resource constraint is the slope of the supporting line to P, and finding where this point supports the set C requires the solution of the Lagrangian problem (2). In many instances this Lagrangian problem will be much easier to solve than the original problem: For example, if the set S places no restrictions on the variable x (i.e., is the entire space), then the Lagrangian subproblem is an unconstrained minimization problem. Therefore the algorithmic appeal of this method is that it often decomposes the overall problem into two easily solved problems—a linear program and a Lagrangian subproblem—to be solved sequentially. In addition the method offers considerable flexibility since we are free to choose which part of the problem to retain as part of the explicit constraints $g(x)$ and which to include in the implicit decision set S. Different choices give different algorithms.

Nondifferentiable Optimization   Let us examine the polygonal case of the geometric version of the problem with a target line TL a bit more closely (see figure 7.7). Recall that we measured the distance from a given point X to a separating line L as the length of the line segment from X to the intercept of the supporting line L and the target line TL. In the dual problem, we wish to maximize over u to find the highest possible intersection. Lets see how this intercept varies with u. Suppose that the a separating line L supports the polygon P at point W which is at a horizontal distance h from the target line (see figure 7.7). Then if u changes and W *continues to*

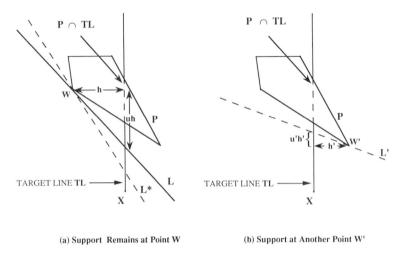

(a) Support Remains at Point W   (b) Support at Another Point W'

Figure 7.7
Dual objective function can be nondifferentiable

be the point of support for a new line L^* with slope $u + \Delta u$, the height of this intersection (the distance from X to L along the target line) changes by $h\Delta u$. That is, as long as W remains the point of support, the dual objective value is *linear* in u. But if for some other slope, the line $L = L'$ supports the polygon at another point W' at a horizontal distance h' from the target line (see figure 7.7), then the dual objective changes linearly with u at a slope h' instead of h. Consequently the dual objective function is not differentiable; instead, it is piecewise linear. This fact makes the dual optimization problem potentially difficult to solve. In general, it cannot be solved by classical methods of optimization based upon derivatives. It requires new methods of solution.

Issues such as this spawned an entirely new and important field in mathematical programming, the study of optimization problems with nondifferentiable functions (for either costs or constraints, or both). This kindling of new developments is one of the ways that duality theory has had a profound influence on the development of mathematical programming.

Other Types of Duality   The duality we have considered uses separating lines (planes). Other choices may be possible. For example, we might attempt to separate a given point and set by a quadratic function of the form $\gamma = \text{constant} + uy + uy^2$. Doing so would change the form of the Lagrangian problem. Instead of being linear in the constraint values $g(x)$ as in (2), it would now be quadratic. This form of the Lagrangian dual function has several potential advantages. It could provide a better approximation to the set C of attainable outcomes and, therefore, be preferred computationally. Or, it might permit us to extend the duality theory to accommodate nonconvex sets C (either locally or globally). These possibilities have prompted the mathematical programming community to extend the notion of duality and Lagrangians (to the theory of "augmented Lagrangians"). Thus, once again, modern duality has stimulated entirely new lines of inquiry.

Computational Fixed Points

Calculation of Fixed Points   The concept of fixed points pervades much of mathematics. It has proved to be useful in many ways, for example, in establishing the existence of solutions to differential equations or the existence of equilibrium solutions in many contexts of economics. And yet the computation of fixed points is relatively new. This theory emanated out of a related theory known as complementarity in mathematical programming. From the perspective of the mathematical programming community, the resulting algorithms have been particularly novel because they rely on a different type of convergence proof. Rather than use some descent function (usually the objective function) to monitor an algorithm's progress and establish convergence, the convergence results for these algorithms invoke a purely combinatorial argument for the solution of a very smooth (continuous) problem.

The following lighthearted problem and accompanying drawings (figures 7.8a and 7.8b) illustrate this argument.[4]

AVOIDING GHOSTS   I eased through the front door of the allegedly haunted house. Just as a ghost appeared, the front door slammed behind me. He spoke "You are now locked inside our house, but it is your fate that except for this room which has one open door, every other room with a ghost has two open doors." I thought, "Is there a room without a ghost?"

Figure 7.8a shows the problem we face. We solve it as follows: Since the room we are in originally has an open door, we pass through it, closing it behind us. If the room we enter had only one open door (which we just closed behind us), then by the prescription of the ghost who spoke, the room has no ghost, and our search has ended. If the room has a ghost,

Figure 7.8a
The haunted house

however, then it must still have another door (which is open). We pass
through this door, closing it behind us, and continue in this fashion. Now
we observe that we could never repeat a room, for doing so would imply
that this room had three open doors. Moreover, assuming that the front
door that we entered was the only outside door, we never leave the haunted
house. But then since the number of rooms is finite, we must eventually,
find a room without a ghost. Figure 7.8b shows the path we took in this
example to reach this room.

How does this problem relate to fixed points or to mathematical programming? Figure 7.9 shows one very simple example. Suppose we wish
to minimize the differentiable function $f(x)$ shown in the top of this figure.
Doing so is equivalent to finding a point where the derivation $g(x)$ of the
function is zero. But solving $g(x) = 0$ is equivalent to solving $h(x) = g(x) +
x = x$, that is, of finding a point where the function $y = h(x)$ crosses the
forty-five-degree line $y = x$. If we assume that $h(0) < 0$ (i.e., $g(0) < 0$) and

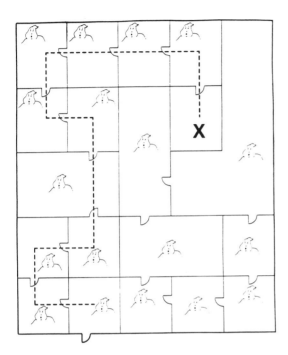

Figure 7.8b
Algorithm for the haunted house

$h(1) > 1$ (i.e., $g(1) > 0$) as in the figure, then the mean value theorem of elementary calculus assures us that the problem has a solution. Let us see how to compute such a solution approximately by using the path-following procedure of the ghost problem (which in this example is very simple). We first impose a finite grid of points on the interval $0 \le x \le 1$, including the end points $x = 0$ and $x = 1$ in this grid. Then we mark each point x with $h(x) \le x$ as a square and every point x with $h(x) \ge x$ as a circle (we choose a circle or a square arbitrarily if $h(x) = x$). By our assumption, the point $x = 0$ is a square and the point $x = 1$ is a circle. Now as we consider the points in the grid from left to right, we must at some point move from a square to a circle. If we use many evenly spaced grid points, then these two transition points must be very near each other. Thus we have found two nearby points y and z, with $h(y) \ge y$ and $h(z) \le z$. Consequently each of these points, or a weighted combination of them such as $\frac{1}{2}y + \frac{1}{2}z$, is an approximate fixed point of $h(x)$ and thus an approximate minimizing point of $f(x)$.

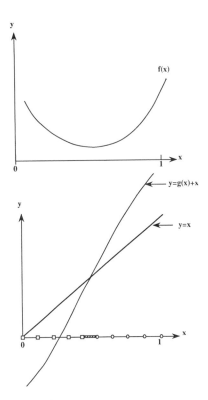

Figure 7.9
Fixed points and optimization

An extension of this argument applies to higher dimensions as well. For example, suppose we wish find a fixed point of the multivalued function $h(w, y, z)$ of three variables w, y, and z defined over the region $S = \{(w, y, z) : w + y + z = 1, w \geq 0, y \geq 0, z \geq 0\}$, which is usually referred to as a simplex. That is, we wish to find a point (w^*, y^*, z^*) for which the three component functions h_1, h_2, and h_3 of h satisfy

$$h_1(w^*, y^*, z^*) = w^*,$$

$$h_2(w^*, y^*, z^*) = y^*,$$

$$h_3(w^*, y^*, z^*) = z^*.$$

Suppose further that for every point (w, y, z) in S, the three components of h are nonnegative and sum to one; that is, the function h maps the simplex onto itself. (A proper transformation or scaling of the data often permits

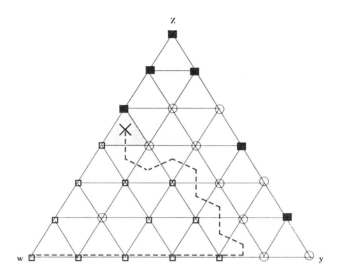

Figure 7.10
Computing approximate fixed points

us to assume that the problem satisfies this "retention property." Later we illustrate one such transformation.)

We represent the problem domain, the simplex S, as follows: Consider an equilateral triangle with vertices labeled w, y, and z. At the vertex labeled w, the variable w is 1. On the edge e of the triangle opposite this vertex, w has the value 0. Everywhere in between, the value of w is determined by linear interpolation as measured by the distance from the edge e to a line parallel to e that passes through the vertex w. The values of y and z are specified similarly with respect to their designated vertex and opposite side; thus every point in the triangle represents a point in the underlying simplex. Now superimpose a triangular grid on T as shown in figure 7.10. We will mark each point $x = (w, y, z)$ on this grid as follows:

as a (hollow) square if $h_1(w, y, z) \leq w$,

as a circle if $h_2(w, y, z) \leq y$,

as a solid square if $h_3(w, y, z) \leq z$,

choosing arbitrarily again from the relevant choices when ties arise. In fact, if any point could be marked as either a square, a circle, or a solid square, then it satisfies all three of these inequalities. But since the three components of h must add to one and w, y, and z add to one as well, all three of the inequalities must be satisfied as an equality. Therefore, if we can find a small triangle whose three vertices are marked as a square, a circle, and a solid square, then, assuming that h is continuous, we have found an approximate fixed point. The point that is the weighted average of these three vertices, for example, approximately satisfies the three prior inequalities.

Figure 7.10 shows how to find a fixed point using the ghost "in-and-out" path-following argument. We start at the vertex w marked with a square and move on the line toward the vertex y marked with a circle until, as in our previous example, we find two consecutive vertices marked with a square and a circle. Then we move into the little triangle adjacent to these two vertices. If its third vertex were marked as a solid square, we would be done. In the illustration, it is marked as a circle. So it has two edges (doors) marked with both a square and a circle. We have entered the triangle from one of these edges, so we leave it from the other moving to the adjacent triangle. We then keep moving from one triangle to the next passing though the square–circle edges. As shown in the figure, the path leads to a fully marked triangle, and hence to an approximate fixed point.[5]

By refining the grid (the triangular decomposition of the large simplex), we can find an approximate solution to within any desired degree of accuracy.

This method, or a higher-dimensional analogue of it, can solve a wide variety of problems. Let us consider three illustrations.

Equilibrium   Figure 7.11 shows a typical rendering of a classical problem in competitive economic equilibrium:

COMPETITIVE ECONOMIC EQUILIBRIUM PROBLEM   Find a price p at which the market "clears," that is, at which the demand $D(p)$ for a good equals its supply $S(p)$.

Suppose, as in this figure, that the demand function is invertible; that is, if $D(p) = d$, we can solve for p uniquely as $p = D^{-1}(d)$. Then the economic equilibrium conditions $S(p) = D(p)$ can be written in fixed point form as

$$D^{-1}(S(p)) = p.$$

Another, very useful, viewpoint is possible. We can regard the equilibrium problem as the following (equivalent) optimization problem (and therefore solve it using methods of nonlinear programming):

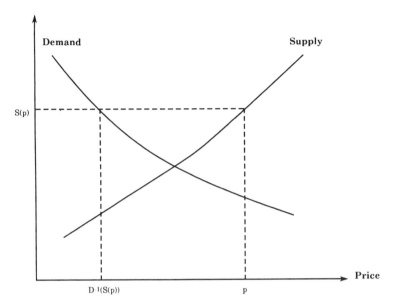

Figure 7.11
Fixed points model economic equilibrium

$$\text{minimize } F(p) = \int_0^p [S(\theta) - D(\theta)]d\theta$$

subject to $p \geq 0$.

If the optimal solution p^* to this problem were positive, then by elementary calculus the derivative of the objective function $F(p)$ at the optimal solution p^* must be zero, or

$$\frac{dF(p)}{dp} = S(p^*) - D(p^*) = 0,$$

which is the desired equilibrium condition $S(p^*) = D(p^*)$. Note, however, that if $p^* = 0$, then the optimization optimality condition becomes $dF(p)/dp \geq 0$ (i.e., locally we cannot improve the objective function by moving away from $p^* = 0$), which models a "free good" version of equilibrium: In equilibrium, supply can exceed demand if the market price p^* of a good is zero.

   In some circumstances it is also possible to state a multiple product generalization of this competitive equilibrium problem as an equivalent optimization problem. In the simplest such situation the supply and demand for each good depends upon the price of only that good (the goods are not complements or substitutes), and we can solve the equivalent optimization problem for each product j separately with its own supply and demand curves, $S_j(p_j)$ and $D_j(p_j)$. More generally, whenever the excess supply function $E(p) \equiv S(p) - D(p)$ is integrable, that is, is the gradient of some function $F(p)$, we can solve the problem by minimizing $F(p)$ over $p \geq 0$. Unfortunately, the integrability stipulation imposes requirements on the demand function that are too restrictive in many applications.[6] In these situations, however, the problem can still be solved as a fixed point problem.

Suppose, for simplicity, that we have three goods and, for the moment, that the problem structure implies that the equilibrium price of each good is positive so that the excess supply of each good j must be zero. Then we can formulate the problem as a fixed point problem, $h(p) = p - E(p) = p$ (we have elected to append a negative sign before $E(p)$ as a convenience to ease our later modeling of a version of the problem in which some equilibrium prices can be zero). In multiple dimensions economists formulate the problem with prices chosen so that their components sum to one (a convenient normalization). Therefore we can again work on the simplex S we introduced previously. We could solve this problem using the fixed point ghost method described in the last subsection if $h(p)$ satisfied the retention property; that is, if for each point p in a simplex S, $h(p)$ also were in S. A problem transformation will permit us to satisfy this restriction: Rather than defining $h(p)$ as $p - E(p)$, define it in two steps as

$$q_j(p) = \max[0, p_j - E_j(p)] \qquad \text{for } j = 1, 2, 3$$

and

$$h_j(p) = \frac{q_j(p)}{q_1(p) + q_2(p) + q_3(p)}.$$

The definition of each q_j implies that the components of h are nonnegative, and the normalization from q to h ensures that the components of h always sum to 1. Now note that if each price p_j^* of an equilibrium solution p^* is positive, then p^* is a fixed point for the modified map h. Indeed, if $p^* - E(p^*) = p^*$, or equivalently, $E(p^*) = 0$, and each component of p^* is positive, then $q(p^*) = p^* - E(p^*) = p^*$. Since the components of p^* sum to one, so do the components of $q(p^*)$ and thus $h(p^*) = q(p^*) = p^*$ and p^*

is a fixed point. A similar argument in the other direction shows that if p^* is a fixed point with all positive components, then $E(p^*) = 0$ and so p^* is an equilibrium solution.

This approach applies even more generally, since we need not assume that the equilibrium price p^* has all positive components in order to assert that the fixed point problem finds an equilibrium solution. The free good version of the equilibrium conditions would permit the jth component $E_j(p^*)$ of the excess supply function to be nonzero: if $p_j^* = 0$, $E_j(p^*)$ can be nonnegative. Note, however, that as stated with the modified form of $h(p)$, the fixed point problem models this situation, for if $q_j(p^*) = p_j^* = 0$, then $\max[0, p^* - E_j(p^*)] = \max[0, -E_j(p^*)] = 0$, and therefore $E_j(p^*) \geq 0$ as required. So even in general circumstances fixed point computations will solve the competitive equilibrium problem.

Complementarity Problems   The previous example illustrates how fixed points can model certain complementary conditions of the form $xF(x) = 0$; that is, either x is 0 or the function value $F(x)$ is zero (in the last two examples, the function F was a component of the excess supply function). In fact the transformation we defined previously (for $q(x)$) permits us to establish an equivalence between the fixed point problem and the following generic problem:

NONLINEAR COMPLEMENTARITY PROBLEM   Find a vector x^* satisfying the conditions

$$x^* \geq 0,$$

$$F(x^*) \geq 0,$$

$$x^*F(x^*) = 0.$$

In this formulation x is an n-dimensional vector and $F(x)$ is a multivalued function with n scalar component functions $F_1(x)$, $F_2(x)$, ..., $F_n(x)$. Note that the first two conditions imply that the condition $x^*F(x^*) = 0$ is equivalent to the n separate conditions $x_j^*F_j(x^*) = 0$ for $j = 1, 2, \ldots, n$.

These types of conditions arise very frequently in practice. The following two examples are illustrative:

1. *Spatially separated economic markets.* Consider the distribution of natural gas between a geographically dispersed supplier and consumer. (Agricultural goods, oil, and financial instruments are other examples.) If the

supplier and consumer were located together, then equilibrium prices would satisfy the classical "supply-equal-demand" conditions of the previous example. But now transporting natural gas from the supplier to the consumer incurs a transportation cost. If the price p of gas at the well-head plus the transportation cost t were to exceed the price q at the consumer location, then shipping loses money and the supplier will not ship anything: if $F_1(x) = p + t - q > 0$, then the shipment y would be 0 (in this setting x has three components y, p, and q, i.e., $x = (y, p, q)$). If $p + t < q$ (i.e., $F_1(x) < 0$), the supplier makes excess profits, which by standard economic theory is not sustainable. Therefore in equilibrium $F_1(x) \geq 0$ and $yF_1(x) = 0$.

Now consider y as the induced demand at the supply point and as the induced supply at the demand point. Then the excess supply-demand complementarity conditions of the previous example become

$$F_2(x) = S(p) - y \geq 0 \quad \text{and} \quad pF_2(x) = 0,$$

$$F_3(x) = y - D(q) \geq 0 \quad \text{and} \quad qF_3(x) = 0.$$

Thus, if $x = (y, p, q)$ and $F(x) = (F_1(x), F_2(x), F_3(x))$, the economic equilibrium conditions become the nonlinear complementarity problem.

Several enhancements are possible. For example, natural gas might have multiple suppliers and consumers, or a complicated underlying distribution network. The problem might also involve many commodities, or complex alternative production technologies. Each of these embellishments leads to a more intricate version of this basic model. One set of such models have been used extensively for public policy. In the United States, for example, a model like this formed the heart of the Project Independence model used by the Department of Energy.

2. *Traffic equilibria.* Suppose that individuals starting from their homes in a suburban community wish to travel as quickly as possible to their workplaces in the central business district. Suppose further that the people in this community can take one of two routes: a rural route or a thoroughfare. The following behavioral principle, named in honor of the traffic engineer who first articulated it, has become a standard modeling assumption for this situation:

WARDROP'S USER EQUILIBRIUM PRINCIPLE   The routes taken by all individuals traveling between the same origin and destination in a transportation system have the same travel time, which is less than the travel time of any alternate route.

In our simple setting this principle states that (a) all individuals can travel on the rural route at a travel time that is less than that of the thoroughfare, (b) all individuals can travel on the thoroughfare at a travel time that is less than that of the rural route, or (c) individuals can split their trips between the rural route and thoroughfare so that the travel times on the two route are the same.

To model this situation formally, let h_1 denote the number of travelers who use the rural route, and let h_2 denote the number of travelers who use the thoroughfare. Furthermore let $t_1(h_1)$ and $t_2(h_2)$ denote the travel time incurred by the travelers on the rural route and on the thoroughfare; note that due to congestion, these travel times depend upon the number of travelers who use these routes. With these definitions the travel times u incurred by travelers will satisfy the following conditions:

$$t_1(h_1) - u \geq 0, \qquad [t_1(h_1) - u]h_1 = 0,$$

$$t_2(h_2) - u \geq 0, \qquad [t_2(h_2) - u]h_2 = 0.$$

The inequalities in these expressions state that the travel time u from the suburban community to the central business district is no larger than the travel time on either of the available paths. The equalities state that if the flow on either path is positive, then the travel time on that path must equal the travel time u between the community and central business district.

These stipulations look like nonlinear complementarily conditions: the inequalities state that some function $f_j(x)$ is nonnegative and the equalities state that the product of this function and a variable x_j of the vector $x = (h_1, h_2, u)$ is zero. In addition, however, the flow must satisfy the mass balance condition

$$h_1 + h_2 = D,$$

stating that the total number of trips made on the two available paths must equal the demand D for trips between the suburban community and the business district. Note that if each travel time function $t_1(\cdot)$ and $t_2(\cdot)$ is positive for any values of flows on these paths, as is the case in practice, we can rewrite the demand requirement as the complementarity condition

$$h_1 + h_2 - D \geq 0 \quad \text{and} \quad [h_1 + h_2 - D]u = 0,$$

since, by necessity, $u > 0$. With the addition of these (somewhat artificial) conditions, each variable h_1, h_2, and u has an associated nonlinear complementarity requirement, and the problem becomes a nonlinear complementarity problem.

In larger transportation systems with many origins and destinations, the underlying model is much the same. Each path has an associated delay function that might depend upon the full vector of path flows, and each origin and destination has a set of nonlinear complementarity conditions like those for our one-origin, one-destination example. This model, with many refinements and enhancements, has become an important planning tool; transportation authorities in many cities throughout the world use versions of it. For example, the Urban Mass Transit Administration in the United States requires that communities conduct an equilibrium impact analysis prior to their receiving federal funds for transportation projects.

Optimization   We next consider a rather general optimization problem

minimize $\{F(x) : x \in C\}$

that requires the minimization of a differentiable function $F(x)$ of a vector x over a specified ground set C. Recall from calculus that the directional derivative of F at a point x in the direction d is the inner product $g(x)d$ of the gradient $g(x)$ of F and the direction d. This observation leads us to formulate the following local optimization condition for characterizing an optimal solution x^* of the optimization problem:

$$g(x^*)(x - x^*) \geq 0 \qquad \text{for all } x \in C. \tag{OPT}$$

This condition states that the function F increases in the direction $d = x - x^*$ from x^* pointing to any other feasible point x.

The optimality condition OPT has a very nice geometric interpretation that, not coincidentally, is similar to the geometry of duality we introduced previously in section 7.3 (see figure 7.12). Note that if x^* satisfies the

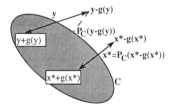

Figure 7.12
Nonlinear programming optimality conditions as fixed points

optimality condition, then in two dimensions the plane $g(x^*)(x - x^*) = 0$ contains x^* and all points x in C lie on one-half of this plane. Equivalently, by our interpretation of geometric duality in section 7.3, x^* is the closest point in C to $x^* - g(x^*)$. Suppose that for any point y, we define $P_C(y)$ as the closest point in C to y (analysts also call this point the projection of y onto C). Then any solution x^* to the optimality condition OPT also solves the fixed point problem

$$x^* = P_C(x^* - g(x^*)),$$

and conversely any solution to this fixed point problem is a solution to the optimality condition OPT. If the ground set C is bounded, it can typically be embedded in a simplex so that the in-and-out ghost-avoiding algorithm will find a fixed point and therefore find a point satisfying the local optimality condition.

Note that the optimization, equilibrium, and complementarity examples we have discussed are similar. We might view the optimality conditions for mathematical programs as local equilibrium conditions. Many nonlinear complementarity problems are equilibrium problems as well. As these observations indicate, in a sense, fixed points and equilibria might be viewed as synonymous. Numerous other examples support this viewpoint. In particular, many problems in the physical sciences are similar: What is the equilibrium mixture of a collection of gasses mixed together, or, what is equilibrium state of a mechanical structure? Computational fixed point theory has provided a general-purpose and unifying tool for studying these problems and for computing equilibrium solutions.

The computational fixed point theory we have described has influenced the mathematical programming community and provided it with new results in a number of ways:

• This theory is so general that it has broad applicability. In particular, the theory imposes very modest requirements on the problem data: essentially only continuity of the underlying functions and some growth (or boundedness) conditions to ensure a form of the retention property.

• The development of computational methods for fixed points has prompted the community to broaden its scope and study a number of important equilibrium problems that it might not have otherwise viewed as mathematical programming.

• The theory has provided new linkages between operation research and some classical topics in pure mathematics such as degree theory in algebraic topology.

• Fixed points have posed a number of modeling challenges and have led to several very significant applications.

As stated, however, the theory is somewhat limited; recognizing these limitations, the mathematical programming community has set out to resolve a number of technical challenges:

• What is the best way to triangularize the problem domain (find the partitioning with the fewest triangles, or the triangularization that leads to most rapid convergence)?

• How fast does the algorithm converge for different classes of problems? Does it wind its way among the problem domain or does it, even in the limit, approach an equilibrium in a special way (e.g., linearly)?

• After solving for an approximate solution, in order to find a more accurate solution, can we restart the method conveniently using information gathered by prior computations, or need we restart the procedure from scratch with a more refined grid?

• Because of its combinatorial search strategy, the algorithm is very general but is limited in the size problem it can solve (generally, 50 variables is a limit, although in some cases a couple hundred of variables is tractable). How can it be modified to solve larger problems? Can the method exploit special structure such as any linearity of the underlying functions? Can it be modified to provide for problem decomposition?

The last two topics on this list, in particular, have generated entire bodies of research.

Deformation Theory   The question of how to efficiently restart fixed point algorithms has led to an important field of inquiry in mathematical programming, known as deformation (or homotopy) theory, which has its roots in numerical analysis and algebraic topology. Essentially, this solution approach considers two problems: the one we wish to solve and other (possibly artificial problem) that can be solved easily, often by inspection. The deformation solution strategy then considers a sequence of problems that "deform" the simple problem into the given one. For example, to solve a system of equations $f(x)$ in the vector x, we might start with the trivial system $x = 0$ and consider the family of problems $\theta f(x) + (1 - \theta)x = 0$ indexed by the scalar parameter θ. Solving for $\theta = 0$ is trivial, and solving for $\theta = 1$ solves the given problem. Deformation methods permit us to move parametrically and iteratively from the solution at $\theta = 0$ to the one at $\theta = 1$.

Iterative Methods Rather than always solving fixed point problems by the combinatorial fixed point algorithm, researchers have devised other methods, particularly iterative methods. For example, as we saw in solving the local optimality condition OPT, we could solve the fixed point problem

$$x^* = P_C(x^* - g(x^*)).$$

An iterative method might attempt to solve the problem as follows: Starting with an initial feasible solution y in C, find the projection z of $y - g(y)$ onto C (i.e., the closest point z in C to $y - g(y)$).[7] If $z = y$, then y is a fixed point, and we have solved the problem. Otherwise, we repeat this computation, starting with the point z. Note that this algorithm repeatedly solves an optimization problem of finding a closest point in a set C to a specified point. The algorithm is known to converge if it starts sufficiently close to a fixed point.

Another way to develop an iterative method is to formulate and solve a series of embedded optimization problems. For example, when solving for a competitive equilibrium with an excess supply function $E(p_1, p_2, p_3)$ for three goods, we might use a "diagonalization algorithm." Given a tentative set of prices q_1, q_2, q_3, we approximate the excess supply function of each good as follows:

$$E_1^a(p_1, p_2, p_3) = E_1(p_1, q_2, q_3),$$

$$E_2^a(p_1, p_2, p_3) = E_2(q_1, p_2, q_3),$$

$$E_3^a(p_1, p_2, p_3) = E_3(q_1, q_2, p_3).$$

With the approximation, the modified excess supply function E_j^a for each good j depends only upon that good's price p_j. Therefore, as we have seen in this section, we can solve the approximation problem as three separate one-dimensional optimization problems. After solving the approximation problem and finding new approximate prices p^a, we repeat the procedure with p^a in place of q. This algorithm is known to converge as long as the excess demand function $E(p)$ satisfies certain diagonal dominance conditions (in a particular technical sense, the effect of p_j in $E_j(p)$ should dominate the effects of the other prices). Practitioners have applied this type of algorithm with remarkable success even when they have no guarantee that problem map satisfies the diagonal dominance condition.

Many other forms of iterative methods are possible. These methods are close relatives of classical iterative methods for solving systems of linear and nonlinear equations such as the noted Gauss-Jordan, Gauss-Seidel, and Newton iterative methods. In particular, these methods have spawned new algorithms and theory for problems of the form of OPT, which have become known as variational inequalities and arises in many forms in game theory and equilibrium analysis.

In the last two decades each of the topics we have mentioned concerning the extensions and refinements of fixed point theory has engendered considerable research that has enriched the mathematical programming community and related fields such as economics.

Emergence of Combinatorial Optimization

Computational integer programming has undergone significant changes in the last four decades, from the use of ad hoc heuristic procedures, dynamic programming for small-scale problems, and specialized branch and bound methods in the 1950s and 1960s to the development of integer programming decomposition, a theory of heuristics, and a theory of integer polyhedra. In this section we elaborate on some of these themes.

As we have previously noted, prior to 1967 the mathematical programming community had already developed novel methods for solving two important offshoots of linear programming: integer programming and network flows. These methods included branch and bound, cutting planes, and "group-theoretic procedures" for integer programming, and specialized "labeling" type methods (and interpretations of the simplex method) for shortest paths, maximum network flows, and other network flow problems, including the classic assignment problem. In a few instances researchers had also developed very successful specialized methods for solving certain discrete optimization problems, most notably the celebrated minimal spanning tree problem (the problem of finding a set of arcs of minimum cost that connect all the nodes in a network) and the network matching problem (the problem of finding a set of arcs of minimum cost that pairs up, or matches, the nodes of a network). In addition attempts to unify and extend these results had produced a fertile new theory known as matroids; by generalizing the notion of linear dependence in linear algebra, this theory was able to establish intimate connections between several of these methods and had revealed the essential underlying combinatorial structure that these algorithms relied upon.

The operation research community had greeted some of these methods, particularly new methods for solving integer programs, with great enthusiasm and anticipation. And yet, for the most part, this promise was unrealized: the mathematical programming community had only limited success in solving the wide range of large-scale discrete optimization problems arising in practice. Some of these pre-1967 contributions did, however, set important foundations and foreshadow a subsequent intellectual reformation: the emergence of the dynamic new field of combinatorial optimization and a renaissance in computational integer programming. These new developments can be traced to several sources, especially to an emerging important interplay between mathematical programming and computer science and an emerging set of new methods, paradigms, and theory. In this section we briefly review a few of these later developments.

Network Flows Although research in network flows prior to 1967 had borne considerable fruit, subsequent research has greatly enhanced both our understanding of this problem class and our ability to solve the large-scale problems routinely met in practice. Figure 7.13 highlights one issue that has prompted major advances on the theoretical front.

This figure represents a small example of the classical maximum flow problem. The number next to each arc is its capacity for carrying flow; we wish to find the maximum flow from the source node s to the terminal

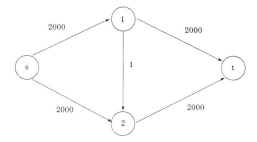

Figure 7.13
Network with arc capacities

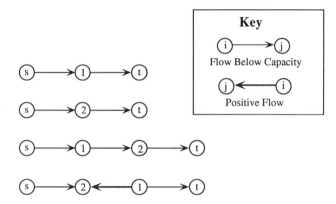

Figure 7.14
Possible augmenting paths

node t, while maintaining conservation of flow (flow in = flow out) for all other nodes in the network. The following, now standard, insight and its ramifications and elaborations were instrumental for developing network flow theory in the 1950s. In order to find the maximum flow, we can incrementally load the network along paths from the source to the sink. The paths, called augmenting paths, have the form shown in figure 7.14. Any augmenting path joins the source s to the terminal t; each (forward) arc on this path directed from s to t has its current flow below the arc's flow capacity, and each arc with the opposite orientation (reverse arc) has a positive flow in the current solution. Note that if we add a small amount of flow to each of the forward arcs and subtract this same amount of flow from the reverse arcs, then we increase the flow from s to t, and maintain conservation of flow at the intermediate nodes. The method finds such an augmenting path and sends as much flow on it as possible until some arc on the augmenting path becomes saturated, that is, until either the flow on some forward arc reaches capacity, or the flow on some reverse arc becomes zero.

For the example in figure 7.13, we can complete the procedure with just two flow changes. Send 2,000 units along path $s-1-t$ and then 2,000 units along path $s-2-t$. This solution must now solve the problem since the flow of every arc out of the source is saturated; since we can't send any more than 4,000 units of flow out of the source to any place else in the network, we can't possibly send more than this amount of flow from the source to the terminal node.

So far, so good. But now suppose, at the first step, we had chosen the path $s-1-2-t$ and saturated it by sending 1 unit of flow along its arcs. Next we might choose the path $s-2-1-t$ and saturate it with one unit of flow as well. (At this point arc $1-2$ again carries no flow.). If we continued in this way, alternately selecting the path $s-1-2-t$ and $s-2-1-t$, the algorithm would find the optimal flow, but now after 4,000 flow changes. In this instance the choice of paths has had a pronounced effect upon the algorithm's performance. The original methods for solving the maximum flow problem did not distinguish between these alternative choices. Motivated by this type of example, however, researchers were able to improve upon the basic method by utilizing a couple of different solution strategies:

1. by choosing to augment at each step along the augmenting path containing the fewest number or arcs;

2. by choosing to augment at each step along augmenting paths with relatively large incremental flow carrying capacity.

Note that, for this example, these two approaches would both lead us to choose the paths $s-1-t$ and $s-2-t$ first, and thus avoid the incremental "unit at a time" additions in flow from the source to the terminal. Sketching the arguments as to why these methods are guaranteed to improve the algorithm's performance might be instructive.

Suppose we always augment using a path P with the fewest number of arcs. Further suppose that arc $i-j$ becomes saturated with the current flow change on path P. The next augmenting path cannot use arc $i-j$ in that direction because it has become saturated. If it also doesn't use arc $j-i$, then the next path was available at the current step. Therefore it must contain as many arcs as the current path. As a result the number of flow changes that we can make using paths with as many arcs as P and without using any saturated arc in its reverse direction is at most A, the number of arcs in the network. It is not too hard to show that if we use an arc $j-i$ in the reverse direction at some subsequent step, then the augmenting path Q must contain at least two more arcs than P.[8] Consequently, after at most A flow changes, augmenting paths must increase by at least two arcs. Since no path can contain any more arcs than the number of nodes N in the network, the total number of flow changes can be no more than $A*N/2$, independent of the capacities associated with the arc. Therefore the capacity 2,000 in the example could become one million or any other number, and the method would still require no more than this number of flow changes.

Let's briefly consider another method, one that seeks out relatively large flow changes. Suppose we round the capacity data in the example to units of 1,000, dropping any fractions. Thus the capacity of arc 1–2 becomes zero, and all the other arcs retain their current capacity. In this instance we essentially eliminate arc 1–2 and thus find the correct optimal flow with only two flow changes. If, however, the 2,000-unit capacities had been 2,222 instead, the rounded capacity of these arcs would have been 2,000 and two flow changes would not, as yet, have solved the problem. If we next refine the rounding approximation by keeping two places of accuracy, but start with the solution from the first phase with 2,000 units on paths $s-1-t$ and $s-2-t$, then two more flow changes would find the next approximate solution with flows of 2,200 on both these paths. Continuing with an approximation with three and then four significant digits will solve the problem in four more flow changes. The arc 1–2 plays a role only at the last step, and at this point, since we are merely making single unit flow changes, this arc cannot obstruct any relatively large flow changes. Indeed, at each step of the approximation, the total incremental capacity we are adding to the network can be no more that the number of arcs A times the current significant digit (e.g., $100 * A$ when we add the hundred digit to the capacity data). Since each flow change adds at least this significant digit amount or more of flow from s to t, the number of flow changes for each significant digit is at most A. If U denotes the largest capacity in the network, then the number of significant digits required is $\log_{10}(U)$; therefore the overall algorithm requires at most $A \log_{10}(U)$ flow changes. Again, we have improved the algorithm's performance.

The fewest arc and scaling algorithms bound the number of flow changes by $A * N/2$ and $A \log_{10}(U)$. If $N/2 < \log_{10}(U)$, that is, $10^{N/2} < U$, the first algorithm gives the better bound; if $N/2 > \log_{10}(U)$, the second method provides the better bound.

More careful analysis would permit us to improve upon these results even further. Nevertheless, even this illustrative discussion has highlighted several points about progress in network flows and combinatorial optimization; it has illustrated

1. the type of progress made on analyzing methods for solving fundamental core problems in network flows;

2. the kind of combinatorial insight (e.g., for the algorithm based upon fewest arcs in an augmenting path) that underlies many advances in this field; and

3. the idea of scaling (the process of approximating data to significant digits and iteratively refining the approximation) which has proved useful in analyzing many algorithms, and represents an important interplay between data manipulation and algorithm performance.

Some of these ideas will surface again in our subsequent discussion.

Lagrangian Relaxation   The duality theory we discussed in section 7.3 is well rooted in the study of continuous mathematics. One of the major computational discoveries in the last twenty years, however, has been that the same type of approach can be used with considerable success to solve a wide variety of problems in discrete optimization. Indeed, this type of solution strategy, and its manifestations in several specific application domains, has now become one of the staples of discrete optimization.

To illustrate this solution approach, and to suggest the computational power of duality theory for discrete optimization, consider a shortest path problem for the network shown in figure 7.15, but with the additional constraint that the optimal path must use exactly four arcs. The objective in this problem is to find the shortest path from node 1 to node 6 with respect to the distances specified next to each arc. Although a dynamic programming approach will solve this problem quite efficiently, for purposes of illustration, assume that we are unaware of this procedure or that we don't have ready access to computer code for it, but that we can easily solve a shortest path problem without the constraint restricting the number of arcs to be used. In a practical problem setting, each arc might have both a travel cost and travel time (which for our example is 1 for each arc), and we might wish to find the least-cost path between a given pair of nodes with the stipulation that the travel time on the chosen path does exceed a prescribed limit (which in our example is 4 and must be met exactly). There is no known efficient dynamic programming procedure for solving this more general problem.

In any event we might attempt to solve the problem as follows. Instead of directly imposing the constraint limiting the number of arcs in the chosen path, we will charge a toll u for the use of any arc. Consequently the cost on any arc (i,j) becomes the original cost c_{ij} plus the toll u. For any choice

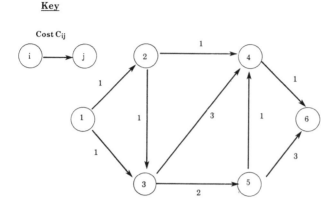

Path	Length (number of arcs)	Cost
1-2-4-6	3	3
1-3-4-6	3	5
1-3-5-6	3	6
1-2-3-4-6	4	6
1-2-3-5-6	4	7
1-3-5-4-6	4	5
1-2-3-5-4-6	5	6

Figure 7.15
Constrained shortest path problem

of the toll, we can solve the problem as a (derived) shortest path problem with the modified costs.

This approach is reminiscent of the economic pricing concept we introduced in our discussion of duality in section 7.3. Indeed, as shown in figure 7.16, this toll setting approach is but one manifestation of mathematical programming duality. In this figure we have plotted the attainable combinations of costs and resource outcomes (the seven dots); in this instance each dot represents a combination of cost and number of arcs used by one of the seven paths joining nodes 1 and 6. For any choice of the toll u, the derived shortest path problem has the interpretation offered in our earlier discussion: we move the "pricing" line with slope $-u$ downward across the set of attainable cost and resource outcomes to its lowest point; note that

1. as in the general theory of mathematical programming duality discussed in section 7.3, for each choice of the toll u, the lowest pricing line with slope

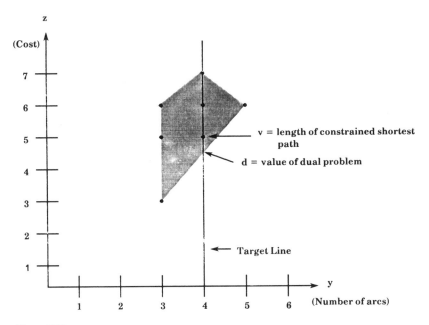

Figure 7.16
A duality gap

$-u$ containing one of the attainable outcomes intersects the target line (i.e., the vertical line representing number of arcs equal to 4) at a point below any feasible solution to the original problem; therefore the vertical value of the intersection is a lower bound on the optimal cost to the constrained shortest path problem; and

2. for this example, the best lower bound of value $4\frac{1}{2}$, obtained by the toll choice $-u^* = 1\frac{1}{2}$, is smaller than the optimal objective value of 5 for the constrained shortest path problem.[9] Because the set of attainable outcomes is a finite set, and hence is not convex, we encounter a *duality gap* between the value of the lower-bounding Lagrangian dual problem and the original problem.

Notice from figure 7.16, that with a toll of $u^* = -1\frac{1}{2}$, two paths, 1–2–4–6 and 1–2–3–5–6, one containing three arcs and the other containing five arcs, tie as shortest paths. These paths correspond to the two points that lie on the supporting line to the attainable set of outcomes at $u^* = -1\frac{1}{2}$. Also note that if we send $\frac{1}{2}$ unit of flow on each of these paths, then the average number of arcs used is exactly 4. Moreover the cost of sending $\frac{1}{2}$

unit on each of the paths 1–2–4–6 and 1–2–3–5–6 is $(\frac{1}{2})(3) + (\frac{1}{2})6 = 4\frac{1}{2}$. By permitting ourselves to split flow, we are replacing the integer program of finding the shortest constrained path with its linear programming relaxation. Equivalently, in figure 7.16 we are replacing the seven outcome points with the convex polyhedron that they define; we are convexifying the problem by taking convex combinations of its outcomes. This observation is completely general and identifies an important interpretation of dualization that characterizes duality gaps.

CONVEXIFICATION AND DUALIZATION EQUIVALENCE PRINCIPLE   The optimal value to the Lagrangian dual of a mathematical program equals the optimal value of the convexified version of the problem, which is defined by taking convex combinations of the set of attainable outcomes.

This result explains how a duality gap arises in terms of the structure of the original problem: a duality gap is equivalent to a gap between a given problem and its convexification.

The shortest path example we have considered is representative of a broad class of applications of Lagrangian relaxation to discrete optimization problems. In general, when applied to such problems, the toll setting, or Lagrangian relaxation, approach will be a lower-bounding procedure; the duality gap between the values of Lagrangian dual problem and the original problem will typically prohibit the Lagrangian dual from finding the optimal solution to the original problem (rather it will find the optimal value of the convexified problem). Nevertheless, Lagrangian relaxation has proved to be an effective solution strategy in a wide variety of applications. Analysts use it, like linear programming relaxation, as a lower-bounding procedure in branch and bound. In addition they use it as a "smart" (smart because it solves an embedded optimization subproblem for any choice of the toll u) heuristic procedure for finding near-optimal solutions. For example, if we used Lagrangian relaxation to solve the time-constrained shortest path problem, for some choices of the Lagrangian dual variable u, the solution to the derived shortest path problem might satisfy the travel time constraint. This solution is optimal with respect to the derived costs but not necessarily for the original costs; nevertheless, it might have a good solution value with respect to the original costs and therefore might be a good solution to the original problem.

One of the greatest advantages of Lagrangian relaxation is its flexibility. Often it is possible to dualize different constraints in a particular problem to obtain different Lagrangian subproblems, each of which is easier to solve than the original problem. These subproblems might have different characteristics: for example, one might be easier to solve than another, or one might provide a better lower bound than another. Because of this flexibility and because the method frequently provides quite good lower bounds (within 5 to 10 percent of the optimal value of original problem), it has become a very effective solution approach for solving a wide variety of applications.

Polyhedral Combinatorics   In principle, it is possible to convert and solve any integer program as a linear program. If we enumerate all the feasible integer points and take their convex hull, then all the extreme points of the resulting polyhedron will be feasible integer points. Therefore, any method for solving linear programs, such as the simplex method, that finds an optimal extreme point will solve the integer program. This observation is very alluring since it suggests the use of the extraordinary computational power of linear programming to solve integer programs.

Unfortunately, in its most rudimentary form, this approach is severely limited. In particular, the number of feasible integer solutions to the problem and the number of inequalities in the resulting linear programming formulation can be enormous (grow exponentially in the problem's size). On the other hand, typically we need only a small number of these inequalities (equal to dimension of the problem) to represent the optimal solution to the resulting linear program. These two observations prompted several important discoveries in the 1960s:

1. The development of cutting plane methods for solving integer programming. These methods solved the linear programming relaxation of the integer program and then, based upon some elementary properties of integers, were able to use the structure of an optimal linear programming basis to find a valid inequality for the integer program that cuts away the fractional linear programming solution. In combinatorial optimization this identification has now become known as the "separation problem." These cutting plane methods had one particularly nice theoretical feature: with mild assumptions imposed upon the problem structure, they were guaranteed to solve the problem after adding only a finite number of cuts.

2. The recognition that specialized combinatorial algorithms could solve certain important classes of problems very efficiently (in a number of steps that grow as a polynomial in the problem's size) even though their linear

programming formulation contains an exponential number of constraints. For example, the usual formulation of the minimal spanning tree problem that we introduced at the outset of section 7.3 contains an exponential number of constraints. Yet a greedy-type solution strategy solves this problem very efficiently (the algorithm orders the arcs by increasing costs and in one pass through this ordered list chooses arcs one at a time unless an arc forms a circuit with those already chosen, in which case the method discards the arc).

Unfortunately, experience in the 1960s showed that both of these approaches for solving integer programming were limited. General cutting plane approaches converged very slowly and did not provide an effective computational engine for solving large-scale applications. The specialized algorithms did lead to elegant theory and to very effective algorithms for solving several important classes of problems, most notably the matching problem and certain matroid optimization problems. These discoveries are among the crowning achievements of combinatorial optimization. But the development of similar theory and algorithms did not emerge for many other problem contexts because the success of the approach requires inherent combinatorial structure not found in other problems.

Nevertheless, these developments did have important consequences that have led more recently to a renewal in computational and theoretical integer programming:

1. The specialized combinatorial applications that can be solved efficiently occur often as subproblems of more complex models. Therefore, as discussed in the last section, methods such as Lagrangian relaxation can exploit the special embedded structure algorithmically.

2. The specialized algorithms demonstrated the potential advantages of developing a deep understanding of the polyhedral structure of integer programs, a field of study that has become known as *polyhedral combinatorics*. For the cases of spanning trees, matching problems, and certain matroid problems, researchers were able to fully describe the convex hull of the underlying integer polyhedra and to use this knowledge to develop new combinatorial methods or interpret older methods in suggestive new ways. Even though the integer programming formulations for each of these problems grows exponentially in the problem's size (the number of constraints is exponential in the number of nodes of the underlying

network), researchers were able to use the problem's special structure to devise algorithms whose running time was guaranteed to grow only polynomially in the problem's size!

The last fact, which demonstrated an important interplay between inherently discrete problems and linear programming, attracted many outstanding individuals to work on problems in polyhedral combinatorics, and set the stage for recent advances in integer programming computations. In particular, it prompted the research community to take a fresh look at the cutting plane methods of the 1960s and to begin to work toward a better understanding of the significance of "good" problem formulations in solving integer programs effectively.

Figure 7.17 illustrates one particularly important concept that has proved to be instrumental in solving integer programs. This figure shows the feasible points of an integer program together with an enclosing polyhedron defined by the problem's linear programming relaxation. The figure also shows two types of cuts that separate an extreme point of the linear programming relaxation from the set of feasible integer points. One cut separates the extreme point but is far removed from the convex hull of the integer points; the other cut, on the other hand, defines one of the faces of

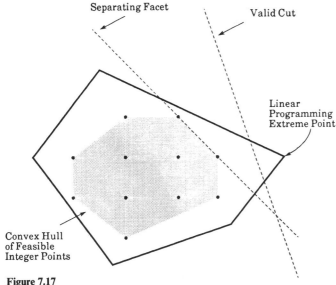

Figure 7.17
Cuts and facets

this convex hull. Therefore not only does it separate the fractional linear programming extreme point, but it is, in a certain technical sense, one of the strongest possible such separating cuts (its intersection with the convex hull of integer points has dimension one less than the dimension of the convex hull). Researchers refer to these special cuts as facets of the integer program (or of its convex hull).

Recent computational experience has shown that the addition of facets can be very effective in improving the performance of cutting plane approaches to solving integer programs. In a wide variety of applications in production planning, economic planning, and even physics, this approach has permitted researchers to solve to optimality problems that they never could before.

The facet generation approach does have one particularly important limitation. For most integer programs, the task of describing all of the facets of the integer program or of solving the separation problems of finding a facet that will cut away each point lying outside the convex hull of the feasible integer points is hopeless (in fact existing theory shows that the general separation problem is as hard as solving the general integer programming problem itself). As a result analysts typically devise algorithms for finding only a subset of facets and embed the facet-generating approach within branch and bound: when the algorithm for solving the separation problem does not find a separating facet, the algorithm reverts to branch and bound.

In addition researchers have found that using cuts that are "strong" but not necessarily facets can be very effective. Consider, for example, the following constraints for an integer programming:

$9x + 5y \le 30$,

$3x + 6y \le 23$,

$x \ge 0$ and integer,

$y \ge 0$ and integer.

Figure 7.18a shows the feasible region described by the linear programming relaxation of these constraints as well as the convex hull of the integer points. Now instead of finding the convex hull of the feasible integer points, suppose that we find the convex hull of the feasible region described by each (structural) constraint individually; that is, we consider the problem as being composed of two single constraint, knapsack problems:

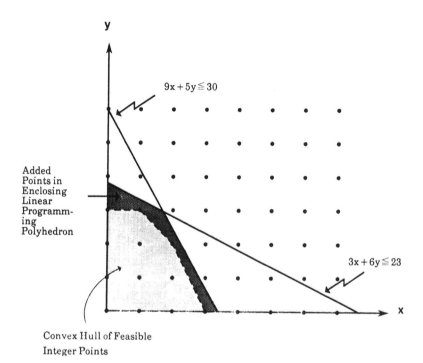

Figure 7.18a
Linear programming relaxation of an integer program

$9x + 5y \le 30$, $3x + 6y \le 23$,

$x \ge 0$ and integer, $x \ge 0$ and integer,

$y \ge 0$ and integer, $y \ge 0$ and integer.

Since the feasible region defined by any subset of constraints always contains the feasible region of the overall problem, the convex hulls of the feasible points of each knapsack problem, and so the intersection of these convex hulls as well, contains the desired convex hull of the integer points. Figure 7.18b shows how the intersection of these convex hulls approximates the convex hull of the overall problem better than the linear programming relaxation of the problem.

This observation has the following algorithmic implication. Suppose that we can find facets for a subset of the overall problem (e.g., the facet $y + 2x \le 6$ of the first knapsack problem in our numerical example). Then

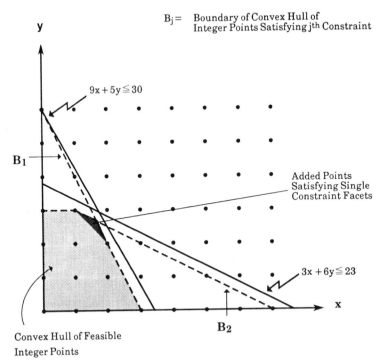

Figure 7.18b
Tightening and LP relaxation by adding facets defined by single constraints

we can use these facets as cutting planes for the overall problem. This approach has the advantage of permitting analysts to develop computational tools and polyhedral theory for subproblems that arise frequently in practice which they can then use to solve more complex problems. Researchers have used this approach successfully to solve a wide variety of problems. As but one illustration, one Lanchester Prize winning paper[10] has successfully used facets based upon single constraints, as in our example, to solve several large-scale applications, including the design of automotive car lines to meet the U.S. government's regulations imposing minimum average fleet mileage for new automobiles.

Perhaps the most dramatic illustration of the power of polyhedral methods is the progress researchers have made in solving the ubiquitous traveling salesman problem. Prior to the early 1970s the largest traveling salesman problem researchers had solved (with a guarantee of optimality) contained

48 cities. At that time the development of Lagrangian relaxation methods permitted researchers to solve problems with up to about 100 cities. Polyhedral methods using facets for cutting away fractional solutions pushed this limit to over 300 cities. Indeed, these successes were instrumental in spearheading interest in Lagrangian relaxation methods and in renewing interest in cutting plane methods for solving integer programs. Recently, using supercomputers, researchers have reported on the solution of problems with over 500 cities, and in one case problems with over 2,000 cities.

Analysis of Heuristics and Approximation Methods   Heuristics have always been a valuable solution strategy for solving optimization problems. In the 1950s and 1960s researchers and practitioners developed heuristic methods for solving a wide variety of applications such as determining the location of warehouses in retail distribution systems. Nevertheless, because these heuristics were not accompanied by parallel theoretical developments and because the research and practitioner communities had no particularly good way to certify the success of most heuristics, the study of heuristics did not attract widespread academic attention. The advent of computational complexity theory in the early 1970s, which showed that essentially all of the known, computationally elusive discrete optimization problems were computationally equivalent and equally difficult to solve, however, changed this perspective and induced researchers to devote more energy to the design and analysis of heuristics as well as methods for solving problems approximately.

This change in focus led to many informative new results. Unfortunately, this new wave of research did not lead to a unifying theory of heuristics. Therefore, in this exposition, we can only hint at the results in this problem domain. Generally, researchers have studied heuristics from three different perspectives:

1. empirical analysis.
2. probabilistic (and statistical) analysis, and
3. worst case analysis.

We will discuss two simple, yet representative, examples drawn from the third category which is perhaps most closely aligned with the type of advances in combinatorial optimization that we have considered previously in this subsection. Basically, worst case analysis develops performance guarantees: when a heuristic is applied to a particular class of problems,

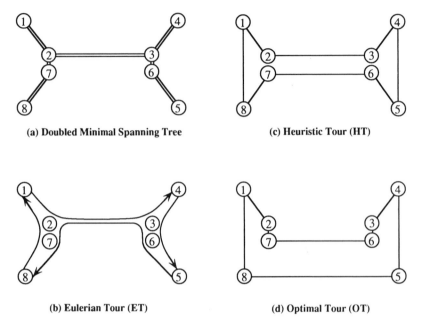

(a) Doubled Minimal Spanning Tree   (c) Heuristic Tour (HT)

(b) Eulerian Tour (ET)   (d) Optimal Tour (OT)

Figure 7.19
Doubled minimal spanning tree heuristic

the analysis provides an a priori warranty specifying how poorly it can perform.

A Traveling Salesman Problem Heuristic   Figure 7.19 illustrates an eight-node example of the well-known traveling salesman problem. The distance between any two nodes is the planar distance separating them; we wish to find a tour of minimal length that starts at node 1, passes through each node, and returns again to node 1. Figure 7.19d shows the optimal tour for this simple example.

No one has yet devised a "good" algorithm for solving planar traveling salesman problems like our example. By good we mean a method requiring a number of computations that grows only polynomially in the number of nodes. In order to be able to find an optimal solution and verify that it solves any problem, all known optimization methods require, in some instances, an exponential number of computations.

Figure 7.19 illustrates a very fast heuristic method. Note that if we eliminate any arc from the optimal tour in figure 7.19d, then the tour becomes a minimal spanning tree. Therefore the cost $C(OT)$ of the optimal tour OT is always as large as the cost $C(MST)$ of the minimal tree MST, which is very easy to detect. Let's see how to use this observation to develop a fast heuristic method with an a priori performance guarantee. We first form a new graph by doubling every arc of the minimal spanning tree as shown in figure 7.19a. Note that because we have doubled every arc, every node now has an even number of adjacent arcs. As is well known from elementary graph theory, any such graph always has an Eulerian tour, that is a tour that starts and returns to node 1 and passes through each arc exactly once. For example, if we pass though the arcs in figure 7.19a by always moving along the previously unused arc that leads to the smallest adjacent node number, we obtain the Eulerian tour ET shown in figure 7.19b. Now we can transform the Eulerian tour into a traveling salesman tour by "short-circuiting" the Eulerian tour whenever it repeats a node. For example, instead of going from node 4 to node 3 to node 6 and then to node 5 in the Eulerian tour, from node 4, we go directly to node 5. Similarly, instead of going from nodes 6 to 3 to 2 to 7 in the Eulerian tour, we go from node 6 to node 7 directly: we also replace the segment $8-7-2-1$ by the single arc $8-1$. This short-circuiting procedure produces the heuristic tour HT shown in Figure 7.19c.

Since short-circuiting in the plane can never increase the length of any segment of the tour (by the "triangle inequality"), we know that $C(HT)$ is no larger than $C(ET)$. Collecting our observations provides the desired performance guarantee:

$$C(HT) \leq C(ET) \leq 2C(MST) \leq 2C(OT).$$

Thus the tour produced by the heuristic can be no more than twice as long as the optimal tour. Our performance guarantee is 200 percent. This result is comforting in that it provides a guarantee of how badly the heuristic can perform. The bound of 200 percent is too loose to be of considerable value in practice though. Fortunately, many heuristics perform much better than their worst case performance guarantee. Also, for some problems, researchers have developed better guarantees—bounds in the range of 105 to 120 percent. Nevertheless, even when the bound is not very tight, worst case analysis has proved to be of value because it has led to insight that has, in many instances, inspired new algorithms with better worst case and empirical behavior. For example, the factor of two in this analysis arises because we doubled the minimal spanning tree in order to obtain a graph with an even number of arcs adjacent to every node. Another way of accomplishing this same objective would be to add to the spanning tree a matching connecting those of its nodes that are adjacent to an odd number of arcs. This type of approach has permitted researchers to develop a heuristic with a performance guarantee of 150 percent. This analysis is somewhat more complicated than the analysis of the double minimal spanning tree heuristic, and so we will not describe the details.

A Knapsack Problem Heuristic   Suppose that we wish to solve the classical binary knapsack problem:

$$\text{maximize } \sum_{j=1}^{n} v_j x_j$$

$$\text{subject to } \sum_{j=1}^{n} w_j x_j \le b,$$

$$x_j = 0 \text{ or } 1, \qquad j = 1, 2, \ldots, n.$$

In this formulation w_j is the weight of the jth item, b is the maximum weight the knapsack can hold, and v_j is the value of the ith item. We assume that all of the weights w_j and the knapsack capacity b are integers. A dynamic programming approach will solve this problem: let $z_k(q)$ denote the optimal value to the problem when the knapsack weight is q (an integer), and we restrict the solution to using only the first k items $1, 2, \ldots, k$. Since we either use the kth item or not, the following dynamic programming recursion is valid:

$$z_k(q) = \begin{cases} z_{k-1}(q) & \text{if } w_k > q, \\ \max\{z_{k-1}(q), v_k + z_{k-1}(q - w_k) & \text{if } w_k \le q, \end{cases}$$

with $z_0(q) = 0$ for all $q \ge 0$. Note that $z_n(b)$ is the optimal value of the original problem. Since solving for $z_k(q)$ for a fixed value of k and for $q = 1, 2, \ldots, b$ requires a total of $3b$ comparisons, subtractions and additions, the overall algorithm requires $3bn$ operations.

In many instances, b will be sufficiently small so that this algorithm is efficient. However, if b is large, say of the order 10^n, the algorithm will require an exponential number of computations. In these instances b contains at most n significant decimal digits. For concreteness, suppose that $n = 10$ and b is 9,238,730,054. Let's see how to use the idea of scaling that we introduced earlier to solve the problem approximately. Suppose we scale and round the weights w_j and knapsack capacity b by using only units of one million. That is, we drop any digits up to the hundred of thousands. The modified value of b is 9,238. When applied to the modified problem, the dynamic programming algorithm requires at most only 3(10)(9238) computations, far less than the computational requirement of 3(10)(9,238,730,054) for the original problem. We have reduced the computations by a factor of one million!

Using dynamic programming, we have solved an approximate problem exactly. How does the approximate problem relate to the original problem? First, the solution generated by solving the approximate problem need not be feasible for the original problem; it is, however, nearly feasible in the following sense: If any variable x_j is one in the solution of the approximate problem, then by introducing all the significant digits of w_j, we can add additional weight of at most 999,999 to the knapsack. Therefore, since the problem contains $n = 10$ variables and the knapsack has 730,054 additional units of capacity, the maximum excess weight of this solution is $EW = 999,999(10) - 730,054$ which is about 0.1 percent of the given knapsack capacity of 9,238,730,054. Thus we have a worst case bound on the amount of infeasibility for the solution to the approximate problem.

By modifying this procedure slightly, we can also obtain a bound on the optimal objective function value of the original problem. Suppose that when scaling, we round b up to the next highest value of one million before applying the algorithm. Then since, as measured in units of millions, the weights in the modified problem are less than their values in the original problem and the knapsack capacity in the modified problem is larger than that in the original problem, any feasible solution to the original problem is feasible to the modified problem as well. Consequently the optimal objective function value of the modified problem is an upper on the value of the original problem.

In summary, dynamic programming as implemented with the scaling technique has permitted us to develop an efficient algorithm to obtain an optimal solution to an approximate version of the original problem, as well as a worst case bound on the degree to which the approximate solution might violate the knapsack problem. This procedure might be useful in practice in situations in which the knapsack is "soft" and can be an violated slightly. The procedure is not entirely satisfactory, though, because it need not generate a feasible solution to the original problem. Researchers have, however, been able to modify the procedure slightly (by interchanging the roles of the objective function and constraint) so that the scaling/ dynamic programming technique will generate a feasible solution with a performance bound on the value of the objective function generated by the approximation procedure.

The two examples we have presented have highlighted a few key ideas:

1. As illustrated by both these examples, sometimes it is useful to relax some feature of a problem's specification to obtain a related problem that is easier to solve.

2. Combinatorial insight might permit us to analyze the relationship between the original and relaxed problems in order to obtain performance guarantees on the solutions generated by a heuristic.

3. Since the computational requirements of some algorithms are affected the size of the underlying problem data, it might be possible to obtain an approximate solution by using ideas of scaling.

We have not exhausted all possible ways to exploit these ideas. For example, we might be able to devise heuristic solutions and bounding procedures by using an underlying dual problem, or by applying a heuristic to a dual formulation of a problem. Or, duality might play an important role in analyzing a problem and in obtaining performance guarantees.

We have described one type of analysis, worst case, of heuristics. Researchers have also adopted several other modes of analysis. For example, rather than considering the conservative approach of seeking out performance guarantees, they have analyzed probabilistic or statistical versions of problems, typically with the aim of finding the average error of solutions generated by a heuristic. This type of analysis often raises complex modeling and analysis issues that lie at the interface of combinatorics and probability. (As but one illustration, what is the proper underlying probabilistic model for a problem?) We will not pursue these issues in this discussion.

7.4   Notes and References

The following selected references, as well as those that we have already cited in the text, amplify on the themes we have presented and contain many citations to the research literature.

Topics Covered in the Chapter

Applications   As we have indicated previously, the journal *Interfaces* publishes extensive material on applications of operations research/management science. Many of these studies rely on mathematical programming. Another useful source of applications is the OR Practice section of the journal *Operations Research*.

Stephen Bradley, Arnoldo Hax, and Thomas Magnanti's text *Applied Mathematical Programming* describes many applications, particularly those that arise in business settings. H. P. William's book *Modeling Building in Mathematical Programming* discusses a variety of modeling issues.

Convexity and Duality   R. Tyrrell Rockafellar and Josef Stoer and Christoph Witzgall's books *Convex Analysis* and *Convexity and Optimization in Finite Dimensions I* are standard references on convexity and duality. For a treatment of augmented Lagrangians, see Dimitri Bertsekas's book *Constrained Optimization and Lagrangian Multiplier Methods*. Jeremy Shapiro and Peter Whittle's texts *Mathematical Programming: Structures and Algorithms* and *Optimization under Constraints* treat mathematical programming duality in a manner similar to our exposition.

Fixed Points and Equilibrium   Standard sources are the books *Computation of Economic Equilibria* by Herbert Scarf and Terje Hansen and *Pathways to Solutions, Fixed Points and Equilibria* by C. B. Garcia and Willard Zangwill, as well as the monograph *The Computation of Fixed Points and Applications* by Michael Todd.

For more information on urban traffic equilibria, see *Urban Transportation Networks* by Yosef Sheffi, and for a classic treatment of spatially separated economic markets, see *Spatial and Temporal Price and Allocation Models* by T. Takayama and G. G. Judge.

Combinatorial Optimization   The recent textbooks *Integer and Combinatorial Optimization* by George Nemhauser and Laurence Wolsey and *Theory of Linear and Integer Programming* by Alexander Schrijver provide modern, comprehensive treatments of integer programming and combinatorial optimization that discuss each of the topics that we have introduced (and much more). *Combinatorial Optimization: Networks and Matroids* by Eugene Lawler and *Combinatorial Optimization: Algorithms and Complexity* by Christos Papadimitriou and Kenneth Steiglitz are other influential texts.

The collection of surveys in *The Traveling Salesman Problem: A Guided Tour of Combinatorial Optimization*, edited by Eugene Lawler, Jan Karel Lenstra, Alexander Rinnooy Kan, and David Shmoys, provides a thorough treatment of the traveling salesman problem, tracing progress on the problem as well as the problem's central role in the development of the field of combinatorial optimization.

For an up-to-date discussion of network flow algorithms, see *Network Flows* by Ravindra Ahuja, Thomas Magnanti, and James Orlin. The text *Matroid Theory* by D. A. J. Welsh contains a wealth of references on the matroid literature.

Other Topics

This limited discussion could not possibly do justice to the full range of activities in mathematical programming. And yet, hopefully, the exposition has highlighted several important key ideas and given something of a flavor of the remarkable progress that the mathematical programming community has made in the second twenty years of the field's existence as a recognized scientific discipline.

We might point out a few references to the two major themes—interfaces with computer science and linear programming—that we have identified, but not discussed, in this chapter.

Interfaces with Computer Science   As we have observed in the text, the field of computational complexity theory has had a profound influence on the directions of mathematical programming in the last two decades. Not only has complexity theory added considerably to our ability to assess the inherent difficulty of many problems in mathematical programming, but it has also been an instrumental force in stimulating much activity in the very broad field of analysis of algorithms. Michael Gary and David Johnson's monograph *Computers and Intractability: A Guide to the Theory of NP-Completeness* gives an encyclopedic account of results in this field through 1979.

Another major development at the interface between computer science and mathematical programming has been the increased recognition of the importance of data structures and careful data manipulation in the implementation of mathematical programming algorithms. One of the most notable examples of this interplay was the development by Fred Glover, Darwin Klingman, and their colleagues in the early 1970s of new implementations of the network flow algorithms. These algorithms, which exploit the problem's special underlying data structure, run about two orders of magnitude faster than implementations of generic linear programming codes. The books *Algorithms for Network Programming* by Jeffery Kennington and R. V. Helgason and *Network Flows* by Ravindra Ahuja, Thomas Magnanti, and James Orlin discuss these contributions.

Linear Programming Although researchers have continued to make numerous contributions to the field of linear programming from the field's inception in the late 1940s, throughout the 1960s, and much of the 1970s, the community made little progress in improving upon the basic computational approach of the simplex method or in explaining why the method was so effectively in practice. Then, almost out of nowhere, researchers made three startling contributions:

1. A new method, known as either Khachian's algorithm or the ellipsoid method, based upon the idea of enclosing a polyhedra in a series of shrinking ellipsoids. This method provided the first polynomial time algorithm for solving linear programs. Computational experience has shown that the approach is not competitive with the simplex method for solving linear programs; nevertheless, by establishing that linear programs could be solved in polynomial time, the discovery and analysis of this method did resolve one of the most fundamental theoretical issues in mathematical programming. (The method has also proved to be effective in solving certain nonlinear programs.)

2. New probabilistic analysis of the simplex method that has shed considerable light on the method's average case performance and provided a partial theoretical justification for the impressive computational results users of the method have experienced in practice.

3. A new method, known as either Karmarkar's algorithm or the projective algorithm, for solving linear programs by intelligently moving through the interior of the feasible region rather than along the boundary as in the simplex method. The original version of this method used ideas from projective geometry and the notion of a surrogate objective function to monitor the algorithm's progress. Later developments have added many enhancements and refinements to the method and established important connections between the method and traditional iterative methods of nonlinear programming. Although the mathematical programming community

has yet to fully understand the algorithm's computational capabilities, the algorithm does seem to be competitive with the simplex method on many problems.

Perhaps the most startling aspect of Khachian's and Karmarkar's algorithms is that they have successfully used methods from nonlinear programming for analyzing and solving linear programs. Many years of prior investigation had suggested that successful methods for linear programs should, like the simplex method, rely on approaches from computational linear algebra and exploit the underlying combinatorial structure of the polyhedra that describe linear programs (in particular, the character and structure of extreme points).

For a fuller discussion of Khachian and Karmarkar's algorithms, the reader might consult the two books *Integer and Combinatorial Optimization* and *Theory of Linear and Integer Programming* that we have cited previously in the context of combinatorial optimization. The second of these books also contains a nice discussion of the advances researchers have made in the probabilistic analysis of the simplex method. In *Geometric Algorithms and Combinatorial Optimization*, Martin Groetshel, Lazlo Lovasz, and Alexander Schrijver thoroughly analyze the ellipsoid method and the wide-ranging implications that it has for combinatorial optimization.

The Future

In looking toward the future, it might be instructive to think back to twenty years ago. As we have seen, during the last twenty years the mathematical programming community has developed entire new fields of inquiry. Who might have imagined the developments of computational fixed points, combinatorial optimization, or computational complexity theory? Who might have imagined the surprising new discoveries in linear programming? On the other hand, might we in 1967 have guessed that researchers would have solved the general integer programming problem or that we might today be routinely solving large-scale nonlinear programs, perhaps even those with nonconvexities?

Certainly, we can look forward to new developments that build upon improved computational hardware such as the design and use of parallel processing algorithms. Also we can certainly imagine continued progress on many of the themes we have addressed in this chapter. And we should expect a few surprises.

But maybe the best way to think about the future is the heartening thought that if the next twenty years are as exciting and productive as the last twenty, then we can look ahead with much anticipation.

Notes

The evolution of CORE as a major and vital research center for mathematical programming would not have been possible without the broad vision of its founder Jacques Drèze or the dedication and hospitality of its mathematical programming research staff Guy De Ghellinck, Etienne Loute, Yves Smeers, Jean Philippe-Vial, and Laurence Wolsey. Like so many other visitors to CORE over the last twenty years, I am grateful to these individuals for making my yearlong stay there in 1976 so pleasurable and professionally rewarding.

I am also grateful to Robert Freund and James Orlin for their insightful comments and advice on earlier versions of this chapter.

1. Each year, the journal *Interfaces* publishes papers describing the applications that are finalists for this prize competition. The studies summarized in our discussion appear in the following four papers:

Walter Bell et al., "Improving the Distribution of Industrial Gases with an On-line Computer-ized Routing and Scheduling Optimizer," *Interfaces* 13 (December 1983), 4–23.

Darwin Klingman, Nancy Phillips, David Stieger, and Warren Young, "The Successful Deployment of Management Science throughout Citgo Petroleum Corporation," *Interfaces* 17 (January–February 1987), 4–25.

Bruce Goeller and the PRAWN Team, "Planning the Netherlands' Water Resources," *Interfaces* 15 (January–February 1985), 3–33.

Mark Lembersky and Uli Chi, "Weyerhaeuser Decision Simulator Improves Timber Profits," *Interfaces* 16 (January–February 1986), 6–15.

2. Because the discussion in this chapter must necessarily be continued to fit within the scope of this twentieth-anniversary volume, we will discuss only the first three of these themes. The first two are intimately related to the type of interactions between mathematical programming and economics that CORE has nourished. The third topic is one that has been a major research thrust at CORE.

3. In keeping with mathematical programming conventions, we let the first component of vectors representing combinations of problem outcomes be costs even though our graphical representations will measure costs along the vertical axis.

4. This story is the lead paragraph of B. Curtis Eaves's paper "Properly Labeled Simplexes" in *Studies in Applied Mathematics* 10, 71–93, published by the Mathematical Association of America's Studies in Applied Mathematics, Georges B. Dantzig and B. Curtis Eaves, editors.

5. The algorithm's behavior can be much more complex. As an illustration, if we change the second and third points on the line from w to y in this example from squares to circles, the algorithm would move immediately from the line wy into one of the small triangles; after six more steps it would return to the line again, from which point we would continue moving toward y and repeat the same steps as in the example in figure 7.10. The effectiveness of the algorithm depends upon its ability to avoid massive "snaking" between lower and higher dimensions as in the modified example.

6. Recall from calculus that if a function $F(p)$ is twice continuously differentiable, then its matrix of second derivatives must be symmetric; that is, $d^2F(p)/dp_idp_j = d^2F(p)/dp_jdp_i$ for all i and j. In our setting this condition would imply the symmetry condition $dE_j(p)/dp_i =$

$dE_i(p)/dp_j$ which will not be valid in many circumstances. Note that in the separable case in which $E_j(p) = E_j(p_j)$ for all j, $dE_j(p)/dp_i = 0$ for all $i \neq j$ so that the matrix of second derivatives of F will be diagonal and therefore symmetric.

7. Actually, to avoid moving away from a fixed point as the algorithm converges, we might use $y - \theta g(y)$, for a suitably small scalar θ, in place of $y - g(y)$.

8. Intuitively, the path Q must contain a leg to node j, the arc $j-i$, and a leg from node j to the terminal t. The two legs, in total, must contain at least one more arc than path P and the path Q contains arc $j-i$ as well.

9. Since the minimum cost path $1-2-4-6$ without any restriction on the number of arcs contains only three arcs, we need to encourage the use of more arcs; therefore, instead of adding a positive toll, we reduce the cost of each arc by using a negative toll.

10. Harlan Crowder, Ellis Johnson, and Manfred Padberg, "Solving Large-Scale Zero-One Linear Programming Problems," *Operations Research* 31 (1983), 803–834.

References

The list of source material is far from comprehensive. The references are limited to books and monographs that have historical significance as well as those that might serve as a useful guide to the literature.

Ahuja, R., T. L. Magnanti, and J. Orlin. *Network Flows*. Forthcoming.

Avriel, M. 1976. *Nonlinear Programming: Analysis and Methods*. Englewood Cliffs, NJ: Prentice-Hall.

Bazaraa, M., and C. M. Shetty. 1979. *Nonlinear Programming Theory and Algorithms*. New York: Wiley.

Bertsekas, D. 1982. *Constrained Optimization and Lagrange Multiplier Methods*. New York: Academic Press.

Bradley, S., A. Hax, and T. Magnanti. 1977. *Applied Mathematical Programming*. Reading, MA: Addison-Wesley.

Charnes, A., and W. Cooper. 1961. *Management Models and Industrial Applications of Linear Programming*. New York: Wiley.

Dantzig, G. 1963. *Linear Programming and Extensions*. Princeton, NJ: Princeton University Press.

Debreu, G. 1959. *Theory of Value*. New York: Wiley.

Dorfman, R., P. Samuelson, and R. Solow. 1958. *Linear Programming and Economic Analysis*. New York: McGraw-Hill.

Fiacco, A., and G. McCormick. 1968. *Nonlinear Programming: Sequential Unconstrained Minimization Techniques*. New York: Wiley.

Ford, L., and D. Fulkerson. 1962. *Flows in Networks*. Princeton, NJ: Princeton University Press.

Gale, D. 1960. *The Theory of Linear Economic Models*. New York: McGraw-Hill.

Garcia, C. B., and W. Zangwill. 1981. *Pathways to Solutions, Fixed Points, and Equilibria*. Englewood Cliffs, NJ: Prentice-Hall.

Garfinkel, R., and G. Nemhauser. 1972. *Integer Programming*. New York: Wiley.

Gary, M., and D. Johnson. 1979. *Computers and Intractability: A Guide to the Theory of NP-Completeness*. San Francisco: Freeman.

Gass, S. 1958. *Linear Programming*. New York: McGraw-Hill.

Gill, P., W. Murray, and M. Wright. 1981. *Practical Optimization*. New York: Academic Press.

Groetshel, M., L. Lovasz, and A. Schrijver. 1988. *Geometric Algorithms and Combinatorial Optimization*. Berlin: Springer-Verlag.

Kennington, J., and R. V. Helgason. 1980. *Algorithms for Network Programming*. New York: Wiley.

Lasdon, L. 1970. *Optimization Theory for Large Systems*. New York: Macmillian.

Lawler, E. 1976. *Combinatorial Optimization: Networks and Matroids*. New York: Holt, Rinehart and Winston.

Lawler, E., J. K. Lenstra, A. Rinnooy Kan, and D. Shmoys. 1985. *The Traveling Salesman Problem: A Guided Tour of Combinatorial Optimization*. New York: Wiley.

Luenberger, D. 1969. *Optimization by Vector Space Methods*. New York: Wiley.

Luenberger, D. 1973. *Introduction to Linear and Nonlinear Programming*. Reading, MA: Addison-Wesley.

Mangasarian, O. 1969. *Nonlinear Programming*. New York: McGraw-Hill.

Nemhauser, G., A. H. G. Rinnooy Kan, and M. J. Todd. 1989. *Optimization*. Vol. 1. Handbooks in Operations Research and Management Science. Amsterdam: North-Holland.

Nemhauser, G., and L. Wolsey, 1988. *Integer and Combinatorial Optimization*. New York: Wiley.

Papadimitriou, C., and K. Steiglitz. 1982. *Combinatorial Optimization: Algorithms and Complexity*. Englewood Cliffs, NJ: Prentice-Hall.

Rockafellar, R. T. 1970. *Convex Analysis*. Princeton, NJ: Princeton University Press.

Scarf, H., and T. Hansen. 1973. *Computation of Economic Equilibria*. New Haven, CT: Yale University Press.

Schrijver, A. 1986. *Theory of Linear and Integer Programming*. New York: Wiley.

Shapiro, J. 1979. *Mathematical Programming: Structures and Algorithms*. New York: Wiley.

Simmonard, M. 1962. *Programmation Linéaire*. Paris: Dunod. (English transl. by W. Jewell. 1966. *Linear Programming*, Englewood Cliffs, NJ: Prentice-Hall.)

Sheffi, Y. 1985. *Urban Transportation Networks: Equilibrium Analysis with Mathematical Programming Methods*. Englewood Cliffs, NJ: Prentice-Hall.

Stoer, J., and C. Witzgall. 1970. *Convexity and Optimization in Finite Dimensions I*. Berlin: Springer-Verlag.

Takayama, T., and G. G. Judge. 1971. *Spatial and Temporal Price and Allocation Models*. Amsterdam: North Holland.

Todd, M. 1976. *The Computation of Fixed Points and Applications*. Lecture Notes in Economics and Mathematical Systems, 124. Berlin: Springer-Verlag.

Welsh, D. A. J. 1976. *Matroid Theory*. London: Academic Press.

Whittle, P. 1971. *Optimization under Constraints*. New York: Wiley.

Williams, H. P. 1978. *Model Building in Mathematical Programming*. New York: Wiley.

Zangwill, W. 1969. *Nonlinear Programming: A Unified Approach*. Englewood Cliffs, NJ: Prentice-Hall.

Zoutendijk, G. 1960. *Methods of Feasible Directions*. Amsterdam: Elsevier.

COMMENTS
ETIENNE LOUTE

My comments focus on some aspects of the interaction between mathematical programming and two other fields, namely, computer science and numerical analysis. The relationships among those three fields have been of primary importance for the development of mathematical programming over the last twenty years. This situation is likely to persist in the future. I will not make comments about a field where there has been a lot of interaction, mostly of a theoretical nature, between mathematical programming and computer science over the last fifteen years, namely, computational complexity.

Emergence of Mathematical Programming Systems

It is through its use supported by hardware and software that mathematical programming has an impact on the real world and proves its usefulness. From the mid-1950s up to the mid-1970s most implementation efforts were devoted to linear programming and mixed integer programming (MIP) within commercial packages called Mathematical Programming Systems (MPS) and available exclusively on mainframes. They are all based on a revised simplex LP engine. Most of these packages still use data structures designed by William Orchard Hays in the mid-1960s. They were continuously improved up to the late 1970s. Data scaling procedures, sophisticated pivot selection rules, basis inverse compact representation, and efficient update, branching strategies for MIP are the result of these improvements and are today considered as among its standard features. The range of applicability has been considerably enlarged: yesterday a few hundred constraints allowed an LP problem to qualify as a "large" one; today's large problems have several thousand constraints if not more than ten thousand. This extension of applicability is partially explained by the algorithmic improvements quoted earlier. It also owns much to continuous improvement of operating systems software. During their development age, from 1960 to 1980, MPS have pushed operating systems to the frontier of their limits. It can be considered that at that time solving a large LP (and particularly MIP) problem was the most demanding computer job, with equal emphasis on data management and numerical computations outside the world of engineering, chemistry, and physics.

Note that the pace of improvement of MPS has somewhat slowed down during the last six years at least in the algorithmic aspects. Most recent developments concentrate on data preprocessing for MIP use, integration with data base systems, and improvement of modeling systems as companion systems of MPS. Initially conceived as simple matrix generation tools, modeling systems implement powerful modeling languages with capabilities going beyond the requirements of current MPS. They are central to decision support systems. A trend is now to view MPS as a component of complex decision support systems.

A significant fact in the MPS would of the last six years has been their transfer to supermini computers, that is, to 32 bits machines. In general, they are somewhat stripped down versions of mainframe MPS with more emphasis on interactivity. The cost of mainframe MPS limits their use to large firms or organizations. Supermini MPS are more affordable but still too expensive for small entities. The next step, currently in progress, is MPS on workstations. It brings the power of yesterday mainframe MPS to the fingertips of a single user. However, it seems that workstation users would benefit from MPS of different design, taking advantage of te hardware, particularly of fast graphic capabilities.

It is striking to find out that MPS have hardly invaded the world of nonlinear programming. Their intrusion is mainly limited to quadratic and separable programming. In both cases the algorithms implemented are extensions of the simplex algorithm so as to make use of the LP engine the heart of the MPS. There are several explanations for this situation: Nonlinear problems are less amenable to standard formulation; it is far more difficult to ensure stability and robustness of solution techniques; computational effort is difficult to predict and increases more rapidly with size for problems in continuous variables. There are also nontechnical reasons. Developing an MPS from scratch is a costly undertaking that must be estimated in man-years of development. The same is true for adding general nonlinear programming capabilities. It is difficult to assess the market response for such capabilities. Note that for the same reasons very few MPS offer classical extensions of linear programming, for example, treatment of special structures beyond generalized upper bounds and decomposition approaches.

Two paths of potential improvement can be foreseen for future MPS: One is the use of special computer architecture such as pipe-lining and parallelism; another is the adoption of new nonsimplex approaches for linear programming, possibly based on special computer architectures. Needless to say these nonsimplex approaches will be considered only if they prove to be significantly more efficient.

Emergence of Experimental Computer Implementations

The fact that among the numerous algorithms proposed in the mathematical programming literature very few are made available through commercial MPS has stimulated the development of high quality software for experimental purposes in the academic world. Two contributions of different nature are worth citing. One is MINOS created by Michael Saunders and Brice Murtagh in 1977, and continuously improved since then at the Stanford System Optimization Laboratory. MINOS offers a capability of solving nonlinear programming models at an unprecedented level of applicability. Another contribution is XMP by Roy Marsten. It is a mathematical programming toolbox useful for any algorithm related to linear programming. The toolbox approach is very useful for implementing new algorithms and very few MPS offer something similar. When considered for solving LP problems, both XMP and MINOS offer the equivalent of a simplified LP engine of a commercial MPS without all the wealth of data management procedures. Both are written in highly standardized FORTRAN for portability. Their authors should be praised for making the sources available to the research community at a nominal cost. Papers that have used either MINOS or XMP count in the hundreds. The acknowledgment of good implementations of algorithms as well as of ideas, concepts, and computer systems related to model generation and model solution reports (GAMS due to Alexander Meeraus is an example) is widespread in the mathematical programming community. A recently created prize, the William Orchard Hays prize, has been awarded to Michael Saunders for his work. This is an encouragement for the development of similar high quality work, particularly in the promising field of projective approaches for linear programming based on Karmarkar's algorithm.

Emergence of Mathematical Programming on Microcomputer

The wide acceptance since the early 1980s of the microcomputer by companies of all sizes has triggered frantic efforts to implement operations research methods on this kind of hardware. Today dozens of packages offer linear programming capabilities on microcomputers. Nonlinear programming capabilities are also commonplace. The level of implementation of mathematical programming algorithms is quite open. For the simplex algorithm, it goes from full tableau formulation up to basis inverse compact representation. However, on the average it is inferior to experimental systems such as MINOS. These packages are undoubtedly very useful on two counts: They are very convenient for teaching purposes; they offer mathematical programming problem solving capabilities—at least in the small to medium size range—cheaply. They are highly interactive and easy to use. For some packages, another element of attractiveness is an interface between an LP solver and a spreadsheet package. On the other hand, because packages for microcomputers are generally not distributed in source form, the quality of their implementation is difficult to assess. They are blackbox systems and hence of limited use for testing algorithmic ideas. Current memory limitations—640K for MS-DOS machines—restrict their range of applicability. It is quite likely that if more memory were available, some codes would simply break down because of limited accuracy control.

The next generation of hardware will offer microcomputers with graphic workstation capabilities at today's microcomputer cost. New programming standards are emerging on these machines: use of bit-mapped interface with pointing devices, control given through events as generalization of menus. Programming within such standards will not be possible anymore if one relies on handcrafting techniques based on traditional procedural languages such as FORTRAN or PASCAL. Developers should look at new software development techniques, such as object-oriented languages.

Growing Importance of Numerical Analysis Techniques

While mathematical programming is borrowing from numerical analysis a lot of well-known and standard techniques such as matrix factorization and least squares, it is also shedding light on problems that have been rather ignored in this field, namely, factorization in a dynamic context. Linear programming with the revised simplex algorithm exemplifies this situation. Each iteration requires solving a square system of linear equations with two different right-hand sides. All direct methods for solving systems of linear equations use some sort of matrix factorization, with a computational cost depending on the cube of the order of the matrix (for dense systems). With the revised simplex algorithm, from one iteration to the next, only one column changes in the coefficient matrix (the basis matrix). The column change is a special case of a rank one change. There was a lot of incentive to avoid a refactorization from scratch. Economical updates have been proposed (with a cost in the square of the system size) in the mathematical programming literature, sometimes without paying much attention to numerical stability. More recently, error analysis involving quite elaborate techniques and the stability problem have been taken care of by contributions from numerical analysis.

Nonlinear programming has had its share of new and interesting problems: the factorization and update of approximate Hessians, computation and updating of eigenvalues within arc methods, etc.

The mathematical programming literature contains numerous and significant contributions to the problem of solving large sparse asymmetric systems of equations. The concept of "supersparse" systems is an outgrowth of linear programming computational techniques. It implies in addition to sparsity, few different values. This can be exploited through special data structures. Data structure techniques for sparse matrices have largely benefited from the development of linear programming techniques over the last twenty years.

COMMENTS: MATHEMATICAL PROGRAMMING IN THE NEXT TWENTY YEARS
ALEXANDER H. G. RINNOOY KAN

Despite many achievements over the past twenty years, several fundamental issues in mathematical programming continue to challenge researchers. Three such challenges were proposed at the twentieth anniversary of CORE and are summarized below.

Introduction

The survey by Tom Magnanti provides impressive evidence of all that has been achieved in the area of mathematical programming during the first twenty years of CORE's existence. When CORE was founded, the simplex method had barely gained recognition as a computational tool, and nonlinear, stochastic, and integer programming were in their infancy. Today the picture has changed almost beyond recognition. Perhaps the most spectacular transformation has been that of integer programming into the broad area of combinatorial optimization. Interestingly enough, nonlinear programming has recently reasserted its importance through the emergence of new, definitely noncombinatorial techniques for linear programming, while the interface between stochastics and optimization continues to represent largely virgin territory. Researchers at CORE have been in the forefront of several important developments. Undoubtedly, the Institute's staff and its stream of distinguished visitors will continue to contribute to the development of mathematical programming, as the paradigm of optimization makes a successful appearance in more and more disciplines.

Quality

One of the mysteries of mathematical programming is that certain algorithms work as well in practice as they do. For each of those algorithms, it is not hard to construct theoretical examples on which they perform very poorly indeed; yet computational experiments confirm repeatedly that these unfortunate examples simply do not occur in practice.

Any theoretical explanation of this phenomenon would have to involve probability theory in some form, but the probabilistic analysis of algorithms, in which the behavior of an algorithm is studied as a random phenomenon defined by a probability distribution over the class of problem instances, is fraught with theoretical difficulties.

The excellent performance of the simplex method is the prime example of such a mystery. Here a virtuoso probabilistic analysis by Borgwardt (1982a,b), Smale (1983a,b), and then by Adler, Haimovich, Karp, Megiddo, and others has shed some light on the phenomenon, but its conclusions are highly dependent on the starting definition of what constitutes a random linear program and do not fully match the computational behavior observed in practice.

There are many other examples. Branch-and-bound methods also frequently combine a notoriously poor performance in the worst case with quite acceptable average behavior, but a probabilistic analysis has only been feasible for highly structured problems, as in recent work by Ahn et al. (1988) on the uncapacitated location problem. The polyhedral combinatorics approach, in which a rough approximation of the convex hull of feasible solutions frequently suffices to solve complicated integer programs as linear programs, also belongs in this category: The success of the computational studies carried out at CORE and elsewhere remains to be explained. Finally, decomposition methods, such as Benders' (1962) and cross decomposition have been applied successfully by Geoffrion and

Graves (1974), Van Rooy (1983), and others, but conditions under which a favorable outcome can be expected remain anybody's guess. One suspects that it may require at least twenty more years for a satisfactory answer to appear.

Randomization

A second, equally puzzling phenomenon that appears in various subareas of mathematical programming is the power of randomization as an algorithmic device. There is no inherent reason why computations that are partially guided by the outcome of statistical experiments should be effective in practice, but frequently they are. Algorithms that flip coins can usually be proved to achieve asymptotic global convergence in some probabilistic sense, but frequently turn out to be already competitive for problems of modest size.

Methods for global minimization of real functions that have many local minima provide a striking example. The simple idea of applying a local minimization routine to an appropriate subset of a random sample of feasible solutions works amazingly well in practice and is vastly preferable to a variety of deterministic approaches. Simulated annealing provides another success story in the area of combinatorial optimization: The idea to generalize local improvement schemes by allowing a deteriorating step with a probability going to zero is surprisingly powerful in practice. Algorithms that identify redundant constraints as those that are not hit by a succession of randomly directed shots from inside the feasible region outperform many deterministic methods designed for the same purpose. Further away from mathematical programming, the story repeats itself on problems such as primality testing and pattern recognition.

The tools for a convincing explanation of why randomization helps will have to come from theoretical computer science. In the meantime algorithm designers are likely to encounter new situations in which the principle applies.

Parallelism

In twenty years parallel computation has evolved from theoretical fiction to practical fact. The issue is no longer if parallel computation will be used, but only when it will become available to the average user. Before then, the mathematical programming community had better develop some good ideas on how to exploit this new possibility.

It is curious to observe how few genuinely new algorithmic approaches have appeared in the first phases of this exploration. In nonlinear programming, one obviously would want to extend the customary one-dimensional (line) search to a multidimensional one, and that has been worked out in detail. Stochastic linear programming offers obvious possibilities in that many similarly structured linear programs can be solved simultaneously, and this is indeed currently being explored. In combinatorial optimization, computer scientists have come up with clever devices to speed up the solutions of easy problems (i.e., those solvable in sequential polynomial time), but the use of parallelism to solve hard (NP-complete) problems has barely been investigated.

Of course, it is precisely in the latter context that one would hope for a dramatic contribution. Decomposition and partitioning approaches are both natural tools to solve large, complicated mathematical programs and natural targets for parallellization. The optimal design of a parallel implementation, involving the right mix of centralized control and decentralized computing, offers an interesting modeling challenge in itself.

Conclusion

In twenty years of mathematical programming, as many interesting new questions have arisen as old problems have been solved. This is a tribute to the vitality of this area of research and a challenge for scientists at CORE who will have ample opportunity to strengthen the reputation of the institute as they pursue new directions of research. Could it be true that we ain't seen nothing yet?

References

Adler, I., Karp, R. M., and Shamir, R. 1983a. "A Family of Simplex Variants Solving an $m \times d$ Linear Program in $O(\min(m^2, d^2))$ Expected Number of Pivot." Report No. UCB/CSD 83/158, Computer Science Division, University of California, Berkeley, CA.

Adler, I., Karp, R. M., and Shamir, R. 1983b. "A Simplex Variant Solving an $m \times d$ Linear Program in Expected Number of Pivot Steps Depending on d Only." Report No. UCB/CSD 83/157, Computer Science Division, University of California, Berkeley, CA.

Adler, I., Megiddo, N., and M. J. Todd. 1984. "New Results on the Average Behavior of Simplex Algorithms." *Bulletin of the American Mathematical Society* 11:378–382.

Ahn S., Cooper, C., Cornuejols, G., and A. M. Frieze. 1988. "Probabilistic Analysis of a Relaxation for the k-Median Problem." *Mathematics of Operations Research* 13:1–31.

Benders, J. F. 1962. "Partitioning Procedures for Solving Mixed Variables Programming Problems." *Numerische Mathematik* 4:76–94.

Borgwardt, K. -H. 1982a. "Some Distribution-Independent Results about the Asymptotic Order of the Average Number of Pivot Steps of the Simplex Method." *Mathematics of Operations Research* 7:441–462.

Borgwardt, K. -H. 1982b. "The Average Number of Pivot Steps Required by the Simplex-Method is Polynomial." *Zeitschrift für Operations Research* 26:157–177.

Geoffrion, A. M., and G. Graves. 1974. "Multicommodity Distribution System Design by Benders Decomposition." *Management Science* 20:822–844.

Haimovitch, M. 1983. "The Simplex Method is very Good!—On the Expected Number of Pivot Steps and Related Properties of Random Linear Programs." Preprint.

Megiddo, N. 1986. "Improved Asymptotic Analysis of the Average Number of Steps Performed by the Self-Dual Simplex Algorithm." *Mathematical Programming* 35:140–172.

Smale, S. 1983a. "The Problem of the Average Speed of the Simplex Method." In: *Mathematical Programming, The State of the Art—Bonn 1982*, edited by A. Bachem, M. Grötschel, and B. Korte. Springer: Berlin. 530–539.

Smale, S. 1983b. "On the Average Number of Steps in the Simplex Method of Linear Programming." *Mathematical Programming* 27:241–262.

Van Roy, T. J. 1983. "Cross Decomposition for Mixed Integer Programming." *Mathematical Programming* 25:46–63.

8 On the Relationship between the Search Directions in the Affine and Projective Variants of Karmarkar's Linear Programming Algorithm

John E. Mitchell and Michael J. Todd

8.1 Introduction

We consider the directions used in Karmarkar's (1984) projective linear programming algorithm and in its affine variant (Vanderbei et al. 1986), and show when they are equivalent. The projective algorithm we consider is closely related to those developed by Anstreicher (1986), Gay (1987), de Ghellinck and Vial (1986), Gonzaga (1989), Jensen and Steger (1985), and Ye and Kojima (1987), among others. We show that if either the affine or the projective direction is nonpositive, then they are equivalent, and we give a general expression for the projective direction in terms of the affine direction. In addition we present a condition that shows when it is possible to use the affine direction and still ensure a constant decrease in Karmarkar's potential function, thus preserving polynomial convergence.

Our original problem is written

minimize $c_0^T x$

subject to $A_0 x = b,$ $\qquad\qquad\qquad\qquad\qquad\qquad\qquad\qquad$ ($\tilde{\text{P}}_0$)

$\qquad\qquad x \geq 0,$

where c_0 and x are n-vectors, b is a m-vector, and A_0 is m by n.

The affine variant of the algorithm works directly on this formulation. In order to develop the projective algorithm, we homogenize to obtain

minimize $c_0^T x$

subject to $[A_0 | -b] \begin{pmatrix} x \\ \xi \end{pmatrix} = 0,$

$\qquad\qquad [0|1] \begin{pmatrix} x \\ \xi \end{pmatrix} = 1,$ $\qquad\qquad\qquad\qquad\qquad$ (P_0)

$\qquad\qquad x, \xi \geq 0,$

where ξ is a scalar.

At iteration k we have a strictly positive solution $(x_k^T, 1)^T$ to (P_0) and a lower bound z_k on its value. We define X_k to be the diagonal matrix with elements the entries of x_k, so $X_k e = x_k$, where e denotes a vector of ones of the appropriate dimension. Then e is a feasible solution to the rescaled problem

minimize $c^T x$

subject to $[A|-b]\begin{pmatrix} x \\ \xi \end{pmatrix} = 0,$

$$[0|1]\begin{pmatrix} x \\ \xi \end{pmatrix} = 1,$$ (P)

$x, \xi \geq 0,$

where $A = A_k := A_0 X_k$ and $c = c_k := X_k c_0$.
   We can similarly rescale $(\tilde{P}_0)$ to get

minimize $c^T x$

subject to $Ax = b,$ $(\tilde{P})$

$x \geq 0.$

Then $x = e$ is a feasible solution to $(\tilde{P})$.
   Let

$$y_{\mathrm{AFF}} = (AA^T)^{-1} Ac.$$ (1)

Then the affine direction is defined to be

$$d_{\mathrm{AFF}} = -P_A c = -c + A^T y_{\mathrm{AFF}},$$ (2)

where P_M denotes projection onto the nullspace of M. Thus d_{AFF} is a feasible direction for $(\tilde{P})$.
   The projective iteration consists of three steps:

i. Obtain a new lower bound $z = z_{k+1} \geq z_k$.
ii. Let

$$\begin{pmatrix} d \\ \delta \end{pmatrix} = -P_{[A|-b]}\begin{pmatrix} c \\ -z \end{pmatrix}.$$ (3)

Choose steplength α, and set

$$x = e + \frac{\alpha d}{d_{\mathrm{siz}}}, \qquad \xi = 1 + \frac{\alpha \delta}{d_{\mathrm{siz}}},$$

where

$$d_{\text{siz}} = \left\| \begin{matrix} d \\ \delta \end{matrix} \right\|_2 .$$

iii. Normalize so $\xi = 1$:

$$x_{k+1} \leftarrow \frac{X_k x}{\xi}, \qquad \xi \leftarrow 1.$$

Notice that this direction differs from that defined in Gonzaga (1989) in that we do not project onto the simplex $e^T x = n + 1$ in step ii.

We can also define a third direction, the affine direction corresponding to problem (P),

$$\begin{pmatrix} d'_{\text{AFF}} \\ \delta'_{\text{AFF}} \end{pmatrix} = -P_{\left(A \mid -b \atop 0 \mid 1\right)} \begin{pmatrix} c \\ -z \end{pmatrix}.$$

PROPOSITION 1   This third direction is equivalent to the affine direction d_{AFF}, in that $d'_{\text{AFF}} = d_{\text{AFF}}$ and $\delta'_{\text{AFF}} = 0$.

Proof   Since

$$\begin{pmatrix} A & -b \\ 0 & 1 \end{pmatrix} \begin{pmatrix} A^T & 0 \\ -b^T & 1 \end{pmatrix} = \begin{pmatrix} AA^T + bb^T & -b \\ -b^T & 1 \end{pmatrix}$$

and

$$\begin{pmatrix} AA^T + bb^T & -b \\ -b^T & 1 \end{pmatrix}^{-1} = \begin{pmatrix} (AA^T)^{-1} & (AA^T)^{-1}b \\ b^T(AA^T)^{-1} & 1 + b^T(AA^T)^{-1}b \end{pmatrix},$$

we find that

$$\begin{pmatrix} d'_{\text{AFF}} \\ \delta'_{\text{AFF}} \end{pmatrix} = \begin{pmatrix} -c \\ z \end{pmatrix}$$

$$+ \begin{pmatrix} A^T & 0 \\ -b^T & 1 \end{pmatrix} \begin{pmatrix} (AA^T)^{-1} & (AA^T)^{-1}b \\ b^T(AA^T)^{-1} & 1 + b^T(AA^T)^{-1}b \end{pmatrix} \begin{pmatrix} A & -b \\ 0 & 1 \end{pmatrix} \begin{pmatrix} c \\ -z \end{pmatrix}$$

$$= \begin{pmatrix} -c + A^T y_{\text{AFF}} \\ 0 \end{pmatrix}$$

$$= \begin{pmatrix} d_{\text{AFF}} \\ 0 \end{pmatrix}. \qquad \blacksquare$$

8.2   Relating the Affine and Projective Directions

In this section we give a sufficient condition for the affine and projective directions to be equivalent, express the projective direction in terms of the affine one, and give a general class of directions that contains both.

The projective direction is defined to be

$$
\begin{pmatrix} d(z) \\ \delta(z) \end{pmatrix} = -P_{[A|-b]} \begin{pmatrix} c \\ -z \end{pmatrix}
\tag{3}
$$

when we take z to be our lower bound z_{k+1}. Hence, after some algebraic manipulation using

$$
(AA^T + bb^T)^{-1} = (AA^T)^{-1} - \frac{ww^T}{1 + b^Tw}
$$

with

$$
w = (AA^T)^{-1}b,
$$

we obtain

$$
d(z) = -c + A^T y_{\text{AFF}} + \frac{(z - b^T y_{\text{AFF}})}{1 + b^T(AA^T)^{-1}b} A^T(AA^T)^{-1}b,
\tag{4}
$$

$$
\delta(z) = \frac{(z - b^T y_{\text{AFF}})}{1 + b^T(AA^T)^{-1}b}.
\tag{5}
$$

The dual problem to (P) is

$$
\max_{y,z} z
$$

$$
\text{s.t.}\quad A^T y \le c,
\tag{D}
$$

$$
-b^T y + z \le 0.
$$

Following Todd and Burrell (1986), we set

$$
y(z) = (\tilde{A}\tilde{A}^T)^{-1}\tilde{A}^T \begin{pmatrix} c \\ -z \end{pmatrix},
\tag{6}
$$

where $\tilde{A} = [A|-b]$.

If $(y(z_k), z_k)$ is feasible in (D), then we choose z_{k+1} to solve

$$\max_{z} \; z$$

$$\text{s.t.} \quad A^T y(z) \le c, \tag{D'}$$

$$-b^T y(z) + z \le 0;$$

otherwise we set $z_{k+1} \leftarrow z_k$. Note that $z_{k+1} \ge z_k$.

Observe that

$$y(z) = (AA^T)^{-1} Ac - \frac{b^T(AA^T)^{-1}Ac}{1 + b^T(AA^T)^{-1}b}(AA^T)^{-1}b$$

$$+ \frac{z}{1 + b^T(AA^T)^{-1}b}(AA^T)^{-1}b$$

$$= y_{\text{AFF}} + \frac{(z - b^T y_{\text{AFF}})}{1 + b^T(AA^T)^{-1}b}(AA^T)^{-1}b$$

$$= y_{\text{AFF}} + \delta(z)(AA^T)^{-1}b,$$

and thus $y(b^T y_{\text{AFF}}) = y_{\text{AFF}}$. We also note that

$$z - b^T y(z) = \frac{z - b^T(AA^T)^{-1}Ac}{1 + b^T(AA^T)^{-1}b}$$

$$= \frac{z - b^T y_{\text{AFF}}}{1 + b^T(AA^T)^{-1}b} = \delta(z). \tag{7}$$

We define a class $\mathcal{D}$ of feasible directions

$$\mathcal{D} = \left\{ -P_{[A|-b]} \begin{pmatrix} c \\ -z \end{pmatrix} : z \in \mathbf{R} \right\}.$$

Thus $\mathcal{D}$ is just the set of directions $\begin{pmatrix} d(z) \\ \delta(z) \end{pmatrix}$ defined in (3); in particular, the projective direction belongs to $\mathcal{D}$. It should also be noted that Ye (1985) uses the direction

$$-P_{[A|-b]} \begin{pmatrix} c \\ c^T e \end{pmatrix}$$

which is in $\mathcal{D}$.

THEOREM 2   The direction $\begin{pmatrix} d_{\text{AFF}} \\ 0 \end{pmatrix}$ is in $\mathcal{D}$.

Proof The result follows directly from (4) and (5), setting $z = b^T y_{\text{AFF}}$. ∎

The direction d_{AFF} is a feasible direction from $x = e$ in $(\tilde{P})$, whereas the projective direction is a feasible direction from $x = e$, $\xi = 1$ in (P) (except that we need to rescale in order to satisfy the final constraint). To relate these two, we find a feasible direction d_{PRO} from $x = e$ in $(\tilde{P})$ that is equivalent to the projective direction. From equations (2), (4), and (5) we have

$$d(z) = d_{\text{AFF}} + \delta(z) A^T (AA^T)^{-1} b,$$

$$\delta(z) = \frac{z - b^T y_{\text{AFF}}}{1 + b^T (AA^T)^{-1} b}.$$

If we take a step of length $\alpha = \beta d_{\text{siz}}$ in the direction $\begin{pmatrix} d(z) \\ \delta(z) \end{pmatrix}$, then our new point in the transformed space, writing d for $d(z_{k+1})$ and δ for $\delta(z_{k+1})$, is

$$x = e + \beta d, \qquad \xi = 1 + \beta \delta,$$

and a radial projection gives

$$x' = \frac{e + \beta d}{1 + \beta \delta}, \qquad \xi' = 1;$$

so our equivalent step in $(\tilde{P})$ from $x = e$ is

$$d' = \frac{e + \beta d}{1 + \beta \delta} - e$$

$$= \frac{\beta}{1 + \beta \delta} (d_{\text{AFF}} - \delta(e - A^T (AA^T)^{-1} b)).$$

By reparametrizing the step length, we find that the direction is

$$d_{\text{PRO}} := d_{\text{AFF}} - \delta(e - A^T (AA^T)^{-1} b). \tag{8}$$

It can be shown that the directions defined in Gonzaga (1989) and Anstreicher (1986) do give the direction d_{PRO} from $x = e$ in $(\tilde{P})$, provided the same lower bound is used.

THEOREM 3   If z is updated and the bounding dual constraint in (D') is the final one, then the projective direction and the affine direction are equivalent.

Proof   From equation (3)

$$\delta = z_{k+1} - b^T(\tilde{A}\tilde{A}^T)^{-1}\tilde{A}\begin{pmatrix} c \\ -z_{k+1} \end{pmatrix}$$

$$= z_{k+1} - b^T y(z_{k+1})$$

$$= 0 \qquad \text{from the hypothesis of the theorem.}$$

Hence from equation (8), $d_{\text{PRO}} = d_{\text{AFF}}$. ∎

We now give necessary and sufficient conditions for the hypothesis of theorem 3 to hold.

THEOREM 4   Given that we update the lower bound z, the tight constraint in (D') is the last one if and only if $d_{\text{PRO}} \leq 0$.

Proof   From (7),

$$d_{\text{PRO}} = d_{\text{AFF}} - \delta(e - A^T(AA^T)^{-1}b)$$

$$= d - \delta e \qquad \text{from equation (4).}$$

Now $d = -c + A^T y(z) \leq 0$ from our choice of z, and similarly $\delta = z - b^T y(z) \leq 0$. Hence, if the last constraint in (D') is tight, we have $\delta = 0$ and so $d_{\text{PRO}} \leq 0$. Conversely, if it is not tight, we have $\delta < 0$ while, from our choice of z, $d_j = 0$ for some j, so d_{PRO} has a positive component. ∎

COROLLARY 5   Assume that z is updated. If $d_{\text{PRO}} \leq 0$, then $d_{\text{PRO}} = d_{\text{AFF}}$.

Proof   The result follows directly from theorems 3 and 4. ∎

To complement corollary 5, we prove the following theorem:

THEOREM 6   Assume that z is updated; then, if d_{AFF} is nonpositive, $d_{\text{AFF}} = d_{\text{PRO}}$.

Proof   Notice that under the hypothesis of the theorem $b^T y_{\text{AFF}}$ is feasible in (D'), since

$$c - A^T y(b^T y_{\text{AFF}}) = c - A^T y_{\text{AFF}} = -d_{\text{AFF}} \geq 0$$

and

$$b^T y_{\text{AFF}} - b^T y(b^T y_{\text{AFF}}) = b^T y_{\text{AFF}} - b^T y_{\text{AFF}} = 0.$$

We also observe from (7) that $z - b^T y(z)$ is a strictly increasing function of z, and thus, since $b^T y_{AFF} - b^T y(b^T y_{AFF}) = 0$, $b^T y_{AFF}$ is optimal for (D'). Hence from (5), $\delta = 0$, and so from (8), $d_{PRO} = d_{AFF}$. ∎

It is clear from the proof of theorem 6 that $b^T y_{AFF}$ gives an upper bound on the solution of (D'), and therefore, if we update z, $z \le b^T y_{AFF}$.

8.3   Decrease in Karmarkar's Potential Function

We now consider the issue of polynomial convergence when using the direction d_{AFF}. Thus we define Karmarkar's potential function

$$f(x, \xi; c, z) = (n + 1)\ln(c^T x - z\xi) - \sum_{j=1}^{n} \ln x_j - \ln \xi. \tag{9}$$

THEOREM 7   Assume that $b^T y_{AFF} < c^T e$.

(i) For a given α $(0 < \alpha < 1)$, we can guarantee a decrease of

$$\alpha - \frac{\alpha^2}{2(1 - \alpha)}$$

in $f(x, \xi; c, b^T y_{AFF})$ when moving in the direction d_{AFF}.

(ii) Let

$$\beta = \frac{c^T e - b^T y_{AFF}}{c^T e - z}.$$

We can guarantee a decrease of ε in $f(x, \xi; c, z)$ by moving in the direction d_{AFF}, provided

$$\beta \ge \max\left\{\frac{1}{n + 2}(n + 1 + \varepsilon + \sqrt{(2\varepsilon)}), \frac{\varepsilon + \sqrt{(2\varepsilon)}}{2}\right\}.$$

Proof   We define the direction

$$\begin{pmatrix} \bar{d} \\ \bar{\delta} \end{pmatrix} = \begin{pmatrix} d_{AFF} \\ 0 \end{pmatrix} - \frac{e^T d_{AFF}}{n + 1}\begin{pmatrix} e \\ 1 \end{pmatrix}, \tag{10}$$

so

$$(e^T \quad 1)\begin{pmatrix} \bar{d} \\ \bar{\delta} \end{pmatrix} = 0.$$

Because f is constant on rays, if we can guarantee a decrease of ε in the direction $\left(\dfrac{\bar{d}}{\bar{\delta}}\right)$, then we can guarantee a decrease of ε in the direction d_{AFF}.

Now

$$(c^T, -z)\left(\frac{\bar{d}}{\bar{\delta}}\right) = c^T d_{\text{AFF}} - (c^T e - z)\frac{e^T d_{\text{AFF}}}{n+1}$$

$$= -\|d_{\text{AFF}}\|_2^2 - (c^T e - z)\frac{e^T d_{\text{AFF}}}{n+1}. \tag{11}$$

Note also that

$$c^T e - b^T y_{\text{AFF}} = c^T e - c^T A^T (AA^T)^{-1} Ae$$

$$= -e^T d_{\text{AFF}} \tag{12}$$

and

$$\left\|\frac{\bar{d}}{\bar{\delta}}\right\|_2^2 = \|d_{\text{AFF}}\|_2^2 - \frac{(e^T d_{\text{AFF}})^2}{n+1}. \tag{13}$$

Define

$$\rho = \left\|\frac{\bar{d}}{\bar{\delta}}\right\|_2.$$

Let

$$f_1(x, \xi; c, z) = (n+1)\ln(c^T x - z\xi),$$

$$f_2(x, \xi; c, z) = \sum_{j=1}^n \ln x_j + \ln \xi,$$

so

$$f(x, \xi; c, z) = f_1(x, \xi; c, z) - f_2(x, \xi; c, z).$$

It is essentially shown in Karmarkar (1984) that by taking a step of length α in the direction $\left(\dfrac{\bar{d}}{\bar{\delta}}\right)$, we can guarantee that $f_2(x, \xi; c, z)$ does not decrease by more than $\alpha^2/2(1 - \alpha)$.

(i) We show that by taking a step of length α in the direction $\left(\dfrac{\bar{d}}{\bar{\delta}}\right)$, we obtain a decrease of at least α in $f_1(x, \xi; c, b^T y_{\text{AFF}})$.

Note that, from equation (11),

$$(c^T, -b^T y_{AFF}) \begin{pmatrix} \overline{d} \\ \overline{\delta} \end{pmatrix} = -\|d_{AFF}\|_2^2 - (c^T e - b^T y_{AFF}) \frac{e^T d_{AFF}}{n+1}$$

$$= -\|d_{AFF}\|_2^2 + \frac{(e^T d_{AFF})^2}{n+1} \qquad \text{from (12)}$$

$$= -\rho^2 \qquad \text{from (13)}.$$

We also observe that

$$\rho \geq |\overline{\delta}| = \left| \frac{e^T d_{AFF}}{n+1} \right|. \tag{14}$$

Hence

$$\frac{-1}{\rho}(c^T, -b^T y_{AFF}) \begin{pmatrix} \overline{d} \\ \overline{\delta} \end{pmatrix} = \rho$$

$$\geq \left| \frac{e^T d_{AFF}}{n+1} \right|$$

$$= \frac{1}{n+1}(c^T e - b^T y_{AFF}) \qquad \text{from (12)}.$$

Thus

$$(c^T, -b^T y_{AFF}) \left(\begin{pmatrix} e \\ 1 \end{pmatrix} + \frac{\alpha}{\rho} \begin{pmatrix} \overline{d} \\ \overline{\delta} \end{pmatrix} \right) \leq \left(1 - \frac{\alpha}{n+1} \right) (c^T e - b^T y_{AFF}).$$

Therefore by taking a step of length α in the direction $\begin{pmatrix} \overline{d} \\ \overline{\delta} \end{pmatrix}$, we obtain a decrease of at least α in $f_1(x, \xi; c, b^T y_{AFF})$, and consequently a decrease of at least $\alpha - (\alpha^2/2(1 - \alpha))$ in $f(x, \xi; c, b^T y_{AFF})$.

(ii) Let α be our steplength in the direction $\begin{pmatrix} \overline{d} \\ \overline{\delta} \end{pmatrix}$. If we can guarantee a decrease of $\gamma\alpha$ in $f_1(x, \xi; c, z)$, then we obtain a decrease of at least

$$g(\gamma, \alpha) := \gamma\alpha - \frac{\alpha^2}{2(1 - \alpha)}$$

in $f(x, \xi; c, z)$. We wish to obtain conditions on β to ensure that there exist γ and α giving $g(\gamma, \alpha) \geq \varepsilon$. For a given $\gamma > 0$,

$$\hat{\alpha}(\gamma) := 1 - \frac{1}{\sqrt{(1 + 2\gamma)}}$$

is the steplength that maximizes $g(\gamma, \alpha)$. To ensure a decrease of ε in $g(\gamma, \alpha)$, it is sufficient to have γ large enough so that $g(\gamma, \hat{\alpha}(\gamma)) \geq \varepsilon$. It is easily checked that

$$\gamma \geq \hat{\gamma} := \varepsilon + \sqrt{(2\varepsilon)}$$

suffices. Thus, to obtain the desired reduction, we only need

$$(c^T, -z)\left(\binom{e}{1} + \frac{\hat{\alpha}(\hat{\gamma})}{\rho}\binom{\bar{d}}{\bar{\delta}}\right) \leq \left(1 - \frac{\hat{\gamma}\hat{\alpha}(\hat{\gamma})}{n+1}\right)(c^T, -z)\binom{e}{1}, \tag{15}$$

or, simplifying (15),

$$\frac{\rho\hat{\gamma}}{n+1}(c^T e - z) \leq -c^T\bar{d} + z\bar{\delta}. \tag{16}$$

Observe that

$$c^T e - z = \frac{1}{\beta}(c^T e - b^T y_{\text{AFF}})$$

$$= -\frac{1}{\beta}e^T d_{\text{AFF}} \qquad \text{from (12),}$$

and so, from (11), (13), and (12),

$$(c^T, -z)\binom{\bar{d}}{\bar{\delta}} = -\|d_{\text{AFF}}\|_2^2 - (c^T e - z)\frac{e^T d_{\text{AFF}}}{n+1}$$

$$= -\rho^2 - \left(\frac{1}{\beta}(-e^T d_{\text{AFF}}) + e^T d_{\text{AFF}}\right)\frac{e^T d_{\text{AFF}}}{n+1}$$

$$= -\rho^2 + \frac{1 - \beta}{\beta}\frac{(e^T d_{\text{AFF}})^2}{n+1}. \tag{17}$$

Hence, after dividing through by $(e^T d_{\text{AFF}})^2$, (16) can be rewritten

$$\frac{\rho^2}{(e^T d_{\text{AFF}})^2} + \frac{\hat{\gamma}}{\beta(n+1)}\frac{\rho}{e^T d_{\text{AFF}}} - \frac{(1 - \beta)}{\beta(n+1)} \geq 0. \tag{18}$$

Let

$$\mu = -\frac{\rho}{e^T d_{\mathrm{AFF}}}.$$

Note that we have assumed $e^T d_{\mathrm{AFF}} < 0$. Then, by writing (18) in terms of μ, we obtain

$$\mu^2 - \frac{\hat{\gamma}}{\beta(n+1)}\mu - \frac{(1-\beta)}{\beta(n+1)} \geq 0. \tag{19}$$

We know from (14) that $\mu \geq 1/(n+1)$. Hence (15) holds if β is sufficiently large so that $1/(n+1)$ is no smaller than the positive root of (19), that is,

$$\frac{\hat{\gamma}}{\beta(n+1)} + \sqrt{\left(\frac{\hat{\gamma}^2}{\beta^2(n+1)^2} + \frac{4}{n+1}\left(\frac{1-\beta}{\beta}\right)\right)} \leq \frac{2}{n+1}.$$

Thus we can obtain a decrease of ε in $f(x,\xi;c,z)$ by moving in the direction d_{AFF} if

$$\beta \geq \max\left\{\frac{\hat{\gamma}}{2}, \frac{1}{n+2}(n+1+\hat{\gamma})\right\}$$

$$= \max\left\{\frac{1}{n+2}(n+1+\varepsilon+\sqrt{(2\varepsilon)}), \frac{\varepsilon+\sqrt{(2\varepsilon)}}{2}\right\}. \quad\blacksquare$$

Let z be our current lower bound on the value of (P). Theorem 7(i) shows that we can obtain a decrease of $\frac{1}{5}$ in $f(x,\xi;c,b^T y_{\mathrm{AFF}})$ by moving in the direction d_{AFF}, and thus, as shown in Todd and Burrell (1986), if $z > b^T y_{\mathrm{AFF}}$, then we also obtain a decrease of $\frac{1}{5}$ in $f(x,\xi;c,z)$. Now suppose that $z < b^T y_{\mathrm{AFF}}$. Theorem 7(ii) suggests that we may need

$$\frac{b^T y_{\mathrm{AFF}} - z}{c^T e - z}$$

to be $O(1/n)$ in a worst case to be assured of a drop in the potential function $f(x,\xi;c,z)$ when moving in the direction d_{AFF}. We present an example to show that this observation is valid.

Example

Let

$$c^T = (-1, -1, 1, \ldots, 1),$$

$$A = (n, 5n-12, 6, \ldots, 6), \qquad b = 12(n-2).$$

Then $Ac = 0$, so $y_{AFF} = 0$ and $b^T y_{AFF} = 0$. Note that the current value is $c^T e = n - 4$ and that the optimal value is $z^* = -12 + 24/n$ achieved at $x^* = (12(n-2)/n, 0, \ldots, 0)$. (We assume that $n > 4$.)

Now $d_{AFF} = -c$, and so $\|d_{AFF}\| = \sqrt{n}$. If we take a step of length $\beta = \alpha \|d_{AFF}\|$ in the direction d_{AFF}, then our new point is

$$x = e + \alpha d_{AFF}, \qquad \xi = 1.$$

The potential function at this point is

$$\varphi(x) := f(x, \xi; c, z)$$

$$= (n+1)\ln(c^T e + \alpha c^T d_{AFF} - z) - 2\ln(1 + \alpha) - (n-2)\ln(1 - \alpha)$$

$$= (n+1)\ln(n - 4 - \alpha n - z) - 2\ln(1 + \alpha) - (n-2)\ln(1 - \alpha).$$

Then

$$\frac{d\varphi}{d\alpha} = \frac{-n(n+1)}{n - 4 - \alpha n - z} - \frac{2}{1 + \alpha} + \frac{n-2}{1 - \alpha},$$

and so

$$\frac{d\varphi}{d\alpha}(0) = \frac{1}{n - 4 - z}(-9n + 16 - (n-4)z).$$

As shown in Todd and Burrell (1986), φ has at most one stationary point, and if it has one, it is a minimizer. Note that $(d\varphi/d\alpha)(0) \geq 0$ if $z \leq (-9n + 16)/(n - 4)$. Therefore, for such z, we cannot get any decrease in $f(x, \xi; c, z)$ by moving in the direction d_{AFF}. For $n \geq 24$, we have $(-9n + 16)/(n - 4) \geq -10$, and so we cannot get any decrease in $f(x, \xi; c, z)$ for $z \leq -10$; in particular, we cannot obtain a decrease in $f(x, \xi; c, z^*)$ since $z^* \leq -11$. Notice that in this case we have

$$\frac{b^T y_{AFF} - z^*}{c^T e - z^*} \leq \frac{12}{n + 8}, \qquad \text{clearly } 0\left(\frac{1}{n}\right).$$

It would therefore appear unlikely that we can prove polynomial convergence of the affine variant of Karmarkar's algorithm purely by considering his potential function.

Note

John Mitchell's research was partially supported by the U.S. Army Research Office through the Mathematical Sciences Institute of Cornell University. Michael Todd's research was partially supported by NSF Grant ECS-8602534.

References

Anstreicher, K. 1986. "A Monotonic Projective Algorithm for Fractional Linear Programming." *Algorithmica* 1:483–498.

Gay, D. 1987. "A Variant of Karmarkar's Linear Programming Algorithm for Problems in Standard Form." *Mathematical Programming* 37:81–90.

de Ghellinck, G., and J. P. Vial. 1986. "A Polynomial Newtonian Method for Linear Programming." *Algorithmica* 1:425–453.

Gonzaga, C. 1989. "Conical Projection Algorithm for Linear Programming." *Mathematical Programming* 43:151–173.

Karmarkar, N. 1984. "A New Polynomial Algorithm for Linear Programming." *Combinatorica* 4:373–395.

Steger, A. 1985. "An Extension of Karmarkar's Algorithm for Bounded Linear Programming Using Dual Variables." M.Sc. Thesis, Department of Applied Mathematics and Statistics, State University of New York at Stony Brook, Stony Brook, NY.

Todd, M., and B. Burrell. 1986. "An Extension of Karmarkar's Algorithm for Linear Programming Using Dual Variables." *Algorithmica* 1:409–424.

Vanderbei, R., M. Meketon, and B. Freedman. 1986. "A Modification of Karmarkar's Linear Programming Algorithm." *Algorithmica* 1:395–407.

Ye, Y. 1985. "K-Projection and Cutting-Objective Method for Linear Programming." Presentation at 12th Mathematical Programming Symposium, EES Department, Stanford University, Stanford, CA.

Ye, Y., and M. Kojima. 1987. "Recovering Optimal Dual Solutions in Karmarkar's Polynomial Algorithm for Linear Programming." *Mathematical Programming* 39:305–317.

9 Two-Terminal Steiner Tree Polyhedra

Michael O. Ball, Wei-Guo Liu, and William R. Pulleyblank

Given a directed graph G, a source node s and demand nodes t and r, a (directed) two-terminal Steiner tree is a minimal tree containing s, r, and t and whose arcs are directed from s toward r and t. We describe several different linear programming formulations of the problem of finding a minimum weight two-terminal Steiner tree, for the case of nonnegative weights. These include a "compact" representation, in which the number of inequalities and variables is polynomial in the size of G and all coefficients have values $0, 1, -1$, and a "natural" formulation having one variable for each arc of G but an exponential number of constraints whose coefficients can take on arbitrary values. We relate these formulations to the convex hull of the incidence vectors of the two-terminal Steiner trees as well as the dominant of this polytope.

9.1 Introduction

Let $G = (V, E)$ be a directed graph, and let s, t, r be three distinct nodes, where we think of s as a "source" node and t and r as "demand" nodes. A *two-terminal Steiner tree* in G (with respect to s, t, and r) is a minimal tree T in G that contains s, t, and r for which all the arcs are directed away from s. Thus its arc set is the union of the arc sets of directed paths in G from s to t and from s to r. Therefore the only nodes of G that can be incident with exactly one arc of T are s, t, and r, but even one of these nodes need not have degree one in the tree. See figure 9.1 for an illustration of the possible "topographies" of a two-terminal Steiner tree. We let uv denote the arc having tail u and head v. Suppose that each arc uv of G has a weight c_{uv}. We wish to find a directed Steiner tree for which the sum of the arc weights is minimum. If we permit negative cost arcs then the problem is NP-hard. For if we wish to determine, in a directed graph $G = (V, E)$, whether there exists a directed Hamilton path joining node s to node t, we can add a new node r and a new arc sr and then find a minimum cost two-terminal Steiner tree, where we give each arc a cost of -1. There will exist such a tree having cost $-|V|$ if and only if the desired Hamilton path exists.

A more general problem is that of finding a minimum cost k-terminal Steiner tree, where we now have a single source node s and a set $D \subseteq V \setminus \{s\}$ of demand nodes, where $|D| = k$. Even if we restrict our attention to nonnegative arc costs, this problem is NP-hard (Karp 1972) if we permit k

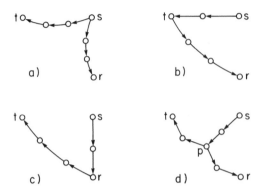

Figure 9.1
Two-terminal Steiner trees

to grow with $|V|$. However it can be solved easily in polynomial time if the number of demand nodes is sufficiently small or sufficiently large (see Hakimi 1971 also Lawler 1976). For suppose that we require $|D| \geq |V| - \rho$ for some fixed ρ. For each subset S of $V\backslash D$ containing s we construct a minimum cost spanning arborescence rooted at s on the subgraph of G induced by $D \cup S$. This can be done polynomially (Edmonds 1967). The number of these graphs is $2^{\rho-1}$ and the minimum over all of these will be the optimum solution.

If $|D| \leq \rho$ for fixed ρ, we can employ a similar method. For every pendent node of each Steiner tree must be a node of D and a tree having at most $\rho + 1$ pendent nodes can have at most $\rho - 1$ nodes having degree greater than two. So we consider each set W of at most $\rho - 1$ nodes from $V\backslash(D \cup \{s\})$. We find shortest paths between all pairs of nodes in $W \cup D$. We then construct an auxiliary graph on the node set $W \cup D \cup \{s\}$, taking these path lengths as arc costs, and find a minimum weight spanning arborescence rooted at s. The optimal solution will be the minimum of these, over all choices of W. Since there are fewer than $|V\backslash D|^\rho$ choices for W, again this total procedure is polynomial.

In two-terminal problems we can give a particularly simple instance of this procedure by observing that each of the topographies of figures 9.1a, b, c is a special case of that of figure 9.1d. A two-terminal Steiner tree consists of arc disjoint paths from s to some "splitter" node p plus paths from p to each of t and r. Figures 9.1a, b, c correspond to the cases $p =$

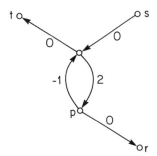

Figure 9.2

s, t, r, respectively. Thus the problem is solved by the following procedure:

For each $v \in V$ compute

$d^s(v) = $ cost of a shortest path from s to v,

$d^t(v) = $ cost of a shortest path from v to t,

$d^r(v) = $ cost of a shortest path from v to r.

Choose p so that $d^s(p) + d^t(p) + d^r(p)$ is minimized. The minimum cost two-terminal Steiner tree consists of shortest paths from s to p, from p to t, and from p to r.

This algorithm will correctly solve the problem if all arc costs are nonnegative. For in this case our choice of p ensures that shortest paths can be chosen that are internally disjoint, and so give the desired tree.

Note, however, that the nonexistence of negative cycles, a sufficient condition for the values $d^s(v)$, $d^t(v)$, and $d^r(v)$ to exist for all v, does not ensure a correct solution (see figure 9.2). The unique two-terminal Steiner tree has cost 2. However, if p is chosen as indicated, we will have $d^s(p) = 2$, $d^t(p) = -1$, and $d^r(p) = 0$, giving us a sum of 1.

We define a *two-terminal Steiner net* to be the union of directed paths in G from s to some node p and from p to t and r. The example of figure 9.2 is a two-terminal Steiner net. The preceding algorithm correctly finds a minimum cost two-terminal Steiner net, provided that no negative cycles exist. If all edges have nonnegative cost, then some zero cost arcs can be removed from a minimum cost two-terminal Steiner net to obtain a minimum cost two-terminal Steiner tree. If all arc costs are strictly positive, then every minimum cost Steiner net is a minimum cost Steiner tree.

It is easy to give an integer programming formulation of the minimum Steiner tree problem, even for general sets D of demand nodes when all arc costs are nonnegative. For each arc uv, we define a $0 - 1$ variable x_{uv} with the interpretation

$$x_{uv} = \begin{cases} 0 & \text{if } uv \text{ is not in the Steiner tree;} \\ 1 & \text{if } uv \text{ is in the Steiner tree.} \end{cases}$$

If all arc costs are nonnegative, then the problem becomes

minimize $\sum\limits_{uv \in E} c_{uv} x_{uv}$

$x_{uv} \in \{0, 1\}$ for all $uv \in E$,

$\sum (x_{uv} : u \in S, v \in V \backslash S) \geq 1$ for all $S \subseteq V$

such that $s \in S$ and $D \backslash S \neq \emptyset$.

Moreover, Prodon et al. (1985) showed that if G is series-parallel, then the linear relaxation of this problem has integer extreme solutions, for general D. However, for general graphs, this will not be the case, even for two-terminal problems. Figure 9.3 gives a particularly simple example. If $c_{st} = c_{sr} = c_{uv} = 1$ and all other $c_{ij} = 0$, then the linear relaxation has value $\frac{3}{2}$, whereas the integer program has value 2. Ericson et al. (1988) give a polynomial algorithm for the k-terminal Steiner tree problem for planar graphs with all terminals on a single face. This example also satisfies their conditions. Thus it would seem that the examination of stronger linear programming formulations is merited.

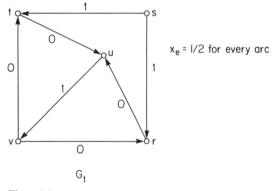

G_1

Figure 9.3

Our goal in this chapter is to treat the two-terminal problem for general graphs. We will give several different linear programming formulations of the problem. The first is obtained "directly" from the preceding algorithm, the second from the first by Gaussian elimination and the last from the second by projection.

Grötschel et al. (1981) proved essentially that whenever we have a class of optimization problems such that each instance can be solved polynomially, we "implicitly" have available a complete linear programming description of the problem. However, it remains a challenge to obtain this linear programming formulation explicitly, for particular instances. In addition it would be of great interest to have an automatic method for obtaining a linear programming formulation directly from a polynomial optimization algorithm. The results presented here are intended as a modest step in that direction.

9.2   Shortest Paths and Gaussian Elimination

We begin with the following linear program:

Maximize z

subject to

$$z \quad -d^s(u) \qquad -d^t(u) \qquad -d^r(u) \qquad \leq 0 \qquad \text{for all } u \in V,$$

$$-d^s(u) + d^s(v) \qquad\qquad\qquad \leq c_{uv} \qquad \text{for all } uv \in E,$$

$$d^t(u) - d^t(v) \qquad\qquad \leq c_{uv} \qquad \text{for all } uv \in E,$$

$$d^r(u) - d^r(v) \leq c_{uv} \qquad \text{for all } uv \in E,$$

$$d^s(s) = d^t(t) = d^r(r) = 0.$$

It is easy to see that if G has no negative cost arcs, then the optimum solution to this linear program gives the value of the optimum solution to the two-terminal Steiner tree problem. Moreover, if c is integer, then there exists an optimal solution which is integer valued. For it is a standard result of network flow theory that a feasible solution exists for the system

$$d(u) - d(v) \leq c_{uv} \qquad \text{for all } uv \in E,$$

$$d(t) = 0,$$

if and only if there are no negative cycles. And in this case $d(u)$ can be no greater than the length of a shortest path in G from u to t (see, e.g., Lawler 1976). (Both results follow by summing the inequalities for the arcs in a cycle or path.) Consequently, for each node u, $d^s(u) + d^t(u) + d^r(u)$ is no greater than the sum of the distances from s to u, u to t, and u to r and so the optimum value of z can be at most the smallest of these sums over all u. But if we let $d^s(u)$, $d^t(u)$, $d^r(u)$ be the distances, and let z be the smallest such sum of distances, exactly as computed by the algorithm of the previous section, then we get a feasible solution which attains this maximum value.

Let $A = (a_{ij} : i \in V, j \in E)$ be the node-arc incidence matrix of G, where we let $a_{ij} = +1$ if the tail of arc j is node i, and we let $a_{ij} = -1$ if the head of arc j is node i. Let I be an identity matrix, and let 1 be a vector all of whose components have value 1. The previous linear program can be rewritten as

maximize z

$$
\begin{aligned}
\text{subject to } z \cdot 1 \quad -d^s I \quad -d^t I \quad -d^r I \;\; &\le 0 \\
-d^s A \qquad\qquad\qquad &\le c \\
d^t A \qquad\qquad &\le c \\
d^r A \;\; &\le c
\end{aligned}
\tag{1}
$$

$$d^s(s) = d^t(t) = d^r(r) = 0.$$

For any $v \in V$, let $\varepsilon^v \in \mathbf{R}^V$ be the vector defined by

$$
\varepsilon_i^v = \begin{cases} 0 & \text{if } i \ne v, \\ 1 & \text{if } i = v. \end{cases}
$$

The dual linear program can be written as

minimize $cx^s + cx^t + cx^r$

$$
\begin{aligned}
\text{subject to } -Ax^s \qquad\qquad\qquad &-Iu = -\varepsilon^s \\
Ax^t \qquad\qquad &-Iu = -\varepsilon^t \\
Ax^r \quad -Iu &= -\varepsilon^r \\
1 \cdot u &= 1
\end{aligned}
\tag{2}
$$

$$x^s, x^t, x^r, u \ge 0.$$

(We obtain this form by observing that imposing the constraints $d^s(s) = d^t(t) = d^r(r) = 0$ on (1) is equivalent to deleting these variables from the formulation. This then is equivalent to deleting the corresponding constraints from the system (2). Since these constraints are linear combinations of other constraints, instead of deleting them, we can leave them in and define the right-hand sides to be the same linear combinations of the other right-hand sides.)

Since, as we observed, (1) has an integer optimum for any integer c for which an optimum exists, the system (2) is *totally dual integral* so all extreme solutions of (2) are integral valued (Edmonds and Giles 1984; Hoffman 1974). Hence every extreme solution can be interpreted as follows. For some node p, $u_p = 1$ but for all other nodes v, $u_v = 0$. The x^s variables constitute a flow from s to p of one unit; the x^t and x^r variables constitute flows of one unit from p to t and r, respectively. The objective value is minimized when the sums of the costs of these three unit flows is minimized. (Compare this with the algorithm of the previous section.)

Finally, we add "aggregate" variables

$$x_{uv} = x_{uv}^s + x_{uv}^t + x_{uv}^r$$

for all $uv \in E$. These new variables are unconstrained and each occurs in a unique equation, so our resulting system still has only integral extreme points. Let

$$P(G; s, t, r) = \{(x, x^r, x^s, x^t, u):$$

$$
\begin{array}{rrrrrl}
-Ix + & Ix^s + & Ix^t + & Ix^r & & = 0 \\
& -Ax^s & & & -Iu = & -\varepsilon^s \\
& & Ax^t & & -Iu = & -\varepsilon^t \quad\quad (3) \\
& & & Ax^r & -Iu = & -\varepsilon^r \\
& & & & 1 \cdot u = & 1
\end{array}
$$

$$x^s, x^t, x^r, u \geq 0\}.$$

Then $P(G; s, t, r)$ is a polyhedron with integral extreme points. Moreover $P(G; s, t, r)$ can be expressed as the sum of a polytope $N(G; s, t, r)$ and a cone $C(G; s, t, r)$. This cone is obtained by replacing the right-hand sides of the equations in (3) with 0. It is easy to see that $C(G; s, t, r)$ has a generator corresponding to each directed cycle of G—let x and one of x^s, x^t, x^r be the incidence vector of this cycle, and let all other variables be zero. Moreover, by our above remarks, if $(\hat{x}, \hat{x}^s, \hat{x}^t, \hat{x}^r, \hat{u})$ is a vertex of $P(G; s, t, r)$, that is, a vertex of $N(G; s, t, r)$, then it is obtained from a Steiner net as described above. This implies the following:

THEOREM 1   *The linear program, minimize cx, subject to $(x, x^r, x^s, x^t, u) \in P(G; s, t, r)$, satisfies the following:*

(i) If G has directed cycles for which the sum of the arc costs is negative, then the minimum is unbounded.

(ii) If there are no negative cycles with respect to c, then the x variables in an extreme optimum solution will be the incidence vector of a minimum cost Steiner net.

(iii) If $c \geq 0$, then the x variables in an extreme optimum solution will be the incidence vector of a minimum cost two-terminal Steiner tree.

We have achieved our objective of obtaining a linear programming formulation of the minimum cost two-terminal Steiner problem. Moreover both the number of variables and the number of constraints are polynomial in the size of G. However, we have many "superfluous" variables — x^s, x^t, x^r, and u. Most of the remainder of this chapter consists in describing how to eliminate them.

Eliminating auxiliary variables from a linear system is equivalent to projecting the associated polyhedron onto the subset of variables we wish to retain. Our projection approach has two parts. In this section we use Gaussian elimination to eliminate the x^s and u variables. (This is possible because of the equations in our system.) In the next section we project away the x^t and x^r variables.

THEOREM 2   *The following linear system defines the projection of $P(G; s, t, r)$ onto the x, x^t, x^r variables:*

$$-Ix + Ix^t + Ix^r \leq 0$$

$$-Ax \qquad\qquad\qquad \leq \varepsilon^t + \varepsilon^r - \varepsilon^s$$

$$-Ax + Ax^t \qquad\qquad = \varepsilon^r - \varepsilon^s \qquad\qquad\qquad (4)$$

$$-Ax + \qquad + Ax^r = \varepsilon^t - \varepsilon^s$$

$$x^t, x^r \geq 0.$$

Proof We start with the linear system (3). The constraint matrix and right-hand side have the following block form:

1:	$-I$	I	I	I	0	0
2:	0	$-A$	0	0	$-I$	$-\varepsilon^s$
3:	0	0	A	0	$-I$	$-\varepsilon^t$
4:	0	0	0	A	$-I$	$-\varepsilon^r$
5:	0	0	0	0	1	1

We consider the partition of the rows into the five sets, as indicated in the figure. We subtract the row sets 3 and 4 from the row set 2, add the row set 1 multiplied by A to row set 2, and obtain the following:

1:	I	I	I	I	0	0
2:	$-A$	0	0	0	I	$-\varepsilon^s + \varepsilon^t + \varepsilon^r$
3:	0	0	A	0	$-I$	$-\varepsilon^t$
4:	0	0	0	A	$-I$	$-\varepsilon^r$
5:	0	0	0	0	1	1

We now add the resulting row set 2 to each of 3 and 4 and subtract the sum of the rows in row set 2 from the single row that makes up row set 5. This gives the following:

1:	$-I$	I	I	I	0	0
2:	$-A$	0	0	0	I	$-\varepsilon^s + \varepsilon^t + \varepsilon^r$
3:	$-A$	0	A	0	0	$-\varepsilon^s + \varepsilon^r$
4:	$-A$	0	0	A	0	$-\varepsilon^s + \varepsilon^t$
5:	0	0	0	0	0	0

We can now interpret x^s and u as slack variables for the rows in row set 1 and 2, respectively, and we obtain the asserted equivalent form of the problem. ■

Thus we have obtained a second linear programming formulation of our problem involving substantially fewer variables.

Note that the second set of inequalities of (4) gives constraints only involving the x variables. For a set $S \subseteq V$, we let $\delta^+(S)$ denote the set of arcs having tails in S and heads not in S, and $\delta^-(S)$ denote the set of arcs having heads in S and tails not in S. We let $\delta^+(u)$ and $\delta^-(u)$ abbreviate $\delta^+(\{u\})$ and $\delta^-(\{u\})$ for $u \in V$. Then the second set of inequalities (4) is

$$-x(\delta^+(u)) + x(\delta^-(u)) \leq \begin{cases} 1 & u = t \text{ or } r, \\ -1 & u = s, \\ 0 & \text{otherwise.} \end{cases} \tag{5}$$

We call these *degree constraints*.

9.3   Projection and a Natural Formulation

The following technique, introduced in Balas and Pulleyblank (1983), uses the same principle as Bender's decomposition: Let

$P = \{(x, u) \in \mathbf{R}^{E \cup F}:$

$\quad Ax + Bu \leq c$

$\quad A'x + B'u = c'$

$\quad x \in Q, u \geq 0\}$

for some set Q. The projection X of P onto the space of the x variables is defined by

$X = \{x \in \mathbf{R}^E : \text{there exists } u \in \mathbf{R}^F \text{ such that } (x, u) \in P\}.$

Let $W = \{(w, w') : wB + w'B' \geq 0, w \geq 0, w' \text{ unrestricted}\}$. Let G be any set of generators of the cone W. That is, each $(w, w') \in W$ must be a positive linear combination of a finite set of members of G. Then

$X = \{x \in Q : (wA + w'A')x \leq wc + wc' \quad \text{for all } (w, w') \in G\}.$

Since every polyhedral cone has a finite set of generators, this provides a finite linear system whose solution set is X.

When applying this method, the difficult part is obtaining a finite set G of generators. When this has been obtained, the final linear system can be obtained immediately. The following is a useful and standard characterization.

PROPOSITION 1   Let $W = \{w : wB \geq 0\}$ be a cone, and let $G \subseteq W$. Then G is a set of generators of W if and only if the following conditions hold:

(i) Any $w \in W$ satisfying $wB = 0$ must be a linear combination of members g of G, each of which satisfies $gB = 0$.

(ii) For any $w \in W$ such that $wB \neq 0$, there must be some $g \in G$, also satisfying $gB \neq 0$, such that for any column b of B such that $wb = 0$, we also have $gb = 0$.

This means that, when dealing with W we can first consider the vectors w satisfying $wB = 0$. Our set of generators must include a basis for this linear space. Then we can consider the vectors w satisfying $wB \neq 0$. We obtain a sufficient set of these by ensuring that we have a representative for each maximal proper subset of the rows of B, such that some member of W satisfies the corresponding homogeneous equations.

If the only solution to $wB = 0$ is the zero vector, then W is said to be *pointed*. Suppose W is pointed, and let B' be a maximal subset of the columns of B such that $wB' = 0$, $wB'' > 0$ has a nonzero solution, where B'' is the submatrix consisting of the columns not in B'. Then $R = \{w \in W : wB' = 0\}$ forms an *extreme ray* of W. Then G is a set of generators of W if and only if G contains one member of each extreme ray.

Now we apply the projection method to the system of theorem 2. In this case our cone W becomes

$$W = \{(y, z, w) : yA \quad + wI \geq 0$$

$$zA + wI \geq 0$$

$$w \geq 0, \ y, z \text{ unrestricted}\}.$$

We can rewrite this cone in matrix form as

$$(y, z, w) \begin{pmatrix} A & 0 & 0 \\ 0 & A & 0 \\ I & I & I \end{pmatrix} \geq 0.$$

Since, for a connected directed graph G, each row of A is the negative of the sum of the other rows, we can choose an arbitrary value for one component of y and z, respectively. We require $y_r = 0$ and $z_t = 0$. By adding these two equations to W, we obtain a pointed cone, namely,

$C = \{(y, z, w) : y \in \mathbf{R}^V, z \in \mathbf{R}^V, w \in \mathbf{R}^E,$

$y_u - y_v \qquad\qquad + w_{uv} \geq 0 \qquad$ for all $uv \in E,$

$\qquad z_u - z_v \quad + w_{uv} \geq 0 \qquad$ for all $uv \in E,$

$\qquad\qquad\qquad w \;\geq 0$

$\qquad$ and $y_r = 0, z_t = 0\}.$

Therefore C can be generated by a set consisting of one element of each extreme ray. The constraint produced by a member (y, z, w) of C is

$$\pi x \geq \pi_0, \tag{6}$$

where

$\pi_{uv} = y_u - y_v + z_u - z_v + w_{uv} \qquad$ for all $uv \in E$

and

$\pi_0 = y_s + z_s.$

The "natural form" of the two-terminal Steiner tree polyhedron, the projection of $P(G; s, t, r)$ onto the x variables, is then

$T(G; s, t, r) = \{x \in \mathbf{R}^E :$

$$x(\delta^-(u)) - x(\delta^+(u)) \leq \begin{cases} -1 & u = s, \\ 1 & u = t \text{ or } r, \\ 0 & u \in V \backslash \{s, t, r\}, \end{cases}$$

$\pi x \geq \pi_0 \qquad$ for one member (y, z, w) of each extreme ray of $C,\Big\}$
$\qquad\qquad$ where π is defined as above

Hence the remaining problem is to determine the extreme rays of C. We first develop some necessary conditions for a ray to be extreme, as well as eliminate some constraints that are obviously redundant. In section 9.4 we will show that, for complete digraphs, all the rays satisfying the conditions given in this section generate facet-inducing inequalities for $T(G; s, t, r)$.

The following describes the extreme rays for the trivial case $y = 0$ and $z = 0$. For any $j \in E, \varepsilon^j \in \mathbf{R}^E$ is defined by

$$\varepsilon_k^j = \begin{cases} 1 & \text{for } k = j, \\ 0 & \text{for } k \in E \setminus \{j\}. \end{cases}$$

PROPOSITION 2   The vector $(0, 0, w) \in C$ belongs to an extreme ray if and only if $w = \alpha \varepsilon^{uv}$ for $uv \in E$ and $\alpha > 0$.

By formula (6), the vector $(0, 0, \varepsilon^{uv})$ for all $uv \in E$ produce the nonnegativity constraints

$$x_{uv} \geq 0 \qquad \text{for all } uv \in E. \tag{7}$$

Next we consider the case that $(y, z) \neq 0$. In particular, we will show that if (y, z, w) belongs to an extreme ray of C and $(y, z) \neq 0$, then the w variables are uniquely determined by the values of y and z.

LEMMA 1   If (y, z, w) belongs to an extreme ray of C and $(y, z) \neq 0$, then, for each arc uv, at least one of the following is true:

(i) $w_{uv} = 0$.

(ii) $y_u - y_v + w_{uv} = 0$.

(iii) $z_u - z_v + w_{uv} = 0$.

Proof   If all three are false for the arc uv, then let

$$\lambda = \min\{w_{uv}, y_u - y_v + w_{uv}, z_u - z_v + w_{uv}\}.$$

Let $\hat{w} = w - \lambda \varepsilon^{uv}$. We can easily check that $(y, z, \hat{w}) \in C, (y, z, \hat{w}) \neq 0$ since $(y, z) \neq 0$, and at least one more inequality corresponding to uv holds as an equation. This contradicts (y, z, w) belonging to an extreme ray. ∎

For any assignment of y, z values to the node set such that $y_r = 0$ and $z_t = 0$, we can let

$$w_{uv} = \max\{0, y_v - y_u, z_v - z_u\} \tag{8}$$

to obtain a member (y, z, w) of C. This member may not belong to an extreme ray, but lemma 1 shows that, for any member of an extreme ray with $(y, z) \neq 0$, (8) holds.

Consider an assignment of y and z to the node set V such that $y_r = 0$ and $z_t = 0$. We can extend our definition of w and π to all pairs of nodes. For any pair u, v of nodes, we let

$$w_{uv} = \max\{0, y_v - y_u, z_v - z_u\}, \tag{9}$$

$$\pi_{uv} = y_u - y_v + z_u - z_v + w_{uv}, \tag{10}$$

$$\pi_0 = y_s + z_s.$$

LEMMA 2   If $y, z \in \mathbf{R}^V$ and w, π are defined by (9) and (10), then π satisfies the triangle inequality, namely,

$$\pi_{uv} \leq \pi_{ui} + \pi_{iv} \qquad \text{for any } u, v, i \in V.$$

Proof   Without loss of generality, suppose that $w_{uv} = y_v - y_u$. Since $w_{ui} \geq y_i - y_u$ and $w_{iv} \geq y_v - y_i$, we have $w_{uv} \leq w_{ui} + w_{iv}$. Therefore

$$\pi_{ui} + \pi_{iv} = y_u - y_v + z_u - z_v + w_{ui} + w_{iv}$$

$$\geq y_u - y_v + z_u - z_v + w_{uv}$$

$$= \pi_{uv}. \quad \blacksquare$$

For a vector $\pi \in \mathbf{R}^E$ and a scalar π_0, if $\pi x \geq \pi_0$ is valid, then we let $F(\pi, \pi_0)$ denote the set of Steiner nets whose incidence vector x satisfy $\pi x = \pi_0$. For a subgraph H, we let $\pi(H)$ denote the value $\sum (\pi_{uv} : uv \text{ is an arc of } H)$.

Our next lemma shows that we need only consider a subset of the possible values for y and z.

LEMMA 3   Suppose that $y, z \in \mathbf{R}^V$ satisfy $y_r = z_t = 0$, and let w, π, π_0 be defined by (9) and (10). If the constraint $\pi x \geq \pi_0$ is not redundant for $T(G; s, t, r)$ and is not equivalent to a degree constraint (5) or a nonnegativity constraint, then

$$0 \leq y_v \leq y_s = y_t \quad \text{and} \quad 0 \leq z_v \leq z_s = z_r \qquad \text{for all } v \in V. \tag{11}$$

Proof   We prove the result for complete graphs. For if G is a spanning subgraph of the complete graph K_n, then $T(G; s, t, r)$ is the face of $T(K_n, s, t, r)$ obtained by requiring $x_j = 0$ for all arcs j of K_n not in G. Therefore a linear system sufficient to define $T(G; s, t, r)$ can be obtained from one that defines $T(K_n, s, t, r)$ by deleting the variables corresponding to the arcs of K_n not in G. All the resulting inequalities will satisfy (11), if they satisfy this for K_n.

So assume that $G = (V, E)$ is complete, that is, $uv \in E$ for all $u, v \in V$. Since $\pi x \geq \pi_0$ is not redundant and not a degree constraint, for any $v \in V$ there exists a vector $x^v \in T(G; s, t, r)$ such that $\pi x^v = \pi_0$ and

$$
x^v(\delta^+(v)) - x^v(\delta^-(v)) >
\begin{cases}
1 & \text{if } v = s, \\
-1 & \text{if } v = t, r, \\
0 & \text{otherwise.}
\end{cases}
$$

Because every vector in $T(G; s, t, r)$ is the sum of a convex combination of incidence vectors of Steiner nets and a positive combination of the incidence vectors of directed cycles, each of which satisfies $x(\delta^+(v)) - (\delta^-(v)) = 0$ for all $v \in V$, we can assume that x^v is a vertex of $T(G; s, t, r)$; that is, x^v is the incidence vector of a Steiner net having splitter node v. Let $Y^v = \{sv, vt, vr\}$. By lemma 2, $\pi_0 = \pi x^v \geq \pi(Y^v)$. Since $\pi(T) \geq \pi_0$ is valid for every Steiner net T, equality must hold, that is,

$$
(y_s - y_v + z_s - z_v + w_{sv}) + (y_v - y_t + z_v - z_t + w_{vt})
$$

$$
+ (y_v - y_r + z_v - z_r + w_{vr})
$$

$$
= y_s + z_s,
$$

and so $(w_{sv}) + (y_v - y_t + w_{vt}) + (z_v - z_r + w_{vr}) = 0$. Since each of the summands is nonnegative, they must all be zero. Therefore

$$
y_s \geq y_v \quad \text{and} \quad z_s \geq z_v \quad \text{for all } v \in V, \tag{12}
$$

$$
y_v \leq y_t \quad \text{and} \quad z_v \leq z_r \quad \text{for all } v \in V. \tag{13}
$$

When $v = s$, from (13) we have $y_t \geq y_s$ and $z_r \geq z_s$. When $v = t$ in (12), we have $y_s \geq y_t$ and $z_s \geq z_t = 0$. When $v = r$ in (12), we have $y_s \geq y_r = 0$ and $z_s \geq z_r$.

Let $v \in V \backslash \{s\}$. Our proof is complete if we show that $y_v \geq 0$, $z_v \geq 0$. Let T^v be the Steiner tree with arc set $\{sr, rv, vt\}$. We first show that $\pi(T^v) = \pi_0$. If there exists a Steiner net $T \in F(\pi, \pi_0)$ that contains rv, then by lemma 2, $\pi(T) \geq \pi(T^v)$. Since we must have $\pi(T^v) \geq \pi_0$, this gives the desired result. Suppose that no such T exists. Since $\pi x \geq \pi_0$ is not equivalent to a nonnegativity constraint, there exists $\hat{x} \in T(G; s, t, r)$ satisfying $\pi \hat{x} = \pi_0$, and $\hat{x}_{rv} > 0$. Therefore there exists a directed cycle P having incidence vector $\hat{x}$ which contains rv, and moreover $\pi \hat{x} = 0$, since any positive multiple of $\hat{x}$ can be added to $\hat{x}$ and we remain in $T(G; s, t, r)$. Since $\pi x \geq \pi_0$ is not equivalent to the degree constraint corresponding to r, there is a Steiner net $\tilde{T} \in F(\pi, \pi_0)$ for which r is the splitter node. Therefore $\pi(\tilde{T}) = \pi_0$. By lemma 2, $\pi_{sr} + \pi_{rt} \leq \pi(\tilde{T})$, so since $\{sr, rt\}$ is the arc set of a Steiner tree, we have $\pi_{sr} + \pi_{rt} = \pi_0$. But the portion of P from v to r, followed by the arc rt is a path from v to t. Therefore, by lemma 2, $\pi_{vt} \leq \pi\tilde{x} - \pi_{rv} + \pi_{rt} = \pi_{rt} - \pi_{rv}$. Hence $\pi(T^v) = \pi_{sr} + \pi_{rv} + \pi_{vt} \leq \pi_{sr} + \pi_{rt} = \pi_0$, so in fact $T^v \in F(\pi, \pi_0)$, a contradiction that establishes the claim.

Since $\pi_{sr} + \pi_{rv} + \pi_{vt} = \pi_0$, we have $y_s - y_t + z_s - z_t + w_{sr} + w_{rv} + w_{vt} = y_s + z_t$. Since $y_t = w_{sr} = 0$,

$$(-y_v + w_{rv}) + (y_v - y_t + w_{rt}) = 0.$$

Since both summands are nonnegative, we have $y_v = w_{rv} \geq 0$, as required. A similar argument shows that $z_v \geq 0$. ∎

We can now restrict our attention to those vectors in C that satisfy (11). Thus, based on the y values, we can form a partition $V_0, V_1, \ldots, V_m$ of V with $y_u = y_v$ for all $u, v \in V_k$. V_0 contains r, and all other v such that $y_v = 0$, V_1 contains all v with the smallest nonzero y_v value, etc., until V_m which contains s and t and all other v with maximum y_v value.

Similarly, we can partition V into $V^0, V^1, \ldots, V^n$ based on the values of the z variables.

For $(y, z, w) \in C$, we call V_i the ith y-level and V^i the ith z-level of (y, z, w).

We let V_i^j denote the node set $V_i \cap V^j$, and call it a block of (y, z, w). Note that although each y- or z-level is nonempty, a block may be empty.

For two nodes u and v in G, the y-distance between u and v is defined as

$$d_y(u, v) = |y_u - y_v|.$$

Also, for any $u \in V$, we let $d_y(u)$ denote $d_y(u, u_0)$ for some $u_0 \in V_0$. Similarly, we define z-distance

$$d_z(u, v) = |z_u - z_v|,$$

and

$$d_z(u) = d_z(u, u_0) \qquad \text{for some } u_0 \in V^0.$$

An arc uv is called a slope if $y_u \leq y_v$, $z_u \leq z_v$, and u, v are not in the same block. That is, at least one inequality must be strict. A slope is called an upper slope, a diagonal, or a lower slope, if

$$d_y(u, v) \geq d_z(u, v),$$

$$d_y(u, v) = d_z(u, v),$$

or

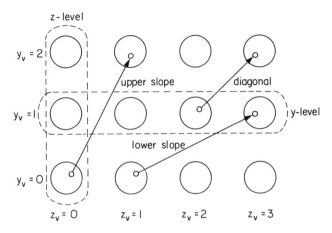

Figure 9.4

$d_y(u, v) \geq d_z(u, v),$

respectively (see figure 9.4).

Let $(\hat{y}, \hat{z}, \hat{w})$ and (y, z, w) be two members of C. We say that $(\hat{y}, \hat{z}, \hat{w})$ dominates (y, z, w) if the following are satisfied:

1. $y_v \leq y_u$ implies that $\hat{y}_v \leq \hat{y}_u$, and $z_v \leq z_u$ implies that $\hat{z}_v \leq \hat{z}_u$.

2. If uv is a diagonal, upper slope, or lower slope of (y, z, w), then uv is a diagonal, upper slope, or lower slope of $(\hat{y}, \hat{z}, \hat{w})$, respectively.

If the set of diagonals of $(\hat{y}, \hat{z}, \hat{w})$ properly includes the set of diagonals of (y, z, w), then we say that $(\hat{y}, \hat{z}, \hat{w})$ *strictly dominates* (y, z, w).

The next lemma shows that we do not need to include any dominated members of C in our set of generators of extreme rays.

LEMMA 4   If both (y, z, w) and $(\hat{y}, \hat{z}, \hat{w})$ in C satisfy (8) and $(\hat{y}, \hat{z}, \hat{w})$ dominates (y, z, w), then the equality set of (y, z, w) is a subset of the equality set of $(\hat{y}, \hat{z}, \hat{w})$.

Proof   Let $uv \in E$. If $w_{uv} = 0$, then $y_u \geq y_v$, $z_u \geq z_v$. Hence $\hat{y}_u \geq \hat{y}_v$ and $\hat{z}_u \geq \hat{z}_v$. This implies that $\hat{w}_{uv} = 0$.

If $y_u - y_v + w_{uv} = 0$, then we have three cases:

1. If $w_{uv} = 0$, then $y_u = y_v$. So we have $\hat{y}_u = \hat{y}_v$ and $\hat{w}_{uv} = 0$. Then $\hat{y}_u - \hat{y}_v + \hat{w}_{uv} = 0$.

2. If $w_{uv} > 0$, and $z_u \geq z_v$, then $y_u < y_v$, and so $\hat{y}_u \leq \hat{y}_v$ and $\hat{z}_u \geq \hat{z}_v$. Thus $\hat{y}_u - \hat{y}_v + \hat{w}_{uv} = 0$.

3. If $w_{uv} > 0$ and $z_u < z_v$, then uv is an upper slope of (y, z, w). So uv is also an upper slope of $(\hat{y}, \hat{z}, \hat{w})$. Thus again $\hat{y}_u - \hat{y}_v + \hat{w}_{uv} = 0$.

Similarly, $z_u - z_v + w_{uv} = 0$ implies that $\hat{z}_u - \tilde{z}_v + \hat{w}_{uv} = 0$. ∎

Lemma 4 indicates that we may find a set of generators of C with $(y, z) \neq 0$ by finding a set of vectors each of which is not strictly dominated by any other vector in C. Given a $(y, z, w) \in C$, we now proceed to define a cone Q. We will characterize undominated (y, z, w)'s in terms of properties of Q.

For a set $S \subseteq V$, we let $\delta(S)$ denote $\delta^+(S) \cup \delta^-(S)$. The cut $\delta_y(i) = \delta(\bigcup \{V_j : j \geq i\})$ is called the ith y-level cut. Similarly, $\delta_z(i) = \delta(\bigcup \{V^j : j \geq i\})$ is called the ith z-level cut. We let d_y^i denote the common value of $d_y(u, v)$, for all $u \in V_i$ and $v \in V_{i-1}$, and let d_z^i denote $d_z(u, v)$, $u \in V^i$ and $v \in V^{i-1}$. For an arc uv, let p^{uv} be the vector in $\mathbf{R}^{m+n}$ defined by

$$p_i^{uv} = \begin{cases} d_y^i & \text{if } 1 \leq i \leq m, \text{ and } uv \in \delta_y(i), \\ -d_z^{i-m} & \text{if } m + 1 \leq i \leq m + n, \text{ and } uv \in \delta_z(i - m), \\ 0 & \text{otherwise.} \end{cases}$$

Let P be the matrix having a row equal to p^{uv} for each slope uv. We have a natural row decomposition of P into

$$P = \begin{pmatrix} P_d \\ P_u \\ P_l \end{pmatrix},$$

where the rows of P_d, P_u, and P_l correspond to diagonals, strict upper slopes and strict lower slopes, respectively.

Consider the following cone:

$$Q = \{\lambda \in \mathbf{R}^{m+n} : P_d \cdot \lambda = 0,$$

$$P_u \cdot \lambda \geq 0,$$

$$P_l \cdot \lambda \leq 0,$$

$$\lambda \geq 0\}.$$

Since $\lambda = 1$ belongs to Q, any nonnegative vector, for which all components are equal belongs to Q. We call these the *trivial* members of Q.

Let $(y, z, w) \in C$ have y-levels $V_0, V_1, \ldots, V_m$ and z-levels $V^0, V^1, \ldots, V^n$. Then any nonnegative vector $\lambda \in \mathbf{R}^{m+n}$ determines a new vector $(\hat{y}, \hat{z}, \hat{w}) \in C$ by

$$\hat{y}_u = \begin{cases} 0 & \text{for all } u \in V_0, \\ \sum (\lambda_i d_y^i : 1 \leq i \leq j), & \text{for all } u \in V_j, \end{cases}$$

$$\hat{z}_u = \begin{cases} 0 & \text{for all } u \in V^0, \\ \sum (\lambda_{m+i} d_z^i : 1 \leq i \leq j), & \text{for all } u \in V^j, \end{cases} \tag{14}$$

$$\hat{w}_{uv} = \max\{0, \hat{y}_v - \hat{y}_u, \hat{z}_v - \hat{z}_u\}.$$

By the definition of Q and formula (14), we have the following:

LEMMA 5   Suppose that (y, z, w) and $(\hat{y}, \hat{z}, \hat{w})$ are both in C. $(\hat{y}, \hat{z}, \hat{w})$ dominates (y, z, w) if and only if $(\hat{y}, \hat{z}, \hat{w})$ is determined by (14) for some $\lambda \in Q$.

Combining lemmas 4 and 5, we have the following:

PROPOSITION 3   If (y, z, w) belongs to an extreme ray of C, then Q has only trivial members.

Proof   If $\lambda \in Q$ is nontrivial, then it determines, by (14), a ray $(\hat{y}, \hat{z}, \hat{w}) \neq 0$. By lemma 5 $(\hat{y}, \hat{z}, \hat{w})$ dominates (y, z, w) and by lemma 4 $(\hat{y}, \hat{z}, \hat{w})$ has a equality set no smaller than that of (y, z, w). Finally, since λ is not trivial, $(y, z, w) \neq \alpha(\hat{y}, \hat{z}, \hat{w})$ for any $\alpha \geq 0$. This contradicts (y, z, w) being extreme. ∎

Thus, if (y, z, w) belongs to an extreme ray, P has rank $m + n - 1$. Moreover we have the following:

PROPOSITION 4   If (y, z, w) belongs to an extreme ray, then rank $(P_d) = m + n - 1$.

Proof   If rank $(P_d) < m + n - 1$, then there exists a nontrivial solution to $P_d \cdot \lambda = 0, \lambda \geq 0, \lambda \in \mathbf{R}^{m+n}$. We can scale λ so that $\lambda \leq 1$. Let $(\hat{y}, \hat{z}, \hat{w})$ be given by (14). Since $\lambda \leq 1$, we know $d_y(u, v) \geq d_{\hat{y}}(u, v)$, and $d_z(u, v) \geq d_{\hat{z}}(u, v)$, for any two nodes u, v. We call a strict slope uv *odd*, if

$$(d_y(u, v) - d_z(u, v))(d_{\hat{y}}(u, v) - d_{\hat{z}}(u, v)) < 0.$$

Otherwise, we call uv *even*. If there is no odd slope, then λ is a nontrivial member of Q, so by proposition 3 (y, z, w) is not extreme. For any slope uv and any τ satisfying $0 \leq \tau \leq 1$, we define

$$\xi_{uv}(\tau) = (d_y(u, v) - d_z(u, v))\{[d_y(u, v) - \tau(d_y(u, v) - d_{\hat{y}}(u, v))]$$

$$- [d_z(u, v) - \tau(d_z(u, v) - d_{\hat{z}}(u, v))]\}.$$

If uv is a strict slope, then $\xi_{uv}(0) > 0$. If uv is even, then $\xi_{uv}(1) \geq 0$. And because ξ_{uv} is a linear function of τ, we have $\xi_{uv}(\tau) > 0$, for any $\tau \in (0, 1)$. If uv is odd, then $\xi_{uv}(1) < 0$. So there exists $\tau_{uv} \in (0, 1)$ satisfying $\xi_{uv}(\tau_{uv}) = 0$. Then for an odd slope uv and any $\tau \in [0, \tau_{uv})$, we have $\xi_{uv}(\tau) > 0$. Let

$$\tau_0 = \min\{\tau_{uv} : uv \text{ is an odd slope}\}.$$

Then $0 < \tau_0 < 1$, and for any strict slope, $\xi_{uv}(\tau_0) \geq 0$. Let

$$y_u^* = \begin{cases} 0 & \text{if } u \in V_0, \\ d_y(u) - \tau_0(d_y(u) - d_{\hat{y}}(u)) & \text{if } u \in V_i \text{ for } i \geq 1; \end{cases}$$

$$z_u^* = \begin{cases} 0 & \text{if } u \in V^0, \\ d_z(u) - \tau_0(d_z(u) - d_{\hat{z}}(u)) & \text{if } u \in V^i \text{ for } i \geq 1; \end{cases}$$

and

$$w_{uv}^* = \max\{0, y_v^* - y_u^*, z_v^* - z_u^*\}.$$

Then for $u \in V_j, j \geq 1$,

$$y_u^* = (1 - \tau_0)d_y(u) + \tau_0 d_{\hat{y}}(u)$$

$$= (1 - \tau_0)d_y(u) + \tau_0 \sum(\lambda_i d_y^i : 1 \leq i \leq j)$$

$$= \sum(((1 - \tau_0) + \lambda_i \tau_0)d_y^i : 1 \leq i \leq j).$$

Similarly, for $u \in V^j, j \geq 1$,

$$z_u^* = \sum(((1 - \tau_0) + \lambda_{i+m}\tau_0)d_z^i : 1 \leq i \leq j).$$

If we let

$$\lambda_i^* = (1 - \tau_0) + \tau_0\lambda_i, \qquad i = 1, \ldots, m + n,$$

then (y^*, z^*, w^*) is determined by λ^* using (14). Since λ^* is a convex combination of 1 and λ, we know that $P_d\lambda^* = 0$. And for every slope uv, we have $(p^{uv} \cdot 1)(p^{uv} \cdot \lambda^*) = (d_y(u, v) - d_z(u, v))(d_{y^*}(u, v) - d_{z^*}(u, v)) = \xi_{uv}(\tau_0) \geq 0$.

Therefore λ^* is in Q and is obviously nontrivial. This contradicts (y, z, w) being extreme. ∎

We now consider some particular rays and the corresponding constraints.

Suppose that $y \neq 0$ but $z = 0$, and suppose that there are $m + 1$ y-levels ($m \geq 1$). Since there is only one z-level, the only slopes in this case are upper slopes. So we have $Q = \mathbf{R}_+^m$. By proposition 3, if (y, z, w) belongs to an extreme ray, then $m = 1$, that is, there are exactly two y-levels.

Therefore we have

$$y_v = \begin{cases} 0 & v \in V_0, \\ \alpha & v \in V_1, \end{cases}$$

where $\alpha > 0$, and by lemma 3, $s, t \in V_1, r \in V_0$. Thus

$$\pi_{uv} = y_u - y_v + w_{uv} = \begin{cases} \alpha & u \in V_1 \text{ and } v \in V_0, \\ 0 & \text{otherwise,} \end{cases}$$

and

$$\pi_0 = y_s = \alpha.$$

The constraints are

$$x(\delta^+(S)) \geq 1 \qquad \text{for all } S \subseteq V, \text{ such that } s, t \in S \text{ and } r \in \bar{S}.$$

Similarly, in the case that $y = 0, z \neq 0$, we obtain the constraints:

$$x(\delta^+(S)) \geq 1 \qquad \text{for all } S \subseteq V, \text{ such that } s, r \in S \text{ and } t \in \bar{S}.$$

We call these constraints the *cut constraints*.

The next simple case is that both y and z have exactly two levels, that is, $m = 1$ and $n = 1$. By proposition 4, if (y, z, w) belongs to an extreme ray, then rank $(P_d) = 1$. But the only way an arc uv can be a diagonal is when $u \; V_0^0$ and $v \in V_1^1$. Hence, if we let (S, T) denote the set of all arcs uv with $u \in S, v \in T$, then $(V_0^0, V_1^1) \neq \varnothing$ and every arc in (V_0^0, V_1^1) is a diagonal. Thus we have

$$y_v = \begin{cases} 0 & \text{for all } v \in V_0, \\ \alpha & \text{for all } v \in V_1, \end{cases}$$

and

$$z_v = \begin{cases} 0 & \text{for all } v \in V^0, \\ \alpha & \text{for all } v \in V^1, \end{cases}$$

where $\alpha > 0$. We can set α to 1; then we obtain

$$\pi_{uv} = \begin{cases} 2 & uv \in (V_1^1, V_0^0), \\ -1 & uv \in (V_0^0, V_1^1), \\ 1 & uv \in \delta^+(V_1) \cup \delta^+(V^1) \backslash (V_1^1, V_0^0). \\ 0 & \text{otherwise,} \end{cases}$$

and

$$\pi_0 = 2,$$

where $s \in V_1^1, t \in V_1^0, r \in V_0^1$, and $(V_0^0, V_1^1) \neq \emptyset$. See figure 9.5. We call these (2×2) *constraints*.

More generally, we have $(m + 1) \times (n + 1)$ *constraints*. Each is generated by a vector $(y, z, w) \in C$ that satisfies

1. for any $v \in V_i^j$, $y_v = i$ for $i = 0, 1, \ldots, m$ and $z_v = j$ for $j = 0, 1, \ldots, n$, where $m, n \geq 1$, and

2. the arc set (V_{i-1}^{j-1}, V_i^j) is nonempty for all $i \in \{1, 2, \ldots, m\}$ and $j \in \{1, 2, \ldots, n\}$.

Then any arc in (V_{i-1}^{j-1}, V_i^j) is a diagonal. It is easy to see rank $(P_d) = m + n - 1$. For $u \in V_i^j$ and $v \in V_h^k$, we have

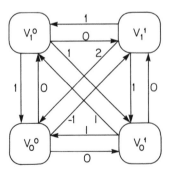

Figure 9.5
The (2×2) constraints

$$\pi_{uv} = \begin{cases} (k-j)+(h-i), & \text{if } k \geq j \text{ and } h \geq i, \\ k-j, & \text{if } k \geq j \text{ and } h \leq i \text{ or } k \leq j, h \leq i \text{ and } j-k \leq i-h, \\ h-i, & \text{if } h \geq i \text{ and } k \leq j \text{ or } k \leq j, h \leq i \text{ and } j-k \geq i-h, \end{cases}$$

and $\pi_0 = m + n$. So for an $(m + 1) \times (n + 1)$ constraint, the coefficients belong to the set

$$\{-m, -(m-1), \ldots, 0, 1, \ldots, m+n\}$$

if $m \leq n$.

We note that the cut constraints together with the degree constraints are sufficient to provide a valid integer programming formulation of the minimum cost two terminal Steiner tree problem when all costs are nonnegative. That is,

$$\text{minimize} \sum_{uv \in E} c_{uv} x_{uv}$$

subject to (5), (15), (15'), and $x_{uv} \in \{0, 1\}$ for all $uv \in E$ is a valid integer programming formulation. It is interesting to note that the linear programming relaxation of this integer program has only integer extreme point solutions for the graph of figure 9.3, whereas the cut-based Steiner tree formulation given in section 9.1 does not.

While the cut constraints and the $m \times n$ constraints have a relatively "nice" structure, we note that more complicated constraints also exist.

Let M be an $m \times n$ integer matrix, and let W be the cone $\{Mx \geq 0\}$. If we let K be the maximum determinant of a square submatrix of M, then there exists an integral generating set for W such that no component of any member of this generating set is greater than K^2. If M is an $m \times n$ matrix all of whose entries are $0, \pm 1$, then no submatrix can have determinant greater than $(\min(m, n))!$. Therefore we now can give a finite description of $T(G; s, t, r)$ based on this determinant bound. But this upper bound on the coefficient size grows exponentially with respect to the size of the graph, and the number of inequalities is very large because of the large number of possible y, z values. However, the following example shows that we cannot avoid this exponential behavior:

Let G_1 and G_2 be as in figure 9.6. In general, G_i be obtained from G_{i-1} by adding two new nodes and having a diagonal uv such that the π value of uv is the sum of the π values of the largest diagonals in G_{i-1} and G_{i-2} (see figure 9.7). It is easy to check that the diagonals indicated in the figure

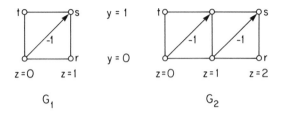

Figure 9.6
G_1 and G_2

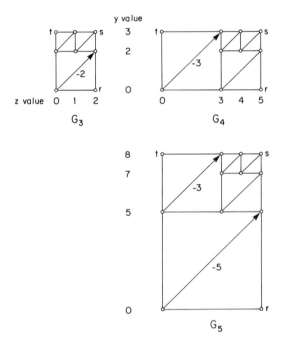

Figure 9.7
The exponentially growing coefficients

9.7 correspond to the linearly independent rows in P_d, that is, the indicated (y, z) and w determined by (8) satisfy the conditions in proposition 4. In general, G_i has $2(i + 1)$ nodes and a coefficient in the corresponding inequality equal in magnitude to the ith Fibonacci number, which grows exponentially with i. In the next section we will show that these inequalities are essential.

9.4   The Facets

In section 9.3, we described a large relatively complex linear system sufficient to define $T(G; s, t, r)$. In this section we restrict out attention to complete graphs and show that all of the inequalities in the system are facet inducing and hence essential. Note that the restriction to complete graphs is not important in the sense that just as every graph is a subgraph of a complete graph, for any $G = (V, E)$, $T(G; s, t, r)$ is the face of $T(K_n, s, t, r)$ for $n = |V|$ obtained by requiring $x_{uv} = 0$ for all (u, v) such that $uv \notin E$.

The system we obtained is the following:

$$T(G; s, t, r) = \{x \in \mathbb{R}^E : x_e \geq 0, \qquad \text{for all } e \in E; \tag{16}$$

$$x(\delta^+(u)) - x(\delta^-(u)) \geq \begin{cases} -1 & u = t, r, \\ 1 & u = s, \\ 0 & \text{otherwise;} \end{cases} \tag{17}$$

$$\pi x \geq \pi_0, \tag{18}$$

where $\pi_{uv} = y_u - y_v + z_u - z_v + w_{uv}$ for all $uv \in E$ and $\pi_0 = y_s + z_s$; y and z are vectors of nonnegative integers that satisfy $y_u \leq y_s = y_t, z_u \leq z_s = z_r, y_r = z_t = 0$; $w_{uv} = \max\{0, y_v - y_u, z_v - z_u\}$ for all $uv \in E$; and the condition in proposition 4 is satisfied$\}$.

First, we characterize the Steiner trees contained in $F(\pi, \pi_0)$ where $\pi x \geq \pi_0$ is an inequality (18).

An arc uv is called y-decreasing (y-increasing) if $y_v \leq y_u$ ($y_v \geq y_u$) and a path is called y-decreasing (y-increasing) if all arcs in it are y-decreasing (y-increasing). We define z-decreasing and z-increasing similarly.

A path is weakly y-decreasing and z-increasing (weakly y-increasing and z-decreasing) if every arc in the path is either a lower (upper) slope or a y-decreasing and z-increasing (y-increasing and z-decreasing) arc (see figure 9.8).

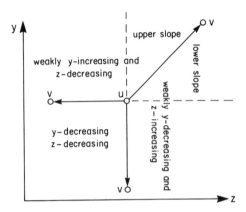

Figure 9.8

For a y-decreasing and z-decreasing arc uv, we have $w_{uv} = 0$ and $\pi_{uv} = y_u - y_v + z_u - z_v$.

For a weakly y-decreasing and z-increasing arc uv, we have $w_{uv} = z_v - z_u$ and $\pi_{uv} = y_u - y_v$.

For a weakly y-increasing and z-decreasing arc uv, we have $w_{uv} = y_v - y_u$ and $\pi_{uv} = z_u - z_v$. Therefore we have the following:

LEMMA 6   Let P be a directed $u - v$ path.

(i) If P is y-decreasing and z-decreasing, then

$$\pi(P) = y_u - y_v + z_u - z_v.$$

(ii) If P is weakly y-decreasing and z-increasing, then

$$\pi(P) = y_u - y_v.$$

(iii) If P is weakly y-increasing and z-decreasing, then

$$\pi(P) = z_u - z_v.$$

LEMMA 7   Let $\pi x \geq \pi_0$ be a constraint (18). Let T be a two-terminal Steiner tree with splitter node u. Then T is in $F(\pi, \pi_0)$ if and only if

(i) the path P_{su} from s to u in T is y-decreasing and z-decreasing.

(ii) the path P_{ur} from u to r in T is weakly y-decreasing and z-increasing.

(iii) the path P_{ut} from u to t in T is weakly y-increasing and z-decreasing.

Proof Suppose the conditions hold. By lemma 6, we have

$$\pi(T) = \pi(P_{su}) + \pi(P_{ur}) + \pi(P_{ut})$$

$$= (y_s - y_u + z_s - z_u) + (y_u - y_r) + (z_u - z_t)$$

$$= y_s + z_s = \pi_0.$$

Now we prove the necessity of our conditions. This we do by establishing five claims:

Claim 1 Any $s - u$ path P that is not y-decreasing and z-decreasing has

$$\pi(P) > y_s - y_u + z_s - z_u.$$

We prove by induction on the number of arcs in P. If P contains no more than one arc (which includes the case $u = s$), then, by lemma 3, it is always y-decreasing and z-decreasing. So the claim is trivially true. Now suppose that it is true for paths having no more than k arcs, and suppose that P has $k + 1$ arcs. Let v be the predecessor of u in P and let P' be the subpath of P from s to v.

Case 1 If P' is not y-decreasing and z-decreasing, then by induction,

$$\pi(P) > y_s - y_v + z_s - z_v.$$

Hence

$$\pi(P) = \pi(P') + \pi_{vu}$$

$$> y_s - y_u + z_s - z_u + w_{vu}$$

$$\geq y_s - y_u + z_s - z_u.$$

Case 2 If P' is y-decreasing and z-decreasing, then, by lemma 6,

$$\pi(P') = y_s - y_v + z_s - z_v.$$

But then vu cannot be y-decreasing and z-decreasing, so $w_{vu} > 0$. Hence

$$\pi(P) = \pi(P') + \pi_{vu}$$

$$> y_s - y_u + z_s - z_u.$$

Claim 2 If P_{su} is not y-decreasing and z-decreasing, then T is not in $F(\pi, \pi_0)$.

By lemma 2, $\pi(P_{ur}) \geq \pi_{ur}$. By lemma 3, $z_u \leq z_r$ and $y_u \geq y_r = 0$. So

$\pi(P_{ur}) \geq \pi_{ur} = y_u.$

Similarly,

$\pi(P_{ut}) \geq \pi_{ut} = z_u.$

Hence, by claim 1,

$$\pi(T) = \pi(P_{su}) + \pi(P_{ur}) + \pi(P_{ut})$$

$$> y_s - y_u + z_s - z_u + z_u + y_u$$

$$= y_s + z_s = \pi_0.$$

Claim 3   Any $u - r$ path P that is not weakly y-decreasing and z-increasing has

$\pi(P) > y_u.$

We prove by induction on the number of arcs in P. When $u = r$, P is y-decreasing and z-increasing, and the claim is trivially true. Suppose that the claim is true for paths having no more than k arcs, and suppose that P has $k + 1$ arcs. Let v be the successor of u in P, and let P' be the subpath of P from v to t.

Case 1   If P' is not weakly y-decreasing and z-increasing, then, by induction, $\pi(P') > y_v$. Then

$$\pi(P) = \pi_{uv} + \pi(P)$$

$$> y_u - y_v + z_u - z_v + w_{uv} + y_v$$

$$\geq y_u.$$

Case 2   If P' is weakly y-decreasing and z-increasing, then, by lemma 6, $\pi(P') = y_v$. But then uv is neither y-decreasing and z-increasing nor a lower slope. There are two possibilities:

(i) uv is y-decreasing and strictly z-decreasing. Then

$w_{uv} = 0$

and

$\pi_{uv} = y_u - y_v + z_u - z_v > y_u - y_v$

(ii) uv is z-decreasing and strictly y-increasing, or uv is a strict upper slope. Then

$$y_u - y_v + w_{uv} = 0$$

and

$$z_u - z_v + w_{uv} > 0.$$

Hence

$$\pi_{uv} > y_u - y_v.$$

So, in both cases, we have

$$\pi(P) = \pi_{uv} + \pi(P') > y_u - y_v + y_v = y_u.$$

We establish the following by methods similar to these used to prove claim 2:

Claim 4   If P_{ur} is not weakly y-decreasing and z-increasing, then T is not in $F(\pi, \pi_0)$.

Symmetrically, we obtain the following:

Claim 5   If P_{ut} is not weakly y-increasing and z-decreasing, then T is not in $F(\pi, \pi_0)$.

This completes the proof. ∎

Using this lemma, for each inequality (16)–(18), we can construct a member x of $T(G; s, t, r)$ such that the inequality is slack. Therefore $T(G; s, t, r)$ is of full dimension. Moreover, for $|V| \geq 5$, let $ax \geq \alpha$ be an inequality (16) or (17). For each other inequality $\phi x \geq \phi_0$ (16)–(18), we can construct $x \in T(G; s, t, r)$ such that $ax = \alpha$ but $\phi x > \phi_0$. This shows that each inequality (16) and (17) induces a distinct facet.

THEOREM 3   Every constraint $\pi x \geq \pi_0$ of (18) induces a distinct facet.

Proof   We prove this result by showing that, for any constraint $\phi x \geq \phi_0$ of (16)–(18), there exists a two-terminal Steiner net T such that $T \in F(\pi, \pi_0)$ but $T \notin F(\phi, \phi_0)$.

From lemma 7 we know that

(i) for every arc $e = uv$, $v \neq s$, there is a tree $T \in F(\pi, \pi_0)$ containing e, and

(ii) for every node $u \in V$, there is a tree $T \in F(\pi, \pi_0)$ such that u is the splitter node of T.

For any arc vs, if $y_s - y_v \geq z_s - z_v$, then $w_{vs} = y_s - y_v$; hence $\pi_{vs} = z_v - z_s$. So, if we let $T_{vs} = \langle sv, vr, vs, st \rangle$, then

$$\pi(T_{vs}) = (y_s - y_v + z_s - z_v) + y_v + (z_v - z_s) + z_s = \pi_0.$$

Symmetrically, if $z_s - z_v \geq y_s - y_v$, then $T = \langle sv, vt, vs, sr \rangle$ is in $F(\pi, \pi_0)$. Hence for any arc vs, we have a Steiner net $T_{vs} \in F(\pi, \pi_0)$ such that $vs \in T_{vs}$. Therefore $F(\pi, \pi_0)$ is not contained in $F(\phi, \phi_0)$, where $\phi x \geq \phi_0$ is an inequality (16) or (17).

Now let $\pi x \geq \pi_0$ and $\phi x \geq \phi_0$ be two constraints (18) produced by (y, z, w) and (y', z', w'), respectively. Suppose that $F(\pi, \pi_0) \subseteq F(\phi, \phi_0)$. We are going to prove that $F(\pi, \pi_0) = F(\phi, \phi_0)$, and in fact $\pi x \geq \pi_0$ is a positive multiple of $\phi x \geq \phi_0$.

Claim 1   If $y_u \leq y_v$, then $y'_u \leq y'_v$.

Case 1   If we also have $z_u \leq z_v$, then vu is y-decreasing and z-decreasing. By lemma 7,

$$T = \langle sv, vu, ur, ut \rangle \in F(\pi, \pi_0).$$

Hence $T \in F(\phi, \phi_0)$. By the necessity part of lemma 7, vu is y'-decreasing and z'-decreasing, that is, $y'_u \leq y'_v$.

Case 2   If we have $z_u > z_v$, then, uv is y-increasing and z-decreasing. Hence

$$T = \langle su, uv, vt, ur \rangle \in F(\pi, \pi_0) \subseteq F(\phi, \phi_0).$$

By lemma 7, uv is either *y'-increasing and z'-decreasing or an upper slope of* (y', z', w'). In both cases uv is y'-increasing, that is, $y'_u \leq y'_v$.

Similarly, we can prove the following:

Claim 2   If $z_u \leq z_v$, then $z'_u \leq z'_v$.

By claims 1 and 2, if uv is a slope of (y, z, w), then uv is also a slope of (y', z', w'). Moreover, if uv is an upper slope, then by lemma 7, $T = \langle su, ur, uv, vt \rangle \in F(\pi, \pi_0) \subseteq F(\phi, \phi_0)$. Since uv is a slope of (y', z', w'), by lemma 7, uv is an upper slope of (y', z', w'). Therefore we have the following:

Claim 3   If uv is an upper slope of (y, z, w), then uv is an upper slope of (y', z', w').

Similarly, we have the following:

Claim 4   If uv is a lower slope of (y, z, w), then uv is a lower slope of (y', z', w'). Combining claims 3 and 4, we have our final claim.

Claim 5   If uv is a diagonal of (y, z, w), then uv is a diagonal of (y', z', w').

Hence, (y', z', w') dominates (y, z, w). By lemma 5, (y', z', w') is determined by a $\lambda \in Q$. But, since (y, z, w) satisfies the condition of proposition 4, Q has only one trivial member. So $(y', z', w') = k(y, z, w)$, where k is a nonnegative number. Therefore (ϕ, ϕ_0) is a positive multiple of (π, π_0). ∎

9.5   Conclusions

We have given three different linear programming formulations of the problem of finding a minimum cost two-terminal Steiner tree for the case that all arcs have nonnegative cost. (See theorems 1 and 2 and the linear system given by (16)–(18)). The formulation of theorem 2 is the simplest, in that it has only $3|E|$ variables and $|E| + 3|V|$ constraints. We call such a formulation, in which the number of variables and constraints is polynomial in the size of the input of the original problem, a *compact* formulation.

The formulation (16)–(18) of $T(G; s, t, r)$ is a *natural* formulation in that it has the minimum possible number of variables, one for each arc of the graph. However, as we have seen, both the number of inequalities and the magnitudes of the coefficient in these inequalities can grow exponentially with the size of the input. Nevertheless, in general, these formulations may be more useful computationally when they are used with constraint generation techniques.

We conclude by discussing this formulation (16)–(18) of $T(G; s, t, r)$ from a polyhedral point of view. Suppose we are given G, s, t, and r. Consider the following four polyhedra:

T = the convex hull of the incidence vectors of the two-terminal Steiner trees,

N = the convex hull of the incidence vectors of the two-terminal Steiner nets,

C = the cone generated by the incidence vectors of all directed cycles in G,

P = the nonnegative orthant in $\mathbf{R}^E$.

When we permit negative cost arcs, then optimizing over T or N includes the problem of determining when a directed graph has a directed Hamiltonian path, so it is probably very difficult to give a reasonable description of a linear system sufficient to define T or N.

The polyhedron $T(G; s, t, r)$ we studied is equal to $N + C$. As we saw, if G has no negative cost cycles (i.e., directed cycles the sum of whose arc costs is negative), then minimizing over $T(G; s, t, r)$ is equivalent to minimizing over N. If G has no negative cost arcs, then minimizing over N is equivalent to minimizing over T.

The dominant of T or N, denoted by $\mathrm{dom}(T)$, $\mathrm{dom}(N)$ is the polyhedron obtained by adding P. That is, $\mathrm{dom}(T) = T + P$; $\mathrm{dom}(N) = N + P$. These polyhedra also have the property that if all arc costs are nonnegative, then minimizing over them is equivalent to minimizing over T or N.

However, in a sense they are not as good as $N + C$ or $T + C$, for if any arc has negative cost, then the minimum over the dominant is unbounded, while there must be a negative cycle for the minimum over $N + C$ or $T + C$ to be unbounded. However, the fact that $N + C$ has a complex polyhedral description does not in itself guarantee that $\mathrm{dom}(N)$ or $\mathrm{dom}(T)$ must have a complex description. In particular, the inequalities we generate usually contain negative coefficients, which means that they are not valid for the dominant. It can, however, be shown that the inequalities in our defining system for $T(G; s, t, r)$ also induce facets of T, so that in this sense they are intrinsic to the problem, and are not simply a byproduct of extending by C instead of P.

Finally, we exhibit a family of facet-inducing inequalities for $\mathrm{dom}(T)$ that show that this polyhedron also has nonsimple facets.

Consider the graph G_1 of figure 9.3 and the constraint.

$$x_{st} + x_{sr} + x_{ab} \geq 2. \tag{19}$$

There are only three Steiner trees in this graph, namely,

$$T_1 = \langle st, sr \rangle,$$

$$T_2 = \langle st, ta, ab, br \rangle,$$

$$T_3 = \langle sr, ra, ab, bt \rangle.$$

All of them satisfy (19) with equality. We can easily prove that (19) is a facet-inducing inequality for the dominant of the two-terminal Steiner tree polytope of G_1. For example, we can list $|E| = 7$ affinely independent

vectors in the face induced by (19) by giving the incidence vectors of the
following sets:

$$T_1, T_1 \cup \{ta\}, T_1 \cup \{ra\}, T_1 \cup \{br\}, T_2, T_3, T_1 \cup \{bt\}.$$

Note that a new arc appears in each of the first six trees and that, while
the first six satisfy $x(\delta^-(t)) = 1$, the last one does not.

We can glue two copies of G_1 together to obtain the graph G_2 (figure 9.9)
and obtain the following valid constraint:

$$x_{st_1} + x_{sr} + x_{a_1b_1} + x_{t_1t} + x_{t_1b_1} + x_{a_2b_2} \geq 3. \tag{20}$$

Using the same method as for G_1, we can easily prove that (20) is again
facet inducing. This glueing process can be carried out in a number of ways.
For example, we can construct G_3 as shown in figure 9.10.

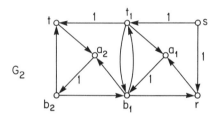

Figure 9.9

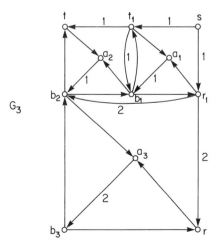

Figure 9.10

The constraint has the right-hand side equal to 5, and the positive coefficients are shown in the figure. Still the constraint induces a facet. This proces can be continued as long as desired. From the examples we can also see that the exponentially large coefficients can occur in some facet-inducing constraints of the dominant.

It may be of particular interest to consider the case where G is acyclic. In this case $N + C = N$ and $T + C = T$. Hence, for any set of arc costs, we can find a minimum cost two-terminal Steiner net, and if arc costs are nonnegative, there will also exist a minimum cost Steiner tree (see Liu 1988).

Note

Supported by the joint research project "Combinatorial Optimization" of the Natural Science and Engineering Research Council Canada (NSERC) and the German Research Association (Deutsche Forschungsgemeinschaft, SFB 303), plus an NSERC operating grant.

References

Balas, E., and W. Pulleyblank. 1983. "The Perfect Matchable Subgraph Polytope of a Bipartite Graph." *Networks* 13:495–516.

Edmonds, J. 1967. "Optimum Branchings." *Journal of Research of the National Bureau of Standards* 71B:233–240.

Edmonds, J., and R. Giles. 1984. "Total Dual Integrality of Linear Inequality Systems." In *Progress in Combinatorial Optimization*, edited by W. R. Pulleyblank for the Silver Jubilee Conference, University of Waterloo, 1982. Toronto: Academic Press, 117–129.

Erickson, R. E., C. L. Momma, and A. F. Veinott. 1988. "Minimum-Concave-Cost-Network Flows." *Mathematics of Operations Research* (forthcoming).

Grötschel, M., L. Lovász, and A. Schrijver. 1981. "The Ellipsoid Method and its Consequences in Combinatorial Optimization." *Combinatorica* 1:169–197 [corrigendum: 4(1984):291–295].

Hekimi, S. 1971. "Steiner's Problem in Graphs and Its Implications." *Networks* 1:113–133.

Hoffman, A. J. 1974. "A Generalization of Max-Flow–Min-Cut." *Mathematical Programming* 6:352–359.

Karp, R. M. 1972. "Reductibility among Combinatorial Problems." In *Complexity of Computer Computations*, edited by R. E. Miller and J. W. Thatcher, New York: Plenum, 85–104.

Lawler, E. 1976. *Combinatorial Optimization: Networks and Matroids*. London: Holt, Rinehart and Winston.

Liu, W.-G. 1988. "Extended Formulations and Polyhedral Projection." Ph.D. dissertation. University of Waterloo.

Prodon, A., T. M. Liebling, and H. Gröfflin. 1985. "Steiner's Problem on Two-Trees." Technical Report RO 850315. Lausanne: Département de Mathématiques, Ecole Polytechnique Féderale.

10 Solving Arborescent Linear Programs with Nested Decomposition

Olivier Janssens de Bisthoven and Etienne Loute

Linear programming used as a modeling technique in large-scale organizations leads to very large problems by today's standards, particularly when multidivisional, dynamic, and stochastic aspects are taken into account. We consider a solution technique based on a recursive use of primal decomposition applied to an arborescent organization of the problem data. Data structuring is discussed in the chapter. We briefly recall the basics of nested decomposition, focusing on implementation aspects, namely, computational data structures and computational strategies. We point out ways to circumvent the problem raised by the reconstruction of the solution in terms of the original variables. A full-scale implementation based on a modular commercial LP software is presented along with numerical experience.

10.1 Introduction

When linear programming is used as a modeling technique in a large organization, the following process is frequently observed: first, static models for specific or typical entities of the organization are set up; then these submodels are either linked or expanded over time. When sufficiently refined, static submodels usually fit in the medium-size LP problem class, that is, from a few hundred to close to a thousand rows (size classification is traditionally based on the number of rows). Most models in that class are sparse, that is, only a few percent of the constraint matrix entries are nonzero.

Linked and time-phased submodels give rise to large-size LP problems, that is, from a few thousand to close to ten thousand row. In addition to sparseness with a density of nonzero elements less than 1 percent, the constraint matrix has its nonzero elements naturally grouped in some submatrices. Such a matrix is said to be *block structured*, or to exhibit a *block structure*. For example, a *multidivisional* or *multiregional* version of a static model has the block structure depicted in figure 10.1, a block structure referred to as *block-angular* or *primal block-angular*. A *dynamic, multiperiod*, or *time-phased* version of a model will exhibit the block structure of figure 10.2, the so-called *staircase structure*. If there is a time lag of more than a period for the variables within the constraints of a particular period,

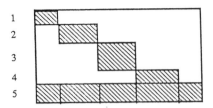

Figure 10.1

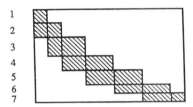

Figure 10.2

this may result in extra subdiagonals of blocks. A complete *lower block triangular* matrix can be obtained when the time lag is maximum.

Linking time-phased submodels gives rise to even larger problems, a class that one would call very large-size LP with a number of rows exeeding 10,000. Figure 10.3 depicts the block structure of a model resulting in linking two-divisional models over three periods. One might query the usefulness and tractability of such models. Generating and managing their data is a tremendous task (a 20,000 by 40,000 constraint matrix with a nonzero density of 0.1 percent has 800,000 nonzero elements). However, most of the data collection and validation can be done when tuning up the submodels. Setting up the full models only requires generating and validating the data used in the linkage. The usefulness of a refined submodel formulation and solution is frequently questioned. Working with aggregated submodels is not always an effective alternative because it requires going through a new data validation process and then provides a solution that is not always implementable or even meaningful. Aggregation contributes to drastic changes in the solution under sensitivity analysis, whereas such changes are smoothed in a refined formulation. Note that it is frequent that little information is ever used from the solution of a very large detailed model.

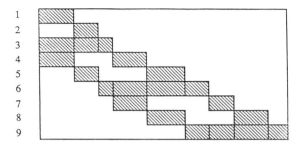

Figure 10.3

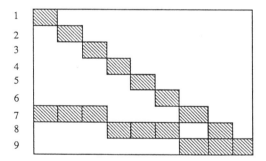

Figure 10.4

Dealing with uncertainty, particularly in time-phased models, leads potentially to extremely large problems. Indeed, the recourse formulation in stochastic linear programming with discrete random data leads to a block structured matrix whose transpose in similar to the matrix depicted in figure 10.4 (a three-period model with two and three realizations of the random data at the second and third periods, respectively).

Improving solution techniques for LP problems is a very popular research subject, particularly methods that are not based on the simplex method. However, practically all currently available software (academic or commercial) implements variants of the revised simplex algorithm with a product from representation for the basis inverse and with a column-oriented internal data representation. Medium-size problems are easily solved, even on microcomputers, with most codes. Solving large-size problems is beyond the capabilities of academic codes. Good commercial packages used on superminis or mainframes are adequate. Once the number of row grows above 10,000, most solvers run into numerical trouble if they do not reach their logical limits (i.e., typically, maximum number of rows) which are frequently hard-wired in the code (when written in assembler). A modeler who generates a very large-size LP must be aware of this.

This situation is difficult to accept, particularly when the problem has a nice block structure. Unless new nonsimplex-based methods offer a breakthrough, there are basically two approaches to improve the solution process by exploiting a block structure. The first one is to specialize the revised simplex algorithm to the particular block structure, which means a particular substitute for the basis inverse with an appropriate update. However, unless special pricing techniques are used, the number of simplex iterations remains unchanged and no gain can be expected for what is the major part in the computational burden of each iteration, that is, pricing out the nonbasic variables. Another major drawback is that the compact basis inverse schemes for block structured problems are quite elaborate. Since the basis inverse data structures are central to any revised simplex code, a major recoding effort must be undertaken, with a resulting code of an order of magnitude more complex. A completely different approach, called decomposition, consists of replacing the solution of the original problem by the repeated solution of a series of coordinated smaller problems, called subproblems, until an optimal coordination is obtained. Subproblems are naturally related to the blocks of the problem block structure. This approach offers several advantages. Most of the computational effort is in solving the subproblems. Because they are from medium to maybe large size, one can rely on existing software. Only the coordination scheme requires development of specific software. Since the data has to be generated on a subproblem basis, it is quite possible to use generators specific to different submodels. A major drawback is that decomposition methods to not lend themselves easily to postoptimal analysis. For a modeling team facing the prospect of very large-size problems, decomposition currently seems the only viable approach.

This chapter describes the development of a nested decomposition method up to its computer implementation. The resulting code, named LIFT/2, has been used in economic studies to solve problems, that were otherwise not tractable due to their size. In section 10.2 we use a graph model of the problem block structure to define an arborescent organization of the blocks to which nested decomposition can be applied (section 10.3).

Section 10.4 is devoted to implementation aspects, in particular data structures. We present in the same section various computational strategies
aimed at speeding up convergence. The construction of a nested decomposition code, using algorithmic tools of a modular mathematical programming commercial package, is discussed in section 10.5. Computational
experience is reported in section 10.6.

10.2 Block-Structured Matrices

Let A be an $m \times n$ matrix with $M = \{1, \ldots, m\}$ its set of row indices and
$N = \{1, \ldots, n\}$ its set of column indices. A_{MN} denotes the entire matrix.
Given M_K a subset of M and N_k a subset of N, $A_{M_k N_k}$ denotes the submatrix
of A whose elements are common to rows of indices in M_k and to columns
of indices in N_k.

A *block structure* of a matrix A_{MN} is a set of pair of subsets of M and N,
$\mathscr{B} = \{(M_k, N_k) | k \in P\}$ such that

1. $N_k \subseteq N$ and $N_k \neq 0 \ \forall k \in P$.

2. $M_k \subseteq M$ and $M_k \neq 0 \ \forall k \in P$. Moreover $\{M_k | k \in P\}$ is a partition of M.

3. The nonzero elements of A must be contained in the submatrices $A_{M_k N_k}$,
$k \in P$.

The set P appearing in the definition of $\mathscr{B}$ is the set of block indices:
$P = \{1, \ldots, p\}$ with $p \leq m$. Because $\{M_k | k \in P\}$ must be a partition of M,
this definition is row oriented. We do not need a column oriented definition.
Hence we use the term "block structure" instead of "row block structure."
As an example of a block structure consider $\mathscr{B} = \{(M_k, N_k) | k \in P\}$, where
$N_p = N$ and $N_i \cap N_j = 0$ for $i, j \in P \setminus \{p\}$, $i \neq j$. This is the primal block
angular structure as illustrated by figure 10.1 with $p = 5$. The hacked
submatrices correspond to the submatrices $A_{M_k N_k}$. A staircase block structure corresponds to the case where the sets N_k in the definition of $\mathscr{B}$ verify
$N_i \cap N_j = 0 \ \forall_{i,j} \in P$ with $|i - j| \geq 1$.

Identifying a particular block structure by appropriate row and column
permutation and grouping is a problem that is not considered here (e.g.,
see Weill and Kettler 1971). This is not an easy problem to tackle. We
assume a block structure comes naturally from the model behind the
problem. However, we will consider some restructuring within a given
block structure, such as merging blocks in larger ones.

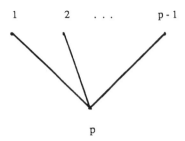

Figure 10.5

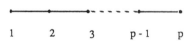

Figure 10.6

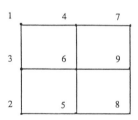

Figure 10.7

With a block structure $\mathscr{B}$ of a matrix A_{MN}, we associate an undirected graph $\Gamma(P, R)$, called the *the overlapping graph* of the block structure. The nodes of the graph are associated with the blocks and the set of edges R is defined as follows:

$$R = \{(s, t) | s \in P, t \in P, s \neq t \text{ and } N_s \cap N_t \neq 0\}.$$

Overlapping graphs corresponding respectively to a block angular structure and to a staircase structure are depicted in figures 10.5 and 10.6. For a full lower block triangular matrix, the overlapping graph is a complete graph. Figures 10.7 and 10.8 give the overlapping graph corresponding respectively to the multidivisional and multiperiod structure of figure 10.3 and to the three-period stochastic structure of figure 10.4.

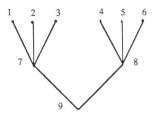

Figure 10.8

The solution technique developed in the next section require a particular ordering of the block structure. We denote by "$\geq$" a partial order on the set P (i.e., a reflexive antisymmetric and transitive binary relation in P). Given s and t in P, "$s \geq t$" (or "$t \leq s$") is equivalently read s is a successor of t, s follows t and t precedes s or t is a predecessor of s. With the symbol $\succ$ ($\prec$) used as relational operator the meaning is the same with in addition s and t distinct. The partially ordered set P will be written $(P, \geq)$ whenever it will be necessary to indicate the partial order being used.

Two sets can be defined for each k in $(P, \geq)$. These are, respectively, P_k *the set of predecessors of k in P,*

$$P_k = \{\kappa | \kappa \in P, k \geq \kappa\},$$

and S_k *the set of successors of k in P,*

$$S_k = \{\kappa | \kappa \in P, \kappa \geq k\}.$$

We denote by $\bar{P}_k$ and $\bar{S}_k$, respectively, the sets $P_k \backslash \{k\}$ and $S_k \backslash \{k\}$.

A partial order is said to be *hierarchical* if for any $k \in P$, the set of its successors S_k is a chain. A *chain* is a subset of $(P, \geq)$ whose elements are all related, that is, a totally ordered set. It is evident that hierarchical orders in P induce hierarchical orders in any subset of P. From now on, we consider only hierarchical orders.

An element t of P is said to be *minimal* if for all $k \in P$ either t and k are not related or $t \leq k$. $P_{\min}$ is defined to be the set of all minimal elements of P. The definition of a *maximal* element and the definition of $P_{\max}$ are similar.

Given any $k \in P \backslash P_{\max}$, k^+ designates an element of P such that $k \prec k^+$ and such that there exist no element κ of P satisfying $k \prec \kappa \prec k^+$. By definition of a hierarchical order this element must be unique. k^+ is said to immediately succeed k or to be a *superordinate* of k in $(P, \succeq)$.

For $k \notin P_{\min}$ it is useful to define the set SUB_k of its immediate predecessors (also called *subordinates* of k):

$$\mathrm{SUB}_k = \{\kappa | \kappa \in P, \kappa^+ \text{ and } k \text{ are identical}\}$$

For notational symmetry with SUB_k, the set of subordinates of k, we denote by SUP_k the set of superordinates of k that either is empty or contains one element (i.e., k^+).

It is convenient to associate with the ordered set P a directed graph $T(P, V)$ whose nodes correspond to the elements of P and which has the following set of arcs:

$$V = \{(k^+, k) | k \in P \backslash P_{\max}\}.$$

An arc (k^+, k) is directed from k^+ to k. Because the order is hierarchical $T(P, V)$ cannot contain cycles. It is fact a forest that reduces to a tree when it has only one component.

As we consider hierarchical orders in P, the set of block indices of a block structure, we want the following condition to be satisfied: For any $(s, t) \in R$, the set of edges of the overlapping graph of the block structure, the elements s and t are related (i.e., there is a chain in $(P, \succeq)$ that contains s and t). In other words, whenever blocks share variables in a block structure, they must be related. A hierarchical order satisfying this condition is said to be *feasible* with respect to R. A total order is always feasible with respect to R. $\mathcal{O}(R)$ will denote the set of all admissible orders in P, that is, the set of all hierarchical partial orders in P, feasible with respect to R.

Orders in $\mathcal{O}(R)$ are given in figures 10.9 to 10.12. An obvious admissible order for a block angular structure is given by the tree with directed arc corresponding to the overlapping graph which is also a tree (figure 10.9). Figure 10.10 gives four admissible orders for the seven-period staircase structure of figure 10.2. Note the depth of the trees which ranges from 3 to 7, the *depth* being the maximum number of elements of a chain in the ordered set.

Zviagina (1973) defines as optimal an admissible order with minimum depth. She gives a dynamic programming algorithm for finding an optimal admissible order. In section 10.3 where we make use of admissible orders to implement nested decomposition, we will give guidelines for choosing a "good" order on computational grounds. Figures 10.11 and 10.12 depict

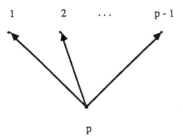

Figure 10.9

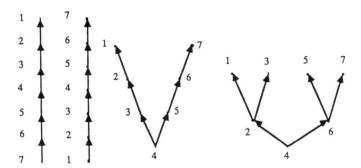

Figure 10.10

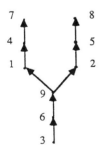

Figure 10.11

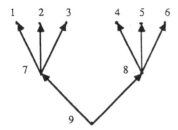

Figure 10.12

admissible orders, respectively, for the block structures of figures 10.3 and 10.4. Note that in the latter case the directed tree is identical to the tree of events of the stochastic programming approach.

10.3   Applying Nested Decomposition to Arborescent Linear Programs

Arborescent Linear Programs

An *arborescent linear program* is a linear programming problem with a block structured constraint matrix for which an admissible hierarchical order has been chosen. The term "arborescent linear program" has been coined by Kallio and Porteus (1977). Without loss of generality, we can assume that the graph associated with the order is connected—that is, it is a tree. Indeed, the problem would otherwise be separable, and the analysis developed hereafter could be applied to each part. We rearrange the constraint matrix in such a way that a block of rows is always below its predecessors. The blocks of the block structure are renumbered accordingly, with p being the only element in $P_{\max}$ and 1 an element in $P_{\min}$. We denote by A_{st} the submatrix corresponding to $A_{M_s N_t^*}$ with the set N_t^* defined as follows:

$$N_t^* = N_t \setminus \left(\bigcup_{\tau < t} N_\tau \right).$$

The set N_t^* corresponds to the columns of the block t that do not also belong to a predecessor of this block. Some of the subsets N_t^* can be empty, and hence the corresponding submatrices A_{st}. Moreover $A_{st} = 0$ for $s < t$ because of our block numbering scheme in the matrix.

The block structured (LP) problem can now be stated as follows:

$$\text{(LP)} \begin{cases} \text{minimize} & z = \sum_{t=1}^{p} c_t x_t & \text{(LP.1)} \\[2ex] \text{subject to } \sum_{t=1}^{s} A_{st} x_t = b_s, & s = 1, \ldots, p, & \text{(LP.2)} \\[2ex] & x_t \geq 0, t = 1, \ldots, p, & \text{(LP.3)} \end{cases}$$

where c_t is a known $(1 \times n_t)$ vector, x_t is an unknown $(n_t \times 1)$ vector, A_{st} is an $(m_s \times n_t)$ known matrix, b_s is a known $(m_s \times 1)$ vector, n_t and m_s are, respectively, equal to $|N_t^*|$ and $|M_s|$,

$$A = \begin{bmatrix} A_{11} & \cdots & A_{1p} \\ \vdots & & \vdots \\ A_{p1} & \cdots & A_{pp} \end{bmatrix}, \quad b = \begin{bmatrix} b_1 \\ \vdots \\ b_p \end{bmatrix},$$

so that A is a known $(m \times n)$ matrix and b a known $(m \times 1)$ vector with $m = \sum_{t=1}^{p} m_t$ and $n = \sum_{t=1}^{p} n_t$. Allowing empty blocks of columns in the partitioning of A (they correspond to empty sets N_t^*), we can consider that A exhibits a lower block triangular structure.

Theoretical Background of Decomposition Approaches

The nested decomposition algorithm proposed here for solving the problem is constructed by applying three techniques among a set of problem manipulation techniques and computational strategies as classified by Geoffrion (1970) and upon which most large-scale mathematical programming are built. The presentation of the following subsections is borrowed from Kallio and Porteus (1977):

1. Successive projection is applied to the problem. It amounts to a dynamic programming reformulation.

2. Each stage problem of the dynamic programming approach is transformed in an extremal problem by using *inner linearization* also known as the Dantzig-Wolfe decomposition principle for linear programming, Dantzig and Wolfe (1960).

3. Extremal problems are made tractable by using *restriction*.

The resulting algorithm is an extension of the Ho and Manne (1974) or Glassey (1973) nested primal decomposition algorithm for staircase block structures. Ament et al. (1981) extend the Ho and Manne algorithm to lower triangular block structures where the hierarchical order is a total one. The implementation presented here is directly derived from the one presented in Ament et al. Instead of solving the original problem, one repeatedly solves in a coordinated manner a series of smaller subproblems until optimal coordination is reached. The subproblems are ordered according to the hierarchical order chosen for the block structure. Each subproblem acts effectively as a master problem with respect to its subordinate subproblems and acts as a column generation subproblem with respect to its superordinate subproblem.

Note that the idea of such an algorithm as outlined by Kallio and Porteus, can be traced to the book of Dantzig (1963, pp. 466–470) where a nested decomposition scheme is proposed for solving staircase LP problems with the minimal depth ordering tree. Broise, Huard, and Sentenac (1968) should be credited for an early and comprehensive work on nested decomposition that went somewhat unnoticed. Their theoretical framework is not as firmly grounded as in Kallio and Porteus (1977). The advantages of their approach, based on an early simplex implementation, were offset by dramatic improvements in simplex techniques in the 1970s (compact basis inverse representations, new pricing techniques). Today, simplex implementations have reached a high level of sophistication, and there is little hope for future improvement on conventional computers. Computers with parallel architecture could be more beneficial to a nested decomposition approach than to the standard simplex approach.

As pointed by Kallio and Porteus (1977), other nested decomposition schemes can be devised if one uses *outer linearization* instead of inner linearization, such as nested Benders decomposition (Birge 1985). Our reasons for adopting the nested Dantzig-Wolfe decomposition scheme are mainly related to implementation and efficiency aspects as explained in the next section.

Successive Projection

It is convenient to give the following interpretation Kallio and Porteus (1977) to the problem (LP): the block index t represents the division t, x_t its vector of activity level, b_s the vector of resources to which division s is commited, and b the vector of all resources to be produced. If $A_{st} \neq 0$, then division t is a predecessor of division s and contributes to resources to which division s is commited.

Using the partition of the vector of unknown in vectors of divisional activities x_t, we can successively project the original problem onto spaces of divisional activities. Adopting a recursive dynamic programminglike formulation as in as in Bellman (1957) and Nemhauser (1974), we end up with the following formulation:

$$(DP_s) \quad z_s(r^s) = \inf_{r^t \in \mathbf{R}^m, t \in \mathrm{SUB}_s} \left\{ \inf_{x_s \geq 0} \left[c_s x_s + \sum_{t \in \mathrm{SUB}_s} z_t(r^t), \right. \right.$$

$$\left. \left. \text{subject to } A_s x_s + \sum_{t \in \mathrm{SUB}_s} r_t = r_s \right] \right\},$$

for each $s \in P$, where

$$A_s = \begin{bmatrix} A_{1s} \\ \vdots \\ A_{ps} \end{bmatrix}$$

and r^s is an $(m \times 1)$ vector. The vector r^s can be interpreted as the resource contribution of the divisions in P_s (i.e., s and all its predecessors). It consists of what is produced by s, $A_s x_s$, and of $\sum_{t \in \mathrm{SUB}_s} r^t$, the sum of what is contributed by its subordinates and their predecessors. The divisions in the set $\bar{S}_s$ (i.e., the superordinate division of s and its successors) request a resource contribution r^s from the divisions in P_s. This contribution can be partitioned as

$$r^s = \begin{bmatrix} r^s_1 \\ \vdots \\ r^s_p \end{bmatrix},$$

with r^s_t an $(m_t \times 1)$ vector for each $t \in P$. For $t \in \bar{S}_s$, r^s_t consists of resources to which division t is commited and which are requested from the divisions in P_s. For $t \in P_s$, r^s_t consists of resources to which divisions in P_s are commited. For other t, the corresponding vector r^s_t is zero. A vector $r \in \mathbf{R}^m$ is said to be a feasible request for s, if $r_t = b_t$ for each $t \in P_s$. In other words, all resources to which division s and its predecessors are committed are provided.

Given a request r^s submitted to the divisions in P_s, $z_s(r^s)$ denotes the minimal cost of providing r^s by division s and its predecessors. It consists of $c_s x_s$ the cost for the division s itself, and of $\sum_{t \in \mathrm{SUB}_s} z_t(r^t)$, the sum of the minimal cost for the subordinates of s.

Setting the problem (DP_p) with a feasible vector r_p (i.e., b) produces $z_p(b)$ which is the optimal value of the objective function of (LP). We call (DP) this problem equivalent to (LP) and defined recursively by the previous formulation.

Equivalent Extremal Problem

In a search for a more tractable form for the recursive problem (DP), it is useful to consider an equivalent formulation as an extremal problem. This formulation is based on the set H_s, the hypergraph of $z_s(\cdot)$,

$$H_s = \{(q,r) \in \mathbf{R}^{m+1} | q \geq z_s(r)\},$$

and C_s the following subset of H_s

$$C_s = \{(q,r) \in H_s | r_t = b_t \text{ for all } t \in P_s \text{ and } z_s(r) < +\infty\}.$$

Both sets are defined for all s in P. For $(q,r) \in H_s$, the scalar q is an upper bound on the minimal cost supported by the division s and its predecessors for satisfying the requested resource vector r. If (q,r) belongs to C_s, then r is a feasible request for s. It is well known that for each s, C_s is a convex polyhedron in $\mathbf{R}^{m+1}$.

If we take into account the arborescent structure of (LP) in the recursive formulation of (DP), we can replace the constraints in (DP_s) by $A_{us} x_s + \sum_{t \in \mathrm{SUB}_s} r_u^t = r_u^s$ for all $u \in S_s$ with the feasibility of r^t for t, for all $t \in \mathrm{SUB}_s$. Moreover $\inf\{q^t | (q^t, r^t) \in C_s\}$ can be substituted for $z_t(r^t)$. This leads to the following formulation of (DP_s) for each s. Given r^s, find x_s in $\mathbf{R}^{n_s}$, and for each t in SUB_t, find $q^t \in \mathbf{R}$ and $r^t \in \mathbf{R}^m$ so as to

$$(\mathrm{DP}'_s) \quad \begin{cases} \text{minimize} \quad c_s x_s + \sum_{t \in \mathrm{SUB}_s} q^t, \\[2mm] \text{subject to } A_{us} x_s + \sum_{t \in \mathrm{SUB}_s} r_u^t = r_u^s \quad \text{for all } u \in S_s, \\[2mm] \qquad\qquad (q^t, r^t) \in C_t \quad \text{for all } t \in \mathrm{SUB}_s, \\[2mm] \qquad\qquad x_s \geq 0. \end{cases}$$

The advantage of this formulation is that the sets C_t can be inner or outer linearized (Kallio 1975). In our implementation we have used an inner linearization for representing C_t:

$$C_t = \left\{ \sum_j \lambda_{tj}(q^t, r^t)^j \,\middle|\, \sum_j \delta_{tj}\lambda_{tj} = 1, \lambda_{tj} \geq 0 \text{ for all } j \right\},$$

where λ_{tj} is a nonnegative weight on the extreme point or extreme ray $(q^t, r^t)^j$ of C_t, and δ_{tj} is 1 or 0, depending upon $(q^t, r^t)^j$ is an extreme point or an extreme ray. The summation over j is a summation over the extreme points and rays of C_t which exist in a finite number, say, h_t. By using the expression of (q^t, r^t) as a weighted combination, we obtain the following equivalent formulation for each problem (DP_s). For a given r^s, find $x_s \in \mathbf{R}^{n_s}$, $\lambda_t \in \mathbf{R}^{h_t}$ for all $t \in SUB_s$, so as to

$$(DP'_s) \begin{cases} \text{minimize} \quad c_s x_s + \sum_{t \in SUB_s} q_t \lambda_t, \\[2mm] \text{subject to } A_{us} x_s + \sum_{t \in SUB_s} R_{ut} \lambda_t = r^s_u \qquad \text{for all } u \in S, \\[2mm] \qquad\qquad\qquad\quad \delta_t \lambda_t = 1 \qquad \text{for all } t \in SUB_s, \\[2mm] \quad x_s \geq 0, \\[2mm] \qquad\qquad\qquad\quad \lambda_t \geq 0. \end{cases}$$

The extremal problem (DP'_p), also noted (DP'), being equivalent to (DP), is still equivalent to (LP), although it is practically untractable because it requires the explicit knowledge of an enormous number of columns. Assume that we know only a few of them. We can state a problem where we restrict to zero most of weight variables and allow to become positive only the weights corresponding to the known columns. By solving this problem, called restricted master problem, we get an upper bound that approximates $z_p(b)$. By selecting an appropriate subset of columns in (DP'), we can state a problem that will produce exactly the value $z_p(b)$.

Restriction and Column Generation

Let (SP^k_p) denote a restricted master problem which corresponds to (DP') where only k_p columns are known explicitly. As in the Dantzig-Wolfe decomposition algorithm a column generation scheme based on the simplex multipliers π^k_t can be developed. It consists of computing the reduced cost of a column that is not known explicitly. Looking for the column with the smallest reduced cost amounts to setting up a subproblem for each $t \in SUB_p$. Each one is an extremal problem to which restriction can be applied with the same column generation scheme.

This leads us to consider the following series of subproblems where each subproblem corresponding to $t \in P \backslash P_{\min}$ is a restricted master problem with its k_t columns known explicitly obtained in the course of the algorithm. Find $x_s \in \mathbf{R}^{n_s}$, $\lambda_t^k \in \mathbf{R}^{k_t}$ for all $t \in \mathrm{SUB}_s$, so as to

$$(\mathrm{SP}_s^k) \begin{cases} \text{minimize} \left(c_s + \displaystyle\sum_{u \in \bar{S}_s} \pi_u^k A_{us} \right) x_s + \displaystyle\sum_{t \in \mathrm{SUB}_s} \left(q_t^k + \displaystyle\sum_{u \in \bar{S}_s} \pi_u^k R_{ut}^k \right) \lambda_t^k, \\[2ex] \text{subject to } A_{ss} x_s + \displaystyle\sum_{t \in \mathrm{SUB}_s} R_{st}^k \lambda_t^k = b_s, \qquad\qquad\qquad \pi_s^k \\[2ex] \qquad\qquad\qquad\qquad \delta_t^k \lambda_t^k = 1 \qquad \forall t \in \mathrm{SUB}_s, \quad \sigma_t^k \\[1ex] \qquad x_s \geq 0, \\[1ex] \qquad\qquad\qquad\qquad \lambda_t^k \geq 0, \qquad \forall t \in \mathrm{SUB}_s, \end{cases}$$

where q_t^k is a known $(1 \times k_s)$ vector, R_{ut}^k a known $(m_u \times k_t)$ matrix, δ_t^k an $(1 \times k_t)$ vector of 0 and 1, and λ_t^k a vector $(k_t \times 1)$ of unknowns. The jth component of q_t^k and the coefficients of the jth columns of the submatrices R_{ut}^k for $u \in S_s$ are the same as the corresponding components of an extreme point or ray (q, r) of C_t. π_s^k is an $(1 \times m_s$ vector denoting the dual price vector on the resources to which division s is commited, whereas σ_t^k is the dual price associated to the convexity row for the subordinate division t of s. The index k denotes a cycle or grand iteration of the algorithm during which the sth subproblem is *queried*. For $s \in P_{\max}$, that is, $s = p$, it consists of finding $x_p \in \mathbf{R}^{n_p}$ and

$$(\mathrm{SP}_p^k) \begin{cases} \text{minimize} \quad c_p x_p + \displaystyle\sum_{t \in \mathrm{SUB}_p} q_t^k \lambda_t^k, \\[2ex] \text{subject to } A_{pp} x_s + \displaystyle\sum_{t \in \mathrm{SUB}_p} R_{pt}^k \lambda_t^k = b_p, \qquad\qquad\qquad \pi_p^k \\[2ex] \qquad\qquad\qquad\qquad \delta_t^k \lambda_t^k = 1, \qquad \forall t \in \mathrm{SUB}_p, \quad \sigma_t^k \\[1ex] \qquad x_p \geq 0, \\[1ex] \qquad\qquad\qquad\qquad \lambda_t^k \geq 0, \qquad \forall t \in \mathrm{SUB}_p. \end{cases}$$

This last subproblem acts exclusively as a master problem, whereas all subproblems corresponding to divisions s in $P_{\min}$ act as pure column generation subproblems where we have to find x_s in $\mathbf{R}^{n_k}$ so as to

$$(SP_s^k) \quad \begin{cases} \text{minimize} \left(c_s + \sum_{u \in \bar{S}_s} \pi_u^k A_{us} \right) x_s \\ \text{subject to } A_{ss}x_s = b_s, \qquad \pi_s^k, \\ \qquad\qquad x_s \geq 0. \end{cases}$$

A Conceptual Algorithm, Convergence, and Bounds

Assume, for the moment, that at the first cycle of the algorithm, each subproblem (SP_s^1) contains enough extreme point or extreme ray columns to be feasible. It is convenient to define the following recursive procedure:

Procedure *SolveSub(s)*
  Solve (SP_s^k).
If (SP_s^k) is solved to optimality, **then**,
    unless $s = p$, make of the current solution an extreme point proposal
    (if profitable) for $(SP_{s^+}^{k+1})$.
    Moreover, unless $s \in P_{\min}$, send dual price to $(SP_t^k) \; \forall t \in S_s$.
If (SP_s^k) is unbounded from below, **then**,
    if $s = p$, **then stop** (the original problem is unbounded)
    else make an extreme ray proposal for $(SP_{s^+}^{k+1})$.
If $s \notin P_{\min}$, then $\forall t \in SUB_s$ *SolveSub(t)*.

The nested decomposition algorithm is then

For $k = 1, 2, \ldots$
  SolveSub(p)
If no proposal has been generated by any subproblem (SP_s^k),
    i.e., $z_s^{k*} - \sigma_{s^+}^k = 0, \; \forall_s \prec p$, **then stop.**

The profitability criterion for generating a column for (SP_{s^+}) from the current solution $(x_s^*, \ldots, \lambda_t^{k*}, \ldots)$ for (SP_s^k) is $z_s^k - \sigma_{s^+}^k < 0$, which expresses the negativity of the candidate column reduced cost with respect to the current basic solution of (SP_{s^+}). It can be shown that the coefficient and the column vector appended, respectively, to $q_{s^+}^k$ and $R_{s^+}^k$ are, respectively,

$$c_s x_s^* + \sum_{t \in SUB_s} q_t^k \lambda_t^{k*},$$

$$A_s x_s^* + \sum_{t \in SUB_s} R_t^k \lambda_t^{k*}.$$

A similar expression of the appended column holds if $(x_s^*, \ldots, \lambda_t^{k*}, \ldots)$ is an extreme ray for (S_s^k).

The convergence of this algorithm is guaranted if nondegeneracy is assumed in all subproblems. The proof derives from Dantzig and Wolfe (1961), Glassey (1973), and Ho and Manne (1974); it consists of showing that sets of basic variables for all subproblems cannot be repeated but only a finite number and cannot reappear after a basis change occurs in any subproblem. It follows from weak duality that when each subproblem (SP_s^k) is solved to optimality, the set of dual price vectors π_s^k constitutes a dual and $\sum_{s=1}^{P} \pi_s^k b_s$ is a lower bound on $z_p(b)$.

Initialization and Solution Reconstruction

To initiate the algorithm, it is necessary to make feasible each subproblem (SP_s^k). This will be done for a particular subproblem (SP_s^k) after making feasible all its subordinate subproblems. We call this initialization phase phase 1. Its algorithm is based on the following procedure:

Procedure   *MakeFeasible(s)*

If $s \notin P_{\min}$, **then** $\forall t \in SUB_s$, *MakeFeasible(t)*.

Set the objective function to the infeasibility form of (SP_s^k).

Apply the nested decomposition algorithm to the arborescent linear
    program corresponding to the divisions $t \in P_s$.

If the value of the infeasibility form is not zero, **then stop**.

The phase 1 algorithm is then simply: *MakeFeasible(p)*. It either terminates with a feasible starting solution or signals infeasibility for the original problem.

Solution reconstruction is an important practical issue in primal decomposition algorithms. It is well known that when overall optimality is reached, it is not possible to produce the final value of the primal variables. Only the objective function value and the dual variables values are directly available. Ho and Manne (1974) address the problem of reconstructing a solution in term of the original variables for nested decomposition applied to staircase problems. We follow their approach for the case of arborescent problems.

A first method assumes that all solutions to (SP_s^k) used to generate proposals are kept explicitly. A particular solution consists of an $(n_s \times 1)$

vector x_s^k (the superscript k indicates the corresponding cycle) and of the catenation of $(k_s \times 1)$ vectors $\lambda_t^k \ \forall t \in \text{SUB}_s$, denoted by $\bigcup_{t \in \text{SUB}} \lambda_t^k$. Because the decomposition algorithm weighs solutions from subproblems, x_s^k cannot be substituted for x_s in the original problem solution, except when $s = p$. Weights must be applied to x_s^j for $j = 1, \ldots, k$ to find the right vector x_s, denoted by y_s. The first method uses a recursive scheme to simultaneously construct the $(n_s \times 1)$ vector y_s and a set of $(k_s \times 1)$ weighing vectors $\mu_t \ \forall t \in \text{SUB}_s, \ \forall s \in P$:

$$\begin{cases} y_p = x_p^k, \\ \mu_t = \lambda_t^k \qquad \forall t \in \text{SUB}_p, \end{cases}$$

$$\begin{cases} y_s = \sum_j \mu_{sj} x_s^j, \\ \mu_t = \sum_j \mu_{sj} \lambda_t^j \qquad \forall t \in \text{SUB}_s, \end{cases}$$

where all vectors λ_t^j are expanded with zero components to match the dimension of λ_t^k and the summation over j is over the number of components of λ_t^k. The proof requires tedious algebraic manipulations and is omitted for brevity (it generalizes the proof in Ho 1974).

Storing explicit solutions of subproblems is somewhat prohibitive by its storage and data management requirements (even on auxiliary memory support) compared to proposals. The latter are likely to be more compact because they are mapping of subproblem solutions into the coupling rows. Moreover their data management as columns of a linear program is automatically provided as a regular service of an LP package. For these reasons a reconstruction scheme based only on proposal data is more practical. Such a scheme, called by Ho and Manne a "Phase 3 procedure," amounts to solving a series of modified subproblems.

Assume that global optimality is detected at cycle k of the nested decomposition algorithm. Then $y_p = x_p^k$ is part of the solution. For all $t \in \text{SUB}_p$, $q_s^k \lambda_s^k$ are requested contributions from the division s and its predecessors, respectively, to the overall objective function and to the resources to which division p is committed (i.e., respectively q^s and r^s in the formulation of (DP_p')). If we pose $y_p = x_p^k$ and $\mu_s = \lambda_s^k \ \forall s \in \text{SUB}_p$, we can state the following subproblems: For all $s \in \text{SUB}_p$, find $y_s \in \mathbf{R}^{n_s}$ and $\mu_t \in \mathbf{R}^{k_t}$ for all $t \in \text{SUB}_s$ so as to

$$
\left\{
\begin{array}{ll}
\text{minimize} & \sum_t q_t^k \mu_t + c_s y_s, \\[2mm]
\text{subject to} & \sum_t R_{pt}^k \mu_t + A_{ps} y_s = R_{ps}^k \mu_s, \\[2mm]
& \sum_t R_{st}^k \mu_t + A_{ss} y_s = b_s, \\[2mm]
& \delta_t \mu_t = 1 \qquad \forall t \in \mathrm{SUB}_s.
\end{array}
\right.
$$

This problem has more constraints than (SP$_s^k$). However, it must be feasible and must produce the same objective function value as (SP$_s^k$). If the latter were not true, it would contradict the global optimality reached at cycle k. Note that feasibility and optimality must be reached without proposal generation from subproblems (SP$_t^k$) with $t \in \mathrm{SUB}_s$, provided that all proposals have been kept. Once such a subproblem has been solved, its solution vectors μ_t for all $t \in \mathrm{SUB}_s$ can be used to set similar subproblems. The general formulation of the phase 3 subproblem, denoted by (SY$_s$) is the following: Find $y_s \in \mathbf{R}^{n_s}$, and $\mu_t \in \mathbf{R}^{k_t}$ for all $t \in \mathrm{SUB}_s$ so as to

$$
(SY_s) \quad
\left\{
\begin{array}{lll}
\text{minimize} & \sum\limits_{t \in \mathrm{SUB}_s} q_t^k \mu_t + c_s y_s, & \\[3mm]
\text{subject to} & \sum\limits_{t \in \mathrm{SUB}_s} R_{ut}^k \mu_t + A_{us} y_s = R_{us}^k \mu_s & \forall u \in S_s, \\[3mm]
& \sum\limits_{t \in \mathrm{SUB}_s} R_{st}^k \mu_t + A_{ss} y_s = b_s, & \\[3mm]
& \delta_t \mu_t = 1 & \forall t \in \mathrm{SUB}_s.
\end{array}
\right.
$$

For $s = p$, (SY$_p$) is identical to (SP$_p^k$s), and its solution is at hand. For $s \in P_{\min}$, the terms in μ_t disappear. Note that (SY$_s$) could be stated as a feasibility problem with the objective function value to be attained, $\sum_t q_t^k \mu_t + c_s y_s = q_s^k \mu_s$, stated as a constraint. This formulation is useful if an intermediate global solution is to be produced. An algorithm for phase 3 is simply *Phase*3(p), with the following definition for the recursive *Phase*3($\cdot$) procedure:

Procedure   *Phase*3(s)
   Solve (SY$_s$), save y_s as part of the overall solution.

If $s \notin P_{\min}$, **then**
   for all $t \in \mathrm{SUB}_s$
      send μ_t to (SY$_t$),
      *Phase*3(t)

10.4   Implementation Aspects

The aspects in the design of a decomposition code for a block angular structure are discussed by Ho and Loute (1981) in a paper on an advanced implementation. We briefly recall here the major aspects:

1. the LP solving service,
2. data handling to update and process the subproblems,
3. computational strategies.

LP Solver

Since most of the computational burden of a decomposition approach lies in solving the subproblems, the efficiency of the LP solver is of primary importance. Equally important is the ability to efficiently revise the LP problem data, particularly the addition of columns. At the time the development was undertaken, the revised simplex method (Dantzig 1963) was unquestionably the most efficient approach. Although it is challenged today by methods based on the work of Karmarkar (1984), it remains attractive on several counts. It offers robustness and capability in accommodating data revision, particularly column changes because of column-oriented data structures. Modular implementation of advanced LP systems allowing use at subroutine level are available. Note that the LP routine should include all the features of a state-of-the-art revised simplex routine (Ho and Loute 1981, p. 308).

Data Handling

Modern LP systems are designed around efficient internal data structures. When they are used as the engine of a decomposition algorithm, the coordinating information (i.e., prices and proposals) should be directly accessed without incurring data conversion to a special communication format or, worse, access through files. It is possible to design a data structure for the subproblems that is efficient from the point of view of coordinating information independently upon the LP code used. It is an extension of a tabular form of the subproblem data originally proposed by Beale et al. (1965) for block angular structures and is depicted in figure 10.13. Note that the usual logical columns (i.e., a column or minus a column of the identity matrix for each row depending upon how it is constrained) have been omitted. The coupling rows are present in the subproblem. They

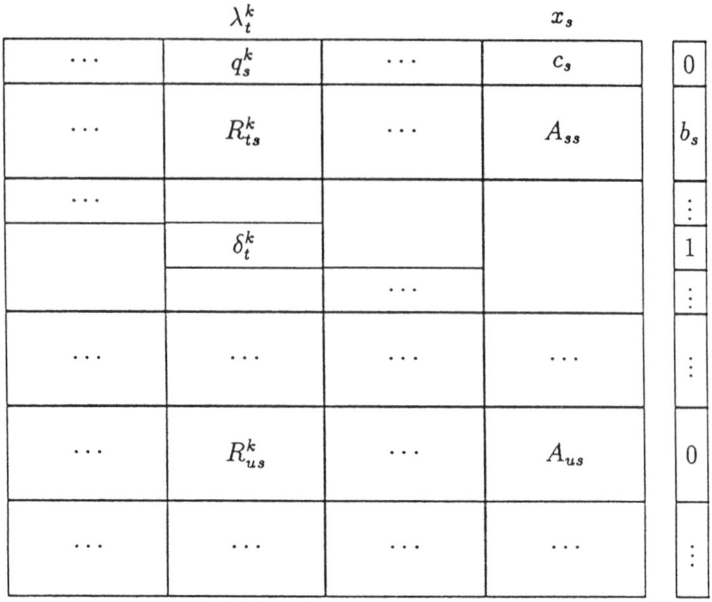

λ_t^k			x_s	
$\cdots$	q_s^k	$\cdots$	c_s	0
$\cdots$	R_{ts}^k	$\cdots$	A_{ss}	b_s
$\cdots$				$\vdots$
	δ_t^k			1
		$\cdots$		$\vdots$
$\cdots$	$\cdots$	$\cdots$	$\cdots$	$\vdots$
$\cdots$	R_{us}^k	$\cdots$	A_{us}	0
$\cdots$	$\cdots$	$\cdots$	$\cdots$	$\vdots$

Figure 10.13

are declared as nonbinding rows. A column-oriented packing scheme is applied to the data of this tabular representation. Access to submatrices data is provided through pointers or linked lists. Note that besides being sparse, the submatrices A_{us} are likely to have rows with all coefficients being zero. R_{us}^k can have a nonzero ith row only when at least one of the submatrices A_{ut} for $t \prec s$ has a nonzero ith row. Thus although our data structure adds $\sum_{u \succ s} m_u$ nonbinding rows, many may be empty in practice and hence do not have to be explicit.

The rationale of this data structure is discussed in Culot and Loute (1980) and Ho and Loute (1981) for the block angular case. Its benefits extend to the arborescent structure. We briefly recall them here.

1. An implicit generation of the subproblem (SP$_s^k$) current objective function through (a) simplex multiplier computation by a BTRAN operation performed on the vector

$$[1, \overbrace{0,\ldots,0}^{m_s}, \overbrace{0,\ldots 0}^{|SUB_s|},\ldots, -\pi_u^k,\ldots],$$

where $u \succ s$, and (b) reduced cost computation as the scalar product of

$$[1, -\pi_s^k, \ldots, -\sigma_t^k, \ldots, -\pi_u^k, \ldots],$$

where $t \in \text{SUB}_s$ and $u \in S_s$, with a nonbasic column.

2. Automatic proposal generation at optimality or in the course of the subproblem optimization (e.g., the coefficients of an extreme point proposal are immediately available as the coupling rows activities).

3. Ease of setup for the phase 3 subproblems (it requires only a revision of the right-hand side and the enforcement of the nonbinding rows as constraints).

Computational Strategies

Computational strategies consist of variants and refinements of an algorithm. They are aimed at reducing the computer resources required by the algorithm or at exchanging a resource for another: elapsed time, CPU time, main memory, I/O activities, and auxiliary memory. They are motivated by heuristics, and their benefits cannot be guranteed on theoretical grounds. Their use and their parameters should be experimentally tuned for specific classes of problems. The range of possible computational strategies depends upon the computer system considered for implementing the algorithm. A machine with a parallel architecture or a network of computers for a distributed implementation is particularly attractive and straightforward when implementing nested decomposition for arborescent linear programs. Our present discussion is limited to conventional architectures.

Cycle Strategies   A cycle in the conceptual algorithm consists of solving each subproblem after its superordinate subproblem. An advantage of this strategy is that if all subproblems are solved up to optimality, a lower bound can be computed. Another possible cycle strategy could be to solve each subproblem after its subordinate subproblems. It has the advantage of immediately reflecting the effect of new proposals up to the subproblem (SP_p^k) during the current cycle. Note that in any strategy, one should only consider the subproblems (SP_s^k) that have new proposals or new prices (i.e., new values in π_u^k for some $u \succ s$ or a new value for σ_s^k), since the last time they were optimized. Such a subproblem is said to be eligible. In fact as Kallio and Porteus (1977) suggest, the notion of "cycle" could be replaced by a list of subproblems where each subproblem is repeated infinitely many times. Among the eligible subproblems the most active ones in the algorithmic process should be solved more frequently. The degree of activity of a subproblem is indicated by the number of simplex iterations between successive resolutions, the number of its proposals that have entered its superordinate subproblem basis, and so on.

Multiproposal Generation Any solution of a subproblem (SP_s^k) that satisfies the candidacy criterion may lead to an improvement in (SP_{s+}^k) and hence can be used to generate a proposal. Empirical evidence show that this strategy can accelerate convergence. To control proposal generation, we have used a mechanism originally proposed by Ho (1978) and used in Ho and Loute (1981). The reader is referred to these papers for the details.

Proposal Purging The size of the subproblems (SP_s^k) for $s \notin P_{\min}$ grows with the cycles, particularly when multiple proposals are generated. It is useful to periodically purge the inactive (nonbasic) ones. However, except in the case of (SP_p^k), an inactive proposal may be needed for the phase 3 algorithm by applying the nested decomposition algorithm to problems of the form (DP_s) with given requirement vectors r_s. The solution reconstruction phase would become prohibitive. We have devised a scheme that allows purging and still allows the use of the original phase 3 algorithm. By attaching to each proposal generated by (SP_s^k) for (SP_{s+}^k), we store, as a bit map, which proposal of (SP_s^k) was basic. Purging is done from (SP_p^k) to the subproblems (SP_s^k) for $s \in P_{\min}$. By doing a logical or on the bit map of the proposal column of (SP_{s+}^k) generated by (SP_s^k), we build a mask that is then used to decide which inactive proposals of (SP_s^k) have to be purged. Bit maps have to be updated to take into account purging.

10.5   An Implementation of the Nested Decomposition Algorithm

The nested decomposition algorithm for arborescent linear programs has been implemented as an extension of LIFT, a code for solving lower block triangular LP problems Ament et al. (1981). This is why we choosed the name LIFT/2 for the new code. LIFT is itself an extension of DE-COMPSX (Ho and Loute 1981), which implements the Dantzig-Wolfe decomposition algorithm for block angular LP problems. The starting point of this continuous stream of development was a powerful commercial mathematical programming system, namely, the IBM product MPSX/370 (IBM 1979). This choice was made about two years after the package was put on the market around 1977. It was considered that the important logic of the algorithm, as well as the handling of the coordinating information, could not be performed by the procedures found in conventional LP packages. Another major requirement was the possibility of repeatedly calling the LP routine from a user control program (we rejected a straight batching of LP jobs as being too inefficient). Finally, an access to internal computational data structures, as well as to modular algorithmic tools for LP (e.g., BTRAN), pricing, FTRAN, CHUZR, etc., was considered mandatory. At that time the MPSX/370 software was the first commercial LP package satisfying our requirement with a state of the art LP technology. Its services can be accessed through a high-level control language called ECL, a PL/I based language extended through macros and PL/I standard preprocessing and completed by a library of algorithmic procedures (IBM 1975, 1979; Slate and Spielberg 1978). Note that a few modifications were brought to the original source of four internal MPSX/370 procedures to fully exploit the tabular representation of the subproblem data structures. A development similar to LIFT/2 could be made on the basis of the FORTRAN LP library XMP due to Marsten (1981). Although it does not match MPSX/370 efficiency, robustness, and commercial support, it has the advantage of being highly portable. Today, there are several examples of embedding of the XMP library in commercial products.

The effort to implement LIFT/2 was moderate because it was built upon the experience of the two previous codes. DECOMPSX was a test bed for several important design decisions and for computational strategies that apply to the three algorithms. The reader is referred to Culot and Loute (1980) and Ho and Loute (1981) for a detailed decription of the code. LIFT required an extension of DECOMPSX data structures to accommodate multiple price vectors and proposals with subvectors corresponding to different coupling blocks. Details about the program can be found in Ament (1980). The total order used in LIFT for ordering the block structure has been relaxed to a hierarchical order in LIFT/2. By allowing more than one subordinate subproblem, we were using what was already available in DECOMPSX for one level of decomposition. LIFT/2 counts 15 external procedures with a total of less than 2,500 lines of ECL. Two libraries of declaration macros are used. We estimate the amount of new code to be less than 20 percent. A major part of it corresponds to the implementation of the proposal purging strategy presented in section 10.4.

LIFT/2 requires the user to input the tree corresponding to the ordering of the block structure as a list of block names along with the name of their superordinate block. The data of each subproblem are entered as a standard MPS file. Whenever a subproblem, say, (SP_t), has a nonzero row in a coupling block A_{ut}, the row must be declared in all subproblems (SP_s) for $t \prec s \prec u$. An MPS file preprocessor has been developed for that purpose. The set of files used by LIFT/2 is the same as in DECOMPSX (see Ho and Loute 1981). In our experiments we have used a version of LIFT/2 dimensioned to handle up to 99 subproblems with up to 1,000 effective coupling rows for each subproblem. Each subproblem could theoretically have up to 16,000 rows, but a practical limit is in the range of 2,000 to 4,000 rows.

10.6   Sample of Experiments

LIFT/2 was developed to provide a solution tool in an energy modeling research project where uncertainty was to be taken into account (Janssens de Bisthoven et al. 1985a, 1985b). Clearly we would not have undertaken this development if we had not benefited from the two previous codes and their related experience. Because they were aimed at answering questions from the modelers rather than at testing the algorithm and its different computational strategies, our experiments are too limited to be considered as an assessment of LIFT/2.

   We report the statistics of the runs on a selection of four typical problems ranging from large to very large (beyond the capability of MPSX/370 itself). The size of the problems is due to their stochastic nature. They are the extensive form of stochastic multistage linear programming problems. The dual of the problem exhibits an arborescent structure where a natural ordering tree is the tree of events. Note that because we solve the dual of the original problem, a reconstruction phase is not necessary. The dimensions of the test problems are summarized in table 10.1. Note that the column statistics do not take into account the logical columns. The density is expressed as a percentage. All the problems are derived from the same generic multistage model. The number of stages is given under the heading "Periods." Discrete random coefficients are considered at some stages for all problems but PGSC0. The number of values considered for such coefficients is 2 or 3. The "Nodes" column indicates the number of nodes of the ordering tree (identical to the tree of events). For PGSC0, it is a chain, whereas for PGSC3 and PGSC4 it is a tree with three branches starting from the root. The tree corresponding to PGSC6 is depicted in figure 10.14.

   Our experiments were carried out on an IBM/370 model 158 under VM/CMS. A 1500K virtual machine was used for the runs. Table 10.2 indicates the number of cycles and the CPU time (in minutes) required for

Table 10.1

Problem	Periods	Nodes	Rows	Columns	Elements	Density
PGSCO	5	5	4,613	4,609	29,132	0.14
PGSC3	6	16	8,918	8,922	67,630	0.0085
PGSC4	11	31	18,975	19,006	160,026	0.044
PGSC6	5	21	12,143	11,676	89,883	0.063

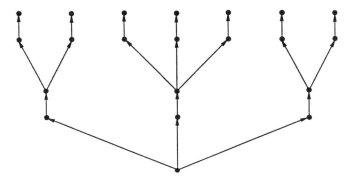

Figure 10.14

Table 10.2

Problem	Numbers of cycles			CPU time			Total CPU time
	Phase 1	Phase 2	Total	Phase 1	Phase 2	Total	
PGSC0	10	21	31	13.1	33.1	46.2	50.3
PGSC3	28	14	42	19.8	37.4	57.2	62.5
PGSC4	62	40	·102	51.7	217.2	274.3	293.9
PGSC6	32	18	50	25.7	57.3	83.0	90.0

Table 10.3

Problem	CPU time in MPSX/370 procedures			
	SETUP	PRIMAL	REVISE	Total
PGSCO	7.8	35.0	1.6	44.4
PGSC3	11.1	41.4	3.1	55.6
PGSC4	111.0	123.1	24.9	259.0
PGSC6	19.5	56.7	5.1	81.3

the feasibility and optimisation phases. The total CPU time column includes the preprocessing and the input time in addition to the phase 1 and phase 2 time. The stopping criterion was a relative gap between primal and dual solution of less than 5×10^{-3}. In all our experiments we used the standard cycle strategy in which a subproblem is solved before its predecessors.

In table 10.3 we indicate the CPU time in the major MPSX/370 procedures during phases 1 and 2: SETUP, REVISE, and PRIMAL. The last column gives the total of the preceeding four and is to be compared to the total of the phase 1 and 2 CPU time in table 18.2. The difference accounts for the processing of the coordination data, prices and proposals. Note that the cumulated SETUP time tends to be of the same order as the PRIMAL time, particularly for the problem PGSC4. The SETUP time can exceed the PRIMAL time during the last cycles when few simplex iterations are performed on most subproblem. This could be improved if MPSX/370 could save and restore the memory image of a subproblem rather than resort to its problem file format. A fine-tuning of the cycle strategy is another possibility of improvement. We would expect an overall CPU time reduction with possibly a larger number of nonstandard cycles.

Note that during the last cycles the objective function value tails off as usually reported in experiences with decomposition methods, but not dramatically. In figure 10.15 we have plotted the objective function and upper bound values against the number of cycles over the last 40 cycles of the problem PGSC4.

We have made some comparisons between LIFT/2 and MPSX/370 used as a standard solver. Based on our experience on this particular class of problems and on another class of problems from soil mechanics, our conclusion is that for problems of less than 5,000 rows, using MPSX/370 leads to faster runs. Between 5,000 and 12,000 rows, LIFT/2 is faster up to

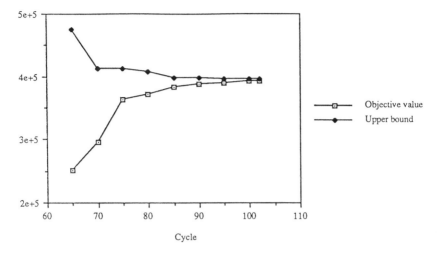

Figure 10.15

halving the CPU time. For larger problems LIFT/2 was for us the only available tool.

References

Ament, D. 1980. "An Implementation of the LIFT Algorithm." Master's thesis, Econometrisch Instituut, Erasmus Universiteit, Rotterdam.

Ament, D., J. Ho, E. Loute, and M. Remmelswaal. 1981. "LIFT: A Nested Decomposition Algorithm for Solving Lower Block Triangular Linear Programs." In *Large-Scale Linear Programming*, Vol. 1, edited by G. B. Dantzig, M. A. H. Dempster, and M. Kallio. Laxenburg, Austria: IIASA, 383–408.

Beale, E. M. L., P. A. B. Hughes, and R. E. Small. 1965. "Experiences in Using a Decomposition Program." *Computer Journal* 8:13–18.

Bellman, R. 1957. "On the Computational Solution of Linear Programming Problems Involving Almost Block-Diagonal Matrices." *Management Science* 3:403–406.

Benichou, M. et al. 1977. "The Efficient Solution of Large-Scale Linear Programming Problems—Some Algorithmic Techniques and Computational Results." *Mathematical Programming* 13:280–332.

Birge, J. 1985. "Decomposition and Partitioning Methods for Multi-Stage Stochastic Linear Programs." *Operations Research* 33:989–1007.

Broise, P., P. Huard, and J. Sentenac. 1968. *Decomposition des programmes mathématiques*. Paris: Dunod.

Culot, B., and E. Loute. 1980. "DECOMPSX System Manual." CORE Computing Report 80-B-02, Université Catholique de Louvain. (In French.)

Dantzig, G. B., and P. Wolfe. 1960. "Decomposition Principle for Linear Programs." *Operations Research* 8:101–110.

Dantzig, G. B., and P. Wolfe. 1961. "The Decomposition Algorithm for Linear Programming." *Econometrica* 29:767–778.

Dantzig, G. B. 1963. *Linear Programming and Extensions*. Princeton, NJ: Princeton University Press.

Geoffrion, A. 1970. "Elements of Large-Scale Mathematical Programming. Part I: Concepts." *Management Science* 16:652–675.

Glassey, C. R. 1973. "Nested Decomposition and Multistage Linear Programs." *Management Science* 20:282–292.

Ho, J. K. 1974. "Nested Decomposition of Large Scale Linear Programs with the Staircase Structure." Technical Report SOL-74-4, System Optimization Laboratory, Department of Operations Research, Stanford University.

Ho, J. K. 1978. "Implementation and Application of a Nested Decomposition Algorithm." In *Computers and Mathematical Programming*, edited by W. White. National Bureau of Standards, 21–30.

Ho, J. K., and A. S. Manne. 1974. "Nested Decomposition for Dynamic Models." *Mathematical Programming* 6:121–140.

Ho, J. K., and E. Loute. 1981. "An Advanced Implementation of the Dantzig-Wolfe Decomposition Algorithm for Linear Programming." *Mathematical Programming* 29:303–326.

IBM. 1975. "Mathematical Programming System Extended/370 (MPSX/370) Logic Manual." LY19-1024-0.

IBM. 1979. "Mathematical Programming System Extended/370 (MPSX/370) Program reference manual." SH19-1095-3.

Janssens de Bisthoven, O., P. Schuchewytsch, and Y. Smeers. 1985a. "Dealing with Uncertain Demand in Power Generation Planning." In *Energy Markets in the Longer-Term: Planning under Uncertainty*, edited by A. Kydes and D. Geraghty. Amsterdam: North Holland, 161–171.

Jannsens de Bisthoven, O., P. Schuchewytsch, and Y. Smeers. 1985b. "Power Generation Planning with Uncertain Demand." In *Numerical Techniques for Stochastic Optimization Problems*, edited by Y. Ermoliev and R. Wets. Laxenburg, Austria: IIASA.

Kallio, M. 1975. "On Large-Scale Linear Programming." Technical Report SOL 75-07, Department of Operations Research, Standford University.

Kallio, M., and E. Porteus. 1977. "Decomposition of Arborescent Linear Programs." *Mathematical Programming* 13:348–356.

Karmarkar, N. 1984. "A New Polynomial Time Algorithm for Linear Programming." *Combinatorica* 4:373–395.

Marsten, R. 1981. "The Design of the XMP Linear Programming Library." *ACM Transactions on Mathematical Software* 7:481–497.

Nemhauser, G. 1974. "Decomposition of Linear Programs by Dynamic Programming." *Naval Research Logistics Quarterly* 11:191–196.

Slate, L., and K. Spielberg. 1978. "The Extended Control Language of MPSX/370 and Possible Application." *IBM Systems Journal* 17:64–81.

Weill, R., and P. Kettler. 1971. "Rearranging Matrices to Block-Angular Form for Decomposition (and Other) Algorithms." *Management Science* 18:98–108.

Zviagina, R. 1973. "Multilevel Decomposition in Linear Programming." *Mathematische Operationsforschung und Statistik* 6:427–443. (In Russian).

III ECONOMETRICS

Introduction to Part III

The Survey Chapter

In his survey of econometrics over the period 1966 to 1986 (chapter 11), Adrian Pagan describes the progress of the discipline in terms of four research topics: "standards," that is, the statistical properties that every estimation should meet; internal "consistency," such as in the specification of the agents' expectations and/or actions, or over time; "robustness" to a departure from the assumptions on which the model rests; and finally, "the individual," that is, the evolution of the field toward more frequent estimations of models of individual behavior.

After a detailed evaluation of these topics, he concludes with a personal view on the econometric theorist's influence on the process of economic investigation. "Quantification is now the norm rather than the exception," he notes on the success side, recognizing even a "persistent tendency toward an excess demand for well-trained econometricians." But he also worries that econometricians might not be economists enough anymore.

Agreeing with this last observation, Michel Mouchart's comment expresses the opinion that more elaborate methodologies are needed for model specification. He mentions, however, three topics where progress has been made, he feels, in this respect. He also stresses the interest of Bayesian thinking in model specification, explaining how it provides a specific approach to both model formulation and the process of learning from the observations.

Jean Waelbroeck's further comments focus on the role played in the progress of econometrics by the enormous development in computer capabilities, both in the past and in the future. For the latter, he foresees that decision modeling will take a substantially increasing place within the econometric discipline.

The Econometrics Seminar Chapters

The chapters that follow deal with a variety of topics: econometric theory and methodology, model specification in demand systems, disequilibrium analysis, and macroeconometric models.

Chapter 12 by David Hendry and Jean-François Richard presents a detailed overview of a recent field in econometric methodology, namely, encompassing theory. The issue is when and whether a model can account for the results obtained by a rival one. Encompassing theory has already reached a considerable level of development in terms of concepts, tools, and techniques. After stating definitions and discussing properties of encompassing, a class of encompassing tests is applied to various examples, including the choice of the regressors problem. Linear dynamic models are formally analyzed, and the treatmemt of exogenous variables in the construction of encompassing tests is discussed. A notion of parsimonious-encompassing is examined, and its properties are discussed within the information matrix framework. Finally, Bayesian notions of encompassing and specificity are analyzed.

The pionneering version of complete systems of demand equations, known as the Rotterdam system, was originally formulated in terms of the first differences in its variables. Chapter 13 by Anton Barten presents a new version of this system in terms of the levels of the variables. This extension is of interest in the analysis of both time series and cross sections of observations. This extension is presented in the framework of a class of competing models, namely, the almost ideal demand system and the CBS demand system, for which also both first differences and level versions are specified and analyzed. An empirical application evaluates the relative merits of the various systems.

In chapter 14 Jean-Pierre Florens and Michel Mouchart present a Bayesian extension to the recent literature on specification tests. Their argument runs against the common view according to which testing and "Bayesianism" are incompatible. After a section on testing in a Bayesian framework in general, specification tests in this context are dealt with in detail, and two examples are treated, namely, the test of the value of regressors in a linear regressive model and a test of exogeneity.

In the field of disequilibrium econometrics, chapter 15 by Peter Kooiman reports on an attempt to estimate excess supply on goods and labor markets, from data provided by business survey reports. Models of the behavior of firms under labor supply, capacity, or demand constraints are specified, and the properties of their estimation are lucidly evaluated.

In chapter 16, the final chapter, Pierre Malgrange presents a method for analyzing a given macroeconometric model, that is, to reveal the model's theoretical underpinnings which are generally hidden behind the numerous and apparently complex equations. The basic idea is to treat the model as if it were a theoretical disequilibrium growth model, but with numerical parameters. The method is illustrated by a thorough application to METRIC, a French quarterly model.

11 Twenty Years After: Econometrics, 1966–1986

Adrian Pagan

11.1 Setting the Scene

What has happened to econometrics in the twenty years since CORE was founded? The external signs of growth are indeed impressive. In 1966 there were probably only three journals to be considered as vehicles for the regular publication of econometric methods—*Econometrica, Journal of the American Statistical Association*, and *The Review of Economics and Statistics*. By 1986 there were at least ten journals doing this, and even a specialist one in *Econometric Theory*. There is other evidence of growth. Johnston's textbook *Econometric Methods* came out in 1963 and ran to some 300 pages. By contrast, the 1984 edition was 568 pages of much smaller print. The 1966 issues of *Econometrica* contained 910 pages, whereas the 1986 issues had 1,503 pages. In 1966 it was probably the case that few members of the public would have even recognized the term econometrics; after the award of two Nobel Prizes in Economics to Tinbergen and Klein for their contributions to econometric modeling, public awareness is now much greater. So, on the external evidence, econometrics has flourished in the last twenty years.

A lot of this growth reflects the rapid advances in computing technology. It has always been true that the type of problems studied and work done in econometrics had been powerfully influenced by the available computation facilities. Techniques such as 2SLS and LIML were developed because it was too expensive to perform FIML; many methods for estimating equations with serial correlation had their origins in a desire to avoid the iterative procedures demanded by maximum likelihood. In 1966 there were no specialist econometric packages available for use; TSP was in the developmental stage, and those wishing to perform econometric analysis were forced to formulate their problems so as to employ the regression routines in packages such as OSIRIS. Thus both theory and practice were conditioned by the computational environment. Mostly what emerged up to 1970 was a second- rather than first-best choice.

All of this has changed dramatically in the last twenty years. Econometric packages have proliferated and have become increasingly easy to use, particularly with the advent of microcomputers. Moreover the modern package can estimate an enormous variety of models; some such as LIMDEP and SHAZAM even allowing users to customize the software.

Consequently the computational constraint has been significantly relaxed, rendering many "shortcuts" developed in the 1960s and 1970s merely of historical interest. Moreover computational advances not only allowed the implementation of complex theoretical work but also enabled solutions to problems too complex for theory—for example, many statistics such as the Durbin-Watson are ratios of quadratic forms in normal variables, and it was found possible to determine the numerical distribution of such quantities even if an analytic expression was intractable (Koerts and Abrahamse 1969; Durbin and Watson 1971).

This chapter will not be directly concerned with the shift described above. Important though it was, it is not primarily an intellectual tale. Furthermore, faced with the fact that the recently completed *Handbook of Econometrics* runs to 2,093 pages, a good proportion of which deals with post-1966 research, some discussion about what is to be excluded from the purview of this chapter is mandatory. My own interests naturally provide a first filter, but I have also adopted the principle of surveying those theoretical ideas that have had (or are likely to have) a significant impact upon the *practice* of econometrics. For this reason I have ignored developments in the fields of estimating markets in disequilibrium, continuous time models, and small sample theory. Excellent surveys of that material already exist in Quandt (1982), Bergstrom (1976), and Phillips (1982). It is my opinion that, for one reason or another, research in these subjects has not yet had the impact upon practitioners that was anticipated in the early stages of their development.

One should perhaps dwell briefly upon two of these omissions— disequilibrium and Bayesian econometrics—as major contributions to these areas were made by CORE researchers during the period. It is hard to deny that disequilibrium econometrics stimulated quite a deal of high-quality research, but I do not believe that much of this work has filtered down to practitioners. Part of the explanation lies in a division of views, roughly along U.S. and European lines, about the utility of economic analysis conducted under the assumption of price-clearing markets. But I also think that many model builders have found it computationally expedient to think of prices as adjusting slowly toward an equilibrium and to rely upon the presence of inventories, etc., to account for any "disequilibrium" effects.

Bayesian analysis suffers from a similar problem. As Poirier (1986) observes, less than 15% of econometrics is done according to strict Bayesian precepts. In my opinion the reasons for this lack of acceptance reside in the difficulties of prior formulation and the computational burden of obtaining a posterior distribution under a realistic prior specification. With the growth of available observations the number of parameters estimated in econometric models has tended to increase, Koenker (1985). At the same time models that are nonlinear in the parameters have become the norm. Such considerations place great demands upon the ability to derive a posterior distribution. Maximizing the likelihood has not been easy in these models, and finding a complete posterior is a far more difficult task. Nevertheless, there are some signs that the Bayesian "way of thinking" is being increasingly favored. Doan et al. (1984) have imposed prior beliefs upon the coefficients of a VAR as a way of reducing the unknown parameters, whereas Geweke (1986) has used the Bayesian approach to estimate models with inequality restrictions, a situation where it is hard to derive distributions of statistics from a frequentist perspective.

Two other self-imposed guidelines operate. First, it is necessary to set the borderline between economic theory and econometrics. Many useful advances were made by the application of duality theory and calculus of variations to a study of business and consumer behavior, and these were reflected in the types of specifications becoming the norm in applied econometric analysis. I have taken this literature as pertaining to economic theory, and have thereby limited my discussion to the estimation issues that arise. Second, one of the distinctive features of much of the work recounted below has been its origins in the mathematical statistics domain. Econometricians have translated these ideas into their own language and concerns. Sometimes the relationship has been symbiotic, with the interest displayed in the technique by our field reawakening interest in it among mathematical statisticians. I have rarely tried to trace the intellectual heritage of the work described below, preferring to only locate the point of its introduction to econometrics.

With all these qualifications made, it is time to set out the structure of the chapter. My title is borrowed from Alexandre Dumas' sequel to his classic "The Three Musketeers." That is a tale of the aging of the four musketeers, and the decline of their zest and vitality; it is a tale in which the events are precipitated by the flawed decisions of twenty years ago at the time of greatest triumph. Above all, it is a tale about a search to right the mistakes of the past. As such it constitutes a powerful metaphor for the changes that have beset econometrics in the past two decades. Twenty years ago, econometrics was probably in its golden age. Since then it has fragmented, particularly after the failure of econometric models in predicting developments following from the first oil price shock, and its spectacular growth is partly a function of the initiation of many searches aimed at rectifying what are now perceived as deficiencies inherent in its concerns at that time.

I have treated the focus of econometrics from 1966–1986 as four "searches": for standards, consistency, robustness, and the individual. It is interesting that, with the exception of the third, almost none of these was on the agenda of econometrics in 1966. That fact emhasizes just how different econometrics has been in the last twenty years to the preceding twenty years. As Pesaran (1986) observes, the postwar developments in econometrics until the 1960s seem a very smooth ascending path, largely being a working out of the Cowles Commission program in which careful attention was paid to the problems of implementation in the light of computational capabilities. By contrast, the last twenty years have witnessed tremendous diversity in econometric research. There is now no longer a single methodology for econometrics, and there is a much greater practical awareness of the limitations of any one. "Search" then seems an apt description of econometrics in the years we cover. The ultimate objective may be clear, but the best route to get there is still to be found.

11.2 The Search for Standards

All modeling activity is based upon a set of conventions whose role it is to reduce a mass of potential outcomes down to a set of what are felt to be important ones. But, at times, these conventions may be seriously at variance with the data under analysis, and it becomes imperative to ascertain the validity of the conventions in any given context. It follows that normal practice should be for the reports on any modeling exercise to contain such discussion. In turn, this implies the need for a set of standards to evaluate the correspondence of conventions with outcomes. Unless such information is provided, any piece of research deserves to be treated with considerable skepticism.

The attempt to delineate such standards was a characteristic of the methodology for the modeling of economic time series advanced by Hendry (1980) and Hendry and Richard (1982). Their taxonomy is exhaustive, but I find it easier to discuss research on standards under five headings that correspond to the five main conventions underlying the general linear regression model:

$$y_t = x_t \beta + u_t. \tag{1}$$

(i) The conditional mean is linear in x_t only.

(ii) The variable x_t is uncorrelated with the error term u_t.

(iii) The conditional variance of the errors is constant.

(iv) The errors u_t exhibit no temporal dependence.

(v) (Sometimes) the errors u_t are normally distributed.

Clearly, there is no reason to suppose that *any* of these assumptions need be correct, and some measure of how accurate they are is desirable. To appreciate just how much of a change in attitude over this matter there has been in the last twenty years, it suffices to compare the paper by Huang in the April 1966 issue of *Econometrica*—a study of the U.S. housing market—with that by Engle et al. (1987) twenty-one years later. In Huang's study almost no evidence is presented on the adequacy of the five assumptions above; each of his estimated equations is accompanied solely by an $\bar{R}^2$. By contrast, Engle et al. incorporate an extensive range of diagnostic tests for failures in the crucial assumptions underlying their work. These two articles probably represent polar cases; some research in 1966 undoubtedly paid more attention to issues (i) through (v) than Huang did, and there are still studies in 1986 failing to be as responsive in meeting a set of standards as Engle et al. are. Nevertheless, the profession has shifted in the latter direction; a comparison of the new editions of Johnston (1964), Kmenta (1986), and Kennedy (1985) with their previous versions makes this abundantly clear.

A summary of developments in this area might be done in a number of ways. One approach is to regard (i) through (v) as statements about the assumed moments of the distribution of the dependent variable y_t; the degree of correspondence with the sample moments then provides the desired measures. Thus, if the conditional mean is postulated as $x_t \beta$, it is natural to ask if it might be augmented to $x_t \beta + z_t \gamma$, that is, if $E(z_t'(y_t - x_t \beta))$ is equal to zero. The "sample" moment for this is $T^{-1} \sum_{t=1}^{T} z_t'(y_t - x_t \hat{\beta})$, where $\hat{\beta}$ is some suitable estimator of β, and this should be close to zero if the maintained model is to be acceptable. I have used this framework elsewhere (Pagan 1984), terming it the "variable addition" strategy. Here I will adopt it to describe the major themes, and some extensions to the treatment will also be indicated.

The Conditional Mean

Ramsey (1969) represents the most influential early contribution to an examination of this topic. He observed that neither the functional form nor the menu of variables appearing in the conditional mean could be asserted with much confidence. To provide some check on the maintained formats he proposed trying to add to the basic model, as z_t variables, polynomials in the regression predictions $\hat{y}_t$(generally $\hat{y}_t^2, \hat{y}_t^3$, and $\hat{y}_t^4$). This became the RESET test. Subsequently, numerous variable addition tests appeared to assess the adequacy of particular aspects of the conditional mean specification. Each was derived by stipulating a plausible alternative model and then checking if the residuals of the maintained model exhibited any pattern that would be consistent with the alternative model being a better representation.

In 1978 Hausman advanced what appeared to be a quite distinct procedure. He advanced the idea that two estimators of the conditional mean parameters (β) be obtained, both being consistent if the maintained model was correct, but with different probability limits if it was incorrect, and that an index of model adequacy could then be based upon the difference in estimates. White (1980b) and Plosser et al. (1982) adopted this philosophy. In the former, OLS estimates of β were compared with weighted least squares values for β, where the weight given to the tth observation was arbitrarily selected. In the second paper, the alternative estimate of β in the comparison came from regressing Δy_t against Δx_t, where Δ is the first difference operator. Both of these proposals are special cases of applying a known transformation matrix F to the matrix version of (1), $y = X\beta + u$, followed by a comparison of $\hat{\beta} = (X'X)^{-1}X'y$ and $\tilde{\beta} = (X'F'FX)^{-1}X'F'Fy$ (for White's case F is diagonal with the chosen weights as elements). Since $y = X\hat{\beta} + \hat{u}$, it follows that $\tilde{\beta} = \hat{\beta} + (X'F'FX)^{-1}X'F'F\hat{u}$ and $\tilde{\beta} - \hat{\beta} = (X'F'FX)^{-1}X'F'F\hat{u}$, making it a test based on $T^{-1}\Sigma z_t'\hat{u}_t = T^{-1}X'F'F\hat{u}$. As such, it is clear that these methods are oriented toward the detection of particular types of departures from the null hypothesis. Breusch and Godfrey (1986) have provided a comprehensive discussion of this.[1]

The nature of x_t

The second area of concern arises from the stochastic nature of x_t. A primary question is whether it is y_t or x_t, which should be the dependent variable in any regression, or which variable is cause and which effect? Significant work has been done on this issue of "causality" since 1969. In that year Granger proposed an "empirical" definition that radically changed what had been an on-going and largely inconclusive debate ever since the Cowles Commission's reports. Granger proposed to define x_t as causing y_t if the ability to predict y_t using the past history of x_t and y_t together was greater than if only the past history of y_t had been exploited. In application this tended to be interpreted as whether the past history of x_t significantly augmented the regression of y_t upon its past values. Sims (1972) produced a modified version of this criterion by adding the requirement that no future values of x_t should have an influence as well.

To say that the idea was popular among applied econometricians would be a vast understatement; an enormous number of inquiries were conducted in this framework during the 1970s on almost every conceivable economic time series. Much of it was very uncritical. As Leamer (1984) points out, the definition is more aptly one of the concept of "precedence," and the "causality" being investigated should be understood in that way. Otherwise, striking conclusions such as "Christmas card sales cause Christmas" (Kennedy 1985, p. 64) are all too likely. Moreover many of these studies were conducted within a strictly bivariate framework, ignoring Granger's own warning about this: "If relevant data have not been included in this set, then spurious causality could arise" (p. 429). A good proportion of those applying the method in a bivariate mode would seem to have totally forgotten one of the earliest maxims of economics statistics courses; ignored "third causes" can be the source of strong bivariate correlations. There was a lot of high-powered mathematics involved in the analysis of this topic, but I come away from a reading of it with the feeling that it was one of the most unfortunate turnings for econometrics in the last two decades, and that it has probably generated more nonsense results than anything else done during that time.

To many econometricians what was of interest in Granger's work was not "causality" *per se* but the idea that it could be used to determine if x_t was "exogenous." The "new classical economists" frequently asserted that x_t was "econometrically exogenous" if and only if x_t was not Granger-caused by y_t, that is, x_t was a function only of its own history (e.g., see Sargent 1976, p. 544), and berated econometricians for not doing such checks (Lucas and Sargent 1981, p. 302). Yet on almost any reasonable definition of "econometrically exogenous," it was difficult to understand why Granger causality was required. For example, if $x_t = \alpha x_{t-1} + \gamma y_{t-1} +$

v_t, where v_t is uncorrelated with u_t, it is not necessary for γ to be zero to ensure that x_t is uncorrelated with u_t. This stance by Sargent (1976) and by Sims et al. (1986) has always puzzled me, and the only way I have made sense of it is to argue that adherents to this position wish to make *no* assumptions about the degree of serial correlation in the error terms. But, I must admit that if this is what Sims (1972) intended in his original discussion of the problem, it is not at all clear.

Confusion over questions of "exogeneity" reigned in applied work during the 1970s and one could almost sense a sigh of relief when Engle et al. (1983) appeared with a simple summary of the main "exogeneity" concepts in the literature. By far the most important theme of the paper was to take the joint density for (y_t, x_t), conditional upon all past data, $f_{t-1}(y_t, x_t; \lambda)$, and ask if it could be factored as $f_{t-1}(y_t/x_t; \lambda_1) \, f_{t-1}(x_t; \lambda_2)$—that is, do the parameters entering in the conditional density also appear in the marginal density for x_t? If not, they termed such a situation one in which x_t was "weakly exogenous" for λ_1; a proposal wholly compatible with the original Cowles Commission idea of exogeneity, as exemplified by Koopmans (1950). Furthermore, if $f_{t-1}(x_t; \lambda_2) = f_{t-1}^*(x_t; \lambda_2)$, where the conditioning in $f_{t-1}^*(\cdot)$ is now upon the past history of x_t alone, Granger causality or "strong exogeneity" prevails. Because of the nested nature of this decomposition, it is immediately apparent that Granger causality is too strong for efficient estimation of λ (or any functions of it).

Still, the question remains, What is an appropriate test for weak exogeneity? A standard reply in many articles has been the presentation of the Wu-Hausman statistic (proposed informally by Durbin 1954). Wu (1973) suggested that a comparison be made between the OLS estimator $\hat{\beta}$ and an instrumental variables estimator $\tilde{\beta} = (Z'X)^{-1}Z'y$. Once again, after substituting $y = X\hat{\beta} + \hat{u}$ into the formula for $\tilde{\beta}$, $\tilde{\beta} - \hat{\beta} = (Z'X)^{-1}Z'\hat{u}$, and therefore the test involves the sample correlation of the instruments with OLS residuals assuming x_t is weakly exogenous. Another interpretation of Wu's proposal is to add Z to the original model, and this is what Hausman (1978) did. From the nature of the sample moment under test, it is apparent that what is being examined is the validity of the instruments, and that in turn is dependent upon the validity of the specification of the marginal density $f_{t-1}(x_t, \lambda_2)$.

Conditional Error Variances

Investigation into the failure of higher-order moment assumptions for the errors was popular, although what progress there was in this area largely involved the reinterpretation of already existing tests, rather than the development of new ones. Thus the design of diagnostic techniques for heteroskedasticity in Breusch and Pagan (1979) and Godfrey (1978b) had antecedents in the literature; the novel element supplied by these papers was the connection with Lagrange multiplier (LM) statistics. All of the tests that were proposed here essentially involved checking if the correlation of some nominated variables z_t with the centered squared errors was zero, that is, was $T^{-1}\Sigma z_i'[(y_t - x_t\beta)^2 - \sigma^2]$ close to zero? In the LM versions, $\theta' = (\beta'\sigma^2)$ were replaced by the OLS estimators $\hat{\theta}$, but, as observed in Pagan (1986), any root $-T$ consistent estimator of θ could be used without affecting the asymptotic power properties of the test, because the limiting distribution of the statistic above does not depend upon the limiting distribution of the θ estimators. However, in small samples the choice may be important, and Evans and King (1985) proposed estimating θ from a weighted regression.

Perhaps the most interesting development under this heading was the recognition that the variance of u_t might be unconditionally constant but nevertheless vary conditionally—for example, the conditional variance $E_{t-1}(u_t^2) = \sigma^2 + \alpha y_{t-1}^2$ has $E(u_t^2)$ as a constant whenever y_t is a covariance stationary process. Engle (1982) popularized this distinction, naming the conditional case autoregressive conditional heteroskedasticity (ARCH). Lately it has become common to compute tests for certain variants of this class of models, particularly those that have $E_{t-1}(u_t^2) = \sigma^2 + \sum_{j=1}^{M} \alpha_j(y_{t-j} - x_{t-j}\beta)^2$; the idea here being that large errors in the past can be expected to create greater uncertainty in present decisions.

Temporal Dependence

Unlike the analysis of the second moment of u_t, work on temporal dependence yielded many new insights. In 1966 the principal way of assessing temporal dependence was with the Durbin-Watson statistic, but it was already known that there were difficulties in applying it to dynamic models in which lagged values of the regressand appeared. The first correct solution to the problem was presented in Durbin (1970). He observed that the Durbin-Watson statistic can be thought of as based upon the sample moment $T^{-1}\Sigma \hat{u}_t\hat{u}_{t-1}$, and so its limiting distribution may well depend upon that of $T^{1/2}(\hat{\beta} - \beta)$. Indeed, this is exactly what happens when x_t contains y_{t-1}, and Durbin's solution was to make an allowance for the fact that β is estimated rather than known.

An appreciation of this principle cleared the way for an extension of the traditional tests for serial correlation to other contexts, such as when $\hat{\beta}$ was an instrumental variable estimator as in Godfrey (1978a). Of course, when the limiting distribution is independent of $T^{1/2}(\hat{\beta} - \beta)$, other choices of $\hat{\beta}$ than the OLS one may be desirable for good small sample performance. Berenblut and Webb (1973) suggested that $\hat{\beta}$ be replaced by $\tilde{\beta}$ formed by regressing Δy_t against Δx_t, while King (1985) adopts an estimate found by regressing $y_t - \lambda y_{t-1}$ against $x_t - \lambda x_{t-1}$, where λ is a prespecified value. He demonstrates that the small sample performance of such a modified statistic is generally superior to that for the Durbin-Watson test.

The other major extension in this area arose from the steady movement of empirical work from yearly to quarterly and even monthly data. Quarterly data meant that variables were likely to exhibit a fourth-order serial correlation pattern, and this makes an examination for only first-order serial correlation inadequate. Ideally, it is desirable to look at the complete autocorrelation function of the residuals, but specialized variants were developed (e.g., for fourth order by Wallis 1972).[2]

Distribution of the Errors

Normality of the errors has traditionally been queried by examining the coefficients of kurtosis and skewness of the residuals. The distribution of these depends upon that of $\hat{\beta}$, and it was Bowman and Shenton (1975) and Bera and Jarque (1981) who provided the requisite adjustments; the latter being particularly interesting in its derivation of the test statistics via the LM principle applied to alternative distributions falling within the Pearson family. As checks on *normality*, these indices are not entirely satisfactory, owing to the existence of distributions, notably Tukey's λ distribution (Joiner and Rosenblatt 1971), which exhibit identical skewness and kurtosis to the normal but which differ in the tails. For regression models, this difference is not of great import, but for models in which the dependent variable is truncated or censored—for example in the Tobit model where only values of y_t corresponding to $x_t\beta + u_t \geq 0$ are observed—it is the shape of the whole distribution that is important. Because of this fact comprehensive tests of normality have appeared in the literature—Heckman (1984) advocated the chi-square test comparing actual and predicted fractiles of empirical distribution functions, and Andrews (1985) generalized this in a number of directions, notably to allow the selection of fractiles to be sample based. Tauchen (1985) has a similar proposal, based on a discrete number of fractiles.

A feature of the 1970s, treated in a later section, was the movement away from the standard regression model to situations involving latent variables or categorical data. Hence there is frequently no continuously measured dependent variable, and it becomes imperative that indices of adequacy be devised from a perspective that is not limited by regression concepts. The most important papers concerned with this task were Tauchen (1985) and Newey (1985). These authors argued that if there exists a vector of functions $m(w_t, \theta)$ (θ being the parameters of the maintained model and w_t the data) with the property that $E(m(w_t, \theta)) = 0$ when the maintained model is valid, then $\hat{\tau} = T^{-1} \Sigma m(w_t, \hat{\theta})$ is a suitable vector of indices to test the adequacy of the original model. As illustrations, $m(w_t, \theta) = z_t'(y_t - x_t \beta)$ would be the choice for specification error in the mean of the regression model, whereas $m(w_t, \theta) = z_t'[(y_t - x_t \beta)^2 - \sigma^2]$ would provide tests for heteroskedasticity in it.

What is the appeal of this approach? Many econometric estimators of θ satisfy a set of equations $T^{-1} \Sigma d(w_t, \theta) = 0$. In the case of maximum likelihood estimation the $d(\cdot)$ are the scores, but, as discussed later, instrumental variable estimators also have this format. Consequently, if $\phi(w, \theta, \tau) = T^{-1} \Sigma [d(w_t, \theta)(m(w_t, \theta) - \tau)]$, the estimates of θ and τ found by setting $\phi(w, \theta, \tau) = 0$ are just $\hat{\theta}$ and $\hat{\tau} = T^{-1} \Sigma m(w_t, \hat{\theta})$, and $\hat{\tau}$ may be treated as a *parameter* in an extended estimation problem. If computer programs are available to solve $T^{-1} \Sigma d(w_t, \theta) = 0$, immediate application to the task of solving $\phi(w, \hat{\theta}, \hat{\tau}) = 0$ is possible, and standard tests of $\tau = 0$ may be performed. Actually, when $\hat{\theta}$ is an MLE, after some suitable partitioning and use of asymptotic theory, both Tauchen and Newey give a simpler test procedure for $\tau = 0$; they regress $m(w_t, \hat{\theta})$ against unity and $d(w_t, \hat{\theta})$, checking if the intercepts in these regressions are zero.[3] If $\hat{\theta}$ is not an MLE, Newey provides an expression for the limiting distribution of $\hat{\tau}$.

By adopting the Newey-Tauchen formulation it is easy to derive indices of inadequacy for cases other than the linear regression model. All that needs be done is to select a suitable $m(\cdot)$ function. To date, the main extensions have been to the situation where the general linear model is the underlying structure but output from it is censored. The dependent variable in (1) becomes a latent variable y_t^* and the actual observations y_t do not equal y_t^* for part of the sample; in the tobit model only nonzero y_t^* are available, whereas in the probit model y_t is binary.

Suppose that it is possible to propose an alternative model differing from the maintained version by the presence of extra parameters ψ. The theory of the E-M algorithm (Dempster et al. 1977) contains the useful result that the actual score with respect to ψ is given by the conditional expectation of the score appropriate to the latent variable model. That is, if L^* is the likelihood of the latent data and L that of the observed data, $\partial \log L/\partial \psi = E(\partial \log L^*/\partial \psi |\text{obs data})$ (Chow 1983 has a good discussion of this). Consequently, a suitable $m(\cdot)$ would be this conditional expectation, and it forms the basis of diagnostic tests given in Bera et al. (1984), Lee and Maddala (1985), and Gourieroux et al. (1985).

One interesting aspect of these developments has been the definition of "generalized residuals," in the sense of Cox and Snell (1968). To get these, consider augmenting (1) with z_t when y_t^* is latent and u_t is n.i.d. (0, 1). From the principle connecting the observed and unobserved scores, $\partial \log L/\partial \psi = E[\Sigma z_t'(y_t^* - x_t\beta)|\text{obs data}] = \Sigma z_t' E[(y_t^* - x_t\beta)|\text{obs data})]$. In the linear regression case the corresponding score would be $\Sigma z_t'(y_t - x_t\beta)$, and it is fitting that $E[(y_t^* - x_t\beta)|\text{obs data})]$, evaluated at $\hat{\beta}$, be regarded as a *generalized* residual. For the probit model $E[(y_t^* - x_t\beta)|\text{obs data}] = y_t F(x_t\beta)^{-1} f(x_t\beta) + (1 - y_t)F(-x_t\beta)f(x_t\beta)$, where $F(\cdot)$ and $f(\cdot)$ are the cumulative normal distribution and standard normal density evaluated at "$\cdot$," and this quantity forms the basis of the diagnostic tests set out in Davidson and MacKinnon (1984). Once the generalized residuals are computed they may be used for checking the assumptions of homoskedasticity, normality, etc., in much the same way as the ordinary residuals were used earlier (Chesher and Irish 1984).[4] Whether it is worth specifically obtaining the generalized residuals is a moot point. Unlike the ordinary residuals, it is hard to interpret plots of them, and so their utility is mainly that of a pedagogic device for explaining the intuition behind diagnostic tests constructed with $m(\cdot)$ as the conditional scores.

Most of the work described above implicitly accords to the maintained hypothesis a special status. The role of alternatives is to expose inadequacies in the current formulation, and they are rarely regarded as being worthy of estimation or reporting. For this reason the alternatives typically reflect statistical rather than economic theory, although it is questionable if the process of econometric modeling is capable of being characterized in this way. Frequently, economic reasoning will supply a number of potential explanations, with no single one capable of being designated as the maintained variant. A method of directly comparing such models is therefore clearly desirable.

This consideration gave rise to a good deal of interest in the question of comparing nonnested models. Dhrymes et al. (1972) mentioned work by

Cox (1961, 1962) when looking at methods for evaluating models, but it was not until after Pesaran's (1974) paper on the choice between two nonnested linear regression models that applications emerged. Thereafter a voluminous literature developed, surveyed in McAleer and Pesaran (1986). Most of it may be treated within the same framework as that utilized previously in the construction of diagnostic tests. It is now necessary, however, to partition θ into θ_1 and θ_2, corresponding to the two models entering the pairwise comparisons. Auxiliary functions are still appended to the set of equations $T^{-1}\Sigma d(w_t, \hat{\theta}) = 0$, and a test statistic based on $\hat{\tau}$ constructed. What complicates the analysis is that $E(d(w_t, \theta)) = 0$ for only a subset of equations, as one of the models is taken to be invalid. Consequently, if $T^{1/2}(\hat{\theta}_1 - \theta_1)$ is $\mathcal{N}(o, v_{11})$, $T^{1/2}(\hat{\theta}_2 - \theta_2^*)$ will be $\mathcal{N}(o, v_{22})$, where θ_2^* is referred to as the "pseudotrue value" of θ_2 (Sawa 1978) and $\Sigma E(d(w_t, \theta_1, \theta_2^*)) = 0$. Derivation of the limiting distributions of τ therefore need to be done carefully but, when $d(w_t, \theta)$ are the scores of each likelihood, analyses of the limiting distribution of $T^{1/2}(\theta_2 - \theta_2^*)$ have been introduced into the econometric literature by White (1982a) and Gourieroux et al. (1984). This theory was applied to $\hat{\tau}$ in Gourieroux et al. (1983) and Mizon and Richard (1986).

What differentiates the contributions to this literature is not the choice of $d(w_t, \theta)$ but the specification of $T^{-1}\Sigma m(w_t, \theta)$.[5] For simplicity, consider the choice between two linear regression models $y_t = x_t\beta + u_{1t}$ and $y_t = z_t\gamma + u_{2t}$. Various selections for $m(w_t, \theta)$ are possible.[6] First, take $m(\cdot) = z_t'(y_t - x_t\beta)$, since the error term $(y_t - x_t\beta)$ should be uncorrelated with any regressor in z_t not in x_t. This yields the F-test for nonnested models. Alternatively, set $m(\cdot)$ to $(z_t\gamma)(y_t - x_t\beta)$, a single auxiliary function, to get the J-test of Davidson and Mackinnon (1981), which is frequently implemented by adding $z_t\hat{\gamma}$ to $y_t = x_t\beta + u_{1t}$ and then testing for its significance.[7] Another choice would be $\Sigma m(w_t, \theta) = L(\gamma) - E_\beta L(\gamma)$, where $L(\gamma)$ is the log likelihood of $y_t = z_t\gamma + u_{2t}$ and $E_\beta L(\gamma)$ is its expectation under the first model. This is the basis of Cox's statistic. Mizon (1984) and Mizon and Richard (1986) have noted that there are many ways to formulate suitable $m(\cdot)$ functions, based upon scores, likelihoods, parameter estimates, etc., and each of these corresponds to asking the question of whether one model encompasses the other with respect to the particular $m(\cdot)$ function adopted.

There is no doubt in my mind that this work on adequacy was vital to improving the standard of applied econometrics. In some respects its role is negative; having a model designed to meet the criteria doesn't mean it is a good model, but having a model that fails them is indicative of a bad one. A major deficiency with econometric research of the 1960s, well exemplified by Huang's paper, was the impossibility of inferring from any reported material whether the model was an adequate representation of the data. Over the years I have been continually impressed by the role of these tests in ferreting out poor models, to such an extent that I now feel very uncomfortable with conclusions drawn on the basis of research that has been subject to little critical assessment through them.

11.3   The Search for Consistency

As mentioned in the introduction, econometric research in the 1970 was frequently stimulated by the perceived failure of large-scale econometric models to predict well after the first oil price shock. One response to this phenomenon would be to claim that such an outcome was inevitable, either because the models had been constructed with a flawed methodology or because very little attention had been paid to whether they met acceptable standards. I certainly believe that there is more than a grain of truth in this judgment. But neither point is specific to large-scale macro models, and it is therefore not surprising that some of the most active research areas in econometrics dealt directly with what were perceived to be inherent weaknesses in the large-scale models. What motivated this research was the desire to make those models internally consistent, with the concomitant belief that restructuring along the new lines would lead to better performance. In making these models consistent, a range of econometric issues arose, some of which were solved and some of which still constitute ongoing research programs. This section distinguishes a number of ways in which internal consistency was sought.

Expectations

The need for consistency first arose from a consideration of the way expectations were normally modeled. Standard empirical macroeconomic models based output decisions upon the ratio of the wage rate to actual prices while, following the modification of the Phillips curve introduced by Friedman and Phelps, the wage rate was determined by price expectations. Suppose these price expectations are represented as a combination of past and present prices, that is, $p_t^e = \sum_{j=0}^{K} w_j p_{t-j} (0 < K < \infty)$. Then any rise in p_t is only partly reflected in p_t^e, wages rise less than prices, and output expands. Workers are "fooled" into supplying more labour even though the actual real wage declines. With the operation of this "Keynesian" mechanism, fiscal policy is expansionary.

Although it is quite plausible that such "mistakes" are made, what was implausible was their persistence, as that can be construed as a defective learning process on the part of economic agents. Believers in "rational economic man" were decidedly uncomfortable with such an implication and proposed that no model should embody the possibility of a consistent pattern of mistakes.

Borrowing Muth's (1961) phrase of "rational expectations," Lucas (1972) argued that expectations in a model should be rational and have the property that they be the predictions of the model for the variable about which expectations are being formed. To present the implications of this viewpoint and to discuss the literature surrounding it, consider the following simple demand and supply model for a commodity:

$$d_t = \alpha p_t + \beta i_t + e_t, \tag{2a}$$

$$s_t = \gamma p_t^e + \delta w_t + \varepsilon_t, \tag{2b}$$

$$s_t = d_t = q_t. \tag{3}$$

Equations (2) and (3) had d_t, s_t, and q_t as quantity demanded, supplied, and transacted, respectively, p_t and p_t^e are actual and expected prices; i_t is real income; w_t the "weather"; e_t and ε_t are zero mean white noise error terms. Older market models of commodities set $p_t^e = p_{t-1}$, but in the new view p_t^e was replaced by $E(p_t|i_t, w_t)$. To find $E(p_t|i_t, w_t)$, get the reduced from equation for p_t,

$$p_t = \pi_1 i_t + \pi_2 w_t + \pi_3 e_t + \pi_4 \varepsilon_t, \tag{4}$$

and take the conditional expectation,

$$p_t^e = E(p_t|i_t, w_t) = \pi_1 i_t + \pi_2 w_t. \tag{5}$$

Notice that there are no systematic mistakes in price expectations in this model since $p_t - E(p_t|i_t, w_t) = \pi_3 e_t + \pi_4 \varepsilon_t = v_t$, is a zero mean white noise.

Econometricians attacked the estimation problems caused by rational expectations (RE) with gusto. McCallum (1976) suggested that $p_t - v_t$ be substituted for p_t^e in (2b), making it

$$s_t = \gamma p_t + \delta w_t + \eta_t, \tag{6}$$

and then estimate (2a), (3), and (6) jointly by two-stage least squares. Others proposed three-stage least squares and FIML (Wallis 1980; Wickens 1982).

Thus the presence of RE's in macroeconomic systems was effectively dealt with by a transformation replacing the expectation by an endogenous variable, followed by an application of a simultaneous equation estimator. But the simplicity of this solution raises a number of technical issues. First, is the new system identified? Although the number of endogenous variables may remain unchanged (p_t was frequently already an endogenous variable before, as it is in (2a)), the number of predetermined variables was generally smaller than when p_t was determined in an extrapolative way. For example, if $p_t^e = p_{t-1}$ in (2b) there would be three potential instruments $\{p_{t-1}, w_t,$ and $i_t\}$ and (2) is overidentified, but in the RE case there are only two, making (2) just identified. With RE's in a system, care must be exercised to ensure that there really are enough available instruments to enable estimation to proceed (Revankar 1980; Pesaran 1981).

Complications arise if (2b) features forward-looking expectations in that it is p_{t+1}^e rather than p_t^e that drives supply decisions. Then η_t in (6) is composed of $\varepsilon_t - \gamma v_{t+1}$ and has the autocorrelation function of an MA(1) process. Although the instrumental variable solution is still available, the MA-type error term should be accounted for in efficient estimation. However, if the composite error term η_t was just replaced by an MA(1), $\xi_t + \alpha \xi_{t-1}$, there is no guarantee that $E(\xi_t | i_t, w_t) = 0$ even though it is true for the individual components. Hence the estimation problem is not a straightforward one and various suggestions were made to improve the efficiency of estimation. Pesaran (1987) and Wickens (1986) provide detailed treatments of this literature, emphasizing that there is a close connection between the estimation problem and the difficulties of finding unique solutions in forward-looking expectations models.

A second issue concerned the possibility of testing if the assumption of RE's was correct. Again, the simultaneous equation perspective provided an affirmative answer. To see why, begin with a single structural equation:

$$y_{1t} = y_{2t}\gamma + x_{1t}\beta + e_t, \tag{7}$$

where y_{2t} are included endogenous variables, x_{1t} are included predetermined variables, and e_t is the disturbance term. The reduced form equations for y_{2t} are

$$y_{2t} = x_{1t}\pi_{21} + x_{2t}\pi_{22} + v_{2t}, \tag{8}$$

enabling substitution for y_{2t} in (7) to give

$$y_{1t} = x_{1t}(\pi_{21}\gamma + \beta) + x_{2t}\pi_{22}\gamma + v_{1t} \tag{9}$$

$$= x_{1t}\pi_{11} + x_{2t}\pi_{12} + v_{2t}, \tag{10}$$

the reduced form equations for y_{1t}. Clearly, the presence of y_{2t} on the right-hand side of (7) induces the restrictions $\pi_{11} = \pi_{21}\gamma + \beta$ and $\pi_{22}\gamma = \pi_{12}$. Since RE's causes an endogenous variable to appear in an equation, it also imposes restrictions between the structural and reduced form parameters. By inserting OLS estimates of π_{ij}, and the 2SLS estimate of γ and β, it is possible to test if $\pi_{11} = \pi_{21}\gamma + \beta$ and $\pi_{22}\gamma = \pi_{12}$. Byron (1970) observed that this was a way of checking the validity of structural specifications, while Hoffman and Schmidt (1981) applied it to the RE situation.

To some extent I think that this approach is not as useful as it might be. Because it essentially compares the restricted and unrestricted reduced form parameters, it is important that the reduced form be general enough to allow for the plausible range of alternative hypotheses. For example, if the alternative in (2b) above is that $p_t^e = p_{t-1}$, the reduced form regressors should include p_{t-1}, whereas it is excluded under the RE formulation. A related difficulty resides in the fact that the choice to be made is really between RE's and some extrapolative mechanism, and this presumably should be done directly rather than via a reduced form. Technically, what is involved are two nonnested models, in that one cannot be found as the limit of the other, and it would be better to do comparisons utilizing the techniques outlined in the preceding section.

Perhaps the most important developments to emerge out of this interest in estimating models with RE's was the refocusing of attention upon the role of economic theory in supplying a set of orthogonality relations between functions of an observed variable and an unknown error term. Sometimes, these relations come from an optimising framework (Kennan 1979). In the context of (2a) and (6), the orthogonality conditions are that $E(z_t\eta_t) = 0$ and $E(z_te_t) = 0$, where $z_t = (w_ti_t)$, since $\eta_t = \varepsilon_t - \gamma v_t$, and as w_t and i_t are both assumed to be in the agents' information set, $E(w_tv_t) = E(i_tv_t) = 0$. A prominent advantage of this approach is that not all of the information used in forming expectations need be specified—a subset of the orthogonality relations is all that is required for consistent estimation. Replacing η_t in (6) by $q_t - (p_tw_t)\begin{pmatrix}\gamma\\\delta\end{pmatrix} = q_t - x_t\phi$, the orthogonality restrictions are $E(z_t'(q_t - x_t\phi)) = 0$. A sample analogue is $T^{-1}\Sigma z_t'(q_t - x_t\phi) =$

0. Solving this last equation for ϕ, assuming that $T^{-1}\Sigma z_t' x_t$ is nonzero, provides the instrumental variables estimator $\hat{\phi} = (\Sigma z_t' x_t)^{-1} \Sigma z_t' q_t$.

Interesting questions arise when there are more orthogonality conditions than parameters ϕ, that is, $\dim(z_t) > \dim(x_t)$. Sargan (1958) demonstrated that within the class of consistent instrumental variable estimators of ϕ, the variance minimising estimator is formed from $z_t = \hat{x}_t$, the predictions from the regression of x_t against all possible instruments. Sargan termed this estimator the generalized instrumental variables estimator (GIVE). What was not fully grasped at the time, although quite clear from Sargan's proof, is that the optimality of GIVE depends crucially upon the assumption of the errors in the orthogonality conditions being i.i.d. $(0, \sigma^2)$—that is, the errors should exhibit no temporal dependence and have a constant conditional variance. To appreciate the restrictiveness of that assumption, suppose that p_{t+1}^e rather than p_t^e was in (2b). Then $E(v_{t+1}|w_t, i_t) = 0$, v_t may be a one-dependent process, and so in turn may η_t. Under such circumstances greater estimator efficiency is possible by combining the instruments in a way that recognizes the temporal dependence in the errors. Cumby et al. (1983), White (1982b), and Hansen (1982) all gave the correct weighting scheme, with the latter describing the estimators as generalized method of moments (GMM), thereby emphasising a connection with the most basic estimation method dealt with in statistics.

GMM was not a major advance over existing estimation methods, but it represented a successful reinterpretation of existing ones and was a concept of enormous power when it came to unifying a scattered literature. As an added bonus, the consistency and asymptotic normality of such estimators was established by White and Hansen for a number of types of variation in economic variables. Applications of the idea to as diverse a range of issues as sequential estimates (Newey 1984), nonlinear RE models (Hansen and Singleton 1982), and multiperiod probit models (Avery et al. 1983) demonstrate this fact.

Consistency in Agents' Actions

Far too many models are built without a consistent framework for agents' actions. It is not uncommon to see separate equations in macro models for prices, output, and labor demand, all deriving from different theoretical perspectives and with little recognition of the fact that these decisions are *interdependent*. Brainard and Tobin (1968) constituted a path-breaking paper setting out the implications of a failure to do so. They were concerned with portfolio allocation models in which the demand for each asset in a portfolio was related to the size of the portfolio and relative returns. Since the sum of all demands must in aggregate equal the size of the portfolio, Brainard and Tobin pointed out that it was impossible to independently specify each equation while retaining consistency. The demand for the nth asset must be a combination of the demand functions for the other $(n - 1)$ assets. Consequently unless care is exercised in specifying demands for the first $(n - 1)$ assets, the format of the derived demand for the n'th asset may be unacceptable.

Macro models exhibit similar problems, arising from the specifications of decisions taken by both the household and business sectors. For the latter it is important to account for prices, output, and employment. Without a consistent framework model performance becomes questionable. To illustrate, in the Australian model, NIF-10S, in some simulations three-quarters of the output response does not require any increase in primary factor usage. With output determined rigidly by a production function, this would be implausible. Actually, in NIF-10S demands are derived from a production function, but the implied restrictions are never enforced. "Consistency" is forthcoming by the presence of a missing factor of production, dubbed "phonium" by Challen and Fitzgerald (1984) (for "off-production-function-onium").

A lack of consistency can show up in other ways. All too often, equations are formulated as relations of flow variables with other flows, ignoring the fact that corresponding to every flow there is a stock. Stock movements would be expected to feedback to flow decisions, and this principle should be reflected in any chosen specification. Failure to do so invariably leads to poor model performance.

Ideally, consistency would be imposed by the derivation of estimable equations from a well-defined optimization process. The movement toward Euler equation methods for this task is a step in that direction. Unfortunately, the quality of economic data is rarely good enough to enable accurate calibration of such precise models. More than that, for the examination of issues, like the effects coming from a tariff change, the data may not even be available. To address issues of this nature "hybrid" models, designed to exhibit a high degree of internal consistency and calibrated partly by econometric models and partly by judgment, have become popular. Examples are the macro models of Rose and Selody (1985), Braynton and Mausskopf (1985), Murphy et al. (1986); micro-based versions encompass the computable general equilibrium models of Piggot and Whalley (1985) and the ORANI model of the Australian economy (Dixon et al. 1982).

I confess to a belief that hybrid modeling is an influential trend in econometrics. The development of microcomputers now makes it possible for a wide range of people to formulate their own model and to easily analyze issues using them. "Personal" rather than "public" models may become dominant in the next decade. Essentially this is a numerical variant of the sort of thing economists have done analytically for years: set up a theoretical model and then compute partial derivatives to assess the consequences of various actions. What the hybrid models add is the possibility of incorporating a richer set of environmental details at the cost of having to specify particular functional forms and parameter values. The role of econometrics in this case is to specify "best-bet" values for the parameters, thereby achieving some correspondence with actual outcomes. If this trend becomes dominant, there will arise the need to describe the sensitivity of model responses to assumed parameter values. This is a very interesting area of research, and largely an untapped one, although the question has been addressed by Kuh et al. (1985), Harrison (1985), Kalaba and Tesfatsion (1985), and Pagan and Shannon (1985).

Steady State Models

"Small is beautiful" became the password in macroeconometric modeling during the past decade. Reduction in dimensionality reflected a growing conviction that whenever difficulties arose within a large model, it was very hard to isolate and understand the causes, whereas a small model might be analyzed quite accurately with the aid of textbook macro models. Dissent was also based on deeper considerations, since it became increasingly obvious that the models deviated quite fundamentally from the consensus view of the properties a good model should possess. Many of these models appeared not to have any steady state solution; once shocked, convergence back to any point or path rarely eventuated. Although this feature may not be important for forecasting applications of models, it is nevertheless disturbing to see a gap emerge between theory and practice.

The first serious attempts to bridge this gap were the models growing out of the International Money Project at the London School of Economics (Bergstrom 1976; Jonson et al. 1977). Basic to their design was the selection of specifications ensuring convergence back to a prespecified growth path after any policy action. Unfortunately, this early attempt at building empirical models with satisfactory steady state operating characteristics had less impact than it might, owing to other features—an emphasis on continuous time and the role of "disequilibrium" money—being accorded more prominence. A new class of models is now emerging—(e.g., Murphy et al. 1986) that emphasizes consistency in actions and extensively utilizes the implicit steady state relations embedded in each of the dynamic relations to assess the long-run consequences of policy changes and to provide measures for desired or equilibrium quantities like the exchange rate and inflation. As these models are still in their infancy, it is too early to pass a definite judgment regarding their lasting impact on econometrics. Nevertheless, I expect it to be substantial.

Achieving Steady State Consistency

Mentioned above was the growing conviction that models should exhibit sensible steady state solutions. What implication does this proposition have for the design of individual equations? A characteristic of time series modeling is the need to allow for the fact that economic actions are characterised by slow adjustment. Thus, if income increases, it takes time for this to be translated into decisions on consumption. If adjustment were immediate, the observed ratio of consumption to income would be constant, and the variance of income would be expected to be close to the variance of consumption. In fact, for Australian data, though the ratio is "constant," the variance of income is some ten times that of consumption. Accounting for this pheonomenon was among the earliest challenges facing econometricians. By 1966 a popular strategy for dealing with it had emerged; the use of the partial adjustment model (PAM):

$$\Delta y_t = (\lambda - 1)y_{t-1} + \beta(1 - \lambda)x_t. \tag{11}$$

If x_t is i.id. (μ, σ^2), it is clear that $E(y_t) = \mu\beta$ and so the ratio of $E(y_t)$ to $E(x_t)$ would be β, but the ratio of the respective variances of y_t and x_t would be $\beta^2(1 - \lambda)/(1 + \lambda)$. Hence, as λ rises toward unity, the variance of y_t could become very small relative to x_t; exactly what is observed in the data.

Although the PAM captures many of the salient characteristics of the data, it has the disadvantage of forcing adjustment to be greatest in the first period, before declining in a geometric progression. Many proposals were made in the years immediately prior to 1966 to relax the restrictive shape of lag distribution associated with the PAM; Griliches (1967) provided a survey of these suggestions which still remains one of the best treatments of the topic. What developments there were after that time largely constituted refinements of the basic ideas. Shiller (1973) and Poirier (1975) modified Almon's (1965) polynomial distributed lag model by allowing deviations from a fixed polynomial order, whereas Godfrey and Poskitt (1975) discussed the determination of polynomial order as testing a sequence of nested hypotheses.

Until the mid-1970s little of this research was concerned with overcoming the deficiencies of the PAM by a direct extension of its philosophy. That was unfortunate, particularly in the new climate of concern over steady state features, since one of the most desirable characteristics of the PAM was the fact that, if x_t was set to $\bar{x}$, y_t would converge to $\beta\bar{x}$. Perhaps it is not surprising then that in 1978 Davidson et al. reintroduced to econometrics a simple generalization of the PAM—error correction mechanisms (ECM's). If $y_t^* = \beta x_t$ is the equilibrium or steady state value of y_t, a simple type of ECM would be

$$\Delta y_t = \alpha_0 \Delta y_t^* + \alpha_1(y_{t-1}^* - y_{t-1}), \tag{12}$$

where $y_t = \log Y_t$, $y_t^* = \log Y_t^*$.

Now the PAM (11) could be rewritten as

$$\Delta y_t = (1 - \lambda)\Delta y_t^* + (1 - \lambda)(y_{t-1}^* - y_{t-1}), \tag{13}$$

showing that the ECM generalizes the PAM by not requiring the impact of disequilibrium effects (α_1) to be equal to those for equilibrium effects (α_0). The "error" is $(y_{t-1}^* - y_{t-1})$, and the "correction" made is $\alpha_1(y_{t-1}^* - y_{t-1})$.

Inspection of (12) reveals that y_t converges to a constant y_t^* as $t \to \infty$ when $|\alpha_1| < 1$ and hints at the possibility of jointly allowing for a wide variety of adjustment schemes while preserving steady state properties by replicating the format as in (14):

$$\Delta y_t = \sum_{j=1}^{p} \alpha_j \Delta y_{t-j}^* + \sum_{j=1}^{q} \beta_j(y_{t-j}^* - y_{t-j}). \tag{14}$$

Notice that two principles interact in the specification (14): the model is *designed* to reproduce desired steady state behavior, and the data are called upon to provide information on the appropriate adjustment path (p, q, α_j, β_j). Segmentation of these tasks preserves the role of the theorist in specifying equilibrium behavior and the econometrician in extracting information on dynamics.[8]

Earlier it was mentioned that the "new" macroeconometric models featured a steady state growth *path*. How does this departure from a target *level* to a growth *rate* impinge upon model design. Return to the PAM in (13), assuming that y_t and x_t are the logs of variables Y_t and X_t, respectively, so that Δy_t^* is the growth rate in Y_t^*. Then

$$\Delta(y_t - y_t^*) = -\lambda\Delta y_t^* + (1 - \lambda)(y_{t-1}^* - y_{t-1}), \tag{15}$$

and $y_t - y_t^*$ will not converge to zero unless $\Delta y_t^* = 0$; that is, when Y_t^* exhibits steady state growth the change in the ratio of Y_t to Y_t^* depends upon this growth rate. Currie (1981) pointed this out, arguing that in many instances it was unacceptable from theory for such "rate of growth effects" to be in evidence in any steady state.

What can be done about this phenomenon? The most popular solution has been to extend the ECM by adding the term $(1 - \alpha_0)\Delta y_{t-1}$ to the RHS of (12) to obtain

$$\Delta y_t = \alpha_0\Delta y_t^* + \alpha_1(y_{t-1}^* - y_{t-1}) + (1 - \alpha_0)\Delta y_{t-1}, \tag{16}$$

$$= -(1 - \alpha_0)\Delta^2 y_t^* + \alpha_1(y_{t-1}^* - y_{t-1})$$

$$+ (1 - \alpha_0)(\Delta y_{t-1} - \Delta y_{t-1}^*) + \Delta y_t^*, \tag{17}$$

where $\Delta^2 y_t^* = \Delta y_t^* - \Delta y_{t-1}^*$.

After subtracting Δy_t^* from both sides of (17) and rearranging, we get

$$y_t - y_t^* = (2 - \alpha_1 - \alpha_0)(y_{t-1} - y_{t-1}^*) - (1 - \alpha_0)\Delta^2 y_t^*$$

$$- (1 - \alpha_0)(y_{t-2} - y_{t-2}^*). \tag{18}$$

In steady state growth $\Delta^2 y_t^* = 0$ and $y_t - y_t^* \to 0$, provided α_1 and α_0 are such that the difference equation is stable. This is Salmon's (1982) solution because (16) could have been expressed as[9]

$$\Delta^2 y_t = \alpha_0(\Delta y_t^* - \Delta y_{t-1}) + \alpha_1(y_{t-1}^* - y_{t-1}). \tag{19}$$

Salmon therefore enforces steady state growth by extending the ECM dynamics from first order in (12) to second order in (18), and some modelers have opted to do this automatically (Murphy et al. 1986). I do not feel this is a good idea, and the implied constraint should at least be tested. When $\Delta y_t^* = \Delta x_t$ (i.e., $\beta = 1$), it is only necessary to test if the coefficient of the introduced variable Δy_{t-1} and that of Δx_t sum to unity in (16). Unfortunately, if $\Delta y_t^* = \beta\Delta x_t$, this solution is no longer available and a nonlinear restriction must be examined, either as in Patterson and Ryding (1984) or Pagan (1985).

What emerges from the above discussion is that the time series behavior of x_t should influence the specification of econometric models. Certainly, something needs to be done to guarantee a steady state equilibrium in the face of differing growth paths, and the fact that most econometric models (both of the single equation and systems of equation variety) have ignored the issue in the past is unsatisfactory. Conceivably, part of the poor performance of models once growth rates were disturbed after the oil price shocks of the 1970s might be accounted for in this way.

This interdependence between model specification and the time series behaviour of x_t might be viewed as unfortunate; it certainly makes life much more difficult than it appeared in the mid-1960s. But, oddly enough, nonstationarity in x_t may even be a benefit. To appreciate this, it is useful to adopt a different reparameterization of the PAM than the ECM variant, namely, that provided by Bewley (1979):

$$y_t = \beta x_t - (1 - \lambda)^{-1} \lambda \Delta y_t. \tag{20}$$

Although (11) and (20) are identical, the reparameterization in (20) proves to be very useful as the coefficient of x_t is the long-run response, whilst that of Δy_t is the mean lag.[10] Suppose now that x_t follows a first-order deterministic time trend and that y_t is regressed against x_t, ignoring entirely Δy_t. From regression theory

$$\hat{\beta} = \beta - \left(\frac{\lambda}{1 - \lambda}\right)(\Sigma x_t^2)^{-1} \Sigma x_t \Delta y_t + o_p(1), \tag{21}$$

so that $\hat{\beta}$ will be consistent if the second term is $o_p(1)$. But the denominator is $O(T^3)$, the numerator is only $O(T^2)$, making $\hat{\beta}$ consistent—that is, long-run information on the system is available by *totally ignoring* the dynamics. This is separation of tasks with a vengeance! Granger and Engle (1987) first drew attention to this remarkable result, although one can see precursors to it in the literature. Kramer (1982), for example, showed that when β was identified, $\hat{\beta}_{OLS}$ would be consistent even if x_t was an endogenous variable, provided the exogenous variables of the system exhibited time trends, and this is just an application of the idea above in that the cross product between x_t and a stationary error term will be of lower order than Σx_t^2.

Not all the news about nonstationarity is good, however, particularly when x_t follows a nonergodic linear process such as an ARIMA process. When $x_t = y_{t-1}$ and $\beta = 1$, Dickey and Fuller (1979) observed that the limiting distribution of $T(\hat{\beta} - 1)$ was not normal, and used simulation methods to tabulate the empirical density function for $T(\hat{\beta} - 1)$. Since many economic times series are well modeled by ARIMA processes, Nelson and Plosser (1982), this suggests that the limiting distribution of the OLS estimator of β could also be nonnormal. In a series of papers Phillips and Durlauf (1986), Park and Phillips (1986), Stock (1987), and Sims, Stock, and Watson (1986) have gone a long way toward establishing the limiting behavior of the suitably standardized OLS estimator when x_t is allowed to be stationary or nonstationary. Suppose that x_t is ARIMA $(p, 1, q)$. Then distributed lag models of the ECM type in (12) can be reparameterized as

$$\Delta y_t = \alpha_0 \beta \Delta x_t + \alpha_1 (x_{t-1} - y_{t-1}) + \alpha_1 (\beta - 1) x_{t-1}, \tag{22}$$

$$= \alpha_0' \Delta x_t + \alpha_1 (x_{t-1} - y_{t-1}) + \alpha_2' x_{t-1}, \tag{23}$$

and the first regressors will be stationary linear processes while the last will be nonstationary. Traditional asymptotic theory then applies to the estimators of α_0' and α_1, but the distribution of the estimator of α_2' is more complex. It is very hard to provide a short summary of the results from those papers, since much depends on whether the x_t processes have a deterministic trend, whether x_t is a scalar or a vector, and whether the processes trend together in a linear fashion (or are co-integrated in Engle and Granger's 1987 terminology). Notice, however, that for many models β will be unity in (20), since this occurs whenever X_t and Y_t are in constant ratio in equilibrium, and therefore all variables in (23) are stationary. Consequently, the fact that x_t follows an ARIMA process is of no importance for the estimation of the reparameterized model. Considerations such as this suggest that the ECM format is a very useful way to express dynamic relations in econometrics, and the parameterization that it adopts can also aid the application of standard statistical theory.

The concept of cointegration has been mentioned above, and it has already had an enormous impact upon econometric theory and practice. Given the fact that many economic series are ARIMA (integrated), how can (1) be interpreted as an equilibrium relation if y_t and x_t are integrated? Engle and Granger (1987) answered that (1) could only be regarded as expressing an equilibrium requirement if u_t was of lower order of integration than y_t and x_t. In such circumstances y_t and x_t were said to be cointegrated and β was the cointegrating vector.

Suppose that y_t and x_t were both ARIMA($p, 1, q$) (or integrated of order one, I(1)). To interpret (1) as an equilibrium, u_t must therefore be $I(0)$ or stationary. Since much economic theory predicts that various series should bear a constant relation to one another in equilibrium (e.g., short- and long-run interest rates, forward and spot exchange rates), a weak test of this theory is whether the series are cointegrated. In turn, such a restriction can be turned into a test for the possibility that u_t is integrated. An obvious way of checking for this is to regress the residuals from the regression of y_t against x_t, $\hat{u}_t$, against $\hat{u}_{t-1}$, and then to test if the coefficient of $\hat{u}_{t-1}$ is unity. If the true value was unity, the distribution of the least squares estimator would not of course be asymptotically normal, as was mentioned previously, and care must be taken to refer this test to an appropriate distribution. Engle and Granger (1987) and Phillips (1987) discuss this test as well as others. As might have been anticipated these techniques have already become part of the standard tool kit of the econometrician analyzing time series data.

11.4   The Search for Robustness

The conclusions drawn from econometric models depend upon the assumptions made in constructing them. As discussed earlier, a lot of attention was paid to methods for evaluating the adequacy of these assumptions. Instead, it might be desirable to try to develop procedures making any conclusions drawn from the research robust to departures from these assumptions. Johnston (1964) commented upon this issue as follows:

Unfortunately, the present stage of development of the subject might be likened to a primitive stage in medicine where a doctor is able to treat only one complaint at time: he can reset a broken arm or prescribe for influenza, but if you come to him with both these troubles at once, the poor fellow is baffled and is forced to select one of your ailments, treat that, and leave the other alone. (p. 147)

An account of attempts to produce a "robust" econometrics may be structured as in section 11.2 by concentrating upon the specification of conditional moments. As will become apparent, the primitive stage of medicine has been left, but no definitive cure has yet emerged for multiple ailments, although the search for one is currently being pursued on a number of research fronts.

Making Inferences Robust to the Conditional Mean

Specification of the conditional mean should be the function of economic theory. In practice, however, that theory tends to supply a menu of variables to appear in a relation without indicating how the combination should be performed. Early work in econometrics largely ignored this problem, favoring simple models such as linear in logs or levels, largely because the restricted computational facilities made the estimation of more complex formulations very difficult. Perhaps the earliest reactions against this ad hoc solution arose from the interest of econometricians in estimating price and income elasticities for many commodities. Since consumer theory is one of the oldest and best developed branches of economics, it was well understood that restrictions must exist between these elasticities to ensure consistency with maximizing behavior.

Translating these theoretical insights into practice was a rich source of theoretical work in the late 1960s. Prima facie, estimation looks simple, involving only a system of seemingly unrelated equations with cross-equation restrictions, and that problem had been intensively studied by Zellner (1962) and was familiar from Goldberger (1964). But there was a complication. The dependent variables of the equations summed to a predetermined aggregate, implying that the disturbances had a singular distribution. McGuire et al. (1968) and Powell (1969) showed, however, that this constraint implied that one equation be dropped in estimation, and that the estimation results were invariant to the particular choice of equation. After that, complete systems of demand equations, imposing and testing the restrictions of consumer theory, appeared (Byron 1970; Barten 1969; Deaton 1974). Byron's paper tested the restrictions with the Lagrangian multiplier test statistic, introducing the work of Aitchison and Silvey (1958) into econometrics.

Although this literature was important for reemphasizing the role of economic theory in econometrics, it also required arbitrary decisions upon the nature of the underlying production and utility functions. Byron (1970), for example, estimated a system of loglinear demand functions, the implicit utility function being linear in the logs of quantities. It is not at all surprising then that interest should have arisen in the possibility of beginning with a functional description of the underlying technology that was sufficiently general to yield a good approximation to the actual one. Diewert (1973) introduced the concept of a "flexible functional form" (defined as functions capable of exactly reproducing all derivatives of the unknown function up to second order), and that line of investigation was a persistent theme in production and consumption economics in the 1970s and 1980s. Since many quantities of interest, such as elasticities of substitution, are functions of the first two derivatives, the basic property of a flexible form was an attractive one.

Deaton (1986) has written an excellent survey of the popular flexible functional forms emerging in demand analysis—the AIDS, Rotterdam, and translog models. The latter, set out in Christensen et al. (1973) for production technology, makes the log of output y_t a quadratic function of the log of factors x_t:

$$y_t = y_t^* + x_t \alpha + x_t' B x_t. \tag{24}$$

The translog form (24) was extensively used in empirical research in the last decade (see Jorgenson 1986 for a detailed account). Because α and B are unrestricted, (24) constitutes a flexible form, but that says nothing about the extent to which the approximation is good over a region rather than locally. Wales (1977) found that various curvature properties operating upon an original function were violated by the approximating one. Nevertheless, the translog function does come out of many studies as a good method of approximation.

Can it be improved upon? As (24) may be regarded as a Taylor series approximation to a general function, the direction of improvement would seem to reside in expansions other than Taylor's. Barnett (1983) suggested that the Laurent series expansion, which has terms such as x^k and x^{-k}, could offer superior approximating properties. Documentation of this point is to be found in Barnett et al. (1985), but it is too early to render a judgment on these claims. An alternative approach is to vary the order of approximation with the sample size. Thus Gallant (1982) and Elbadawi et al. (1983) employ a combination of a quadratic approximation and a Fourier series expansion, the number of terms in the Fourier series being a function of the sample size. As anticipated, this strategy eventually recovers the actual conditional mean when sample sizes become very large, provided that data and functions are "well behaved."

What this development portends is a movement toward nonparametric estimation; Gallant's idea of making the degree of parameterization dependent on sample size being an attempt to get the benefits of not adopting an explicit parameterization but retaining all the advantages of a parametric form. For many years it has been known that with a sufficiently large number of observations and i.i.d. data, it is possible to find the expection of y_t conditional upon x_t without specifying the functional form. Rosenblatt (1956) noted that it was possible to consistently estimate a density function at a point by effectively smoothing the empirical density function with a "kernel"; since the regression model specifies a conditional density, it is a natural step to co-opt the same theory to estimate the unknown conditional expectation, and this was done by Nadaraya (1964) and Watson (1964). But the method has been little used in econometrics, probably because of the nature of economic time series and sample sizes.[11] Robinson (1983) showed that the results could be extended to stationary time series obeying certain mixing conditions, and reviews this time series literature in Robinson (1986a). However, it is in the area of data on individual units that the procedure is likely to have its greatest impact, since the complexity and arbitrary nature of the functional forms prescribed go hand in glove with large amounts of data. Moreover, what is central to many of these studies is a query about aspects of the conditional mean.

Making Inferences Robust to the Second Moment

Inferences in econometrics generally demand that an estimate of the variance of estimators be made. Traditionally, it was assumed that the error term in regressions, or the score vector in more advanced cases, had a constant conditional variance. Detailed examination of the validity of this assumption has assumed a position of importance in the past twenty years, although it has to be conceded that responses to evidence of any heteroskedasticity are problematic, as it is a very difficult matter to decide upon a reasonable alternative to the constancy assumption. A number of norms have emerged in econometrics—weighting by a regressor, by the conditional mean, or ARCH type processes (Engle 1982)—but many empirical researchers felt uncomfortable adopting such tightly parameterised solutions.[12] Accordingly, the desirability of making inferences from econometric estimation robust to any type of heteroskedasticity in the innovations is obvious.

Once again, the solution to this problem was known in statistics before its translation into econometrics (Eicker 1967). But it does not seem to have been used in that discipline until White's (1980a) import of it to econometrics. The underlying idea is very simple. From section 11.1 a wide variety of econometric estimators solve $T^{-1}\Sigma \hat{d}_{\theta,t} = T^{-1}\Sigma d_{\theta,t}(\hat{\theta}) = 0$. A first-order

Taylor series expansion around the true value θ_0 yields $T^{1/2}(\hat{\theta} - \theta_0) = A^{-1}T^{-1/2}\Sigma d_{\theta,t} + o_p(1)$, where A is plim $T^{-1}\Sigma \partial d_{\theta,t}/\partial \theta'$ and $d_{\theta,t}$ is evaluated at θ_0. Hence, the variance of $T^{1/2}(\hat{\theta} - \theta_0)$ depends upon $B = E[(\Sigma d_{\theta,t}) (\Sigma d_{\theta,t})']$. When the $d_{\theta,t}$ are independent random variables with bounded variance, a consistent estimator of B is $T^{-1}\Sigma \hat{d}_{\theta,t}\hat{d}'_{\theta,t}$. In the least squares case (1), $d_{\theta,t} = x'_t(y_t - x_t\beta)$ and B is estimated by $T^{-1}\Sigma x'_t x_t(y_t - x_t\hat{\beta})^2$, where $y_t - x_t\hat{\beta}$ will be the least squares residuals.

Of course, this result extends out of the class of independent observations. Whenever $d_{\theta,t}$ is a martingale difference with respect to past data, $E(d_{\theta,t}d'_{\theta,t-k}) = 0$ $\forall k > 0$, and so $E(T^{-1}(\Sigma d_{\theta,t})(\Sigma d_{\theta,t})') = T^{-1}\Sigma E(d_{\theta,t}d'_{\theta,t})$. With suitable restrictions upon the nature of $d_{\theta,t}$, this expectation can be consistently estimated by $T^{-1}\Sigma \hat{d}_{\theta,t}\hat{d}'_{\theta,t}$. The main impact of such an enlargement of the domain of Eicker's and White's conclusion is to allow x_t to contain lagged values of y_t (see Nicholls and Pagan 1983). There can be little doubt that the proposed adjustment to make regression-type inferences robust to heteroskedasticity was a particularly beneficial one for applied econometrics. Its widespread use since 1980, and the fact that it can be adapted to many different situations, has meant that at least one of the ills of econometrics has found a medicine to at least suppress the symptoms.

Robustness to Data Dependence

Economic time series data are rarely independently distributed, and inferences will be affected whenever the quantities $d_{\theta,t}$ are dependent. Sometimes the dependence stems from the theoretical construct, as in the relationship between a future price for three periods into the future $F_{t+3/t}$, and the spot series at that time S_{t+3}. In such cases it is customary to assume that $E(S_{t+3}|\text{data at time } t) = F_{t+3/t}$, making the difference $v_{t+3} = S_{t+3} - F_{t+3/t}$ have the property $E(v_{t+3}|\text{data at time } t) = 0$, which is compatible with v_{t+3} following an MA(2).

Arguments of this sort led to interest in methods for making inferences robust to dependence in $d_{\theta,t}$. What makes the adjustment complex is that $E(T^{-1}\Sigma d_{\theta,t}d'_{\theta,t})$ cannot generally be replaced by $T^{-1}\Sigma E(d_{\theta,t}d'_{\theta,t})$; if $d_{\theta,t}$ was a martingale difference with respect to past data, it could, but that is not true for the future/spot rate example above. When $d_{\theta,t}$ exhibits Kth order dependence, $E(T^{-1}\Sigma d_{\theta,t}d'_{\theta,t})$ might be approximated by $T^{-1}\Sigma E(d_{\theta,t}d'_{\theta,t}) + 2T^{-1}\sum_t\sum_{k=1}^{L}\{E(d_{\theta,t}d'_{\theta,t-k}) + E(d_{\theta,t-k}d'_{\theta,t})\}$, after which this expression is quantified by substituting $\hat{\theta}$ for θ.[13] When K is finite, $L \geq K$ gives an exact result, and a variant of this idea appeared in Hansen and Hodrick (1980). However, if K is not finite, certain restrictions must be imposed if the approximation is to consistently estimate the unknown variance. These restrictions state that the dependence in the data must die out in a particular way, and L must tend to infinity but at a slower rate than K. Domowitz and White (1982) pioneered analysis of this issue, imposing "mixing conditions" upon the $d_{\theta,t}$ and setting $L = o(T^{1/3})$. This last restraint turned out to be slightly incorrect. As shown by Phillips (1987) and Newey and West (1987), $o(T^{1/4})$ is needed. To date, little experience has been accumulated with this procedure, but it represents another promising step on the road to making econometrics more robust to errors in its maintained assumptions.

Robustness to Distributional Assumptions

Robustness of estimators of β in (1) to the distribution of u_t attracted an increasing amount of attention over the period under survey, and a variety of approaches emerged. Because the OLS estimator is robust to the distribution of u_t asymptotically (predictions made with it are not), one response would be to formulate criterion functions, minimization of which would yield consistent asymptotically normal estimators of β that may have better small sample performance. Bassett and Koenker (1978) represent a most important reflection of this theme in econometrics. In their paper the limiting distribution of the estimator of β minimizing the absolute deviations $\sum_{t=1}^{T} |y_t - x_t\beta|$ was found. When $x_t = 1$, making β the location parameter for y_t, this estimator is the median. Other popular location estimates are the α-trimmed means $(1 - 2\alpha)^{-1} \int_{\alpha}^{1-\alpha} F_n^{-1}(u)du$, where F_n is the empirical distribution function of y_t, and the later work generalized this idea to regression models, producing "quantile-regression estimators."

An alternative procedure is to find the MLE that would be appropriate if the true density for u_t were known. Denote this by f_t, so that the log likelihood for (1) would be $L = \sum_{t=1}^{T} L_t = \sum_{t=1}^{T} \log f(y_t - x_t\beta)$. Gallant and Nychka (1987) suggested that $f(u_t)$ be approximated by a series of Hermite polynomials, and that the order of the terms in the expansion be increased with T. They prove consistency of the resulting estimator of β.

Suppose we actually knew $f(u_t)$. Then the MLE of β could be obtained by using the method of scoring, which prescribes the iterative scheme $\hat{\beta}_{(n)} - \hat{\beta}_{(n-1)} = [\sum_{t=1}^{T} (\partial L_t/\partial\beta)(\partial L_t/\partial\beta)']^{-1} \sum_{t=1}^{T} \partial L_t/\partial\beta$, where all derivatives are evaluated with $\hat{\beta}_{(n-1)}$, the estimate of β at the $(n - 1)$th iteration. Since

β_{OLS} is consistent, an estimator that is asymptotically as efficient as the MLE could be found by setting $\hat{\beta}_{(0)} = \hat{\beta}_{\text{OLS}}$. Now the problem with implementing this solution is that $\partial L_t / \partial \beta = x_t' f^{-1}(u_t)(\partial f(u_t)/\partial u_t)$ and f is unknown. However, since $\hat{u}_t = y_t - x_t \hat{\beta}_{\text{OLS}}$ is a consistent estimator of u_t, $f(u_t)$ can be estimated from the empirical density function of $\hat{u}_t$ by some nonparametric method, and the derivative $\partial f(u_t)/\partial u_t$ may also be estimated in the same way (see the survey by Ullah 1988). This strategy, adaptive estimation, implements a proposal of Stone (1975), the utility of which was investigated extensively for econometrics by Manski (1984).

Instead of forming a nonparametric estimate of $f^{-1}(u_t)\partial f(u_t)/\partial u_t$, one might approximate it by a polynomial in u_t. Then the expectation of such terms involves the convolution of x_t with the conditional moments of u_t. Hence it seems reasonable that a GMM estimator of β exploiting the orthogonality conditions between x_t and the centered moments of u_t could yield an estimator of β that is as efficient as the MLE, provided the number of moments is allowed to expand with the sample size. Newey (1988) has proved that this is so, and given an example of its use. The estimator is clearly an attractive one as it can be implemented on existing GMM software.

By and large though robust estimation did not make such impact upon time series based econometrics performed with the linear model (1). In some ways this is surprising. By definition, little is known about the error term in (1), and it might be thought desirable to conduct analysis under a minimal set of conventions. Hausman (1982) probably reflects the opinion of many econometricians upon the matter. He notes that many of the examples used to demonstrate the sensitivity of OLS to distributional assumptions represent the error term as a mixture of random variables, and it is not clear why this is a good description of the errors in econometric models. In practice many of the unusual movements in y_t are the product of events, such as strikes and wars, that may be better captured with constructed variables than regarded as generated from a contaminated normal distribution. Because of this feature, econometricians have tended to "patch up" the linear model and report results from a well-understood alternative. There are exceptions to this rule. For models featuring unit data, where the asymptotic distributions of popular estimators depend upon the actual distribution of the data and are not independent of it as is true of OLS applied to (1), the design of robust estimators has attracted a lot of attention. Attempts to grapple with that problem will be discussed in the following section.[14]

Robustness to System Specification

Economic decisions are interdependent, making it hard to avoid the necessity of posing and answering questions within a systems' framework. This requirement can be troublesome. In estimation it would be unfortunate if estimates of parameter values in one part of a system were rendered incorrect owing to errors made in specifying another part. That issue arose with particular force in the modeling of expectations; it may be easy to list some of the information exploited by agents in forming expectations, but very difficult to make the list complete. Acting as if it was complete normally induces inconsistencies into estimators of the effect of expectations (Nelson 1975). To overcome this, estimators are best formulated from orthogonality relations between the known information set and disturbances. In simultaneous equation parlance, that technique was usually referred to as "truncated two-stage least squares," from the fact that a truncated rather than complete set of predetermined variables was employed as instruments. Brundy and Jorgenson (1971) emphasised this partial approach to estimation in a system.

A legitimate query is whether the problems posed by systems are just those of estimation. Skepticism about this point reached its peak in Sims' (1980) paper. Sims argued that economic theory was just not strong enough to reduce the number of explanators in an equation to the level where estimation was feasible, and hence that the focus of attention should not be upon the structural equations like (7) but "reduced form" equations like (8) and (10). Answering questions by reference to the latter was to be preferred because it safeguarded against false conclusions being reached due to contamination from invalid assumptions made in the specification of the equations constituting the structure.

In fact, Sims proposed for this task, not the classical reduced form, but a high-dimensional vector autoregressive process (VAR) for y_{1t} and y_{2t}. Conceptually, (8) and (10) need only be redefined with x_{1t} and x_{2t} incorporating lagged values of y_{1t}, y_{2t} and any exogenous variables of the system. Sim's arguments and technique are too involved to summarize here. Some feeling for them may be had by observing that (7) imposed restrictions upon the reduced form equations (8) and (10), and so it also implies certain restrictions between VAR coefficients when (8) and (10) are reinterpreted as VAR's. Consequently it is possible to examine propositions about the structure by formulating them as implications for the VAR's. Opinions vary on the worth of doing so, and as Cooley and LeRoy (1985) point out in their excellent critique of this literature, much depends on the objectives of the investigator. Nevertheless, there is a strong case for at least checking if the restrictions on the VAR implied by (7) actually do hold (essentially an action analogous to the classical testing of overidentifiability). I know of no formal attempt to construct a specification error test in this way, although there are examples of informal comparisons of estimated and derived VAR's.

11.5   The Search for the Individual

In 1966 it would have been difficult to find a piece of applied econometrics that did not use time series data. But by 1986 some six out of thirty-five chapters of the *Handbook of Econometrics* pertained to issues rising in the estimation of models for individual behavior. This reorientation was wrought in part, if not totally, by the computer revolution. Confidentiality requirements associated with much unit data collected by official agencies could now be satisfied by releasing data upon magnetic tapes without identifiers, while the large volumes of such data, almost impossible to handle in card format, were easily managed through magnetic storage devices. Moreover the cost of transmitting, recording, constructing, and analyzing large-scale surveys had fallen dramatically as computers became more powerful. This allowed many researchers to collect their own data rather than having to rely upon official data.

Nowhere are these developments more dramatic than in "labor econometrics." From being a rather sleepy minor field in 1966, its vitality in 1986 is evidenced by the two surveys devoted to its output in the *Handbook of Econometrics*. Such rapid development presents difficulties to a surveyer. Unlike the coherence discernible in time series based econometrics, a product of almost a quarter of a century of textbooks and articles aimed at unification, unit-based econometrics has only recently generated equivalent resources, principally Amemiya (1981, 1985), Maddala (1983), and the *Handbook of Econometrics* entries. All of this leaves a strong impression that the dust has not yet settled enough to enable a proper assessment of what is of lasting value and what is ephemereal. Moreover some of the issues discussed individually below can potentially arise in combination, leading to an almost bewildering diversity of models to be analyzed. What follows therefore is even more of a personal selection than my previous sections, and my emphasis on four main themes is unlikely to appeal to all.

Models for the Individual

Prima facie the analysis of unit level data doesn't seem to demand new techniques. Replacing t with i (for the ith unit) in (1) would allow estimation of the linear model with individual data. There may even be some gains, as the absence of a natural ordering for the data makes issues of dependence in u_i less important. Indeed, in much of this literature it is assumed that the u_i are independently distributed. Of course, the switch from a sample of time points to one of units may not be entirely happy, as it may not be possible to conceive of the number of units (N) becoming very large (e.g., if these are states of a federation), thereby restricting the use of asymptotic theory.

Chronologically, the first difficulties encountered by econometricians came when attempts were made to exploit data upon both time series and individual units (panel data) in a bid to get "large samples" by pooling the two types of data. In that context (1) became

$$y_{it} = x_{it}\beta + u_{it} \qquad i = 1, \ldots, N; t = 1, \ldots, T. \tag{25}$$

Equation (25) was soon regarded as inadequate, since it was felt that there were likely to be "individual-specific" effects. Mundlak (1963) generalized (25) to

$$y_{it} = x_{it}\beta + \alpha_i + u_{it}, \tag{26}$$

treating α_i as "fixed effects" parameters to be estimated.

Summing (26) over time and forming sample averages $\bar{y}_i = T^{-1}\sum_{t=1}^{T} y_{it}$, etc., allows the representation

$$\bar{y}_i = \bar{x}_i\beta + \alpha_i + \bar{u}_i, \tag{27}$$

from which it is evident that α_i could be eliminated from (25) by working with mean corrected data, that is, $y_{it} - \bar{y}_i$ and $(x_{it} - \bar{x}_i)$. The fixed effects estimator of β obtained by regressing $y_{it} - \bar{y}_i$ against $x_{it} - \bar{x}_i$ was probably the most common procedure employed for estimation with panel data over the period under review; it was easily implemented via dummy variables, the number of fixed effects could range from unity to N at the choice of the investigator, and it could be augmented to allow for "time-specific" effects.

Perhaps the main complication to emerge was that consistency of $\hat{\beta}$, $\hat{\alpha}_i$ required that both N and T tend to infinity.

Basic to the estimation strategy described above was the elimination of the individual effects by centering upon the unit temporal means. Defining F as the matrix with $1 - T^{-1}$ as the diagonal and $-T^{-1}$ on the off-diagonals means that β was estimated by applying OLS to the transformed model $Fy = FX\beta + Fu$, leading to the query of what other choices for F might also be satisfactory. Suppose that (26) is first differenced to produce

$$\Delta y_{it} = \Delta x_{it}\beta + \Delta u_{it}. \tag{28}$$

This also eliminates any fixed effects. When $T = 2$ mean correction and the first difference methods coincide since $\bar{y}_i = \frac{1}{2}(y_{i1} + y_{i2})$ and therefore $y_{it} - \bar{y}_i = \frac{1}{2}(y_{it} - y_{it-1}) = \frac{1}{2}\Delta y_{it}$.

There are many transformations that will eliminate fixed effects, for example, nth differencing ($n \leq (T - 1)$). For each corresponding choice of F, $\hat{\beta} = (X'F'FX)^{-1}X'F'Fy = (Z'X)^{-1}Z'y$, and $\hat{\beta}$ will be consistent provided the variable Z satisfies the conditions to be a valid instrument, in particular that it be asymptotically uncorrelated with the error Fu. There is one obvious instance where it fails. If $x_{it} = y_{it-1}$, the "dynamic fixed effects model," $z_t = x_{i,t-1} - 2x_{i,t} + x_{i,t+1}$ for the first difference procedure, and thus must be correlated with the error. Bhagava and Sargan (1983) provide a comprehensive account of estimation options in this case.

Rather than treat α_i as fixed, a literature grew up (Balestra and Nerlove 1966; Maddala 1971) that looked at the possibility of making α_i a random variable ($\alpha_i \sim N(0, \sigma_v^2)$), the "random effects" model. Assuming that α_i and x_{it} are independent, $\alpha_i + u_{it}$ becomes the error term in the regression, and its covariance matrix exhibits a particular pattern. Efficient estimation needs to recognize the nonspherical nature of the errors and this leads to the application of GLS, feasible GLS or MLE. Much of this literature was concerned with the relative efficiency of each estimator and with expanding the model to allow for random time effects or serial correlation in the u_{it} (see Amemiya 1985, sec 6.6, for a detailed discussion of these developments). In practice, the random effects model has been little used; perhaps because of the concern, mentioned in Hausman (1978), that the regressors x_{it} cannot be plausibly regarded as independent of the u_{it}.

Although the models described above were advocated for "unit" data, the "units" envisaged were really a collection of agents rather than individuals in the conventional sense of the word. It is perhaps not surprising that the range of estimators employed in the above developments did not fundamentally depart from those used in time series analysis, although the specific details needed to be worked out, and that proved quite challenging. But once data began to become available upon "... choice of occupation, marriage partner, or entry into a product market ... housing choices into 'sub-standard' or 'standard' ... (number of telephone calls) ... freight shipment mode" (McFadden 1984, p. 1396), this had to change, as it rapidly became apparent that the observed data on y_i could not be validly treated as a continuous random variable. Rather than *quantitative responses*, these data sets frequently only yielded *qualitative responses*.

Generally, the best way to characterize these data is as observations upon an indicator variable. In the simplest schemes choice is dichotomous, and the indicator variable y_i can be arbitrarily assumed to be a binary discrete random variable taking the value unity if a decision is made and zero if it is not. Since the decision is probabilistic, the $\Pr\{Y_i = 0\} = F_i$, and it is necessary to describe F_i. This formulation has a long history in biostatistics and psychometrics, and econometricians borrowed substantially from that literature in identifying plausible candidates for F_i. An appealing strategy for doing this is to regard the outcome $y_i = 0$ as occurring whenever some latent variable y_i^* fails to cross a threshold C. Equation (1) may then be employed to model y_i^* as $y_i^* = x_i\beta + u_i$, leading to the determination of $F_i = \text{Prob}\{y_i = 0\} = \text{Prob}\{y_i^* < C\} = \text{Prob}\{x_i\beta + u_i < C\} = \text{Prob}\{u_i < C - x_i\beta\}$. F_i can then be identified with the cumulative distribution function for u_i. Making F the cumulative normal yields the probit model while the logistic gives the logit, but other choices such as exponential or Student's t might be candidates in the search for robustness. Applied studies have, however, rarely departed from the logit or probit forms.

McFadden (1974) recognized the potential of this framework in econometrics. Defining y_{ij}^* as the utility the ith individual gets from the jth alternative action he can take, and treating y_{ij}^* as determined by (1), $y_{ij}^* = x_{ij}\beta + u_{ij}$, a particular action J will be adopted only if y_{iJ}^* exceeds the value of y_{ij}^* for all other j. Clearly the choice between alternative J and any other j depends upon whether $y_{iJ}^* - y_{ij}^* = (x_{iJ} - x_{ij})\beta + u_{iJ} - u_{ij}$ exceeds zero, that is, $\Pr[y_i = 0] = \Pr[y_{iJ}^* - y_{ij}^* < 0] = \Pr[(u_{iJ} - u_{ij}) < -(x_{iJ} - x_{ij})\beta]$. By ascribing densities to the u_{ij} maximization of a random utility function generates the probit or logit models.

As apparent from the details above the framework is applicable to multiple as well as binary choice situations. It was soon discovered that estimation of the probit model in this context was a forbidding task, but that for the logit model was relatively straightforward. Having a utility-maximizing perspective then proved to be invaluable, and McFadden (1974) used it to demonstrate that the multinomial logit model would be compatible with utility maximization only if all the errors u_{ij} were independent; the restriction earning the designation "independence of irrelevant alternatives." This is an unhappy assumption, and it spawned a literature concerned with checking its adequacy (Hausman and McFadden 1984) and with relaxing it. The best-known solution allowing for some dependence among the u_{ij} was the nested logit model described in McFadden (1981). In this construct choices between very similar alternatives are made as if governed by a binary logit model, but these similar alternatives are then aggregated into a composite alternative for a binary comparison with any distinct alternative. A number of applications of this model have appeared (Hausman and McFadden 1984; Small and Brownstone 1982), but it has proved to be computationally demanding.

The above discussion was rooted in the polar extremes for which data are either continuous or discrete, but a combination of the two types is not unusual. Tobin (1958) was interested in applying (1) to data on household durable expenditure and income but found that there were both zero and positive expenditures. A zero expenditure clearly represents a qualitative response, the decision not to purchase, whereas a positive value is a commitment to purchase a specific quantity. To represent the data probabilistically therefore requires a combination of the densities for continuous and discrete random variables; the likelihood for $y_1 \ldots y_N$ will be $\prod_{i \in I_0} F_i \prod_{i \in I_1} f_i$, where f_i is the density for u_i in (1), I_0 are the points for which only a qualitative response occurs, and I_1 represents the remainder. Although zero represents the censoring point above, the "Tobit" model applies whenever y_i^* must pass some threshold value before an action is taken.

Tobin took the f_i to be normal and Amemiya (1973) provided the seminal treatment of the asymptotic properties of the MLE of β and σ^2 for truncated normal regression models, a class that includes the Tobit model. Since 1970 numerous applications of this sort of model have appeared (see Amemiya 1985, ch. 10). Most of the variability here came from generalizations that replaced (1) by more than a single equation or allowed the censoring threshold for one random variable to depend upon another, thereby inducing a type of simultaneity. Amemiya (1985) has proposed that all these contributions be classified into five types depending upon the dimension of y_i^* and the censoring rule employed. Despite this diversity in model form, estimation is rarely by anything but MLE. Thus the interesting aspects of this literature are the applications made rather than the econometric theory employed, although sometimes considerable ingenuity is needed in finding the likelihood.

Perhaps the major concern and challenge to econometric theorists in this area has been one of robustness. Unlike the linear regression context in which the scores derived under a normality assumption continue to have zero expectation under a range of alternative distributions for u_i, this will rarely be true for discrete random variables, inasmuch as the scores involve $\partial F_i / \partial \beta$, and these are a function of F_i itself. Because of that dependence, misspecification of F_i leads to a score with nonzero expectation when evaluated with respect to the true probability measure, and so the MLE of β will be inconsistent. A related difficulty stems from the fact that the scores for β and σ^2 do not have zero covariance even when f_i has been selected correctly; misspecification in either the conditional mean or variance can therefore be expected to affect the consistency properties of the MLE of either set of parameters.

The correct log likelihood to be maximized is

$$\sum_{i=1}^{n} y_i \log(1 - F_i) + (1 - y_i) \log F_i, \tag{29}$$

where F_i is the unknown distribution function of u_i. One might ask therefore if $\log F_i$ can be replaced by a quantity $\bar{F}_i$—and $\log(1 - F_i)$ by $(1 - \bar{F}_i)$—such that maximizing (29) with these substitutions would generate a consistent estimator of β. Manski (1975) set $\bar{F}_i = I[x_i \beta < 0]$, where I is the indicator function and termed the resulting optimand the "score function." This terminology is most unfortunate and would be better described as a "success function" in that it captures the number of successful predictions made if y_i is predicted to be unity whenever $x_i \beta \geq 0$. Restricting the parameter space to $B = \{\beta | \beta' \beta = 1\}$, Manski optimizes by a line search method described in Manski and Thompson (1986), and a complete proof of the strong consistency of the estimator is provided in Manski (1985) provided $F(0) = 0.5$.

An alternative approach would be to consider estimating F_i along with β. For given F_i, the MLE of β is consistent and asymptotically normal, whereas, for given β, consistent and asymptotically normal density estimators of F_i can be obtained by a variety of nonparametric procedures. This suggests that, by iterating between each single estimator, both β and F_i can be jointly determined. Cosslett (1983) described a suitable estimator of F_i and then demonstrated the consistency of $\hat{\beta}$ obtained by maximizing (29) with F_i replaced by its estimator $\hat{F}_i$.

A parallel but more extensive literature has developed upon the robust estimation of Tobit models, the log likelihood of which is (29) with the first term $y_i \log(1 - F_i)$ replaced by $y_i \log f_i$. Fernandez (1986) and Horowitz (1986) used the Kaplan and Meier (1956) estimator of F_i, whereas Duncan (1986) approximates f_i by spline functions. Unfortunately, each of these solutions, as well as those detailed above for qualitative response models, shares a fundamental weakness. The unknown F_i's are being treated as nuisance parameters, and their number tends to infinity with the sample size. Although it is possible to invoke Kiefer and Wolfowitz's (1956) theorem on the consistency of the MLE in the presence of infinitely many incidental parameters to prove consistency of $\hat{\beta}$, no corresponding argument for the limiting distribution of $\hat{\beta}$ is currently available. This failing may make such estimators unattractive to applied researchers whose samples are not large enough to ignore distributional questions.

Given this feature, it is not surprising that estimators have been proposed for censored models that aim to optimize something other than the log likelihood in (29). For Tobit models, the most influential of these has been Powell's (1986) "symmetrically trimmed least squares" estimator of β which minimizes $N^{-1} \sum_{i=1}^{N} (y_i - \max\{\frac{1}{2} y_i, x_i \beta\})^2$; the "symmetry" deriving from the fact that the observations for which $u_i \leq x_i \beta_0$ are discarded, mirroring the natural censoring which has "discarded" observations $u_i \geq -x_i \beta_0$. Powell demonstrated consistency and asymptotic normality for his estimator. Another promising approach has been Ichimura's (1986) method of finding β to minimize $\sum_{i=1}^{N} (y_i - E(y_i|x_i, \beta))^2$. For a given value of β, $E(y_i|x_i, \beta)$ may be recovered by the nonparametric methods of Nadarya (1964) and Watson (1964), so that a suitable iteration scheme will minimize the sum of squares above. Ichimura's proposal applies to both Tobit and Probit models and has also been shown to be consistent and asymptotically normal.

Robustness of estimators to the characteristics of the error term is a crucial requirement for models based on unit data, but the derivation of suitable estimators and the isolation of their properties is a complex and demanding task, upon which some of the best econometric theorists have labored in the first half of the current decade. Progress has been made, but the current stock of estimators is distinguished by incomplete characterization of asymptotic properties and the computer intensity of the associated algorithms. In many ways the situation is reminiscent of that in the early stages of the development of simultaneous equations methodology; it was not MLE that eventually became the preferred option of applied workers, but the method of moments estimators 2SLS and 3SLS, and these were not part of the original proposals made by the Cowles Commission members. Perhaps a similar history will one day be evident here. The next decade should be an exciting one for workers in this field, but it would be premature to hazard a prediction about which orientation will eventually prove to be the dominant one.

Selecting the Individual

Early in elementary statistics courses students are exposed to examples of inferences rendered invalid by a failure to draw a sample randomly, such as the telephone poll predicting Roosevelt's defeat. Perhaps it is not surprising then that, once the data to be analyzed were determined by an investigator, econometricians were forced to analyze the joint issues of sample selection and estimation. Random selection of a population can create no problems for estimation, and the assumption of independence of u_i in (1) is sometimes justified for individual datum on this basis. But there are reasons why one might wish to deviate from this ideal, particularly in the light of cost considerations. If the subject to be studied were the choice by Americans of Belgium as a tourist destination, it would be very costly to randomly sample the complete American population, since the sample size would need to be very large to capture a reasonable number of individuals choosing Belgium. A cheaper method is to randomly sample only those who had booked to travel to Europe at travel bureaus. But this method can have its problems. Cast in terms of (1), individuals in the "travel bureaus sample," may be those with higher than average u_i, and this must therefore be allowed for in estimation.

Two generic types of selection are stressed in the literature. In the first sampling is done on the basis of the characteristics x_i in (1) and is naturally referred to as *exogenous* sampling. Here, if the finite choice set is denoted by C and the choice model specifies $P(j|x_i, \beta), j \in C$ being the jth alternative chosen by the ith individual, the analyst draws a sample $i = 1, \ldots, N$ from a larger population of size N^* according to some density $g(x_i)$. The likelihood of the observed data becomes $\prod_{i=1}^{N} P(j|x_i, \beta)g(x_i)$. When $g(x_i) =$

$f(x_i)$, the actual density for the characteristics, sampling is random; otherwise, it is stratified. Clearly the nature of exogenous sampling is important only if $g(x_i)$ is a function of β; if it is not the score with respect to β depends solely upon the $P(j|x_i, \beta)$, and so the nature of $g(x_i)$ is irrelevant.

The tourist case cited above is different in that the selection is based upon the choices of agents—travel to Europe—and not upon the x_i. Hence Manski and Lerman (1977) called this *choice-based* sampling. Here the investigator predetermines the probability of observing the elements in the choice set, $H(j)$, by the way he selects from the population. Within this class, sampling is done at random. Hence the probability of observing an alternative j and characteristics x_i is $P_c(j, x_i) = P_c(x_i|j)H(j)$, with the c indicating the conditioning feature that sampling was conducted only among those in the population who choose an alternative j. By Bayes' rule $P_c(x_i|j) = P(j|x_i, \beta)p(x_i)|Q(j)$, where $Q(j)$ is the probability that an agent in the population would have adopted alternative j, making the likelihood $\prod_{i=1}^{n}(P(j|x_i\beta) \cdot p(x_i)H(j)|Q(j))$. From this expression it follows that, although $p(x_i)$ and $H(j)$ do not normally enter the score, the fact that $Q(j) = \int_{x_i} P(j|x_i, \beta)p(x_i)dx_i$ means the contribution of $Q(i)$ to the likelihood cannot be ignored.

Potentially, there are a number of unknowns in this likelihood, particularly $p(x_i)$ and $Q(j)$. When $Q(j)$ is known the likelihood to be maximized is $\prod_{i=1}^{n} P(j|x_i, \beta)$, but with β obeying the constraint $Q(j) = \int_{x_i} P(j|x_i, \beta)p(x_i)dx_i$. Manski and Lerman (1977) observed that straight MLE was complex and proposed instead that a consistent estimator of β be found by maximizing $\prod_{i=1}^{n} P(j|x_i, \beta)w(i)$ where the weights $w(i) = H(j)Q(j)$. Later work provided rigorous proofs for the MLE when $Q(j)$ was unknown (Manski and McFadden 1981) and MLE when both $f(x_i)$ and $Q(j)$ are unknown (Manski and McFadden 1981; Cosslett 1981).

From all of this it is apparent that the freedom of an investigator to construct his sample complicates estimation. But even if the sample has not been manipulated by the econometrician, does this mean that it may be regarded as randomly selected? Just as the debate over rational expectations showed that it is not satisfactory to consider agents as reacting passively to any policy changes, rather they will actively optimize in the face of such changes, so too it is necessary to consider that the inherited sample is the outcome of optimizing decisions, and therefore it may be unrepresentative of the population. That is, although the error term in (1) has a zero mean when the complete population is examined, or a random sample of it is chosen, the sample presented to a researcher could well have "high" or "low" u_i individuals deleted from it, as such agents' optimizing decisions remove them from the sample entirely. Such a process is referred to as "self-selectivity." Its consequences are to force the remaining u_i's to have a nonzero mean, so that a regression of observations on y_i against x_i will produce an inconsistent estimator of β.

As might be expected given its origin in individual choice behavior, self-selectivity is a pervasive phenomenon with economic data collected on units. Initially, it was highlighted in wage equations seeking to explain wages earned by women y_i as a function of characteristics x_i from data on wage-earners. This represents a sample from a larger population that includes non-wage-earners, that is, those who do not work. If the participation decision is done optimally, it occurs only if the actual wage exceeds some reservation wage $\bar{y}_i$. Hence all individuals whose u_i is less than $\bar{y}_i - x_i\beta$ will be "self-selected" out of the sample, and the individuals remaining in the sample will have an excessive number of "high" u_i's. Although Roy (1951) drew attention to this issue in discussing the choice of individuals between two occupations, hunting and fishing, on the basis of comparative advantage, it was the work of Gronau (1974), Lewis (1974), and Heckman (1974) upon the earnings equation described above that brought home the phenomenon with great force to econometricians.

In its greatest degree of generality, when (1) describes a latent variable, self-selectivity is an extreme case of choice-based sampling, and could be treated from that perspective. However, more direct analysis exploiting some of its specific features has been the preferred way of proceeding. Accordingly, in the context of the labor econometrics example cited above, if the reservation wage is a function of variables z_i, that is, $\bar{y}_i = z_i\gamma$, then $P(u_i \leq \bar{y}_i - x_i\beta) = P(u_i \leq z_i\gamma - x_i\beta)$. Individuals located in the work force are those for whom u_i exceeds $z_i\gamma - x_i\beta$, and the error term for the sample of wage earners is truncated. Assuming that the underlying error u_i is n.i.d. $(0, \sigma^2)$, Amemiya (1973) demonstrated that the expected value of the error for those in the sample was $\sigma^2\varphi(\sigma^{-1}(z_i\gamma - x_i\beta))/\Phi(\sigma^{-1}(z_i\gamma - x_i\beta))$, where φ is the standard normal density and Φ is the cumulative standard normal. Knowledge of the mean of this error makes it possible to force the regression on the sample data to have a zero mean by the simple expedient of augmenting the regressors in (1) by $\varphi(\cdot)/\Phi(\cdot)$.

Heckman (1976) used this solution, estimating $\sigma^{-1}\gamma$ and $\sigma^{-1}\beta$ by applying a probit model to data on individuals both in and out of the work force and then constructing regressors $\hat{\phi}$ and $\hat{\Phi}$ from these estimates. This two-stage solution is very elegant, is simple to apply, and has found favor in many contexts. Apart from its use of strong distributional assumptions to find the appropriate correction to the mean, its major disadvantage is the need to allow for the fact that $\hat{\phi}$ and $\hat{\Phi}$ are estimated quantities when calculating the covariance matrix of $\hat{\beta}$, but programs such as LIMDEP now automatically provide this adjustment. The literature on self-selectivity is vast, both in terms of applications and in terms of extending the theory to handle simultaneity (Kenny et al. 1979), latent variables (Lee 1979), missing data (Griliches et al. 1978), and nonnormality (Olsen 1982; Lee 1982). A comprehensive examination of this literature is beyond this survey. However, Amemiya (1985) and Maddala (1985) provide excellent reviews of this literature.

The Duration of Events

Once unemployment rose sharply after the first oil price shock, and proved to be unusually persistent, examination of its causes became an important issue among economists. Before long it was realized that the unemployment rate was a stock variable and therefore that its behavior was compatible with many different under!ying flows. Knowledge of the nature of the flows was crucial to any conclusions drawn from unemployment experience and to the appropriate policy responses. To see why, suppose that there are twelve individuals in the work force, but an unemployment survey taken each month for a year reveals that one person is unemployed in each of these months, giving a constant 8.5 percent unemployment rate. Now this rate could come about in many different ways. Polar cases are when one person is unemployed for the whole twelve months and when each of the twelve is unemployed for one of the twelve months. In the first case, the average duration of unemployment for an individual rises from one to twelve months over the year, whereas in the latter it remains at one month. Theories of the cause of unemployment, and responses to it, must therefore have a very clear picture of both the stock and flow dimensions of this series.

In a stationary labor market, where the number of persons entering unemployment equals the number leaving, the unemployment rate can be decomposed as the product of the proportion of the labor force entering unemployment during the period, the average duration of unemployment, and the frequency (or number of spells) of unemployment. As a prelude therefore to the analysis of unemployment experience, it is important to estimate the average duration of unemployment. Moreover many economic theories concerned with entry and exit into unemployment make strong predictions about the determinants of the period of unemployment for an individual. Hence there was a considerable demand for and interest in the analysis of series on duration data. Strengthening this tendency was the fact that statistics existed on a number of other types of duration data besides unemployment, such as strikes and employment tenure, and so any techniques developed could be readily transferred.

Statisticians have been concerned with the analysis of duration data in biostatistics and reliability theory for many years, meaning that a well-established pool of techniques could be initially imported into econometrics, as was done by Lancaster (1979) in an early presentation. Basic to this literature was the notion of a hazard function derived as follows. If S is defined as the length of a spell of (say) unemployment and treated as a random variable with cumulative distribution function $F(s) = 1 - P(S > s)$, and density $f(s)$, the exit probability out of the unemployed state will be

$$h(s) = \frac{f(s)}{1 - F(s)}. \tag{30}$$

$h(s)$ is the hazard function, and it remains to specify how the exit probability $h(s)$ will vary with individual characteristics and spell length.

In the simplest models $h(s)$ is set to a constant. Estimation is then very simple since (30) can be solved to yield $F(s) = 1 - e^{-hs}$ and $f(s) = h(1 - e^{-hs})$. With data on completed spell lengths for N individuals $S_1, \ldots, S_N$, the likelihood is just $\prod_{i=1}^{N} f(s_i)$, and the unknown parameter can be estimated by maximizing the likelihood.

But it is unlikely that $h(s)$ can be taken to be constant for data on economic agents. First, it would be expected that the escape probability from unemployment should depend upon individual characteristics such as age, education, sex, etc. A minimal respecification for the hazard function would be to allow it to vary with individuals—$h_i = h(x_i \beta)$, where x_i is a vector of characteristics. This modifies the density to a conditional one $f(s_i|x_i) = h(x_i \beta)(1 - e^{-h(x_i \beta)s_i})$. Estimation by MLE is still fairly straightforward and, as the references in Amemiya (1985) and Heckman and Singer (1986) attest, the most favored strategy. In fact, since $f(s_i|x_i)$ is a conditional density, and $h(x_i \beta)$ is unknown, it might be more appropriate, when N is large, to estimate the density by nonparametric methods, particularly the kernel estimator mentioned in section 11.4. Although this density may be poorly estimated by such procedures for regions where few x_i are available, if interest is really in statistics such as average duration ($E(S/X)$), nonparametric methods are probably the most effective way of estimation.

Where problems really arise, however, is when h is allowed to be a function of s—the possibility that the exit probability depends upon the period of time spent in the state—and a recognition that individuals may have differing hazard rates due to unobserved characteristics (neglected heterogeneity). Both of these complicate estimation immensely, and research has been devoted to finding expressions for $h_i(s)$ that are both tractable and flexible.

Many proposals have been made to allow the hazard to vary with s. In his germinal piece on duration analysis, Lancaster (1979) specified $h(s)$ as $\alpha s^{\alpha-1}\exp(x_i\beta)$, whereas Flinn and Heckman (1982) allow for a general Box-Cox transformation on s, thereby relating $h(s)$ to $(s^\lambda - 1)/\lambda$. Other suggestions have been polynomials in s, ranging from a quadratic (Tuma 1976) to ninth order (Kennan 1985). Just as in the production function literature detailed in section 11.4, there is a continuing search for more flexible ways of modelling the dependence of $h(s)$ upon s, and some cross-fertilization from the earlier literature might be profitable, for example, Gallant's Fourier series expansions appeal as a flexible form. Nonparametric methods could also be adapted, but if the dependence is complex large numbers of observations will be required.

This is clearly an area with an evident need to investigate the adequacy of any assumed form of duration dependence, that is, $\partial h/\partial s$. Since estimation has always been done by MLE, diagnostic tests are simply set up by the score test or Newey/Tauchen approaches mentioned in section 11.2. Kiefer (1985) represents one of the few attempts to construct standards in this area. He takes the maintained hazard function to be $h_i = \exp(x_i\beta)$ giving $f(s_i) = h_i\exp(-s_ih_i)$, and then considers the class of alternative densities $f^*(s_i) = f(s_i)(1 + \sum_{j=2}^n \alpha_j L_j((\exp x_i\beta)s_i))$, where $L_j(\cdot)$ are the jth Laguerre polynomials. His alternative covers the exponential, gamma, Weibull and Pareto alternatives for $f^*(s_i)$. Both the gamma and Weibull distributions have had use (Salant 1977; Lancaster 1985). Kiefer constructs LM tests for $\alpha_2, \ldots, \alpha_n$ being zero, based on the restricted scores

$$\partial\log\frac{\sum_{i=1}^n f^*(s_i)}{\partial\alpha_j}\bigg|_{\alpha_j=0} = L_j(\exp(x_i\beta)s_i), \qquad j = 2,\ldots,n. \tag{28}$$

A much more difficult effect to control for has been unobserved heterogeneity, and attempts to do so have been a major concern of researchers. Neglect of individual heterogeneity has been proven to induce a negative bias into estimates of duration dependence, the most precise statement of this contention being Heckman and Singer (1986, p. 1205). Lancaster (1979) recognized the issue and wrote the hazard rate as the product of $\alpha s^{\alpha-1} \exp(x_i\beta)$ and a random variable v_i that was identically and independently distributed as a gamma $(1, \sigma^2)$ random variable. To get the density of s_i, he integrated out the v_i, and this strategy has been followed by others, although sometimes replacing the gamma distribution with the beta. Unfortunately, as Heckman and Singer (1986, p. 1710) emphasize, parameter estimates are very sensitive to the specification of a density for v_i, and the need for nonparametric analysis here is paramount. Heckman and Singer (1984) adapted Kiefer and Wolfowitz's (1956) nonparametric MLE for mixtures of distributions. What is at issue here is that treating u_i as random with unknown density induces an infinite number of incidental parameters into the model. Once again, this makes it hard to establish limiting distributions, and it might be better to employ less efficient estimators—for example one might follow Ichimura and minimize $\Sigma(s_i - E(s_i/x_i))^2$ with respect to α and β.

If one is to stick with parametric procedures, checks for their adequacy would seem mandatory. Lancaster (1985) has been very active in the design of diagnostic tests for such a task, deriving a score test for $\sigma^2 = 0$ against an approximation to the true density suggested by a Taylor series expansion. His test is a very simple one, being based on the generalized residuals, which in his duration model are identified with the integrated hazard function evaluated at the MLE's under the null hypothesis.

In practice, it is even harder to estimate duration models than described above, since data is rarely available on completed spells. Incomplete spells with unknown initiation (left-censoring) and termination (right-censoring) dates are the norm rather than the exception. Adjustment of the likelihood for this effect is feasible, but it means that a conversion must be effected from the estimated density of incomplete spells to that for completed ones.

Faced with all of these difficulties, as well as the presence of multiple as well as single spell data, official applications of duration data have tended to use the simplest possible models. Thus statistics on average completed duration have normally been derived by assuming constant hazard functions and gamma-distributed heterogeneity. Probably this will change as software to estimate the more complex models becomes generally available, but at the moment the very youth and vigor of this area of econometric research has been a powerful inhibitor to the widespread adoption of the techniques that it has thrown up.

From Micro to Macro

The emergence of data upon individual units not only changes the range of models needed in the tool kit of an econometrician; it fundamentally changed the way in which enquiry could proceed. Because many issues are inherently microeconomic in nature, such as tax reform and the impact of employment subsidies, use of aggregate data to investigate them misses the diversity in responses of individuals. It might even be argued that the diversity of responses is paramount, as it is the marginal rather than the average response revealed in aggregate figures that an economist seeks. Accordingly, the impact of tax reform upon labor supply may be very strong upon individuals with high marginal tax rates but very hard to detect in any aggregate data where such individuals constitute only a small fraction of the population. Moreover data on individuals can supply data sets rich in different environmental conditions, and studying behavior for the total range might be very informative for the generation and calibration of theories.

Thus there is a strong case for utilizing micro data to investigate macro issues, and research has flourished with the aim of doing just that. By far the most ambitious effort in this direction was initiated by Orcutt (1957) and extended in Orcutt et al. (1961, 1976). In these reports the micro decisions of individuals are determined by the conditional probabilities of action; information that the models discussed in section 11.5 were designed to provide. With the conditional probability known, a random draw is made to determine the actual outcome for any individual. Summation of individual histories is then performed to yield outcomes upon macro aggregates. The framework is an appealing one, although in its present version it tends to ignore general equilibrium considerations, mainly concentrating upon supply side decisions and sociological phenomena. A tax reform, for example, would generate effects upon prices and quantities in many markets, whereas in most of these models the computed effects would largely relate to labor/leisure choices, participation decisions, etc. Undoubtedly, these strands could be integrated, but no successful variant has yet appeared.

The micro-simulation approach effectively sidesteps what has always been a conundrum in economics; optimizing theory is about an individual but many of the interesting questions are about aggregates. Most macro-econometric analysis has always invoked the "representative agent," but the availability of data on units means an opportunity to explore more rigorous ways of moving from the individual to the "state." Micro-simulation does this numerically, and thereby avoids a set of questions about the process of aggregation that have always bothered econometricians: Should data be pooled under the assumption of a common underlying model? What meaning can be attached to parameter estimates from a pooled sample? How is a macromodel calibrated from time series data built up from those appropriate at a lower degree of disaggregation? Each of these queries has stimulated a modicum of interesting and useful research in the last two decades.

If (1) were such that β varied with individuals, that is, $y_i = x_i\beta_i + u_i$, pooling all the data in a single regression would be illegitimate. But estimating (1) with dummy variables to allow for each slope coefficient to shift leaves too many unknown parameters. Zellner (1969) suggested a way out of this impasse, by treating the coefficients β_i as realizations from a p.d.f. with mean $\bar{\beta}$ and variance V, that is, $\beta_i = \bar{\beta} + v_i$ where $v_i \sim (0, V)$. Then $y_i = x_i\bar{\beta} + (u_i + x_iv_i)$, a linear model with heteroskedasticity to which OLS can be applied to find a consistent estimator of $\bar{\beta}$, after which various estimators of V (Hildreth and Houck 1968; Swamy 1970) can be computed from the regression residuals. This formulation, known as the random coefficients regression model, is essentially a generalization of the random effects model; the latter could be interpreted as arising from a randomly varying intercept. Zellner proposed that a test of $V = 0$ would be a suitable test of aggregation bias, and this procedure has had some use.[15]

A promising attack was made on the second question in a series of papers by Stoker (1984, 1986). Suppose that $y_i = F(x_i, \beta)$ is the underlying micro relationship and that x_i is distributed across agents as $p(x|\tau)$. Macroeconomic theory might be regarded as being concerned with the response of $\mu_y = E(y_i)$ to a change in $\mu_x = E(x_i)$, that is, $\partial\mu_y/\partial\mu_x$, as this captures the idea of the representative or average reaction. Can this information be extracted from a regression of y_i against x_i? By the chain rule $(\partial\mu_y/\partial\mu_x) = (\partial\mu_x/\partial\tau)^{-1}(\partial\mu_y/\partial\tau)$, provided $\partial\mu_x/\partial\tau$ is nonsingular. Now $\int x\,\partial p/\partial\tau\,dx = \int x(\partial\log p/\partial\tau)p(x)dx = E(dx) = V_{dx}$, where d is the score $\partial\log p/\partial\tau$ and V_{dx}

is the covariance of d with x. Similarly $\partial\mu_y/\partial\tau = V_{dy}$, making $\partial\mu_y/\partial\mu_x = V_{dx}^{-1} V_{dy}$, which is asymptotically equivalent to the IV estimator of the coefficient of x_i in the linear model relating y_i to x_i and where d_i is the instrument used. When $p(x|\tau)$ is a member of the exponential family, the IV estimator just becomes the OLS estimator. Hence a sensible macroeconomic interpretation can be given to a linear cross-sectional regression even though the underlying micro relationship is a nonlinear one that is not preserved in the aggregate data. To be sure, special assumptions are needed to get this outcome, principally that all variation in θ can be ascribed to μ_x, but Stoker's focus upon what can be learned about the average response is an important contribution to our understanding of what can be learned from aggregate data. It is interesting to note that in his example in Stoker (1986), the OLS estimator gives a good estimate of $\partial\mu_y/\partial\mu_x$, even though $p(x|\theta)$ is not in the exponential family.

A final attempt to build a bridge between macro and micro analysis comes if it is assumed that functions aggregate and an examination is made of how a macro relation estimated from time series would be build up from a series of micro relations. Using panel data is an ideal way of doing this; if the sample size is large enough, aggregating over all individuals in the panel should generate time series resembling those in the social accounts. Then, by varying the level of aggregation, it is possible to see how much information is hidden by the time series regressions.

Unfortunately, panel data are rare, and unlikely to be consistently available for long periods of time. By their very nature statistical agencies are happier collecting randomly chosen samples from a population in each time period rather than attempting to trace the same set of individuals over time. What exists then are repeated surveys upon the same actions of a different group of individuals over time. Household expenditure surveys are the classic illustration. To obtain these data, individuals cannot be tracked but cohorts can—that is, we can follow the actions of the "age 21–25" cohort as it ages through its representative groups. Estimation proceeds in much the same way as in the fixed effects model, and Deaton (1985) has a comprehensive discussion of how this is done, dealing particularly with the statistical problems arising from the possession of sample rather than population values for each cohort. More work utilizing this framework would seem desirable if we are to fully understand many macroeconomic phenomena.

11.6   The Achievements: A Personal View

How do we take the measure of the achievements of econometrics over this period? For a discipline aiming to provide tools for the analysis of data, some productivity measure is appropriate. To what extent then have the econometric theorists' work of the past twenty years become part of the process of economic investigation and the training of an economist?

Based on this criterion econometrics would have to be credited as an outstanding success. It is hard to find an official report or inquiry by a private or academic group that does not use many, or most, of the techniques discussed above whenever a model is appropriate. Econometric tools are routinely used in forecasting and policy assessment tasks, and a majority of these were developed in the past twenty years.

One of the problems in being more precise about this feature is the fact that the techniques and methods of econometrics have become part of the milieu. It is easy to forget that procedures readily understood and used by undergraduate students were once dimly understood and hotly debated by some of the best minds of the day.

The judging of achievement inevitably involves contrast and comparison. Over a period of twenty years this would be best done by interviewing a time-traveling economist displaced from 1966 to 1986. I came into econometrics just after the beginning of this period, so I have some appreciation for what has occurred. But because I have seen the events gradually unfolding, the effects upon me are not as dramatic. Nevertheless, let me try to be a time-traveler and comment on the perceptions of a 1966'er landing in 1986. My first impression must be of the large number of people who now have enough econometric and computer skills to formulate, estimate, and simulate highly complex and nonlinear models. Someone who could do the equivalent tasks in 1966 was well on the way to an academic chair. My next impression would be of the widespread use and purchase of econometric services in the academic, government, and private sectors. Quantification is now the norm rather than the exception. A third impression, gleaned from a sounding of the job market, would be a persistent tendency toward an excess demand for well-trained econometricians. The economist in me would have to acknowledge that the market judges the products of the discipline as a success.

Yet amid all this light there are dark corners. Ted Hannan, in an interview I did with him for *Econometric Theory* in 1985, said about the

Cowles Commission program, "In fact, its been a little bit of a failure, I'm afraid." Equivalent statements appear from time to time in the financial press or as presidential addresses by eminent people. Some of this may be sour grapes, but in other cases it runs deeper. There is a nagging feeling that current econometric practice is in some way deficient and that its approach distracts attention away from the economic history and data issues that should be paramount. "In house" criticisms have centered upon whether the probability model adopted by the Cowles Commission is well designed for the types of analysis we typically are forced to do. Leamer (1983) has been a vigorous promoter of this view, and much of that philosophy was shared by the econometricians at CORE in their research on Bayesian econometrics and statistics (Drèze and Richard 1984). By and large this remains a minority view, not because the philosophy does not appeal, but because the preferred alternative has been more conceptual than practical. I feel very strongly that the failure of CORE's admirably conceived Bayesian Regression Program stemmed from the fact that it was a very unfriendly piece of software. Leamer's greater success with his SEARCH program is attributable, in my opinion, to its greater flexibility and ease of use. It will be interesting to see if Bayesian econometrics has a much greater impact if programs can be designed so as to make analysis in this framework relatively easy. Here the interactive capabilities of the personal computer would seem to be a fertile base upon which to build an alternative style of doing econometrics.

"Outsider" reservations are based on a perspective that characterizes econometric theory as a search for optimal procedures in a hypothetical environment that doesn't capture reality or, worse, fails to address the essential economic issues. My empathy with some aspects of this belief has steadily grown in the last decade. Econometrics, which began with people who were excellent mathematicians, developed a startling lack of rigor in the 1950s and 1960s, prompting Malinaud's letter on the topic to the editor of the *International Economic Review* in 1971. Since then we have swung the other way, perhaps too far. Today there is a growing group of econometricians who would appear to regard their peer group as mathematical statisticians, and whose reading is more likely to be the *Annals of Statistics* than the *American Economic Review*. In the hands of extremely skilled people, such as Peter Phillips and Hal White, a lot can be, and has been, learned from this orientation, but it is nowhere near as effective or useful when done by those with lesser skills. Moreover it is worrying that the group of econometricians who can double as reputable economists—for example, Jerry Hausman, Jim Heckman, and Angus Deaton—does not seem to be gaining new recruits. Associated with this tendency has been the virtual demise, to the detriment of the profession, of the old-style economic statistician who was concerned with index numbers, national accounts, etc. Because of the disappearance of such individuals these topics, prominent in courses twenty years ago, have faded out of the curriculum. "Theory wise, data foolish" is sometimes all too true of our graduates today.

In some ways the notion of achievement is a very personal one, and the best indicator is how the participants feel about it twenty years later. These twenty years for me were exciting times, and I am glad to have made some contribution to the range of tools currently available to assist economic modeling. I firmly believe that econometrics weathered the storms created by flexible exchange rates, supply side shocks, money market deregulation, etc. much better than I would have expected if told of the likelihood of these events in 1966, and it has produced creative responses to them. This chapter has tried to exposit those responses. Much remains to be done, and it is that which should make the next twenty years just as exciting and productive as the last.

Notes

1. Hausman's principle is much more widely applicable than to just the linear regression model, and one of its most popular applications has been in checking the independence from irrelevant alternatives assumption in the multinomial logit model (Hausman and McFadden 1984).

2. Although little used, the investigation of nonlinear patterns in residuals may be important in certain contexts. Thus evidence on the "efficient markets hypothesis" should not be based solely on the detection of *linear* patterns of autocorrelation; the hypothesis rules out nonlinear ones as well. I have found evidence of a nonlinear weekly effect in stock market data in Pagan (1978) and Hinich and Patterson (1985) who reach a similar conclusion.

3. Both authors assume that $d(w_t, \theta)$ and $m(w_t, \theta)$ are independently distributed random variables. However, it is only necessary that such quantities be martingale differences.

4. Since $E((y_t^* - x_t \beta)|\text{obs data}) = E(u_t|\text{obs data})$, the moments cf u_t can be found as in Amemiya (1973), and it is these which are employed.

5. An exception is Singleton (1985) who looked at $\hat{\theta}$ coming from the GMM estimators discussed later.

6. In what follows comparisons are done with $y_t = x_t \beta + u_{1t}$ as the maintained model, but the process needs to be reversed as well since there is no reason to give it any special status.

7. Adjustments to the J-test, aimed at getting a closer correspondence of asymptotic theory with small behavior can be found in Godfrey and Pesaran (1983). In Pagan (1984) I suggested a way of finding the type I error of the J-test by Monte Carlo methods, but James MacKinnon has pointed out to me that the argument given there is incorrect.

8. Nickell (1985) has shown the ECM format to be an optimal response for certain types of behavior in x_t. It should also be emphasized that steady state behavior for stock/flow variables is naturally enforced by the presence of a stock disequilibrium term. Carland and Pagan (1979) impose steady state behavior upon an output equation by including a term representing the departure of inventories from their equilibrium levels, while Hendry and von Ungern-Sternberg (1979) argue for an "integral effect" of liquid asset balances upon consumption behavior.

9. There is more than one way of getting this result (Pagan 1985), including adjusting the constant terms in equations, a method favored in the type of models formulated in Bergstrom (1976). Others reduce to the condition prescribed by Currie (1981) that the "mean lag" response of y_t to y_t^* should be zero.

10. As mentioned in Hendry and Pagan (1980) there are many other reparameterizations which could be performed.

11. Stock (1985) estimates the conditional mean in an analysis of environmental policy, whereas Pagan and Ullah (1988) calculate the conditional variance as a measure of risk. Of course spectral analysis is a case of nonparametric density estimation and that has had quite a bit of use.

12. Recently Robinson (1986b) and Newey (1989) have shown that fully efficient estimators of β in (1) can be constructed when σ_t^2 is unknown by performing weighted least squares with weights $\hat{\sigma}_t^{-1}$, where $\hat{\sigma}_t^2$ is the nonparametric estimate of the conditional variance.

13. Note $\hat{\theta}$ must be consistent, and this means that $T^{-1}\Sigma d_{\theta,t} \overset{P}{\to} 0$ is needed, thereby restricting the type of model that this trick is applicable to.

14. Robustness to variation in the data points x_t was also a subject of study, principally by Krasker and Welsch (1982) in their "bounded influence" estimators, which effectively down-weight influential observations. Koenker (1982) argues that this is largely a response to a failure in the linearity assumption. It may well be that these points are the informative ones (e.g., they may come from a new regime) so that automatic reweighting seems dangerous.

15. The idea of treating the coefficients as characterized by a p.d.f. over individuals was also exploited by Trivedi (1985) in studying how lag distributions such as that of Koyck's can arise as a result of aggregation, even though individual units' dynamic behavior is not governed by such simple forms.

References

Aitcheson, I., and S. D. Silvey. 1958. "Maximum Likelihood Estimation of Parameters Subject to Restraints." *Annals of Mathematical Statistics* 29:813–828.

Almon, S. 1965. "The Distributed Lag between Capital Appropriations and Expenditures." *Econometrica* 33:178–196.

Amemiya, T. 1973. "Regression Analysis When the Dependent Variable Is Truncated Normal." *Econometrica* 41:997–1016.

Amemiya, T. 1981. "Qualitative Response Models: A Survey." *Journal of Economic Literature* 19:1483–1536.

Amemiya, T. 1985. *Advanced Econometrics*. Cambridge, MA: Harvard University Press.

Andrews, D. 1985. "Random Cell Chi-square Diagnostic Tests for Econometric Models: I. Introduction and Applications." Cowles Foundation Discussion Paper 762.

Avery, R. B., L. P. Hansen, and V. J. Hotz. 1983. "Multiperiod Probit Models and Orthogonality Condition Estimation." *International Economic Review* 24:21–35.

Balestra, P., and M. Nerlove. 1966. "Pooling Cross-Section and Time Series Data in the Estimation of a Dynamic Model: The Demand for Natural Gas." *Econometrica* 34:585–612.

Barnett, W. A. 1983. "New Indices of Money Supply and the Flexible Laurent Demand System." *Journal of Business and Economic Statistics* 1:7–23.

Barnett, W. A., Y. W. Lee, and M. D. Wolfe. 1985. "The Three Dimensional Global Properties of the Miniflex Laurent, Generalized Leontief, and Translog Flexible Functional Forms." *Journal of Econometrics* 30:3–31.

Barten, A. P. 1969. "Maximum Likelihood Estimation of a Complete System of Demand Equations." *European Economic Review* 1:7–73.

Bassett, G. W., and R. W. Koenker. 1978. "The Asymptotic Distribution of the Least Absolute Error Estimator." *Journal of the American Statistical Association* 73:618–622.

Bera, A. K., and C. M. Jarque. 1981. "An Efficient Large Sample Test for Normality of Observations and Regression Residuals." Working Papers in Economic and Econometrics 49, Australian National University.

Bera, A. K., C. M. Jarque, and L. F. Fee. 1984. "Testing for the Normality Assumption in Limited Dependent Variable Models." *International Economic Review* 25:563–578.

Berenblut, I. I., and G. I. Webb. 1973. "A New Test for Autocorrelated Errors in the Linear Regression Model." *Journal of the Royal Statistical Society B* 35:33–50.

Bergstrom, A. R. 1976. *Statistical Inference in Continuous Time Economic Models.* Amsterdam: North Holland.

Bewley, R. 1979. "The Direct Estimation of the Equilibrium Response in a Linear Dynamic Model." *Economic Letters* 3:357–362.

Bhagava, A., and J. D. Sargan. 1983. "Estimating Dynamic Random Effects Models from Panel Data Covering Short Periods." *Econometrica* 51:1635–1659.

Bowman, K. O., and L. R. Shenton. 1975. "Omnibus Countour for Departure from Normality Based on $\sqrt{b_1}$ and b_2." *Biometrika* 62:243–250.

Brainard, W. C., and J. Tobin. 1968. "Pitfalls in Financial Model Building." *American Economic Review* 58:99–122.

Braynton, F., and E. Mauskopf. 1985. "The MPS Model of the United States Economy." Mimeo, Board of Governors of the Federal Reserve System.

Breusch, T. S., and L. J. Godfrey. 1986. "Data Transformation Tests." *The Economic Journal* 96(supplement):47–58.

Breusch, T. S., and A. R. Pagan. 1979. "A Simple Test for Heteroscedasticity and Random Coefficient Variation." *Econometrica* 47:1287–1294.

Byron, R. P. 1970. "The Restricted Aitken Estimation of Sets of Demand Relations." *Econometrica* 47:1287–1294.

Byron, R. P. 1974. "Testing Structural Specification Using the Unrestricted Reduced Form." *Econometrica* 38:816–830.

Brundy, J. M., and D. W. Jorgenson. 1971. "Efficient Estimation of Simultaneous Equations by Instrumental Variables." *Review of Economics and Statistics* 53:207–224.

Carland, D. J., and A. R. Pagan. 1979. "A Short-Run Econometric Model of the Japanese Wool Textile Industry." *Economic Record* 55:317–327.

Challen, D. W., and V. W. Fitzgerald. 1984. "Dynamic Features of the NIF-10S Model." In *Proceedings of the Conference on the NIF-10 Model*, Australian Government Publishing Service, 186–233.

Chesher, A. D., and M. Irish. 1984. "Residuals and Diagnostics for Probit, Tobit and Related Models." Discussion Paper 84/152, University of Bristol.

Chow, G. C. 1983. *Econometrics*. New York: MacGraw-Hill.

Christensen, L. R., D. W. Jorgenson, and L. J. Lau. 1973. "Transcendental Logarithmic Production Functions." *Review of Economics and Statistics* 55:28–45.

Cooley, T. F., and S. F. Le-Roy. 1985. "Atheoretical Macroeconomics: A Critique." *Journal of Monetary Economics* 16:283–308.

Cosslett, S. R. 1981. "Maximum Likelihood Estimation for Choice Based Samples." *Econometrica* 49:1289–1316.

Cosslett, S. R. 1983. "Distribution-Free Maximum Likelihood Estimator of the Binary Choice Model." *Econometrica* 51:765–782.

Cox, D. R. 1961. "Tests of Separate Families of Hypotheses." In *Proceedings of the Fourth Berkeley Symposium on Mathematical Statistics and Probability*, Vol. 1, 105–123.

Cox, D. R. 1962. "Further Results on Tests of Separate Families of Hypotheses." *Journal of the Royal Statistical Society B* 24:406–424.

Cox, D. R., and E. J. Snell. 1968. "A General Definition of Residuals." *Journal of the Royal Statistical Society B* 30:248–275.

Cumby, R. E., J. Huizinga, and M. Obstfeld. 1983. "Two-Step Two-Stage Least Squares Estimation in Models with Rational Expectations." *Journal of Econometrics* 21:333–335.

Currie, D. 1981. "Some Long-Run Features of Dynamic Time Series Models." *The Economic Journal* 91:704–715.

Davidson, J. E. H., D. F. Hendry, F. Srba, and J. S. Yeo. 1978. "Econometric Modelling of the Aggregate Time-Series Relationships between Consumers Expenditure and Income in the United Kingdom." *The Economic Journal* 88:661–692.

Davidson, R., and J. G. MacKinnon. 1981. "Several Tests for Model Specification in the Presence of Alternative Hypotheses." *Econometrica* 49:781–793.

Davidson, R., and J. G. MacKinnon. 1984. "Convenient Specification Tests for the Logit and Probit Models." *Journal of Econometrics* 25:241–262.

Deaton, A. S. 1974. "The Analysis of Consumer Demand in the United Kingdom, 1900–1970." *Econometrica* 42:341–367.

Deaton, A. S. 1985. "Panel-Data from Time Series of Cross-Sections." *Journal of Econometrics* 30:109–126.

Deaton, A. S. 1986. "Demand Analysis." In *Handbook of Econometrics*, Vol. 3, edited by Z. Griliches, and M. D. Intriligator. Amsterdam: North Holland, 1768–1839.

Dempster, A. P., N. M. Laird, and D. B. Rubin. 1977. "Maximum Likelihood from Incomplete Data Via the E-M Algorithm." *Journal of the Royal Statistical Society B* 39:1–22.

Dixon, P. B., B. R. Parmenter, J. M. Sutton, and D. P. Vincent. 1982. *ORANI: A Multisectoral Model of the Australian Economy*. Amsterdam: North Holland.

Dhrymes, P. J., et al. 1972. "Criteria for Evaluation of Econometric Models." *Annals of Economic and Social Measurement* 1:291–324.

Dickey, D. A., and W. A. Fuller. 1979. "Distribution of the Estimators for Autoregressive Time Series with a Unit Root." *Journal of the American Statistical Association* 74:427–431.

Diewert, W. E. 1973. "Functional Forms for Profit and Transformation Functions." *Journal of Economic Theory* 6:284–316.

Doan, T., R. Litterman, and C. Sims. 1984. "Forecasting and Conditional Projection Using Realistic Prior Distributions." *Econometric Reviews* 3:1–100.

Domowitz, I., and H. White. 1982. "Misspecified Models with Dependent Observations." *Journal of Econometrics* 20:35–58.

Drèze, J. H., and J. -F. Richard. 1984. "Bayesian Analysis of Simultaneous Equation Systems." In *Handbook of Econometrics*, Vol. 1, edited by Z. Griliches and M. D. Intriligator. Amsterdam: North Holland, 517–598.

Duncan, G. M. 1986. "A Semi-Parametric Censored Regression Estimator." *Journal of Econometrics* 31:5–34.

Durbin, J. 1954. "Errors in Variables." *Review of the International Statistical Institute* 22: 23–32.

Durbin, J. 1970. "Testing for Serial Correlation in Least Squares Regression When Some of the Regressors Are Lagged Dependent Variables." *Econometrica* 38:410–421.

Durbin, J., and G. Watson. 1971. "Testing for Serial Correlation in Least Squares Regression, III." *Biometrika* 58:1–19.

Eicker, F. 1967. "Limit Theorems for Regressions with Unequal and Dependent Errors." In *Proceedings of the Fifth Berkeley Symposium on Mathematical Statistics and Probability*, Vol. 1, 59–82.

Elbadawi, I. A., A. R. Gallant, and G. Souza. 1983. "An Elasticity Can Be Estimated Consistently without a Priori Knowledge of Functional Form." *Econometrica* 52:1731–1751.

Engle, R. F. 1982. "Autoregressive Conditional Heteroscedasticity with Estimates of the Variance of UK Inflations." *Econometrica* 50:987–1007.

Engle, R. F., D. F. Hendry, and J. -F. Richard. 1983. "Exogeneity." *Econometrica* 51:277–304.

Engle, R. F., D. M. Lillien, and R. P. Robins. 1987. "Estimating Time Varing Risk Premia in the Term Structure: The ARCH-M Model." *Econometrica* 55:391–408.

Engle, R. F., and C. W. J. Granger. 1987. "Dynamic Model Specification with Equilibrium Constraints: Co-integration and Error Correction." *Econometrica* 55:251–278.

Evans, M., and M. L. King. 1985. "A Point Optimal Test for Heteroscedastic Disturbances." *Journal of Econometrics* 27:163–178.

Fernandez, L. 1986. "Nonparametric Maximum Likelihood Estimation of Censored Regression Models." *Journal of Econometrics* 32:35–57.

Flinn, C., and J. Heckman. 1982. "Models for the Analysis of Labor Force Dynamics." In *Advances in Econometrics* 1, edited by R. Basmann and G. Rhodes. New York: Academic Press, 35–95.

Gallant, A. R. 1982. "Unbiased Determination of Production Technologies." *Journal of Econometrics* 20:211–245.

Gallant, A. R., and D. W. Nychka. 1987. "Semi-nonparametric Maximum Likelihood Estimation." *Econometrica* 55:363–390.

Godfrey, L. G. 1978a. "A Note on the Use of Durbin's *h* Test When the Equation Is Estimated by Instrumental Variables." *Econometrica* 46:225–228.

Godfrey, L. G. 1978b. "Testing for Multiplicative Heteroskedasticity." *Journal of Econometrics* 8:227–236.

Godfrey, L. G., and M. H. Pesaran. 1983. "Small Sample Adjustments for the *J*-test." Working Paper in Economics and Econometrics 84, Australian National University.

Godfrey, L. G., and D. S. Poskitt. 1975. "Testing the Restrictions of the Almon Technique." *Journal of the American Statistical Association* 70:105–108.

Goldberger, A. S. 1964. *Econometric Theory*. New York: Wiley.

Gourieroux, C., A. Monfort, and A. Trognon. 1983. "Testing Nested or Non-nested Alternatives." *Journal of Econometrics* 21:83–115.

Gourieroux, C., A. Monfort, and A. Trognon. 1984. "Pseudo Maximum Likelihood Methods: Theory." *Econometrica* 42:681–700.

Gourieroux, C., A. Monfort, and A. Trognon. 1985. "A General Approach to Serial Correlation." *Econometric Theory* 1:315–340.

Granger, C. W. J. 1969. "Investigating Causal Relations by Econometric Models and Cross-Spectral Methods." *Econometrica* 37:424–438.

Griliches, Z. 1967. "Distributed Lags: A Survey." *Econometrica* 35:16–49.

Griliches, Z., B. H. Hall, and J. A. Hausman. 1978. "Missing Data and Self-selection in Large Panels." *Annales de l'INSEE* 30-31(Supplement): *The Econometrics of Panel Data*:137–176.

Gronau, R. 1974. "Wage Comparisons—A Selectivity Bias." *Journal of Political Economy* 82:1119–1143.

Hansen, L. P. 1982. "Large Sample Properties of Generalized Method of Moments Estimators." *Econometrica* 50:1029–1054.

Hansen, L. P., and R. J. Hodrick. 1980. "Forward Exchange Rates as Optimal Predictors of Future Spot Rates: An Econometric Analysis." *Journal of Political Economy* 88:829–853.

Hansen, L. P., and K. J. Singleton. 1982. "Generalized Instrumental Variables Estimation of Nonlinear Rational Expectations Models." *Econometrica* 50:1269–1286.

Harrison, G. W. 1985. "Sensitivity Analysis and Trade Policy Modelling." In *General Equilibrium Trade Policy Modeling*, edited by T. N. Srinivasan, and J. Whalley. Cambridge, MA: MIT Press.

Hausman, J. A. 1978. "Specification Tests in Econometrics." *Econometrica* 46:1251–1272.

Hausman, J. A. 1982. "Comment." *Econometric Reviews* 1:271–277.

Hausman, J. A., and D. McFadden. 1984. "Specification Tests for the Multinomial Logit Model." *Econometrica* 52:1219–1240.

Heckman, J. 1974. "Shadow Prices, Market Wages and Labour Supply." *Econometrica* 42:679–694.

Heckman, J. 1976. "The Common Structure of Statistical Models of Truncation, Sample Selection, and Limited Dependent Variables and a Simple Estimator for such Models." *Annals of Economic and Social Measurement* 5:475–492.

Heckman, J. 1984. "The χ^2 Goodness of Fit Statistic for Models with Parameters Estimated from Microdata." *Econometrica* 52:1543–1547.

Heckman, J., and B. Singer. 1984. "A Method for Minimizing the Impact of Distributional Assumptions in Econometric Models for Duration Data." *Econometrica* 52:271–320.

Heckman, J., and B. Singer. 1986. "Econometric Analysis of Longitudinal Data." In *Handbook of Econometrics*, Vol. 3, edited by Z. Griliches, and M. D. Intriligator. Amsterdam: North Holland, 1689–1763.

Hendry, D. F. 1980. "Econometrics—Alchemy or Science." *Economica* 47:387–406.

Hendry, D. F., and J. -F. Richard. 1982. "On the Formulation of Dynamic Models in Econometrics." *Journal of Econometrics* 20:3–33.

Hendry, D. F., and A. R. Pagan. 1980. "A Survey of Recent Research in Distributed Lags." Mimeo, Australian National University.

Hendry, D. F., A. R. Pagan, and J. D. Sargan. 1984. "Dynamic Specification." In *Handbook of Econometrics*, Vol. 2, edited by Z. Griliches, and M. Intriligator. Amsterdam: North Holland.

Hendry, D. F., and T. von Ungern-Sternberg. 1979. "Liquidity and Inflation Effects on Consumers' Expenditure". In *Theory and Measurement of Consumers' Behaviour*, edited by A. S. Deaton. Cambridge: Cambridge University Press.

Hildreth, C., and J. P. Houck. 1968. "Some Estimators for a Linear Model with Random Coefficients." *Journal of the American Statistical Association* 63:584–595.

Hinich, M. J., and D. M. Patterson. 1985. "Identification of the Coefficients in a Non-linear Time Series of the Quadratic Type." *Journal of Econometrics* 30:269–288.

Hoffman, D. L., and P. Schmidt. 1981. "Testing the Restrictions Implied by the Rational Expectation Hypothesis." *Journal of Econometrics* 15:265–287.

Horowitz, J. L. 1986. "A Distribution-Free Least Squares Estimator for Censored Linear Regression Models." *Journal of Econometrics* 32:59–84.

Huang, D. S. 1966. "The Short-Run Flows of Non-farm Residential Mortgage Credit." *Econometrica* 34:433–459.

Ichimura, H. 1986. "Estimation of Single Index Models." Mimeo, Massachusetts Institute of Technology.

Johnston, J. 1964. *Econometric Methods*. New York: McGraw-Hill.

Joiner, B. K., and J. R. Rosenblatt. 1971. "Some Properties of the Range in Samples from Tukey's Symmetric Lambda Distributions." *Journal of American Statistical Association* 66:394–399.

Jonson, P. D., E. R. Moses, and C. R. Wymer. 1977. "The RBA Model of the Australian Economy." In *Conference in Applied Economic Research*. Sydney: Reserve Bank of Australia.

Jorgenson, D. W. 1986. "Econometric Methods for Modeling Producer Behaviour." In *Handbook of Econometrics*, Vol. 3, edited by Z. Griliches, and M. D. Intriligator. Amsterdam: North Holland, 1841–1915.

Kalaba, R., and L. Tesfatsion. 1985. "Nonlocal Comparative Statics, Automatic Derivatives, and Nonlinear Filtering: Recent Developments at USC." MRG Working Paper M8518, University of Southern California.

Kaplan, E. L., and P. Meier. 1958. "Nonparametric Estimation from Incomplete Observations." *Journal of the American Statistical Association* 53:467–481.

Kennan, J. 1979. "The Estimation of Partial Adjustment Models with Rational Expectations." *Econometrica* 47:1441–1456.

Kennan, J. 1985. "The Duration of Contract Strikes in U. S. Manufacturing." *Journal of Econometrics* 28:5–28.

Kenny, L. W., L. F. Lee, G. S. Maddala, and R. P. Trost. 1979. "Returns to College Education: An Investigation of Self-Selection Bias Based on the Project Talent Data." *International Economic Review* 20:751–765.

Kennedy, P. 1985. *A Guide to Econometrics* 2d ed. Oxford: Blackwell.

Kiefer, N. M. 1985. "Specification Diagnostics Based on Laguerre Alternatives for Econometric Models of Duration." *Journal of Econometrics* 28:135–154.

Kiefer, J., and J. Wolfowitz. 1956. "Consistency of the Maximum Likelihood Estimator in the Presence of Infinitely Many Incidental Parameters." *Annals of Mathematical Statistics* 27: 887–906.

King, M. L. 1985. "A Point Optimal Test for Autoregressive Disturbances." *Journal of Econometrics* 27:21–37.

Koenker, R. W. 1982. "Robust Methods in Econometrics." *Econometric Reviews* 1:213–255.

Koenker, R. 1988. "Asymptotic Theory and Econometric Practice." *Journal of Applied Econometrics* 3:139–147.

Koenker, R. W., and G. W. Bassett. 1978. "Regression Quantiles." *Econometrica* 46:33–50.

Koerts, J., and A. P. J. Abrahamse. 1969. *On the Theory and Application of the General Linear Model*. Rotterdam: Rotterdam University Press.

Koopmans, T. C. 1950. "When Is an Equation System Complete for Statistical Purposes?" In *Statistical Inference in Dynamic Economic Models*, edited by T. C. Koopmans. New York: Wiley.

Kmenta, J. 1986. *Elements of Econometrics* 2d ed. London: Macmillan.

Kramer, W. 1982. "On the Consequences of Trend for Simultaneous Equation Estimation." *Economics Letters* 14:23–30.

Krasker, W. S., and R. E. Welsch. 1982. "Efficient Bounded-Influence Regression Estimation." *Journal of the American Statistical Association* 77:595–604.

Kuh, E., J. W. Neese, and P. Hollinger. 1985. *Structural Sensitivity in Econometric Models*. New York: Wiley.

Lancaster, T. 1979. "Econometric Methods for the Duration of Unemployment." *Econometrica* 47:939–956.

Lancaster, T. 1985. "Generalized Residuals and Heterogeneous Duration Models." *Journal of Econometrics* 28:155–169.

Leamer, E. 1983. "Let's Take the Con out of Econometrics." *American Economic Review* 73:31–44.

Leamer, E. 1984. "Vector Autoregressions for Causal Inference." *Carnegie-Rochester Conference Series on Public Policy* 22:255–303.

Lee, L. F. 1979. "Identification and Estimation in Binary Choice Models with Limited (Censored) Dependent Variables." *Econometrica* 47:977–996.

Lee, L. F. 1982. "Some Approaches to the Correction of Selectivity Bias." *Review of Economic Studies* 49:355–372.

Lee, L. F., and G. S. Maddala. 1985. "The Common Structure of Tests for Selectivity Bias, Serial Correlation, Heteroscedasticity and Non-normality in the Tobit Model." *International Economic Review* 26:1–20.

Lewis, H. G. 1974. "Comments on Selectivity Biases in Wage Comparisons." *Journal of Political Economy* 82:1145–1155.

Lucas, R. E. 1972. "Econometric Testing of the Natural Rate Hypothesis." In *The Econometrics of Price Determination Conference*, edited by O. Eckstein. Washington: Board of Governors of the Federal Reserve System.

Lucas, R. E. 1976. "Econometric Policy Evaluation: A Critique." In *The Phillips Curve and Labour Markets*, Carnegie-Rochester Series on Public Policy 1. Amsterdam: North Holland.

Lucas, R. E., and T. J. Sargent. 1981. "After Keynesian Macroeconomics." In *Rational Expectations and Econometric Practice*, edited by R. E. Lucas and T. J. Sargent. University of Minnesota Press, 295–320.

McAleer, M., and M. H. Pesaran. 1986. "Statistical Inference in Non-nested Econometric Models." *Applied Mathematics and Computation* 20 (3/4): 271–311.

McCallum, B. 1976. "Rational Expectations and the Natural Rate Hypothesis: Some Consistent Estimates." *Econometrica* 44: 43–52.

McFadden, D. 1974. "Conditional Logit Analysis of Qualitative Choice Behavior." In *Frontiers in Econometrics*, edited by P. Zarembka. New York: Academic Press, 105–142.

McFadden, D. 1981. "Econometric Models of Probabilistic Choice." In *Structual Analysis of Discrete Data with Econometric Applications*, edited by C. F. Manski and D. McFadden. Cambridge, MA: MIT Press, 198–272.

McFadden, D. L. 1984. "Econometric Analysis of Qualitative Response Models." In *Handbook of Econometrics*, Vol. 2, edited by Z. Griliches and M. D. Intriligator. Amsterdam: North Holland, 1395–1457.

McGuire, T. W., J. W. Farley, R. E. Lucas, and R. L. Winston. 1968. "Estimation and Inference for Linear Models in Which Subsets of the Dependent Variable Are Constrained." *Journal of the American Statistical Association* 63: 1201–1213.

Maddala, G. S. 1971. "The Use of Variance Components Models in Pooling Cross-Section and Time Series Data." *Econometrica* 39: 341–358.

Maddala, G. S. 1983. *Limited-Dependent and Qualitative Variables in Econometrics*. Cambridge: Cambridge University Press.

Maddala, G. S. 1986. "Disequilibrium, Self-Selection, and Switching Models." In *Handbook of Econometrics*, Vol. 3, edited by Z. Griliches and M. D. Intriligator. Amsterdam: North Holland, 1634–1688.

Manski, C. F. 1975. "The Maximum Score Estimation of the Stochastic Utility Model of Choice." *Journal of Econometrics* 3: 205–228.

Manski, C. F. 1984. "Adaptive Estimation of Non-linear Regression Models." *Econometric Reviews* 3: 145–194.

Manski, C. F. 1985. "Semiparametric Analysis of Discrete Response: Asymptotic Properties of the Maximum Score Estimator." *Journal of Econometrics* 27: 313–333.

Manski, C. F., and T. S. Thompson. 1986. "Operational Characteristics of Maximum Score Estimation." *Journal of Econometrics* 32: 85–108.

Manski, C. F., and S. R. Lerman. 1977. "The Estimation of Choice Probabilities from Choice-Based Samples." *Econometrica* 45: 1977–1988.

Manski, C. F., and D. McFadden. 1981. "Alternative Estimators and Sample Designs for Discrete Choice Analysis." In *Structural Analysis of Discrete Data with Econometric Applications*, edited by C. F. Manski and D. McFadden. Cambridge, MA: MIT Press, 2–50.

Mizon, G. E. 1984. "The Encompassing Approach in Econometrics." In *Econometrics and Quantitative Economics*, edited by D. F. Hendry and K. F. Wallis. Oxford: Blackwell.

Mizon, G. E., and J. -F. Richard. 1986. "The Encompassing Principle and Its Application to Testing Non-nested Hypotheses." *Econometrica* 54: 657–678.

Mundlak, Y. 1963. "Estimation of Production and Behavioral Functions from a Combination of Time Series and Cross Section Data." In *Measurement in Economics*, edited by C. F. Christ. Stanford: Stanford University Press.

Murphy, C. W., I. A. Bright, R. J. Brooker, W. D. Greeves, and B. K. Taplin. 1986. *A Macroeconometric Model of the Australian Economy for Medium-Term Policy Analysis*. Canbera: Office of the Economic Planning Advisory Council.

Muth, J. F. 1961. "Rational Expectations and the Theory of Price Movements." *Econometrica* 29:315–335.

Nadaraya, E. A. 1964. "On Estimating Regression." *Theory of Probability and Its Applications* 9:141–142.

Nelson, C. E. 1975. "Rational Expectations and the Estimation of Econometric Models." *International Economic Review* 16:555–561.

Nelson, C. R., and C. I. Plosser. 1982. "Trends and Random Walks in Macroeconomic Time Series: Some Evidence and Implications." *Journal of Monetary Economics* 10:139–162.

Newey, W. K. 1984. "A Method of Moments Interpretation of Sequential Estimators." *Economics Letters* 14:201–206.

Newey, W. K. 1988. "Maximum Likelihood Specification Testing and Conditional Moment Tests." *Econometrica* 53:1047–1070.

Newey, W. K. 1988. "Adaptive Estimation of Regression Models via Moment Restrictions." *Journal of Econometrics* 38:301–339.

Newey, W. K. 1989. "Efficient Estimation of Models with Conditional Moment Restrictions." *Econometrica*, forthcoming.

Newey, W. K., and K. D. West. 1987. "A Simple, Positive Semi-Definite, Heteroskedasticity and Autocorrelation Consistent Covariance Matrix." *Econometrica* 55:703–778.

Nicholls, D. F., and A. R. Pagan. 1983. "Heteroscedasticity in Models with Lagged Dependent Variables." *Econometrica* 51:1233–1242.

Nickell, S. 1985. "Error Correction, Partial Adjustment and All That: An Expository Note." *Oxford Bulletin of Economics and Statistics* 47:119–130.

Olsen, R. 1982. "Distribution Tests for Selectivity Bias and a More Robust Likelihood Estimator." *International Economic Review* 23:223–240.

Orcutt, G. 1957. "A New Type of Socio-Economic System." *Review of Economics and Statistics* 58:773–797.

Orcutt, G., M. Greenberger, J. Korbel, and A. Rivlin. 1961. *Microanalysis of Socioeconomic Systems: A Simulation Study*. New York: Harper and Brothers.

Orcutt, G., et al. 1976. *Policy Exploration through Microanalytic Simulation*. Washington: The Urban Institute.

Pagan, A. R. 1978. "Some Simple Tests for Nonlinear Time Series Models." CORE Discussion Paper 7812, Université Catholique de Louvain, Louvain-la-Neuve.

Pagan, A. R. 1984. "Model Evaluation by Variable Addition." In *Econometrics and Quantitative Economics*, edited by D. F. Hendry and K. F. Wallis, Oxford: Blackwell, 103–133.

Pagan, A. R. 1985. "Time Series Behaviour and Dynamic Specification." *Oxford Bulletin of Economics and Statistics* 47:199–211.

Pagan, A. R. 1986. "Two Stage and Related Estimators and Their Applications." *Review of Economic Studies* 53:517–538.

Pagan, A. R., and J. Shannon. 1985. "Sensitivity Analysis for Linearised Computable General Equilibrium Models." In *New Developments in Applied General Equilibrium Analysis*, edited by J. Piggott, and J. Whalley. Cambridge: Cambridge University Press.

Pagan, A. R., and A. Ullah. 1988. "The Econometric Analysis of Models Involving Risk Terms." *Journal of Applied Econometrics* 3:87–105.

Park, J., and P. C. B. Phillips. 1986. "Statistical Inference in Regressions with Integrated Processes: Parts I and II." Mimeo, Yale University.

Patterson, K. D., and J. Ryding. 1984. "Dynamic Time Series Models with Growth Effects Constrained to Zero." *The Economic Journal* 94:137–143.

Pesaran, M. H. 1974. "On the General Problem of Model Selection." *Review of Economic Studies* 41:153–171.

Pesaran, M. H. 1981. "Identification of Rational Expectation Models." *Journal of Econometrics* 16:375–398.

Pesaran, M. H. 1986. "Econometrics." In *The New Palgrave. A Dictionary of Economics.* London: Macmillan, 1987.

Pesaran, M. H. 1987. *The Limits to Rational Expectations.* Oxford: Blackwell.

Phillips, P. C. B. 1982. "Exact Small Sample Theory in the Simultaneous Equations Models." In *Handbook of Econometrics,* Vol. 1, edited by Z. Griliches and M. D. Intriligator. Amsterdam: North Holland.

Phillips, P. C. B. 1987. "Time Series Regression with Unit Roots." *Econometrica* 55:277–302.

Phillips, P. C. B., and S. N. Durlauf. 1986. "Multiple Time Series Regression with Integrated Processes." *Review of Economic Studies* 53:473–496.

Piggott, J., and J. Whalley. 1985. *U.K. Policy and Applied General Equilibrium Analysis.* Cambridge: Cambridge University Press.

Plosser, C. I., G. W. Schwert, and H. White. 1982. "Differencing as a Test of Specification." *International Economic Review* 23:535–552.

Poirier, D. J. 1975. "Spline Lags: Why the Almon Lag Has Gone to Pieces." In *The Econometrics of Structural Change,* edited by D. J. Poirier. Amsterdam: North Holland.

Powell, A. A. 1969. "Aitken Estimators as a Tool in Allocating Predetermined Aggregates." *Journal of the American Statistical Association* 64:913–922.

Powell, J. L. 1986. "Symmetrically Trimmed Least Squares Estimation for Tobit Models." *Econometrica* 54:1435–1460.

Quandt, R. E. 1982. "Econometric Disequilibrium Models." *Econometric Reviews* 1:1–63.

Ramsey, J. B. 1969. "Tests for Specification Errors in Classical Linear Least-Squares Regression Analysis." *Journal of the Royal Statistical Society B* 31:350–371.

Revankar, N. S. 1980. "Testing of the Rational Expectations Hypothesis." *Econometrica* 48:1347–1363.

Robinson, P. M. 1983. "Non-parametric Estimators for Time Series." *Journal of Time Series Analysis* 4:185–207.

Robinson, P. M. 1986. "Non-parametric Methods in Specification." *Economic Journal* (Supplement) 96:134–141.

Robinson, P. M. 1987. "Asymptotically Efficient Estimation in the Presence of Heteroscedasticity of Unknown Form." *Econometrica* 55:875–891.

Rose, D. E., and J. G. Selody. 1985. "The Structure of the Small Annual Model." Technical Report 40, Bank of Canada.

Rosenbiatt, M. 1956. "Remarks on Some Nonparametric Estimates of a Density Function." *Annals of Mathematical Statistics* 27:832–837.

Roy, A. D. 1951. "Some Thoughts on the Distribution of Earnings." *Oxford Economic Papers* 3:135–146.

Salant, S. 1977. "Search Theory and Duration Data: A Theory of Sorts." *Quarterly Journal of Economics* 91:39–57.

Salmon, M. 1982. "Error Correction Mechanisms." *The Economic Journal* 92:615–629.

Sargan, J. D. 1958. "The Estimation of Economic Relationships Using Instrumental Variables." *Econometrica* 26:393–415.

Sargent, T. J. 1976. "A Classical Macroeconomic Model for the United States." *Journal of Political Economy* 84:207–237.

Sawa, T. 1978. "Information Criteria for Discriminating among Alternative Regression Models." *Econometrica* 46:1273–1291.

Shiller, R. J. 1973. "A Distributed Lag Estimator Derived from Smoothness Priors." *Econometrica* 41:775–788.

Sims, C. A. 1972. "Money, Income and Causality." *American Economic Review* 62:540–552.

Sims, C. A. 1980. "Macroeconomics and Reality." *Econometrica* 48:1–48.

Sims, C. A., J. H. Stock, and M. Watson. 1986. "Inference in Linear Time Series Models with Some Unit Roots." Mimeo, Stanford University.

Singleton, J. J. 1985. "Testing Specifications of Economic Agents' Intertemporal Optimum Problems in the Presence of Alternative Models." *Journal of Econometrics* 30:391–413.

Small, K. D., and D. Brownstone. 1982. "Efficient Estimation of Nested Logit Models: An Application to Trip Timing." Research Memorandum 296, Princeton University.

Stock, J. H. 1985. "Nonparametric Policy Analysis." Mimeo, Harvard University.

Stock, J. 1987. "Asymptotic Properties of Least Squares Estimators of Co-intergrating Vectors." *Econometrica* 55:1035–1056.

Stoker, T. M. 1984. "Completeness, Distribution Restrictions and the Form of Aggregate Functions." *Econometrica* 52:887–908.

Stoker, T. M. 1986. "Aggregation, Efficiency and Cross-Section Regression." *Econometrica* 54:171–188.

Stone, C. J. 1975. "Adaptive Maximum Likelihood Estimation of a Location Parameter." *Annals of Statistics* 3:267–284.

Swamy, P. A. V. B. 1970. "Efficient Inference in a Random Coefficient Regression Model." *Econometrica* 38:311–323.

Tauchen, G. 1985. "Diagnostic Testing and Evaluation of Maximum Likelihood Models." *Journal of Econometrics* 30:415–443.

Tobin, J. 1958. "Estimation of Relationships for Limited Dependent Variables." *Econometrica* 26:24–36.

Tuma, N. 1976. "Rewards, Resources and the Rate of Mobility: A Non-stationary Multivariate Stochastic Model." *American Sociological Review* 41:338–360.

Trivedi, P. K. 1985. "Distributed Lags, Aggregation and Compounding: Some Econometric Implications." *Review of Economic Studies* 52:19–36.

Ullah, A. 1988. "Nonparametric Estimation of Econometric Functionals." *Canadian Journal of Economics* 21:625–658.

Wales, T. J. 1977. "On the Flexibility of Flexible Functional Forms: An Empirical Approach." *Journal of Econometrics* 5:183–193.

Wallis, K. F. 1972. "Testing for Fourth Order Autocorrelation in Quarterly Regression Equations." *Econometrica* 40:617–636.

Wallis, K. F. 1980. "Econometric Implications of the Rational Expectations Hypothesis." *Econometrica* 48:49–73.

Watson, G. S. 1974. "Smooth Regression Analysis." *Sankhya Series A* 26:359–372.

White, H. 1980a. "A Heteroskedasticity-Consistent Covariance Matrix Estimator and a Direct Test for Heteroskedasticity." *Econometrica* 48:817–838.

White, H. 1980b. "Using Least Squares to Approximate Unknown Regression Functions." *International Economic Review* 21:149–170.

White, H. 1982a. "Maximum Likelihood Estimation of Misspecified Models." *Econometrica* 50:1–25.

White, H. 1982b. "Instrumental Variables Regression with Independent Observations." *Econometrica* 50:483–500.

Wickens, M. W. 1982. "The Efficient Estimation of Econometric Models with Rational Expectations." *Review of Economic Studies* 49:817–838.

Wickens, M. W. 1986. "The Estimation of Linear Models with Future Rational Expectations by Efficient and Instrumental Variable Methods." Center for Economic Policy Research Discussion Paper 111, London.

Wu, D. M. 1973. "Alternative Tests of Independence between Stochastic Regressors and Disturbances." *Econometrica* 41:733–750.

Zellner, A. 1962. "An Efficient Method of Estimating Seemingly Unrelated Regressions and Tests for Aggregation Bias." *Journal of American Statistical Association* 57:348–368.

Zellner, A. 1969. "On the Aggregation Problem: A New Approach to a Troublesome Problem." In *Economic Models, Estimation and Risk Programming: Essays in Honor of Bernhard Tintner*, edited by K. A. Fox, J. K. Sengupta, and G. V. L. Narasimham. New York: Springer Verlag, 365–374.

COMMENTS
MICHEL MOUCHART

General Comment

I first want to thank and to congratulate Adrian Pagan for his brilliant exposition: for so many provoking comments, for the depth and spread of his overview, for the complementarity and the guiding hand to the 2,000-page *Handbook of Econometrics*, and for his bravery to publicly expose what he considers important and relevant for the practice of econometrics and what he does not. In particular, he resisted the temptation of confronting the various chapters in the *Handbook of Econometrics* with the econometric activity at CORE, neither did he fall into the trap of trying to evaluate the divergence and the convergence of approaches at CORE, in Europe or in the world. Pagan rather provides us with his view of the last twenty years' achievements which he regards as most relevant for the practice of econometrics; thus he has excluded, for instance, disequilibrium models, demand and consumption analysis, macromodeling, at variance with our experience at CORE.

The Next Twenty Years

Rather than commenting on a personal evaluation of past achievement, let me try to indicate the kind of progresses I am expecting for the next twenty years. I want to pay particular attention to some developments we have seen in the last ten years at CORE and in several other research institutions, particularly on this side of the Atlantic.

Essentially I believe that an important challenge for the near future will be the development of *methodological help for model specification.* A good deal of Pagan's survey is concerned with contributions that either design innovative specifications or improve inference procedures for given models, the frontier of this last field being surveyed under the heading of "the search for robustness." This suggests an ordering of procedures: economic theory would first provide a model, and thereafter econometric (or statistical?) theory would provide inferential procedures that consider data and model as given. This is at variance from common practice where typically a decision maker asks a question such as, what will be (the order of) the magnitude of a particular variable if some decision is taken and coincidentally a particular event occurs? Then even the choice of data to be analyzed requires methodological guidance and the model finally regarded as suitable is (almost?) never the same as the first one envisaged; imagine, as an example, that two econometricians, one "neoclassical," the other one "neo-Keynesian," were asked to construct predictions for the level of unemployment next year; they will most likely analyze different data and build different models to answer the same question, and any evaluation of their respective output should take into account their entire road from data collection to the evaluation of their predictive distribution (or interval). A crucial role of methodology is precisely to design safeguards that avoid transforming a data-based model selection into a data-mining procedure. I tend to believe that improving inferences upon parameters of a given model often becomes of secondary relevance in empirical works or, put differently, making due allowance, at the inference phase, for the model search is often more important and more difficult than optimizing inference for a given model.

Let me suggest some topics where progresses in this direction have been made in the recent past and where further progresses are definitely called for:

1. *The interaction between economic theory and observation.* From an empirical point of view a basic concern of theoretical construct is to provide a ("sufficient") summary of a very large body of observations (over time and space), with the main tools being the search for structural stability, the search for structural invariance (such as stationarity or exchangeability), and the search for (conditional) independence. Although already present in the Cowles Commission's time-honored monographs and in the numerous procedures for testing parametric stability, stationarity, exchangeability, or independence, this concern remains one of the most difficult to be handled in a systematic way because the crucial question is, How should theory and facts adjust to each other?

2. *The microeconomic foundations of macroeconomics.* This intellectually challenging problem has received a lot of attention in the last decade. It concerns a suitable probabilistic approach to aggregation that should bridge the economic and the statistical analysis. In particular, the economist's concern for flexible form of latent structures such as utility functions naturally convey the statistician's interest in nonparametric procedures for the analysis of observables such as demand functions. As pointed out by Pagan, this attitude has recently gained an increasing attention thanks to the new availability of micro data along with the recent developments in computer technology. But in addition to the problem of interpersonal structural stability comes the one of averaging individual characteristics and of describing the process of diffusing global constraints, namely, constraints active on aggregates but not on specific individuals; as an example, consider the credit-rationing policy in financial markets. I tend to believe that these efforts should also lead to put in agreement the "homo economicus" (i.e., optimizing behavior) with the "homo sociologicus" (i.e., environment determined and/or determining).

3. *Designing a progressive strategy for model specification.* Furthering this objective appears to be the cornerstone of much econometric thinking in many places, here and elsewhere. The problem is to formally describe such a strategy and analyze its properties. Progress has been achieved through

the idea of stepwise reduction of models. The role of marginalizing and of conditioning has now become clear, and this framework has proved to be useful in handling such concepts as exogeneity or causality and in showing, in particular, the crucial difference between the stage of inference, given the model, and the stage of model building. Thus weak exogeneity (i.e., cut in the sequential model) is a useful structure to simplify inferences for a given model, whereas noncausality combined with weak exogeneity can be used to obtain strong exogeneity which involves the same cut in both the initial and the sequential model: This is a useful structure for model building, the first stage of which is to establish conditions that validate a starting point. This approach of successive model reduction has proved its usefulness, inter alia, in handling linear models both in the IID case and in the dynamic case. But future progress should be expected in various nonlinear situations, in particular, under conditions of partial observability such as censored data (disequilibrium model, discrete indicators, etc.). The very same approach of model reduction has motivated the research around the concept of encompassing.

Let me conclude these comments by some remarks on the *role of Bayesian thinking in model specification*. If we agree that a model is a device to extract information from observation (the "no model–no inference" paradigm), the Bayesian method provides an approach to modeling and learning.

The *Bayesian approach to modeling* considers every quantity as stochastic; this is true for observables, nonobservables, or those not yet observed, and the distinction between parameters or unobserved quantities is ancillary. The only relevant classification relies on the available information, that is, which quantities are considered to be reliable messages: ("reliable") observations or accepted restrictions on the parameter space are treated the same way (by conditioning), whereas the unknown quantities of interest such as parameters of interest or future realization are all treated the same way (by being expressed through a probability distribution conditional on the available information). Our experience is that this approach effectively helps to provide a simple coherent view that clarifies difficult issues and sweeps away irrelevant problems.

The *Bayesian approach to learning* through observations consists of thinking systematically in probabilistic terms, be it through the posterior distribution for inference or through the predictive distribution. This provides a clear and easy-to-understand treatment of nuisance parameters, thus avoiding, for instance, the well-known paradoxes in conditional testing. Nevertheless, statistical thinking should not be reduced to Bayesian computation. I tend to believe that the Bayesian approach is ideally suited to develop coherent thinking in statistics (and for an economist isn't it natural to look for coherence or rationality?) even when most our computations are, at best, approximations of what would be deemed as ideal. Surely the Bayesian programs developed at CORE are still not friendly, and much progress should also be expected in this field for the near future. But in spite of this these programs are already useful for comparing a "pure" sampling theory analysis with a "pure" Bayesian analysis; we should nevertheless accept that pure routine Bayesian analysis is still not the rule for today!

Finally, let me emphasize *two points of contact between Bayesian and sampling theory methods*. The first one is well known and has been alluded to before: maximum likelihood estimators may be often interpreted as asymptotic approximations of the posterior mode and the posterior distributions often converge to the limiting distribution of some maximum likelihood estimator. This is useful both for approximating Bayesian results and for interpreting sampling theory results. Another point of contact is presently under development and is a treatment of hypothesis testing as a device that allows a statistician to confront his doubts about his model. Were he sure of the null hypothesis, then he would constrain his inference to the null hypothesis and the idea of specification test is precisely to look for "acceptable hypothesis." Such a doubt naturally affects the sampling theorist as well as the Bayesian statistician, and the paper presented by J. P. Florens at this colloquium is a step toward building another bridge between these two approaches to statistical inference.

I expect that developments in the near future will stress the complementary rather than the mutually exclusive character of these two approaches; so we might arrive at a position where no statistician would be allowed to ignore one of the two.

Acknowledgment

I want to express my deep gratitude to R. Schuler for quite illuminating discussions on an earlier version of these comments.

COMMENTS
JEAN WAELBROECK

I will try to complement Adrian Pagan's erudite presentation rather than comment on it. But I will be indelicate and borrow the Three Musketeers device that he has used to present his ideas.

I will, however, adopt an unabashedly model-centered perspective. I apologize in advance if what I say implies that modeling is the shining star around which econometrics and its related disciplines should revolve. But like most apologists, I will be hypocritical. Indeed, is not this view of econometrics the correct one? Does it not, for example, reflect the vision of the founders of the Econometric Society?

I will begin by underlining the preeminent role of "the Machine" in the progress of econometrics: The computer, with its hundred thousand demon bits and bytes and registers, has been the driving force that has kept econometrics interesting and exciting. When in the late 1930s Leonid Kantorovitch wrote a strange book on the management of a sawmill that was the first presentation of linear programming, he was lucky that in the USSR pretty much anything that is apolitical can get into print, for his method was useless at a time when even the electric office calculator was only a gleam in some engineer's eye. Is a count possible of the "clever but too expensive" methods of econometrics which, thanks to the demons' handywork, have become the essential tools of every serious applied researcher.

I do not know how clearly my three musketeers—Koopmans, Klein, and Theil—predicted how the power of computers would grow as they devised what I will call the Cowles Rotterdam research agenda. Today's students have difficulty in imagining the limitations that we faced, limitations that, as rereading of the original Cowles monographs reveals, were very much in the minds of the musketeers. Clearly, they did not suspect that in less than a generation, full information methods would be at the behest of every student.

To dramatize this progress, I will use three examples; two are personal. When in 1962 I used my first large body of data, the only computer available was a machine at the Institut National de Statistique, which went by the colorful name of "Le Tigre." It had 300 bytes of RAM—as much power but far less convenient than today's hand calculators. I was lucky that it was kindly programmed for me in machine language by a friendly

Fonds National de la Recherche Scientifique researcher, who was to become Belgium's leading specialist in the theory of computer languages.

In 1965, while I was a MIT, a student who had been trained by Daniel Suits of Michigan explained that as part of the technical baggage that he had had to acquire was an ability to invert a 5×5 matrix in fifteen minutes, using the Gauss Doolittle method. Knowing that most of my students would not have access to a computer once they had left the university, I came close to following that example. It was also in those years that one of Holland's eminent economists, Wouter Tims, spent fifteen hours a day for months inverting the 65×65 matrix of his famous model of Pakistan using an electric calculator that could add but not multiply.

Vingt ans après, it is as though we have entered another age. An age in which a wide range of packaged programs drop steadily in price as they compete for the attention of users, each with a powerful computer on his desk alongside his ballpoint pen and writing pad.

All of this is well known. But we should not forget the other, less visible source of strength of econometrics: that its structure has kept the simple elegance that it had in the days when the musketeers were having their first adventures. An enormous amount of research has been done since then, and there has been vast progress, but we have retained the ability to relate this intellectual wealth to a limited number of well-tested statistical concepts that order our knowledge and enable us to understand quickly what any new method does differently, and hopefully better, than existing ones.

What we have *vingt ans après* is thus something of a triumph, a culmination of the master plan that was mapped out in the 1950s: a very broad range of estimation methods to grasp whatever meaning is hidden in the poor data that economists live with, a coherent logical framework to organize these techniques within our minds, and computers that are so powerful that pretty much all of this methodology can be implemented on the powerful machines that sit next to our ballpoint pens. So what is left?

There is of course always another idea to be properly written up. There are always assistant professors looking for tenure, and econometric journals to publish the papers that will get it for them. But what is left that interests others than the members of our coterie? What econometric progress shall we boast of when to these twenty years have been added another twenty?

What "the Machine" can do will be decisive, but this we can only infer. We have vague ideas about fifth generation parallel computers, of a gigantic world data base, of vastly superior data free from the ambiguities of statistical questionnaires because the datum is captured by tapping actual transactions, of data bases that couple econometric results with the underlying data so that users, if they wish, can easily redo the estimates according to their insights and tastes.

Is this a pipedream? I do not think so. Today's capabilities would have seemed more incredible when CORE was founded. What is certain is two things: that computing power will be vastly greater than today's, and that the computer will be more personal than the most user friendly computers of today.

It is convenient at this point to return to Adrian Pagan's *Three Musketeers* device. As every reader of Alexandre Dumas knows, the three musketeers numbered four. I can never remember who the three were and who was the fourth, but I do know that the fourth musketeer of econometrics lived in Belgium and that twenty years ago, in leisurely and productive discussions with acolytes, he was inventing CORE.

In their minds was an agenda that differed in revolutionary ways from the Cowles Rotterdam agenda. I shall designate this as the Jimmy Savage research agenda. This program provided the raison d'être for an institution that is predicated on a harmonious balance between the three servants of decision making: econometrics, operations research, and mathematical economics. Thus CORE's basic concern would be models, in the true sense of that term. In econometrics, the area surveyed by Pagan's paper, CORE planned to invest heavily in the development of Bayesian methods as the most promising way of integrating data analysis into the modeling of decisions.

As always, reality hasn't quite matched the original dream. Contacts between econometricians, operations researchers, and mathematical economists have not been as close as had been hoped for. The Bayesian gamble may have at times resembled a lone quest for the Holy Grail as the overwhelming majority of the profession rallied round the less adventurous Cowles Rotterdam agenda.

Well, thanks to mysterious powers which his virtue evoked, Parsifal did find the Holy Grail, and I will conclude this discussion by venturing the view that thanks to the computer, the lone search will become the central question of mainstream econometrics. Whether in the process the purity of Bayesian thinking will be debased by eclecticism à la Leamer is not for me to say. But I suspect that something like that is bound to happen because advocates of Bayesian econometrics have failed to establish a following among applied econometricians, and this is partly due to the excessive preoccupation of the Bayesian school with fine theoretical points concerning the subtleties of flat priors, and the like. From a lost manuscript which I stumbled onto amid the ruins of the Abbey of Villers, I have learned that Parsifal, when at last he had found the Holy Grail, was deeply saddened by the dents and scratches in it.

What is the alternative? The Cowles Rotterdam approach, which views econometrics as a discipline separate from modeling, has by now been exhausted. As Pagan tells us, Sims, Granger, and others who have sought to sever econometrics from modeling have been unsuccessful. I believe that the time has arrived to revive the Jimmy Savage program that CORE has pioneered.

That now is the time to make this structural change, which the fourth musketeer had very clearly in mind when he devised the structure of CORE, is evidenced by the continuing, and apparently boundless, progress of the computer. We are entering an age of powerful, personal computers. Computational power will help to overcome a major block to the Bayesian approach, the high cost of calculating complicated integrals. This cost, which already has fallen drastically, is bound to decrease by another order of magnitude.

More important, in the wake of personal computing will come personal models, and the model builder and model user will often be the same person. The Cowles Rotterdam separation of econometric estimation from decision making was appropriate when teams of specialists were required to build and operate models. We are moving away from this situation, as shown, for example, by Ken Wallis' remarkable achievement in making all British models accessible to users throughout the British Isles. In twenty years from now the pressure of "personal model builders" will force econometricians to integrate far more intimately econometrics into decision modeling than most of the people in this room would accept.

While being cautious, I hope to have given the impression of being bold. Professional forecasters learn by experience, by the art of seeming reckless while never losing sight of the escape hatch through which they can slip out of mistakes. I especially did not predict that the future of econometrics will be Bayesian. The one thing I did predict, for which, should my forecast turn out to be wrong, I will submit to being strung up on the gallows with a hood as food for crows, is that if econometrics is to remain an interesting and progressive science, it will have to become far more integrated into the modeling of decisions.

A *mot de la fin* comes to mind. When older and wiser we meet to celebrate the fortieth anniversary and my forecast has proved true, what institution would be better placed as a venue of economic science, twenty years hence of its triple-barreled hunt for truth in the thickets of decision analysis?

12 Recent Developments in the Theory of Encompassing

David F. Hendry and Jean-François Richard

12.1 Introduction

One model is said to encompass another if the former can account for, or explain, the results obtained by the latter. Such a notion has long been accepted as a natural aspect of the research strategy in many sciences, though surprisingly rarely formalized. A number of recent developments in the econometric literature, however, have opened the way to formalizations of the notion of encompassing and the object of this chapter is to report on progress to date as well as to outline areas of further research.

Initially, applications of encompassing informally explored the implications of each of two models (denoted by M_1 and M_2 below) for the other, but such exercises lacked formal test statistics (see, e.g., Hendry and Anderson 1977 and Davidson et al. 1978). The motivation behind these exercises was the development of a progressive research strategy that would ensure that successive models not only explained new phenomena but also accounted for previous results. To formalize an explicit concept of population encompassing, Hendry and Richard (1982) exploited the property that knowledge of the data generating process (DGP) entails knowledge of (and hence encompasses) models derived from it. Since any empirical model must be derived from the underlying DGP, any two rival models M_1 and M_2 are always indirectly related even though neither need be a special case of, or embedded in, the other. The first example in section 12.4 illustrates this idea which is closely linked to the notions of separate families of hypotheses and nonnested tests, based on the pioneering work of Cox (1961, 1962). Such tests, which view M_1 and M_2 as distinct entities to be tested against each other, have found increasing usage in econometrics (see MacKinnon 1983 for a survey and a discussion of the relevant literature). One advantage of the encompassing approach is to offer an alternative perspective on nonnested tests as focusing on the issue of whether each model can account for the error variance of the other. A more general concept of parameter encompassing follows and is analyzed in Mizon (1984) and Mizon and Richard (1986) who develop systematic formulae for generating test statistics germane to any given hypotheses on the parameters of each model. Since each model views the other as being incorrectly specified, the literature on estimating misspecified models naturally provides useful techniques for investigating the behavior of encompassing test statistics (see White 1982 and Gouriéroux et al. 1984, inter alia).

Finally, formal encompassing tests are progressively appearing in computer software (such as PC-GIVE; see Hendry 1986). Thus, the concepts, tools, and techniques have reached a sufficiently mature level that the field as it stands merits an overview: that is the purpose of this chapter.

The chapter is organized as follows. In section 12.2, the general analytical framework is explained followed by a more extensive discussion and exposition in section 12.3 and two simple examples of encompassing in section 12.4. Then a Monte Carlo approach to evaluating encompassing is introduced in section 12.5 and parsimonious encompassing in section 12.6, and these ideas are developed in greater detail for the choice of regressors problem in section 12.7, including an extension to a general stationary stochastic process. The relation to the information matrix framework is discussed in section 12.8 leading to a more formal analysis of linear dynamic models in section 12.9. Section 12.10 briefly develops a Bayesian approach to encompassing and section 12.11 concludes and summarizes the paper.

12.2   Parametric Encompassing

Let Y_T^1 denote a sample of T observations on a random variable y in $\mathbb{R}^l$. The economy which has generated Y_T^1 and to which we refer below as the data generating process (DGP) is an entity of considerable complexity, the actual functioning of which is only partially understood. Hence the *axiom of correct specification* formalized by Leamer (1978), which requires of any given model that it exactly represent the revelant aspects of the DGP, is not an adequate basis for applied studies. Rather empirical models are simplified representations of the underlying DGP, and hence inherently misspecified though hopefully capturing the salient features of the DGP pertinent to the given problem. Essential to our argument is the fact that models can be construed as (implicit) reparametrizations of the DGP by marginalizing, conditioning, transforming, linearizing, and so on, as is obvious in a Monte Carlo context (see Hendry and Richard 1982 for further discussion of this issue).

Let the DGP be denoted by $\mathscr{H}$. It is convenient to assume that $\mathscr{H}$ can be represented by a joint data density $D(Y_T^1|\theta)$ parametrized by a vector of unknown parameters $\theta \in \Theta$, many of which could be "transient" in the sense that they are only relevant to a subperiod or "incidental" in that they are not directly parameters of interest. At this stage of the discussion, Y_T^1 includes all the variables that are retained in the modeling process, whether endogenous or exogenous, though we will discuss below how exogeneity assumptions affect our analysis.

Now let M_1 be a tentative empirical model of $\mathscr{H}$. Since patently mis-specified models would usually fail to encompass rival models, it is sug-gested that M_1 should already satisfy whatever design criteria are part of one's modeling strategy (see, e.g., Hendry and Richard 1982 where we dis-cuss a number of criteria that are thought to be of relevance for dynamic econometric models). Having achieved that objective, one may wish to confront M_1 with "fresh" evidence as provided by a rival model, say, M_2, and to analyze whether M_1 can mimic the encompassing capability which the DGP will always manifest.

M_1 and M_2 are represented by the density functions $f(Y_T^1|\alpha)$ and $g(Y_T^1|\delta)$, respectively, where α and δ are finite-dimensional, identifiable, and suffi-cient parametrizations within their respective models (see, e.g., Madansky 1987, ch. 2). The Bayesian framework we discuss in section 12.10 provides substance to our statement of parameter sufficiency.

In order to formalize the notion of encompassing, we have to make explicit the interpretation of α and δ as (derived) transformations of θ, and furthermore to discuss the interpretation of δ within the context of M_1. In a sampling theory framework we can usefully adopt a Monte Carlo based interpretation whereby parameters are conflated with plim's of their estimators, avoiding thereby ambiguities that would arise from the use of inconsistent estimators. This does not restrict the scope of application of our notion of encompassing since, as we discuss below, we can always apply our analysis to aspects of M_2 that were not considered by its proprietor and hence base our investigation on whatever estimator is thought to be relevant in our understanding of the salient features of M_2.

Thus let $\tilde{\alpha}$ and $\tilde{\delta}$ denote estimators which are consistent within their respective models so that

$$\text{plim}_{M_1} \tilde{\alpha} = \alpha, \qquad \text{plim}_{M_2} \tilde{\delta} = \delta, \tag{1}$$

possibly at the cost of redefining parameters and/or estimators in such a way that (1) holds. If the DGP were known, we could conceptually trace the sequences of transformations and reductions that lead to the formulations of M_1 and M_2, thus obtaining α and δ as explicit functions of θ. Practical alternatives would rely upon the use of Monte Carlo and response surface techniques, as described, for example, in Hendry (1984), for obtaining numerical approximations of these functions by showing how α or δ vary when θ is changed. From either route we obtain

$$\alpha_\theta = \text{plim}_{\mathscr{H}}\, \tilde{\alpha}, \qquad \delta_\theta = \text{plim}_{\mathscr{H}}\, \tilde{\delta}. \tag{2}$$

The distinction between (1) and (2) is important. In the former the estimators are each selected in the belief that their associated model is correct, in which case the parameter vectors α and δ result. In fact $\mathscr{H}$ is correct. So α and δ depend on the population parameters θ in (2). However, a third possibility arises. If M_1 is treated as the DGP (tentatively), then it entails a prediction as to what $\tilde{\delta}$ would become in large samples:

$$\delta_\alpha = \text{plim}_{M_1}\, \tilde{\delta}. \tag{3}$$

Then δ_α provides a reinterpretation of δ within M_1 and is known as the pseudotrue value (see Sawa 1978 or Gouriéroux et al. 1984). If M_1 encompasses M_2 (denoted $M_1 \mathscr{E} M_2$), then δ_α, or an estimate denoted $\delta_{\tilde{\alpha}}$, should coincide with what M_2 actually finds. This idea leads to two notions of encompassing that relate to the population and the sample, respectively, and we consider these in the reverse order.

The statistic

$$\tilde{\phi} = \tilde{\delta} - \delta_{\tilde{\alpha}} \tag{4}$$

compares the actual value of $\tilde{\delta}$ which M_2 obtained with an estimate of its plim on M_1 and embodies the essence of the notion of "parametric encompassing" as discussed in Richard and Mizon (1986) (note that we are considering cases with sufficient parameterizations).

DEFINITION 1 (Sampling) M_1 *(parametrically) exactly encompasses M_2 with respect to $\tilde{\delta}$ if $\tilde{\phi} = 0$ (for almost any value of the sample).*

In practice, exact encompassing will be difficult to achieve, but definition 1 leads directly both to a measure of deficiency (or failure to encompass) based on $\text{plim}_{M_1} |\tilde{\phi}|$ (or the expectation when that is computable), and to a test procedure based on $\sqrt{T}\,\tilde{\phi}$ (using the sampling distribution of $\tilde{\phi}$ on M_1).

If, in particular, the limiting distribution of $\sqrt{T}\,\tilde{\phi}$ on M_1 is $N(0, V_\alpha(\phi))$, a Wald encompassing test (WET) statistic with respect to $\tilde{\delta}$ is given by

$$\eta_w(\tilde{\delta}) = T\tilde{\phi}' V_{\tilde{\alpha}}^+(\phi)\tilde{\phi} \xrightarrow[M_1]{\mathscr{L}} \chi^2(\rho), \tag{5}$$

where $\rho = \text{rank } V_{\tilde{\alpha}}(\phi)$ and $V_{\alpha}^{+}(\phi)$ denote the Moore-Penrose inverse of $V_{\alpha}(\phi)$ (thus allowing for the fact the latter can be singular; as discussed in Marsaglia 1964, the algebra of singular normal distributions naturally relies upon the notion of Moore-Penrose inverse). WET statistics with respect to other M_2 statistics than the complete vector $\tilde{\delta}$ are defined in a similar way.

Alternatively, within the context of the underlying DGP $\mathcal{H}$, encompassing can be reformulated in terms of the population parameters. Let $\delta_{\alpha_\theta} = \text{plim}_{\mathcal{H}} \, \delta_{\tilde{\alpha}}$, and

$$\phi_\theta = \delta_\theta - \delta_{\alpha_\theta} = \text{plim}_{\mathcal{H}} \, \tilde{\phi} \tag{6}$$

DEFINITION 2 (Population) M_1 *(parametrically) population encompasses* M_2 *with respect to* δ_α *iff* $\phi_\theta = 0$.

Let

$$\theta \in \Theta_1 = \{\theta | \phi_\theta = 0\}. \tag{7}$$

Then population encompassing entails an implicit test on θ. In Mizon and Richard (1986), where θ indexes a class $\mathcal{M}$ of models, which consists of M_1 and alternatives to M_1 but does not necessarily include the DGP, Θ_1 is called the implicit null hypothesis associated with the statistic $\eta_w(\tilde{\delta})$. In, say, a Monte Carlo study of the properties of encompassing test statistics, $\mathcal{M}$ and $\mathcal{H}$ would be conflated with the process from which the random drawings are generated so that definition 2 could be applicable. Figure 12.1 summarizes our discussion of encompassing and as above, $M_1 \mathcal{E} M_2$ reads as M_1 encompasses M_2.

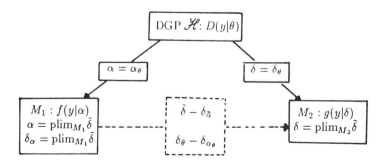

Figure 12.1

In the rest of the chapter we will rarely draw an explicit distinction between sampling and population encompassing. The distinction matters only insofar as some of the properties we discuss in section 12.3 are easily established for population encompassing but may not hold on small samples for parametric encompassing.

12.3 Discussion

The notion of parametric encompassing formulated above offers a number of conceptually attractive features that can be usefully discussed before we address the more technical issues related to its application.

First, the notion that a "later" model should be able to explain the findings of "earlier" ones is widely accepted in the methodology of science (see, e.g., Popper 1963 or Lakatos 1978) and characterizes *progressive* research strategies. For example, relativity theory provides a framework in which the major constituents of Newtonian gravitational theory can be explained as well as "anomalies" or other phenomena that were beyond the reach of the latter. The finding that a model M_1 cannot encompass a model M_2 indicates that M_2 incorporates *specific* features of the DGP that are not suitably accounted for by M_1. Either M_1 is therefore *rejected* or, more constructively, such evidence may contribute toward improving M_1 whenever these specific features are relevant to the objectives of the proprietor of M_1 (in which case other ways of testing M_1 than using M_2 must be sought).

Next, encompassing provides us with an integrating concept for modeling. It rightly emphasises model *comparison* over model *choice* since in practical situations all contending models are inherently misspecified and more is learned from analyzing their respective strengths and weaknesses, than by simply seeking to select any single one of them. Also the same basic techniques apply whether M_1 and M_2 are nested or nonnested. If, in particular, M_c denotes a (minimal) model that nests M_1 and M_2, we discuss below conditions under which the fact that M_1 encompasses M_2 is necessary *and* sufficient for M_1 to encompass M_c. Heuristically, M_c reflects specific evidence against M_1 only insofar as M_2 also does so. In turn, this suggests an invariance principle for selecting tests, namely, to ensure that test properties are not influenced by features that are *common* to the two models.

Furthermore we will see that encompassing can eventually be construed as a test-generating procedure (as discussed, e.g., by Mizon 1984 or Mizon and Richard 1986). This is illustrated below in the context of the choice of regressors problem and also in section 12.8 where Hausman (1978) specification tests are reinterpreted within the encompassing framework. This generating capacity should not be viewed as an end in itself but rather as a way of illustrating the flexibility of the encompassing notion. More important, it suggests that the choice between alternative test procedures could be based on their respective encompassing interpretation, attention being paid to those features of the contending models that are *relevant* to the proprietor of M_1, and deemphasising such notions as that of power against an artifical sequence of local alternatives. This is not meant to imply that considerations of power are unimportant, but that they are only one aspect of a general modeling strategy.

Also the concept of parsimonious encompassing, which we discuss below, sets a natural limitation to model reduction exercises (the well-known issue of parsimony in the face of limited sample evidence), the objective of which is to construct "simple" models that can still encompass the major features of "larger" models.

Third, it is essential to evaluate any empirical model outside of its design procedure. Specifically, the careful design of a model should essentially exhaust the direct data evidence, and the resulting model should satisfy by construction all the design criteria against which it has been tested. Hence it is indispensable that the ex post validation of a model be based on fresh information. Postsample prediction tests provide us with one possible route but require the availability of new data. Alternatively, a model M_2 that has been formulated by other investigators will typically incorporate features that were not specifically examined by the proprietor of M_1—unless obviously M_2 is nested within M_1—and so M_2 provides "fresh" evidence for evaluating M_1. By exploiting such evidence, the encompassing approach can be extremely useful for the ex post validation of M_1.

Another indication of the flexibility of the notion of encompassing lies in the fact that various levels of analysis can be considered, notwithstanding the development of the appropriate procedures. For example, encompassing subsumes three distinct facets, namely, *specification* encompassing (explaining the results actually obtained by another model; see, e.g., Hendry and Richard 1982); *misspecification* encompassing (predicting features of another model of which its proprietor is unaware; see Hendry and Anderson

1977); and *selection* encompassing (explaining why an inappropriate or inadequate model was chosen in preference to the encompassing model; see Davidson et al. 1987). The first two facets follow the dichotomy in Mizon (1977), and the approach adopted in section 12.2 essentially covers the first aspect. However, the second one follows by extending the scope of the analysis to a broader choice of statistics than those initially examined within the context of M_2 or, alternatively, by enlarging M_2 within a model that incorporates the additional features—such as changing coefficients or residual autocorrelation—that are to be subjected to encompassing by M_1. Although it was one of the motivations behind early encompassing applications, formalization of the third aspect remains for further research.

We would expect encompassing to generate a partial ordering on models. However, it is well-known that pseudotrue values are not transitive. Hence parametric encompassing, as introduced in definitions 1 and 2, is itself nontransitive. Conceptually at least, transitivity can be recovered at the cost of modifying definitions 1 (and 2) in the following way:

DEFINITION 1′ (Sampling) M_1 *exactly encompasses* M_2 *with respect to* $\tilde{\delta}$ *iff there exists a function* δ_α *such that* $\tilde{\delta} - \delta_{\tilde{\alpha}} = 0$ *(for almost any value of the sample).*

Definition 2 is left formally unchanged except that δ_α is selected in accordance with definition 1′.

In fact the Bayesian notion of encompassing that we introduce in section 12.10 generalizes definition 1′ in the usual way in that estimators are replaced by posterior densities and (exact) functions by transition probabilities.

If we explicitly distinguish between parametric encompassing in definition 1 and, say, encompassing in definition 1′, we see that parametric encompassing is sufficient but not necessary for encompassing. The two notions coincide if M_1 happens to be the DGP. The application of definition 1′ when M_1 is not the DGP raises major practical issues, though our discussion in section 12.10 suggests ways of constructing approximate δ_α functions as degenerate (large samples) limit probability densities. Hence, though some of our comments implicitly apply to the broader definition 1′, in practice we will restrict our attention to the more operational definition 1 which, as already discussed, has considerable interest on its own and is likely to provide useful approximations to the underlying δ_α when M_1 itself closely approximates the DGP.

At a different level, when δ is a sufficient parameterization for M_2, encompassing with respect to $\tilde{\delta}$ is said to be "complete." As mentioned earlier and as discussed in Mizon (1984) and Mizon and Richard (1986) in greater detail, incomplete or partial encompassing with respect to a statistic $\tilde{b}$, which is *not* in one-to-one correspondence with $\tilde{\delta}$, can also usefully be considered. We may wish, in particular, to draw a distinction between *historical* encompassing (M_2 being a "sequential" model describing how a vector x_t is generated at time t conditionally on its past, emphasis being set on such notions as Granger noncausality and innovation errors), *current* encompassing (focusing on the choice of exogenous or instrumental variables in M_2), and *forecast* encompassing (examining whether or not the M_1 forecasts encompass the M_2 forecasts). This trichotomy reflects more than just alternative choices of the focus of interest, and in particular the issue of different exogeneity claims between rival models raises complicated problems. However, forecast encompassing does entail a reduction of information since it can be implemented only after the outcomes are realized, in which case historical encompassing is applicable in principle. Obviously, if $\tilde{b}$ is a function of $\tilde{\delta}$, then complete encompassing entails encompassing with respect to $\tilde{b}$, but the converse will generally not be true (unless the rank of the covariance matrix of the encompassing difference $\tilde{b} - b_{\tilde{a}}$ equals that of $V_{\tilde{a}}(\phi)$). Presently historical encompassing has been the main area of interest though work is in progress in the two other areas (see Govaerts et al. 1978b and Chong and Hendry 1986, respectively).

We note finally that the choice of regressors problem has been the main area of application of our recent work on encompassing, partially for considerations of analytical tractability and partially also because this has been a major area of discussion (and controversy) in the recent literature on nonnested hypotheses testing and model choice. Other examples of applications are provided in the course of the chapter, and much of the discussion in sections 12.4 and 12.5 applies to a wide range of potential applications.

12.4 Two Simple Examples

A Univariate Normal Process

Let $\{Y_t\}$ $(t = 1, \ldots, T)$ denote a sequence of independent identically distributed normal random variables. M_1 is defined as

$$M_1 : Y_t \sim IN(\mu, 1). \tag{8}$$

The alternative to be encompassed is

$$M_2 : Y_t \sim IN(0, \sigma^2). \tag{9}$$

These two models are nonnested except at $\mu = 0$ or $\sigma^2 = 1$. A (minimal) nesting model associated with M_1 and M_2 is naturally defined as

$$M_c : Y_t \sim IN(m, s^2). \tag{10}$$

The ML (or pseudo-ML) estimators associated with these three models are

$$\tilde{\mu} = \tilde{m} = \bar{Y} = \frac{1}{T} \sum_{t=1}^{T} Y_t, \qquad \tilde{\sigma}^2 = \frac{1}{T} \sum_{t=1}^{T} Y_t^2, \qquad \tilde{s}^2 = \frac{1}{T} \sum_{t=1}^{T} (Y_t - \bar{Y})^2. \tag{11}$$

The pseudotrue values of interest on M_1 are

$$m(\mu) = \mu, \qquad \sigma^2(\mu) = 1 + \mu^2, \qquad s^2(\mu) = 1, \tag{12}$$

and the corresponding encompassing differences, as defined in (4), are

$$\tilde{\phi}_1 = \tilde{\sigma}^2 - \sigma^2(\tilde{\mu}) = \tilde{s}^2 - 1, \tag{13}$$

$$\tilde{\phi}_2 = \begin{pmatrix} \tilde{m} - m(\tilde{\mu}) \\ \tilde{s}^2 - s^2(\tilde{\mu}) \end{pmatrix} = \begin{pmatrix} 0 \\ \tilde{s}^2 - 1 \end{pmatrix}. \tag{14}$$

The first component of $\tilde{\phi}_2$ is identically zero so that the corresponding WET statistic, as defined in (5), has only one degree of freedom. In fact

$$M_1 \mathscr{E} M_2 \Leftrightarrow M_1 \mathscr{E} M_c \Leftrightarrow \tilde{s}^2 = 1, \tag{15}$$

and an *exact* test is available since the distribution of $\tilde{s}^2$ on M_1 is

$$\tilde{s}^2 \underset{M_1}{\sim} \frac{1}{T-1} \chi^2(T-1). \tag{16}$$

If we wish instead to examine whether M_2 encompasses M_1 or M_c, the pseudotrue values of interest on M_2 are

$$\mu(\sigma^2) = m(\sigma^2) = 0, \qquad s^2(\sigma^2) = \sigma^2 \tag{17}$$

leading to the following expressions for the corresponding encompassing differences:

$$\tilde{\phi}_3 = \tilde{\mu} - \mu(\tilde{\sigma}^2) = \bar{Y} \tag{18}$$

$$\tilde{\phi}_4 = \begin{pmatrix} \tilde{m} - m(\tilde{\sigma}^2) \\ \tilde{s}^2 - s^2(\tilde{\sigma}^2) \end{pmatrix} = \begin{pmatrix} \bar{Y} \\ -T\bar{Y}^2 \end{pmatrix}. \tag{19}$$

The WET statistic associated with $\tilde{\phi}_4$ has only one degree of freedom and

$$M_2 \mathscr{E} M_1 \Leftrightarrow M_2 \mathscr{E} M_c \Leftrightarrow \mu = 0. \tag{20}$$

On M_2, $\tilde{\mu}$ is distributed as

$$\tilde{\mu} \underset{M_2}{\sim} N\left(0, \frac{\sigma^2}{T}\right) \tag{21}$$

and the corresponding WET statistic is

$$\eta_w(\tilde{\mu}) = \frac{T\tilde{\mu}^2}{\tilde{\sigma}^2} \underset{M_2}{\overset{\mathscr{L}}{\to}} \chi^2(1). \tag{22}$$

Its exact distribution could be analyzed using standard finite sample techniques or Monte Carlo simulation. This simple example incorporates a number of features that will be the focus of our interest in the following sections, including singularities in V_α, equivalence between encompassing a nonnested alternative and a minimal nesting model, and finite sample results versus asymptotic ones.

Log Versus Linear Models

The choice between additive and multiplicative models has received a lot of attention in statistics (see the pioneering work of Cox 1962). A simple version of this problem can be used to illustrate the flexibility of an asymptotic approach to encompassing but also its limitations, thereby introducing the discussion in section 12.5.

The model M_1 is defined as

$$M_1 : y_t = \ln Y_t = \beta + u_t, \qquad u_t \sim IN(0, \sigma^2), \tag{23}$$

with parameter $\alpha = (\beta, \sigma^2)$. The alternative to be encompassed is

$$M_2 : Y_t = \gamma + v_t, \qquad v_t \sim IN(0, \tau^2) \tag{24}$$

with parameter $\delta = (\gamma, \tau^2)$. The ML estimator of α and the pseudo ML estimator of δ are given by

$$\tilde{\beta} = \bar{y} = \frac{1}{T}\sum_{t=1}^{T} y_t, \qquad \tilde{\sigma}^2 = \frac{1}{T}\sum_{t=1}^{T}(y_t - \bar{y})^2, \tag{25}$$

$$\tilde{\gamma} = \bar{Y} = \frac{1}{T}\sum_{t=1}^{T} Y_t, \qquad \tilde{\tau}^2 = \frac{1}{T}\sum_{t=1}^{T}(Y_t - \bar{Y})^2. \tag{26}$$

On M_1, the pseudotrue value $\delta_\alpha = (\gamma_\alpha, \tau_\alpha^2)$ of δ is given by the two-component expression:

$$\gamma_\alpha = \exp\left(\beta + \frac{1}{2}\sigma^2\right), \tag{27}$$

$$\tau_\alpha^2 = \gamma_\alpha^2(e^{\sigma^2} - 1). \tag{28}$$

A couple of comments are worth making before we derive the asymptotic distribution of the encompassing difference $\sqrt{T}\tilde{\phi}$:

1. Since M_1 is a multiplicative model, σ is the percentage standard error, and the analogous measure for M_2 is

$$\tau_\alpha \cdot \gamma_\alpha^{-1} = (e^{\sigma^2} - 1)^{1/2} = \left(\sigma^2 + \sum_{i=1}^{\infty}\frac{\sigma^{2i}}{i!}\right)^{1/2} > \sigma. \tag{29}$$

This is the criterion proposed by Sargan (1964) which is seen here as a *necessary* condition for $M_1\mathscr{E}M_2$. It remains necessary for $M_1\mathscr{E}M_2$ if the arithmetic mean γ_α is replaced by the geometric mean

$$g_\alpha = \exp\left(\beta + \frac{1}{2T}\sigma^2\right) \cong e^\beta. \tag{30}$$

In practice, the statistic computed is $\tilde{\tau}\cdot(\tilde{\sigma}e^{\tilde{\beta}})^{-1}$ to be compared to unity. Its properties are difficult to analyze, but its expectation on M_1 to $0_p(1/T)$ is given by

$$\tau_\alpha \cdot (\sigma e^\beta)^{-1} = \sigma^{-1}\cdot e^{\sigma^2/2}\cdot(e^{\sigma^2} - 1)^{1/2}. \tag{31}$$

This depends only on σ^2 and for small σ^2, (31) is very close to unity (e.g., 1.002 for $\sigma = 0.05\,\%$) so sampling fluctuations around its mean seem likely to dominate its behavior as a selection criterion. Even so, the criterion (29) is closely analogous to the variance dominance condition for linear regression models in Hendry and Richard (1982).

2. The sampling variances of $\tilde{\sigma}^2$ and $\tilde{\tau}^2$ on M_1 are tedious to evaluate. The

asymptotic derivation simplifies if $\tilde{\sigma}^2$ and $\tilde{\tau}^2$ are replaced by the control variates

$$\bar{\sigma}^2 = \frac{1}{T} \sum_{t=1}^{T} u_t^2 = \frac{1}{T} \sum_{t=1}^{T} (y_t - \beta)^2, \tag{32}$$

$$\bar{\tau}^2 = \frac{1}{T} \sum_{t=1}^{T} v_{t\alpha}^2 = \frac{1}{T} \sum_{t=1}^{T} (Y_t - \gamma_\alpha)^2, \tag{33}$$

the differences being $0_p(1/T)$. On M_1,

$$\text{Var}(\sqrt{T}\bar{\sigma}^2) = 2\sigma^4, \qquad \text{Var}(\sqrt{T}\tilde{\gamma}) = \tau_\alpha^2, \tag{34}$$

$$\text{Var}(\sqrt{T}\bar{\tau}^2) = \tau_\alpha^4 \cdot (e^{4\sigma^2} + 2e^{3\sigma^2} + 3e^{2\sigma^2} - 4), \tag{35}$$

$$\text{Cov}(\sqrt{T}\tilde{\gamma}, \sqrt{T}\bar{\tau}^2) = \gamma_\alpha \tau_\alpha^2 \cdot (e^{\sigma^2} - 1)(e^{\sigma^2} + 2). \tag{36}$$

A proof of formulae (35) and (36) is given in the appendix. The derivation of the asymptotic distribution of $\sqrt{T}\tilde{\phi}$ on M_1 now follows from theorem 1 in Mizon and Richard (1986), and we have

$$\sqrt{T}\tilde{\phi} \overset{\mathscr{L}}{\underset{M_2}{\to}} N[0, (V_\alpha(\sqrt{T}\tilde{\delta}) - D_\alpha V_\alpha(\sqrt{T}\tilde{\alpha})D_\alpha')], \tag{37}$$

where $V_\alpha(\sqrt{T}\tilde{\delta})$ is given by formulae (35) and (36) and

$$V_\alpha(\sqrt{T}\tilde{\alpha}) = \begin{pmatrix} \sigma^2 & 0 \\ 0 & 2\sigma^4 \end{pmatrix}, \tag{38}$$

$$D_\alpha = \frac{\partial \delta_\alpha}{\partial \alpha'} = \begin{pmatrix} \gamma_\alpha & \frac{1}{2}\gamma_\alpha \\ 2\tau_\alpha^2 & \gamma_\alpha^2(2e^{\sigma^2} - 1) \end{pmatrix}. \tag{39}$$

Interestingly, if we use Taylor series expansions for the polynomials in (σ^2, e^{σ^2}) which appear in the expression of $V_\alpha(\sqrt{T}\tilde{\phi})$, the leading factor is found to be

$$V_\alpha(\sqrt{T}\tilde{\phi}) \cong \frac{1}{6}\gamma_\alpha^2 \sigma^6 \begin{pmatrix} 1 \\ 6\gamma_\alpha \end{pmatrix} (1 \quad 6\gamma_\alpha). \tag{40}$$

Hence, for small σ, the asymptotic covariance matrix of $\sqrt{T}\tilde{\phi}$ is near singular, and the ("complete") WET statistic for $\tilde{\delta}$ essentially conveys no more information than the one degree of freedom WET statistic for $\tilde{\gamma}$. Equally important, we note that $\delta_{\tilde{\alpha}}$ is a biased estimator of δ_α and that, though the bias is $0(1/T)$, the effect can be large relative to the sampling variance of $\sqrt{T}\tilde{\phi}$.

These two remarks suggest that when σ is small, we should correct the encompassing test statistic for bias. Although an exact test statistic can be derived numerically by means of the Monte Carlo procedure we discuss in section 12.5, the numerical efficiency of that procedure is greatly increased if a control variate is available for $E_1(\gamma_{\tilde{a}})$ (E_1 is the expectation under M_1). Such control variates are easily obtained since, taking advantage of the independence between $\tilde{\beta}$ and $\tilde{\sigma}^2$ on M_1, we have successively

$$
E_1(\gamma_{\tilde{a}}) = \gamma_\alpha \cdot E_1[\exp(\tilde{\beta} - \beta)] E_1 \left[\exp \frac{1}{2}(\tilde{\sigma}^2 - \sigma^2) \right]
$$

$$
= \gamma_\alpha \cdot \exp \frac{\sigma^2}{2T} \left[\left(1 - \frac{\sigma^2}{2T} \right)^{T/2} \cdot \exp \frac{1}{2} \sigma^2 \right]^{-1} \tag{41}
$$

At an earlier stage of our investigations we used the following (approximately) unbiased estimator for γ_α:

$$
\gamma_\alpha^* = \gamma_{\tilde{a}} \cdot \exp \left[-\frac{\tilde{\sigma}^2}{2T} \left(1 + \frac{\tilde{\sigma}^2}{2} \right) \right], \tag{42}
$$

and Monte Carlo simulations suggested that this yielded a better-behaved statistic than that based on $\gamma_{\tilde{a}}$ (for $\sigma \leq 0.05$ and $T \leq 100$).

We will not derive encompassing test statistics for M_2 versus M_1 since the fact that M_2 can generate values of Y_t which do not belong to the support of M_1 raises obvious conceptual problems and may require truncation of the support of M_2 (see the discussion in Cox 1962, secs. 6 and 9).

12.5   A Monte Carlo Approach to Encompassing Analysis

The motivation for discussing a general Monte Carlo procedure for evaluatting encompassing test statistics is threefold:

1. We wish to emphasize that the range of applicability of the notion of encompassing is broad since all that is required is the capacity for drawing random samples from M_1—notwithstanding the treatment to be given to exogenous variables, an issue we discuss in section 12.9.

2. The discussion indicates when analytical results can contribute substantially to reducing the burden of computation and, thereby, provides guidance in the analysis of specific classes of models. Some of the notions

introduced in section 12.9 in the context of linear dynamic models are directly motivated by this consideration;

3. As discussed in the second example of section 12.4, WET statistics based on the asymptotic distribution of $\sqrt{T}\tilde{\phi}$ may occasionally perform poorly in small samples, in which case the (numerical) evaluation of its finite sampling distribution may prove crucial.

Precisely because of items (1) and (2), definition 2 may be inapplicable even though the DGP is known to the investigator. Intermediate cases will exist in which encompassing statistics can be evaluated numerically for the population, even though explicit analytical solutions cannot be obtained. Here, however, we focus on the use of Monte Carlo methods to obtain the (approximate) empirical distribution of $\tilde{\phi}$.

Conditionally on an arbitrary value of α—typically set at an estimated value $\tilde{\alpha}$ as in (5)—the generation of $\tilde{\phi}_i$, the ith random drawing $(i = 1, \ldots, N)$ of $\tilde{\phi}$, requires the following steps:

Step 1. Conditional on α, a random sample Y_i is drawn from M_1 and the corresponding estimates $\tilde{\alpha}_i$ and $\tilde{\delta}_i$ are evaluated.

Step 2. The evaluation of $\delta(\tilde{\alpha}_i)$ then requires an inner loop of auxiliary drawings whereby P random samples $Y_{i(j)}$ for $j = 1, \ldots, P$ are drawn from M_1 where α is now set at $\tilde{\alpha}_i$, and the corresponding estimates $\delta_{i(j)}$ are computed. An approximation of $\delta(\tilde{\alpha}_i)$ is then given by

$$\overline{\delta}(\tilde{\alpha}_i) \cong \frac{1}{P} \sum_{j=1}^{P} \tilde{\delta}_{i(j)}. \tag{43}$$

Step 3. The ith random drawing of $\tilde{\phi}$ is then

$$\tilde{\phi}_i = \tilde{\delta}_i - \overline{\delta}(\tilde{\alpha}_i). \tag{44}$$

Numerical confidence intervals may then be constructed from the empirical distribution of $\tilde{\phi}$ and the test requires examining whether or not the actual value of $\tilde{\phi}$ falls within such an interval. The burden of computation lies in step 2 which requires NP auxiliary random drawings and can be largely reduced if an (asymptotic) analytical expression is available for $\delta(\alpha)$. Such an expression could be used directly in which case step 2 is deleted from the algorithm. Alternatively if, as in the second example of section 12.4, the quality of an asymptotic expression is under scrutiny, an asymptotic approximation for $\delta(\tilde{\alpha}_i)$ can be used as a control variate for $\overline{\delta}(\tilde{\alpha}_i)$ in (43).

Econometrics

The use of such control variates, combined with other variance reduction techniques such as antithetic variables, might contribute to substantially reducing the burden of computation in step 2.

It would equally be useful if "response surfaces" could be evaluated for $\delta(\alpha)$. We doubt, however, that this procedure will prove very practical since $\delta(\alpha)$ is typically a complicated and highly nonlinear function of α, as the simplest dynamic or nonlinear examples quickly reveal. Thus the effort needed to establish good approximations to $\delta(\alpha)$ is likely to be disproportionally high relative to the benefits and would be better devoted to determining $\delta(\alpha)$ analytically for the relevant model class.

12.6 Parsimonious Encompassing

It follows from our discussion in section 12.2 that if M_2 is nested within M_1, then M_1 automatically encompasses M_2 at least in the population sense of definition 2 since sampling fluctuations could still occasionally result in M_1 failing to parametrically encompass M_2. It follows that, conceptually at least, M_1 could always be made to encompass rival models by extending it into a more general nesting model. However, this possibility is of little interest in worlds where limited sample evidence enforces parsimony in model specification.

More relevant to the point is the issue of whether or not a "simple" model M_1 encompasses a "larger" model M_2 within which it is nested. If such were the case, then M_1 would meet our requirement for parsimony relative to M_2 and still reproduce all the salient features of M_2. Hence the notion of parsimonious encompassing which we define as follows:

DEFINITION 3 M_1 *parsimoniously encompasses* M_2 *if and only if*

i. M_1 *encompasses* M_2,

ii. M_1 *is nested within* M_2.

The notation $M_1 \mathscr{E}_p M_2$ will be used in such cases. We need not be more specific at this stage of the discussion about the precise technical meaning of nesting. A definition that proves operational in the context of encompassing is proposed in section 12.8 where we discuss an asymptotic analysis based on the algebra of information matrices.

Beyond the fact that parsimony is indispensable in worlds of limited sample evidence, two additional reasons for emphasizing parsimonious encompassing will emerge from the discussion in the rest of the chapter. First, the algebra of the encompassing test statistics—and, in particular the derivation of the pseudotrue values—can be substantially simple when M_1 is nested within M_2. More fundamentally we will establish conditions under which $M_1 \mathscr{E} M_2$ if *and only if* $M_1 \mathscr{E}_p M$, where M_c is a "minimal" model nesting both M_1 and M_2. The heuristic interpretation of this result is that M_2 and M_c can only be equally "specific" against M_1. The first example of section 12.4 illustrated the argument, and other examples are provided below.

12.7 The Choice of Regressors Problem

The choice of regressors problem has received much attention in the econometric literature (see, e.g., Pesaran 1984). It offers the advantage that analytical results can be obtained for the case where the regressors are "fixed." It usually takes the form

$$M_1 : y = X\beta + u, \qquad u \sim N(0, \sigma^2 I_T), \qquad \alpha = (\beta, \sigma^2), \tag{45}$$

$$M_2 : y = Z\gamma + v, \qquad v \sim N(0, \tau^2 I_T), \qquad \delta = (\gamma, \tau^2), \tag{46}$$

where X and Z are $T \times k$ and $T \times l$ matrices of regressors. Our analysis in this section is *conditional* on X and Z, which are therefore assumed to be *strongly* exogenous in the terminology of Engle et al. (1983). We postpone a discussion of the exogeneity issue until section 12.9 in order to clarify other ideas first, but the importance of assuming no feedback from y_t onto later x_t or z_t must be obvious.

For the ease of presentation we shall also assume that the matrix $W = (X \quad Z)$ has full column rank, that is, that M_1 and M_2 contain no common regressors. As shown in Mizon and Richard (1986) and discussed in Florens et al. (1987b), the extension to the case where X and Z contain common regressors is straightforward and does not affect the validity of the results we discuss here, merely complicating the algebra.

M_1 and M_2 are *implicitly* nested within the model M_c defined as

$$M_c : y = Wa + e, \qquad e \sim N(0, v^2 I_T), \qquad d = (a, v^2), \tag{47}$$

where a is partitioned conformably with W into $a = (b, c)$. The ML estimators $\tilde{\alpha}$ and the pseudo ML estimators $\tilde{\delta}$ and $\tilde{d}$ are given by

$$\tilde{\beta} = (X'X)^{-1}X'y, \qquad T\tilde{\sigma}^2 = y'M_X y, \qquad M_X = I - X(X'X)^{-1}X', \qquad (48)$$

$$\tilde{\gamma} = (Z'Z)^{-1}Z'y, \qquad T\tilde{\tau}^2 = y'M_Z y, \qquad M_Z = I - Z(Z'Z)^{-1}Z', \qquad (49)$$

$$\tilde{a} = (W'W)^{-1}W'y, \qquad T\tilde{v}^2 = y'M_W y, \qquad M_W = I - W(W'W)^{-1}W'. \quad (50)$$

Encompassing of M_2

The so-called nonnested case is discussed in Mizon and Richard (1986), to which the reader is referred for details. The (finite sample) pseudotrue values of $\tilde{\delta} = (\tilde{\gamma}, \tilde{\tau}^2)$ on M_1 are

$$\gamma_\alpha = (Z'Z)^{-1}Z'X\beta, \qquad T\tau_\alpha^2 = (T - l)\sigma^2 + \beta'X'M_Z X\beta. \qquad (51)$$

The asymptotic covariance matrix of the encompassing difference $\tilde{\phi} = \sqrt{T}(\tilde{\delta} - \delta_{\tilde{a}})$ can be written as

$$V_\alpha(\tilde{\phi}_1) = T\sigma^2 \cdot A(Z'Z)^{-1}Z'M_X Z(Z'Z)^{-1}A', \qquad (52)$$

where

$$A' = (I_l : -\frac{2}{T}Z'X\beta). \qquad (53)$$

Hence the following asymptotic equivalence holds on M_1 (*as* denotes "almost surely"):

$$\sqrt{T}(\tilde{\tau}^2 - \tau_{\tilde{a}}^2) \overset{as}{\underset{M_1}{\sim}} -2\beta'\left(\frac{X'Z}{T}\right)\sqrt{T}(\tilde{\gamma} - \gamma_{\tilde{a}}). \qquad (54)$$

The following WET statistics are of interest for our purposes:

1. $\eta_W(\tilde{\delta})$, the "complete" WET statistic as defined in (5) is asymptotically distributed as $\chi^2(l)$ on M_1;

2. $\eta_W(\tilde{\gamma})$, the WET statistic relative to $\tilde{\gamma}$, is given by

$$\eta_W(\tilde{\gamma}) = \tilde{\sigma}^{-2} \cdot y'M_X Z(Z'M_X Z)^{-1}Z'M_X y \overset{as}{\underset{M_1}{\sim}} \chi^2(l); \qquad (55)$$

3. $\eta_W(\tilde{\tau}^2)$, the WET statistic relative to $\tilde{\tau}^2$, is asymptotically distributed as $\chi^2(1)$ on M_1.

Also let F_c^2 denote the "conventional" F-test statistic associated with the null hypothesis $c = 0$ on M_c. Following (55), F_c^2 is related to $\eta_W(\tilde{\gamma})$ by the identity

$$lF_c^2 \equiv \frac{T-k-l}{T}\eta_W(\tilde{\delta})\left[1 - \frac{1}{T}\eta_W(\tilde{\delta})\right]^{-1}. \tag{56}$$

The main findings in Mizon and Richard (1986) can be summarised as follows:

1. The complete WET statistic $\eta_W(\tilde{\delta})$ is asymptotically equivalent on M_1 to the WET statistic $\eta_W(\tilde{\gamma})$ relative to the regression coefficient $\tilde{\gamma}$. So l, the number of regressors *specific* to M_2, corresponds to the maximum number of degrees of freedom for tests of whether $M_1 \mathcal{E} M_2$—and also M_c, as we discuss below.

2. The WET statistic $\eta_W(\tilde{\gamma})$ is equivalent to the conventional F-test statistic F_c^2 in the sense that the identity (56) can be used to derive the *exact* sampling distribution of $\eta_W(\tilde{\delta})$. The large sample equivalence reads as $lF_c^2 \underset{M_1}{\overset{as}{\sim}} \eta_W(\tilde{\delta})$.

3. A vast range of one degree of freedom nonnested test statistics of M_1 versus M_2 are asymptotically equivalent on M_1 to the WET statistic $\eta_W(\tilde{\tau}^2)$. Among these are the Cox (1961) generalized likelihood ratio test statistic, the J-test statistic in Davidson and MacKinnon (1981), the T_x-statistic in Godfrey (1983), and the one-degree-of-freedom test statistic in Pesaran (1974).

Parsimonious Encompassing of M_c

The notion of parsimonious encompassing outlined in section 12.6 and its application to the choice of regressors problem are discussed more fully in Florens et al. (1987a). Their main findings are briefly summarized here. We note first that the pseudotrue value associated with $\tilde{d}$ takes the simple form

$$d_\alpha' = (b_\alpha' : c_\alpha' : v_\alpha^2) = (\beta' : 0' : \sigma^2). \tag{57}$$

Hence the encompassing difference relative to $\tilde{a}$ is given by

$$\sqrt{T}\tilde{\phi}_2 = \sqrt{T}\begin{pmatrix} \tilde{b} - \tilde{\beta} \\ \tilde{c} \end{pmatrix}$$

$$= \begin{pmatrix} -(X'X)^{-1}X'Z \\ I_l \end{pmatrix}(Z'M_XZ)^{-1}Z'Z \cdot \sqrt{T}(\tilde{\gamma} - \gamma_{\tilde{a}}). \tag{58}$$

The asymptotic normal distribution of the encompassing difference $\sqrt{T}(\tilde{v}^2 - \tilde{\sigma}^2)$ is degenerate as a result of the fact that the asymptotic covariance matrix of $\sqrt{T}\tilde{v}^2$ and $\sqrt{T}\tilde{\sigma}^2$ is given by $2\sigma^4 ii'$, where $i' = (1 \quad 1)$

and hence is singular in the direction $(1 \quad -1)$. In fact it can be shown that

$$T(\tilde{v}^2 - \tilde{\sigma}^2) \underset{M_1}{\overset{as}{\sim}} \tilde{c}'Z'M_X Z\tilde{c}. \tag{59}$$

Here again no encompassing test statistic of M_1 versus either M_2 or M_c has more degrees of freedom than there are regressors specific to M_2. Hence we now restrict out attention to the WET statistics associated with the regression coefficients $\tilde{a}$.

Following, for example, Florens et al. (1987a; see also Mizon 1984, in particular for his discussion of Hausman 1978 tests), we can distinguish three basic types of WET statistics of M_1 relative to M_c, using a superscript "$+$" to distinguish them from the WET statistics relative to M_2:

1. the *complete* WET statistic $\eta_W^+(\tilde{a})$,

2. the *simplification* WET statistic $\eta_W^+(\tilde{c})$,

3. the *Hausman* WET statistic $\eta_W^+(\tilde{b})$.

The following equivalences hold on M_1:

1. The simplification WET statistic is equivalent to the WET statistic relative to $\tilde{\gamma}$, both being asymptotically equivalent to the complete WET statistic relative to M_2 and M_c:

$$\eta_W^+(\tilde{a}) \underset{M_1}{\overset{as}{\sim}} \eta_W^+(\tilde{c}) \equiv \eta_W(\tilde{\gamma}) \underset{M_1}{\overset{as}{\sim}} \eta_W(\tilde{\delta}). \tag{60}$$

2. The Hausman WET statistic is asymptotically equivalent to the conventional Hausman (1978) specification test for the hypothesis $c = 0$ on the maintained hypothesis M_c. Following (58), it is also asymptotically equivalent to the WET statistic relative to $(X'X)^{-1}X'Z\tilde{c}$. Hence, as shown by Holly (1982), the use of the Hausman specification test entails a loss of degrees of freedom relative to the complete test when $k < l$, the two being equivalent when $k \geq l$ and rank $X'Z = l$.

Additional Comments

The class of WET statistics we have discussed unifies a vast collection of test statistics that have been introduced in the literature on testing nested and nonnested hypotheses. The two approaches are fully reconciled and, as we have shown, are implicitly equivalent at least in the context of the choice of regressors problem. A generalisation of this equivalence is discussed in section 12.8.

It seems to us that the choice between the various encompassing test statistics should primarily be a matter of deciding which are the salient features of M_2 or M_c that M_1 ought to encompass. We have demonstrated that all the information relevant for a *specification* encompassing analysis is contained in the WET statistic relative to the vector of regression coefficients associated with the regressors which are *specific* to M_2 and, hence, to M_c. In contrast, neither the variance encompassing test statistics nor (when $k \geq l$) the Hausman WET statistic exploit all the relevant information, leading to the usual power trade-off from degrees of freedom versus noncentrality. Note that the simplification WET statistic relative to the *entire* vector $\tilde{c}$ (or $\tilde{\gamma}$) is invariant to the addition or deletion of common regressors in M_1 and M_2, whereas the variance and Hausman WET statistics are clearly not. Hence the F_c^2-test seems to be the maximal invariant test and focuses explicitly on the *specific* features of M_2 under M_1. As is well known, the Hausman WET statistic is sensitive to the orthogonality between X and Z and breaks down when $\lim \frac{1}{T} X'Z = 0$. Also considerations of numerical tractability might affect our choice when dealing with larger and possibly nonlinear models. It might well be that complete parametric encompassing would require a prohibitive amount of computation, but simpler forms of one degree of freedom (variance) encompassing tests could still be evaluated at a reasonable cost.

One might obviously wish to investigate the properties of the various WET statistics when M_1 is false, although doing so on the basis of a sequence of local alternatives, as is often done in the literature on nonnested hypotheses testing, is hardly relevant to the domain of application of the encompassing principle. Results can be established under the assumption that M_c is the DGP. The variance WET statistics are then distributed as noncentral χ^2 with noncentrality parameters which are all functions of the encompassing difference $\sqrt{T}(\tilde{\gamma} - \gamma_{\tilde{a}})$ so that if $\gamma \neq \gamma_\alpha$, M_1 does not encompass M_2. Since, however, the degrees of freedom *and* the noncentrality parameters differ between statistics, the power functions are not rankable. Little can be said about the properties of the various WET statistics when the DGP differs from M_c.

We note that, as in section 12.4, the pseudo ML estimators of the variances τ^2 and v^2 are biased estimators of the corresponding pseudotrue values; hence we may wish to replace the variance estimators in formulae

(48) through (50) by the corresponding unbiased OLS estimators. It then follows from (51) that $\tau_a^2 > \sigma^2$ (a derivation of this inequality in the "population" sense is given below) so that, as discussed in Hendry and Richard (1982) within the choice of regressors problem, *variance dominance* is a necessary condition for encompassing.

The use of the conventional F-test statistic F_c^2 has often been criticized in the literature on nonnested hypotheses testing on the grounds that the nesting model M_c is "artificial." Our analysis invalidates this claim since it demonstrates that M_c is "implicit" in the encompassing comparison between M_1 and M_2 in that $M_1 \mathscr{E} M_2$ if and only if $M_1 \mathscr{E}_p M_c$, and hence that F_c^2 is the only statistic invariant to altering components of M_2 common with M_1.

The above analysis is based upon a set of fairly restrictive assumptions, including linearity, normality, fixed regressors, and strong exogeneity. Our current research aims at relating these assumptions and a number of results are noted below. The main areas of investigation are

1. linear dynamic models,

2. weakly exogenous regressors,

3. endogenous regressors (instrumental variables techniques),

4. nonlinear models.

Before discussing some of these issues we conclude the present section by reinterpreting the algebra of the pseudotrue values associated with the choice of regressors problem within the context of a joint stationary process, thereby setting the scene for our analysis of linear dynamic models in section 12.9.

A Joint Stationary Framework

The assumption that the regressors X and Z are fixed can be relaxed and, in fact, full analytical tractability is preserved if (45) and (46) are embedded in a joint stationary process whereby x_t, y_t, and z_t are assumed to be independent random drawings from the *joint* model M_c, which for ease of presentation is conflated with the DGP $\mathscr{H}$:[1]

$$\overline{M_c} : \begin{pmatrix} y_t \\ x_t \\ z_t \end{pmatrix} \sim N \left(\begin{pmatrix} 0 \\ 0 \\ 0 \end{pmatrix}, \begin{pmatrix} \sigma_{yy} & \sigma_{yx} & \sigma_{yz} \\ \sigma_{xy} & \Sigma_{xx} & \Sigma_{xz} \\ \sigma_{zy} & \Sigma_{zx} & \Sigma_{zz} \end{pmatrix} \right) . \tag{61}$$

Let θ denote the column expansion of the lower triangular part of the covariance matrix Σ in (61) which is left unrestricted except for the usual symmetry and positivity constraints.

Two points are worth making at this stage of the discussion:

1. The general formulation of $\overline{M}_c$ *preserves* the weak exogeneity of x_t for α in (45) and of z_t for δ in (46) since, as discussed in Richard (1980) and in Engle et al. (1983), weak exogeneity within the unrestricted multivariate normal process is paramount to declaring which parameters are of interest.

2. However, as soon as the pseudotrue values of $\tilde{\delta}$ in M_2 and $\tilde{d}$ in M_c have to be marginalized with respect to x_t and z_t, they no longer depend solely on the parameter α in M_1. Hence M_1 has to be "enlarged" into a model $\overline{M}_1$ that includes a model of the exogenous process but preserves the restrictions that characterize M_1 itself. In the case under consideration, $\overline{M}_1$ is nested within $\overline{M}_c$ by the restriction that y_t and z_t are independent, *conditionally* on x_t, that is,

$$\overline{M}_1 : \sigma_{zy} = \Sigma_{zx}\Sigma_{xx}^{-1}\sigma_{xy}. \tag{62}$$

The implications of this enlargement of M_1 into $\overline{M}_1$ are discussed in a broader context in section 12.9.

We can now obtain all the pseudotrue values which are relevant to the encompassing framework illustrated in figure 12.1:

$$\beta_\theta = \Sigma_{xx}^{-1}\sigma_{xy}, \qquad \sigma_\theta^2 = \sigma_{yy} - \sigma_{yx}\beta_\theta, \tag{63}$$

$$\gamma_\theta = \Sigma_{zz}^{-1}\sigma_{zy}, \qquad \tau_\theta^2 = \sigma_{yy} - \sigma_{yz}\gamma_\theta, \tag{64}$$

$$\begin{pmatrix} b_\theta \\ c_\theta \end{pmatrix} = \begin{pmatrix} \Sigma_{xx} & \Sigma_{xz} \\ \Sigma_{zx} & \Sigma_{zz} \end{pmatrix}^{-1} \begin{pmatrix} \sigma_{xy} \\ \sigma_{zy} \end{pmatrix}, \qquad v_\theta^2 = \sigma_{yy} - \sigma_{yx}b_\theta - \sigma_{yz}c_\theta, \tag{65}$$

whereas, under $\overline{M}_1$, as defined by the restriction (62), we have

$$\gamma_\alpha = \Pi\beta, \qquad \tau_\alpha^2 = \sigma^2 + \beta'\Omega\beta, \tag{66}$$

where $\Pi = \Sigma_{zz}^{-1}\Sigma_{zx}$ and $\Omega = \Sigma_{xx} - \Sigma_{xz}\Pi$. Also

$$b_\alpha = \beta, \qquad c_\alpha = 0, \qquad v_\alpha^2 = \sigma^2. \tag{67}$$

Hence the (population) encompassing differences of interest to us are

$$\gamma_\theta - \gamma_{\alpha\theta} = \Sigma_{zz}^{-1} \sigma_{zy|x}, \tag{68}$$

$$\tau_\theta^2 - \tau_{\alpha_\theta}^2 = (\sigma_{yz} - \sigma_{yz|x})\Sigma_{zz}^{-1}(\sigma_{zy} - \sigma_{zy|x}) - \sigma_{yz}\Sigma_{zz}^{-1}\sigma_{zy}, \tag{69}$$

$$b_\theta - b_{\alpha_\theta} = -\Sigma_{xx}^{-1}\Sigma_{xz}\Sigma_{zz|x}^{-1}\sigma_{zy|x}, \tag{70}$$

$$c_\theta = \Sigma_{zz|x}^{-1}\sigma_{zy|x}, \tag{71}$$

$$v_\theta^2 - v_{\alpha_\theta}^2 = \sigma_{yz|x}\Sigma_{zz|x}^{-1}\sigma_{zy|x}, \tag{72}$$

where $\sigma_{zy|x} = \sigma_{zy} - \Sigma_{zx}\Sigma_{xx}^{-1}\sigma_{xy}$.

Formulae (68) through (72) bear a direct resemblance to those obtained by Mizon and Richard (1986) in their discussion of the implicit null hypothesis associated with a variety of nonnested hypotheses test statistics. They contribute to explaining both the relationship between the various WET statistics we have obtained earlier in this section and, in particular, the fact that these statistics are all functions of the difference $\tilde{\gamma} - \gamma_{\tilde{\alpha}}$. The ML estimators of the parameters $(\beta, \sigma^2, \Sigma_{xx}, \Sigma_{xz}, \Sigma_{zz})$ in $\overline{M}_1$ are given by the OLS estimators $(\tilde{\beta}, \tilde{\sigma}^2)$ in (48) together with the sample moment matrices $\dfrac{1}{T}X'X, \dfrac{1}{T}X'Z$ and $\dfrac{1}{T}Z'Z$. Hence the WET statistics associated with the *joint* model $\overline{M}_1$ coincide with those we obtained for the *conditional* model M_1, where X and Z are held fixed. We will discuss below whether this equivalence extends to the linear *dynamic* choice of regressors problem.

We note in passing that formula (66) has been derived in Hendry and Richard (1982) under a "projection" approach, whereby the model M_1 is completed by the "auxiliary data description" relating together the two sets regressors

$$x_t|z_t \sim N(\Pi z_t, \Omega) \tag{73}$$

and the z's are kept fixed. As indicated by (66), this is all that is required to find the pseudotrue values γ_α and τ_α^2, and furthermore, in the case under consideration, the corresponding WET statistics are the same whether or not they are derived conditionally on the z's.

In conclusion of this section we briefly indicate how the joint approach enables us to formalize the notion of misspecification encompassing that was evoked in section 12.3. Let us, for example, assume that a covariance analysis suggests that the covariance matrix Σ_{xz} has changed at some point of time during the sample period. The proprietor of M_1 being satisifed with the claim that β is invariant with respect to this change would then infer that γ_α—which reflects his interpretation of γ—should vary along with Σ_{xz}, even though the proprietor of M_2 may not have thought of that possibility. This would provide M_1, with the basis of an encompassing test for a change in $\tilde{\gamma}$ where the sample subdivision would be chosen according to the change in the exogenous process reflected by Σ_{xz}.

12.8   An Information Matrix Generalization

The question of how general is the equivalence between the notion of encompassing a rival model and that of encompassing an implicit nesting model has been addressed in a recent paper by Florens et al. (1987a) within the context of a *joint* model of all the variables in M_1 and M_2 (possibly defined initially as conditional submodels and extended into joint models for the purpose of the analysis as in section 12.7).

Let Y denote a (sample) matrix of random variables. The models M_1 and M_2 are assumed to be represented by their respective data densities $f(Y|\beta)$ and $g(Y|\gamma)$.[2] Let M_c denote a "minimal" implicit nesting model characterized by the data density $h(Y|a)$. In the course of the discussion we will be more specific about the relationship between M_c and (M_1, M_2). As in section 12.7 it proves convenient to conflate M_c with the DGP $\mathcal{H}$ since allowing for a broader class of DGP does not affect the derivation of the parametric encompassing test statistics. Estimators are denoted by a tilde ("$\sim$") and, as in section 12.2, estimators are assumed to be consistent within their respective models, that is,

$$\text{plim}_{M_1}\, \tilde{\beta} = \beta, \quad \text{plim}_{M_2}\, \tilde{\gamma} = \gamma, \quad \text{and} \quad \text{plim}_{M_c}\, \tilde{a} = a. \tag{74}$$

The basic assumptions that condition our analysis can be qualified as follows:

ASSUMPTION 1 M_c is a minimal nesting model in the sense that a can be partitioned in $a = (b, c)$ in such a way that

i. M_1 is associated with the restriction $b = 0$,

ii. $M_1^\perp$ is defined as the model associated with the restriction $c = 0$, then

$$M_1^\perp \subset M_2 \subset M_c, \tag{75}$$

where $\subset$ reads as "is nested within."

To ease notation, we restrict attention to the case where $M_2 = M_1^\perp$, but if $(M_1 \mathcal{E}_p M_c \Leftrightarrow M_1 \mathcal{E} M_1^\perp)$, then $(M_1 \mathcal{E}_p M_c \Leftrightarrow M_1 \mathcal{E} M_2)$. A proof goes as follows:

Proof (i) If $M_1 \mathcal{E}_p M_c$, then $M_1 \mathcal{E} M_2$ since $M_2 \subset M_c$. (ii) If $M_1 \mathcal{E} M_2$, then $M_1 \mathcal{E} M_1^\perp$ since $M_1^\perp \subset M_2$, and hence $M_1 \mathcal{E}_p M_c$. ∎

ASSUMPTION 2   On M_c, $\tilde{a}$ is asymptotically equivalent to the ML estimator of a and, under the usual regularity assumptions, its asymptotic distribution is

$$\sqrt{T}(\tilde{a} - a) \xrightarrow[M_1]{\mathscr{L}} N(0, I_{aa}^{-1}), \tag{76}$$

where I_{aa} is the information matrix. Also on M_1, $\tilde{\beta}$ is asymptotically equivalent to the constrained ML estimator of a subject to the restriction $c = 0$ so that

$$\sqrt{T}\tilde{\beta} \underset{M_1}{\overset{as}{\sim}} \sqrt{T}(\tilde{b} + I_{\beta\beta}^{-1} I_{\beta 0} \tilde{c}), \tag{77}$$

where I_{aa} has been partitioned conformably with $a = (b, c)$ and

$$I_{aa}|_{a=(\beta:0)} = \begin{pmatrix} I_{\beta\beta} & I_{\beta 0} \\ I_{0\beta} & I_{00} \end{pmatrix}. \tag{78}$$

Under assumption 2, the asymptotic distribution of the encompassing difference $\sqrt{T}(\tilde{a} - a_{\tilde{\beta}})$ on M_1 is

$$\sqrt{T}\begin{pmatrix} \tilde{b} - \tilde{\beta} \\ \tilde{c} \end{pmatrix} \xrightarrow[M_1]{\mathscr{L}} N\left(\begin{pmatrix} 0 \\ 0 \end{pmatrix}, \begin{pmatrix} I_{\beta\beta} & I_{\beta 0} \\ I_{0\beta} & I_{00} \end{pmatrix}^{-1} - \begin{pmatrix} I_{\beta\beta}^{-1} & 0 \\ 0 & 0 \end{pmatrix} \right). \tag{79}$$

Hence as in section 12.7 we find that on M_1

1. the complete WET statistic $\eta_W^+(\tilde{a})$ is asymptotically equivalent to the simplification WET statistic $\eta_W^+(\tilde{c})$,

2. the Hausman WET statistic $\eta_W^+(\tilde{b})$ is asymptotically equivalent to the WET statistic relative to $I_{\beta\beta}^{-1} I_{\beta 0} \tilde{c}$.

Our third assumption aims at clarifying the relationship between $\tilde{\gamma}$ and $\tilde{a}$ *under M_c* and, hence, as a special case under M_1, exploiting the fact that M_2 is nested within M_c. Though a clarification of this issue remains on our research agenda, none of the definitions of nested hypotheses that we have found in the literature (see, e.g., the discussion in Pesaran 1987) seems to fit our purpose exactly. Hence we opt for formulating assumption 3 directly in terms of the relationship between $\tilde{\gamma}$ and $\tilde{a}$. A "strong" version of assumption 3 reads as follows:

ASSUMPTION 3A   The estimator $\tilde{\gamma}$ is an *exact* function of the unconstrained estimator $\tilde{a}$, say:

$$\tilde{\gamma} = \lambda(\tilde{a}), \tag{80}$$

where λ is differentiable and $\partial\lambda/\partial\theta'$ evaluated at $\theta = (\beta:0)$ has full (row) rank.

It is difficult to assess exactly how restrictive assumption 3a is. It will be satisfied whenever $\tilde{\theta}$ is a sufficient statistic within M_c as would be the case within the exponential family of distributions. Under assumptions 1 to 3a it can be shown that the simplication WET statistic $\eta_W^+(\tilde{c})$ is equivalent to the WET statistic $\eta_W(\tilde{\gamma})$ so that all the results that have been obtained for the (static) choice of regressors problem apply in this broader context. See Florens et al. (1987a) for details and proof.

Our discussion in section 12.9 indicates, however, that assumption 3a cannot always be satisfied in the context of linear dynamic models, but a weaker (asymptotic) version of it can always be met.

ASSUMPTION 3B   Under M_c,

$$\text{plim}_{M_c} \tilde{\gamma} = \lambda(a) \tag{81}$$

where λ satisfies the same differentiability and rank conditions as in assumption 3a.

Under this weaker assumption the simplicity of the algebra of pseudotrue values is fully preserved and we have, in particular,

$$\gamma_\beta = \lambda(\beta, 0), \quad \gamma_a = \lambda(a), \quad \text{and} \quad a_\beta = (\beta:0), \tag{82}$$

so that, following definition 2, the equivalence between the *population* concepts of encompassing (M_2) and parsimonious encompassing (M_c) is preserved. Note, however, that under assumption 3b the WET statistics $\eta_W^+(\tilde{c})$ and $\eta_W(\tilde{\gamma})$ are *no longer* equivalent under M_1 since the difference $\tilde{\gamma} - \lambda(\tilde{a})$ may include factors of order $0(T^{-1/2})$ that cannot be neglected in the evaluation of the asymptotic covariance matrix of the encompassing difference $\sqrt{T}(\tilde{\gamma} - \gamma_{\tilde{\beta}})$.

The distinction between assumptions 3a and 3b plays a crucial role in our analysis of the linear dynamic choice of regressors problem.

12.9   Encompassing in Linear Dynamic Stationary Models

In our discussion of the choice of regressors problem in section 12.7, the
regressors in M_1 were assumed to be *strongly* exogenous (in the terminology of Engle et al. 1983 and hence were held "fixed" throughout the
analysis. We now wish to consider cases where the regressors include lagged
y's and also variables that are only *weakly* exogenous, being Granger-
caused by y (see Granger 1969). As already evoked in section 12.7 the
latter extension requires the "completion" of M_1 by an auxiliary description of the exogenous process—at least within a sampling theory
framework—and thereby raises novel issues which we wish to discuss
first.

Our analysis of the linear dynamic model is largely based on the work
of Govaerts (1987a, b) and Govaerts et al. (1988a, b).

Weak Exogeneity and Completion of M_1

The issue of exogeneity naturally arises within the framework of encompassing when the model of interest M_1 takes the form of a (sequential)
conditional model associated with a "partial" likelihood function of the
form

$$M_1 = L_1(\alpha; Y_T^1, X_T^1) = \prod_{t=1}^{T} f(y_t | x_t, Y_{t-1}, X_{t-1}, \alpha), \qquad (83)$$

where x_t is a vector of current dated variables that are assumed to be *weakly*
exogenous for the parameter of interest α and (Y_{t-1}, X_{t-1}) regroups the past
observations on y and x up to period $t - 1$, including the initial conditions
that are assumed here to be known.

Following Engle et al. (1983) the assumption that x_t is weakly exogenous
for α ensures that "all the sample information concerning the parameters
of interest (α) can be obtained from the partial likelihood function L_1".
Within a Bayesian framework it entails that if α is a priori independent of
the parameters of the sequential process whereby the x's are generated (e.g.,
λ in formula 84), then the posterior density of α which, by definition is
conditional on Y_T^1 and X_T^1, is proportional to the product of the prior
density of α with the partial likelihood function L_1 as defined in (83) (see,
e.g., Florens and Mouchart 1985 for further discussion). This explains
why the Bayesian notion of encompassing we discuss in section 12.10
easily accommodates weakly exogenous variables. Within the context of

our sampling theory's notion of encompassing, however, the treatment of weakly exogenous variables raises two important issues.

First, the assumption that the x's are weakly exogenous does *not* imply that they can be treated as "fixed" regressors (unless it is assumed in addition that y does not Granger-cause x so that the x's are strongly exogenous, an assumption we do not wish to impose here). Hence, even though efficient estimators of α can be derived from the partial likelihood function L_1 alone—whose first-order partial derivatives can be construed as estimator generating equations (EGE), as in Hendry (1976)—their sampling distributions remain to be interpreted within the *joint* probability space of Y_T^1 and X_T^1. It follows that the statement that α and $\delta(\alpha)$ can be interpreted as plims on M_1 *only* does not make sense any more since X_T^1 cannot be held fixed.

More precisely, let M_e denote the (implicit) marginal sequential model associated with the partial likelihood function L_e defined as

$$M_e : L_e(\lambda; Y_T^1, X_T^1) = \prod_{t=1}^{T} f_e(x_t | Y_{t-1}, X_{t-1}, \lambda), \tag{84}$$

and let $\overline{M}_1$ denote the joint (or completed) model consisting of M_1 together with M_e. Under the weak exogeneity assumption of x for α *and* under (implicit) suitable regularity conditions,[3] the ML estimators $\tilde{\alpha}$ and $\tilde{\lambda}$ (or asymptotically equivalent versions thereof) will typically be asymptotically *independently* normally distributed *under* $\overline{M}_1$, say,

$$\sqrt{T}\begin{pmatrix} \tilde{\alpha} - \alpha \\ \tilde{\lambda} - \lambda \end{pmatrix} \xrightarrow[\overline{M}_1]{\mathscr{L}} N\left(0, \begin{pmatrix} I_{\alpha\alpha}^{-1} & 0 \\ 0 & I_{\lambda\lambda}^{-1} \end{pmatrix}\right), \tag{85}$$

where, in particular,

$$I_{\alpha\alpha} = -E_{\overline{M}_1}\left[\frac{1}{T}\frac{\partial^2 L_1}{\partial\alpha\partial\alpha'}\right]. \tag{86}$$

It will often be the case that the evaluation of $I_{\alpha\alpha}$ does not require a detailed specification of M_e, even though the expectation in (86) is taken under $\overline{M}_1$. This is the context under which we will operate below.

A second difficulty arises within the encompassing framework, where we are now discussing the properties of a statistic $\tilde{\delta}$ which is associate with a rival model M_2, say,

$$M_2 : L_2(\delta; Y_T^1, X_T^1) = \prod_{t=1}^{T} g(y_t | x_t, Y_{t-1}, X_{t-1}, \delta). \tag{87}$$

It proves convenient for the purpose of the present discussion to assume that the variables y and x are given the same status within M_1 and M_2. It should, nevertheless, be obvious that evaluating the properties of $\tilde{\delta}$ on M_1 alone requires that the variables in $\tilde{\delta}$ be given an unambiguous status under M_1 but that this status need not coincide with the one given under M_2. Hence the models under consideration may differ also in their partitioning between endogenous and exogenous variables. Further discussion of this issue goes beyond the objective of the present chapter but is on our research agenda.

The key issue at this stage of our discussion lies in the fact that as soon as y Granger-causes x, the pseudotrue value of $\tilde{\delta}$ has to be evaluated under the completed model $\overline{M}_1$ and generally depends on both α and λ, say,

$$\delta(\alpha, \lambda) = \text{plim}_{\overline{M}_1} \tilde{\delta}, \tag{88}$$

even though x is weakly exogenous for α. Hence the evaluation of WET statistics relative to M_2 requires the completion of the conditional model of interest M_1 into a joint model $\overline{M}_1$ by means of a (nuisance) marginal completing model M_e. Such marginal models are often inherently difficult to formulate and, hence, are likely to be misspecified so that the issue of the robustness of the encompassing analysis against the choice of M_e naturally arises. We wish, in particular, to protect ourselves against the possibility that $\overline{M}_1$ fails to encompass M_2 purely as the result of a misspecification of the completing model M_e.

In this chapter we will approach the issue of robustness in the following way. We (implicitly) consider a class $\mathcal{M}$ of potential *joint* models that could eventually be used as DGP's for a Monte Carlo investigation of the properties of various WET statistics. We next define a subclass $\mathcal{M}_1$ of $\mathcal{M}$ by the property that a joint model $\overline{M}_1$ belongs to $\mathcal{M}_1$ if and only if M_1 is a valid conditional submodel of $\overline{M}_1$ (i.e., if M_1 is "true" on $\overline{M}_1$). In practice, we will consider a class $\mathcal{M}_e$ of completing models that could be associated with M_1, in which case $\mathcal{M}_1$ is given by

$$\mathcal{M}_1 = \{M_1\} \times \mathcal{M}_e. \tag{89}$$

Hence the choice of a completing model M_e in $\mathcal{M}_e$ is equivalent to the choice of a joint model $\overline{M}_1 = (M_1, M_e)$ in $\mathcal{M}_1$.

Assume now we have chosen a specific completing model M_e^0 in $\mathcal{M}_e$ and have evaluated the corresponding encompassing difference, say,

$$\tilde{\phi}_0 = \tilde{\delta} - \delta_0(\tilde{\alpha}, \tilde{\lambda}). \tag{90}$$

By construction, $\tilde{\phi}_0$ has zero plim on $\overline{M}_1^0 = (M_1, M_e^0)$. The question then arises of whether or not it has also zero plim under *any* model in $\mathcal{M}_1$.

DEFINITION 4 $\tilde{\phi}_0$ is $\mathcal{M}_1$-consistent if and only if

$$\text{plim}_{\overline{M}_1} \tilde{\phi}_0 = 0, \qquad \forall \overline{M}_1 \in \mathcal{M}_1. \tag{91}$$

Clearly a completing model M_e^0 that ensures that the encompassing difference $\tilde{\phi}_0$ is $\mathcal{M}_1$-consistent for a "broad" class of completing models ensures robustness within that class against misspecification of M_e^0. We will demonstrate in section 12.9 that within the context of the linear dynamic choice of regressors problem, $\mathcal{M}_1$-consistency can *always* be achieved for a class of completing models consisting of VAR models for the x's.

There are other ways of approaching the issue of robustness, some of which may be more specific to the problem under consideration. One can, in particular, examine whether there exists a completing model M_e^0 such that the WET statistic associated with the corresponding encompassing difference $\tilde{\phi}_0$ coincides with the WET statistic derived under a set of stronger simplifying assumptions. In the context of the choice of regressors problems, we have shown in section 12.9 that if all the regressors in the completing models (83) and (87) are treated as "fixed" regressors, then the WET statistic for the regression coefficients in M_2 takes the form of the "conventional" F-test statistic. The question then arises of whether, in the more general dynamic case, there exists a completing model M_e^0 such that the WET statistic associated with $\tilde{\phi}_0$ coincides with that F-test statistic. If so, we will say that $\tilde{\phi}_0$ is *moment-efficient* (on $\mathcal{M}_1$). Moment efficiency entails robustness in the sense that it provides us with a set of sufficient conditions under which the F-test statistic, which was initially obtained under a set of "fixed" regressors assumptions, remains a valid WET statistic, even though these assumptions are relaxed. Moment-efficiency implies $\mathcal{M}_1$-consistency but, in contrast with the latter, cannot always be achieved. We will also introduce a weaker notion of asymptotic $\mathcal{M}_1$-efficiency that can always be obtained. It no longer guarantees the equivalence between the WET statistic and the F-test statistic, for reasons that are closely related to those we discussed in connection with formula (81) but still results in a considerable simplification of the algebra of the pseudotrue values.

The Dynamic Choice of Regressors Problem

The two competing linear dynamic regression models are[4]

$$M_1 : y_t = \beta_0' x_t + \sum_{i=1}^{p} \beta_i' w_{t-i} + u_t, \qquad u_t \sim IN(0, \sigma^2), \tag{92}$$

$$M_2 : y_t = \gamma_0' x_t + \sum_{i=1}^{p} \gamma_i' w_{t-i} + v_t, \qquad v_t \sim IN(0, \tau^2), \tag{93}$$

where $w_t = (y_t : x_t')$ and x_t is weakly exogenous for the parameters of M_1. The two models implicitly differ by the linear restrictions that are imposed on the β and the γ coefficients, but these need not be explicited for the object of our discussion. Let β and γ denote the unrestricted elements in $(\beta_0, \langle \beta_i \rangle)$ and $(\gamma_0, \langle \gamma_i \rangle)$, respectively. The parameters of the two competing models are $\alpha = (\beta, \sigma^2)$ and $\delta = (\gamma, \tau^2)$, respectively. Lag lengths are assumed to be finite and initial conditions to be known.

The class $\mathcal{M}_e$ of completing models used in the rest of this section consists of models of the form:

$$M_e : x_t = \sum_{i=1}^{p} \Phi_i w_{t-i} + \varepsilon_t, \qquad \varepsilon_t \sim IN(0, \Sigma_\varepsilon), \tag{94}$$

where the Φ_i's are assumed to be unrestricted except for entire columns of zero restrictions that enable us to exclude components of w_{t-i} from the list of regressors in M_e. It follows that the parameters $\lambda = (\langle \Phi_i \rangle, \Sigma_\varepsilon)$ of the completing model can be estimated by ordinary least squares. More general cases, where sets of regressors differ across equations in (94), raise no conceptual problems within our framework, which only requires the estimators $\tilde{\alpha}$ and $\tilde{\lambda}$ to be functions of the second-order moments of the w's but lead to substantial *analytical* complications. Let $\underline{\alpha} = (\alpha, \lambda)$ denote the parameters of the completed model $\overline{M}_1 = (M_1, M_e)$, which is a VAR model of the form

$$M_1 : w_t = \sum_{i=1}^{p} \Pi_i w_{t-i} + v_t, \qquad v_t \sim IN(0, \Omega_{11}), \tag{95}$$

whose parameters $(\langle \Pi_i \rangle, \Omega_{11})$ are functions of $\underline{\alpha}$.

The essence of the argument lies in the finding that the encompassing difference $\tilde{\delta} - \delta_{\tilde{\alpha}}$ is a function of the estimators of the second-order moments of the w's, hence its asymptotic distribution can be derived from that of these estimators, as given in Hannan (1970). We briefly outline the derivation of the appropriate Jacobian. Details are found in Govaerts (1987a).

The VAR model (94) is first rewritten in its companion form

$$f_t = D f_{t-1} + \eta_t, \qquad \eta_t \sim IN(0, \psi), \tag{96}$$

where $f_t' = (w_t' \ldots w_{t-p}')$ and

$$D = \begin{pmatrix} \Pi_1 \ldots \Pi_p & \vdots & 0 \\ \cdots\cdots\cdots\cdots & \vdots & \cdots \\ I & \vdots & 0 \end{pmatrix}. \tag{97}$$

Under the implicit assumption that the roots of D lie within the unit circle, namely, that the model (94) is stationary, the covariance matrix ψ is the solution of the identity

$$\psi = \Omega + D\psi D', \qquad \text{with} \quad \Omega = \begin{pmatrix} \Omega_{11} & \vdots & 0 \\ \cdots\cdots & \vdots & \cdots \\ 0 & \vdots & 0 \end{pmatrix} \tag{98}$$

and hence is itself a function of $\underline{\alpha}$. The notation $\psi_{\underline{\alpha}}$ or $\psi(\underline{\alpha})$ will be used whenever the dependence of ψ on $\underline{\alpha}$ is important for the flow of the argument.

The *unrestricted* moment estimator of ψ, say, $\tilde{\psi}$, is given by

$$\tilde{\psi} = \frac{1}{T} \sum_{t=1}^{T} f_t f_t'. \tag{99}$$

Hannan (1970) demonstrates that if the process (96) is stationary, then the column expansion of $\sqrt{T}(\tilde{\psi} - \psi_{\underline{\alpha}})$ is asymptotically normally distributed, say,

$$\sqrt{T} \, \text{Vec}(\tilde{\psi} - \psi_{\underline{\alpha}}) \xrightarrow[M_1]{\mathscr{L}} N(0, C). \tag{100}$$

The expression for C is given in Hannan (1970) and Govaerts (1987b) discusses efficient ways of evaluating it numerically using a Jordan form decomposition of D. The estimators $\tilde{\underline{\alpha}}$ and $\tilde{\delta}$ are functions of $\tilde{\psi}$, say,

$$\tilde{\underline{\alpha}} = a(\tilde{\psi}), \qquad \tilde{\delta} = d(\tilde{\psi}). \tag{101}$$

Hence the pseudotrue value $\delta_{\underline{\alpha}}$ is

$$\delta_{\underline{\alpha}} = d(\psi(\underline{\alpha})) \tag{102}$$

and the encompassing difference $\tilde\delta - \delta_{\tilde a}$ is itself a function of $\tilde\psi$:

$$\tilde\delta - \delta_{\tilde a} = d(\tilde\psi) - d(\psi(a(\tilde\psi))) \overset{\text{say}}{=} h(\tilde\psi). \tag{103}$$

Let H denote the matrix of partial derivatives of h with respect to Vec ψ evaluated at $\psi = \psi_\alpha$. It follows by application of Hannan's theorem that the encompassing difference $\sqrt{T}(\tilde\delta - \delta_{\tilde a})$ is asymptotically normally distributed as

$$\sqrt{T}(\tilde\delta - \delta_{\tilde a}) \underset{M_1}{\overset{\mathscr{L}}{\to}} N(0, HCH'). \tag{104}$$

Focusing now on the issue of robustness we discussed in section 12.9, we quickly discover that the entire issue essentially depends on whether or not the specification of $\overline{M}_1$ places restrictions on the estimator of the second-order moment matrices of the regressors in M_1 and M_2. More specifically, let X and Z denote the matrices of regressors in M_1 and M_2, respectively, all regressors being listed independently of their status as lagged endogenous or current and lagged exogenous variables. The unrestricted estimator of the second-order moment matrix of X and Z is

$$\tilde{Q} = \frac{1}{T}\begin{pmatrix} X'X & X'Z \\ Z'X & Z'Z \end{pmatrix} = S\tilde\psi S', \tag{105}$$

where S is an appropriate selection matrix. Hence the plim of $\tilde{Q}$ on $\overline{M}_1$ is

$$Q(\underline{\alpha}) = S\psi(\underline{\alpha})S' \tag{106}$$

and the restricted (ML) estimator of the second-order moment matrix of X and Z is

$$Q(\tilde a) = S\tilde\psi(\tilde a)S'. \tag{107}$$

The comparison between $\tilde{Q}$ and $Q(\tilde a)$ provides the key to our understanding how the presence of lagged endogenous and weakly exogenous variables in X and Z affects the results we derived for the static case in section 12.7. Heuristically, there should be no changes if the specification of $\overline{M}_1$ places no restriction on $\tilde{Q}$, hence the following definition:

DEFINITION 5   *The complete model $\overline{M}_1^0 = (M_1, M_e^0)$ is moment efficient on $\mathscr{M}_1$ relative to M_2 if and only if*

$$\tilde{Q} \equiv Q(\tilde a). \tag{108}$$

It can be shown that, under moment efficiency, the algebra of the encompassing differences *and* of their covariance matrices is essentially similar to that of the static case and, in particular, that the simplification WET statistic against M_2 coincides with the conventional F-test statistic (up to a scalar transformation as in (56).

A weaker property is that of asymptotic-moment efficiency, relative to the entire class $\mathcal{M}_1$ of complete models.

DEFINITION 6   *The complete model* $\overline{M}_1^0 = (M_1, M_e^0)$ *is asymptotically moment efficient on* $\mathcal{M}_1$ *relative to* M_2 *if and only if*

$$\tilde{Q} \underset{M_1}{\overset{as}{\simeq}} Q(\tilde{\alpha}), \qquad \forall \overline{M}_1 \in \mathcal{M}_1. \tag{109}$$

Asymptotic moment-efficiency preserves the simplicity of the algebra of pseudotrue values. However, for reasons already explained in connection with our discussion of formula (81), the algebra of the covariance matrices of the encompassing differences is now affected by the presence of a term of order $0(T^{-1/2})$ and is more complicated than under moment-efficiency. In particular, the equivalence between the simplification WET statistic and th conventional F-test statistic no longer holds, *even* asymptotically. It is obvious that moment-efficiency entails asymptotic moment-efficiency. It can also be shown that the latter entails $\mathcal{M}_1$-consistency.

The important question is that of whether or not, given a pair of models M_1 and M_2, there exists a completing model M_e that guarantees either moment-efficiency or at least asymptotic moment-efficiency. (Ex post verification that either of these two properties holds for a specific choice of M_e is conceptually at least, straightforward.) Govaerts (1987a) proposes an algorithm based on a systematic comparison of the two lists of regressors in M_1 and M_2, the outcome of the algorithm being a list of regressors defining a so-called "minimal completing model" which we denote here M_e^m (see also Govaerts et al. 1988a for further discussion).

The minimal completing model M_e^m has a number of interesting features:

1. If M_1 and M_2 are such that there exists a completing model M_e under which (M_1, M_e) is moment-efficient on $\mathcal{M}_1$, then (M_1, M_e^m) is also moment efficient on $\mathcal{M}_1$.

2. The model (M_1, M_e^m) is asymptotically moment efficient on $\mathcal{M}_1$, and hence the corresponding encompassing difference is $\mathcal{M}_1$-consistent.

3. M_e^m is minimal in the sense that its list of regressors is included in that associated with any other model M_e that satisfies either (1) or (2).

It follows from the above discussion that unless the proprietor of M_1 has objective reasons to select a specific completing model M_e, much is to be said in favour of selecting M_e^m as the completing model, thus achieving robustness within the class of VAR completing models.

We conclude our discussion of the dynamic case by mentioning another property, which was proposed by Govaerts (1987a), in an attempt to reinterpret within the dynamic framework the "projection approach" used by Hendry and Richard (1982) in the static case (see formula (73)).

DEFINITION 7   *The complete model $\overline{M}_1^0 = (M_1, M_e^o)$ is projection efficient if and only if*

$$(Z'Z)^{-1}Z'X = [Q_{ZZ}(\tilde{\alpha})]^{-1}Q_{ZX}(\tilde{\alpha}), \tag{110}$$

$$\frac{1}{T}[X'X - X'Z(Z'Z)^{-1}Z'X] = Q_{XX}(\tilde{\alpha}) - Q_{XZ}(\tilde{\alpha}) \cdot [Q_{ZZ}(\tilde{\alpha})]^{-1}Q_{ZX}(\tilde{\alpha}), \tag{111}$$

where $Q(\tilde{\alpha})$ is partitioned conformably with $\tilde{Q}$ in (105).

Moment-efficiency entails projection efficiency which, in turn, entails $\mathscr{M}_1$-consistency. Projection-efficiency is neither necessary nor sufficient for asymptotic moment-efficiency. Under projection efficiency the simplification WET-statistic against M_2 is asymptotically equivalent to the convention F-test statistic (while the two statistics were equivalent under moment-efficiency). However, and somewhat intriguingly, projection-efficiency is not necessarily obtained under M_e^m even when there exists a completing model under which it holds.

12.10   The Bayesian Notions of Encompassing and Specificity

General Principle

As usual within the Bayesian framework, the data densities associated with the models M_1 and M_2 are completed by prior densities on the corresponding spaces. From the resulting joint densities, predictive densities on the observations are obtained by marginalizing with respect to the (unknown) parameters, and posterior densities on the parameters are obtained by conditioning on the observations. The notation for the two

Table 12.1

	M_1	M_2
Sample	$y \in Y$	$y \in Y$
Parameters	$\alpha \in A$	$\delta \in D$
Sampling density	$f(y|\alpha)$	$g(y|\delta)$
Prior density	$\mu(\alpha)$	$v(\delta)$
Predictive density	$f(y)$	$g(y)$
Posterior density	$\mu(\alpha|y)$	$v(\delta|y)$

models is given in table 12.1, where for notational convenience Y_T^1 is replaced by y.

The prior densities $\mu(\alpha)$ and $v(\delta)$ need not be "coherent" with each other since they are specific to each individual model proprietor and hence are typically based on different information sets.

The object of the encompassing exercise for the proprietor of M_1 is to examine whether or not his *own* posterior density on δ, which must be constructed in a way that is "coherent" with his probability on $Y \times A$, coincides with $v(\delta|y)$ as derived by the proprietor of M_2. The critical step is that of reinterpreting δ within the context of M_1. Florens et al. (1987b) suggest that is would be natural for the proprietor of M_1 to assume first that α is a sufficient parameter for characterizing the data density of y, that is, that y and δ are independent, conditionally on α or, in terms of densities, that

$$f(y|\alpha, \delta) \equiv f(y|\alpha). \tag{112}$$

Under this assumption the proprietor of M_1 only needs to specify a transition probability from A to D in order to complete his own probability assessment on the product space $Y \times A \times D$. For the purpose of the present exposition, we will assume that this transition probability can be represented by a conditional density $\lambda(\delta|\alpha)$, which can be degenerate—for example, a Dirac density in such special cases as that where δ is thought to be an exact function of α. The corresponding joint density on $Y \times A \times D$ is then given by

$$\pi(y, \alpha, \delta) = f(y|\alpha) \cdot \lambda(\delta|\alpha) \cdot \mu(\alpha). \tag{113}$$

The predictive and posterior densities associated with this joint density are given by

$$\pi(y) \equiv f(y), \qquad \pi(\alpha, \delta | y) = \mu(\alpha | y) \cdot \lambda(\delta | \alpha) \tag{114}$$

$$\pi(\delta | y) = \int_A \mu(\alpha | y)\lambda(\delta | \alpha)d\alpha, \tag{115}$$

but as the result of assumption (112), the transition density λ is unaffected by sample information

$$\lambda(\delta | \alpha, y) \equiv \lambda(\delta | \alpha). \tag{116}$$

Formula (115) is central to the Bayesian notion of encompassing and indicates that, under assumption (112), the proprietor of M_1 derives his own posterior density on δ directly from his posterior density on α via the transition probability $\lambda(\delta | \alpha)$.

The Bayesian notion of encompassing we propose below is then naturally based on a comparison between the two posterior densities $\pi(\delta | y)$ and $v(\delta | y)$. Such comparisons critically depend on the choice of the transition density $\lambda(\delta | \alpha)$. There might be cases where $\lambda(\delta | \alpha)$ would correspond to a genuine prior probability assessement by the proprietor of M_1, assuming he can unambiguously interpret δ within M_1. Alternatively, we may consider a class Λ of conditional density functions and examine whether or not there exist functions within Λ that meet our requirements. The definitions that follow are relative to such a class Λ that can be left unspecified as long as we do not discuss specific examples and can eventually consist of a single, preassigned density function.

DEFINITION 8 M_1 (*exactly*) *encompasses* M_2 *if and only if there exists a transition probability* $\lambda \in \Lambda$ *such that*

$$v(\delta | y) = \int_A \mu(\alpha | y)\lambda(\delta | \alpha)d\alpha \tag{117}$$

almost surely in Y.

Within a strict Bayesian framework "almost surely" is naturally understood as being relative to the predictive density $f(y)$, though, as illustrated by the example we discuss below and as discussed further in Florens et al. (1987b), the data density $f(y | \alpha)$ can occasionally be substituted for $f(y)$.

It is unlikely that condition (117) will often be met in practice, if only because the prior densities $\mu(\alpha)$ and $v(\delta)$ will typically be "incoherent" with each other in the sense that $v(\delta)$ differs from the derived prior density $v_*(\delta) = \int_A \mu(\alpha)\lambda(\delta | \alpha)d\alpha$. In such a case the proprietor of M_1 might consider replacing the prior v, which he views to be "incoherent" with his *own* prior beliefs, by the "coherent" prior v_*. Hence the notion of coherent encompassing we now define (and where, for notational convenience, v and v_* are conflated with each other by means of condition (118)).

DEFINITION 9 M_1 coherently encompasses M_2 if and only if there exists a transition probability $\lambda \in \Lambda$ such that

i. M_1 exactly encompasses M_2 under λ,

ii. v is "coherent" with μ in the sense that

$$v(\delta) = \int_A \mu(\alpha)\lambda(\delta|\alpha)d\alpha. \tag{118}$$

The Bayesian notion of encompassing we have just introduced has considerable conceptual appeal in that it can be reinterpreted as a notion of "sufficiency among models" that is dual to the notion of "sufficiency (among statistics)," as defined, for example, in LeCam (1964). Specially, in terms of density functions, a statistic s would be sufficient for a statistic t, conditional on a parameter α if and only if there existed a transition density function ρ such that

$$f(t|\alpha) = \int_S g(s|\alpha)\rho(t|s)ds. \tag{119}$$

Comparing together formulae (117) and (119), we recognize a fundamendal duality between sufficiency, in the sense of LeCam, and encompassing, in that the two notions simply interchange parameters and observations. This suggests, in particular, that we might be able to transpose within the context of encompassing results that have been established in a vast literature on sufficiency. This is the object of our current research.

In the same spirit, exactly as LeCam uses a notion of deficiency to measure a lack of sufficiency, we can introduce a notion of specificity to measure a lack of encompassing. More precisely, the specificity of M_2 relative to M_1 will be defined as a measure of "divergence" between the posterior densities $v(\delta|y)$ and $\pi(\delta|y)$. There are many ways in which such a measure can be defined, a number of which are discussed in Florens et al. (1987b). For the purpose of the present discussion we can restrict ourselves to a measure based on an appropriate norm.

Specifically, for any given (vector) function h of the parameter δ, we can first evaluate the difference between the posterior expectations of h under $v(\delta|y)$ and $\pi(\delta|y)$, namely,

$$\psi_h(y) = \int_D h(\delta)[v(\delta|y) - \pi(\delta|y)]d\delta. \tag{120}$$

Let $\| \ \|_p$ denote an L_p-norm on the sample space Y relative to a density function, say, $f(y|\cdot)$, which as discussed above can be either the predictive density $f(y)$ or the data density $f(y|\alpha)$.

DEFINITION 10   *The p-specificity of M_2 relative to M_1, with respect to a function h on D, a class Λ of transition probabilities and a density $f(y|\cdot)$ on Y is*

$$\sigma_h(M_2; M_1) = \inf_{\lambda \in \Lambda} \|\psi_h(y)\|_p, \tag{121}$$

where $\psi_h(y)$ is defined in formula (120) together with (117).

In the spirit of LeCam, we might wish to consider a class $\mathscr{H}$ of functions h such as, at a conceptual level at least, the class of all bounded functions on D.

DEFINITION 11   *The p-specificity of M_2 relative to M_1, with respect to a class $\mathscr{H}$ of functions on D, a class Λ of transition probabilities, and a density $f(y|\cdot)$ on Y is*

$$\sigma_{\mathscr{H}}(M_2; M_1) = \sup_{h \in \mathscr{H}} [\sigma_h(M_2; M_1)]. \tag{122}$$

Not only does the evaluation of specificity prove of interest on its own in that, for example, it can lead to the construction of Bayesian tests of encompassing in the spirit of Florens and Mouchart (chapter 14) but also, in the absence of a genuine conditional prior density λ, there is much to be said in favor of using the transition that solves the optimization problem (121). If, in particular, h is the identity function $h(\delta) = \delta$, a heuristic argument runs as follows: If $\mathscr{M}_1$ is (a valid reduction of) the DGP then the posterior densities $\mu(\alpha|y)$ and $v(\delta|y)$ converge a.s. toward Dirac densities, attaching mass one, respectively, to α and $\delta(\alpha)$ (see, e.g., Berk 1966, 1970 regarding the convergence of v). In such a case the transition λ that solves (121) itself converges toward a Dirac distribution with mass one at $\delta = \delta(\alpha)$— under the implicit assumption that the latter is included in the closure of Λ—and the specificity of $\mathscr{M}_2$ relative to $\mathscr{M}_1$ tends to zero.

If we except such simple cases as the linear choice of regressors problem we discuss below, the optimization problem (121) will generally prove to be intractable. We are presently investigating the property of a class of transition probabilities that are easier to evaluate than the optimal one and yet have the same limiting behavior. One such property is the transition probability:

$$l(\delta|\alpha) = \int_Y v(\delta|y)f(y|\alpha)dy, \tag{123}$$

which can be viewed as a Bayesian extension of the sampling theory notion of pseudotrue values as defined in (3).

Finally, note that the treatment of (weakly) exogenous variables raises no problems within the Bayesian framework since posterior densities are, by definition, *conditional* on the sample. Hence, under the assumption that the parameter of the exogenous process are a priori independent of α and δ, the posterior densities $\mu(\alpha|y)$ and $v(\delta|y)$ are proportional to the product of the relevant prior densities and the corresponding partial likelihood functions, as defined respectively in (83) and (84). Furthermore it seems natural in such a case to allow for the possibility that the transition probability λ might be conditional on the exogenous variables x. All the definitions we have proposed above are easily adapted to this new situation, and in particular, formula (115) is replaced by

$$\pi(\delta|x, y) = \int_A \mu(\alpha|x, y)\lambda(\delta|\alpha, x)d\alpha \tag{124}$$

An Example

Let us reconsider the choice of regressors problem as stated in formulae (45) and (46) under the additional simplifying assumption that the variances σ^2 and τ^2 are known. The case where the variances are unknown is discussed in Florens et al. (1987b) and raises technical problems that go beyond the objectives of the present discussion.

The parameters α and δ are conflated with the regression coefficients β and γ, respectively. We assume further that the prior densities $\mu(\beta)$ and $v(\gamma)$ belong to the class of normal conjugate (NC) priors (as defined, e.g., in Zellner 1971):

$$\mu(\beta) = f_N^k(\beta|\beta_0, \sigma^2 M_0^{-1}), \qquad v(\gamma) = f_N^l(\gamma|\gamma_0, \tau^2 N_0^{-1}), \tag{125}$$

where $f_N^p(x|\mu, \Sigma)$ denotes the normal density function for a vector $X \in \mathbb{R}^p$ with mean vector $\mu \in \mathbb{R}^p$ and covariance matrix $\Sigma \geq 0$. The corresponding posterior densities are

$$\mu(\beta|y) = f_N^k(\beta|\beta_*, \sigma^2 M_*^{-1}), \qquad v(\gamma|y) = f_N^l(\gamma_*, \tau^2 N_*^{-1}), \tag{126}$$

with

$$M_* = M_0 + X'X, \qquad N_* = N_0 + Z'Z, \tag{127}$$

$$M_*\beta_* = M_0\beta_0 + X'y, \qquad N_*\gamma_* = N_0\gamma_0 + Z'y. \tag{128}$$

Within the present context it seems natural to define Λ as the class of conditional normal density functions of the form

$$\Lambda(\gamma|\beta) = f_N^l(\gamma|C\beta + c, V), \tag{129}$$

with $C \in \mathbb{R}^{l \times k}$, $c \in \mathbb{R}^l$, and $V \geq 0$. These densities are implicitly conditional on X and Z, hence C, c, and V can be functions of X and Z. Under (126) and (129) the derived posterior density $\pi(\gamma|y)$ is given by

$$\pi(\gamma|y) = f_N^l(\gamma|C\beta_* + c, V + \sigma^2 C M_*^{-1} C'). \tag{130}$$

Exact encompassing would then require the existence of (C, c, V) such that

$$\gamma_* = C\beta_* + c \quad \text{and} \quad V + \sigma^2 C M_*^{-1} C' = \tau^2 N_*^{-1} \tag{131}$$

almost surely in Y. Necessary and sufficient conditions for (131) are

$$(N_*^{-1}Z' - C M_*^{-1} X')y \underset{\text{a.s.}}{=} 0 \quad \text{and} \quad \tau^2 N_*^{-1} \geq \sigma^2 C M_*^{-1} C'. \tag{132}$$

For large enough samples or, equivalently, under "noninformative" prior densities, these conditions simplify to

$$[(Z'Z)^{-1}Z' - C(X'X)^{-1}X']y \underset{\text{a.s.}}{=} 0 \quad \text{and} \quad (Z'Z)^{-1} \geq \frac{\sigma^2}{\tau^2} C(X'X)^{-1}C'. \tag{133}$$

In section 12.7 we found that the condition $(Z'Z)^{-1}Z'M_x y \underset{\text{a.s.}}{=} 0$ was necessary and sufficient for population encompassing, together with the necessary variance dominance condition $\tau^2 \geq \sigma^2$. It now appears that these conditions also guarantee (asymptotic) exact encompassing when C, c, and V are chosen as follows:

$$C = (Z'Z)^{-1}Z'X, \qquad c = 0, \tag{134}$$

$$V = (\tau^2 - \sigma^2)(Z'Z)^{-1} + \tau^2(Z'Z)^{-1}Z'M_x Z(Z'Z)^{-1}. \tag{135}$$

When the conditions (132) do not hold, we can evaluate the specificity of M_2 relative to M_1 under the following specifications:

1. the function h is the identity $h(\gamma) \equiv \gamma$ so that

$$\psi(y) = \gamma_* - (C\beta_* + c); \tag{136}$$

2. $p = 2$, and the L_2-norm is characterized by an $l \times l$ matrix $Q \geq 0$;

3. the density on Y is normal with mean μ_y and covariance matrix V_y, where $\mu_y = X\beta$ and $V_y = \sigma^2 I_T$ if we use the data density, or $\mu_y = X\beta_0$ and $V_y = \sigma^2(I_T + XM_0^{-1}X')$ if we use instead the predictive density.

Formula (136) indicates that we are only comparing posterior means so that the covariance matrix V in (129) can be chosen arbitrarily. We can, in particular, set it equal to zero in which case λ degenerates into a Dirac distribution. The usual algebra of expectations of quadratic forms leads to the following operational expression for the L_2-norm of $\psi(y)$:

$$\|\psi(y)\| = [c_* - c + (C_* - C)\beta_\Delta]'Q[c_* - c + (C_* - C)\beta_\Delta] + tr\, Q\Phi_* \tag{137}$$

where

$$\beta_\Delta = M_*^{-1}(M_0\beta_0 + X'\mu_y), \tag{138}$$

$$c_* = N_*^{-1}[N_0\gamma_0 - Z'X(X'X)^{-1}M_0\beta_0], \tag{139}$$

$$C_* = N_*^{-1}Z'X(X'X)^{-1}M_*, \tag{140}$$

$$\Phi_* = \Sigma_* + (C - C_*)M_*^{-1}X'V_yXM_*^{-1}(C - C_*)', \tag{141}$$

$$\Sigma_* = \sigma^2 N_*^{-1}Z'M_\times ZN_*^{-1}. \tag{142}$$

We note that c_*, C_*, and Σ_* are the same whether we use the data density of the predictive density. The norm in (137) is minimized by taking $C = C_*$ and $c = c_*$ so that

$$\sigma_2(M_2; M_1) = tr\, Q\Sigma_* \tag{143}$$

The expression $C_*\beta_* + c_*$ can be interpreted as a Bayesian pseudotrue value and can be rewritten as

$$C_*\beta_* + c_* = N_*^{-1}(N_0\gamma_0 + Z'Z\gamma_{\tilde{a}}), \tag{144}$$

where $\gamma_{\tilde{a}} = (Z'Z)^{-1}Z'X\tilde{\beta}$ is the sampling theory estimated pseudotrue value. Note the functional analogy between the Bayesian pseudotrue value (144) and the posterior mean γ_*, as given in (128). Finally the "approximate" transition probability (123) is given by

$$l(\gamma|\beta) = f_N^l(\gamma|N_*^{-1}(N_0\gamma_0 + Z'X\beta), \tau^2 N_*^{-1} + \sigma^2 N_*^{-1}Z'ZN_*^{-1}). \tag{145}$$

12.11   Conclusion and Summary

The theory of encompassing was analyzed above in a series of models, ranging from simple normal densities through choice of regressors problems to dynamic systems. In each case the basic principle was to derive from one model an explanation or prediction of certain aspects of a contending model and contrast that with the result actually obtained by that rival model. The resulting discrepancy was then evaluated relative to the uncertainty involved, usually via a statistical test whose distribution was known at least in large samples under the null of the first model encompassing the second.

Since alternative explanations of empirical phenomena are relatively common in economics, it seems natural to seek to reconcile disparate findings in order to reduce the proliferation of claimed results. As a research *strategy*, encompassing seems closely linked to progressivity in so far as it is transitive and antisymmetric. "Completely" encompassed models can be viewed as being redundant, in that they provide no additional specific information about the given sample, or in a more Popperian spirit as being rejected by the encompassing model since there exist specific features for which they cannot offer an account. Moreover encompassing predictions are not restricted to known features of existing rival models but include predicting aspects of their models of which the proprietors may be unaware. In so far as new or unexpected phenomena are anticipated, models acquire excess corroborated content. As a research *tactic*, encompassing provides a basis for model comparisons, as well as integrating a large and diverse literature covering nested and nonnested hypothesis tests. By evaluating models against the specific features of work developed by others, an objective check on model design is available to help detect spurious or incomplete findings. By clarifying the interpretation of many tests as checks for particular encompassing features, their interrelationships and respective advantages and drawbacks are highlighted independently of any dichotomies between nested and nonnested, or specification and misspecification, classes of tests. Moreover many well-established results reappear in the encompassing framework, albeit with a somewhat altered perspective (e.g., Sargan's 1964 criterion for log versus linear appears as a necessary condition; variance dominance is necessary but not sufficient for encompassing in linear regressions; and the F-test is both a Wald encompassing test and a simplification test in that context). Finally, the role of encompassing is equally clear in both classical and Bayesian approaches, yielding interesting "duality" results in the latter.

Many technical issues and extensions remain to be developed, some of which were noted in the chapter. Prominent items on the research agenda include exogeneity encompassing (see Govaerts et al. 1987b), extensions to nonlinear models (see Ghysels and Hall 1987 for an application to orthogonality conditions in Euler equation approaches), forecast encompassing (see, e.g., Chong and Hendry 1986), and nonstationary processes (as analyzed in Engle and Granger 1987). Using both analytical and Monte Carlo techniques, several of these problems seem likely to be resolved in the near future.

Appendix: A Proof of Formulae (35) and (36)

The observations y_t being i.i.d. on M_1, we could use the formulae in White (1982) to evaluate the asymptotic covariance matrix of $\tilde{\gamma}$ and $\tilde{\tau}^2$ on M_1. Alternatively, exact results are directly obtainable for $\tilde{\gamma}$ and $\tilde{\tau}^2$ since, on M_1,

$$E(Y_t^r) = e^{r\beta + r^2\sigma^2/2} = \gamma_\alpha^r \cdot e^{(r^2-r)\sigma^2/2}, \qquad r \geq 0, \tag{A1}$$

from which

$$E[(Y_t - \gamma_\alpha)^3] = \gamma_\alpha^3 (e^{\sigma^2} - 1)^2(e^{\sigma^2} + 2) = \gamma_\alpha \tau_\alpha^2 (e^{\sigma^2} - 1)(e^{\sigma^2} + 2),$$

$$E[(Y_t - \gamma_\alpha)^4] = \gamma_\alpha^4 (e^{6\sigma^2} - 4e^{3\sigma^2} + 6e^{\sigma^2} - 3).$$

The proof follows from the fact that

$$\mathrm{Cov}(\sqrt{T}\tilde{\gamma}, \sqrt{T}\tilde{\tau}^2) = \frac{1}{T} E\left[\sum_{t=1}^{T} (Y_t - \gamma_\alpha) \cdot \sum_{t=1}^{T} (Y_t - \gamma_\alpha)^2 \right]$$

$$= E[(Y_t - \gamma_\alpha)^3]$$

$$\mathrm{Var}(\sqrt{T}\tilde{\tau}^2) = \frac{1}{T} E\left[\sum_{t=1}^{T} (Y_t - \gamma_\alpha)^2 \right]^2 - T\tau_\alpha^4$$

$$= \frac{1}{T} E\left[\sum_{t=1}^{T} (Y_t - \gamma_\alpha)^4 + \sum_t \sum_{s \neq t} (Y_t - \gamma_\alpha)^2 (Y_s - \gamma_\alpha)^2 \right]$$

$$- T\tau_\alpha^4.$$

$$= E(Y_t - \gamma_\alpha)^4 - \tau_\alpha^4 \qquad \blacksquare$$

Notes

This chapter surveys a topic to which Jean-Pierre Florens, Bernadette Govaerts and Grayham Mizon have contributed substantially, and we have drawn freely on our current research with them. They have considerably influenced our own views of encompassing, but we retain sole responsibility for our errors and shortcomings. The chapter has been presented at several workshops and has benefited from comments by several participants. In particular, Jean-Pierre Florens, Bernadette Govaerts, Robert Marshall, Grayham Mizon, Michel Mouchart, Quang Vuong, Clive Granger, and Hall White have helped to clarify earlier shortcomings. We are grateful to S. Johansen for many helpful comments. Financial support from the ESRC under grant B0022012 and from the NSF under grant SES-8708615 is gratefully acknowledged.

1. Conflating $\overline{M}_c$ with the DGP $\mathscr{H}$ enables us to obtain analytical expressions for the population encompassing differences $\delta_\theta - \delta_{\alpha}$ and, in the process, to gain an understanding of the nature of the encompassing approach. Note that the derivation of the WET statistics is *not* affected by our choice of a DGP since it only requires the evaluation of plims under M_1. There are no conceptual limitations in selecting more general DGP's, such as for the purpose of investigating the properties of various WET statistics when M_1 is "false," though in such cases the evaluation of the population encompassing differences might have to be conducted numerically, for example, by means of the Monte Carlo procedures described in section 12.5.

2. For ease of comparison, the parameters associated with the models M_1, M_2, and M_c are denoted throughout this section by the letters associated with the *regression* coefficients in section 12.7 (leaving aside the variances).

3. Results have been established, for example, under the assumption that the x's are identically independently distributed (see, e.g., Gouriéroux et al. 1984). In section 12.9 we will require that $\overline{M}_1$ describe a linear dynamic stationary stochastic process. Much remains to be done to cover cases where the x's might be generated by a nonstationary and/or explosive process, though the recent literature on the analysis of "cointegrated" processes opens the way for extensions.

4. Given our convention about restrictions being kept implicit, it proves notationally convenient to impose a common lag length for M_1, M_2, and M_e.

References

Berk, R. H. 1966. "Limiting Behavior of Posterior Distributions When the Model Is Incorrect." *Annals of Mathematical Statistics* 37:51–58.

Berk, R. H. 1970 "Consistency a Posteriori." *Annals of Mathematical Statistics* 41:894–906.

Chong, Y. Y., and D. F. Hendry. 1986. "Econometric Evaluation of Linear Macro-economic Models." *The Review of Economic Studies* 53:671–690.

Cox, D. R. 1961. "Tests of Separate Families of Hypotheses." In *Proceedings of the Fourth Berkeley Symposium on Mathematical Statistics and Probability.* Vol. 1, 105–123.

Cox, D. R. 1962. "Further Results on Tests of Separate Families on Hypotheses." *Journal of the Royal Statistical Society* B24:406–424.

Davidson, J. E. H., Hendry, D. F., Srba, F., and J. S. Yeo. 1978. "Econometric Modelling of the Aggregate Time-Series Relationship between Consumers Expenditure and Income in the United Kingdom." *Economic Journal* 88:661–692.

Davidson, R., and J. G. MacKinnon. 1981. "Several Tests for Model Specification in the Presence of Alternative Hypotheses." *Econometrica* 49:781–793.

Engle, R. F., Hendry, D. F., and J. F. Richard. 1983. "Exogeneity." *Evonometrica* 51:277–304.

Engle, R. F., and C. W. J. Granger. 1987. "Co-integration and Error Correction: Representation, Estimation and Testing." *Econometrica* 55:251–276.

Florens, J. P., and M. Mouchart. 1985. "Conditioning in Dynamic Models." *Journal of Time Series Analysis* 6:15–34.

Florens, J. P., Hendry, D. F., and J. F. Richard. 1987a. "An Information Matrix Approach to Parsimonious Encompassing." ISDS Discussion Paper 8709, Duke University.

Florens, J. P., Hendry, D. F., and J. F. Richard. 1987b. "Encompassing and Specificity." ISDS, Duke University. Mimeo.

Ghysels, E., and A. Hall. 1987. "Testing Non-nested Euler Conditions with Quadrature Based Methods of Approximations." University of Montreal. Mimeo.

Godfrey, L. G. 1983. "Testing Non-nested Models after Estimation by Instrumental Variables or Least-Squares." *Econometrica* 51:355–365.

Gouriéroux, C., Monfort, A., and A. Trognon. 1984. "Pseudo-Maximum Likelihood Methods: Theory." *Econometrica* 52:681–700.

Govaerts, B. 1987a. "Application of the Encompassing Principle to Linear Dynamic Models." Ph.D. dissertation. Université Catholique de Louvain.

Govaerts, B. 1987b. "A Note on a Method to Compute the Asymptotic Distribution of the Sample Second-Order Moments of Dynamic Linear Normal Variables." CORE Discussion Paper 8709, Louvain-la-Neuve: CORE.

Govaerts, B., Hendry, D. F., and J. F. Richard 1988a. "Application of the Encompassing Principle to the Linear Dynamic Choice of Regressors Problem." ISDS, Duke University. Mimeo.

Govaerts, B., Hendry, D. F., and J. F. Richard 1988b. "Encompassing in Linear Dynamic Stationary Processes." Nuffield College, Oxford. Mimeo.

Granger, C. W. J. 1969. "Investigating Causal Relations by Econometric Models and Cross-Spectral Methods." *Econometrica* 37:424–438.

Hannan, F. J. 1970. *Multiple Time Series*. New York: Wiley.

Hausman, J. A. 1978. "Specification Tests in Econometrics." *Econometrica* 46:1251–1272.

Hendry, D. F. 1976. "The Structure of Simultaneous Equations Estimators." *Journal of Econometrics* 4:51–85.

Hendry, D. F. 1984. "Monte Carlo Experimentation in Econometrics." In *Handbook of Econometrics*, edited by Z. Griliches and M. D. Intriligator. Vol. 2, ch. 16. Amsterdam: North Holland.

Hendry, D. F. 1986. "The Use of PC-GIVE in Econometrics Teaching." *Oxford Bulletin of Economics and Statistics* 48:87–98.

Hendry, D. F., and G. J. Anderson. 1977. "Testing Dynamic Specification in Small Simultaneous Systems: An Application to a Model of Building Society Behavior in the United Kingdom." In *Frontiers in Quantitative Economics*, edited by M. D. Intriligator. Vol. 3A, 361–383. Amsterdam: North Holland.

Hendry, D. F., and J. F. Richard. 1982. "On the Formulation of Empirical Models in Dynamic Econometrics." *Journal of Econometrics* 20:3–33.

Hendry, D. F., and J. F. Richard. 1983. "The Econometric Analysis of Economic Time Series." *International Statistical Review* 51:111–163.

Holly, A. 1982. "A Remark on Hausman's Specification Test." *Econometrica* 50:749–760.

Lakatos, I. 1978. *The Methodology of Scientific Research Programmes*, edited by J. Worrall and G. Currie. Vol. 1. Cambridge: Cambridge University Press.

Leamer, E. E. 1978. *Specification Searches: Ad-hoc Inference with Non-experimental Data.* New York: Wiley.

LeCam, L. 1964. "Sufficiency and Approximate Sufficiency." *Annals of Mathematical Statistics* 35:1419–1455.

MacKinnon, J. G. 1983. "Model Specification Tests against Non-nested Alternatives. *Econometric Review* 2:85–110.

Madansky, A. 1976. *Foundations of Econometrics.* Amsterdam: North Holland.

Marsaglia, M. 1964. "Conditional Means and Covariances of Normal Variables with Singular Covariance Matrix." *Journal of the American Statistical Society* 49:1203–1204.

Mizon, G. E. 1977. "Model Selection Procedures. " In *Studies in Modern Economic Analysis*, edited by M. J. Artis and A. R. Nobay. Ch. 4. Oxford: Basil Blackwell.

Mizon, G. E. 1984. "The Encompassing Approach in Econometrics." In *Econometrics and Quantitative Economics*, edited by D. F. Hendry and K. F. Wallis. Ch. 6. Oxford: Basil Blackwell.

Mizon. G. E., and J. F. Richard. 1986. "The Encompassing Principle and Its Application to Testing Non-nested Hypotheses." *Econometrica* 54:657–678.

Peraran, M. H. 1974. "On the General Problem of Model Selection." *Review of Economic Studies*, 41:153–171.

Pesaran, M. H. 1987. "Global and Partial Non-nested Hypotheses and Asymptotic Local Power." *Econometric Theory* 3:69–97.

Popper, K. R. 1963., *Conjectures and Refutations.* London: Routledge & Kegan Paul.

Sargan, J. D. 1964. "Wages and Prices in the United Kingdom: A Study in Econometric Modelling." In *Econometric Analysis for National Economic Planning*, edited by P. E. Hart, F. Mills, and J. K. Whitaker. London: Butterworks. Reprinted in *Econometrics and Quantitative Economics*, edited by D. F. Hendry and K. F. Wallis. Ch. 6. Oxford: Basil Blackwell.

Sawa, T. 1978. "Information Criteria for Discriminating among Alternative Regression Models." *Econometrica* 46:1273–1292.

White, H. 1982. "Maximum Likelihood Estimation of Misspecified Models." *Econometrica* 50:1–26.

Zellner, A. 1971. *An Introduction to Bayesian Inference in Econometrics.* New ͺ ork: Wiley.

13 Toward a Levels Version of the Rotterdam and Related Demand Systems

Anton P. Barten

13.1 Introduction

The theory of demand for the individual consumer implies a set of properties (constraints) on the elasticities of demand with respect to income (or total expenditure) and prices. For at least two reasons it is desirable to take these properties into account in empirical work: The first is the reduction in the number of independent coefficients to be estimated. The second is the ability to obtain predictions with estimated versions of the demand relations that make sense from a theoretical point of view. This last possibility is attractive also if one works with data for the whole economy rather than for a single consumer. Indeed, without the fiction of the representative consumer, it is difficult to give any meaning to empirical results for an aggregate of consumers.

Besides the homogeneity condition the constraints on the elasticities pertain to more than one demand function at a time. To take the constraints into account in a proper way, one has to formulate and estimate a complete system of demand equations, which in principle describes how the consumer allocates his budget over all desirable goods and services.

The Theil (1965) formulation of what is known as the Rotterdam demand system amounts to a convenient and simple transformation of demand elasticities into constants that satisfy, or can be made to satisfy, the theoretical constraints. They can be directly estimated. Of course, the Rotterdam system is not the only demand system that (1) can or does incorporate constraints from theory, (2) is relatively easy to estimate and interpret, and (3) is potentially flexible (i.e., allows for nontrivial interactions among commodities, such as specific substitution or complementarity). Still, the Rotterdam system is not a priori dominated by any other system, and it is therefore useful to increase its applicability.

Indeed, as originally formulated, the Rotterdam specification applies to a system in terms of the logarithmic first differences in quantities, prices, and incomes. This limits its practical use to the analysis of time series data. Even for that type of data more refined dynamics are difficult to capture using first differences of the major determinants. Moreover there are cross sections of observations with (sometimes imputed) price variation, which can only be meaningfully handled by a system in terms of the levels of the variables. Such a system with a Rotterdam-type parametrization appears to be a useful tool for demand analysis. It is the purpose of this chapter to present such a system.

The first-difference version of the Rotterdam system is one of a class of systems to which the almost ideal demand system (AIDS) of Deaton and Muellbauer (1980)—in first differences—and the CBS demand system of Keller and Van Driel (1985) also belong. For the levels version of the Rotterdam system, a similar class can be formulated. The counterpart of the AIDS first-difference equation in this class is not quite the same as the levels version of AIDS proposed by Deaton and Muellbauer, although its parametrization is the same.

It is useful to start with a presentation of the constraints on the elasticities which are derived from demand theory. This is the topic of section 13.2. Section 13.3 takes up the case of convenient parametrization in systems in terms of first differences. We then turn to a discussion of the choice of levels versions for these systems. Alternative approaches are also considered. Such systems are used to generate information about quantities demanded, expenditure shares, and the like. For some of these systems, such simulation is not trivial, as is shown in section 13.6. Some insight about the relative merits of the various systems can be gained from an empirical application, which one finds in section 13.7. The last section is devoted to concluding remarks.

13.2 Constraints on Elasticities

As a starting point we use the double-logarithmic demand function

$$\ln q_i = \alpha_i + \eta_i \ln m + \sum_j \mu_{ij} \ln p_j, \qquad i, j = 1, \ldots, n, \tag{1}$$

where q_i is the (positive) quantity of good i and p_i its (positive) price, and m is total expenditure defined as

$$m = \sum_j p_j q_j. \tag{2}$$

The η_i are income or expenditure elasticities; the μ_{ij} are the price elasticities. There is no fundamental reason why these elasticities are constant (i.e., independent of m and the p_j). The same is true for the intercept α_i.

Frisch (1959) states a set of properties that the η_i and the μ_{ij} should satisfy if they are to reflect utility-maximizing behavior. These properties involve the budget shares, w_i, defined as

$$w_i = \frac{p_i q_i}{m}, \tag{3}$$

that is, the share of expenditure on good i in total expenditure. Clearly

$$\sum_i w_i = 1. \tag{4}$$

The first set of properties are those of *adding-up*:

$$\sum_i w_i \eta_i = 1 \quad \text{(Engel aggregation)}, \tag{5}$$

$$\sum_i w_i \mu_{ij} = -w_j \quad \text{(Cournot aggregation)}. \tag{6}$$

These properties guarantee that explained demand satisfies the budget identity (2). Next is the *homogeneity* condition:

$$\sum_j \mu_{ij} = -\eta_i, \tag{7}$$

which is derived from the linear homogeneity in m and the p_j of the budget identity (2).

Further properties can be conveniently formulated in terms of the *Slutsky* or compensated price elasticity, defined as

$$\varepsilon_{ij} = \mu_{ij} + \eta_i w_j, \tag{8}$$

which reflects the substitution effect of price changes, with utility kept constant. Note that adding-up conditions (5) and (6) imply an adding-up condition for the Slutsky elasticities,

$$\sum_i w_i \varepsilon_{ij} = \sum_i w_i \mu_{ij} + \sum_i w_i \eta_i w_j = -w_j + w_j = 0 \quad \text{(Slutsky aggregation)}, \tag{9}$$

while it follows from homogeneity condition (7) and from (4) that

$$\sum_j \varepsilon_{ij} = \sum_j \mu_{ij} + \eta_i \sum_j w_j = -\eta_i + \eta_i = 0 \tag{10}$$

which is the homogeneity condition for the Slutsky elasticities.

An additional property is that of Slutsky *symmetry*:

$$w_i \varepsilon_{ij} = w_j \varepsilon_{ji}. \tag{11}$$

The *negativity* property (not mentioned by Frisch) amounts to

$$\sum_i \sum_j x_i w_i \varepsilon_{ij} x_j < 0, \tag{12}$$

for all x_i that are not constants. These two properties derive from continuity and strong quasi-concavity properties of the utility function.

A further property is not purely theoretical. If the preference ordering can be represented by a utility function that is a sum of n functions $h_i(q_i)$, then

$$\varepsilon_{ij} = \varphi \eta_i (\delta_{ij} - \eta_j w_j), \tag{13}$$

with φ being the reciprocal of what Frisch terms "money flexibility," and δ_{ij} a Kronecker delta. Equation (13) states what is known as the (complete) *want* or *preference independence property*. The linear expenditure system (LES), for instance, is characterized by such independence. Property (13) is attractive in the sense that besides income elasticities η_i, one needs only one other magnitude, φ, to determine all Slutsky elasticities. This extreme reduction in parameters corresponds to an extremely rigid representation of interactions among goods in the preference order. Whether this is acceptable depends on the empirical context.

Apart from the homogeneity property, the constraints mentioned above involve budget shares, which are in principle and in practice variable. The constraints for constant elasticities cannot be applied to variable budget shares. If one is only interested in saving degrees of freedom, one could work with constant elasticities, using a single set of w_i in the constraints. That means, inter alia, that (2) is not respected for the explained q_j except for the sample point for which the selected w_i are valid. It is clearly more desirable to work with a parametrization that allows the use of constraints without impairing the simulation properties of the demand equations.

13.3   Parametrization

The choice of constraints underlying the Rotterdam demand system can be conveniently explained, starting from a double-logarithmic demand function in differential form

$$d\ln q_i = \eta_i \, d\ln m + \sum_j \mu_{ij} \, d\ln p_j, \tag{14}$$

with the η_i and the μ_{ij} being, as before, income and price elasticities, respectively. Note that (14) is not simply (1) in differential form unless η_i and μ_{ij} are constants.

An alternative version of (14) is obtained by using the Slutsky elasticities defined in (8):

$$d\ln q_i = \eta_i(d\ln m - \sum_j w_j\,d\ln p_j) + \sum_j \varepsilon_{ij}\,d\ln p_j. \tag{15}$$

In view of (2),

$$d\ln m = \sum_j w_j\,d\ln q_j + \sum_j w_j\,d\ln p_j. \tag{16}$$

Writing

$$d\ln Q = \sum_j w_j\,d\ln q_j, \tag{17a}$$

$$d\ln P = \sum_j w_j\,d\ln p_j, \tag{17b}$$

we have from (16)

$$d\ln m = d\ln Q + d\ln P. \tag{18}$$

We may then also write (15) as

$$d\ln q_i = \eta_i\,d\ln Q + \sum_j \varepsilon_{ij}\,d\ln p_j. \tag{19}$$

The second term in (19) represents the substitution effect of price changes, with utility kept constant. The first term represents the change in demand because of a change in utility. To see this, we make use of the second law of Gossen: $\partial u(q)/\partial q_j = \lambda p_j$, where $u(q)$ is the utility function and λ a (positive) Lagrange multiplier. Then $w_j = (1/\lambda m)\partial u(q)/\partial \ln q_j$, and

$$d\ln Q = \sum_j w_j\,d\ln q_j = \left(\frac{1}{\lambda m}\right)\sum_j \left(\frac{\partial u(q)}{\partial \ln q_j}\right)d\ln q_j$$

$$= \left(\frac{1}{\lambda m}\right)du. \tag{20}$$

The $d\ln Q$ variable can be seen as the change in the logarithm of real income.

The Rotterdam Specification

By multiplying both sides of (19) by w_i and using

$$b_i = w_i\eta_i, \tag{21}$$

$$s_{ij} = w_i\varepsilon_{ij}, \tag{22}$$

we obtain

$$w_i \, d\ln q_i = b_i \, d\ln Q + \sum_j s_{ij} \, d\ln p_j. \tag{23}$$

Note that the sum over i of the variable on the left-hand side is equal to the log change in real income.

From (5) we have as an adding-up property,

$$\sum_i b_i = 1 \quad \text{(Engel aggregation)}, \tag{24}$$

while the s_{ij} satisfy

$$\sum_i s_{ij} = 0 \quad \text{(Slutsky aggregation)}, \tag{25}$$

$$\sum_j s_{ij} = 0 \quad \text{(homogeneity)}, \tag{26}$$

$$s_{ij} = s_{ji} \quad \text{(symmetry)}, \tag{27}$$

$$\sum_i \sum_j x_i s_{ij} x_j < 0 \quad \text{(negativity, } x_i, x_j \neq \text{constant)}, \tag{28}$$

$$s_{ij} = \varphi b_i (\delta_{ij} - b_j) \quad \text{(preference independence)}. \tag{29}$$

All of these constraints are formulated in terms of constants only. The two adding-up conditions (24) and (25) guarantee satisfaction of (17a) for the $d\ln q_i$.

As follows from (21), the b_i represent the (constant) marginal propensities to consume since

$$b_i = w_i \eta_i = \frac{p_i q_i}{m} \frac{\partial \ln q_i}{\partial \ln m} = p_i \frac{\partial q_i}{\partial m} = \frac{\partial (p_i q_i)}{\partial m}. \tag{30}$$

They are also called marginal budget shares in order to distinguish them from the w_i, the (average) budget shares. Constant b_i mean linear Engel curves with convergence of the b_i and the w_i for increasing values of m. Negative b_i, indicating inferior goods, are difficult to reconcile with this type of asymptotic behavior. There are clearly limits to the validity of the Rotterdam specification.

In the transition from differentials to time subscripted finite differences, the w_i on the left-hand side of (23) is replaced by

$$\bar{w}_{it} = \frac{w_{i,t} + w_{i,t-1}}{2}, \tag{31}$$

and a disturbance term (v_{it}) is added. Eventually, we may add an intercept (a_{i0}) and other variables (Δz_{kt}) representing shifts in demand caused by determinants other than income and the prices. The final specification is

$$\bar{w}_{it} \Delta\ln q_{it} = b_i \Delta\ln Q_t + \sum_j s_{ij} \Delta\ln p_{jt} + (a_{i0} + \sum_k a_{ik}\Delta z_{kt}) + v_{it}, \tag{32}$$

with

$$\Delta\ln Q_t = \sum_j \bar{w}_{jt} \Delta\ln q_{jt}. \tag{33}$$

Given this definition and adding-up conditions (24) and (25), we have the additional adding-up conditions

$$\sum_i v_{it} = 0, \tag{34}$$

$$\sum_i a_{il} = 0, \qquad l = 0, 1, \ldots. \tag{35}$$

The CBS Specification

Keller and van Driel (1985) propose a specification that treats the s_{ij} of (22) and the

$$c_i = w_i(\eta_i - 1) \tag{36}$$

as constants, but not the b_i. Their version—the CBS version—of (23) reads

$$w_i(d\ln q_i - d\ln Q) = c_i d\ln Q + \sum_j s_{ij} d\ln p_j. \tag{37}$$

Here the c_i satisfy the adding up condition

$$\sum_i c_i = 0 \tag{38}$$

as can be readily verified.

The dependent variable in (37) is $w_i d\ln(q_i/Q)$. Note that the sum of these variables over i equals zero and that $d\ln(q_i/Q)$ basically is the deviation of the relative change in q_i from the average relative quantity change.

As is obvious from (36) and (21) $c_i = b_i - w_i$, with the b_i being the (now variable) marginal propensity to consume and w_i, as before, the average propensity to consume good i. A positive c_i means $b_i > w_i$ or an income elasticity larger than one (i.e., i is a luxury good). A negative c_i means that η_i is smaller than one (i is a necessity). In general, $c_i = \partial w_i/\partial\ln m$. A negative value of c_i implies that for increasing m, w_i turns negative, which is inadmissible. For positive c_i, w_i may become larger than unity, which is also inadmissible. It is clear that the CBS specification (and for the same reason, the AIDS specification) cannot claim global validity, except for the trivial case of $c_i = 0$ for all i.

Another disadvantage of the CBS specification is that preference independence cannot be specified in terms of constants as in the Rotterdam case.

The CBS estimating equation in terms of first differences takes the form

$$\bar{w}_{it} \Delta \ln\left(\frac{q_{it}}{Q_t}\right) = c_i \Delta \ln Q_t + \sum_j s_{ij} \Delta \ln p_{jt} + (a_{i0}^c + \sum_k a_{ik}^c \Delta z_{kt}) + v_{it}^c, \tag{39}$$

with additional adding-up properties similar to (34) and (35). Note that the sum over i of the dependent variables equals zero.

The AIDS Specification

In their development of the almost ideal demand system (AIDS), Deaton and Muellbauer (1980) employ as constants the c_i defined by (36) and the r_{ij}, which are defined as

$$r_{ij} = w_i(\varepsilon_{ij} + \delta_{ij} - w_j) = s_{ij} + w_i \delta_{ij} - w_i w_j. \tag{40}$$

Using this expression to eliminate the s_{ij} from the right-hand side of (37), we obtain with some rearrangement

$$w_i(d\ln q_i - d\ln Q + d\ln p_i - d\ln P) = c_i d\ln Q + \sum_j r_{ij} d\ln p_j, \tag{41}$$

where $d\ln P$ is defined as in (17b).

The variable on the left-hand side is, in view of (18),

$$w_i(d\ln q_i + d\ln p_i - d\ln m) = w_i d\ln w_i, \tag{42}$$

which is the relative change in the expenditure share of good i multiplied by the expenditure share of i itself. Since

$$w_i d\ln w_i = w_i \left(\frac{dw_i}{w_i}\right) = dw_i, \tag{43}$$

this variable is simply the change in the expenditure share of good i.

It is easily verified from (40), (4) and from (25) through (27) that the r_{ij} satisfy

$$\sum_i r_{ij} = 0 \qquad \text{(AIDS aggregation)}, \tag{44}$$

$$\sum_j r_{ij} = 0 \qquad \text{(homogeneity)}, \tag{45}$$

$$r_{ij} = r_{ji} \quad \text{(symmetry).} \tag{46}$$

There is no counterpart of the negativity condition (28) in terms of constant parameters. It is also not possible to specify preference independence in constants only.

It follows from (40) and (22) that the Slutsky elasticities ε_{ij} can be expressed in terms of the r_{ij} and the (variable) w_i, w_j by

$$\varepsilon_{ij} = \left(\frac{r_{ij}}{w_i}\right) - \delta_{ij} + w_j. \tag{47}$$

Transition to finite differences, addition of a disturbance term, and eventually an intercept and additional variables results in the AIDS estimating equation:

$$\Delta w_{it} = c_i \Delta \ln Q_t + \sum_j r_{ij} \Delta \ln p_{jt} + (a_{i0}^A + \sum_k a_{ik}^A \Delta z_{kt}) + v_{it}^A, \tag{48}$$

with the same types of additional adding-up properties as the other two systems. As in the CBS system the dependent variables add up to zero.

A further qualification is in order. In their presentation of AIDS, Deaton and Muellbauer use two alternatives to specify $d\ln P$. The first is consistent with the expenditure function on which their derivation of AIDS is based and involves the r_{ij}. The second is an approximation of that concept and is the same as the one used here, namely, (17b). The main reason for using it here is to have a system which is linear in the unknown coefficients and which has also, as will become clear in the next subsection, the same variables on the right-hand side as in the two other systems.

A Class of Systems

Note that as far as variables are concerned, the right-hand sides of the demand equations of the three systems are basically equal. Since the dependent variables are different, the coefficients on the right-hand side are interpreted differently across these three systems.

A natural extension to a class of systems can be obtained by taking a convex combination of the dependent variables for each system:

$$(1 - \theta_2)\bar{w}_{it}\Delta \ln q_{it} - \theta_1 \bar{w}_{it} \Delta \ln Q_t + \theta_2 \Delta w_{it}$$

$$= d_i \Delta \ln Q_t + \sum_j t_{ij} \Delta \ln p_{jt}(a_{i0}^M + \sum_k a_{ik}^M \Delta z_{kt}) + v_{it}^M, \tag{49}$$

with $0 \leq \theta_1 \leq 1$, $0 \leq \theta_2 \leq 1$. For $\theta_1 = \theta_2 = 0$, we have the Rotterdam system. For $\theta_1 = 1$ and $\theta_2 = 0$, the CBS system prevails, whereas $\theta_1 = 0$ and $\theta_2 = 1$ result in the AIDS. The coefficients d_i and t_{ij} are related to the coefficients of the original systems by

$$d_i = (1 - \theta_1 - \theta_2)b_i + (\theta_1 + \theta_2)c_1, \tag{50}$$

$$t_{ij} = (1 - \theta_2)s_{ij} + \theta_2 r_{ij}. \tag{51}$$

The properties of these coefficients derive from those for the b_i, c_i, s_{ij}, and r_{ij}. Note that

$$\sum_i d_i = (1 - \theta_1 - \theta_2) \tag{52}$$

and that the negativity property does not hold for t_{ij} with $\theta_2 \neq 0$.

It can be shown that for increasing m, with $0 < 1 - \theta_1 - \theta_2 \leq 1$, the w_i tend to $d_i/(1 - \theta_1 - \theta_2)$, that is, to a constant as in the Rotterdam system. The a_{i0}^M, a_{ik}^M, v_{it}^M satisfy the usual adding up properties. We can express the income elasticities as

$$\eta_i = \frac{d_i}{w_i} + (\theta_1 + \theta_2), \tag{53}$$

and the Slutsky elasticities as

$$\varepsilon_{ij} = \frac{t_{ij}}{w_i} - \theta_2(\delta_{ij} - w_j). \tag{54}$$

It can be verified that with symmetry and homogeneity imposed on the estimation of the t_{ij} the elasticities satisfy all properties implied by demand theory (except negativity for $\theta_2 \neq 0$), even for values of θ_1 and θ_2 outside the $[0, 1]$ interval.

The appeal of (49) is that it can leave somewhat more to be determined by data than would be the case for each of the constituent "elementary" systems while remaining consistent with theory.

13.4   Levels Version

In the preceding section we discussed parametrization in the context of a system in terms of log changes in the system's variables. This context, however, is accidental. What matters is the way in which the elasticities are transformed into constants that satisfy theoretical constraints.

The same approach will be taken to arrive at corresponding levels versions. We will start with a variant of the double-logarithmic demand function (1), namely,

$$\ln q_i = \alpha_i + \eta_i \ln Q' + \sum_j \varepsilon_{ij} \ln p_j, \tag{55}$$

where $\ln Q'$ is a real income variable which we will define later. The ε_{ij} are Slutsky elasticities, which were defined by (8).

Multiplying both sides of (55) by w_i and using Rotterdam specifications (21) and (22), we obtain

$$w_i \ln q_i = a'_{i0} + b_i \ln Q' + \sum_j s_{ij} \ln p_j, \tag{56}$$

with properties (24) through (29) for the b_i and s_{ij}. The a'_{i0} is an additional intercept.

Given adding-up properties (24) and (25), we may write

$$\sum_i w_i \ln q_i = \sum_i a'_{i0} + \ln Q', \tag{57}$$

which in fact defines $\ln Q'$. Using this definition in (56), we can write

$$w_i \ln q_i = \left(a'_{i0} - b_i \sum_j a'_{j0}\right) + b_i \sum_j w_j \ln q_j + \sum_j s_{ij} \ln p_j. \tag{58}$$

With

$$a_{i0} = a'_{i0} - b_i \sum_j a'_{j0} \tag{59}$$

and

$$\ln Q = \sum_i w_i \ln q_i, \tag{60}$$

demand equation (58) can be reformulated as

$$w_i \ln q_i = a_{i0} + b_i \ln Q + \sum_j s_{ij} \ln p_j. \tag{61}$$

It follows from (59) that

$$\sum_i a_{i0} = 0. \tag{62}$$

Clearly, $\ln Q$ is a logarithmic quantity index number and thus a natural measure for real income. Its price counterpart is defined as

$$\ln P = \sum_i w_i \ln p_i. \tag{63}$$

We can verify that:

$$\ln m = \ln Q + \ln P - \ln W, \tag{64}$$

with

$$\ln W = \sum_i w_i \ln w_i \tag{65}$$

which contrasts with (18), the corresponding relation for differentials. Here the factor-reversal test is not satisfied. The usual interpretation of real income as deflated nominal income (in this case m/P) does not correspond to this treatment of Q. Note, however, that the (logarithmic) difference $\ln W$ is usually nearly a constant. Its terms, $w_i \ln w_i$, are less variable than w_i, which itself is only variable insofar as preferences are not homothetic. Their sum is at most zero and at least $-\ln n$, with n being the number of goods considered.

However, replacing $\ln Q$ by $\ln(m/P)$ in (61) is not desirable. The adding-up condition will not be satisfied by the full system. There is moreover, no particular reason to prefer $\ln(m/P)$ as the real income indicator over $\ln Q$. The latter has the advantage of being a quantity concept, and thus a real magnitude.

Expression (61) is proposed as the levels version of the Rotterdam system. To it, of course, disturbance terms and eventually other demand determinants are added. To obtain the levels version of the CBS system, we simply replace b_i in (61) by $c_i + w_i$. The result is

$$w_i \ln\left(\frac{q_i}{Q}\right) = a_{i0}^C + c_i \ln Q + \sum_j s_{ij} \ln p_j. \tag{66}$$

On the left-hand side, we have q_i/Q. Here Q can also be seen as a weighted geometric average of the quantities. So q_i/Q is the ratio of q_i to the average of the q_j's. Note that the sum of the variables on the left-hand side equals zero. The intercepts will also add up to zero.

Substituting (40) for s_{ij} in (66) gives the counterpart of (41):

$$w_i(\ln q_i - \ln Q + \ln p_i - \ln P) = a_{i0}^D + c_i \ln Q + \sum_j r_{ij} \ln p_j. \tag{67}$$

The variable on the left-hand side can also be written as

$$w_i(\ln w_i - \ln W) = w_i \ln\left(\frac{w_i}{W}\right). \tag{68}$$

We have here the ratio of w_i to the (weighted geometric) average of the budget shares. Since $w_i/W = (p_iq_i)/(PQ)$, we may also say that it is the ratio of expenditure on i to the (weighted geometric) average of expenditures. Note also that (68) adds up to zero as does the intercept in (67).

Expression (67) can be considered the natural levels counterpart of the AIDS first difference equations. However, the AIDS equations of Deaton and Muellbauer's original proposal are formulated differently. Their levels analogue of (41) is

$$w_i = a_{i0}^A + c_i \ln Q + \sum_j r_{ij} \ln p_j, \tag{69}$$

with the constants a_{i0}^A adding up to one. In fact, as we have already mentioned when presenting the first differences version of AIDS, Deaton and Muellbauer use m/P^* rather than Q, where P^* is either a price index involving the r_{ij} or P as defined by (63). Here the use of Q instead of deflated income is motivated by the desire to have the right-hand side the same as in the other systems. We will therefore consider (69) as our levels version of AIDS. To avoid confusion, equation (67) is taken to represent a separate system, which we will call the W-system.

By construction, the four systems just presented have the same variables on their right-hand sides. Convex combinations of their left-hand sides then also constitute demand systems in levels.

13.5 Alternative Approaches

Another way to derive levels counterparts for the Rotterdam and CBS systems would be to start from AIDS specification (69). Replacing r_{ij} by the right-hand side of (40) and rearranging terms results in an alternative CBS-type equation:

$$w_i\left(1 - \ln\left(\frac{p_i}{P}\right)\right) = a_{i0}^E + c_i \ln Q + \sum_j s_{ij} \ln p_j, \tag{70}$$

where now the variable on the left-hand side and the intercepts add up to one. The dependent variable can also be written as

$$w_i\left(1 + \ln\left(\frac{q_i}{Q}\right) - \ln\left(\frac{w_i}{W}\right)\right) \tag{71}$$

which makes it more comparable to the left-hand variable of (66).

Next, replacing the c_i in (70) by $b_i - w_i$ gives an alternative Rotterdam-type equation:

$$w_i\left(1 - \ln\left(\frac{p_i}{P}\right) + \ln Q\right) = a_{i0}^F + b_i \ln Q + \sum_j s_{ij} \ln p_j. \tag{72}$$

Its dependent variable is equal to

$$w_i\left(1 + \ln q_i - \ln\left(\frac{w_i}{W}\right)\right), \tag{73}$$

which sums up to $1 + \ln Q$. Note that also in this case the intercepts a_{i0}^F add up to one.

The presence of $1 - \ln(w_i/W)$ in both dependent variables (71) and (73) make these alternatives less intuitively plausible. Still, similarity of the right-hand sides of (70) and (72) with those of the systems of the previous section suggests that the class of systems considered there may be extended further. However, we will not discuss them further here.

Another approach to defining cross-sectional demand systems has been explored by Theil (1983). He basically uses the first differences approach. The variables are taken as first differences from one of the observation units. The various systems could be rather easily converted into proper levels versions were it not that $\bar{w}_{ic}$ appears in $\ln Q_c = \sum_i \bar{w}_{ic}(\ln q_{ic} - \ln q_{is})$ and in the dependent variables of the Rotterdam and CBS systems. Here s refers to the observation unit used as the standard from which the differences are taken and c refers to the unit described. Thus $\bar{w}_{ic} = (w_{ic} + w_{is})/2$. We cannot simply write the differences as differences between two terms of which one is constant across c. The estimation results will generally depend on the observation unit used as standard. It is not clear which unit should be taken as standard.

In such a system we could of course replace $\Delta \ln Q_c$ by $\ln Q_c - \ln Q_s$ with $\ln Q_c = \sum_i w_{ic} \ln q_{ic}$ as in (60). Likewise, we could replace the left-hand side variable of the Rotterdam system by $w_{ic} \ln q_{ic} - w_{is} \ln q_{is}$ and that of the CBS system by $w_{ic} \ln (q_{ic}/Q_c) - w_{is} \ln(q_{is}/Q_s)$. Reordering of terms brings us back to the levels version of the previous section with somewhat more elaborate intercepts. The results will not depend on the unit used as standard. In fact there is no need to single out any unit for that purpose.

If we can use the original Theil approach to choose one unit as the standard one, we have another set of three demand systems with mutually related parametrizations. Their right-hand sides contain the same variables. However, these are not the same as those of the level versions of section 13.4.

13.6 Simulation

By estimating demand systems, we obtain information about coefficients, elasticities, or partial derivatives. The final use of demand systems is to provide information about the quantities demanded. Given m and the prices, knowledge of the budget shares is equivalent. The left-hand sides of the Rotterdam and CBS specifications are not simple functions of the quantities and/or budget shares. Their derivation from the calculated values of the right-hand sides deserves some discussion in view of the possibility of comparing their ability to correctly simulate the actual quantities or budget shares. In this context simulation does not refer to the use of artificial random data generation processes.

The case of AIDS seems to create few problems. The left-hand variable of its levels version is the budget share itself. Assuming that the prices are exogenously given, there are two possible simulations: with Q given and m not, and the reverse of this. If Q is given, the w_i are easily calculated for given values of the coefficients in (69). To solve for Q, however, we need m. This variable is endogenously determined by (64) by using the calculated w_i as weights in (63) and (65). To apply (69) when m rather than Q is given, we proceed first by calculating Q, for which (64) can also be employed. Now, the w_i needed for (63) and (65) are not available. An iterative solution procedure is needed, starting from provisional values for w_i, calculating $\ln Q$, applying (69) to obtain new values for w_i, which serve as the starting values for the new round. This sequence is repeated until successive changes in w_i become smaller in absolute value than some specified minimum. Usually a few iterations are sufficient for this purpose.

Simulation of budget shares and quantities demanded for AIDS in first differences does not create any additional problems. Note that there is no guarantee that simulated w_i stay within the interval between zero and one.

They will add up to one, but some w_i may be negative and others larger than unity.

Simulating with Rotterdam system (61) requires further treatment of the left-hand side variable $w_i \ln q_i$. We will first transform it into an expression in w_i:

$$w_i \ln q_i = w_i(\ln w_i - \ln p_i + \ln m) = w_i(\ln w_i + z_i), \tag{74}$$

with $z_i = \ln m - \ln p_i$. Let y_i be the calculated value of the right-hand side of (61). We then look for the w_i that solves

$$w_i(\ln w_i + z_i) = y_i. \tag{75}$$

Such a solution might not exist. The left-hand side reaches for $w_i = \exp(-1 - z_i)$, its minimum of $-\exp(-1 - z_i)$. If y_i is less than this value, there is no solution to (75). If y_i is larger, there are two solutions: one larger than $\exp(-1 - z_i)$, and the other smaller. The latter will always be non-negative; the larger may be greater than unity and hence be inadmissible. If there are two admissible solutions, a choice has to be made. Often one of the two solutions is rather improbable, leaving one acceptable solution. This, however, cannot be guaranteed in general.

A further aspect of simulation with (61) is similar to the one discussed for AIDS. If Q is given rather than m, there is no problem in obtaining y_i, but we need to calculate m to arrive at z_i. Therefore an iterative procedure is needed. If m is given rather than Q, the reverse happens: z_i can be readily found, but to obtain y_i, we need to calculate Q first, for which w_i are needed. Here also an iterative solution procedure has to be used.

From the point of view of simulation, Rotterdam variant (72) has a simpler left-hand side variable. There are no multiple solutions. Iteration is needed to determine P and, if m is given, to determine Q. Solutions for w_i outside the 0–1 interval may occur.

The possibility of no solution or a two-valued solution also arises in the case of the Rotterdam system in first differences. The situation is slightly different from that of (75) because the equation to be solved is

$$\bar{w}_{it}(\ln w_{it} + z_{it}) = y_{it}, \tag{76}$$

with $\bar{w}_{it}$ on the left-hand side. Here $z_{it} = \ln m_t - \ln p_{it} - \ln q_{i,t-1}$, whereas y_{it} is calculated from the right-hand side of (32) by setting $v_{it} = 0$. The simulation can be made more straightforward when in (76) if $\bar{w}_{it}$ is replaced by predetermined $w_{i,t-1}$.

Similar problems and possibilities exist for the various versions of the CBS system.

From the discussion of determining m if Q is given, it is clear that m is the expenditure needed to pay for the optimal bundle given Q. It is the left-hand side variable of the expenditure function. By simulating with varying prices and constant Q, we can numerically generate price index numbers as the ratios of the m's needed to obtain $\ln Q$ in the two price systems.

13.7 Comparing Empirical Performance

Demand systems are tools for the empirical analysis of consumer behavior. To compare their empirical performance seems natural. However, it is not possible to draw general conclusions from the results for a particular sample or a set of samples. Still, some experimentation can be informative.

Our experiments will involve only the levels versions (61), (66), and (69) of the Rotterdam system, the CBS system, and AIDS, respectively. The comparison should shed some light on the relative merits of the particular parametrizations. The matrix of price coefficients s_{ij} of the Rotterdam and CBS systems will be estimated without imposing negativity condition (28) to maintain comparability with AIDS where such a condition cannot be implemented.

The Data

The three systems are estimated for a cross section of 34 countries in 1975. The U.N. International Comparison Project (ICP) has collected price and quantity data for 151 categories of consumer demand, which have been published by Kravis, Heston, and Summers (1982). The countries of the sample range from (poor, e.g., Malawi) to rich (e.g., the United States). Their price systems show considerable variation. These data seem well suited to tests of empirical performance.

For our purpose the 151 categories of consumer demand are more than is necessary. We have aggregated them into eight major groups. One of these is food. Its budget share ranges from 68 percent for Sri Lanka to 16 percent for the United States—an indication of the wide range of variability in this data set.

It is obvious that the differences in demand behavior across this set of countries have to be attributed to more than differences in prosperity and price structure. One source of difference is that of climate; another is that of the age composition of the population. Altogether six additional variables, taken from Barten and Summers (1986), have been used to account for other determinants of demand than average income and prices. They are mean annual temperature, the average temperature of the coldest month, the average temperature of the warmest month, the percentage of children under 15 years of age, the Gini index of inequality of the income distribution, and the logarithm of the population size. Note that the ICP is already expressed in per capita terms. Population size as an additional variable includes possible economies of scale. These six variables are selected from a class of twelve. The desire not to waste degrees of freedom limited their number to six.

There are many reasons why any demand system would be inadequate to describe the variation in behavior across countries. Demand systems reflect characteristics of individual consumer demand, whereas the data refer to countries in the aggregate. In spite of the enormous effort of the ICP to arrive at comparable data, there is still much disparity. The additional variables are perhaps also not representative enough to absorb explainable variation across countries. The omitted variables could be correlated with the income and price variables causing biases in coefficient estimators. More reasons for the inadequacy in describing behavior can be advanced. Still it is interesting to find out the extent to which the data agree with the proposed models.

The Coefficients of Determination

The DEMMOD computer program has been used to estimate systems of demand equations by maximum likelihood procedures as described in Barten (1969) and Barten and Geyskens (1975). This program calculates the R^2 for each commodity group. But all equations are estimated jointly, and the R^2's are not maximized. Still, they may serve as a simple measure of relative fit (see table 13.1). A simple inspection of the R^2's in table 13.1 shows that CBS scores best, followed by Rotterdam, with AIDS being the weakest.

Information Inaccuracy

One could argue that the R^2's are not really comparable across the three systems because the left-hand side variables differ. One way to test comparability is to let the estimated version of each system generate budget

Table 13.1
Coefficients of determination (R^2)

Commodity group	Rotterdam system	CBS system	AIDS
1. Food	0.811	0.829	0.892
2. Clothing and footwear	0.726	0.910	0.656
3. Housing and fuel	0.699	0.723	0.575
4. Household furnishings and operations	0.788	0.890	0.698
5. Medical care	0.904	0.892	0.890
6. Transport and communications	0.824	0.898	0.689
7. Education	0.507	0.748	0.566
8. Remainder	0.809	0.789	0.687

Table 13.2
Average information accuracy

System	Full sample	Reduced sample
Rotterdam	0.0326	0.0326
CBS	0.1785	0.1172
AIDS	0.0141	0.0141

shares (see the preceding section) and then to compare the simulated budget shares with the actual ones.

A useful aggregate measure of the divergence between observed and predicted budget shares is Theil's (1967) concept of information inaccuracy, which is defined as

$$I_c = \sum_i w_{ic}(\ln w_{ic} - \ln \hat{w}_{ic}), \qquad (77)$$

where w_{ic} refers to the observed and $\hat{w}_{ic}$ to the calculated budget shares for commodity i and country c. For our purpose we will use the average information inaccuracy:

$$I = \frac{\sum_c I_c}{34}. \qquad (78)$$

The results are given in table 13.2.

A lower value for I means better performance. From table 13.2 it is clear that AIDS dominates the other two systems. The CBS system is particularly weak. Calculating predicted shares for AIDS did not cause any problems.

For the Rotterdam and CBS systems, the work was less simple. The simulation failed to converge for at least one country using the Rotterdam system and for no less than thirteen countries using the CBS system. Omitting these countries from the calculation of I gives the results of the last column of table 13.2. The picture has not changed drastically.

It is not clear whether this remaining divergence in predictive behavior is due to shortcomings in the simulation procedure, or to the fact that predicting w_{ic} is just what AIDS is optimizing, or even to the superiority of the AIDS parameterization for this type of data.

Income and Price Elasticities

Another way to compare the three systems is to evaluate the implied income and price elasticities to see to what extent they correspond to theoretical and intuitive prior ideas. For all three system, the elasticities are not estimated as such but they can be calculated from the estimated coefficients and the budget shares for a particular country. In this case the elasticities are evaluated for Italy because its budget shares correspond closely to the average elasticities for the whole sample.

In table 13.3 are listed the values of the elasticity of demand for a commodity with respect to Q, the "income" elasticity, and in table 13.4 the

Table 13.3
Income elasticities for Italy

Commodity group	Rotterdam system	CBS system	AIDS
1. Food	0.38	0.81	0.86
	(0.59)	(0.11)	(0.09)
2. Clothing and footwear	0.85	1.10	0.99
	(0.71)	(0.06)	(0.11)
3. Housing and fuel	2.46	1.27	1.24
	(0.92)	(0.14)	(0.14)
4. Household furnishings and operations	1.97	0.96	1.18
	(1.03)	(0.12)	(0.17)
5. Medical Care	1.35	1.04	1.12
	(0.60)	(0.08)	(0.08)
6. Transport and communications	1.85	1.21	1.13
	(0.70)	(0.08)	(0.12)
7. Education	−0.63	0.74	0.71
	(1.06)	(0.17)	(0.16)
8. Remainder	0.81	1.14	1.02
	(0.88)	(0.13)	(0.13)

values of the Slutsky elasticity of demand for a commodity with respect to its own price. In parentheses under the elasticity values are the standard errors.

Form table 13.3 it appears that the income elasticities for CBS and AIDS are rather similar, as one would expect of the same type of parametrization for the effect of real income. Also the standard errors are roughly equal. All of the elasticities turn out to be close to unity. This reflects the fact that the underlying c_i are close to zero.

As indicated in section 13.3, the nonzero c_i cause problems for asymptotic behavior. With zero c_i, such problems are avoided. The present sample with its wide variation in Q ($Q_{max}/Q_{min} = 12.6$) seems to force the c_i toward zero.

Zero c_i suggest linear Engel curves. The Rotterdam system should agree with that. The results of table 13.3 are not in accordance with this expectation. There is a substantial and unusual variation in the Rotterdam income elasticities, which is suspicious. Moreover the standard errors are fairly large. The Rotterdam specification does not seem to adjust very gracefully to the wide variation in Q and in the budget share of this particular sample.

The inadequate performance of the Rotterdam system reveals itself also in the estimated values of the own Slutsky elasticities. Only three out of

Table 13.4
Own Slutsky elasticities for Italy

Commodity group	Rotterdam system	CBS system	AIDS
1. Food	2.67 (0.95)	−0.19 (0.09)	−0.18 (0.15)
2. Clothing and footwear	−2.04 (0.92)	−0.93 (0.08)	−1.06 (0.07)
3. Housing and fuel	1.65 (0.87)	−0.38 (0.12)	−0.51 (0.13)
4. Household furnishings and operations	−2.14 (1.25)	−1.07 (0.17)	−1.19 (0.21)
5. Medical Care	2.44 (0.56)	−0.34 (0.08)	−0.44 (0.07)
6. Transport and communications	1.99 (0.91)	−0.62 (0.11)	−0.46 (0.07)
7. Education	0.49 (0.77)	−0.78 (0.13)	−0.70 (0.11)
8. Remainder	−2.31 (1.43)	−1.00 (0.23)	−1.03 (0.17)

the eight elasticities have the theoretically expected negative sign. The two other systems have no problem with the negativity of the own Slutsky elasticity. Here also the Rotterdam elasticities are large in absolute value, like the corresponding standard errors.

Despite the different parametrizations of price coefficients for CBS and AIDS, the implied elasticity values for Italy are rather close. They are roughly comparable in size to what one usually obtains for such elasticities for highly aggregate commodity groups with few, if any, close substitutes.

The difference between the Rotterdam and the CBS Slutsky elasticities is then even more surprising since they are based on the same parametrization. The difference in the specification of the effect of real income appears to be dominating.

A More Formal Test

The comparisons discussed so far have been descriptive. It is not easy to assess the statistical significance of differences in performances. Note that the systems considered are not nested. The well-established theory of model selection when the various alternatives are nested cannot be applied.

The present set of systems distinguishes itself from the usual context of nonnested model selection by having the same right-hand sides. This property can be conveniently exploited.

Consider, for example, the following linear combination of the Rotterdam and CBS dependent variables:

$$(1 - \theta)w_{ic} \ln q_{ic} + \theta w_{ic} \ln \left(\frac{q_{ic}}{Q_c}\right). \tag{79}$$

For a given value of θ, we can estimate the coefficients on the right-hand side in the usual way and obtain a (maximum) likelihood value. Clearly, for $\theta = 0$, we have the maximum likelihood value for the Rotterdam system, and for $\theta = 1$, the maximum likelihood value for the CBS system.

We can, of course, also estimate θ itself by maximum likelihood procedures. Under either hypothesis it will be a consistent estimator of 0 or 1, respectively. The greater proximity to one of these values in finite samples is then seen as a rejection of the empirical validity of the other.

In the present case θ was estimated by maximizing the likelihood function concentrated on θ only. The square root of the reciprocal of the second-order derivative of the quadratic approximation evaluated at the maximizing value for θ serves as its standard error.

Table 13.5
Logarithmic likelihood values and test statistics

Rotterdam/CBS		Rotterdam/AIDS		CBS/AIDS	
θ	ln L	θ	ln L	θ	ln L
0	245	0	245	0	742
1	742	1	683	1	683
1.14	818	1.18	1062	0.21	751
(0.01)		(0.00)		(0.01)	

The same approach can be used for the pairwise comparison between the Rotterdam system and AIDS and between the CBS system and AIDS. Note that this test is symmetric for the two alternatives in each pair—that is, replacing θ by $1 - \xi$ in (79) will simply reverse the roles of the two alternatives, but the optimizing ξ will be one minus the optimizing θ.

The results for the optimizing θ values are given in table 13.5, together with (in parentheses) their standard errors and the corresponding logarithmic likelihood values. To complete the picture, the logarithmic likelihood values for the elementary systems are given as well.

From the table 13.5 it is obvious that the Rotterdam system is dominated by both the CBS system and AIDS. The optimizing θ values are in both comparisons closer to one than to zero. The small standard errors reflect the sharp peak in the likelihood function at the relevant point. (They may overstate the small sample precision of the optimizing θ values.) The 0.21 value for θ in the CBS/AIDS comparison may be interpreted as a rejection of AIDS.

We might argue that the substantial increases in the likelihoods when θ is estimated suggests the rejection of all three systems in favor of some hybrid system. It might very well be that each system is too rigid in its parametrization and that some simple relaxation may improve the empirical performance drastically. It is beyond the scope of this chapter to investigate this approach further.

A Final Evaluation

The various comparisons of the three systems have not created an entirely clear picture. The Rotterdam system appears to be the least satisfactory as far as coefficients estimates and likelihood value are concerned. The CBS system does not fare well in simulation. The R^2's of AIDS are relatively weak. Still, apart from the simulation problem, CBS seems to be best. AIDS is a close runner-up. The specification of the effect of real income appears to be crucial.

As mentioned at the beginning of this section, these conclusions are specific for the data set used and do not necessarily carry over to an application of levels versions to, for instance, time series data.

13.8   Concluding Remarks

We started with specifications for the Rotterdam, CBS, and almost ideal demand systems for first differences in the logarithm of the relevant variables and derived analogous systems for the levels of the logarithms of those variables. In each system the right-hand side was the same but not the left-hand side. Nevertheless, even with the same coefficients, more than one variant could be used on the left-hand sides.

The Rotterdam parametrization uses constant marginal budget shares and constant price coefficients that are simple transformations of the Slutsky elasticities and therefore easy to interpret. The price coefficients of AIDS are less convenient in that respect. AIDS takes the difference between the marginal and average budget shares as constant. The CBS system uses the same type of income coefficients as AIDS and the Rotterdam type of price coefficients.

The constant marginal budget shares used in the Rotterdam system imply constant average shares for high budget levels. Similarly, keeping the difference between the marginal and average budget shares constant (AIDS and CBS) is only possible for high budget levels if this difference is zero. Equal marginal and average budget shares means that both are constant. In this respect the three systems are less different than appears on first sight.

The 1975 ICP cross section of 34 countries displays considerable variation in the variables. It has a wide (real) income range and widely varying budget shares. Because the variations in budget shares cannot be attributed to differences in price structures and determinants other than (real) income, one might expect all three systems not to describe these data well. But it appears that the CBS specification has hardly any problem with this. Its implied values for income elasticities are close to one, however, suggesting independence of the budget shares from income. For AIDS a similar conclusion can be made. The Rotterdam specification seems to agree less well with these data. This is no doubt due to the use of constant marginal budget shares.

The development of the various systems has also introduced hybrid forms—linear (convex) combinations of the underlying elementary systems. These might offer better adjustment to the data, although somewhat less suitable interpretation of the results. However, as our experiments indicate, there is still room for improvement of the empirical performance of the various elementary systems.

Note

The author is indebted to Leon Bettendorf for his assistance on the empirical applications. He also thanks an anonymous referee for his constructive remarks. The author remains solely responsible for possible errors. Research for this project was supported by the Belgian Science Foundation (FKFO) and the Research Fund of the Katholieke Universiteit Leuven.

References

Barten, A. P. 1969. "Maximum Likelihood Estimation of a Complete System of Demand Equations." *European Economic Review* 1:7–73.

Barten, A. P., and E. Geyskens. 1975. "The Negativity Condition in Consumer Demand." *European Economic Review* 6:227–260.

Barten, A. P., and R. Summers. 1986. "An International Demand Model with Varying Tastes." Paper presented at the Eurostat Seminar on the 'Use of Purchasing Power Parities', 17–20 November 1986.

Deaton, A., and J. Muellbauer. 1980. "An Almost Ideal Demand System." *American Economic Review* 70:312–326.

Frisch, R. 1959. "A Complete Scheme for Computing All Direct and Cross Demand Elasticities in a Model with Many Sectors." *Econometrica* 27:177–196.

Keller, W. J., and J. van Driel. 1985. "Differential Consumer Demand Systems." *European Economic Review* 27:375–390.

Kravis, I. B., A. Heston, and R. Summers. 1982. *World Product and Income, International Comparisons of Reals Gross Product.* Baltimore: Johns Hopkins University Press.

Theil, H. 1965. "The Information Approach to Demand Analysis." *Econometrica* 33:67–87.

Theil, H. 1967. *Economics and Information Theory.* Amsterdam: North Holland.

Theil, H. 1983. "World Product and Income: A Review Article." *Journal of Political Economy* 91:505–517.

14 Bayesian Specification Tests

Jean-Pierre Florens and Michel Mouchart

14.1 Introduction

Following the pioneering work of Hausman (1978) the recent econometric literature gives evidence of significant developments in the analysis of the so-called *specification tests*, with an important application to testing the exogeneity of some variables in an econometric model (see, e.g., Hausman and Taylor 1981; Holly 1982; Holly and Sargan 1982; Nakamura and Nakamura 1981; or Wu 1973, 1974). A general presentation of this kind of testing procedure can be found in Hausman (1978), Holly and Monfort (1986), or in Monfort (1982), but we briefly recall the general principles of this approach in the first part of this introduction.

We consider a *statistical experiment* in which the *sample space* is S and the family of sampling probabilities is denoted P^a, where a is an element of the *parameter space* A. Let us assume that $\tilde{b}$ and $\tilde{c}$ are two vector-valued functions defined on A. The principle of the specification tests is to test an hypothesis characterized by a particular value c_0 of $\tilde{c}$ through its implications on the inference on $\tilde{b}$ by comparing $\hat{b}(c_0)$ and $\hat{b}$, estimators of $\tilde{b}$ using or not the hypothesis on $\tilde{c}$. A convenient interpretation is obtained by assuming that $\tilde{b}$ represents parameters of interest while the components of $\tilde{c}$ may be viewed as nuisance parameters (as far as they are not functions of $\tilde{b}$). In particular, if $A \subseteq \mathbb{R}^k$ and $a = (b, c)$, $\hat{b}(c_0)$ and $\hat{b}$ may be obtained by the maximum likelihood method, constraining or not c to be equal to a particular value c_0. Under usual regularity conditions, we have, under the null hypothesis:

$$\sqrt{n}(\hat{b} - b) \xrightarrow{\mathscr{L}} N(0, \Sigma^a)$$

$$\sqrt{n}(\hat{b}(c_0) - b) \xrightarrow{\mathscr{L}} N(0, \Omega^a)$$

$$\sqrt{n}(\hat{b} - \hat{b}(c_0)) \xrightarrow{\mathscr{L}} N(0, V^a)$$

where the asymptotic variances Σ^a and Ω^a are derived from the computation of the information matrix, and with $V^a = \Sigma^a - \Omega^a$ as shown by Hausman (1978). A natural test statistic is then $n(\hat{b} - \hat{b}(c_0))'(V^a)^+(\hat{b} - \hat{b}(c_0))$ asymptotically distributed, under the null hypothesis, as a χ^2 variate (where V^+ is the Moore-Penrose inverse of V). Conditions for the asymptotic equivalence of this test and the usual tests (Wald, likelihood-ratio or score tests) are given in Holly and Monfort (1986).

The objective of this chapter is to analyze the specification test approach in a Bayesian framework. Several considerations motivate this work. First, the Bayesian analysis enriches the class of test statistics by allowing one to take into account nondogmatic prior informations or by suggesting new procedures like the comparison of the whole posterior distributions on the parameters of interest conditionally or not to the hypothesis being tested. Second, the Bayesian approach allows the statistician to introduce the hypothesis to be tested as a conditioning on the parameter space considered as a probability space. This analysis, in terms of *conditioning* instead of *restrictions*, is known to be relevant in practice as far as it provides a natural solution to Borel-Kolmogorov type of paradoxes (see Kolmogorov 1956, p. 51; Florens, Mouchart, and Richard 1974, p. 422; or Florens, Mouchart and Rolin 1984, sec. 1.3.3.B). The last interest is more general: testing and "Bayesianism" are too often considered as incompatible, and we want to illustrate how the testing philosophy can be used by a Bayesian statistician. The approach of this chapter may be viewed as an alternative to the use of posterior odds (see, e.g., Zellner 1971) and is deemed to be closer to the traditional testing philosophy while staying within a Bayesian framework.

Section 14.2 is devoted to present the main lines of the approach we suggest for testing within a Bayesian framework. This section covers a field more general than the specification test in the sense recalled above and exposits general ideas on Bayesian tests. Section 14.3 is concentrated on the specification tests viewed as a comparison between marginal and conditional inference and presents three different approaches for such a comparison. Some examples illustrate the discussion in these two sections, but in section 14.4 two particular problems are treated in more detail. We have chosen two very standard ones: the test of a particular value of some coefficients in a linear regression model and the test of an exogeneity property.

14.2   Bayesian Testing

Doubt in Bayesian analysis

Traditional *Bayesian models* are specified through a unique probability measure, Π, on a product space, $A \times S$, where A is the parameter space and S is the sample space. This model is typically built from a "prior probability" μ on A and a family of "sampling probabilities" P^a on S

indexed by $a \in A$. Bayesian techniques are based on the dual decomposition of Π into a "predictive probability" P on S and a family of "posterior probabilities" μ^s on A. Under technical conditions ensuring that the families P^a and μ^s become regular conditional probabilities, a *Bayesian experiment* may be synthetically described through

$$\Pi_{A \times S} = \mu_A \otimes P_S^a = P_S \otimes \mu_A^s. \tag{1a}$$

As far as notation is concerned, $\otimes$ represents a Markovian product extending (through Neveu 1970, prop. 3.2.1.) the product of two independent probabilities; Π, μ, and P systematically denote probability measures on $A \times S$, A, and S, respectively; upper indices denote conditioning, and lower indices denote marginalizing. As a matter of fact, lower indices will be suppressed in case of trivial marginalizing (i.e., marginalizing through identities). Thus formula (1a) can also be written as

$$\Pi = \mu \otimes P^a = P \otimes \mu^s. \tag{1b}$$

Note also that the lowercase letters in the upper indices indicate (regular) conditional probabilities defined through a family of probability measures that are indexed by (almost all) points of a set, whereas the capital letters suggest the set supporting the probabilities. More precise interpretation of formula (1a) may be obtained by reading both lowercase and capital letters as σ-fields on the product space $A \times S$ (see Florens et al. 1984).

In dominated experiments the symmetric decomposition of the joint probability becomes

$$\pi(a, s) = \mu(a)p(s|a) = p(s)\mu(a|s) \tag{1c}$$

where $\pi(a, s)$ is the joint density, $p(s|a)$ and $p(s)$ are the data and the predictive densities, and $\mu(a)$ and $\mu(a|s)$ are the prior and the posterior densities. Note that in this chapter any equalities involving conditional expectations and densities hold almost surely only with respect to the joint probability Π. This caveat will, however, be systematically omitted in what follows.

A characteristic feature of Bayesian methods is to probabilize *all* elements of a statistical problem (i.e., both parameters and observations) through a joint probability Π representing a "state of information" at a given instant. Taking Π as a starting point, an *information structure* may be viewed as a function defined on $A \times S$—that is, $\tilde{m} : A \times S \rightarrow M$, where M is the set of possible *message* given by $\tilde{m}$. Thus any new information, or messages, is formalized as the knowledge of the value $m_0 \in M$ of some function $\tilde{m}$. Note that the set M is, in general, arbitrary. When such a message is not questioned, Π is eventually conditioned on the value of that message. In this approach an exact restriction on the parameter space is represented by the value c_0 of a function $\tilde{c}: A \to C$ and is handled by revising Π into Π^{c_0}, and the observation of a sample is represented by the value t_0 of a statistic $\tilde{t}: S \to T$ and used to revise into Π^{t_0}. Parametric inference (respectively, prediction) is eventually characterized by the transformation $\mu \to \mu^{t_0}$ (resp., $P \to P^{t_0}$). In these case $M = C$ (resp., $M = T$), and defining $\tilde{c}$ (resp., $\tilde{t}$) on A (resp., S) rather than on $A \times S$ simply means that if $\tilde{c}$ (resp., $\tilde{t}$) were defined on $A \times S$ rather than on A (resp., T), the value of $\tilde{c}(a, s)$ (resp., $\tilde{t}(a, s)$) would depend on a (resp., s) only. Note that a slightly more general approach would consider the information structure as a σ-field $\mathcal{M}$ of subsets of $A \times S$; typically that σ-field would be the one generated by the function $\tilde{m}$.

Let us now consider situations where the message m_0 is perceived as questionable. It should be stressed that such doubts symmetrically regard the message m_0 and the Bayesian model characterized by $\Pi_{A \times S}$; in other words, the doubt questions whether message (m_0) and model (Π) "conform" to each other. For instance, "surprising" (from the point of view of the predictive distribution) observations may lead us to question the prior probability as well as the sampling process. This situation may be formalized as follows:

A partition (M_0, M_1) of M is called a *critical partition of level* α if $\Pi(M_0) = 1 - \alpha$ and $\Pi(M_1) = \alpha$ (with the usual convention that $\Pi(M_j)$ stands for $\Pi(\tilde{m}^{-1}(M_j), j = 0, 1)$ along with the interpretation "any message m_0 falling in M_0 will be *accepted* in the sense that Π will eventually be revised into Π^{m_0}, whereas any message m_0 falling in M_1 will be *rejected* in the sense that Π will not be revised into Π^{m_0} but first be respecified in order to deal with the apparent conflict between m_0 and Π."

The following examples may help to illustrate this idea. In each cases we specify Π through $(s|a) \sim N(a, 1)$ and $a \sim N(0, 1)$ so that $s \sim N(0, 2)$ and $(a|s) \sim N(\frac{1}{2}s, \frac{1}{2})$.

EXAMPLE 1 *In this example the "message" is an observation, that is, $M = S$. Let us consider $M_1 = \{s \in S; |s| \ge \sqrt{2}z_{\alpha/2}\}$ when $z_{\alpha/2}$ is the $(\alpha/2)$ fractile of a $N(0, 1)$ variate. The interpretation may be that upon observing a value of s "far" from his (predictive) expectation (e.g., $s = 10$ or 100 or 1000, etc.), a statistician whose beliefs are represented by Π might be quite surprised and might reasonably be led to question Π (more specifically, P, his predictive* *probability) and/or s. One may also view* M_1 *as representing the set of observations to be considered as "outliers" with the interpretation that inference (or prediction) to be based on observations falling in* M_1 *should eventually consider a respecification of* Π *before being operated.*

EXAMPLE 2   *This example presents a situation of hypothesis testing before an observation has been obtained. Let us consider* $M = A$ *and* $M_1 = \{a \in A; |a| \geq z_{\alpha/2}\}$. *The interpretation may be that under a given specification of* Π, *the statistician, being told that "a is exactly equal to 10 (or 100 or ...)," might reasonably question whether the message* $a = 10$ *(or 100, or ...) conforms with his model* Π *(in this case, with his prior probability).*

EXAMPLE 3   *The final example presents a more natural situation of testing a hypothesis (here, a specific value of a) in the presence of a given observation. Let us now consider* $M = A \times S$ *and* $M_1 = \{(a,s) \in A \times S; [a - \frac{1}{2}s]^2 > \frac{1}{2}\chi^2_{1;\alpha}\}$, *where* $\chi^2_{1;\alpha}$ *is the* α-*fractile of a* χ^2 *variable with one degree of freedom. The interpretation may be that in observing a sample* s_0 *and being told that the value of a is* a_0, *our statistician might be quite surprised if, relative to the posterior variance,* a_0 *is "very far" from* $E(a|s_0)$.

The last example suggests that the nonconformity of the message (a_0, s_0) with Π may lead us to treat a_0 and s_0 differently; in particular, it might be reasonable, in some cases, to "accept" s_0 (e.g., because s_0 is not very far in the tail of the predictive probability) and to "reject" a_0 once s_0 has been accepted. This topic is precisely the object of next section.

Bayesian Testing as Treatment of Unreliable Messages

In the sampling theory of hypothesis testing, a crucial equation concerns the role of the alternative hypothesis. This role is minor in most nonparametric tests or in specification tests, as shown in White (1982), where the question is whether an observed data conforms with an hypothesized model (see also Newey 1985 for extensions of White's paper and for an explicit introduction on alternative hypotheses). In such a context the power function is barely relevant, and the conclusion of the test is in the spirit of either go on with the model or give it up. This situation is very close to example 1. In a slightly more general setup, the message $\tilde{m} : A \times S \to M$ would be represented through a function $\tilde{m}_* : S \to M$ such that $\tilde{m}(a,s) = \tilde{m}_*(s)$, $\forall(a,s)$, and the level of the critical partition (M_0, M_1) would depend on only the predictive probability P on S. This suggests a strategy for the Bayesian specification, to systematically control the predictive behavior of the data. This issue will not be pursued here.

We will rather proceed to an analysis of parametric testing. In a Bayesian framework a hypothesis (a "null" hypothesis) is viewed as a value c_0 of a function $\tilde{c}$ defined on only the parameter space, and we will write C for the range of $\tilde{c}$. Let us now consider the hypothesis $\tilde{c}(a) = c_0$ as a message. Clearly, this message can be questioned, in the prior distribution, before any observation has been obtained: this is the meaning of example 2 and will not be elaborated here. The more interesting situation is, as in example 3, to consider a compound message $m_0 = (c_0, t_0)$, where $t_0 = \tilde{t}(s)$ is the realization of a statistic and $c_0 = \tilde{c}(a)$ represents a hypothesis. Without loss of generality we will now restrict the attention to the case in which the message has the form $m_0 = (c_0, s_0)$, where $c_0 = \tilde{c}(a)$ and s_0 is a particular realization of the sample. (If t_0 were different from s_0, one could first marginalize the sampling probability on $\tilde{t}(s)$.)

The critical partition defined above is usually defined through a *test function* $\tilde{d}$ which is a positive real-valued random variable defined on $C \times S$ such that the critical region M_1 is equal to the subset of $C \times S$ defined by $M_1(\alpha) = \{(c, s) | \tilde{d}(c, s) > \eta_\alpha\}$, where η_α is the critical value of level α (i.e., such that $\Pi(M_1(\alpha)) = \alpha$)) and $\tilde{d}$ is a measure of discrepancy between (c, s) and Π.

A class of test functions may be introduced by considering a *parameter of interest* that is defined by a function $\tilde{b}$ from the parameter space A to a space B. If we denote $b = \tilde{b}(a)$, then $\mu(b|s_0)$ and $\mu(b|s_0, c_0)$ represent the posterior distributions of b given the realization s_0 of the sampling process and given both $s = s_0$ and $\tilde{c}(a) = c_0$, respectively. These two probabilities are easily derived from Π. Note that in some cases (e.g., when there are common elements in $\tilde{b}(a)$ and $\tilde{c}(a)$) the distribution of b given c and s could be partially or totally degenerate, but for simplicity, we note this distribution by its density (with respect to a degenerate measure if necessary). In most circumstances one would "accept" the part s_0 of the message m_0 and question the part c_0 of m_0. Thus $\mu(b|s_0)$ would represent the information on b given the unquestionable part of the message, whereas $\mu(b|s_0, c_0)$ would incorporate the questionable part of the message; the test function would then be built through a comparison between these two posterior distributions. Different kinds of comparison will be introduced later, but first we want to distinguish between two situations.

If $\tilde{b}(a) = \tilde{c}(a)$ or, somewhat more generally, if $\tilde{b}(a)$ is a function of $\tilde{c}(a)$, the posterior distribution of b given s_0 and c_0 is a Dirac measure that is independent of the sampling result. Equivalently, in such a case $b(a)$ is perfectly known under the hypothesis $\tilde{c}(a) = c_0$. This case may be called a *significance testing problem*.

A *specification testing problem* arises when $\tilde{b}(a)$ is not a function of $\tilde{c}(a)$. This definition is analogous to the definition used by Hausman (1978), Hausman and Taylor (1981), Holly (1982), etc. An important example is when $\mu(b|s_0)$ is dominated by $\mu(b|s_0, c_0)$, that is, when any null set for $\mu(b|s_0, c_0)$ is also a null set for $\mu(b|s_0)$. Then comparisons of $\mu(b|s_0)$ and $\mu(b|s_0, c_0)$ through divergences may be meaningfully evaluated.

Null and Alternative Models

Let $\tilde{d}$ be a test function. We want to study the distribution and some properties of $\tilde{d}$ as a random variable in order to find the critical value (analysis of $\tilde{d}$ under the null model) or its power and consistency properties (analysis of $\tilde{d}$ under alternative models).

The null model unambiguously defines the restriction $\Pi_{C \times S}$ of the joint probability Π on $C \times S$, but the properties of $\tilde{d}$ under $\Pi_{C \times S}$ may be considered under three different points of view. In a *strictly Bayesian* approach, the distribution or the properties of $\tilde{d}$ are derived from the joint probability $\Pi_{C \times S}$, and both c and s are considered as random. In a *posterior analysis*, $\tilde{d}$ is examined relative to the posterior distribution of c given s. This viewpoint is coherent with the absence of doubt about the observed value of s. The last approach may be called *pseudoclassical*, and it examines $\tilde{d}$ with respect to the sampling probability integrated with respect to $\mu(a|c)$. If $\tilde{c}(a) = a$, this approach almost mimics the usual classical one in the sense that the Bayesian model is used for defining only $\tilde{d}$. If $\tilde{c}(a) \neq a$, this analysis differs from the classical one by the treatment of the parameters that are not in $\tilde{c}(a)$: they are integrated here out with respect to the prior distribution on a given c.

EXAMPLE 4 *We extend somewhat the previous examples. Let us assume that* $(s|a) \sim N(a, (\sigma^2/n))$ *and* $a \sim N(a^p, \sigma^{p2})$. *Then* $(a|s) \sim N(a^*, \sigma^{*2})$, *and* $s \sim N(a^p, (\sigma^2/n) + \sigma^{p2})$, *where*

$$a^* = \left(\left(\frac{1}{\sigma^{p2}} \right) + \left(\frac{n}{\sigma^2} \right) \right)^{-1} \left(\left(\frac{a^p}{\sigma^{p2}} \right) + \left(\frac{n}{\sigma^2} \right) s \right),$$

$$\sigma^{*2} = \left(\left(\frac{1}{\sigma^{p2}} \right) + \left(\frac{n}{\sigma^2} \right) \right)^{-1}.$$

Here the superscript p and the asterisk (*) denote parameters of the prior and posterior distributions, respectively.

Let us now consider the message $m_0 = (a_0, s_0)$ in which case $\tilde{c}(a) = a$. Moreover we suppose $\tilde{b}(a) = a$. The test function is deduced from the properties of the difference $a^* - a$. We can easily check that $a^* - a$ is distributed as $N(0, \sigma^{*2})$ with respect to the joint distribution and to the posterior distribution but $a^* - a$ given a is $N((\sigma^{*2}/\sigma^{p2})(a^p - a), (n\sigma^{*4}/\sigma 2))$. A suitable test function is then $(a^* - a)2/\sigma^{*2}$ which follows a $\chi^2_{(1)}$-distribution in small samples both under the joint probability and under the posterior distribution, whereas its sampling distribution (i.e., given a) is also distributed as $\chi^2_{(1)}$ but only asymptotically.

Knowledge of the null hypothesis is sufficient to evaluate the level of a critical partition, but the usual theory of hypothesis testing requires explicit alternative models when analyzing power or consistency. We follow Newey's (1986) approach. Let g be a function from $C \times \Gamma$ into C, where Γ is a set such that there exists an element γ_0 in Γ satisfying $g(c, \gamma_0) = c$ for any $c \in C$. We can now define $\{\Pi^\gamma_{C \times S} : \gamma \in \Gamma\}$, a family of probabilities on $C \times S$, such that

$$\Pi^\gamma_{C \times S} = \mu_C \otimes P_S^{g(c, \gamma)},$$

$$\Pi^{\gamma_0}_{C \times S} = \Pi_{C \times S} = \mu_C \otimes P_S^c.$$

An interesting development of this approach can be obtained when Γ is a group operating on C through g, in which case γ_0 would be the unit element, but we will not pursue this here.

EXAMPLE 5   This example is an extension of example 4. Let us choose $\Gamma = \mathbb{R}$ and $g(a, \gamma) = a + \gamma$, where $\gamma_0 = 0$. Thus $\Pi^\gamma_{A \times S}$ is characterized by the prior probability $N(a^p, \sigma^{p2})$ and by the probability on S given a and γ, which is $N(a + \gamma, (\sigma^2/n))$. Then, under Π^γ, $\tilde{d}(a, s) = (a^* - a)^2/\sigma^{*2}$ is a noncentral $\chi^2_{(1)}$ with a noncentrality parameter equal to γ^2. Γ is a new parameter set, and the hypothesis to be tested is now $\gamma = \gamma_0$. But the enlarged model introducing γ as a parameter has two particular features. First, Γ is not endowed with a prior measure, and second, a large part of the test procedure does not involve Γ.

14.3   Bayesian Specification Tests

We start with a Bayesian model characterized by a proability Π on $A \times S$ and with two functions $\tilde{b}$ and $\tilde{c}$ defined on A and taking their values in B and C. Here $b = \tilde{b}(a)$ is the parameter of interest, and the message is a pair $m_0 = (c_0, s_0)$ consisting of a particular value of $\tilde{c}(a)$ and of the sample. We want to test the value c_0 by comparing the posterior distribution of b given $s = s_0$ and given both $s = s_0$ and $c = c_0$. We successively consider three kinds of comparisons. We first compare the conditional expectations $E(b|s_0)$ and $E(b|c_0, s_0)$; next we compare the whole posterior distributions $\mu(b|s_0)$ and $\mu(b|c_0, s_0)$. Finally, we present a comparison based on an encompassing point of view using a Bayesian notion of pseudotrue value.

Comparison between Marginal and Conditional Posterior Expectations

We want to examine the properties of $\xi(c, s) = E(b|c, s) - E(b|s)$ as a function of c and s. Typically a test function would have the form $[E(b|c, s) - E(b|s)]' H [E(b|c, s) - E(b, s)]$, where H is a suitably chosen SPDS matrix. Such a procedure may be viewed as a Bayesian counterpart to the classical analysis of specification tests (as in Hausman and Taylor 1981; or Holly 1982): $E(b|s_0)$ replaces the (unconstrained) maximum likelihood estimator of b, and $E(b|c_0, s_0)$ replaces the maximum likelihood estimator constrained by the hypothesis to be tested.

EXAMPLE 6   *Let us assume that* $a \in \mathbb{R}^k$ *with* $a = \binom{b}{c}$, *and suppose that a is distributed a posteriori as* $N(a^*, \Sigma^*)$. *Partitioning* a^* *and* Σ^* *into*

$$a^* = \begin{pmatrix} b^* \\ c^* \end{pmatrix} \quad and \quad \Sigma^* = \begin{pmatrix} \Sigma^*_{bb} & \Sigma^*_{bc} \\ \Sigma^*_{cb} & \Sigma^*_{cc} \end{pmatrix},$$

we have $E(b|s_0) = b^*$ *and* $E(b|c_0, s_0) = b^* + \Sigma^*_{bc}(\Sigma^*_{cc})^{-1}(c_0 - c^*)$; *thus the difference* $E(b|s_0, c_0) - E(b|s_0)$ *is equal to* $\Sigma^*_{bc}(\Sigma^*_{cc})^{-1}(c_0 - c^*)$. *Note that if* $\Sigma^*_{bc} = 0$ *(i.e., if b and c are a posteriori independent), this function is 0 for any* c_0 *and* s_0.

The remark given at the end of the preceding example can be generalized: if b and c are a posteriori independent, $E(b|s)$ and $E(b|c, s)$ are almost surely ("a.s." henceforth) equal (in s and c), and the difference between these two expectations is a.s. zero. Then any hypothesis on c will be accepted. This result is, however, not paradoxical because, if b and c are a posteriori independent, the value of c is irrelevant for the inference on b; it is therefore natural that in situations where testing is motivated by only the inference on b, specification testing becomes inoperative under such a posterior independence.

Let us now examine the properties of ξ under the null model $\Pi_{C \times S}$.

PROPOSITION 1   *Under* $\Pi_{C \times S}$, *we have*

i. $E(\xi|s) = 0$,

ii. $E(\xi) = 0$. ∎

The proof is a trivial application of the properties of conditional expectation. Note that the property $E(\xi|a) = 0$ does, in general, not hold with a proper prior probability unless b and c are a posteriori independent (see example 6).

The next result about the variance of ξ is a Bayesian version of a property first remarked by Hausman (1978) in a sample theory framework. We denote by Σ, Ω, and V the variances (for the joint distribution Π) of $(b - E(b|s))$, $(b - E(b|c,s))$, and $\xi(c,s)$ and by Σ^*, Ω^*, and V^* the posterior variances of these three random vectors. These variances are assumed to be finite. Let us remark that the expectations of these three vectors are zero with respect to both the joint probability and the posterior probability. Thus, for example, we have

$$\Sigma = E((b - E(b|s))(b - E(b|s)')),$$

$$\Sigma^* = E[(b - E(b|s)(b - E(b|s))'|s].$$

PROPOSITION 2   *We have*

i. $V^* = \Sigma^* - \Omega^*$,

ii. $V = \Sigma - \Omega$.

Proof

$$(b - E(b|s))(b - E(b|s))' = (b - E(b|c,s))(b - E(b|c,s))'$$
$$+ (b - E(b|s))(E(b|c,s) - E(b|s))'$$
$$+ (E(b|c,s) - E(b|s))(b - E(b|s))'$$
$$+ (E(b|c,s) - E(b|s))(E(b|c,s) - E(b|s))'.$$

The two intermediate terms vanish by taking the expectation (w.r.t. Π) or the expectation given s on both sides of this equality, and the two properties follow. ∎

Note that proposition 2 is exact (i.e., not asymptotic) for the joint distribution of (c,s) and for its posterior distribution. Furthermore we cannot exhibit a similar result for the sampling variances in small sample.

EXAMPLE 7   *We continue the example 6. Clearly, we have*

$$V^* = V(\xi|s) = \Sigma_{bc}^*(\Sigma_{cc}^*)^{-1}\Sigma_{cb}^*,$$

$$\Sigma^* = V(b|s) = \Sigma_{bb}^*,$$

$$\Omega^* = V[b - E(b|c,s)|s] = \Sigma_{bb}^* - \Sigma_{bc}^*(\Sigma_{cc}^*)^{-1}\Sigma_{cb}^*.$$

The property i of the proposition 2 is checked by taking the expectation (on s) of the three matrices.

The last property of ξ on the null model $\Pi_{C \times S}$ is about its asymptotic behavior. We just give a result on its almost sure limit, and we do not analyze the asymptotic distribution of this random variable. Let us now consider a model with a sample size equal to n in which the sample is denoted s_n and ξ_n is defined as in a one-short experiment by $\xi_n = E(b|s_n) - E(b|c,s_n)$. The parameter c is said to be *exactly estimable* if there exists a sequence of estimators $\hat{c}_n$ such that

$$\mu\{a|\hat{c}_n \to c(a) \quad P^a\text{-a.s.}\} = 1.$$

It can be proved that this condition is actually equivalent to the condition

$$\mu\{a|E(c|s_n) \to c(a) \quad P^a\text{-a.s.}\} = 1$$

(see Florens et al. 1984, ch. 7). Given this definition, the result is the following:

PROPOSITION 3   *If c is exactly estimable, then*

$$\mu\{a|\xi_n \to 0 \quad P^a\text{-a.s.}\} = 1$$

or equivalently

$$\xi_n \to 0 \quad \Pi_{C \times S}\text{-a.s.}$$

Proof   The proof is a simple application of general results about limits of posterior expectations which are detailed in Florens et al. (1984, ch. 7). We just sketch the argument and refer the reader to this reference for more details. If s represents the infinite sequence of the sample $s = (s_1, s_2, \ldots)$, the property

$$E(b|s_n) \to E(b|s) \quad \Pi_{C \times S}\text{-a.s.}$$

follows from the martingale convergence theorem. Similarly we get

$E(b|c, s_n) \to E(b|c, s)$ $\Pi_{C \times S}$-a.s.

The hypothesis of exact estimability of c implies that, asymptotically, c is a.s. a function of s, and then

$E(b|c, s) = E(b|s)$ $\Pi_{C \times S}$-a.s.

Therefore $\xi_n \to 0$ $\Pi_{C \times S}$-a.s., and this property is equivalent to the first one given in the proposition. ∎

A general exposition of the properties of ξ on an alternative model and particularly the study of its asymptotic behavior requires more technical arguments (in particular, invariance structures appear very useful) and are out of the scope of this chapter. We will illustrate this point by the following example:

EXAMPLE 8   *Let us assume that the sample of size n is summarized by $\bar{x} = (\bar{y}, \bar{z})' \in \mathbb{R}^2$ with $[(\bar{y}, \bar{z})'|b, c) \sim N[(b, c)', n^{-1}\Sigma]$, where Σ is a known matrix. If the prior probability of $a = (b, c)'$ is $N(a^p, \Sigma^p)$, the posterior distribution is normal, and we get the same result as in example 6, with*

$$a^* = [(\Sigma^p)^{-1} + n\Sigma^{-1}]^{-1}[(\Sigma^p)^{-1}a^p + n\Sigma^{-1}\bar{x}),$$

$$\Sigma^* = [(\Sigma^p)^{-1} + n\Sigma^{-1}]^{-1}.$$

It is obvious to verify that the asymptotic behaviour of $\xi_n = \Sigma_{b,c}^*(\Sigma_{cc}^*)^{-1}(c_0 - c^*)$ is asymptotically identical to that of $\Sigma_{bc}(\Sigma_{cc})^{-1}(c_0 - \bar{z})$ relative to any of the probabilities Π, P^a, or μ^s. Thus on the null model $\xi_n \to 0$ a.s. in the sampling process (for almost all c_0) or in the joint process. If the alternative model is defined by $(\bar{x}|b, c) \sim N[(b, c + \gamma), n^{-1}\Sigma]$, the function ξ_n has an almost sure limit equal to $\Sigma_{bc}(\Sigma_{cc})^{-1}\gamma$.

We conclude this discussion by summarizing the suggested test procedure. A natural test function is given by $\tilde{d}_n(s_n, c) = [E(b|s_n) - E(b|c, s_n)]'$ $H[E(b|s_n) - E(b|c, s_n)]$. If we want to make a posterior analysis, H is naturally taken to be equal to $(V^*)^+$, and this function $\tilde{d}$ has a mean equal to the rank of V^*. This result remains true if H is taken to be equal to V^+ under a joint probability analysis. If the posterior distribution of a is normal, the posterior distribution of $\tilde{d}_n$ is a χ^2. This will also be approximatively the case in asymptotic models in which, under usual regularity conditions, the posterior probability is approximatively normal (see De

Groot 1970, ch. 10). In these cases the distributions of $\tilde{d}_n$, derived from the joint distribution on the parameters and the observations or from the sampling distribution, are also χ^2 with the same degrees of freedom, and the three different viewpoints asymptotically coincide.

The analysis of $\tilde{d}_n$ under an alternative hypothesis does not raise specific problems. For instance, if the posterior expectation under an alternative hypothesis only differs from the posterior expectation under the null hypothesis by a constant added to the posterior expectation, $\tilde{d}_n$ is distributed, under this alternative hypothesis, as a noncentral χ^2 probability. The extension of this argument to an asymptotic case, assuming asymptotic posterior normality and replacing the alternative hypothesis by a suitable sequence of hypotheses, can easily be done using standard techniques of asymptotic statistics.

Comparison between Marginal and Conditional Probabilities

We will now explore another criterion for the comparison between the inferences on b marginally or conditionally on c. Let $\mu(b|s_0)$ and $\mu(b|c_0, s_0)$ be the two posterior distributions given a particular realization of the sample s_0 and given s_0 and the hypothesis c_0, respectively. We will compare these two probabilities by means of φ-divergences.

Let us recall that if P and Q are two probabilities characterized by their densities f and g with respect to a common dominating measure and if φ is a nonnegative convex function, normalized by $\varphi(1) = 0$, the φ-divergence of P with respect to Q is defined by $E_Q[\varphi(f/g)] = \int \varphi(f/g)dQ$. The divergences were first systematically studied by Csiszar (1967a, 1967b) and some computations relevant for Bayesian statistics can be found in Florens and Scotto (1984). Note that the divergences are not distances except for some particular cases.

Let us examine in detail example 6. Assuming that $a = (b \quad c)'$ is a posteriori distributed as $N(a^*, \Sigma^*)$, we may deduce the following marginal and conditional posterior distributions:

$(b|s) \sim N(b^*, \Sigma^*_{bb})$,

$(b|s, c) \sim N(b^* + \Sigma^*_{bc}(\Sigma^*_{cc})^{-1}(c - c^*), \Sigma^*_{bb \cdot c})$,

where $\Sigma^*_{bb \cdot c} = \Sigma^*_{bb} - \Sigma^*_{bc}(\Sigma^*_{cc})^{-1}\Sigma^*_{cb}$. We have now to select a particular divergence, namely, a particular function φ. In the normal family, the choice of $\varphi(x) = x \log x$ is convenient; for such a specification of φ, the divergence is identical to the Kullback information measure. Specifically, the computation of

$$\int \log \frac{\mu(b|c,s)}{\mu(b|s)} \cdot \mu(b|c,s) db$$

gives

$$\tilde{d}(c,s) = \tfrac{1}{2}\{\log|\Sigma_{bb}^*| - \log|\Sigma_{bb \cdot c}^*| + \mathrm{tr}(\Sigma_{bb}^*)^{-1}\Sigma_{bb \cdot c}^* - k_b$$
$$+ (c - c^*)'(\Sigma_{cc}^*)^{-1}\Sigma_{cb}^*(\Sigma_{bb}^*)^{-1}\Sigma_{bc}^*(\Sigma_{cc}^*)^{-1}(c - c^*)\},$$

where k_b is the dimension of b.

The properties of this test function under the posterior null probability are summarized in the following proposition:

PROPOSITION 4

i. *Conditionally on* s, $2(\tilde{d}(c,s) - K)$, *where* $K = \log|\Sigma_{bb}^*| - \log|\Sigma_{bb \cdot c}^*| + \mathrm{tr}(\Sigma_{bb}^*)^{-1}\Sigma_{bb \cdot c}^* - k_b$, *is a linear combination of* k_b *independent* $\chi_{(1)}^2$ *random-variables. The coefficients* λ_i, $i = 1, \ldots, k_b$ *of this linear combination are the solutions of the determinental equation* $|\lambda \Sigma_{cc}^* - \Sigma_{cb}^*(\Sigma_{bb}^*)^{-1}\Sigma_{bc}^*| = 0$.

ii. $E(\tilde{d}(s,s)|s) = \tfrac{1}{2}\{\log|\Sigma_{bb}^*| - \log|\Sigma_{bb \cdot c}^*|\}$.

iii. $V(\tilde{d}(c,s)|s) = \tfrac{1}{2}\sum_{i=1}^{k_b} \lambda_i^2$.

Proof. (i) Let us define x and A through $2\tilde{d}(c,s) - K = x'Ax$, where

$$x = (\Sigma_{cc}^*)^{-1/2}(c - c^*)$$

$$A = (\Sigma_{cc}^*)^{-1/2}\Sigma_{cb}^*(\Sigma_{bb}^*)^{-1}\Sigma_{bc}^*(\Sigma_{cc}^*)^{-1/2}.$$

Clearly $(x|s) \sim N(0, I)$. Let us now consider a spectral decomposition of A, namely, $A = Q'\Lambda Q$ with Q orthogonal and $\Lambda = \mathrm{diag}(\lambda_1, \ldots, \lambda_{k_b})$. Clearly $y = Qx$ is also distributed conditionally on s, as $N(0, I)$, and the λ_i's $(i = 1, \ldots, k_b)$ are the solutions of the given determinantal equation. Thus $x'Ax = y'\Lambda y = \Sigma \lambda_i y_i^2$ when y_i^2 are i.i.d. $\chi_{(1)}^2$ random variables.

Part (ii) follows from $E(x'Ax|s) = \mathrm{tr}A = \mathrm{tr}(\Sigma_{bb}^*)^{-1}(\Sigma_{bb \cdot c}^* - \Sigma_{bb}^*)$. Part (iii) directly follows from part (i). ■

We do not detail the properties of $\tilde{d}(c,s)$ conditionally on s under an alternative hypothesis in which case the posterior distribution of c would be $N(c^* + \gamma, \Sigma_{cc}^*)$. The distribution of $2(\tilde{d}(c,s) - K)$ becomes a linear combination of noncentral $\chi^2_{(1)}$ random variables whose moments can be computed without difficulty.

An Encompassing Approach to Bayesian Specification Tests

We present the general principles of a Bayesian approach to encompassing before considering its application to specification tests. Our definition follows that given in Mizon and Richard (1986), Florens and Mouchart (1985b), and Florens, Mouchart, and Scotto (1983) (see also in this volume chapter 12 by Hendry and Richard). Let us consider two Bayesian models defined on the same sample space S and on two different parameter spaces E and F. Because these models analyze finite sample sizes, it is not very restrictive to assume that the predictive distributions have the same null sets (or are equivalent). These models have sampling densities $p(s|e)$ and $q(s|f)$, prior densities $m(e)$ and $n(f)$ from which are derived the predictive densities $p(s)$ and $q(s)$ and the posterior densities $m(e|s)$ and $n(f|s)$.

Thus we consider two Bayesian models characterized, in terms of densities, by

$$\pi_1(e, s) = m(e)p(s|e) = p(s)m(e|s),$$

$$\pi_2(f, s) = n(f)q(s|f) = q(s)n(f|s).$$

The basic idea of a Bayesian encompassing of model 2 by model 1 is that the learning on f, the parameter of model 2, may be reproduced only by model 1 after a suitable extension. More precisely, model 1 is said to encompass model 2 if there exists a distribution of f conditionally on e, of density $\delta(f|e)$ such that

$$n(f|s) = \int m(e|s)\delta(f|e)de$$

which means that the posterior distribution of f, obtained naturally in model 2 as $n(f|s)$, may also be reproduced, independently of s, from the posterior distribution of model 1. The role of the transition $\delta(f|e)$ may be viewed as follow: If we want, in general, to extend model 1 into a probability π_* on $E \times F \times S$, we would need a conditional distribution on f given (e, s):

$$\pi_*(e, f, s) = \pi_1(e, s) \cdot \delta_*(f|e, s).$$

In the extended model the inference on f would be characterized by

$$k_*(f|s) = \int m(e|s)\delta_*(f|e,s)de.$$

Up to now, the transition δ_* is arbitrary. Bayesian encompassing actually embodies two ideas: (1) In the extended model, parameter e is sufficient, that is, f and s are independent given e with respect to π_* (thus $f \perp\!\!\!\perp s|e; \pi_*$) and therefore $\delta_*(f|e,s)$ does not depend on $s : \delta_*(f|e,s) = \delta(f|e)$. (2) The extended model reproduces the inferences on f obtained from model 2, that is, $k_*(f|s) = n(f|s)$. If such a transition δ does not exist, we look for an approximate transition $\delta(f|e)$ that minimizes the expectation on s (i.e., w.r.t. the predictive probability $p(s)$) of the divergence between $n(f|s)$ and $\int m(e|s)\delta_*(f|e)de$.

Note that the transition $\delta(f|e)$ may be viewed on a Bayesian pseudotrue value of f in the following sense. In sampling theory, a pseudotrue value of a statistic may be viewed as follows: Consider an estimation $\tilde{t}(s)$ for some function $\tilde{c}(f)$; in model 2, $\tilde{t}(s)$ would be a reasonable estimation of $\tilde{c}(f)$ if, for instance, $E_2(\tilde{t}(s)|f) = \tilde{c}(f)$ or if $\tilde{t}(s_1,\ldots,s_n) \to \tilde{c}(f)$ in $q(s|f)$-probability or $q(s|f)$-a.s. for any f. But viewed from model 1, the statistic $\tilde{t}(s)$ will actually "estimate" some function $\tilde{b}(e)$ in the sense that $E_1(\tilde{t}(s)|e) = \tilde{b}(e)$ or $\tilde{t}(s_1,\ldots,s_n) \to \tilde{b}(e)$ in $p(s|e)$-probability or $p(s|e)$-a.s., for any e and $\tilde{b}(e)$ has been called a "pseudotrue" value of $\tilde{t}(s)$ (with the understanding that $\tilde{c}(f)$ would be its "true value" if model 2 were true). Thus $\tilde{b}(e)$ may be viewed as the function of e, which, in model 1, is "closest" to the statistic $\tilde{t}(s)$. In a Bayesian framework that function of e, defined relatively to a specific function $\tilde{c}(f)$ of f, becomes a distribution of f considered as a function of e that is, a transition, and this transition makes the inference on f in model 2 the closest possible to the inference on f in model 1.

In this chapter we will not derive the general testing procedure obtained from the encompassing approach; we rather apply this concept to the specification problem only where, as mentioned before, a message on (c,s) is treated by a comparison between $\mu(b|c,s)$ and $\mu(b|s)$. In that context it was implicitly assumed that the parameter of interest b had the same meaning in the model conditional on c as in the marginal model. In the encompassing approach to specification tests, the parameter of interest is now considered differently in these two models: this aspect is stressed by denoting the parameter of interest by β in the marginal model and by b in the model conditional to c. Therefore the two models of the encompassing approach are now written as

$$\pi_1(b, s|c_0) = \mu(b|c_0)p(s|b, c_0) = p(s|c_0)\mu(b|s, c_0),$$

$$\pi_2(\beta, s) = \mu(\beta)p(s|\beta) = p(s)\mu(\beta|s),$$

where π_1 and π_2 are both derived from the same Bayesian model characterized by $\pi(a, s)$. The Bayesian pseudotrue value, characterized by a conditional distribution $\delta(\beta|b, c_0)$, may be viewed as a reinterpretation of β within the first model that brings $\mu_1(\beta|s, c_0)$ the nearest to $\mu(\beta|s)$, where $\mu_1(\beta|s, c_0)$ in the posterior distribution of β in the model characterized by the knowledge of c_0, that is,

$$\mu_1(\beta|s, c_0) = \int \mu(b|s, c_0)\delta(\beta|b, c_0)db.$$

This approach may be illustrated by the following example where all the distributions are normal.

EXAMPLE 9   *Let us take the same framework as in example 8. We now consider the model given c_0 (with a posterior probability on $(b|s, c_0)$ being $N(b^* + \Sigma_{bc}^*(\Sigma_{cc}^*)^{-1}(c_0 - c^*), \Sigma_{bb\cdot c}^*))$ and the marginal model (with a posterior probability on $(\beta|s)$ being $N(b^*, \Sigma_{bb}^*))$ as distinct models. We look for a conditional distribution of β given b and c_0. For the sake of simplicity, we limit our search of pseudotrue value to the particular class of normal distributions, that is, $(\beta|b, c_0) \sim N(M_0 b + m_0, V_0)$, where M_0, m_0, V_0 are (possibly) functions of c_0 that have to be computed as follows: The posterior distribution of β in the model characterized by the knowledge of c_0 is then $N(M_0 b^* + M_0\Sigma_{bc}^*(\Sigma_{cc}^*)^{-1}(c_0 - c^*) + m_0, M_0\Sigma_{bb\cdot c}^*M_0' + V_0)$. We compute a divergence between this distribution and the distribution of β. A simple result is obtained by choosing the Kullback information measure, which is equal to*

$$\tfrac{1}{2}\{\log|\Sigma_{bb}^*| - \log|M_0\Sigma_{bb\cdot c}^*M_0' + V_0| + tr(\Sigma_{bb}^*)^{-1}(M_0\Sigma_{bb\cdot c}^*M_0' + V_0)$$

$$- k_b + [M_0 b^* + M_0\Sigma_{bc}^*(\Sigma_{cc}^*)^{-1}(c_0 - c^*) - b^* + m_0]'$$

$$(\Sigma_{bb}^*)^{-1}[M_0 b^* + M_0\Sigma_{bc}^*(\Sigma_{cc}^*)^{-1}(c_0 - c^*) - b^* + m_0]\}.$$

We now have to compute the expectation of this quantity with respect to the predictive probability of the null model, that is, with respect to the distribution of s given $c = c_0$. In general, Σ^* and b^* may be both functions of s, and this computation may be tedious. It requires in any case the specification of the whole joint distribution on b and s (given c). However, a sample result is obtained if the posterior variance Σ^* is assumed to be constant and if it is *equal to the predictive variance of* (b^*, c^*) *given* c_0; *such a situation occurs as a limit case when the prior precision tends to zero or when the sample size tends to infinity. In this case it can be checked that the optimal choice is given by* $M_0 = I$, $m_0 = \Sigma_{bc}^*(\Sigma_{cc}^*)^{-1}(c_0 - E(c^*|c_0))$ *and* $V_0 = \Sigma_{bc}^*(\Sigma_{cc}^*)^{-1}\Sigma_{cb}^*$ *in which case the first four terms of the divergence vanish. In order to obtain a simple formula, we moreover assume that* $E(c^*|c_0) = c_0$, *which is natural in a noninformative context. Then, for the optimal choice of* M_0, m_0, *and* V_0, *the divergence between the posterior probabilities becomes*

$$d = (c_0 - c^*)'(\Sigma_{cc}^*)^{-1}\Sigma_{cb}^*(\Sigma_{bb}^*)^{-1}\Sigma_{bc}^*(\Sigma_{cc}^*)^{-1}(c_0 - c^*).$$

In this context d is naturally used as a test function for the assumption $c = c_0$. In this particular case (joint normal distribution on the parameter and the sample and noninformative prior probability), the test function obtained through an encompassing viewpoint is identical to that obtained in the comparison of posterior means presented earlier in this section. However, the comparison between the posterior distributions without a transformation by a pseudotrue value is different. The argument is easy to understand: in the normal framework conditioning on c reduces uniformly the variance and introduces a difference between the marginal and the conditional probabilities whatever the value of c_0 is. This difference is taken into account in the function $\tilde{d}$ and appears in the pseudotrue value of the encompassing approach. The pseudotrue value of β given b is not a function. Rather it is really a probability centered on b, and its variance is exactly the decrease of variance obtained by conditioning. This example shows the interest of the Bayesian approach to pseudotrue values considered as transition probabilities instead of functions as in the classical analysis. Note that if Σ^* had the form $n^{-1}\Sigma$ (where n is the sample size), the Bayesian pseudotrue value would converge to the classical pseudotrue value, which, in this case, is the identity. Note that the identity of the test functions derived from the comparison of posterior expectations and from the encompassing analysis is evidently a particular feature of the joint normal model with noninformative prior probability and cannot be generalized.

14.4. Two Examples: The Selection of Regressors and an Exogeneity Test

This final section is devoted to applications of the preceding tests in two "standard" econometric problems: the selection of regressors in a linear regression model and a test of exogeneity which is equivalent, in a linear model, to uncorrelatedness between an explanatory variable and the residual.

EXAMPLE   10   Let us consider a standard regression model

$$y = X\beta + u = X_1\beta_1 + X_2\beta_2 + u, \qquad (u|X, \beta, \sigma^2) \sim N(0, \sigma^2 I_T),$$

in which a particular value of β_2 will be tested by its consequences on the inference on β_1. The prior probability is the natural conjugate prior commonly used in this model and is characterized by

$$(\beta|\sigma^2, X) \sim N(\beta^p, \sigma^2 \Sigma^p)$$

$$(\sigma^2|X) \sim \text{IW}(\sigma^{p2}, v^p)$$

where IW stands for an Inverted Whishart distribution, which is preferred here to an inverted gamma distribution because the extension to multi-variate models becomes easier, and v^p stands for the degrees of freedom (see, e.g., Zellner 1971, app. 1 and 2). It is well known that the posterior distribution is

$$(\beta|\sigma^2, y, X) \sim N(\beta^*, \sigma^2 \Sigma^*),$$

$$(\sigma^2|y, X) \sim \text{IW}(\sigma^{*2}, v^*),$$

where

$$\Sigma^* = [(\Sigma^p)^{-1} + X'X]^{-1},$$

$$\beta^* = [(\Sigma^p)^{-1} + X'X]^{-1}[(\Sigma^p)^{-1}\beta^p + X'y],$$

$$v^* = v^p + T,$$

$$v^*\sigma^{*2} = v^p\sigma^{p2} + (y - X\beta^p)'(I - X\Sigma^*X')(y - X\beta^p).$$

We decompose β^* and Σ^* according to the decomposition of β into β_1 and β_2.

Following the test procedure presented in section 14.3, we focus on the function $\xi = \Sigma^*_{12}(\Sigma^*_{22})^{-1}(\beta_2 - \beta_2^*)$, which is equal to a weighted difference between the posterior mean of β_1 marginally and conditionally on β_2. The posterior distribution of ξ is Student with 0 mean, v^* degrees of freedom, and a variance covariance matrix equal to

$$\frac{v^*}{v^* - 2}\sigma^{*2}\Sigma^*_{12}(\Sigma^*_{22})^{-1}\Sigma^*_{21}.$$

A natural test statistic is then based on

$$\frac{1}{k_1 \sigma^{*2}} \zeta' (\Sigma^*_{12}(\Sigma^*_{22})^{-1} \Sigma^*_{21})^{-1} \xi,$$

which has a posterior distribution $F(k_1, v^*)$ (see Zellner 1971) on the null hypothesis. With a noninformative prior distribution, β_2^* and σ^{*2} are equal to the OLS estimators $\hat{\beta}$ and $\hat{\sigma}^2$, $\Sigma^* = (X'X)^{-1}$ and $v^* = T - k$; in such a case the test statistic reduces to a statistic considered in the classical literature (see Holly and Monfort 1982).

We may also adopt a test based on the comparison of the whole posterior distributions described in section 14.3 and follow two approaches.

In the first one we consider β_1 as the parameter of interest, and we compare the posterior distribution of β_1 marginally and conditionally to β_2. These two distributions are both multivariate Student, and no usual divergence gives analytic results. However, it has been remarked (Florens and Scotto 1984) that the computation of the Hellinger distance (defined as a φ-divergence with $\phi(x) = (\sqrt{x} - 1)^2$) reduces to the computation of the normalization constant of a poly-t distribution (Drèze 1977) which can be obtained numerically in a very efficient way (Richard and Tompa 1980). If the sample size is large, the normal approximation on the posterior distribution of β can be used. Then the test procedure can be performed analytically as described in section 14.3.

A second approach consists of considering β_1 and σ^2 as the parameters of interest, and we have to compare the marginal and conditional distributions of β_1 and σ^2. These two distributions are both Inverted Wishart normal distributions, and the Hellinger distance between these probabilities can be computed analytically. This computation is not reproduced here, nor is the analysis of its properties (see Florens and Scotto 1984).

The analysis of this example, from an encompassing viewpoint, is an application of the case where σ^2 is known, which is treated in section 14.3. Indeed, in this case the Bayesian model of β and y is jointly normal, and the results at the end of section 14.3 apply. But, if σ^2 were unknown, finding the pseudotrue value would involve tedious calculations that go beyond the scope of this chapter. A study of this problem is presented in Florens, Hendry, and Richard (1989).

EXAMPLE 11   We will restrict our presentation of the Bayesian exogeneity test to a special case. However, the arguments can be extended to more general cases without difficulty except for matrix manipulations and numerical computations. We consider the following model:

$$y_t = \alpha x_t + u_t,$$

$$x_t = w_t' \delta + \varepsilon_t.$$

In this model, it is well known (see Florens et al. 1979) that x_t is exogenous (in the sense of Engle et al. 1983 or Florens and Mouchart 1985a, ex. 2.10) if u_t and x_t are uncorrelated in the sampling. We adopt the following parametrization of the model: the vector of the parameters a is equal to $(\alpha, \delta, \sigma^2, \lambda. \tau^2)$, where σ^2, λ, and τ^2 are unambiguously defined through the equality

$$V\begin{pmatrix} u_t \\ \xi_t \end{pmatrix} = \begin{pmatrix} \sigma^2 & \sigma^2 \lambda \\ \sigma^2 \lambda & \tau^2 + \lambda^2 \sigma^2 \end{pmatrix}.$$

The sampling model is then characterized by

$$\left(\begin{matrix} x_t \\ y_t \end{matrix} \middle| w_t, a \right) \sim IN\left[\begin{pmatrix} w_t' \delta \\ \alpha w_t' \delta \end{pmatrix}, \begin{pmatrix} \tau^2 + \lambda^2 \sigma^2 & \alpha \tau^2 + (\alpha \lambda^2 + \lambda)\sigma^2 \\ \alpha \tau^2 + (\alpha \lambda^2 + \lambda)\sigma^2 & \alpha^2 \tau^2 + (\alpha^2 \lambda^2 + 2\lambda + 1)\sigma^2 \end{pmatrix} \right].$$

The exogeneity assumption can be written as $\lambda = 0$ in this parameterization. If no assumption is made on λ, the maximum likelihood estimation of α is the LIML estimator (see Florens et al. 1979), and if $\lambda = 0$, the model can be cut as follows:

$$(x_t | w_t, a) \sim (x_t | w_t, \delta, \tau^2) \sim N(w_t' \delta, \tau^2),$$

$$(y_t | x_t, w_t, a) \sim (y_t | x_t, w_t, \alpha, \sigma^2) \sim N(\alpha x_t, \sigma^2).$$

Then, if (δ, τ^2) and (α, σ^2) are "variation free" or a priori independent, x_t is exogenous, and the MLE estimator of α is obtained by OLS in the conditional model. If one wants to make a specification test of the exogeneity assumption, that is, if one wants to test $\lambda = 0$ through the implication of this hypothesis on the estimation of α, one has to compare the LIML and the OLS estimate as described by Hausman (1978).

To simplify this example, we restrict the prior specification to a partially noninformative case. A priori information will be introduced in only the parameters of interest (α and σ^2), and a noninformative measure is specified on $(\delta, \lambda, \tau^2)$. However, it should be noted that the proposition 4.3 of Florens et al. (1979) may be used to consider a larger class of prior distributions, but it requires more technical manipulations. Thus we consider a prior density defined by

$$\mu(\alpha, \sigma^2, \delta, \lambda, \tau^2) \propto \tau^{-(r+3)} f_{\text{IW}}(\sigma^2) f_N(\alpha | \sigma^2),$$

where $f_{\text{IW}}(\sigma^2)$ denote the density of an Inverted Whishart distribution with parameters σ^{p2} and v^p and $f_N(\alpha | \sigma^2)$ denotes a normal density with parameters α^p and σ^2 / h^p. We do not reproduce here the motivation for the choice of the exponent of τ^2 (see, e.g., Drèze 1976).

Using the proposition 5.3 of Florens et al. (1979) and, in particular, the result 5.17, we get the following posterior poly-t distribution of α:

$$\mu(\alpha | x, y, w) \propto \frac{[m_w^{yy} - 2\alpha m_w^{xy} + \alpha^2 m_w^{xx}]^{(T-1)/2}}{[v^p \sigma^{p2} + h^p \sigma^{p2} + y'y - 2\alpha(\alpha^p h^p + x'y) + \alpha^2(h^p + x'x)]^{(T+vp+1)/2}},$$

where

$$\begin{pmatrix} m_w^{xx} & m_w^{xy} \\ m_w^{xy} & m_w^{yy} \end{pmatrix} = \begin{pmatrix} x' \\ y' \end{pmatrix} (I - W(W'W)^{-1} W')(x, y).$$

By means of the Bayesian regression program (BRP) (see Bauwens et al. 1981), the computation of the posterior mean α^* and the posterior variance ω^* of α can be performed without difficulties. Under the exogeneity assumption, or, equivalently, conditionally on λ taking the particular value 0, the posterior distribution of (α, σ^2) is obtained analogously to example 10, and so are α_0^* and ω_0^*, the posterior mean and variance, also obtained. The test statistic is then equal to $(\alpha^* - \alpha_0^*)^2 (\omega^* - \omega_0^*)^{-1}$. If the sample size increases, the approximate normality of the posterior distribution implies that this statistic becomes approximatively $\chi_{(1)}^2$ under the exogeneity hypothesis.

The comparison of the exact posterior distributions on α, whether or not given the exogeneity assumption $\lambda = 0$, cannot be performed analytically using the usual divergence. One can easily verify, however, that the computation of the Hellinger distance between these probabilities leads to the computation of the normalization constant of a poly-t distribution, which can also be computed by BRP.

Note

Comments by N. Capuccio, J. H. Drèze, V. Marimoutou, J.-M. Rolin and L. Simar are gratefully acknowledged and led to improvements in the presentation.

References

Bauwens, L., J. P. Bulteau, P. Gille, L. Longrée, M. Lubrano, and H. Tompa. 1981. "Bayesian Regression Program (BRP)-Users' Manual." CORE Computing Report 81-A01, Université Catholique de Louvain.

Csiszar, I. 1967a. "Information-Type Measures of Difference of Probability Distributions and Indirect Observations." *Studia Scientiarum Mathematicarum Hungria* 2:299–318.

Csiszar, I. 1967b. "On Topological Properties of f-Divergences." *Studia Scientiarum Mathematicarum Hungria* 2:319–329.

De Groot, M. H. 1970. *Optimal Statistical Decisions*. New York: McGraw-Hill,

Drèze, J. H. 1976. "Bayesian Limited Information Analysis of the Simultaneous Equations Model." *Econometrica* 44:1045–1075.

Drèze, J. H. 1977. "Bayesian Regression Analysis Using Poly-t Densities." *Journal of Econometrics* 6:329–354.

Engle, R., D. Hendry, and J. -F. Richard. 1983. "Exogeneity." *Econometrica* 51:227–304.

Florens, J.-P., D. Hendry, and J.-F. Richard. 1989. "Encompassing and Specificity." Duke University, ISDS Discussion Paper 8902.

Florens, J.-P., and M. Mouchart. 1985a. "Conditioning in Dynamic Models." *Journal of Time Series Analysis* 53(1):15–35.

Florens, J.-P., and M. Mouchart. 1985b. "Model Selection: Some Remarks." In *Model Choice*, Proceedings of the 4th Franco-Belgian Meeting of Statisticians (November 1983), edited by J.-P. Florens, M. Mouchart, J. P. Raoult, and L. Simar. Bruxelles, Publications des Facultés Universitaires Saint-Louis, 27–44.

Florens, J.-P., M. Mouchart, and J.-F. Richard. 1974. "Bayesian Inference in Error-in-Variables Models." *Journal of Multivariate Analysis* 4:419–452.

Florens, J.-P., M. Mouchart, and J.-P. Richard. 1979. "Specification and Inference in Linear Model" CORE Discussion Paper 7943, Louvain-la-Neuve: Université Catholique de Louvain.

Florens, J.-P., M. Mouchart, and J. M. Rolin. 1984. *Elements of Bayesian Statistics*. Preliminary version available at CORE, Université Catholique de Louvain and to be published by Marcel Dekker, Inc. (1989).

Florens, J.-P., M. Mouchart, and S. Scotto. 1983. "Approximate Sufficiency on the Parameter Space and Model Selection." In *44th Session of the International Statistical Institute: Contributed Papers*, 12:763–766.

Florens, J.-P., and J. M. Rolin. 1983. "Asymptotic Sufficiency and Exact Estimability in Bayesian Experiments." In *Alternative Approaches in Time Series Analysis*, Proceedings of the 3rd Franco-Belgian Meeting of Statisticians, (November 1982), edited by J.-P. Florens, M. Mouchart, J. P. Raoult, and L. Simar. Bruxelles: Publications des Facultés Universitaires Saint-Louis, 121–142.

Florens, J.-P., and S. Scotto. 1984. "Information Value and Econometric Modelling." South European Economic Discussion Series No 17.

Hausman, J. A. 1978. "Specification Tests in Econometrics." *Econometrica* 46:1251–1271.

Hausman, J. A., and W. E. Taylor. 1981. "A Generalized Specification Test." *Economic Letters* 8:239–245.

Holly, A. 1982. "A Remark on Hausman's Specification Test." *Econometrica*, 50:749–759.

Holly, A., and A. Monfort. 1986. "Some Useful Equivalence Properties of Hausman's Test." *Economic Letters* 20:39–43.

Holly, A., and D. Sargan. 1982. "Testing for Exogeneity within a Limited Information Framework." Cahier No 8204. Cahiers de Recherches Economiques, Université de Lausanne.

Kolmogorov. 1956. *Foundations of Probability* (trans.). New York: Chelsea Publishing Co.

Metivier, M. 1972. *Notions fondamentales de la théorie des probabilités*. Paris: Dunod.

Mizon, G., and J. -F. Richard. 1986. "The Encompassing Principle and Its Application to Nonnested Hypothesis." *Econometrica* 54:657–678.

Monfort, A. 1982. *Cours de statistique mathématique*. Paris: Economica.

Nakamura A., and M. Nakamura. 1981. "On the Relationships among Several Specification Error Tests Presented by Durbin-Wu and Hausman." *Econometrica* 49:1583–1588.

Neveu, J. 1962. *Bases mathématiques du calcul des probabilités*. Paris: Masson.

Newey, W. K. 1985. "Maximum Likelihood Specification Testing and Conditional Moment Tests." *Econometrica* 53:1047–1070.

Richard, J.-F., and H. Tompa. 1980. "On the Evaluation of Poly-*t* Density Functions." *Journal of Econometrics* 12:335–351.

White, H. 1982. "Maximum Likelihood Estimation of Misspecified Models." *Econometrica* 50:1–25.

Wu, D. 1973. "Alternative Tests of Independence Between Stochastic Regressors and Disturbances." *Econometrica* 41:733–750.

Wu, D. 1974. "Alternative Tests of Independence between Stochastic Regressors and Disturbances: Finite Sample Results." *Econometrica* 42:529–546.

Zellner, A. 1971. *An Introduction to Bayesian Inference in Econometrics*. New York: Wiley.

15 Estimating Average Excess Supply on Goods and Labor Markets from a Cross Section of Business Survey Reports

Peter Kooiman

15.1 Introduction

In this chapter I analyze a cross section of business survey reports of industrial firms in the Netherlands. Among other things these firms report on the types of constraints met in production. They also give an estimate of their degree of (physical) capacity utilization. These data are analyzed by means of a simple disequilibrium model for single-input/single-output firms. The basic assumption of the model is that relative excess supply of labor and demand for output are normally distributed in the population of industrial firms. This assumption allows us to estimate average excess supply of labor and demand for goods from the business survey reports.

In Kooiman (1984) I presented a similar model designed to analyze the results of these business surveys. This model used the aggregation-by-integration methodology for markets in disequilibrium, introduced by Muellbauer (1978). Instead of aggregating over markets in disequilibrium, this technique was used to aggregate over firms in disequilibrium. The main advantage of doing so is that it allows us to deal with spillovers between the labor and goods market at the individual firm level. To calibrate the model, I used aggregate time series of degrees of capacity utilization and proportions of firms reporting to meet capacity, labor, or demand constraints or to operate without constraints. As a result I obtained time series of estimates of two central latent variables in the model that can be interpreted as relative aggregate excess supply of labor and excess demand for goods.

Instead of using these aggregate time series of business survey results, we will analyze here a cross section of individual firm reports. Given the panel structure of the Dutch business survey, it is possible in principle to correct for individual effects by pooling the available cross sections. I have not processed along this line, though, since a separate cross-sectional analysis using a minimum-condition model is computationally quite cumbersome. So we will restrict ourselves to the analysis of the single cross section of about 1,500 reports in the survey of September 1985.

From a cursory inspection of the individual answers to the business survey, it becomes clear that the model used to analyze the aggregate time series cannot be used without modification to analyze micro data. A major part of this chapter consists of a discussion of the discrepancies between our basic model of the firm in disequilibrium and the available data. In trying to bridge the gap between the model and the data, we have to introduce several modifications into the basic disequilibrium framework. These modifications are purely data inspired and have no foundation in economic theory. This is not to say that these modifications cannot be defended. Economic theory simply does not account for all features of the actual data. From the statistical point of view some of the neglected aspects are quite dominant, so in most cases ad hoc modifications cannot be avoided in empirical work.

In section 15.2 we describe and summarize the prominent features of the data used in this chapter. Section 15.3 presents the basic disequilibrium model of the firm, and discusses the discrepancies between the model and the data. In section 15.4 we modify the (statistical) model to account for part of these discrepancies, and we present some estimation results for the group of firms reporting to meet constraints in production. In section 15.6 we discuss how the group of firms reporting to meet no constraints can be included. Estimation results are given here as well. In section 15.6 we tentatively discuss why the estimate of the correlation coefficient of excess supply of labor and excess demand for goods tends to -1. Section 15.7 provides some concluding remarks.

15.2 Some Results of the September 1985 Business Survey

As in all other EEC countries, the Netherlands Central Bureau of Statistics surveys a sample of industrial firms on a monthly basis, asking for current business conditions. Most questions are of a qualitative nature: the emphasis is on timeliness, not on precision. Four times a year, namely, at the end of each quarter, some extra questions are included. We will analyze two of these quarterly questions. One asks for the degree of capacity utilization; the other is concerned with constraints met in production. The actual phrasing of the questions is as follows:

Over the last month the degree of utilization* of the available installations for production was approximately . . . . %
*The degree of utilization could be more than 100% in case of incidental use of multiple shifts or overtime work.

At the moment our production activities meet*
a. no constraints   (Y/N)
b. constraints, predominantly as a consequence of
    —insufficient demand   (Y/N)
    —lack of labor force   (Y/N)
    —lack of capacity of installations for production   (Y/N)
    —other causes, i.e.,. . . . . (Y/N)
    . . . .
* If necessary multiple answers allowed.

The population sampled consists of about 9,000 industrial firms with 10 or more workers employed, including the self-employed. The population surveyed accounts for approximately 92 percent of total industrial employment. In September 1985 the sample size was 1,876. The sample is stratified according to sectors of industry. For each sector it is first checked whether the fifty largest firms account for 80 percent of the sectoral shipments. If so, these, and no other firms, are selected. When it is not the case, the sector is properly sampled, and stratified according to sales level. The probabilities of inclusion are such that very large firms are included anyway. Obviously such a design implies that small firms are either absent or undersampled, so the sample has to be reweighted when sectoral aggregates are computed. Overall industrial aggregates are computed as weighted averages of sectoral results, using value added as weights.

Figure 15.1 displays the average degree of capacity utilization and the weighted proportions of constraints reported in the business surveys from October 1971 to September 1985. We have left out the category of other constraints because it is difficult to interpret and makes the figure less transparent. The break in the series in September 1982 is due to a substantial revision of the survey, both with respect to the selection of respondents and the individual and sectoral weights applied in computing aggregates. The series displayed show a strong cyclical pattern. High degrees of capacity utilization tend to be associated with low proportions of demand constraints and (historically) high proportions of labor and capacity constraints, as may be expected. Also the proportion of firms reporting to be without constraints tends to be large in that case. The recessions triggered by the oil price increases of 1973 and 1979 are clearly visible, as well as the steady recovery of the Dutch industrial sector during the most recent years. At the end of the period displayed, the average degree of capacity utilization is about 85 percent, a value that has not been reported since the end of 1973. Over the cycle we observe an alternating pattern between the

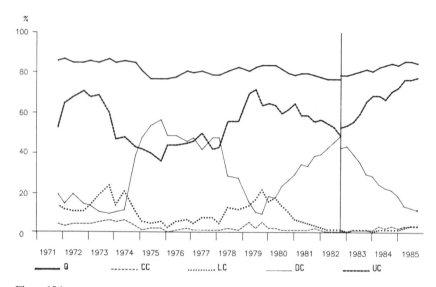

Figure 15.1
Business conditions, manufacturing, October 1971–September 1985. Average degree of
capacity utilization (*q*) and weighted proportions of unconstrained (*uc*), demand
constrained (*dc*), labor constrained (*lc*), and capacity constrained (*cc*) firms

proportions of firms reporting to meet demand constraints and those
reporting to be without constraints. Together these categories consistently
make up between 80 and 90 percent of the answers. The other categories
play a far less prominent role, especially in the most recent years, where
only a few percent of the firms report labor or capacity constraints, with
a slight tendency to increase in the most recent quarters. The unevenness
of the distribution of the answers over the available categories causes
serious problems for the statistical analysis of these data, as we shall see
below.

The results displayed in Figure 15.1 are weighted industry averages. In
the remainder of this chapter we will analyze the raw (i.e., unweighted)
sample. Thus we do not correct for the underrepresentation of small firms
in the sample. The bias involved does not seem to be serious: a visual
inspection of the answers by size group does not show a systematic effect
of firm size on the proportions of constraint "regimes" reported. Table 15.1
summarizes the results of the answers of the September 1985 survey. With
the nonresponse we have singled out the group of firms reporting other
constraints and the firms reporting combinations of constraints, since these

Table 15.1
Distribution of constraints, September 1985 (unweighted)

	Number of firms	Percentage of firms	Average degree of capacity utilization (%)
Capacity constrained	51	3.4	92.8
Labor constrained	62	4.1	88.0
Demand constrained	161	10.8	73.0
Unconstrained	1,221	81.7	86.9
Subtotal	1,495	100	85.6
Other constraints	61	3.3	79.1
Multiple answers	36	1.9	84.4
Nonresponse	284	15.1	—
Sample	1,876		

cannot properly be fitted into the statistical framework to be used later on. We will only deal with the remaining group, consisting of about 82 percent of the raw sample.

As one might expect, the group of firms reporting capacity constraints has the highest degree of capacity utilization on average, whereas the lowest degree is observed with firms meeting insufficient demand. The large group of firms reporting to operate without constraints strongly dominates the overall degree of capacity utilization. Figure 15.2 presents the cumulative distributions of the reported degrees of capacity utilization for the groups of firms reporting capacity, labor, and demand constraints. A similar curve obtains for the group of unconstrained firms. The resolution is too low to allow for its inclusion in the figure: it almost coincides with the curve for the labor-constrained firms. The figure shows that degrees of capacity utilization above 100 percent are exceptional. Less than 2 percent report such values; in most cases these are firms without constraints or with capacity constraints. Because 100 percent capacity utilization is the most frequently reported—more than 20 percent report this value—the distributions are extremely skewed, except for demand-constrained firms. This skewness gives rise to serious statistical complications, as we shall see below.

An interesting aspect of the reported degrees of capacity utilization is that the vast majority of respondents chooses to report rounded values, either in multiples of 10 percent or in multiples of 5 percent. Only 6 percent

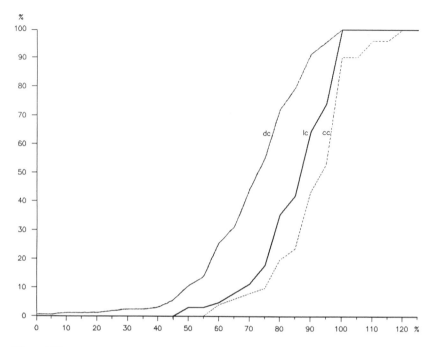

Figure 15.2
Reported degrees of capacity utilization (q) per constraint group (cumulative), September
1985: cc-capacity constraints, lc-labor constraints, dc-demand constraints

of the firms use multiples of 1 percent.[1] This is quite understandable in view
of the fact that the statistical office urges firms to respond as quickly
as possible. The fact that due to rounding the precision of the answers
differs complicates the statistical analysis of the data, however. Figure 15.3
displays the joint distribution of reported degrees of capacity utilization
and constraint group for firms reporting capacity, labor, or demand
constraints. Each point in the figure gives the (absolute) frequency of
the answers falling in centered 5 percent intervals. Again, I have left out
the large group of firms that reported no constraints. If included, they
would dominate to such an extent that the other curves could no longer be
distinguished properly. The distribution of degrees of capacity utilization
reported by unconstrained firms closely resembles the one associated with
the group of labor-constrained firms. The figure clearly demonstrates that
values reported in multiples of 10 percent occur more frequently than
intermediate values. This can indeed be expected when only part of the

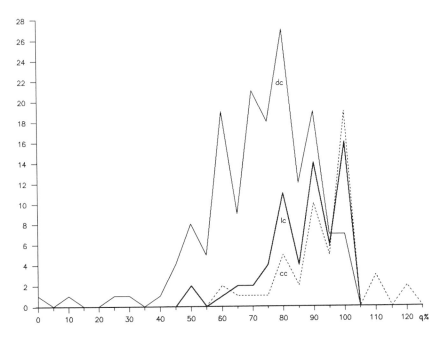

Figure 15.3
Reported degrees of capacity utilization (*q*) and constraint group (jointly), September 1985:
cc-capacity constraints, *lc*-labor constraints, *dc*-demand constraints

respondents rounds to multiples of 5 percent. It also shows that a value
of 75 percent is too frequently reported and a value of 70 percent too
infrequently as compared with the general pattern displayed. Apparently
a value of 75 percent is an "attractive" one to report, which is psycholog-
ically quite understandable. A value of 50 percent is reported too frequently
by the group of labor-constrained firms only.

Figure 15.3 also shows the collapse of the distribution of the reported
degrees of capacity utilization at values larger than 100 percent. In particular, this affects the distributions observed with the capacity-constrained
and the labor-constrained firms. The same applies to the unconstrained
firms, which are not in the figure. Note that values of 105, 115, 125, ...,
percent do not occur at all. Due to rounding, and the infrequency of
reported values larger than 100 or less than 45 percent the available data
can be condensed to the frequencies reported in table 15.2 with almost no
loss of information. The next section of the chapter addresses the question
how these data can be modeled statistically.

Table 15.2
The joint frequency distribution of constraints and degrees of capacity utilization

Degree of capacity utilization (%)	Constraint regime			
	Capacity constraints	Labor constraints	Demand constraints	No constraints
≤ 40	0	0	5	10
45	0	0	4	0
50	0	2	8	12
55	0	0	5	3
60	2	1	19	40
65	1	2	9	18
70	1	2	21	72
75	1	4	18	82
80	5	11	27	182
85	2	4	12	129
90	10	14	19	223
95	5	6	7	122
≥ 100	24	16	7	328

15.3   A Disequilibrium Model for Constraint Regimes

In this section we develop the basic model to be used for the analysis of
the data displayed in table 15.2. It serves as a starting point for subsequent
sections where we introduce some modifications in order to account for
the specific features of the data. The model is a modified version of the one
used in Kooiman (1984) to analyze time series of the average degree of
capacity utilization and proportions of firms reporting different types of
constraints. The model is inspired by disequilibrium, or fix-price theory,
and is based on minimum conditions. The basic idea is that a firm, when
reporting a certain type of constraint, implicitly reveals that other potential
constraints have not been binding.[2] When, for example, a firm reports
demand constraints, we may infer that its level of capacity and the available
supply of labor are large enough to allow for an increase in output when
conditions get better.

Let y_s be the level of full capacity output of a given firm, and let l_d be the
associated level of labor input. We will assume that capital stock is fixed
in the short run and that these entities correspond to the notional supply
of goods and demand for labor of the firm. In its labor market the firm is

confronted with a supply of labor l_s, and in the output market with a demand for output y_d. When labor supply falls short of l_d, the full capacity level of output y_s is not feasible and is replaced by an effective or constrained supply of output y_{sc}, which is a function of l_s. To keep things manageable we will assume that this function is linear through the origin. Moreover, when $l_s \geq l_d$, we require y_{sc} to be equal to y_s so that we have $y_{sc} = (l_s/l_d)y_s$ for $l_s \leq l_d$. The actual output level y of the firm equals

$$y = \min[y_s, y_{sc}, y_d] = \min\left[y_s, \left(\frac{l_s}{l_d}\right)y_s, y_d \right]. \tag{1}$$

The three possibilities for y in this equation correspond to three types of constraints or *regimes*. When y equals y_d, we will assume that the firm reports demand constraints, whereas it reports labor constraints when y equals $(l_s/l_d)y_s$. Equivalently, we will say that the firm is in the *dc*- or *lc*-regime. We cannot be sure what the firm reports when y equals y_s. On the one hand, it can be argued that the firm is without (external) constraints because it is able to realize its notional level of operations, given its productive capacity. On the other hand, since both labor supply and output demand are large enough, an increase in capacity would entail a larger sales level so that the firm may equally well report to be capacity constrained. As in Kooiman (1984) we will assume in this section that the firm reports capacity constraints; we will say that it is in the *cc*-regime. So for the moment we concentrate on firms reporting constraints. In section 15.5 we will modify the basic model of this section to include firms reporting to be without constraints. Figure 15.4 depicts the three possible regimes.

It is obvious to define the degree of capacity utilization q as y/y_s. Dividing equation (1) by y_s, and taking logarithms, we obtain the basic equation of the model:

$$\tilde{q} = \min[0, \tilde{l}, \tilde{y}], \tag{2}$$

where $\tilde{q}$ stands for $\ln q$, and $\tilde{l}$ and $\tilde{y}$ are the relative excess supply of labor and demand for output $\ln(l_s/l_d)$ and $\ln(y_d/y_s)$, respectively.

Since the population of our firms is finite, the empirical distribution of (y_s, y_d, l_s, l_d) is discrete. However, we will assume that it can closely be approximated by a four-dimensional log-normal distribution function. This implies that the empirical distribution of $\tilde{l}$ and $\tilde{y}$ is approximately bivariate normal. Suppose we have a random sample of firms from which

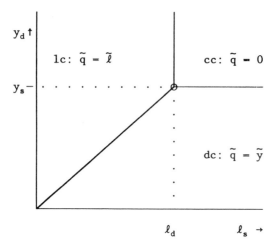

Figure 15.4
Constraint regimes and degrees of capacity utilization

we observe $\tilde{q}$ and the ruling regime $r \in \{cc, lc, dc\}$. From these observations we can estimate the means μ_l and μ_y, the standard deviations σ_l and σ_y, and the correlation coefficient ρ_{ly} of $\tilde{l}$ and $\tilde{y}$ by maximum likelihood. Apart from the additional truncation at 0, $\tilde{q}$ is the minimum of the two random variables $\tilde{l}$ and $\tilde{y}$. The likelihood function is therefore similar to the likelihood function of the endogenous switching model derived by Maddala and Nelson (1974):

$$\left.\begin{aligned}
L &= \prod_{\{i:r_i=cc\}} L_{cc}(i) \cdot \prod_{\{i:r_i=lc\}} L_{lc}(i) \cdot \prod_{\{i:r_i=dc\}} L_{dc}(i), \\
L_{cc}(i) &= \int_0^\infty \int_0^\infty n(\tilde{l}, \tilde{y}) d\tilde{y} d\tilde{l}, \\
L_{lc}(i) &= n_l\{\tilde{q}(i)\} \cdot \int_{\tilde{q}(i)}^\infty n_{y|l}\{\tilde{y}|\tilde{q}(i)\} d\tilde{y}, \\
L_{dc}(i) &= n_y\{\tilde{q}(i)\} \cdot \int_{\tilde{q}(i)}^\infty n_{l|y}\{\tilde{l}|\tilde{q}(i)\} d\tilde{l},
\end{aligned}\right\} \qquad (3)$$

where i denotes sample elements, $n(\tilde{l}, \tilde{y})$ is the joint normal density function of $\tilde{l}$ and $\tilde{y}$, and $n_l(\cdot)$, $n_y(\cdot)$, $n_{l|y}(\cdot|\cdot)$, and $n_{y|l}(\cdot|\cdot)$ are the associated marginal and conditional density functions. Under capacity constraints the only thing we know about $\tilde{l}$ and $\tilde{y}$ is that both are larger than zero. The contribution to the likelihood function is of the (bivariate) probit type in that case: it is the probability that this condition is indeed satisfied. Under labor constraints we observe $\tilde{l}$ as $\tilde{q}$. This gives rise to the first factor in the expression for L_{lc}. We moreover know that $\tilde{y}$ is larger than, or at least equal to, $\tilde{q}$. The second factor gives the probability that this is true, conditionally on the value of $\tilde{l}$ observed. The expression for L_{dc} is similar to the one for L_{lc} with $\tilde{l}$ and $\tilde{y}$ reversed.

Unfortunately the model presented so far cannot directly be used to analyze the data discussed in the previous section. Quite a few features of these data are in direct contradiction with the assumptions underlying the model. We will deal with them in turn:

1. The model does not account for the very significant group of firms reporting to be unconstrained.

2. Using a continuous distribution function the model has probability measure zero for the coincidence of two or more constraints. As a consequence the group of firms reporting multiple constraints cannot be accounted for.

3. The model does not allow for firms reporting "other" constraints.

4. According to the model all firms reporting capacity constraints should also report a degree of capacity utilization of 100 percent. It can be seen from figure 15.3 that this is not the case. In fact more than 70 percent report other values, either lower or higher.

5. The model does not allow for degrees of capacity utilization in excess of 100 percent. Actually about 2 percent of the firms in the sample do report a value larger than 100 percent.

6. The model assumes that $\tilde{q}$ is a continuously measured variable. It is in fact reported as a categorical variable due to rounding. Respondents differ in the precision of the reported values, so that we obtain the peculiar sawtooth shape of figure 15.3. As it stands, the model can only give rise to smooth density functions of $\tilde{q}$ conditional on the ruling regime.

These discrepancies are not all equally important. We have already mentioned that we have put aside observations reporting multiple constraints or other constraints. The frequency of those answers is simply too low to justify complicating modifications of the model.[3] Also the number of firms reporting a degree of capacity utilization in excess of unity is so low that a rather crude solution seemed appropriate: I have simply substituted a value of unity for those observations. To avoid problems with outliers I have also substituted a value of 0.4 for observations reporting degrees of capacity utilization less than 40 percent.[4] Thus we are left with three "hard" problems: how to deal with the unconstrained firms, how to deal with $\tilde{q} < 0$ for capacity constrained firms, and, finally, how to account for rounding in the reported values of $\tilde{q}$. In the remaining sections we will try to solve these problems and will also present some estimation results.

15.4 Estimation Results for Constrained Firms

In this section we will restrict ourselves to the group of firms reporting constraints. We will modify the model developed in the previous section to account for rounding and for degrees of capacity utilization less than unity reported by capacity-constrained firms, and we will discuss some estimation results. In the next section we will deal with the group of unconstrained firms.

The concept of *capacity* is not very well founded in economic theory. When input coefficients are fixed, as in a Leontief technology, it is straightforward to define capacity once the capital–output ratio and the amount of capital installed are given. However, when the possibility of substitution between inputs comes into play, it is by no means clear how capacity should be defined. The issue has been discussed, among others, by Cassel (1937), Klein (1960), Johansen (1968), Forest (1979), Berndt and Morrisson (1981), and Zeelenberg (1986, sec. 7.4). Figure 15.5 illustrates three alternative interpretations: *design* capacity q^d, *profitable* capacity q^p, and *maximum* capacity q^m. The figure displays the usual short-run marginal and average cost functions, SRMC and SRAC, with capital fixed. Both q^d and q^p represent economic concepts of capacity: they are defined by the short-run optimality condition that marginal costs equal output price. The only difference is in the price level taken as a point of reference: either the actual price level p or the short-run equilibrium price level p^*. The maximum capacity level q^m is not an economic but an "engineering" or physical concept: It can formally be defined as the level of output attainable with the available installations, given unlimited amounts of variable inputs (cf., Johansen 1968). As such it is independent of prices, both of the input and of the output of production activities. A remaining ambiguity, however, is to what extent labor has to be counted as a variable input. According to Forest (1979), who surveys the available evidence, the notion of capacity that respondents have in mind when reporting a degree of capacity utilization is most likely a kind of *practical maximum capacity*, defined as "the

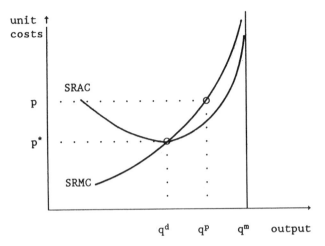

Figure 15.5
Alternative capacity concepts

greatest output that a firm can achieve by using its existing production facilities to the fullest extent possible within the framework of realistic work patterns." Economic conditions only come in "through their influence on customary work patterns" (p. 78). The output level q^m may be interpreted accordingly.

The fact that a significant proportion of the firms reporting capacity constraints also reports a degree of capacity utilization less than unity suggests that two different concepts of capacity are involved. Respondents seem to have a kind of physical capacity measure q^m in mind when reflecting on their degree of capacity utilization: otherwise, the lack of reported degrees over 100 percent cannot be explained. When reporting on constraints met in production, it seems more likely that an economic notion of capacity, such as q^d or q^p, is taken as a point of reference: otherwise, we cannot explain the less than maximal utilization of capacity with firms reporting capacity constraints. According to this view firms report these constraints only when the degree of capacity utilization is in excess of q^d or q^p. In establishing such a reference level considerations of a more practical nature may be involved as well. One may think of occasional breakdowns, inefficient use by inexperienced workers, maintenance, and other phenomena hindering maximal use of the available installations. Also, within one establishment, different production units may operate with different intensity, so that the overall degree of utilization can be less than unity even when capacity constraints dominate the activities of the firm as a whole.

We will therefore relax our assumption that capacity constraints imply q to be equal to unity. Instead, we will introduce a third random variable $\tilde{c}$ which is observed as $\tilde{q}$ only when capacity constraints are binding.[5] From an inspection of figure 15.3 it seems appropriate to assume that $\tilde{c}$ has a spike with mass π_0 at a value of 0, whereas the remaining mass is exponentially distributed[6] on the open interval $(-\infty, 0)$:

$$\Pr(\tilde{c} = 0) = \pi_0,$$

$$e(\tilde{c}) = (1 - \pi_0)\sigma_c^{-1} \exp\left(\frac{\tilde{c}}{\sigma_c}\right), \qquad \tilde{c} < 0,$$

where $e(\cdot)$ is the density function of $\tilde{c}$ for $\tilde{c} < 0$, and π_0 and σ_c are parameters to be estimated. The fraction π_0 represents firms that do indeed produce at the limits of their available capacity. The expectation of $\tilde{c}$ is $-(1 - \pi_0)\sigma_c$; its standard deviation is $(1 - \pi_0)\sigma_c$. To keep our model tractable, we will assume that $\tilde{c}$ is independent from $\tilde{l}$ and $\tilde{y}$.

Equation (2) now transforms into

$$\tilde{q} = \min[\tilde{c}, \tilde{l}, \tilde{y}], \tag{4}$$

and the expressions for $L_{cc}(i)$, $L_{lc}(i)$, and $L_{dc}(i)$ are modified as follows:

$$\left.\begin{aligned}
L_{cc}(i) &= e\{\tilde{q}(i)\} \cdot \int_{\tilde{q}(i)}^{\infty} \int_{\tilde{q}(i)}^{\infty} n(\tilde{l}, \tilde{y}) d\tilde{y} d\tilde{l}, \qquad \text{if } \tilde{q}(i) < 0, \\
&= \pi_0 \cdot \int_{0}^{\infty} \int_{0}^{\infty} n(\tilde{l}, \tilde{y}) d\tilde{y} d\tilde{l}, \qquad \text{if } \tilde{q}(i) = 0, \\
L_{lc}(i) &= n_l\{\tilde{q}(i)\} \cdot \int_{\tilde{q}(i)}^{\infty} n_{y|l}\{\tilde{y}|\tilde{q}(i)\} d\tilde{y} \cdot \left\{\int_{\tilde{q}(i)}^{\infty} e(\tilde{c}) d\tilde{c} + \pi_0\right\}, \\
L_{dc}(i) &= n_y\{\tilde{q}(i)\} \cdot \int_{\tilde{q}(i)}^{\infty} n_{l|y}\{\tilde{l}|\tilde{q}(i)\} d\tilde{l} \cdot \left\{\int_{\tilde{q}(i)}^{\infty} e(\tilde{c}) d\tilde{c} + \pi_0\right\}.
\end{aligned}\right\} \tag{5}$$

Likelihood function (5) still assumes that $\tilde{q}(i)$ is observed as a continuous random variable. Because it is in fact observed as a categorical variable, due to considerable rounding, (5) has to be modified in turn. From now on we will assume that $\tilde{q}(i)$ is a latent continuous random variable, generated according to equation (4). We only observe the interval in which $\tilde{q}(i)$ happens to fall. As in table 15.2, thirteen intervals can be observed. We assume that, independent of the value of $\tilde{q}(i)$ or the ruling regime, a fraction π_5 of the respondents rounds to multiples of 5 percent, whereas $1 - \pi_5$ uses multiples of 10 percent. The 40 percent interval accounts for all the values less than 42.5 percent for the first group and less than 45 percent for the second. Similarly, the 100 percent interval represents values larger than either 97.5 percent for the first group, or 95 percent for the second. The intervals in between are centered at the values 45, 50, ..., 95 percent. The parameter π_5 has to estimated.

Because we have a fully categorical model now, we have to adapt our notation. Let $j = 1, ..., 13$ denote the intervals for $\tilde{q}$. The vectors with elements a_j and b_j contain lower and upper bounds of the 5 percent intervals, that is, $a_1 = -\infty$; $a_j = \ln(0.325 + 0.05 * j)$ for $j = 2, ..., 13$; $b_j = \ln(0.375 + 0.05 * j)$ for $j = 1, ..., 12$; $b_{13} = 0$. Also let $a_0 \equiv a_1$ and $b_{14} \equiv b_{13}$. When the number of observations in regime r and interval j is $N_{r,j}$, the likelihood function is

$$
L = \prod_r \prod_j p_{r,j}^{N_{r,j}}, \qquad r = cc, lc, dc; j = 1, ..., 13,
$$

$$
p_{cc,j} = \pi_5 \cdot \int_{a_j}^{b_j} e(\tilde{c}) \int_{\tilde{c}}^{\infty} \int_{\tilde{c}}^{\infty} n(\tilde{l}, \tilde{y}) d\tilde{y} d\tilde{l} d\tilde{c} + (1 - \pi_5) l_{\text{odd}}(j)
$$

$$
\cdot \int_{1/2a_j + 1/2a_{j-1}}^{1/2b_j + 1/2b_{j+1}} e(\tilde{c}) \int_{\tilde{c}}^{\infty} \int_{\tilde{c}}^{\infty} n(\tilde{l}, \tilde{y}) d\tilde{y} d\tilde{l} d\tilde{c}
$$

$$
+ l_{13}(j)\pi_0 \cdot \int_0^{\infty} \int_0^{\infty} n(\tilde{l}, \tilde{y}) d\tilde{y} d\tilde{l},
$$

$$
p_{lc,j} = \pi_5 \cdot \int_{a_j}^{b_j} n_l(\tilde{l}) \left\{ \int_{\tilde{l}}^{\infty} n_{y|l}(\tilde{y}|\tilde{l}) d\tilde{y} \right\} \left\{ \int_{\tilde{l}}^0 e(\tilde{c}) d\tilde{c} + \pi_0 \right\} d\tilde{l}
$$

$$
+ (1 - \pi_5) l_{\text{odd}}(j)
$$

$$
\cdot \int_{1/2a_j + 1/2a_{j-1}}^{1/2b_j + 1/2b_{j+1}} n_l(\tilde{l}) \left\{ \int_{\tilde{l}}^{\infty} n_{y|l}(\tilde{y}|\tilde{l}) d\tilde{y} \right\} \left\{ \int_{\tilde{l}}^0 e(\tilde{c}) d\tilde{c} + \pi_0 \right\} d\tilde{l},
$$

$$
p_{dc,j} = \pi_5 \cdot \int_{a_j}^{b_j} n_y(\tilde{y}) \left\{ \int_{\tilde{y}}^{\infty} n_{l|y}(\tilde{l}|\tilde{y}) d\tilde{l} \right\} \left\{ \int_{\tilde{y}}^0 e(\tilde{c}) d\tilde{c} + \pi_0 \right\} d\tilde{y}
$$

$$
+ (1 - \pi_5) l_{\text{odd}}(j)
$$

$$
\cdot \int_{1/2a_j + 1/2a_{j-1}}^{1/2b_j + 1/2b_{j+1}} n_y(\tilde{y}) \left\{ \int_{\tilde{y}}^{\infty} n_{l|y}(\tilde{l}|\tilde{y}) d\tilde{l} \right\} \left\{ \int_{\tilde{y}}^0 e(\tilde{c}) d\tilde{c} + \pi_0 \right\} d\tilde{y},
$$

(6)

where the indicator function $\iota_{\mathrm{odd}}(j)$ is 1 when j is odd, and 0 elsewhere, and the indicator function $\iota_{13}(j)$ is 1 when $j = 13$, and 0 elsewhere. The likelihood function is of the multinomial type now: the probabilities $p_{r,j}$ add to unity over the three regimes r and the thirteen intervals j. Each of the terms in (6) obtains by integration over the appropriate interval of the corresponding terms in likelihood function (5), which was associated with a continuously instead of a discretely observed $\tilde{q}$. For odd j the integration has to be performed twice because both respondents using multiples of 5 percent and those using multiples of 10 percent contribute to the mass in these intervals. The intervals in between can only be observed when a 5 percent scale has been used. The terms are weighted with the corresponding fractions π_5 and $1 - \pi_5$.

To evaluate the likelihood function, multiple integrals have to be computed. The value of the exponential integral $\int_a^b e(\tilde{c})d\tilde{c}$ is obtained analytically. I used routine S15ABF of the NAG-library to compute the value of the cumulative normal distribution function. The evaluation of the bivariate normal integral in the expression for $p_{cc,j}$ has been documented in appendix B of Kooiman (1984). For the outer integrations over intervals (a_j, b_j), I used the 10-point Gauss-Legendre quadrature available as routine D01BBF, option D01BAZ of the NAG-library. The quadrature was applied to the range $[12.5\%, 100\%]$ of values of q in 35 separate intervals, each with a width of 2.5 percent. The contribution to the integrals of the left tail, with values of q less than 12.5 percent, is negligible. Values for the left-hand sides of (6) were subsequently obtained by addition of the values obtained for the appropriate subintervals. Thus the integration procedure involves 350 evaluations of the integrand for each of the three available regimes, which makes for relatively accurate results. The computational burden is rather heavy: one evaluation of (6) takes about 2 seconds cpu on a CDC Cyber 170-855 mainframe computer. It was checked whether the sum of the $3 * 13 = 39$ values obtained deviated more than 1 percent from unity. This never occurred.

The maximum of likelihood function (6) was obtained using NAG-library routine E04JBF, with numerical evaluation of first derivatives with respect to the parameters. There are five parameters of interest, namely, the first and second moments of $n(\tilde{l}, \tilde{y})$, and three nuisance parameters σ_c, π_0, and π_5, which we have introduced in this section to account for specific features of the data. Estimation results for the group of firms reporting constraints are in table 15.3. It gives estimates, and asymptotic standard

Table 15.3
Estimation results for firms reporting constraints

Parameter	Estimates (standard deviation)		
μ_l	0.011 (0.021)	0.088 (0.028)	0.164 (0.033)
μ_y	−0.146 (0.021)	−0.128 (0.022)	−0.115 (0.023)
σ_l	0.183 (0.017)	0.213 (0.021)	0.252 (0.026)
σ_y	0.305 (0.019)	0.319 (0.020)	0.333 (0.021)
ρ_{ly}	0 (—)	−0.5 (—)	−0.9 (—)
σ_c	0.106 (0.017)	0.106 (0.017)	0.105 (0.017)
π_0	0.675 (0.064)	0.674 (0.065)	0.670 (0.066)
π_5	0.628 (0.058)	0.629 (0.058)	0.630 (0.059)
$\ln L$	−877.7	−874.7	−869.4

errors, for three fixed values of the correlation coefficient ρ_{ly}. This parameter could not be properly estimated. It invariably tended toward a value of −1, as can be inferred from the values of $\ln L$ displayed in the table.[7] The nuisance parameters σ_c, π_0, and π_5 are seen to be completely insensitive to the value of ρ_{ly} imposed. The distribution of $\tilde{c}$ is fairly concentrated at the theoretical value of 0 associated with full capacity production, as it should be. The spike at this value accounts for about two thirds of the mass and the overall mean $-(1 - \pi_0)\sigma_c \approx -0.03$. About one third of the respondents rounds to multiples of 10 percent in reporting the degree of capacity utilization, the others—more accurately—use multiples of 5 percent. Unfortunately the parameters of interest, relating to the joint distribution of $\tilde{l}$ and $\tilde{y}$, and sensitive to the choice of ρ_{ly}, especially μ_l and σ_l. Because it makes quite a difference whether on average relative excess supply of labor is about 1 percent (if $\rho_{ly} = 0$.) or 16.5 percent (if $\rho_{ly} = -0.9$), the results are virtually useless from the applied point of view, despite the fact that the overall pattern is acceptable. We will return to this issue in section 15.6, where we investigate why ρ_{ly} tends to −1.

15.5   Unconstrained Firms

We still have to deal with firms reporting to operate without constraints. According to the actual phrasing of the business survey questionnaire, firms first have to decide whether they should report to be constrained. If they answer in the affirmative, they must mention the type of constraint. Leaving firms out that report to be without constraints, as we did in the previous section, one in fact analyzes a conditional distribution of $\tilde{c}$, $\tilde{l}$, and $\tilde{y}$. It is obvious that a selection bias will occur: the distribution of excess supplies of labor and goods is not likely to be the same for the group of firms reporting constraints, as it is for the group of firms reporting to be without constraints. This leaves us with the question how the latter group can be included in the model.

There are several options available. We have already noticed in section 15.3 that in our cc-regime firms realize their notional level of activities, so it is quite possible that firms report being unconstrained instead of being capacity constrained when operating in this regime. This gives us the first option: we take the unconstrained and the capacity-constrained firms together and treat them as one group. Unfortunately the available data do not unequivocally support this view. Recalling that the distribution of the reported degrees of capacity utilization of the unconstrained firms is very similar to the one of the labor-constrained firms, it can be inferred from figures 15.2 and 15.3, and table 15.1 that capacity-constrained and unconstrained firms are not the same. As far as the degree of capacity utilization is concerned, they represent different, though possibly partly overlapping, groups.

The second option available it to assume that firms reporting to be unconstrained in fact signal that they are not severely constrained. Such a view entails that the probability of values of $\tilde{y}$ or $\tilde{l}$ (or both) not being too far from 0 is larger than average for those firms. In Kooiman (1984) I proceeded along this line. There it led to the introduction of a fourth region in figure 15.4, as a band between the cc- and dc-regions. Modifying our present model in a similar way we have to include additional random variables determining the boundaries between the new region and the cc- and dc-regions. This entails additional integration steps as well, which is not very attractive since the computational burden is considerable already in our present model. Also, the group of unconstrained firms is very large so that the fourth region is likely to dominate the other regimes completely. Some preliminary computations, which we will not reproduce here, indicate that indeed such an effect obtains, and that unrealistic estimates for the parameters of interest in our model are implied.

A final, and quite straightforward option is to assume that firms indicating to be without constraints only do so because it provides them with an easy way out of the question involved; that is, they are partially nonresponding. In this view firms reporting to be without constraints may in fact be constrained by capacity, by labor supply, or by output demand, just as firms that report such constraints. Such an assumption may be justified by the fact that on a similar question in the French business survey, which did not include the possibility to indicating no constraints, almost all respondents reported constraints.[8] Although we do not observe the type of constraint, we do observe the degree of capacity utilization for those firms, that is, the marginal distribution of q, and this can be used to obtain more precise estimates.

Assuming that the probabilities $p_{r,j}$ introduced before apply to all firms, and not only to firms actually reporting constraints, the likelihood function can easily be obtained, provided the probability P that constraints are reported is independent of both the regime r and the value of $\tilde{q}$. In that case the probability that a randomly chosen firm reports a constraint of type r and an interval j for its degree of capacity utilization is $Pp_{r,j}$; $r = cc$, lc, dc; $j = 1, \ldots, 13$. As a consequence of the independence assumption the probability that such a firm reports being unconstrained, and has a degree of capacity utilization in the interval j, is $(1 - P)(p_{cc,j} + p_{lc,j} + p_{dc,j})$; $j = 1, \ldots, 13$. This yields the following likelihood function:

$$
\left.
\begin{aligned}
L &= P^{N-N_{uc}}(1 - P)^{N_{uc}} \cdot \prod_r \prod_j p_{r,j}^{N_{r,j}}, \qquad r = cc, lc, dc, uc; j = 1, \ldots, 13, \\
p_{uc,j} &= \sum_{r'} p_{r',j}, \qquad r' = cc, lc, dc,
\end{aligned}
\right\} \tag{7}
$$

where $p_{cc,j}$, $p_{lc,j}$, and $p_{dc,j}$ are as in equation (6), N is the sample size, and N_{uc} is the number of firms reporting to be without constraints. Because P is assumed to be independent of $p_{r,j}$, it does not involve the parameters of our model. As a consequence the mechanism determining whether constraints are reported is exogenous, and the likelihood function can be concentrated by first maximizing over (the parameters of) P for given values of the model parameters.[9] As a result we obtain

$$
L^* = \prod_r \prod_j p_{r,j}^{N_{r,j}}, \qquad r = cc, lc, dc, uc; j = 1, \ldots, 13, \tag{8}
$$

as the function to be maximized.[10] Table 15.4 presents the estimation results.

The results in table 15.4 are similar to those in table 15.3. The correlation coefficient tends to a value of -1 again. The values of the nuisance param-

Table 15.4
Estimation results that include unconstrained firms

Parameter	Estimates (standard deviation)		
μ_l	0.011 (0.014)	0.061 (0.018)	0.103 (0.020)
μ_y	-0.009 (0.018)	0.006 (0.019)	0.011 (0.020)
σ_l	0.157 (0.010)	0.179 (0.012)	0.204 (0.013)
σ_y	0.304 (0.014)	0.314 (0.014)	0.318 (0.015)
ρ_{ly}	0 (—)	-0.5 (—)	-0.9 (—)
σ_c	0.086 (0.009)	0.090 (0.010)	0.095 (0.011)
π_0	0.668 (0.055)	0.696 (0.053)	0.717 (0.050)
π_5	0.692 (0.028)	0.691 (0.028)	0.683 (0.027)
$\ln L^*$	-3422.9	-3417.3	-3413.5

eters are relatively stable as before. Standard errors are somewhat smaller due to the increased number of observations. The values obtained for μ_l and σ_l are similar. The main difference is in the value of μ_y, which has increased from about -0.13 to 0 as a consequence of the inclusion of the group of unconstrained firms. Despite this shift in location, the standard deviation σ_y is remarkably stable. I have mentioned before that the distribution of reported degrees of capacity utilization for the group of unconstrained firms almost coincides with the one for the group of labor-constrained firms. This explains why the inclusion of unconstrained firms in the likelihood function does not entail a shift in the distribution of $\tilde{l}$. In figure 15.3 we have seen that demand-constrained firms report lower degrees of capacity utilization on average. In (7) $p_{dc,j}$ has to accommodate not only values for $\tilde{q}$ reported by demand-constrained firms but also—in combination with $p_{lc,j}$ and $p_{dc,j}$—values reported by the large group of unconstrained firms. This explains the shift to the right of the distribution of $\tilde{y}$ when we include the group of unconstrained firms.

It has to be noted, finally, that the residuals, defined as (absolute) differences between sample fractions and the corresponding model proportions, though generally small, display rather systematic patterns, similar to the presence of (severe) serial correlation in the residuals of a time series regression model. Also the introduction of unconstrained firms blows up the residual of the 100 percent cell of the capacity-constrained regime by a factor 3, making it about four times as large as any other residual. This indicates that important specification errors may still be present in the model associated with (7).

One may doubt the validity of the assumption that the probability P is exogenous to the model, which is at the basis of the results in table 15.4. The proportion of firms reporting to be without constraints fluctuates strongly over the cycle: values between 35 and 75 percent occur. This testifies against the exogeneity of P. There is almost no gain in reporting to be unconstrained for firms subject to unequivocal constraints: the reduction in the effort involved in filling in the questionnaire is marginal in that case. Respondents in less clear-cut circumstances may welcome the possibility to avoid figuring out what type of constraint has actually been binding over the past period, though. This brings us back to the second option again, where we assume that unconstrained firms are firms not being severely constrained. Some overlap with capacity constraints, as in the first option, is likely to be present as well. Although no direct information is available, I am inclined to conclude that the three options are all valid: the group of firms under discussion in this section is likely to involve capacity-constrained firms, partially nonresponding firms, and firms signaling not to be severely constrained. It remains to find a proper way to incorporate such a heterogeneous group in our statistical model.

15.6 The Covariance of Excess Supply of Labor and Excess Demand for Goods

In both sections 15.4 and 15.5 we have obtained the puzzling result that the correlation coefficient ρ_{ly} of the relative excess supply of labor $\tilde{l}$ and the relative excess demand for output $\tilde{y}$ tends to -1 when maximizing the likelihood function, so that it cannot be properly estimated. A value of -1 is not acceptable. It entails that the distinction between labor markets and goods markets is redundant: once the labor market position is given, the position of a firm on the goods market is given as well. A negative correlation, though not a perfect one, may not be unreasonable. Growing firms are likely to be those experiencing high levels of demand for output: otherwise, they would not be expanding. Difficulties to recruit sufficient labor to sustain this growth may entail a less than average excess supply of labor. On the other hand, prospering firms are likely to offer more secure positions, so that they may also attract a more than average supply of labor, and a positive correlation might result.

In this section we will try to figure out why ρ_{ly} tends to -1 in our model. As the modifications of the model introduced in sections 15.4 and 15.5 are immaterial for this issue, we will be concerned with likelihood function (3) associated with the model in equation (2). The basic thing to notice is that, apart from the truncation at 0 we observe the minimum of two random variables $\tilde{l}$ and $\tilde{y}$. We observe $\tilde{l}$ ($\tilde{y}$) when it is small relatively to $\tilde{y}$ ($\tilde{l}$). When small values of $\tilde{l}$ ($\tilde{y}$) tend to be associated with large values values of $\tilde{y}$ ($\tilde{l}$), and the minimum of the two is observed, the conditional probabilities $\Pr(\tilde{y} > \tilde{l}|\tilde{l}$ observed$)$ and $\Pr(\tilde{l} > \tilde{y}|\tilde{y}$ observed$)$ tend to be large, so that the probability to observe the given sample tends to be large as well. Although not very precisely so, this basically explains why a tendency may exist for the correlation of $\tilde{l}$ and $\tilde{y}$ to tend to -1, when maximizing the likelihood function.

More formally, Goldfeld and Quandt (1978) have demonstrated that in small samples a tendency may exist for the correlation coefficient to go to -1 in case we observe the minimum of two correlated normal random variables, as in models for markets in disequilibrium. In summarizing their argument, it will become clear that this tendency is likely to be more pronounced in our model due to the additional truncation of $\tilde{q}$ at a value of 0. We start with a nontruncated model, where $\tilde{q}$ is the minimum of the normal variates $\tilde{l}$ and $\tilde{y}$. Assuming the regime observed, as in our model, the likelihood of an observation $\tilde{q}$ on, say, $\tilde{l}$ is $n_l(\tilde{q}) \cdot P(\tilde{y} > \tilde{l}|\tilde{l} = \tilde{q})$; compare the expression for $L_{lc}(i)$ in (3). The first factor, being a marginal density function, does not involve the parameter ρ_{ly}. The second factor, being a conditional probability, does. When ρ_{ly} tends to -1 the conditional distribution of $\tilde{y}$ degenerates as its variance tends to zero. From the usual formulae for the conditional mean of normal variates it can directly be checked that the second factor tends to 1 if and only if the condition

$$\frac{\sigma_l \mu_y + \sigma_y \mu_l}{\sigma_l + \sigma_y} > \tilde{q} \tag{9}$$

is satisfied. The same condition holds when $\tilde{y}$ instead of $\tilde{l}$ is observed. When it holds[11] for all observations in the sample, the second factors are maximal, which explains that in small samples maximizing the likelihood may result in $\rho_{ly} \to -1$.

It is essential that condition (9) hold for all observations. When the reverse inequality sign holds, the probability involved will tend to 0, so one observation suffices to cancel the contributions of all other observations.

When the sample size increases the value of the largest $\tilde{q}$ tends to infinity. In order for condition (9) to hold for all observations, either one of the means has to tend to infinity as well or both variances have to go to 0. This, however, entails very unfavorable values for the first factors in the likelihood, that is the marginals $n_l(\tilde{q})$ and $n_y(\tilde{q})$, so that the tendency for ρ_{ly} to go to -1 will effectively be countered, and anomalous results will no longer occur. It is clear then that the introduction of an additional truncation from above, as in our model (2), may prevent this counteraction from becoming effective. The critical point is whether values of μ_l, μ_y, σ_l, and σ_y exist that both satisfy condition (9) for all observations and allow for a reasonable fit of the marginals $n_l(\cdot)$ and $n_y(\cdot)$.

Figure 15.6 demonstrates that this may indeed be the case with our data. It displays the situation obtained when the joint distribution of $\tilde{l}$ and $\tilde{y}$ has collapsed to a line $\tilde{l} = -c \cdot \tilde{y} + d$; $c, d > 0$. With $d > 0$, condition (9) is satisfied for all observations since $\tilde{q} \leq 0$. When $\tilde{y}$ is observed as $\tilde{q}$, $\tilde{q} < 0$, the associated value of $\tilde{l}$ is automatically given as $-c \cdot \tilde{q} + d$, which is larger than $\tilde{q}$ with probability 1. A similar result obtains when we observe $\tilde{l}$. Projection of the two half-lines on the negative parts of the $\tilde{l}$- and $\tilde{y}$-axes, as indicated in the figure, gives an impression of the resulting conditional

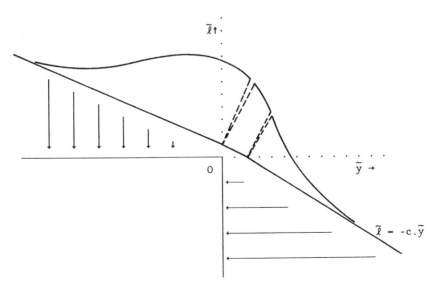

Figure 15.6
A degenerated joint distribution of $\tilde{l}$ and $\tilde{y}$

distributions of $\tilde{q}$ under the dc- and lc-regimes. Comparing the observed distributions of q for these regimes in figure 15.3, it becomes clear that the general pattern of the available data is fairly accurately reproduced this way. The modifications to the model introduced in the first part of section 15.4 do not invalidate this result. Notice that the observations on the cc-regime are represented by the segment of the line $\tilde{l} = -c \cdot \tilde{y} + d$ falling in the positive quadrant.

The analysis given so far demonstrates that the problem under discussion could be due to the size of our sample, but it does not prove that this is indeed the case. Specification errors may be present as well. There can be no doubt that the results of Hartley and Mallela (1977) generalize to our model, so that the parameters of the distribution of $\tilde{l}$ and $\tilde{y}$ are identified and the usual properties of maximum likelihood apply, provided the model has been correctly specified. In that case one may expect the problem to disappear when the sample size is increased, for example by pooling several cross sections. Things may be different, however, when the model is misspecified. To investigate to what extent specification errors play a role, it is desirable therefore to perform some Monte Carlo experiments. Unfortunately estimation of the model is too expensive to allow for a full-fledged stochastic simulation of the small sample properties of the maximum likelihood estimator. So we will be content with a few estimation runs on simulated data only.

We will first compare the actual distribution of the reported degrees of capacity utilization with the theoretical distribution according to the model developed in section 15.4, that is, the distribution associated with likelihood function (6). As the estimates obtained in section 15.4 represent the best possible fit—on the likelihood criterion—of the theoretical distribution to our actual data, I have used these estimates in simulating the model. Figures 15.7 and 15.8 present the results of 100,000 random drawings generated with NAG-library routines G05CAF, G05CBF, G05DBF, and G05DDF. They are based upon the estimates with $\rho_{ly} = 0$ and $\rho_{ly} = -0.9$ given in the first and third colums of table 15.3. Figure 15.9 repeats the central part of figure 15.3 in order to ease a comparison of these simulated distributions with our actual data. Although the difference between figures 15.7 and 15.8 is not spectacular, figure 15.8 fits the distribution of our actual data in figure 15.9 somewhat better than figure 15.7. Going from figure 15.7 to figure 15.8, the maximum of the distribution for the dc-regime shifts from 70 to 80 percent, which is more in line with figure 15.9. Also the dispersion of the

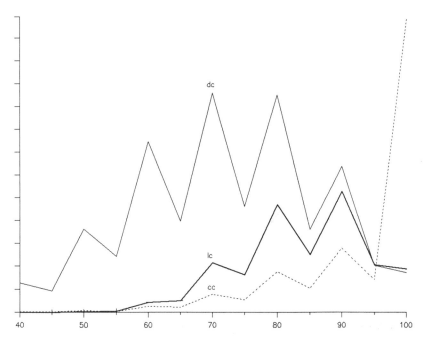

Figure 15.7
The theoretical distribution of reported degrees of capacity utilization (q) with $\rho_{ly} = 0$ (first column of table 15.3, 100,000 random drawings)

distribution for the lc-regime increases, yielding a better fit both at the lower and the upper ends of the scale.

A comparison of figures 15.7 and 15.8 with figure 15.9 also indicates remaining misspecifications. We have already noticed that a 75 percent degree of capacity utilization is observed too frequently, mainly at the cost of the 70 percent category. A more serious discrepancy is observed with the labor-constrained firms at the 100 percent interval. As it stands, the model cannot account for the relatively large number of firms reporting this value. According to our model such a value can only be observed with labor-constrained firms when $\tilde{y} \geq 0$ and $\tilde{c} = 0$. Apparently, the probability involved is too low, probably because $\Pr(\tilde{y} \geq 0)$ is too small. This may either indicate that the joint distribution of $\tilde{l}$ and $\tilde{y}$ is not normal or that the 100 percent interval attracts observations over a wider range of actual $\tilde{q}$ values than our model assumes.

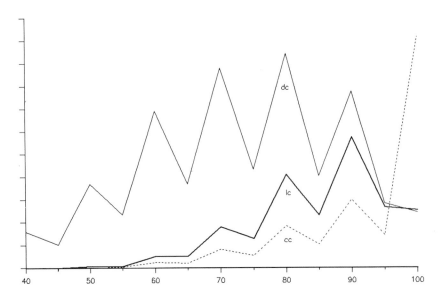

Figure 15.8
The theoretical distribution of reported degrees of capacity utilization (q) with $\rho_{ly} = -0.9$
(third column of table 15.3, 100,000 random drawings)

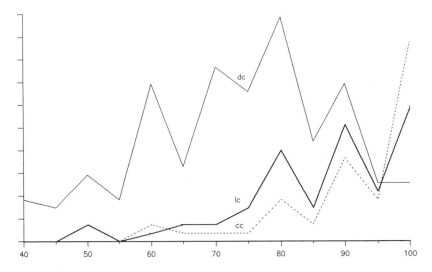

Figure 15.9
The actual distribution of reported degrees of capacity utilization, September 1985

We can also use simulated data to estimate the model. To this end random drawings were generated using the estimates reported in the second column of table 15.3, where $\rho_{ly} = -0.5$ was imposed. Four data sets were created, one based upon 100,000 random drawings, and three based upon 300 random drawings, which is about the size of our sample of firms reporting constraints. Estimation results were as follows: The large sample gave $\hat{\rho}_{ly} = -0.477\,(0.021)$. The three small samples gave $\hat{\rho}_{ly} = +0.27\,(0.72)$, $-0.50\,(0.41)$, and $-0.65\,(0.31)$. No tendency for ρ_{ly} to go to -1 could be detected. These results clearly show that a sample size of 300 is far too small to determine ρ_{ly} with any precision. Given that we never observe $\tilde{l}$ and $\tilde{y}$ together, this may not come as a surprise. Even minor misspecifications may therefore easily lead to the anomalous results that we have obtained.

15.7   Conclusion

The degree of capacity utilization and the kind of constraints met in production, as observed in business surveys, reflect the intensity and the dispersion of disequilibria on goods and labor markets. The model derived in this chapter to estimate the joint distribution of excess supply on goods and labor markets from such data fails in two respects. First, the covariance could not be identified. In maximizing the likelihood function, the correlation coefficient ρ_{ly} of relative excess supply of labor $\tilde{l}$ and relative excess demand for goods $\tilde{y}$ invariably tends to -1 so that the likelihood degenerates. It was shown that such an effect may indeed obtain in our model, because the sample size is too small to determine ρ_{ly} with any precision and some misspecification is likely to be present. Since the estimated mean and variance of excess supply of labor appear to be quite sensitive to the value of ρ_{ly} imposed, the model is only useful when the value of this parameter is known from other sources.

The second unresolved problem is how to deal with the large group of firms reporting to meet no constraints. Although some possibilities to incorporate such a group into the basic disequilibrium framework have been pointed out, no satisfactory solution seems to be available. From the point of view of the firm the distinction between being capacity constrained and being unconstrained is rather vague, and perhaps more a matter of psychology than hard economic facts. It is not unlikely that part of the respondents misused the possibility to indicate being unconstrained as an easy way to skip the question involved. Since it also complicates the analysis of the data, it would perhaps be better to change the phrasing of the question. The French experience shows that it is quite possible to do without an explicit category of "no constraints."

Notes

The views expressed in this chapter are those of the author and do not necessarily reflect the policies of the Netherlands Central Bureau of Statistics. I thank Teun Kloek for his extensive comments on an earlier version of this chapter, which appeared as chapter 5 of my Ph.D. dissertation. All remaining errors are mine.

1. As a consequence the distribution functions in figure 15.2 are in fact stepfunctions. This feature of the data was neglected in the figure to make it more transparent.

2. It is possible in principle that two or more constraints are simultaneously binding. In the model that we will use it has probability measure zero. As can be seen from table 15.1 the fraction of firms actually reporting multiple constraints is very low, and these observations have been removed from the sample.

3. It is possible to account for the firms reporting "other" constraints in a straightforward way, though, by treating them as observations where the information about the regime is missing. We then only use the information that $\tilde{l}$ and $\tilde{y}$ are larger than, or at least equal to the value of $\tilde{q}$ reported. I have not proceeded along this line, as this solution was recognized too late.

4. Notice that some firms report zero degree of capacity utilization; that is, $\tilde{q} = -\infty$! These observations have to be "repaired" (or discarded) anyway.

5. Note that the observations on $\exp(\tilde{c})$ are *not* observations on q^d or q^p. According to our model we only know that the critical level of capacity utilization referred to is less than (larger than) the reported degree of capacity utilization q when capacity constraints are reported (are not reported).

6. I have tried a normal distribution for $\tilde{c}$ as well, both with a separate truncation parameter π_0 as above, and in a Tobit version where the probability that $\tilde{c} = 0$ obtains as the mass of the truncated part of the distribution. The Tobit version was definitely rejected on a likelihood ratio criterion. The truncated exponential seemed to perform as well as the truncated normal. As the normal involves an additional parameter the exponential was preferred.

7. I have not included positive values of ρ_{ly} in the table as no tendency was observed toward such values when maximizing the likelihood function.

8. The only way to indicate being unconstrained in the French survey is by not answering the question involved, that is, by item nonresponse. Also De Leeuw (1979) finds evidence in the survey held by the U.S. Bureau of Economic Analysis that the frequency of the "no change" response is extraordinarily high due to biased reporting, when asking for the change in degrees of capacity utilization over the past quarter. This clearly points at the same sort of phenomenon.

9. When P is treated as a constant it can directly be seen that it is estimated as $1 - N_{uc}/N$, that is, the sample proportion reporting constraints.

10. Note that although (7) is of the multinomial type, (8) is not since the probabilities $p_{r,j}$ do not add to unity. In fact we have $\sum\sum p_{r,j} = 2$ when the summation includes the uc-regime.

11. Goldfeld and Quandt (1978) also show that the correlation may tend to $+1$ as well, provided a condition similar to (9) is satisfied. In our present model this condition is not likely to be met, and such a tendency did not occur; compare note 7.

References

Berndt, E. R., and C. J. Morrison. 1981. "Capacity Utilization Measures: Underlying Economic Theory and an Alternative Approach." *American Economic Review* 71:48–52.

Cassel, J. M. 1937. "Excess Capacity and Monopolistic Competition." *Quarterly Journal of Economics* 51:426–443.

De Leeuw, F. 1979. "Why Capacity Utilization Rates Differ." In *Measures of Capacity Utilization: Problems and Tasks. Staff Studies* 105. Board of Governors of the Federal Reserve System, Washington, 17–56.

Forest, L. R., Jr. 1979. "Capacity Utilization: Concepts and Measurement." In *Measures of Capacity Utilization: Problems and Tasks.* Staff Studies 105, Board of Governors of the Federal Reserve System, Washington, 57–136.

Goldfeld, S. M., and R. E. Quandt. 1978. "Some Properties of the Simple Disequilibrium Model with Covariance." *Economics Letters* 1:343–346.

Hartley, M. J., and P. Mallela. 1977. "The Asymptotic Properties of a Maximum Likelihood Estimator for a Model of Markets in Disequilibrium." *Econometrica* 45:1205–1220.

Johansen, L. 1968. "Production Functions and the Concept of Capacity." In *Recherches récentes sur la fonction de production.* Namur: Ceruna, Facultés Universitaires Notre-Dame de la Paix.

Klein, L. R. 1960. "Some Theoretical Issues in the Measurement of Capacity. *Econometrica* 28:272–286.

Kooiman, P. 1984. "Smoothing the Aggregate Fix-Price Model and the Use of Business Survey Data. *The Economic Journal* 94:899–913.

Maddala, G. S., and F. D. Nelson. 1974. "Maximum Likelihood Methods for Models of Markets in Disequilibrium." *Econometrica* 42:1013–1030.

Muellbauer, J. 1978. "Macrotheory vs. Macroeconometrics: The Treatment of Disequilibrium in Macromodels." Birkbeck Discussion Paper 59, Birbeck College, London.

Zeelenberg, C. 1986. *Industrial Price Formation.* Amsterdam: North Holland.

16 The Structure of Dynamic Macroeconometric Models

Pierre Malgrange

16.1 Introduction

We generally build macroeconometric models for two reasons: to construct explanatory structures able to test a particular theory about the working of an economy, and to produce forecasts with the greatest possible degree of accuracy. The generation of reliable forecasts leads, quite naturally, to a large number of equations in the model. Indeed, a medium size model typically includes two to three hundred equations, whereas a large one might include several thousand. In comparison, a model of fifty or fewer equations is called a "core model" or a "maquette" (i.e., it is a demonstration model unable to deliver "serious" forecasts). This impressively large size has the unfortunate consequence of rendering the working of the model rather opaque to the user. In other words, such models are treated as "black boxes," which conflicts with their other role as stylized explanations of the working of the economy. This has been the major argument against macroeconometric models, since very small size "black boxes" can produce much cheaper and equally accurate forecasts (Sims 1980).

Thus, to defend structural models, there is a need for methods designed to attain satisfactory control of their different mechanisms, and there now exists a substantial set of methods aimed at enlightening various aspects of a model (see, e.g., Hickman 1972; Deleau and Malgrange 1978; Kmenta and Ramsey 1981; Chow and Corsi 1984; Wallis 1984; Kuh et al. 1985).

We present here a method that seeks to reveal the theory embodied in the specification of the model by exploiting the peculiar structure of standard macroeconomic models (which combine standard Keynesian disequilibrium in the short run with dynamic capital accumulation). The basic approach is to treat them as purely deterministic disequilibrium growth models. Starting from a given macroeconomic model, the strategy consists in first looking for a steady state growth path solution and in then trying to interpret this path as an equilibrium path. By a conventional change of coordinates, the steady state growth path is transformed into a steady state, constant through time. The disequilibrium dynamics can then be studied around a well-defined equilibrium state.

This procedure has the advantages of precluding any simulation horizon from the study of the model, and of using linear methods of investigation, which are by far best suited to elucidating the most important features of a model.

We first give a detailed presentation of the methodology, and then illustrate it by applying this approach to METRIC, a French quarterly model. The analysis stems essentially from our previous work (see, e.g., Deleau and Malgrange 1978) and is a synthesis of two unpublished studies of this model (Malgrange 1983; Kuh, Le Van, and Malgrange 1984).

16.2 Methodology

Long-Run Equilibrium

1. Without loss of generality, macroeconometric models may be written in the form:

$$y(t) = f(y(t), y(t-1), x(t); \beta, t),$$ (1)

with

$y(t) = (y_1(t), \ldots, y_n(t))$, an $n \times 1$ vector of endogenous variables,

$x(t) = ((x_1(t), \ldots, x_m(t))$, an $m \times 1$ vector of exogenous variables,

β = a vector of parameters,

t = the time index.

The variables $x(t)$ and $y(t)$ represent levels. Note that we are concerned here only with the deterministic part of the model. As capital accumulation is endogenized in macroeconometric modeling, the consistent concept of "long run," or equilibrium, is that of the steady state growth path (SSGP), a moving equilibrium where the rates of growth of the levels are constant through time.

Formally, we are looking for the following solution to (1):

$$\begin{cases} \bar{x}_i(t) = \bar{x}_i(0)a_i^t, & i = 1, \ldots, m, \\ \bar{y}_j(t) = \bar{y}_j(0)b_j^t, & j = 1, \ldots, n. \end{cases}$$ (2)

Thus a SSGP is the vector of the n initial conditions, $\bar{y}(0)$, and of the n trends $(b_1, \ldots, b_n)$, given $x(0)$ and $(a_1, \ldots, a_m)$, which verify (1) at each date.

2. Some specification constraints on the system (1) are necessary for a SSGP to exist. In many macroeconometric models these constraints are not always satisfied because these models are not typically oriented toward the long run. The usual case is the presence of additive constants in

equations where the evolution of the dependent variable follows a trend. Indeed the relation

$$y(t) = \alpha x(t) + \beta, \tag{3}$$

has no solution of the type (2) except if $a = b = 0$ (no trend) or if $\beta = 0$. It is, however, possible to attain homogeneity without substantially altering the structure of the system; for example, (3) may be reestimated with the constraint $\beta = 0$, or a time-dependent constant $\beta(t)$, consistent with a SSGP, may be introduced. Our past experience suggests that a careful examination of the violations of these long-run constraints may call into question certain aspects of the model's specification.

3. The equilibrium growth factors (b_i) can, in general, be determined before the level $y(0)$, since they all necessarily derive from only three basic exogenously given rates:

γ = rate of growth of (Harrod neutral) technical progress,

ρ = rate of growth of foreign prices in domestic units,

n = rate of growth of population.

All the endogenous *and exogenous* variables of the system must actually grow at a rate determined by γ, ρ, and n: $g = (1 + n)(1 + \gamma) - 1$ for *all* real variables, ρ for *all* prices, and n for *all* variables relative to population, $(1 + g)(1 + \rho) - 1$ for *all* nominal variables, and $(1 + \gamma)(1 + \rho) - 1$ for nominal wage rate. This may readily be seen by considering the relations of a typical macro model, and in particular the various accounting identities.

The only exception to this strong rule occurs in a closed economy (or an open economy with perfectly flexible exchange rates) in which no monetary variable is fixed exogenously. In that case it is easy to see that ρ is then simultaneously determined with initial levels and that the price level is indeterminate. Note that not only the b_i's but also the a_i's must be fixed with γ, n, and ρ; these latter are actually the only 3 degrees of freedom as far as steady state rates of growth are concerned.

4. We are now able to derive the n initial conditions $\bar{y}_j(0)$. Substituting (2) into (1), for $t = 0$, we get

$$\bar{y}_j(0) = f_j\left(\bar{y}_1(0), \ldots, \bar{y}_n(0); \frac{\bar{y}_1(0)}{b_1}, \ldots, \frac{\bar{y}_n(0)}{b_n}; \bar{x}(0); \beta, 0\right), \qquad j = 1, \ldots, n, \tag{4}$$

or equivalently, including the restrictions on rates of growth and dropping the time index t,

$$\varphi(\bar{y}, \bar{x}, \beta, \gamma, n, \rho) = 0. \tag{5}$$

Thus *any solution in y of (5) is the initial condition for a SSGP of (1)* (modified to eliminate long-run heterogeneities). *We observe that the (static) multipliers associated with (5) correspond to the "long run" effect of a sustained unitary multiplicative shock on $\bar{x}$.*

5. The system (5) is actually easier to analyze than a dynamic model, and because of its static nature building reduced size representation by substitutions is straightforward. Consequently we can render its underlying structure and theory more apparent, as will be evident later on.

At this stage note that the static model (5) may display a rather different causal structure, and hence behavior, than its dynamic counterpart (1). This feature comes typically from equations in which the dependent variable is defined in growth rate terms, as it is readily illustrated by considering the following Phillips relation:

$$\frac{W(t) - W(t-1)}{W(t-1)} = \beta_1 + \beta_2 \frac{P(t) - P(t-1)}{P(t-1)} + \beta_3 U_N(t), \tag{6}$$

with $W(t)$, nominal wages, $P(t)$, price level, and $U_n(t)$, unemployment rate. Along a SSGP, (6) becomes

$$(1 + \gamma)(1 + \rho) - 1 = \beta_1 + \beta_2 \rho - \beta_3 U_N. \tag{7}$$

There are two implications of (7): U_N becomes predetermined as a function of the only exogenously given rates of growth and the coefficients of the Phillips curve; and nominal wages, W, must be implicitly determined elsewhere in the model.

The Dynamic Structure

1. A straightforward but important step in tackling the dynamics of the model (1) is to rewrite it in a detrended form using the transformation

$$\begin{cases} \hat{x}_i(t) = a_i^{-t} x_i(t), \\ \hat{y}_j(t) = b_j^{-t} y_j(t), \end{cases} \tag{8}$$

to get

$$\hat{y}(t) = g(\hat{y}(t), \hat{y}(t-1), \hat{x}(t); \gamma, n, \rho, \beta, t). \tag{9}$$

The usual structure of macroeconometric models is such that, after correcting for long-run heterogeneities, time disappears in the system (9) as an explicit variable.

This can be illustrated with reference to the Cobb-Douglas model:

$$q_t = A k_{t-1}^\alpha n_t^\beta \gamma^t,$$

where q_t denotes production, k_t capital, n_t employment, and γ technical progress.

Looking for a SSGP of the form

$$\begin{cases} \bar{q}_t = \bar{q}_0 a^t, \\ \bar{k}_t = \bar{k}_0 b^t, \\ \bar{n}_t = \bar{n}_0 c^t, \end{cases}$$

generates the two long-run conditions:

$$a = b^\alpha c^\beta \gamma, \qquad \text{rates of growth,}$$

$$\bar{q}_0 = A \left(\frac{\bar{k}_0}{b} \right)^\alpha \bar{n}_0^\beta, \qquad \text{initial levels.}$$

The transformation (8) of the initial model, taking into account the long-run constraints, then leads to the following stationary form:

$$\hat{q}_t = \frac{A}{b^\alpha} \hat{k}_{t-1}^\alpha \hat{n}_t^\beta.$$

So, in general, (9) may be rewritten as

$$\hat{y}(t) = g(\hat{y}(t), \hat{y}(t-1), \hat{x}(t); \gamma, n, \rho, \beta). \tag{10}$$

2. The form (10) is especially suited for a careful study of the model we want to work out because it describes a stationary dynamic system fluctuating around a well-defined and time-invariant equilibrium (formula 5).

Simulation methods can be applied over a (very) long time span without risk of large bias, due to nonstationarity (and sometimes no well-defined reference path) in interpreting results. Linear methods are, in general, highly powerful tools for revealing the few important mechanisms driving a given model, and they can be applied rigorously. Indeed, in the neighborhood of the equilibrium of (10) we can approximate by the following linear *stationary* form:

$$\Delta \hat{y}(t) = D\Delta \hat{y}(t) + E\Delta \hat{y}(t-1) + F\Delta \hat{x}(t), \tag{11}$$

where D, E, and F are constant matrices of suitable dimension and Δ, denotes deviations from the equilibrium. Equation (11) generally works well due to the typically weak nonlinearity of macroeconometric models.

Finally, knowledge of the long run permits the study of the model from the present time ($t = 0$) until infinity. It also provides us with a precise definition of the concepts of delays and more generally of the dynamic hierarchy between variables in reaching their asymptotic equilibrium values.

16.3   An Illustration: Application to a Condensed Version of the Metric Model

We now illustrate the above methodology by applying it to a French quarterly forecasting model. We first briefly review how the model was made amenable to analysis using the methodology discussed above, and after presenting the model, we study its long-run implications and its dynamic features.

Derivation of the Model

1. METRIC is a dynamic quarterly model (involving about 900 equations) built and used by the French government to assist in short-term macroeconomic forecasting and economic policy studies (see Artus et al. 1981). Several shorter versions of this model have been built to better understand its properties. In particular, P. Artus constructed a shorter version for pedagogical purposes in 1980; this version, which embedded the same basic behavioral equations as the large-scale version, has unfortunately never been published.

As we noted earlier, the goal of our methodology is to shed light on the specification and the theoretical foundations of a given model. So, as we transform it into a stationary form, according to formula (10), we will simultaneously eliminate the mechanisms whose contributions to the overall behavior of the model are negligible.

2. We will now briefly describe the different steps of these preliminaries. First, the model was made to be consistent with SSGP constraints. For METRIC, this was not a big problem. The corrections introduced a bias that grows over time, but this bias has barely reached 8% after 20 quarters,

and more than four fifths of the bias comes from a faster growth rate for foreign trade than for production in the original model (the EEC integration effect), which conflicts with the requirement of a *unique* growth rate for all quantities.

From the very beginning, numerical values for the three basic long-run growth rates, γ, n, and ρ, were needed. For this illustration, they were chosen to be the average growth rates of the relevant variables within the sample period (1962.1 to 1978.4), leading to

$\gamma = 0.8\%$,

$n = 0.2\%$,

$\rho = 2\%$,

on a quarterly basis.[1]

3. Second, the model was transformed into a stationary dynamic system. An initial sensitivity analysis was undertaken to remove numerically non-significant mechanisms and to consolidate its dynamic structure. The criterion for evaluating the significance of a mechanism was the proximity of selected dynamic multipliers in the initial and modified models.

In the case of METRIC an obvious way to simplify was to omit the financial sector which, in this version of the model, was seen to be of small importance, as shown in figures 16.1 and 16.2. These figures illustrate the dynamic effects of a one-period increase of government spendings on output (Q) and the price level (p) with and without the financial sector.[2]

By this simplication the dynamic order (i.e., the number of lagged variables weighted by the lag length) of METRIC was reduced by roughly one third. The equations for investment (putty-clay structure), and imports and exports (relative price effects), which were responsible for more than half of the remaining lags, were also simplified.

The Model

1. The "maquette" of the METRIC model[3] is given in table 16.1, and the numerical values of the coefficients in table 16.2. The left-hand side of table 16.1 (equations D1 to D25), describes the stationary dynamic model, and the right-hand side (equations S1 to S25) its long-run static counterpart. This set of equations represents, in a conventional Keynesian demand-oriented model, a small open economy with a fixed exchange rate, sluggish

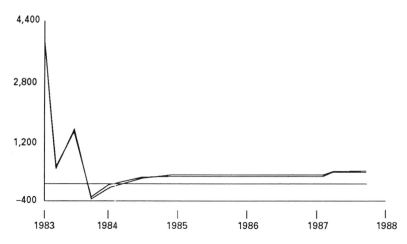

Figure 16.1
Effects of government spendings on Q (10^6 F): financial sector exogenous/endogenous

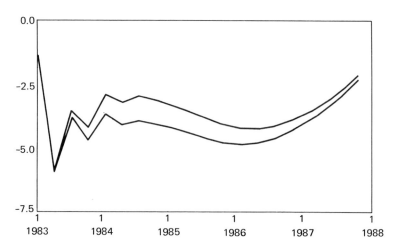

Figure 16.2
Effects of government spendings on p (10^{-3} points): financial sector exogenous/endogenous

Table 16.1
Stationary dynamic version and long-run static version of METRIC

Dynamic version	Static version	Description
D1 $N^d = \alpha_1 + \alpha_2 N^d_{-1} - \sum_0^2 NL_{-1} + \alpha_4\alpha_{3,i}$	S1 $N^d = \beta_1 - \beta_2 L + \beta_3 \underline{N}$	Unemployment
D2 $N^s = \alpha_5 + \alpha_6 N^s_{-1} - \alpha_7 L_{-1} + \alpha_8 L^*$	S2 $N^s = \beta_4 - \beta_5 L + \beta_6 L^*$	Unfilled vacancies
D3 $U_n = \log(N^d/N^s)$	S3 $U_n = \log(N^d/N^s)$	Measure of labor market disequilibrium
D4 $L = \alpha_9 + \alpha_{10} L_{-1} + \alpha_{11} L^*$	S4 $L = \beta_7 + \beta_8 L^*$	Actual employment
D5 $L^* = \alpha_{12}(CC/W)^b(Q - \delta' Q_{-1}) + \delta'' L^*_{-1}$	S5 $L^* = \beta_9(CC/W)^b Q$	Optimal employment
D6 $I = \alpha_{13} I^* + \alpha_{14} I_{-1}$	S6 $I = \beta_{10} I^*$	Actual fixed investment
D7 $I^* = \alpha_{15}(W/CC)^{1-b}(Q - \delta' Q_{-1})$	S7 $I^* = \beta_{11}(W/CC)^{1-b} Q$	Optimal fixed investment
D8 $C = \alpha_{16} + \alpha_{17} C_{-1} + \alpha_{18} R$	S8 $C = \beta_{12} + \beta_{13} R$	Consumption
D9 $R = (\alpha_{19} WL + \alpha_{20} pQ)/p_c$	S9 $R = (\beta_{14} WL + \beta_{15} pQ)/pc$	Real disposable income
D10 $IS = \alpha_{21} + \alpha_{22} IS_{-1} + \sum_0^2 \alpha_{23,i}(D_{-i} - \delta D_{-i-1})$	S10 $IS = \beta_{16} + \beta_{17} D$	Inventory investment
D11 $M = (D + IS)(\alpha_{24} + \alpha_{25} U_c - \varphi_m(L)\log(p_m/p))$	S11 $M = (D + IS)(\beta_{18} + \beta_{19} U_c - \beta_{20}\log(p_m/p))$	Imports
D12 $X = D_e^{\alpha_{26}}\exp(\alpha_{27} - \alpha_{28} U_c + \varphi_x(L)\log(\underline{p_e}/p_x))$	S12 $X = D_e^{\beta_{21}}\exp(\beta_{22} - \beta_{23} U_c)(\underline{p_e}/p_x)^{\beta_{24}}$	Exports
D13 $Q = C + I + IS + \underline{G} + X - M$	S13 $Q = C + I + IS + \underline{G} + X - M$	Actual production
D14 $D = C + I + \underline{G} + X$	S14 $D = C + I + \underline{G} + X$	Aggregate demand out of inventory investment
D15 $U_c = Q/Q^*$	S15 $U_c = Q/Q^*$	Degree of capacity utilization
D16 $Q^* = \alpha_{29}(Q - \delta' Q_{-1})\cdot I/I^* + \delta' Q^*_{-1}$	S16 $Q^* = \beta_{25} Q \cdot I/I^*$	Optimal production capacity
D17 $TC = \alpha_{30} WL + \alpha_{31} W + \alpha_{32} P_{-1} Q_{-1}$	S17 $TC = \beta_{26} WL + \beta_{27} W + \beta_{28} PQ$	Total costs of firms
D18 $p = \alpha_{33}(TC/\sum_0^3 Q_{-i})^{\alpha_{34}} p_{-1}^{1-\alpha_{34}}$	S18 $p = \beta_{29} TC/Q$	General price level
D19 $p_c = \alpha_{35} p_c^{\alpha_{36}} p^{\alpha_{37}} p_m^{1-\alpha_{36}-\alpha_{37}}$	S19 $p_c = \beta_{30} p^{\beta_{31}} p_m^{1-\beta_{31}}$	Consumption price
D20 $p_i = \alpha_{38} p_i^{\alpha_{39}} p^{\alpha_{40}} p_m^{1-\alpha_{39}-\alpha_{40}}$	S20 $p_i = \beta_{32} p^{\beta_{33}} p_m^{1-\beta_{33}}$	Investment price
D21 $p_x = \alpha_{41} p_{x-1}^{\alpha_{42}} p^{\alpha_{43}} \underline{p_e}^{\alpha_{44}} p_m^{1-\alpha_{42}-\alpha_{43}-\alpha_{44}}$	S21 $p_x = \beta_{34} p^{\beta_{35}} p_m^{\beta_{36}} \underline{p_e}^{1-\beta_{35}-\beta_{36}}$	Export price
D22 $p_m = \alpha_{45} p_{m-1}^{\alpha_{46}} \underline{p_e}^{1-\alpha_{46}}$	S22 $p_m = \beta_{37} \underline{p_e}$	Import price
D23 $CC = p_i r$	S23 $CC = p_i \cdot r$	Cost of capital
D24 $\hat{W} = \alpha_{47} + \sum_0^2 \alpha_{48,i}\hat{p}_{c-1} - \sum_0^3 \alpha_{49,i} U_{n-1}$	S24 $U_n = \beta_{38}$	Phillips relation
D25 $r = \alpha_{50} + \alpha_{51} r_{-1} + \alpha_{52}(r_c - \sum_0^2 \alpha_{53,i}\hat{p}_{-1})$	S25 $r = \beta_{39} + \beta_{40} \underline{r_c}$	Long-run real interest rate

Table 16.2
Values of coefficients

$\alpha_1 = -2836.0$	$\alpha_{21} = -630.0$	$\alpha_{41} = 1.092$
$\alpha_2 = 0.275$	$\alpha_{22} = 0.591$	$\alpha_{42} = 0.733$
$\alpha_{3,0} = 0.764$	$\alpha_{23,0} = 0.139$	$\alpha_{43} = 0.180$
$\alpha_{3,1} = -0.217$	$\alpha_{23,1} = 0.114$	$\alpha_{44} = 0.069$
$\alpha_{3,2} = 0.124$	$\alpha_{23,2} = 0.331$	$\alpha_{45} = 1.366$
$\alpha_4 = 0.558$	$\alpha_{24} = -0.0377$	$\alpha_{46} = 0.399$
$\alpha_5 = 380.0$	$\alpha_{25} = 0.281$	$\alpha_{47} = 0.0162$
$\alpha_6 = 0.295$	$\alpha_{26} = 1.074$	$\alpha_{48,0} = 0.50$
$\alpha_7 = 0.0315$	$\alpha_{27} = 4.707$	$\alpha_{48,1} = 0.33$
$\alpha_8 = 0.0165$	$\alpha_{28} = 1.27$	$\alpha_{48,2} = 0.17$
$\alpha_9 = 58.6$	$\alpha_{29} = 1.08$	$\alpha_{49,0} = 1.86 \times 10^{-3}$
$\alpha_{10} = 0.947$	$\alpha_{30} = 0.571$	$\alpha_{49,1} = 1.40 \times 10^{-3}$
$\alpha_{11} = 0.0483$	$\alpha_{31} = 2120.0$	$\alpha_{49,2} = 0.93 \times 10^{-3}$
$\alpha_{12} = 0.0773$	$\alpha_{32} = 0.329$	$\alpha_{49,3} = 0.46 \times 10^{-3}$
$\alpha_{13} = 0.121$	$\alpha_{33} = 4.27$	$\alpha_{50} = 0.654$
$\alpha_{14} = 0.88$	$\alpha_{34} = 0.141$	$\alpha_{51} = 0.757$
$\alpha_{15} = 2.403$	$\alpha_{35} = 1.015$	$\alpha_{52} = 0.276$
$\alpha_{16} = 1477.0$	$\alpha_{36} = 0.720$	$\alpha_{53,0} = 200.0$
$\alpha_{17} = 0.832$	$\alpha_{37} = 0.213$	$\alpha_{53,1} = 120.0$
$\alpha_{18} = 0.156$	$\alpha_{38} = 1.014$	$\alpha_{53,2} = 80.0$
$\alpha_{19} = 0.782$	$\alpha_{39} = 0.717$	
$\alpha_{20} = 0.0843$	$\alpha_{40} = 0.227$	

$b = 0.55$

$\sigma = 0.008$

$\rho = 0.02$

$n = 0.002$

$\delta = 0.02$

$\delta = 0.99$

$\delta' = 0.968$

$\delta'' = 0.976$

$$\varphi_m(L) = \frac{4.46 \times 10^{-3}}{1 - 1.612L + 0.677L^2}$$

$$\varphi_x(L) = \frac{0.0227}{1 - 1.533L + 0.389L^2 + 0.165L^3}$$

Table 16.2 (continued)

$\beta_1 = -3911.0$	$\beta_{15} = 0.0843$	$\beta_{30} = 1.055$
$\beta_2 = 0.926$	$\beta_{16} = -1540.0$	$\beta_{31} = 0.761$
$\beta_3 = 0.770$	$\beta_{17} = 0.0142$	$\beta_{32} = 1.050$
$\beta_4 = 539.0$	$\beta_{18} = -0.0547$	$\beta_{33} = 0.802$
$\beta_5 = 0.0447$	$\beta_{19} = 0.281$	$\beta_{34} = 1.388$
$\beta_6 = 0.0234$	$\beta_{20} = 0.0686$	$\beta_{35} = 0.258$
$\beta_7 = 1103.0$	$\beta_{21} = 1.074$	$\beta_{36} = 0.670$
$\beta_8 = 0.912$	$\beta_{22} = 4.707$	$\beta_{37} = 1.680$
$\beta_9 = 0.102$	$\beta_{23} = 1.27$	$\beta_{38} = 1.771$
$\beta_{10} = 1.014$	$\beta_{24} = 1.107$	$\beta_{39} = 2.691$
$\beta_{11} = 0.0762$	$\beta_{25} = 1.082$	$\beta_{40} = 1.136$
$\beta_{12} = 8792.0$	$\beta_{26} = 571.0$	
$\beta_{13} = 0.929$	$\beta_{27} = 2120.0$	
$\beta_{14} = 0.782$	$\beta_{28} = 0.329$	
	$\beta_{29} = 1.084$	

prices, and wages determinated by a Phillips curve. But due to our earlier simplication, the financial sector of the original METRIC is not included, and neither are survey variables in expectations because of their observed minor influence. It must also be noted that most fiscal and other policy instruments have been fixed and are embedded in the parameters.

2. The first three equations, D1 to D3, describe the working of the employment market; this determines the imbalance in the job market, which is defined as the logarithm of the ratio between unfilled demands for and offers of employment. In the original version of METRIC the employment vacancies equation, D2, is written in first differences to take into account the vintage structure of the technology. However, writing this relationship in levels does not change the working of the model as long as the equation is not perturbed directly.

The four subsequent equations, D4 to D7, derive in a rather standard way from the theory of labor and capital demand by firms facing a putty-clay technology with adjustment costs on both factors. Consumption (D8) depends on real disposable income, R_t, which is consistent with traditional permanent income theory. The inventory investment equation (D10) formalizes a dynamic buffer stock mechanism. Foreign trade (D11 and D12) includes the three classic explanatory variables, corresponding to the "demand pull" effect, the relative price or competitiveness effect, and the capacity utilization or "cost-push" effect.[4]

The (optimal) production capacity (D16) is determined so as to be consistent with the vintage technology, and the ratio between this supply and effective demand, Q, defines the degree of capacity utilization (D15). The production price level is set up by firms, supposed to be in a situation of monopolistic competition, as following a sluggish adjustment path toward the classical markup pricing (D17 and D18). Equations D19 to D22 describe the price structure of the different components of aggregate demand, with a common specification of partial adjustment to a composite index of production and import prices. The cost of capital is defined in a conventional way (D23); note that tax rates are merged with the coefficients. Equation D24 is the standard Phillips curve with lagged indexation of wages to inflation, and the last equation concatenates the traditional "cascade" of interest rates as a relation between the long-run real interest rate and the very short-run money market rate.

The model includes only five explicit exogenous variables:

$\underline{N}$: labor force

$\underline{D}_e$: foreign demand

$\underline{P}_e$: foreign price index

$\underline{G}$: government spending

$\underline{r}_c$: money market interest rate (nominal)

Analysis of the Long-Run Structure

In this section we turn to an analysis of the long-run static version of the maquette. Equations S1–S25 of table 16.1 describe the set of conditions that the initial values of the endogenous variables must satisfy to generate, via D1–D25, a dynamic path that is constant over time (i.e., a steady state). We label this version SSM. Note that SSM has the characteristics of an equilibrium. Also the theoretical aspects of these equations are more transparent than in their dynamic counterparts. In general, static systems are more amenable to size reduction and analytical study.

1. The SSM has the form of a simultaneous equations model which must be solved by a fixed point algorithm for the known values of the five exogenous variables. Table 16.3 lists the long-run levels of the endogenous variables associated with the historical values of the exogenous variables

Table 16.3
Long-run levels, 1979:1

Variable	Symbol	Equilibrium level (1979:1)	Percentage deviation from actual (1979)	Units FF
Consumption	C	161116	−6.55	10^6 FF70
Aggregate demand	D	292169	−4.38	10^6 FF70
Foreign demand	$\underline{D}_e$	1789	—	10^6 FF70
Government spending	$\underline{G}$	41748	—	10^6 FF70
Actual investment	I	28969	−10.95	10^6 FF70
Optimal investment	I^*	28573	−8.91	10^6 FF70
Inventory investment	IS	2624	−50.77	10^6 FF70
Actual employment	L	13201	−4.27	10^3 units
Optimal employment	L^*	13261	−0.45	10^3 units
Imports	M	61933	−0.69	10^6 FF70
Labor force	$\underline{N}$	22915	—	10^3 units
Unemployment	N^d	1508	+21.67	10^3 units
Unfilled vacancies	N^s	256	+62.24	10^3 units
General price level	p	2.101	+3.94	1 in 70
Consumption price	p_c	2.146	+4.26	1 in 70
Foreign price	$\underline{p}_e$	1.102	—	1 in 70
Investment price	p_i	2.153	+4.00	1 in 70
Import price	p_m	1.851	−0.55	1 in 70
Export price	p_x	1.875	ε	1 in 70
Actual production	Q	232860	−5.93	10^6 FF70
Optimal production	Q^*	255512	−6.39	10^6 FF70
Disposable income	R	163879	−8.59	10^6 FF70
Short-run interest rate	$\underline{r}_c$	1.893	—	percent
Long-run interest rate	r	4.843	+7.74	percent
Total costs of firms	TC	451421	−3.15	10^6 FF70
Disequilibrium in goods market	U_c	0.9113	+0.43	units
Disequilibrium in labor market	U_N	1.771	−41.19	percent
Wage rate	W	30.06	ε	10^3 FF
Exports	X	60337	+1.60	10^6 FF70

in 1979:1, as well as the percentage deviations between immediate and long-run levels.

We find that the actual level of production exceeds the long-run level, obtained as the solution to SSM, by almost 6 percent. In other words, for the chosen steady growth rates of quantities, the actual level of production leads its long-run value by about six quarters. The price level is lower by 4 percent—a lag of six months—and employment higher by 4 percent—an advance of twenty quarters. These deviations appear reasonably modest, and this justifies our using the SSGP as a reference path for the analyses of the dynamic model we wish to pursue.

The reasonable gaps between short- and long-run values are not surprising. Indeed, the dynamic model appears to satisfy the mean values of the sample data set—if it is estimated by least squares methods—and so does the long-run model because it is the same model. Thus, by setting exogenous variables to their mean values over the sample data set, we also find the mean values for the endogenous variables of the SSM.

This property, however, is not verified in the maquette because this model was not reestimated after the numerous simplifications and alterations, and the mean value argument is valid only for stationary data with a sufficiently long sample set. Taking growth into account may lead to important biases; in particular, the results may be rather sensitive to the values of the three basic long run growth rates.

For reasons of space, we cannot discuss this topic in detail here;[6] we merely caution the reader to be very careful in interpreting the numerical values of the levels given by SSM as a benchmark for an evaluation of the amplitude of actual disequilibrium.

2. Rewriting SSM in a compact form, familiar to macroeconomists, we observe, first, that all relative prices can be expressed in terms of $\pi = p/p_e$, second that, only the real wages $\omega = W/p$ are required, and, finally, that by combining S6 and S16, U_c becomes a constant. A compressed form for SSM can now be obtained.

The demand for goods derives from equations S6 to S14:

$$Q = C + I + IS + \underline{G} + X - M, \tag{C1}$$

where

$$C = \varepsilon_1 + (\varepsilon_2 \omega L + \varepsilon_3 Q)\pi^{\varepsilon_4},$$

$$I = \varepsilon_5 \left[\left(\frac{\omega}{r}\right) \pi^{\varepsilon_6} \right]^{1-b} Q,$$

$$IS = \varepsilon_7 + \varepsilon_8(C + I + \underline{G} + X),$$
$$X = \varepsilon_9 \underline{D}_e^{\varepsilon_{10}} \pi^{-\varepsilon_{11}},$$
$$M = (\varepsilon_{12} + \varepsilon_{13} \log \pi)(Q + M).$$

or, formally,

$$Q = f_1(\pi, \omega L, \underline{D}_e, \underline{G}) + f_2(\pi, \omega, r)Q. \tag{C1}$$

Firms labor demand is derived from S4 and S5:

$$L = \varepsilon_{14} + \varepsilon_{15}\left[\left(\frac{\omega}{r}\right)\pi^{\varepsilon_6}\right]^{-b} Q = \varepsilon_{14} + f_3(\pi, \omega, r)Q. \tag{C2}$$

Three more equations are necessary to determine π, ω, and r.

The combination of S17 and S18 gives the outcome of the general price level equation:

$$Q = \omega(\varepsilon_{16} + \varepsilon_{17} \cdot L). \tag{C3}$$

Recall from the analysis in the methodological section that in the long run a Phillips curve, such as D24, results in a predetermined "unemployment rate." Combining S1 through S4 with S24, we obtain

$$L = \varepsilon_{18} + \varepsilon_{19}N. \tag{C4}$$

Finally, the interest rate r is given by the simple transcription of S25:

$$r = \varepsilon_{20} + \varepsilon_{21}\underline{r}_c. \tag{C5}$$

Table 16.4 lists the numerical values obtained for this system (C1–C5).

The system of equations (C1) through (C5) describes a monetary economy with markets for output, labor, and bonds. The demand for goods and labor are given by (C1) and (C2). The supply of goods, given monopoly

Table 16.4
Cofficients of the compact model

$\varepsilon_1 = 8792.0$	$\varepsilon_8 = 0.014$	$\varepsilon_{15} = 0.101$
$\varepsilon_2 = 0.608$	$\varepsilon_9 = 23.30$	$\varepsilon_{16} = 3295.0$
$\varepsilon_3 = 0.0656$	$\varepsilon_{10} = 1.074$	$\varepsilon_{17} = 0.887$
$\varepsilon_4 = 0.239$	$\varepsilon_{11} = 1.107$	$\varepsilon_{18} = -8480.0$
$\varepsilon_5 = 0.0722$	$\varepsilon_{12} = 0.201$	$\varepsilon_{19} = 0.946$
$\varepsilon_6 = 0.198$	$\varepsilon_{13} = 0.0687$	$\varepsilon_{20} = 2.691$
$\varepsilon_7 = -1518.0$	$\varepsilon_{14} = 1103.0$	$\varepsilon_{21} = 1.136$

markup behavior by firms, is described by (C3) and is essentially an income distribution relation. Equation (C4) is ambiguous because it is not a supply relation but rather the long-run effect on employment of wage bargaining between firms and unions (i.e., the NAIRU). The resulting employment is, by definition, equal to the labor demanded by firms as given by (C2). Finally, the bonds market is described by (C5), with the implicit assumption that the supply, by the government, clears the market at the given interest rate r.[7] The formal modeling of the demand for bonds is not important if we are mainly interested in the goods and labor markets with regard to the (Keynesian) hierarchical structure of consumer behavior: the savings rate is independent of portfolio decisions with respect to the uses of these savings.

We focus now on the output and labor markets. Observe that (C3) and (C4) correspond to excess supply in both markets: *firms, as monopolistic competitors, produce less than they would were prices rigid,*[8] and the NAIRU clearly suggests a certain amount of involuntary unemployment.

The demand equations (C1) and (C2) must therefore be viewed as "effective" demand, with the usual spillover mechanism between the two markets. The public expenditure multiplier on the demand block, (C1) and (C2), can be computed for rigid prices and wages. In the case of SSM, the value is 1.94; the closed economy multiplier would be twice as high.

To study the incidence of prices, we follow the IS-LM tradition, deriving aggregate demand and aggregate supply in terms of the two relations between output and prices. Here we find, however, the presence of real wages, ω, due to income distribution effects in consumption, C, and in the substitution mechanism between the two factors, L and I.

Basically, (C1) gives the demand schedule, (C4) gives the supply schedule, and (C2) and (C3) help to eliminate L and ω. The outcome for SSM, in terms of log-linearized variations around the equilibrium, is

$$\begin{cases} Q^d = -0.027p + 2.54G, \\ Q^s = 0.22p + 2.41\underline{N}. \end{cases}$$

In the first place, it is easily verified that the slope of the supply function is proportional to the elasticity of the investment price index to the foreign price index, $\varepsilon_6 = 1 - \beta_{33}$. In other words, in the absence of partially imported capital goods, supply curve would be "classical" (i.e., horizontal). Indeed, $\varepsilon_6 = 0$ would imply that labor demand does not depend on π and that, because L is fixed by (C4), the relations (C2) and (C3) jointly determine

Q and ω. Here the flexibility is generated by the Laursen-Metzler relative costs effect (i.e., p_i varies less than p).

The surprisingly strong effect of $\underline{N}$ on Q, at the given prices, is due to the fact that L is much lower than N (L represents wage-earners), augmented by casual numerical specifications details (the constant terms in employment equations). In a theoretical model the elasticity would be 1 rather than 2.41.

Second, the effect of government spending on demand, at given prices and flexible wages, is greater than the multiplier with given prices and wages (2.54 versus 1.94). It is easy to see that the presence of the positive constant terms ε_{14} and ε_{16} in (C2) and (C3) implies an elasticity of L with respect to Q of 0.7, a covariation of ω of 0.45, and consequently an elasticity of ωL amounting to 1.15. Wage increases therefore contribute to increased consumption and investment.

Note also that the demand function is sloped very slightly in the negatively direction. The explanation has to do with the Laursen-Metzler effect on both consumption (ε_4) and investment (ε_6) counteracting the normal negative effect of prices on foreign trade (ε_{11} and ε_{13}), and with an ambiguous resulting sign.

Finally, the complete resolution of the system gives

$$\begin{cases} Q = 2.26\underline{G} + 0.26\underline{N}, \\ p = 10.3\underline{G} - 9.76\underline{N}. \end{cases}$$

The public spending multiplier is substantially larger than in the case of fixed wages and prices (2.26 versus 1.94). In other words, price crowding-out is not even enough to compensate wage crowding-in. Prices are also very sensitive, contrasting sharply with rather small short- and medium-range effects, as we will see below.

3. To conclude this study of the long-run properties of METRIC, it is worth commenting on the theoretical consistency of some properties of SSM exhibited thus far. The long run, as well as the short run, is characterized by excess supply. It is therefore incorrect to say that models are Keynesian in the short run and Walrasian in the long run. Actually the long-run model resembles the model of monopolistic competition as presented by Dixit-Stiglitz (1974), Blanchard-Kiyotaki (1987), and Sneessens (1987).

Another aspect of interest, when analyzing the theoretical specification behind the SSM, is to study its consistency with respect to agents. Indeed, in the IS-LM tradition, model builders generally think in terms of "macro-economic functions" rather than agents behavior. This is a major factor in rendering their construction obscure to an economist trained in micro-economic theory. In the SSM, firms choose the levels of their factor demands, I and L, of their inventory investment IS, and of their output price but do not derive them as the solution to a single optimization problem. A theoretical approach does exist (see, e.g., Maccini 1981), but it has never been tested. However, we do not believe this to be a crucial issue. The usual procedure has the effect of not generating sufficient interdependence in the system.

On the consumers side, it is hard to understand why, in the long run, their marginal propensity to spend out of disposable income is not exactly equal to one (cf., S8, where $\beta_{13} = 0.929$). It appears that their implicit utility function may include more than just consumption, or that consumers are constrained in a way not modeled. Clearly something is missing here such as a monetary (and financial) equation or block of equations[9] in which non-Walrasian theory has been shown to play an essential role.

The "rest of the world" interacts through exports and imports. We first note that the relative price elasticity of X is equal to 1.107, whereas the (implicit) corresponding value for M is 0.414. This might be explained by a monopolistic competition argument, similar to that used for the domestic market. However, these two values seem rather low for such a long period, and their effect is to make the aggregate domestic demand, Q^d, almost horizontal.

Another important point, as far as foreign trade is concerned, is the absence of a balance of payments constraint and of a flexible exchange rate, both of which are rather inconsistent with the notion of the long run. Finally, another potentially crucial constraint not present in the maquette is the government budget constraint. This comes from the fact that the government is viewed as an exogenous agent, and this too is not defensible in the long run.

Dynamic Structure of METRIC

We now turn to a structural analysis of the dynamic properties of our core version of METRIC. Since the methodology used is well known and rather standard, we will focus mainly on the transition between the short and long runs, an aspect not generally pursued when studying macroeconometric models.

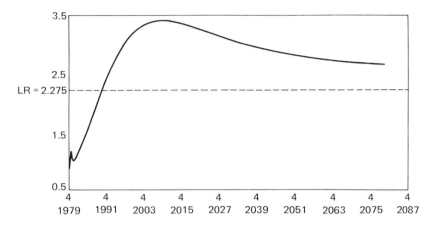

Figure 16.3
Dynamic multipliers: Q

We proceed as follows: After introductory simulations of the model, over 400 periods, we show that it can be represented by a two-block system, each of which, to a large extent, works independently. A final paragraph is devoted to the so-called linear analysis (Kuh et al. 1985) which provides more precise statements about its quantitative time structure.

1. Figures 16.3 to 16.6 describe the dynamic and long-run multipliers associated with a sustained shock on public expenditures (1 percent of Q) as percentage variations of production, Q prices, p, imports, M, and employment, L, respectively.

In figure 16.3 we observe that Q, after attaining a small peak, increases smoothly from 0.8 to 3.4 (this maximum value is obtained in about twenty-five years) and then decreases toward its long-run value, which seems far from being reached after one hundred years (400 periods). There appears to be no tendency toward oscillatory behavior. In figure 16.4 prices first drop significantly and then cross the horizontal axis after a surprisingly long period (seventeen years). This is clearly due to the so-called productivity cycle—a combination of long lags in employment and in prices. The subsequent monotonic increase, although strong, results in prices only half their long-run level after one hundred years. In figure 16.5 the evolution of imports initially resembles (on a magnified scale) the path for Q but is subsequently increasingly influenced by prices, and this prevents an asymp-

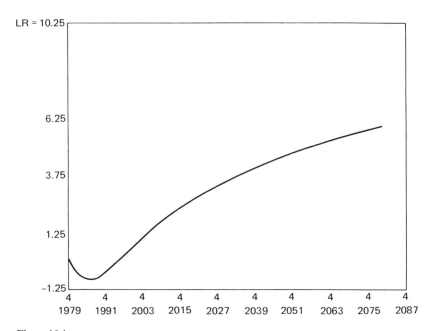

Figure 16.4
Dynamic multipliers: p

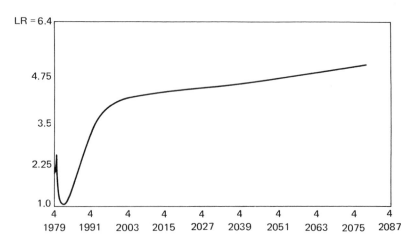

Figure 16.5
Dynamic multipliers: M

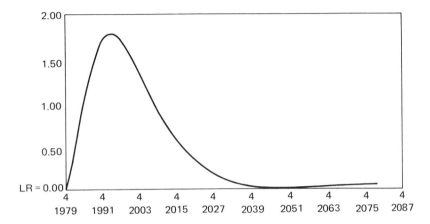

Figure 16.6
Dynamic multipliers: L

totic decrease. Figure 16.6 confirms the previous finding that employment is fixed in the long run; note that it seems to converge faster to its long-run level than do the other variables.

2. The apparent complexity of a macro model is strongly linked to its nonrecursive nature. The first approach to understanding its short-run structure is to obtain an economically meaningful "feedback set." By this we mean the smallest possible subset of endogenous variables of the system such that their exogenization leads to a purely recursive system. Several algorithms implementing this idea are available-in particular, one built by Gilli (1982) and accessible as part of TROLL. The application of Gilli's algorithm to METRIC provided several possible three-variable subsets, among which we chose the subset (W, p, Q). This is very satisfactory finding: As is standard practice for agents to interpret feedback variables as signals necessary in making their plans, we observe that in a Keynesian economy agents need both price and quantity signals.

Thus, in the short run, METRIC can be written as

$$(W, p, Q) = \psi(W, p, Q, [\text{past}]), \tag{12}$$

where other contemporaneous variables, interpreted as intermediate variables, are eliminated by substitution. A vector of "pure" shocks (null in the reference equilibrium), $\overline{\Delta W}, \overline{\Delta p}, \overline{\Delta Q}$ is then added to (12). Following a (log) linearization of (12) around the reference steady state equilibrium, we get

$$
\begin{pmatrix} \Delta W \\ \Delta p \\ \Delta Q \end{pmatrix} = \begin{bmatrix} -0.0003 & 0.105 & 0.0017 \\ 0.105 & -0.1645 & -0.039 \\ 0.086 & -0.033 & -0.089 \end{bmatrix} \begin{pmatrix} \Delta W \\ \Delta p \\ \Delta Q \end{pmatrix} + \begin{pmatrix} \Delta \overline{W} \\ \Delta \overline{p} \\ \Delta \overline{Q} \end{pmatrix}.
\tag{13}
$$

All values are given in percentages, so the matrix is easily interpreted in terms of elasticities.

The solution of (13) yields the ex post matrix:

$$
\begin{pmatrix} \Delta W \\ \Delta P \\ \Delta Q \end{pmatrix} = \begin{bmatrix} 1.009 & 0.091 & -0.002 \\ 0.089 & 0.867 & -0.031 \\ 0.079 & -0.018 & 0.919 \end{bmatrix} \begin{pmatrix} \Delta \overline{W} \\ \Delta \overline{P} \\ \Delta \overline{Q} \end{pmatrix}.
\tag{14}
$$

Diagonal effects appear highly dominant, but cross-effects between wages and prices are nonnegligible. Approximation of (13) by alternative more or less decomposable systems reveals that the system is almost perfectly represented by a configuration in which prices and wages are coupled but are predetermined with respect to production. This representation yields the reduced form:

$$
\begin{pmatrix} \Delta W'' \\ \Delta p'' \\ \Delta Q'' \end{pmatrix} = \begin{bmatrix} 1.010 & 0.091 & 0 \\ 0.091 & 0.867 & 0 \\ 0.077 & -0.010 & 0.918 \end{bmatrix} \begin{pmatrix} \Delta \overline{W} \\ \Delta \overline{p} \\ \Delta \overline{Q} \end{pmatrix}.
\tag{15}
$$

In other words, in conformity with disequilibrium theory, the system is approximately hierarchical in the short run. It can be verified that predetermining quantities rather than prices yield a worse approximation. This finding coincides with that of Kuh et al. (1985) with reference to the American model MQEM. It implies that in computing the short-run effects of quantity shocks on production, we can neglect such effects in the price-wage block, and conversely for prices and wages.[10]

3. We now extend the previous analysis to a dynamic setting to see whether this almost perfect hierarchical structure between prices and quantities would quickly vanish. Table 16.5 lists the dynamic multipliers associated with sustained pure multiplicative shocks to p, W, and Q, over 80 periods. It also lists the long-run values for the entire model (table 16.5a), and for the model that disconnects production and prices (table 16.5b).

Table 16.5
Dynamic interactions

		(a) *Whole model*			(b) *Blocks disconnected*		
		$\Delta\overline{W}$	$\Delta\bar{p}$	$\Delta\overline{Q}$	$\Delta\overline{W}$	$\Delta\bar{p}$	$\Delta\overline{Q}$
1	ΔW	1.009	0.091	−0.002	1.010	0.091	0
	Δp	0.089	0.867	−0.031	0.091	0.867	0
	ΔQ	0.077	−0.018	0.919	0	0	0.919
2	ΔW	2.051	0.300	−0.004	2.042	0.300	0
	Δp	0.259	1.680	−0.044	0.267	1.678	0
	ΔQ	0.225	−0.050	0.964	0	0	0.963
4	ΔW	4.273	0.997	−0.022	4.215	0.996	0
	Δp	0.810	3.192	−0.160	0.852	3.184	0
	ΔQ	0.756	−0.084	1.058	0	0	1.048
8	ΔW	9.372	2.737	−0.125	9.106	2.728	0
	Δp	2.544	5.860	−0.415	2.856	5.831	0
	ΔQ	2.355	−0.094	1.190	0	0	1.140
20	ΔW	29.07	6.326	−0.324	27.35	6.108	0
	Δp	10.42	11.36	−0.913	13.58	10.69	0
	ΔQ	9.327	−2.106	1.705	0	0	1.410
40	ΔW	69.25	5.805	0.288	58.83	4.282	0
	Δp	25.28	14.17	−0.912	34.80	10.20	0
	ΔQ	19.70	−6.635	2.631	0	0	1.709
80	ΔW	176.5	−1.731	3.089	96.25	0.853	0
	Δp	61.44	12.82	0.429	58.78	8.975	0
	ΔQ	33.39	−12.11	3.912	0	0	2.046
∞	ΔW	391.0	−23.06	15.32	∞	∞	0
	Δp	353.0	−3.867	12.20	∞	∞	0
	ΔQ	−21.18	−11.90	2.777	0	0	2.418

From this table it is clear that for 8 to 10 quarters, the real block functions in almost total isolation from prices. Integration in the price-wage loop is slower—about 20 quarters—supporting, over a five year horizon, the assertion that prices are largely predetermined by quantities. Note that the price-wage loop, taken in isolation, (table 16.5b) generates monotonic divergent dynamics, unlike the rather rapid convergence of the real block. However, the very slow convergence of the full model (table 16.5a) and its nonmonotonic behavior show that the interaction between prices and quantities generates asymptotic effects that contradict the effects that we would expect to observe if the analysis were restricted to a medium-run horizon.

4. Further insights into the dynamic behavior of the model result from the computation of its eigenvalues and sensitivity analysis. This is now routine, and particularly easy due to the availability of LIMO software from TROLL (cf., Kuh et al. 1985). This technique amounts to working on a linearized stationary approximation of the system—formula (11)—and to studying its endogenous dynamics—$\Delta \hat{x}(t) = 0$—through the equation

$$\Delta \hat{y}(t) = A \Delta \hat{y}(t - 1), \qquad \text{with } A = (I - D)^{-1} E. \tag{16}$$

Then n eigenvalues, λ_i, of the matrix A are then computed, as well as the sensitivity coefficients:

$$\varepsilon_i(\beta_j) = \frac{\partial |\lambda_i|}{\partial \beta_j} \frac{\beta_i}{|\lambda_i|}, \tag{17}$$

which are the elasticities of the eigenvalues with respect to the various structural coefficients, β_j, of the model embedded in the state matrix A[11].

Table 16.6 summarizes the informations obtained from the computation of the eigenvalues and the sensitivity coefficients.

The first two columns give the magnitude and the periodicity of the 23 nonnegligible eigenvalues, 7 of which are real and positive, 2 real negative, and 14 correspond to 7 complex pairs; 34 nonnegligible eigenvalues were theoretically possible. All lie within the unit circle, implying the (locally) dynamic stability of the system. They are far from equally distributed—almost one-half lies between 0.8 and 1. Observe also that no complex eigenvalue, except perhaps the seventh, can generate oscillations resembling business cycles, and these do not vanish quickly over time. The third column indicates the dying out lag or, more precisely, the date T such that

Table 16.6
Eigenvalues of metric

Number	Magnitude	Periodicity	Dying out lag	Quantities	Prices-wages
1	0.9975	∞	1,200	—	p, W
2	0.9851	473	200	Q, L *, Q*, I	W
3	0.9625	∞	78	Q, Q*, L *, L	—
4	0.9452	112	53	Q*, I, Q, L	W
5	0.8767	158	23	—	XPR, XPR$_{-1}$
6	0.8371	∞	17	C	—
7	0.8202	30	15	—	MPR, MPR$_{-1}$
8	0.7343	7,100	10	—	PX, R, PC
9	0.7175	∞	9	—	PI
10	0.5964	97	6	IS, Q, I, Q*	PC
11	0.3986	∞	3.25	—	PM
12	0.3003	∞	2.50	NS, Q	—
13	0.2760	∞	2.32	ND	—
14	0.2673	(2)	2.27	I, Q, D, D$_{-1}$, D$_{-2}$, IS	—
15	0.2636	15.3	2.25	I, Q, IS, D$_{-2}$, D, D$_{-1}$	—
16	0.2152	(2)	1.95	—	XPR$_{-2}$, XPR$_{-1}$

$\lambda_i^T = 0.05$. It is striking that the first eigenvalue dominates the dynamics after 200 periods but stays active during more than 1,000 periods.

The two last columns summarize the results of the sensitivity analysis as assignments of eigenvalues to lagged state variables. Ignoring technical details, we consider the elasticities:

$$\varepsilon_{i,j,k} = \frac{\partial |\lambda_i|}{\partial a_{j,k}} \frac{a_{j,k}}{|\lambda_i|},$$

which are the sensitivies of the different eigenvalues with respect to the state matrix A. After computing $\eta_{i,k} = \text{Max}_j |\varepsilon_{i,j,k}|$, to sum up influence of the kth lagged variable, only the $\eta_{j,k}$ higher than 0.2 are selected;[12] they are displayed in either column 4 or column 5, depending upon whether the relevant lagged state variable is a quantity or a price.

It can be observed that the only eigenvalues influenced simultaneously by the two blocks are the complex pairs 2, 4 and 10, and that for real eigenvalues, which are easy to assign, there exists a quasi identity between the eigenvalue and the autoregressive term of the relevant variable. This is shown in table 16.7. Denote by **XPR** and **MPR** the dynamic terms of the influence of relative prices on exports and imports, respectively:

$$\begin{cases} \text{XPR} = \varphi_x(L)\log\left(\dfrac{p_e}{p_x}\right), \\[2ex] \text{MPR} = \varphi_m(L)\log\left(\dfrac{p_m}{p}\right). \end{cases}$$

These expressions can be written as (see table 16.2)

$$\begin{cases} \text{XPR} = 1.533\text{XPR}_{-1} - 0.389\text{XPR}_{-2} - 0.165\text{XPR}_{-3} + 0.0227\log\left(\dfrac{p_e}{p_x}\right), \\[2ex] \text{MPR} = 1.612\text{MPR}_{-1} - 0.677\text{MPR}_{-2} + 4.46 \times 10^{-3}\log\left(\dfrac{p_m}{p}\right). \end{cases}$$

If the autoregressive components correspond exactly to the eigenvalues λ_5 and λ_6 for XPR, and λ_7 for MPR, as table 16.6 suggests, this would result in

$$\begin{cases} \text{XPR} = 1.537\text{XPR}_{-1} - 0.391\text{XPR}_{-2} - 0.165\text{XPR}_{-3}, \\ \text{MPR} = 1.606\text{MPR}_{-1} - 0.672\text{MPR}_{-2}. \end{cases}$$

Finally, the two first eigenvalues govern the price-wage loop. Indeed, the second eigenvalue is almost a multiple real root that mixes separate real and nominal phenomena. In isolation, the price-wage dynamics (D18 and D24 of table 16.1) imply both a unitary eigenvalue and a second smaller eigenvalue whose value is very close to one, linked to the speed of price adjustment and to the degree of indexation of wages to prices (see, e.g., Deleau et al. 1984). Consequently the interactions in the maquette between quantities and prices have a slight stabilizing influence.

5. The conclusion that clearly emerges from this section is that the dynamics of the core model are extremely sluggish: for a number of variables, own dynamics are strongly dominant. Thus it is not surprising to find that the quantities and wage-price blocks function essentially independently for more than 10 periods. This is illustrated by the stylized two variables model:

$$\begin{cases} x = \rho_1 x_{-1} + \displaystyle\sum_{i=0}^{n} a_i y_{-i} + \bar{x}, \\[3ex] y = \rho_2 y_{-1} + \displaystyle\sum_{0}^{m} b_i x_{-i} + \bar{y}, \end{cases}$$

Table 16.7

Eigenvalue	Variable	Autoregression
$\lambda_3 = 0.9625$	Q*	$\delta' = 0.968$
$\lambda_6 = 0.8371$	C	$\alpha_{17} = 0.832$
$\lambda_9 = 0.7175$	PI	$\alpha_{39} = 0.717$
$\lambda_{11} = 0.3986$	PM	$\alpha_{46} = 0.399$
$\lambda_{12} = 0.3003$	NS	$\alpha_6 = 0.295$
$\lambda_{13} = 0.276$	ND	$\alpha_2 = 0.275$

where $\rho_2 < \rho_1 < 1$ and $(\sum_0^n a_i) \times (\sum_0^m b_i)$ are nonnegligible, but the a_i's and b_i's are all very small.

In the spirit of the concept of "near decomposability" developed by Ando et al. (1963), one can define a horizon H_1 before which x and y may be analyzed separately, and another horizon H_2 after which the own dynamics of x stabilize, making x a passive variable. Between H_1 and H_2 interactions are increasingly significant, but the lag structure can be simplified. Thus it is possible to build a whole set of simple approximations of the maquette, each valid for different time spans and each telling a different story about the working of the economy.

16.4   Conclusion

The method for analyzing a given macroenometric model presented here seeks to reveal its theoretical underpinnings, which are generally hidden behind its numerous and apparently complex equations. The basic idea is to treat the model as if it were a theoretic disequilibrium growth model, but with numerical parameters instead of formal ones. The procedure involves two steps: first, determining and analyzing the long-run solution in terms of the steady state growth path and, second, analyzing the dynamics on the basis of the stationary representation.

In the case of METRIC we discovered that the inherent formalization of the working of the economy in the long-run equilibrium is not Walrasian but a kind of monopolistic equilibrium, with a rather ambiguous determination of employment. Some elements are missing, however, related to stock-flow relations (consumer and government budget constraints, the balance of payments constraint) and to the monetary aspects of exchange.

The dynamic investigation of METRIC focused mainly on its potential block structure. A strong decomposability, lasting for a surprisingly long time, was found between prices and quantities. This feature is due to the very weak interaction between variables in contrast with the pronounced autoregressive structure of this model, which creates stickiness almost everywhere. It must be stressed that this study deals with the reduction of a specific version of METRIC, and this phenomenon is probably less evident in more recent versions. It would be highly instructive to establish precisely how the model has evolved in this respect.

Notes

This chapter was partly written while the author was visiting CORE and the Département des sciences Economiques at Louvain-la-Neuve. He benefited from many fruitful comments and suggestions, especially from an anonymous referee. V. Barham is gratefully acknowledged for her editorial assistance.

1. Theses growth rates look rather high compared with the performances of the 1980s, but they are consistent with the historical estimation period of the model.

2. This result is rather general; see, for example, Goldberger (1959) for the Klein-Goldberger model or Kuh et al. (1985) for the MQEM model.

3. There are indeed several versions of METRIC. We analyze a reduced version of Artus et al. (1981).

4. The differences in the specifications of exports and imports are unimportant and do not imply different theoretical conceptions.

5. The symbol $\dot{x}$ denotes the rate of growth $(x_t - x_{t-1})/x_{t-1}$ of the variable x.

6. See Deleau, Le Van, and Malgrange (1987) for more discussion of this point.

7. The predetermination of r is not due to economic policy but to the hypothesis of a small open economy.

8. Furthermore the degree of capacity utilization, U_c, is less than 100 percent but can be rationalized, in the present context, by arguments about uncertainty; see, for example, Malinvaud (1987) and Sneessens (1987).

9. We recall that the original core version of METRIC involves a monetary financial block, but it is essentially inactive; see also note 2.

10. Here we consider only pure shocks, perturbing ex ante only one block. But economically meaningful shocks may involve a combination of several pure shocks from different blocks. One typical example is an exchange rate or foreign price shock which ex ante influences exports and imports as well as relative prices, thus generating both quantity and price perturbations.

11. These coefficients are computed formally from the eigenvalues and the associated eigenvectors; see Kuh et al. (1985).

12. This is common practice; see, for example, Deleau-Malgrange (1978), Kuh et al. (1982, 1985), and Schoonbeek (1984) for discussion of this practice.

References

Ando, A., F. M. Fisher, and H. Simon. 1963. *Essays on the Structure of Social Science Models.* Cambridge: MIT Press.

Artus, P., P. Morin, A. Pacaud, C. Peyroux, M. Sterdyniak, and R. Teyssier. 1981. "METRIC, modèle trimestriel de conjoncture." Publication de l'INSEE, Paris.

Blanchard, O. J., and N. Kiyotaki. 1987. "Monopolistic Competition and the Effects of Aggregate Demand." *American Economic Review* 77:647–666.

Chow, G., and P. Corsi. 1982. *Evaluating the Reliability of Macroeconomic Models.* New York: Wiley.

Deleau, M., C. Le Van, and P. Malgrange. 1987. "Le Long terme des modèles macro-économiques." CEPREMAP Working Paper 8729, Paris.

Deleau, M., and P. Malgrange. 1978. *L'Analyse des modèles macroéconomiques quantitatifs.* Paris: Economica.

Deleau, M., P. Malgrange, and P. A. Muet. 1984. "A Study of Short-Run and Long-Run Properties of Macroeconometric Models by Means of an Aggregative Core Model." In *Contemporary Macroeconomic Modelling*, edited by P. Malgrange and P. A. Muet. Oxford: Blackwell, 215–246.

Dixit, A., and J. Stiglitz. 1977. "Monopolistic Competition and Optimum Product Diversity." *American Economic Review* 67:297–308.

Gilli, M. 1982. "TROLL Program CAUSOR: A Program for the Analysis of Recursive and Interdependent Causal Structures." Technical Report 37, MIT, Cambridge.

Goldberger, A. S. 1959. *Impact Multipliers and Dynamic Properties of the Klein-Coldberger Model.* Amsterdam: North Holland.

Hickman, B. G. 1972. *Econometric Models of Cyclical Behaviour.* NBER, Studies in Income and Wealth. Columbia University Press, 36.

Kuh, E., C. Le Van, and P. Malgrange. 1984. "Une Étude de la dynamique structurelle des modèles macroéconomiques." CEPREMAP Working Paper, Paris.

Kuh, E., and J. Neese. 1982. "Econometric Model Diagnostics." In *Evaluating the Reliability of Macroeconomic Models*, edited by G. C. Chow and P. Corsi. New York: Wiley, 119–146.

Kuh, E., and J. Neese. 1982. "Econometric Model Diagnostics." In *Evaluating the Reliability of Macroeconomic Models*, edited by G. C. Chow and P. Corsi. New York: Wiley, 119–146.

Kuh, E., J. Neese, and P. Hollinger. 1985. *Structural Sensitivity in Econometric Models.* New York: Wiley.

Kmenta, J., and J. B. Ramsey. 1981. *Large Scale Macro-Econometric Models.* Amsterdam: North Holland.

Malgrange, P. 1983. "Steady Growth Paths in a Short Run Dynamic Model: The Case of The French Quarterly Model METRIC." CEPREMAP Working Paper 8321, Paris.

Malinvaud, E. 1987. "Capital productif, incertitudes et profitabilité." *Annales d'Economie et de Statistique* 5:1–36.

Schoonbeek, L. 1984. "Coefficient Values and Dynamic Properties of Econometric Models." *Economic Letters* 16:303–308.

Sims, C. 1980. "Macroeconomics and Reality." *Econometrica* 48:1–48.

Sneessens, H. 1987. "Investment and the Inflation-Unemployment Trade-off in a Macro-economic Rationing Model with Monopolistic Competition." *European Economic Review* 31:781–815.

Wallis, K. F. 1984. *Models of the UK Economy: A Review by the ESRC Macroeconomic Modeling Bureau.* Oxford: Oxford University Press.

Index